Current Perspectives on Stemmed and
Fluted Technologies in the American Far West

Current Perspectives on Stemmed and Fluted Technologies in the American Far West

edited by

KATELYN N. MCDONOUGH,
RICHARD L. ROSENCRANCE, *and* JORDAN E. PRATT

The University of Utah Press
SALT LAKE CITY

Copyright © 2024 by The University of Utah Press. All rights reserved.

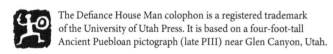 The Defiance House Man colophon is a registered trademark of the University of Utah Press. It is based on a four-foot-tall Ancient Puebloan pictograph (late PIII) near Glen Canyon, Utah.

LIBRARY OF CONGRESS CATALOGING-IN-PUBLICATION DATA

Names: McDonough, Katelyn N., 1988– editor. | Rosencrance, Richard L., 1988– editor. | Pratt, Jordan E., 1993– editor.
Title: Current perspectives on stemmed and fluted technologies in the American Far West / edited by Katelyn N. McDonough, Richard L. Rosencrance, and Jordan E. Pratt.
Description: Salt Lake City : The University of Utah Press, [2024] | Includes bibliographical references and index.
Identifiers: LCCN 2023036711 | ISBN 9781647691431 (hardback) | ISBN 9781647691448 (ebook)
Subjects: LCSH: Projectile points—West (U.S.)—History. | Tools, Prehistoric—West (U.S.) | Stone implements—West (U.S.)—History. | Indians of North America—Implements—West (U.S.) | Indians of North America—West (U.S.)—Antiquities. | Excavations (Archaeology)—West (U.S.) | West (U.S.)—Antiquities.
Classification: LCC E98.I4 C87 2023 | DDC 978.00909—dc23/eng/20230829
LC record available at https://lccn.loc.gov/2023036711

Cover illustration: Projectile points, beginning from top right: (1) Lind Coulee point from the Lind Coulee site, Washington (photo by Richard Rosencrance, used with permission); (2) Haskett point from the Haskett site, Idaho (photo by Richard Rosencrance, used with permission); (3) Channel Islands Amol point from CA-SRI-26, California (photo by Jon Erlandson, used with permission); (4) Lake Mohave point from Lake Mojave, California (photo by Edward Knell, used with permission). The furthest left point is a Clovis point from the Dietz site, Oregon (photo by Richard Rosencrance, used with permission).

Errata and further information on this and other titles available at UofUpress.com

Printed and bound in the United States of America.

Contents

List of Figures	vii
List of Tables	xi
Acknowledgments	xiii
1. A History of Stemmed and Fluted Technology Research in the American Far West Katelyn N. McDonough, Richard L. Rosencrance, *and* Jordan E. Pratt	1

Part I: Stemmed Technologies

2. Western Stemmed Tradition Projectile Point Chronology in the Intermountain West Richard L. Rosencrance, Daron Duke, Amanda Hartman, *and* Andrew Hoskins	21
3. Western Stemmed Tradition Toolstone Conveyance and Its Role in Understanding How Early Populations Settled into the Northwestern Great Basin Geoffrey M. Smith, Dennis L. Jenkins, Derek J. Reaux, Sophia Jamaldin, Richard L. Rosencrance, *and* Katelyn N. McDonough	59
4. Haskett and Its Clovis Parallels Daron Duke *and* Daniel Stueber	79
5. Regional Morphological Homogeneity among Mojave Desert Terminal Pleistocene/Early Holocene Projectile Points Edward J. Knell *and* Mark Q. Sutton	113
6. The Younger Dryas-Aged Stemmed Points from Smith Creek Cave, Nevada Joshua J. Lynch, Caitlin Doherty, Ted Goebel, *and* Pat Barker	132
7. The Western Stemmed Tradition Predates Clovis in the Columbia River Plateau: Archaeological Evidence from the Cooper's Ferry Site Loren G. Davis	153

Part II: Fluted Technologies

8. The Clovis Record in the Far West George T. Jones *and* Charlotte Beck	163
9. Geographic Variability of Far West Fluted Points Michael F. Rondeau, Nicole D. George, *and* John W. Dougherty	184
10. The Ages of Stemmed and Fluted Points in the Great Plains and Rocky Mountains Todd A. Surovell	199

Part III: Broader Interactions

11. Stemmed Points in the Southwest — 219
    CASSANDRA L. KEYES

12. Cultural Transmission and the Interaction of Two Cultural Traditions in the Far West — 240
    CHARLOTTE BECK *and* GEORGE T. JONES

13. A Paleocoastal Western Stemmed Tradition Variant from the California Channel Islands — 262
    JON M. ERLANDSON, TODD J. BRAJE, KRISTINA M. GILL, AMY E. GUSICK, *and* TORBEN C. RICK

Part IV: Moving Forward

14. Across the Continental Divide — 277
    DAVID J. MELTZER

    References — 299

    List of Contributors — 359

    Index — 361

Figures

1.1. Regions of the American Far West discussed in the text. 2
2.1. Map of Western Stemmed Tradition (WST) sites discussed in text. 22
2.2. Type specimens for WST projectile point types. 26
2.3. WST projectile points from the northwest Great Basin with reliably associated radiocarbon ages. 34
2.4. WST projectile points from Danger Cave. 36
2.5. Paleoindian projectile point chronologies of the Intermountain West and Great Plains and Rocky Mountains (GPRM). 56
3.1. Map of Western Stemmed Tradition sites and toolstone sources discussed in the text. 61
4.1. Complete Haskett points from the Old River Bed Delta. 80
4.2. Map of sites discussed in text and the Old River Bed Delta study area. 81
4.3. Display of calibrated Haskett-associated radiocarbon dates and ranges. 87
4.4. Haskett points from Tule Springs. 93
4.5. Haskett point classified as a Lake Mohave point from Fort Irwin. 93
4.6. Fragmented projectile point blade from Fossil Lake site. 99
4.7. Haskett and Clovis artifact silhouettes. 101
4.8. Biface from study area exhibiting overshot flaking. 104
4.9. Obsidian sources (labeled with geographic extents) represented among Haskett projectile points in the study area. 107
5.1. Map depicting the location of Mojave Desert study areas. 114
5.2. Images of Lake Mohave and Silver Lake projectile points from the north-central Mojave Desert. 116
5.3. Percent of north-central region Lake Mohave and Silver Lake points grouped by raw material type. 124
5.4. Box plots depicting the length, width, basal width, and mass of north-central region Lake Mohave points grouped by raw material type. 125
5.5. Map depicting the location of Mojave Desert and Great Basin study areas. 127
5.6. Percent of Great Basin Concave Base (GBCS), Lake Mohave, and Silver Lake points when grouped by Great Basin study area. 128
6.1. Map of the western United States, showing location of Smith Creek Cave in east-central Nevada and locations of other archaeological sites mentioned in the text. 133
6.2. View of Smith Creek Cave in 2019. 134
6.3. Map of Bryan's 1968–1974 excavation at Smith Creek Cave, showing provenience of hearths, dated samples, some of

6.4.	the Western Stemmed bifacial points, and other artifacts. 135 The Western Stemmed bifacial-point fragments from Smith Creek Cave analyzed in this study. 140	9.3. 9.4. 9.5.	Basal width comparisons of fluted point samples. 191 Basal depth comparisons of fluted point samples. 192 Basal indentation index comparisons. 193
6.5.	(a) Biplot of rubidium (Rb) and zirconium (Zr) measures for obsidian artifacts; (b) biplot of rubidium (Rb) and strontium (Sr) measures. 141	10.1. 10.2.	Study area showing sites discussed in the text or providing chronological data. 200 Calibrated continuous 1-sigma radiocarbon dates from fluted and stemmed point components from the Great Plains and Rocky Mountains (GPRM). 202
6.6.	Map of eastern Great Basin showing geographic distribution of obsidians so far identified in the Smith Creek Cave Paleoindian assemblage. 146		
7.1.	Map of the southern Columbia River Plateau region and noted Great Basin sites. 154	10.3.	Calibrated continuous 1-sigma radiocarbon dates averaged by component from fluted and stemmed point components from the GPRM. 208
7.2.	Stemmed projectile points and fragments excavated in situ within LU3 at Cooper's Ferry. 156	10.4.	Localities with stratified fluted and point components from the GPRM shown in order of superposition. 212
7.3.	Chronostratigraphic context of WST projectile point technology and evidence of bifacial reduction debitage at Cooper's Ferry within LU3 in relation to elevation and stratigraphically associated AMS radiocarbon ages. 157	10.5.	Hypothesized cultural time-space relationships between fluted and stemmed points across the western United States. 214
		11.1.	Map of the geographic regions and site locations discussed in the text. 220
7.4.	Timeline comparing initial radiocarbon-dated appearance of cultural occupation in the bottom portion of LU3 (through diagnostic WST artifacts at the Cooper's Ferry site) to long and short Clovis radiocarbon chronologies. 158	11.2. 11.3. 11.4.	Map of the Tularosa Basin, New Mexico. 224 Sample of tapering stemmed points in the Cycyk collection. 226 Box plots comparing mean measurements of each variable for the Cycyk, Jay, Western Stemmed Tradition (WST), and Hell Gap stemmed points. 231
8.1.	Fluted points exhibiting classic Clovis morphology. 165		
8.2.	(a) Biface from the Fenn cache illustrating use of overshot flaking; (b) Clovis blade from the Sunshine Locality, Nevada, illustrating longitudinal curvature. 171	11.5.	Bivariate plots showing the distribution of measurements by variable for the Cycyk, Jay, Western Stemmed Tradition (WST), and Hell Gap points. 235
9.1.	Multi-flute points from Sunshine Well Locality. 185	12.1.	Map of sites and other locations mentioned in text. 241
9.2.	Bi-concave basal cross section. 189	12.2.	The two lithic reduction systems in the Far West. 245

12.3.	Comparison of Lind Coulee, Haskett, and earliest stemmed points from Paisley Cave 5.	250	13.3.	Channel Islands Amol (CIA) point from CA-SRI-26.	267
12.4.	Numbers of Clovis and Sunshine points identified in the analysis by Beck and colleagues (2019b), Folsom points in the Far West, and other Clovis artifacts in the Far West.	252	13.4.	Various Island Paleocoastal Tradition (IPT) crescent forms from CA-SRI-512 and CA-SMI-679.	268
12.5.	Histograms comparing Sunshine and Folsom points.	258	13.5.	Paleocoastal Channel Islands Barbed (CIB) points in situ, associated with bird and marine mammal bones found in a deeply buried, ~11,700 cal BP component at CA-SRI-512.	270
13.1.	Reconstructed paleogeography of Santarosae Island between about 20,000 and 10,000 cal BP.	265	14.1.	Highly simplified tree showing the relationship of Anzick and Spirit Cave to one another.	288
13.2.	Channel Islands Barbed (CIB) projectile points in the collections of the Smithsonian Institution's National Museum of Natural History.	267	14.2.	Cloud model of the overlapping distributions of projectile point types in space and time.	295

Tables

2.1. Western Stemmed Tradition (WST) Type Definitions. 27
2.2. A Summary of Windust Concepts by Researcher. 28
2.3. Chronological ^{14}C Hygiene Scoring System to Evaluate the Existing WST ^{14}C Record. 30
2.4. Reliable Radiocarbon Dates from Western Stemmed Tradition Sites. 38
3.1. Western Stemmed Tradition Sites from Oregon and Nevada Included in This Study. 65
3.2. Source Assignments for Western Stemmed Tradition Artifacts from Fort Rock and Chewaucan Basin Sites. 66
3.3. Source Assignments for Western Stemmed Tradition Artifacts from Additional Fort Rock and Chewaucan Basin Sites. 68
3.4. Source Assignments for Western Stemmed Tradition Artifacts from Southeastern Oregon Lake Basins. 70
3.5. Source Assignments for Western Stemmed Tradition Artifacts from High Rock Country Sites. 72
3.6. Source Assignments for Western Stemmed Tradition Artifacts from Additional High Rock Country Sites. 73
3.7. Frequencies of Local and Nonlocal Toolstone. 74
4.1. Haskett-Associated Radiocarbon Dates. 88
4.2. Descriptive Statistics for Kill Site-Associated Clovis and Folsom Points, Haskett Points, and Agate Basin Points. 100
4.3. Obsidian Source Profile for Western Stemmed Points from Old River Bed Delta Study Area. 106
4.4. Obsidian Sources Represented by Count and Weight for Non-projectile Point Tools in Haskett and Post-Haskett Western Stemmed Tradition Sites in the Study Area. 108
5.1. Frequency of Point Types by Region and Mojave Desert Study Area. 119
5.2. Summary Data for Projectile Points from All Mojave Desert Study Areas. 120
6.1. Details on the Western Stemmed Points in the Smith Creek Cave Assemblage. 138
6.2. Obsidian-Procurement Statistics for Paleoindian Projectile Point Assemblages in the Eastern Great Basin. 148
8.1. Radiocarbon Dates Reported to Be Associated with Fluted Points in the Intermountain West. 174
9.1. Basal Margin Elements. 188
9.2. Flute Scar Configurations. 189
9.3. Other Basal Scars Associated with Flutes. 189
9.4. Flute Scar Relationships. 189
9.5. Base Lateral Margin Relationships. 190
9.6. Basal Cross Sections. 190
9.7. Basal Width. 192
9.8. Basal Depth. 192
9.9. Basal Index (Basal Depth/Basal Width). 193

10.1. Radiocarbon Dates from Plains and Rocky Mountain Fluted (Clovis and Folsom) and Stemmed (Agate Basin, Hell Gap, and Cody) Archaeological Components. 203

10.2. Component-Averaged Radiocarbon Dates from Plains and Rocky Mountain Fluted (Clovis and Folsom) and Stemmed (Agate Basin, Hell Gap, and Cody) Archaeological Components. 209

11.1. Summary of Quantitative Data for Cycyk, Jay, Western Stemmed Tradition (WST), and Hell Gap Points. 230

11.2. Results of the ANOVA/Kruskal-Wallis and T-Tests Comparing Metric Attributes between Cycyk, Jay, Western Stemmed Tradition, and Hell Gap Point Types. 233

12.1. Stage Model Used in Beck and Jones Biface Analysis. 247

12.2. Results of Bivariate Analyses of the Three Classic Subgroups, Far Western Clovis, and Sunshine Fluted Points. 255

13.1. Island Paleocoastal Tradition Sites from the Northern Channel Islands with Diagnostic Technology (Stemmed Points and/or Crescents) and Clearly Associated Radiocarbon Dates. 271

Acknowledgments

This book is a product of many years of research and collaboration. We are grateful to all the contributors for sharing their work and sticking with us as this volume coalesced. We thank University of Utah Press acquisitions editors Reba Rauch and Justin Bracken for their generous and patient guidance through the publishing process, and Anya Martin for her careful copyediting. Many reviewers contributed to the improvement of this volume. David Madsen and an anonymous reviewer provided detailed feedback on the full compiled manuscript. We appreciate their time and acknowledge that their reviews made the volume better. Each chapter was also individually reviewed by two anonymous peers who we thank for their service and constructive comments. We thank the Oregon Humanities Center and the College of Arts and Sciences at the University of Oregon and the Melbern G. Glasscock Center for Humanities Research at Texas A&M University for subvention support. This volume was inspired by the symposium *Current Perspectives on the Western Stemmed Tradition—Clovis Debate in the Far West* at the 84th Annual Meeting for the Society for American Archaeology in Albuquerque, New Mexico. We appreciate everyone who attended and participated in that symposium, many of whom are authors of chapters herein, but several of whom are not: Margaret Helzer, Bryan Hockett, Robert Kelly (discussant), Patrick O'Grady, Thomas Stafford Jr., and Scott Thomas. It is a privilege to work with all these fine people, and we look forward to more collaborations ahead.

1

A History of Stemmed and Fluted Technology Research in the American Far West

KATELYN N. MCDONOUGH, RICHARD L. ROSENCRANCE, *and* JORDAN E. PRATT

The predominance of stemmed projectile points and scarcity of fluted points in the Far West relative to the rest of North America has prompted intrigue and debate for nearly 100 years (Bedwell 1970; Bryan 1980; Butler 1961; Campbell et al. 1937; Cressman 1951; Davis et al. 2019; Jenkins et al. 2012; Layton 1970; Smith and Barker 2017; Smith et al. 2020; Willig et al. 1988). What is the relationship between fluted and stemmed projectile points in Far Western North America? How do they compare chronologically, geographically, and technologically? What does that tell us about the lives and interactions of their makers? How does this inform broader questions regarding when and how the continent was first populated?

These questions and the cross-regional discussion crucial to answering them are what inspired this volume and the symposium at the 2019 Society for American Archaeology meeting in Albuquerque, New Mexico on which it is based. While the chapters that follow do not offer final resolution to such inquiries, they do bring together the work of scholars from different regions, perspectives, and paradigms that move us toward a better understanding.

The Western Stemmed Tradition (WST) or technocomplex refers to a diverse group of stemmed projectile points and associated tool types that collectively span at least 4.5 millennia (ca. 13,500 to 9,000 calendar years [cal BP]). Early stemmed projectile point technologies are found throughout much of North America and parts of South America but are most common and well-understood in the Great Basin and Columbia Plateau (i.e., the Intermountain West). Other early stemmed projectile points are known from the Pacific Coast, Great Plains and Rocky Mountains, Colorado Plateau, Midwest, Southwest, Northeast, Alaska, Mexico, Venezuela, and Chile (Bryan et al. 1978; Chapin 2017; Cruxent and Rouse 1956; Dillehay 1997; Erlandson et al. 2011; Fedje et al. 2008; Fishel 1988; Gruhn 1988; Janetski et al. 2012; Kunz et al. 2003; Lothrop et al. 2016; Mackie et al. 2018; Minor 1984; Sánchez and Carpenter 2016; Surovell, Chapter 10; Tune 2020). Disagreement over WST chronology abounds, even within these pages, but many researchers view recent discoveries at Cooper's Ferry in Idaho (Davis et al. 2019) and the Paisley Caves in Oregon (Jenkins et al. 2012) as compelling evidence that the earliest examples of WST technology are contemporaneous with or anterior to Clovis (Meltzer 2021; Pratt et al. 2020; Waters 2019).

Despite having an early inception and geographic expanse comparable to fluted technology, the WST has historically received much less attention in the archaeological literature. Previous Far West Paleoindian

FIGURE 1.1. Regions of the American Far West discussed in the text. We consider the Great Basin, Columbia Plateau, and areas to the west as the Far West.

period syntheses largely focused on human behavioral adaptations (e.g., Graf and Schmitt 2007; Willig et al. 1988), and despite efforts to examine the chronology, morphology, and geographic variability of WST lithic technology, a comprehensive volume aimed at these issues does not exist for the WST as it does for other Paleoindian technocomplexes (e.g., Amick 1999; Bonnichsen et al. 2005; Clark and Collins 2002; Gingerich 2013, 2018; Holliday et al. 2017; Knell and Muñiz 2013; Smallwood and Jennings 2015). This volume aims to bridge this gap by offering a synthesis of current research and understanding surrounding stemmed and fluted technology in the American Far West. We consider the Far West to be the Great Basin, Columbia Plateau, areas west of the Cascade and Sierra Nevada Mountains, and the Pacific Coast from the Northern Channel Islands to Coastal British Columbia (Figure 1.1).

The tumultuous history of debates about the chronological, technological, and cultural relationships of stemmed and fluted points in the Far West can be summarized into four major periods with a number of seminal works that exemplify the advancements of thought through time. Here we provide a brief overview of major works and themes in Far West Paleoindian research to serve as an historical backdrop and context for the volume.

Pre-1980s Archaeology: The Search for Order

The first claims of Pleistocene-aged stemmed points in the Far West came around the same time as early claims of Pleistocene-aged fluted points in the Great Plains and Southwest. Campbell and colleagues (1937) argued for great antiquity of stemmed projectile points found on desiccated shorelines in the Mojave Desert, suggesting alongside Ernst Antevs that the points dated to the Pleistocene when pluvial lakes last filled the basins. In the northern Great Basin, Cressman and colleagues (1940) used the stratigraphic position of artifacts below Mazama tephra (then hypothesized to be between 10,000 and 4,000 years old but now dated to ~7630 cal BP [Egan et al. 2015]) at the Fort Rock and Paisley caves to argue for deep antiquity of humans there. Cressman later claimed to have found "crudely shaped points or scrapers" in association with a U-shaped house structure and extinct camel and horse remains at Paisley Cave 3 (Cressman 1942:93; see also Jenkins 2007). Though Cressman could only describe the items in very basic terms, he recovered WST points and a crescent in the lower levels of Paisley Caves 1 and 2 (see Cressman 1942:82 and Figure 94e) and noted the similarity of the crescent to "Lake Mohave specimens" (Cressman 1942:82). Cressman ultimately concluded that he had uncovered evidence of people inhabiting central Oregon alongside extinct megafauna species and that central Oregon had been continuously occupied since that time.

Experts of the day and the following decades harshly critiqued and largely discounted the Campbells' and Cressman's claims (Heizer and Baumhoff 1970; Jennings 1986; Krieger 1944; see discussion in Warren and Schneider 2017 and Cressman 1968). Jennings (1986) justifiably questioned the proposed human-extinct fauna co-occurrence on the grounds that Cressman had not adequately documented the association of artifacts with the extinct mammal remains. The scientific community at the time agreed that the Great Basin had no or very little evidence of Pleistocene occupations. Such a situation stood in contrast to the Great Plains where researchers repeatedly confirmed the Pleistocene antiquity of Clovis and Folsom points with their presence in extinct mammal bone beds (Holliday 2000; Meltzer 2015).

As the mid-twentieth century approached, researchers began to document fluted points in surface sites throughout the Far West, mostly in the Great Basin (Davis and Shutler 1969; Tuohy 1968 and references therein). Even the Campbells (Campbell and Campbell 1940; Campbell 1949) found fluted points, although spatially separated from stemmed points, around the margins of pluvial lakes in the Mojave Desert and southwest Nevada. Tuohy (1968) noted that archaeologists ignored the Great Basin because of the apparent lack of fluted points and extinct mammal kill sites. His summary and introduction of a few fluted and stemmed point localities in western Nevada led him to conclude that the earliest stone tool tradition in the area was Clovis, closely followed by Lake Mohave (i.e., stemmed points).

While stemmed points dominate the region, the Far West also has a special place in this history of Clovis/fluted point research. Residents of south-central Idaho inadvertently discovered the first reported Clovis cache during the summer of 1961 (Butler 1963; Butler and Fitzwater 1965). Dubbed the Simon Clovis Cache, it consists of 63 items that include multiple large Clovis projectile points, large bifaces of various stages, and a few other tools such as a graver and several scrapers (Santarone 2014; Woods and Titmus 1985). Many of the items were covered in ocher and are of exquisite craftsmanship and made of seemingly exotic raw materials such as pure quartz crystal. Such characteristics were the first in a pattern of discovery and interpretation repeated with Clovis cache finds in the following decades (see Kilby 2008 and Huckell and Kilby 2014 for current and historic perspectives on Clovis caches). The discovery of the Simon Clovis Cache remains significant in peopling of the Americas research and is one of two Clovis caches in the Far West.

Surveys and excavations throughout the 1950s and 1960s in the Far West continued to recover and record scores of stemmed and fluted projectile points that led to a variety of broad-scale human-ecological models (Bedwell 1970; Butler 1961; Davis 1963; Jennings 1957; Layton 1970; Rice 1965; Swanson et al. 1964). Most notable are the excavations at the Lind Coulee site (Daugherty 1956; Irwin and Moody 1978) and Marmes Rockshelter (Fryxell and Daugherty 1962; Hicks 2004) in Washington; Danger Cave in Utah (Jennings 1957); Bison and Veratic Rockshelters (Swanson et al. 1964), and Wilson Butte Cave (Gruhn 1961) in Idaho; Last Supper Cave (Layton and Davis 1978), Hanging Rock Shelter (Layton 1970), and Smith Creek Cave in Nevada (Bryan 1979); and the Fort Rock and Connley caves in Oregon (Bedwell 1970). All of those sites contained stemmed projectile points dating (although imprecisely) to ~10,000 cal BP or older. Bedwell's (1970, 1973) work pushed the proposed antiquity of stemmed points back further, purporting human occupations (without diagnostics) dating to ~15,000 cal BP at Fort Rock Cave and Haskett points dating to ~13,500 cal BP at the Connley Caves.

The foundations of WST typology and technology come from this era. By 1970, seven of the nine WST types had been defined (see Beck and Jones 2009; Rosencrance 2019), and within another decade numerous researchers had produced robust site- and regional-level analyses of WST lithic assemblages (Davis et al. 1969; Layton 1970; Pendleton 1979; Tuohy 1969, 1974; Tuohy and Layton 1977; Warren 1967). These researchers agreed there were broadly connecting trends of these technologies, but there remained no clear answer on specific cultural history (Rosencrance et al., Chapter 2). Warren and Ranere (1968) provided early criticism to Jennings' (1957) popular Desert Culture concept which contended there was little change in Great Basin lifeways over the past 10,000 years. Armed with analyses of various Haskett sites, Warren and Ranere argued those early lithic assemblages in the Intermountain West were distinct from later assemblages and more akin to Paleoindian technologies elsewhere in North America.

Bedwell's (1970) work in the Fort Rock Basin also played an important role in shaping thought and models about the WST during this time. Primarily relying on robust Haskett assemblages from the Connley Caves, Bedwell's Western Pluvial Lakes Tradition (WPLT) hypothesis suggested foragers living along the Cascade-Sierra Nevada eastern front were focused on or "tethered" to marsh and lacustrine habitats during the late Pleistocene/Early Holocene (LP/EH). He also hypothesized that similarities in stemmed projectile points from the Fort Rock Basin and those in the Snake River Plain and central Washington may be the result of interaction and trade. At the same time, he contrasted his WPLT to the eastern Great Basin record (hence the "western" in WPLT). While we now know the WPLT is oversimplified (Grayson 2011), the model gained much traction with researchers as another contrast to the Desert Culture concept, and for a while, the WPLT was used as a moniker for *all* stemmed point assemblages in the Far West (see various chapters in Willig et al. 1988).

Archaeological investigations in the Far West prior to 1980 established clear evidence that stemmed points resided in the lowest components of the region's stratified sites. Early radiocarbon dating efforts confirmed these sites were quite old, some even possibly as old as the extinct megafauna kills in the Great Plains and Southwest (Haynes 1964), but many questions about context and reliability of those sites persisted. Dated fluted point sites remained enigmatic in the Far West, but most researchers considered them to be Clovis and the basal unit of the region's culture history (Aikens 1978; Haynes 1964; Tuohy 1968). While morphological differences in stemmed and fluted points were obvious, lithic technological and toolstone selection research at the end of this interval found additional differences that set the stage for decades of focused research (Clewlow 1968; Pendleton 1979; Tuohy 1969, 1974).

1980–2000: The Stemmed Point Tradition, Paleoarchaic, and the Growth of Data

In our opinion, Bryan's (1980, see also 1988) Stemmed Point Tradition model marks one of the most important developments in Far Western Paleoindian archaeology of any period. Bryan provided the first sophisticated, continental perspective trying to explain the widespread occurrence of early stemmed projectile point technology in the Far West and beyond. More than taxonomic nomenclature (e.g., the Great Basin Stemmed Series [Tuohy and Layton 1977]), Bryan's (1980) Stemmed Point Tradition is a model that seeks to explain the stemmed point archaeological record as one of cultural relatedness with a chronological trajectory. Although Bryan's (1980) defining technological characteristics are hafting techniques (i.e., basal shape), and to a much lesser degree flaking techniques, more recent lithic technological research continues to support his larger model. Bryan (1980) considered the Stemmed Point Tradition a chronological parallel to what he called the Fluted Point Tradition (i.e., Clovis-Folsom in the Great Plains and other fluted point technologies in the Eastern Woodlands). In his review of radiocarbon data to support that hypothesis, he included a number of sites we now know to be younger than initially thought. Other sites have been reinvestigated and reaffirmed as critical to the chronological side of the debate (see Davis et al. 2019; Lynch et al., Chapter 6; Jenkins et al. 2012; Rosencrance et al. 2019; G. Smith, Felling, Taylor, et al. 2015).

Bryan's (1980) ability to form this model was largely possible from the previous decades of technological description, definition, and syntheses. It is important to note that Bryan's (1980) model was not considered particularly influential at the time or even during the following decades. This is exemplified in the growth of Paleoarchaic as discussed below. We feel, however, that it is Bryan's broader ideas that prevail in the present day.

The seminal work from this period is *Early Human Occupation in Far Western North America: The Clovis-Archaic Interface* edited by Judith Willig, C. Melvin Aikens, and John Fagan (1988). This volume profoundly shaped thought around Paleoindian archaeology of the Far West, particularly in the Great Basin. It was also the first compilation of research concerning stemmed and fluted technologies in western North America and remains impressive for the breadth of subjects and geographic space it encompassed. Viewed through an historical lens, it provides a great summary of present understandings, a wealth of new archaeological data, novel interpretations of lithic technology and settlement patterns, and finally, a large paradigm shift within Far Western Paleoindian research. Many of today's questions about stemmed and fluted technologies are effectively echoes of the research questions and data in that volume—principally, ones of chronology and technology. Willig and Aikens (1988) distinguished "Western Stemmed" and "Western Fluted" in the opening chapter to emphasize those complexes in the Far West (and the peoples' ecological adaptations) from other regions—a modification of Bryan's earlier ideas (1980).

Willig's (1989; Willig and Aikens 1988) introduction of the term "Paleoarchaic" in that volume and in her dissertation was the beginning of a significant paradigm shift. "Paleoarchaic" was meant to shed the big-game subsistence-oriented baggage attached to "Paleoindian" in lieu of a term that was more regionally focused and highlighted the "broad spectrum (Archaic) adaptations among the earliest (paleo) occupants of the Far West" (Willig 1989:14). "Paleoarchaic" implied that the apparent broad-spectrum foraging of early Far West peoples was fundamentally different than the strategies of highly mobile, big-game hunters of the Great Plains (e.g., Clovis and Folsom) and more like subsistence strategies of people in the Great Basin during the Middle and Late Holocene (i.e., the Archaic). In some ways, it can be seen as an outgrowth of the Desert Culture concept (Jennings 1957), but is different than Elston's (1982, 1986) use of "Prearchaic," which highlighted the differences in pre- and post-8000 cal BP lifeways, likening the former to Paleoindian lifeways elsewhere on the continent.

The term "Paleoarchaic" was adopted by many researchers in the following decades (Beck and Jones 1997; Jones and Beck 1999; Jones et al. 2003; Madsen 2007) and is still preferred by some today (Davis et al. 2012; Janetski et al. 2012; Madsen et al., eds. 2015). "Prearchaic" also continues to be used by some (Elston and Zeanah 2002; Elston et al. 2014; Smith 2007) but is essentially equivalent to the use of the term "Paleoindian." The Paleoarchaic concept drove researchers' attention to adaptive subsistence strategies and away from the vexing questions of diachronic stemmed point technology. It also fueled/fuels what we believe to be a somewhat false dichotomy between the WST and other Paleoindian technologies across the continent.

In terms of stemmed and fluted technology relationships, the general perspective throughout *Early Human Occupation in Far Western North America: The Clovis-Archaic Interface* (Willig et al., eds. 1988) was "Clovis-first" with the idea that the WST was a regional development out of Clovis (Carlson 1988; Musil 1988; Tuohy 1988; Wallace and Riddell 1988; Willig and Aikens 1988). Some chapters found the question unsolved and broadly grouped fluted and stemmed sites into the same general period (Price and Johnson 1988; Zancanella 1988). Bryan (1988) stood out as one of the few willing to make an extended argument that stemmed points may be as old as fluted points in the Far West, primarily leaning on his excavations and radiocarbon dates at Smith Creek Cave. Fagan (1988) emphatically distinguished fluted and stemmed lithic technologies from different spatial scatters at the Dietz site, and Warren and Phagan (1988) posited different reduction strategies for stemmed and fluted points from the Mojave Desert. Those studies reaffirmed differences in lithic technology first identified by Pendleton (1979).

Still, nearly every researcher in the monograph grouped stemmed point assemblages and sites as a monolith, perhaps recognizing different types but never considering different forms as possibly representing different periods or adaptations. Lastly, Willig's (1988) chapter exemplifies the important role of pluvial lake histories to estimate relative timings and relationships of stemmed and fluted assemblages. Although many of her interpretations of timing and environments were later challenged (Pinson 2008, 2011), using geomorphology and spatial distribution of surface assemblages to interrogate chronological questions remains an important facet of Paleoindian research in the Far West (Duke 2011, 2015; Duke and King 2014; Madsen et al., eds. 2015; Reaux 2021; Reaux et al. 2018; G. Smith, Felling, Wriston, et al. 2015; Wriston and Smith 2017).

The last major work of this period comes near the end, with Beck and Jones' (1997) review article on the Great Basin's LP/EH paleoecology and archaeology, with an emphasis on research problems and prospects. That work is especially impactful for the swath of questions and data they assemble and synthesize. Compiling, discussing, and hypothesizing about the Great Basin fluted point record—as well as how it may or may not relate to the WST record—was a major focus of the paper. The 1997 paper set the stage for decades of work by Beck, Jones, and their colleagues (2007, 2009, 2010, 2012b, 2013, 2015; Beck, Jones, and Taylor 2019) attempting to address those questions. The six primary questions Beck and Jones (1997) outlined are still primary interests today (see Smith and Barker 2017). They (see also Jones and Beck 1999) emphasized chronology as one of the major questions moving forward, concluding that WST types coexisted for millennia, and fluted points were poorly dated. Lastly, Beck and Jones (1997) provided the first extended argument for a post-Clovis fluted point variant in the Great Basin (see Beck and Jones, Chapter 12; Beck, Jones, and Taylor 2019; Jones and Beck, Chapter 8).

The discovery of the East Wenatchee Clovis Cache marks one of the better known developments in Far West Paleoindian archaeology during this time (Gramly 1993; Mehringer 1988). East Wenatchee represents the furthest west Clovis cache yet discovered and one of the very few occurrences of Clovis materials found in a primary buried context in the Far West. Though the cache is not directly dated, we do know based on the adherence of Glacier Peak tephra to the bottom of at least one Clovis point that the cache postdates ~11,600 ^{14}C BP (~13,440 cal BP; Kuehn et al. 2009). East Wenatchee remains prominent in the minds of many Clovis researchers, and it is even argued to have been left by a Clovis origin population (Fiedel and Morrow 2012; Schroedl 2021), but as noted above the tephra only provides a maximum age for the cache and its actual, younger, age is unknown.

As the twentieth century came to a close, Far West researchers understood that stemmed points dominated the Paleoindian record, that the people who made them probably practiced broad-based subsistence strategies, stemmed points appeared to be technologically different than fluted points, not all fluted points in the Far West were necessarily Clovis, and much work was left to do to sort out the ages of the various techno-complexes.

2000–2010: Expansions of Lithic Technological Research and a Paleoarchaic Rebuff

Far Western stemmed and fluted point research from 2000 to 2010 is defined by an expansion of lithic technological research for both complexes, significant developments in settlement-subsistence models, and increased knowledge of early Pacific coastal sites. Beck and Jones' (2009) extensive study of stemmed and fluted projectile points from the Sunshine Locality remains one of the most thorough and expansive works addressing WST lithic technological questions, including morphological variance, function, breakage, and possible cultural relationships. Graf's (2001) master's thesis is also an important detailed lithic technological organization study that examined an entire toolkit from two discrete WST surface localities. Smith (2006) and Estes (2009) adapted Graf's approach to lithic analysis and applied it to other sizeable stemmed point assemblages, creating a robust set of comparable data. Galm and Gough's (2008) chapter on the Haskett assemblage at Sentinel Gap is a critical example of Haskett reduction and production strategies, maintenance, and hafting techniques that is nearly unmatched for a WST type in the literature (see Duke and Steuber, Chapter 4, for a regional view of Haskett). This list is far from exhaustive but illustrates the increased focus on WST lithic technology during the first decade of the twenty-first century.

Another very important development of this period is the unequivocal recognition of Pleistocene-aged archaeological sites on the Pacific Coast and growing support for a coastal migration by the continent's first inhabitants. Though Fladmark (1979) proposed a model for early coastal migration decades earlier, the "Coastal Migration Theory" remained peripheral to the ice-free corridor paradigm until the late 1990s. Research on the Northern Channel Islands was pivotal to that shift, including the dating of Arlington Springs man to ~13,000 cal BP (Johnson et al. 2002; but see Jazwa et al. 2021) and the discovery of multiple LP/EH sites there

(Erlandson 2010; Erlandson et al. 2007; Erlandson and Jew 2009). As the islands (or *the* island of Santarosae during the Pleistocene) were never connected to the mainland, such evidence indicates an early inception and familiarity with seafaring and marine-oriented lifeways (Erlandson 2002). While identifying early sites on the Pacific Coast remains extremely difficult (Braje et al. 2020; Punke and Davis 2006), Younger Dryas-aged sites from the Oregon coast (Indian Sands [Davis 2006; Hall et al. 2005; Willis 2005]) and Coastal British Columbia (Haida Gwaii [Fedje et al. 2008]) came to light during this time. Work of the decade solidified the importance of examining Far West coastal environments and archaeological evidence in models of the peopling of the Americas (Erlandson et al. 2008).

Paleoindian or Paleoarchaic? Great Basin Human Ecology at the Pleistocene/Holocene Transition, edited by Kelly Graf and Dave Schmitt (2007), is a defining work for this period, as well as one of the seminal works of Far West LP/EH research. This volume reexamined Willig's (1988, 1989; Willig and Aikens 1988) Paleoarchaic model. Contributors presented a wealth of new data such as radiocarbon-dated, stratified records from the Paisley Caves (Jenkins 2007), Bonneville Estates Rockshelter (Goebel 2007; Graf 2007; Hockett 2007; Rhode and Louderback 2007), and Kelvin's Cave (Henrikson and Long 2007). Jenkins (2007) confirmed Cressman's (1942) claims that humans and extinct megafauna coexisted in the northern Great Basin via radiocarbon dating of extinct horse and camel remains associated with cultural materials including coprolites containing human DNA. Henrikson and Long (2007) determined that Kelvin's Cave is a paleontological locality with intrusive later archaeological materials. Other researchers made significant bounds regarding WST lithic technological and settlement patterns using large surface assemblages (Duke and Young 2007; Schmitt et al. 2007; Smith 2007). Subsistence (Hockett 2007; Pinson 2007; Rhode and Louderback 2007) was another key focus of the volume, as is appropriate for the nature of the Paleoarchaic concept. Beck and Jones' (2007) cladistics and morphological analysis made strong distinctions between many Great Basin fluted points and "classic Clovis" points.

From *Paleoindian or Paleoarchaic?* we learned that Great Basin peoples' lithic technological and settlement organization during the LP/EH—characterized by sophisticated, formal lithic toolkits and high residential mobility—was more like other groups in North America during the same period than later Great Basin groups (Haynes 2007). We also began to see evidence that Great Basin LP/EH subsistence strategies included more diverse faunal (Hockett 2007) and botanical (Rhode and Louderback 2007) resources than previously recognized, though Haynes (2007:256) concluded that the diets of the earliest groups remained "unsolved mysteries."

Together, conclusions in the volume were a mixed bag as to whether "Paleoarchaic" or "Paleoindian" is the best term to use. Such a conundrum was not new (Elston and Zeanah 2002), nor is it fully resolved (Elston et al. 2014; Smith and Barker 2017). Regardless, following the publication of the volume, "Paleoarchaic" has fallen out of vogue for some. In any case, we find it unproductive to compare ~4,500 years of lifeways (Paleoarchaic) to ~7,000 years of lifeways (Archaic). One of the key things that came out of this period is a better grip on LP/EH cultural variability that is beyond any singular "Paleoarchaic" lifeway. Most researchers have found it clearer and more appropriate to refer to WST occupations as "Paleoindian." This conclusion comes from the work described above and below, but is also due to the lessened association of "Paleoindian" to strictly refer to Clovis.

2010–2020: Chronology Building and Placement of the WST Within the Peopling of the Americas

The beginning of the past decade is marked by another critical work published by Beck and Jones (2010) in which they formally proposed a hypothesis for distinct populations represented by WST and Clovis users within

North America during the late Pleistocene. They made two primary arguments: (1) WST users were the first to settle the Intermountain West; and (2) those populations predate the advent of Clovis technology anywhere on the continent—seemingly supporting a coastal migration (Beck and Jones 2010, 2013; Erlandson and Braje 2011; Waters 2019). Their paper was disputed primarily because of the radiocarbon dates they considered reliable (Fiedel and Morrow 2012; Goebel and Keene 2014; see also Beck and Jones 2012a, 2013). Goebel and Keene (2014) critically reviewed their dataset by applying a strict radiocarbon hygiene, arguing that most dated WST sites are coeval with or younger than Clovis in the Intermountain West. These two papers are indicative of the larger debate that has flourished since: are WST points older than Clovis in the Far West, and if so, how does that change our interpretations of the peopling process (Brown et al. 2019; Davis et al. 2019; Jenkins et al. 2012; Jenkins et al. 2013)? Other work since 2010 has focused on renewed excavation of sites to assess their ages and further grow our knowledge of WST subsistence and lithic technology.

Evidence for robust Pleistocene occupations of the Pacific Coast and possible relationships with the greater Far West record has grown significantly in the last decade, beginning with work by Erlandson and colleagues (2011) revealing new Younger Dryas-aged sites on the Channel Islands containing small stemmed points and crescents. That work highlights a probable connection with the WST and interior Far West Paleoindian complexes that they expand upon in this volume (Erlandson et al., Chapter 13). While we still lack direct evidence of seacraft (Sutton 2018a), repeated secure evidence on island sites and for deep-sea fishing continues to be found (Des Lauriers et al. 2017; Erlandson et al. 2020; Fedje et al. 2011). Moreover, the recent discovery of likely Clovis-aged footprints in Coastal British Columbia provides long-sought evidence of this age in the coastal corridor (McLaren et al. 2018). The simultaneous growth of interior (see below) and coastal archaeology throughout the Far West has naturally culminated in more serious consideration of a coastal migration as the origin of those similarities than ever before (Braje et al. 2020; Davis and Madsen 2020; Mackie et al. 2013; McLaren et al. 2019). Davis and Madsen (2020) have recently defined several testable hypotheses under the umbrella concept of the Coastal Migration Theory that provide clear avenues for future confirmation or falsification.

The defining developments in the Far West of the past 10 years come from Paisley Caves and Cooper's Ferry, both of which have evidence of WST technology dating to between 13,500 and 13,000 cal BP, and for the presence of humans in the Far West by ~14,500 cal BP and possibly as early as ~16,000 cal BP (Davis et al. 2014; Davis et al. 2019; Gilbert et al. 2008; Hockett and Jenkins 2013; Jenkins et al. 2012; Jenkins et al. 2013; Shillito et al. 2020). As mentioned, this debate really began at the end of the last decade with the initial reporting of stratigraphically consistent, directly dated coprolites with human DNA and extinct mammal remains from Paisley Caves overlapping sometime between ~14,500 and 14,000 cal BP (Gilbert et al. 2008; Jenkins 2007). Jenkins and colleagues (2012; see also Jenkins et al. 2013) presented evidence of a WST basal fragment (and others in the same stratigraphic interval) in an undisturbed indurated silt lens dated to ~13,000 cal BP by a presumably non-cultural twig found 40 cm away from the point. Directly dated coprolites with human DNA stratigraphically bracketing the point(s), other stratigraphically associated lithic artifacts, and multiple columns of radiocarbon dates further attest to the well-stratified nature of the deposits containing the ~13,000-year-old WST points. A typological assignment of the point fragments beyond WST is a matter of debate (see Davis, Chapter 7; Duke and Stueber, Chapter 4; Rosencrance et al., Chapter 2).

Jenkins and colleagues (2012) also report a hearth feature directly dated to ~13,000 cal BP surrounded by lithic debitage, a small biface fragment, and burned bone in Paisley Cave 2. Kennedy's (2018:286) analysis of macrobotanical remains from that hearth yielded a diverse seed assemblage of Boraginaceae, Poaceae, cheno-ams, *Chenopodium, Atriplex, Achnatherum,* and *Sesuvium*—many of which are known plant foods for Indigenous groups of the Great Basin. Such evidence lends further support for the unambiguous cultural origin of this feature.

Critiques of the early evidence from the Paisley Caves have generally focused on whether the earliest dated coprolites can definitely be considered human, or if the presence of human DNA is due to contamination (Fiedel 2014; Goldberg et al. 2009; Haynes 2015; Poinar et al. 2009; Sistiaga et al. 2014). The earlier critiques were met with responses that included a wide range of multi-proxy data, experiments, and details about the excavations (Gilbert et al. 2009; Hockett and Jenkins 2013; Jenkins et al. 2012; Jenkins et al. 2013; Rasmussen et al. 2009; see also Smith and Barker 2017:6–7). To address the latter critiques and present novel data, Shillito and colleagues (2020) obtained human fecal biomarkers in some of the same coprolites containing human DNA, the oldest of which is directly dated to ~14,200 cal BP. Further, their study directly dated a small piece of a bulrush S-twist weft basketry fragment to ~14,500–14,000 cal BP (~95.4% probability). Together, the Paisley Caves >14,000 cal BP evidence consists of directly dated coprolites containing both human fecal biomarkers and human DNA stratigraphically associated with directly dated artifacts that include cut-marked bone (Hockett and Jenkins 2013), a textile (Shillito et al. 2020), a modified bone flesher (Jenkins et al. 2013), and finally, lithic debitage and flake tools.

Work at the Cooper's Ferry site indicates short-stemmed points may date to at least the Clovis period, if not slightly before, on the Columbia Plateau (Davis, Chapter 7; Davis et al. 2014; Davis et al. 2019). Davis and colleagues (2019) reported that the two oldest WST fragments were found stratigraphically within LU3 alongside 25 additional stone tools and over 160 pieces of debitage. They stratigraphically bracket the oldest WST fragment using dated bone fragments that calibrate to between ~13,610–13,275 and 14,690–14,380 cal BP (95.4% probability), with the second point fragment bracketed by calibrated dates of ~13,475–13,060 and 13,610–13,275 cal BP (see Davis, Chapter 7; Davis et al. 2014; Davis et al. 2019 for details, including additional radiocarbon dates). There was also a cultural pit feature (PFA2) with a cache of WST points, tools, debitage, and bone capped with a rock cairn originating at the surface of LU3. A radiocarbon date at the surface of LU3 less than a meter from the pit calibrates to ~13,200 cal BP which Davis (Chapter 7; Davis et al. 2019) argues accurately represents the age of the surface.

Davis and colleagues (2019) also report a hearth feature with bone fragments, debitage, and a flake tool within its margins dated by three overlapping radiocarbon dates to between ~15,200 and 14,100 cal BP (95.4% probability). Another stratigraphically consistent combustion feature, lithic tools, debitage, bone, and a horse (*Equus* sp.) tooth, as well as other dated isolated charcoal and bone fragments, provide additional evidence for pre-14,000 cal BP occupations at Cooper's Ferry. While lacking diagnostic projectile points, Davis and colleagues (2019) suggest the earliest lithic tools at Cooper's Ferry are a flake- and blade-based stone tool tradition similar to Upper Paleolithic assemblages of northeast Asia. They also suggest that the Cooper's Ferry earliest projectile points share "temporal and technological affinity" with stemmed points from Japan, and, as such, they may share an ancestral "cultural connection with Upper Paleolithic Northeastern Asia" (Davis et al. 2019:895; see also Davis et al. 2021:48–49).

Critiques thus far have questioned the Bayesian analysis which suggests the site was first occupied between 16,560 and 15,280 cal BP (Manning 2020), the site's stratigraphic integrity (including in relation to WST points [Fiedel et al. 2021]), and the lithic technological antecedent relationships proposed by Davis and colleagues (Fiedel et al. 2021; Pratt et al. 2020). These critiques have been met with cogent responses that illustrate misconceptions about statistical modeling (Davis et al. 2020) and the nature of the site's deposits and regional archaeological record (Davis et al. 2021). The newest evidence of Cooper's Ferry is very recent, and we expect debate about the site and possible antecedent WST technologies will continue.

New insights from Bonneville Estates Rockshelter have also provided evidence for Clovis-age WST points. Goebel and Keene (2014) build upon the earlier stratigraphic, lithic, and radiocarbon reporting at the site (Goebel 2007; Goebel et al. 2011; Graf 2007) and discuss the occurrence of Haskett points in the same stratum (18b) as different hearth features dated to ~13,000 cal BP and 12,600 cal BP. However, they argue that the Haskett points are a few meters closer to the younger feature. Recently Goebel and colleagues (2021) contend that modeled ages within Stratum 18b indicate the stratum, the hearth features, and WST points date to ~12,950–12,550 cal BP, making them coeval with Clovis. Smith Creek Cave also contains possible evidence for 13,000 cal BP Haskett points, but questions remain about Bryan's (1979) original reporting, and chronological precision is complicated by radiocarbon dates with relatively large (100–200) standard deviations from the hearth charcoal dates (Bryan 1988; Goebel et al. 2007). Lynch and colleagues (Chapter 6) present a new Clovis-age radiocarbon date from the site but conclude that the twig's non-cultural origin still leaves uncertainty about whether it dates human occupations there.

Both the Paisley Caves and Cooper's Ferry sites have provided evidence of human occupations substantially predating the ages associated with WST technology. The paucity of WST, fluted, or other projectile points in the earliest deposits makes it impossible to definitively associate a diagnostic lithic technology with the earliest occupations in the Far West, leaving the door open for variable interpretations of the record (see Davis et al. 2019; Duke and Stueber, Chapter 4; Rosencrance et al., Chapter 2; Surovell, Chapter 10; Waters 2019). Nonetheless, the available evidence at Paisley Caves and Cooper's Ferry suggests that the continent's first inhabitants likely traversed a Pacific Coast route prior to the opening of the ice-free Corridor (Davis and Madsen 2020; but see Potter et al. 2017 and Potter, Baichtal, et al. 2018 for an alternative hypothesis). The timing of a Pacific Coast route is currently supported by biogeographical and aDNA research (Waters 2019), though this conclusion could change with future work in both corridors.

In the last decade our understanding of Younger Dryas-aged WST sites and human lifeways has expanded with clear evidence of robust toolkits that included projectile points, a suite of formal flake tools, osseous technology, cordage, and possibly hide clothing and string (Connolly et al. 2016; Duke 2011; Goebel et al. 2011; Pratt et al. 2020; Rosencrance et al. 2019; Smith and Barker 2017; Smith et al. 2020). New evidence of Younger Dryas-aged WST occupations comes from sites such as the Connley Caves (Jenkins et al. 2017; McDonough et al. 2022; Rosencrance et al. 2022), Cougar Mountain Cave (Jamaldin 2018; Rosencrance et al. 2019), Paisley Caves (Blong et al. 2020; Jenkins et al. 2016; Taylor et al. 2020), Tule Lake Rockshelter (Erlandson, Kennett, Ingram, et al. 2014), Weed Lake Ditch (Pratt 2021; Smith et al. 2020; Wriston 2003), Bonneville Estates Rockshelter (Goebel, Hockett, et al. 2011, 2021; Hockett 2015) and the Wishbone site (Duke et al. 2022). There is a robust, holistic, and emerging picture of life in the Far West during the Younger Dryas that rivals any other region in North America.

We have also learned through renewed fieldwork and dating efforts that some WST sites are younger than previously proposed. Jazwa and colleagues (2021) provided a critical review of the single radiocarbon age on the Buhl burial (Green et al. 1998), showing that there was probably not adequate collagen preservation to produce a reliable radiocarbon date, and even if there was, the input of anadromous fish into her diet (indicated by the $\delta^{15}N$ value) means the existing radiocarbon age calibrates to the late Younger Dryas. Connolly and colleagues (2017) returned to Fort Rock Cave and found the site largely disturbed from previous excavation and looting. They were ultimately unable to confirm an occupation prior to ~10,500 cal BP, though a Younger Dryas occupation is suggested by Haskett points and a bulk charcoal date of 10,200 ± 200 ^{14}C BP (12,610–11,260 cal BP) obtained by Bedwell (1970, 1973). Regardless, there is little evidence the site dates to ~15,000 cal BP as suggested by Bedwell (1970). Keene's (2018) new radiocarbon dates from Veratic Rockshelter are much younger than those obtained by Swanson (1972), calibrating to between ~10,000 and 9500 cal BP, though Keene's dates are from dispersed charcoal in a >50 cm thick deposit with variable WST forms. Future work may be able to further refine the age of the site's earliest occupations. Such examples of renewed fieldwork and collection-based research with chronology building at their forefront have resulted in new outlooks on projectile point, textile, and general cultural chronologies throughout the Far West (Connolly et al. 2016; Rosencrance 2019; Smith et al. 2020).

Throughout the last decade, there also has been vigorous work on WST lithic technology (Beck and Jones 2015b; Davis et al. 2014, 2015, 2017; Davis and Willis 2018; Duke 2011, 2015; Duke and Stueber, Chapter 4; Hartman 2019; Lafayette and Smith 2012; Knell and Becker 2017; Knell et al. 2014; Pratt et al. 2020; Reaux 2021) and toolstone conveyance (Duke 2011; Jamaldin 2018; Jones et al. 2012; Lynch et al., Chapter 6; Newlander 2018; Reaux 2021; Smith 2010, 2011; Smith and Harvey 2018; Smith et al., Chapter 3). Broadly these studies elaborate on previous work, supporting the presence of a diverse WST toolkit that is clearly Paleoindian in nature, embedded within a residentially mobile system with distinguishable patterns between subregions.

We are also beginning to better understand the age and distribution of crescents (Moss and Erlandson 2013; Pratt 2021; Sanchez et al. 2017; Smith et al. 2014), though a definitive answer on their function remains enigmatic (Lenzi 2015). Additional subsistence data continue to support a relatively broad diet, with distinct use of botanical, faunal (both small and large game), and insect foods throughout the LP/EH (Blong et al. 2020; Duke et al. 2018; Hockett et al. 2017; Kennedy 2018; Kennedy and Smith 2016; McDonough et al. 2022; Pellegrini 2014).

Fluted point studies are ongoing, with particular emphasis placed on more gracile "post-Clovis" fluted points (sometimes referred to as Great Basin Fluted, Western Fluted, or "Clovis-like") in comparison to classic Clovis points (Beck and Jones 2010, 2013; Jones and Beck, Chapter 8; Rondeau 2015a; Rondeau et al., Chapter 9). Recently Beck, Jones, and colleagues (2019b) formally introduced the name "Sunshine Fluted," for these points, which they show are morphologically distinct from Clovis points. To them, Western Fluted/Sunshine Fluted points are generally smaller, narrower, have deeper basal concavities, variable numbers of fluting scars, and fine pressure flaking compared to classic Clovis points (Beck and Jones, Chapter 12; Beck, Hughes, and LaPierre 2019; Beck, Jones, and Taylor 2019; Jones and Beck, Chapter 8; see also Rondeau 2015a). Another intriguing pattern identified by multiple researchers is the prevalence of "flute scratching" on obsidian fluted points in the Far West (Beck, Jones, and Taylor 2019; Rondeau 2015a).

Clovis points and associated technologies are still present throughout the region, albeit in relatively low numbers (Beck, Jones, and Taylor 2019; Rondeau 2015a, 2015b), and researchers continue reporting on both new and existing sites north of Arizona, including Heil Pond (Reid 2011, 2017; Reid et al. 2015), Seagull Bay (Speer et al. 2019), Sage Hen Gap (O'Grady et al. 2008, 2009; Thomas et al. 2011), Sheep Mountain (O'Grady et al. 2009; O'Grady et al. 2011; Rondeau 2015b), North

Warner Valley (G. Smith, Felling, Wriston, et al. 2015), Twain Harte (Moratto et al. 2017), Nye Canyon (Rhode et al. 2022), and others. A Clovis point from Blackwater Draw in New Mexico, knapped from obsidian sourced to southwestern Utah, indicates some connection between the southern Plains and the Great Basin (Holen 2004; Madsen et al., eds. 2015). The largest paucity of fluted points anywhere on the continent is still the Columbia Plateau and regions north of the Mojave Desert and west of the Sierra Nevada and Cascade Ranges (Beck, Jones, and Taylor 2019; Rondeau 2015a).

While the cultural relationships between WST, Clovis, and Western/Sunshine Fluted in the Far West are actively debated, multiple researchers propose Clovis points in the Far West represent a distinct human population moving into the region, likely coming from the east (Beck and Jones 2010, 2013, Chapter 12; Davis et al. 2012; Grayson 2011; Jones and Beck, Chapter 8; O'Grady et al. 2012; G. Smith, Felling, Wriston, et al. 2015; Speer et al. 2019). These claims are bolstered by evidence of differential raw material and land-use patterns between Clovis and WST points in the northern Great Basin in areas such as Warner Valley, and sites such as Dietz, Sage Hen Gap, and Sheep Mountain (O'Grady et al. 2012; G. Smith, Felling, Wriston, et al. 2015; Wriston and Smith 2017). Even though more research is needed to fully explain these possible population interactions, this volume presents new hypotheses and explorations of those relationships.

As we round to the present, several key research developments are worth reviewing. In the last two decades, many researchers in the Far West have come to recognize the following: (1) the WST is a clear Paleoindian adaptation associated with high residential mobility and relatively broad-spectrum diets; (2) the WST is at least coeval with Clovis, and occupations older than Clovis are present in the region (although their relationship to WST is not explicitly clear); (3) as we begin to build more robust radiocarbon chronologies, we can tease apart regional point chronologies within the WST; and (4) typological and technological differences are observable between fluted points (both Clovis and post-Clovis) in the Far West.

Researchers are increasingly coming together to define and tackle these central questions. For example, the Wilson Workshop 1 cohosted by the Center for the Study of the First Americans (Texas A&M University), Hakai Institute (British Columbia), and University of Victoria in April 2018 brought together professors, First Nation representatives, graduate students, and professionals to exchange ideas resulting in a special issue of *PaleoAmerica* (Waters, Goebel, and Graf 2020). Smith and colleagues' (2020) overview of Intermountain West Paleoindian research problems and prospects in that issue recognizes that the peopling process is complicated, and therefore a replacement of "Clovis first" with "WST first" is not enough if we want to more broadly understand this event. More work needs to be done, especially to continue building chronologies, investigating sites from variable environmental contexts, and exploring technological and cultural relationships between WST and fluted points (both inter- and extra-regionally). It is clear to us, however, that irrespective of the lack of well-dated fluted points in the region, a critical review of the peopling of the Americas, or continental Paleoindian records, must include research from the Far West and of the WST.

Volume Overview

This volume brings together the work of researchers from across space and paradigms in response to an overarching question: *What is the chronological and morphological relationship between Western Stemmed, Western Fluted, Clovis, and other Paleoindian technocomplexes throughout the continent?* There are many ways to address this mammoth question, and we do so here primarily through the lens of lithic technology. While we don't agree with every conclusion drawn in the following chapters, they all shed new light on questions that have yet to be fully resolved.

The Western Stemmed Tradition

Part 1 focuses on chronology, morphology, regional variation, and conveyance of stemmed technology in the Far West. We recognize that this section is conspicuously longer than others but contend that the imbalance reflects the predominance of WST technology in the early archaeological record of the region.

The chronological and geographical expanse of the WST is vast, and a common assumption is that there is little understanding of change or chronological constraints for the varieties of stemmed points (Beck and Jones 1997; Bryan and Touhy 1999; Goebel and Keene 2014; Smith and Barker 2017). Rosencrance and colleagues (Chapter 2) demonstrate that although many questions remain, our understanding of WST point variability as it relates to chronology has progressed much further than some may think. Using a substantial compilation of radiocarbon dates, the authors constrain the age ranges of certain stemmed point types, including Haskett, which appears to be one of the earliest distinct and widespread WST styles in the Great Basin. They also identify increasing stylistic variation at the onset of the Early Holocene that coincides well with diversification of Paleoindian technology elsewhere in North America.

Chronology is followed by conveyance, as Smith and colleagues (Chapter 3) draw on an extensive collection of provenance data to assess what the movement of toolstone might reveal about human relationships and mobility in the northwestern Great Basin. They find rather similar patterns with both their Pleistocene-aged and Early Holocene-aged samples, which to them suggests people quickly became familiar with the northwestern Great Basin toolstone landscape and established procurement patterns that persisted for thousands of years.

Morphological analysis guides the next two chapters. Duke and Stueber (Chapter 4) compare size, design, and conveyance patterns of Haskett technology with that of Clovis points to address questions of function and the implications for initial settlement of the continent. Their work shows that both projectile styles represent specialized high-tech hunting technology that chronologically converge on the timing of the final megafauna extinctions. The authors highlight the need for refined regional approaches and biogeographic research related to the extinction process to more fully understand the relationship between Haskett and Clovis, and the longer persistence of the former. Knell and Sutton (Chapter 5) statistically characterize the morphological variability of Lake Mohave and Silver Lake projectile points in the Mojave Desert. In addition to assembling the largest database currently available for LP/EH points in the region ($n = 499$), the authors identify several key patterns in regional morphology and delineate testable hypotheses that can be further refined as the database grows. Their morphometric approach is able to quantitatively discriminate between the Lake Mohave and Silver Lake types—something that has eluded researchers for nearly a century.

The WST section concludes with more focused looks at two of the oldest WST assemblages from the Great Basin and Columbia Plateau. First, Lynch and colleagues (Chapter 6) analyze the biface assemblage from Smith Creek Cave and present a radiocarbon date (10,900 ± 30 ^{14}C BP; 12,750–12,885 cal BP) obtained on an uncharred twig from the stemmed-point-bearing Mount Moriah occupation zone. This date reaffirms the presence of Clovis-age deposits at the site initially argued by Bryan (1979, 1988), however, the authors note that the cultural origin of the twig is equivocal and renewed work at the site is needed to confirm or deny Bryan's original claims. Using a suite of analytical techniques including morphometrics, source provenance, and use wear, the authors are able to draw numerous inferences regarding toolstone procurement, reduction techniques, conveyance, and function from the modest Mount Moriah biface assemblage.

Second, Davis' thesis (Chapter 7) is that WST projectile points at Cooper's Ferry in Idaho minimally date to ~11,720 ^{14}C BP (~13,580 cal BP) and are thus centuries older than Clovis technology. He presents details about the context, age, and morphology of these early projectile points, which represent a new WST form that he provisionally calls the *Cooper's Ferry type*. Davis proposes that the age of the Cooper's Ferry points allows for the rejection of the hypothesis that the WST descended from Clovis, at least in the Columbia Plateau, and that the two technologies are unlikely to share a direct evolutionary relationship.

Fluted Technologies

Part II brings together our current understanding of fluted technology in the Far West. Jones and Beck (Chapter 8) provide a thorough synthesis of the historical study and current understanding of fluted points in the region. They begin with a detailed description of Clovis technology which lays necessary context for the following discussion of fluted point variability in the Intermountain West and the failure of some points to meet all Clovis criteria. Their chapter illustrates the danger in projecting perspectives of fluted technologies from the Great Plains and elsewhere to the Far West. Though the age of Far West fluted points continues to elude us, Jones and Beck provide a foundation from which to move forward, ending with a prospectus for future research aimed at clarifying the complex technological and sociocultural landscape that characterized the late Pleistocene.

Rondeau and colleagues (Chapter 9) present one of the first systematic characterizations of the variability described by Jones and Beck (Chapter 8), and their work serves as a prime example of how researchers might progress understandings of Far West fluted technology. Their research uses statistical analyses of morphometric data from four subregional fluted point clusters in the Great Basin, finding considerable variation that may relate to the size and quality of available toolstone and hafting material, as well as the effects of temporal, geographic, and collection method variability.

Surovell (Chapter 10) provides a view from the neighboring region of the Great Plains and Rocky Mountains (GPRM) with his synthesis of radiocarbon and stratigraphic evidence for the relative chronology of fluted and stemmed points there. In stark contrast to the Great Basin and other areas of the Far West, stratified open-air sites in the GPRM have repeatedly demonstrated the superposition of fluted and stemmed points, with the latter replacing the former sometime around 12,200 cal BP. Surovell proposes that if Clovis predates stemmed points in the Far West as it does on the Great Plains, and fluted technology was only in use there for several hundred years, then the rarity of Clovis artifacts in stratified contexts should be expected. The historical context of this research in the GPRM contains important examples and relevant data for unraveling stemmed and fluted relationships in the Far West.

Broader Interactions

Part III considers regional interactions and cultural transmission—perspectives that are essential to making broader connections between site- and subregion-specific studies. Beck and Jones (Chapter 12) build upon their previous work to consider information exchange between different groups who inhabited the Far West during the late Pleistocene. They propose that early WST technology represents the first people in the region and that fluted points signal a later incursion of Clovis makers who likely entered through the Snake River Plain sometime during the early Younger Dryas. They further propose that the first fluted point makers to enter the Far West left behind their own tools but also influenced the way WST groups produced theirs. Ideas for tool production were exchanged indirectly or directly, resulting in a post-Clovis fluted variant in the Far West and a biface reduction system in the WST.

Moving south, Keyes (Chapter 11) uses geometric morphometrics to examine enigmatic stemmed points of the Southwest. Through a comparison of Hell Gap points from the Great Plains and WST points from the eastern Great Basin with a large assemblage of contracting stemmed points from the Tularosa Basin of New Mexico, Keyes finds that the New Mexico assemblage more closely resembles WST points. Her work has important implications for the understanding of stemmed points in the Southwest, particularly the Jay points of the Oshara Tradition, and the rarely considered interaction between the Great Basin and Southwest.

Erlandson and colleagues (Chapter 13) share a view from the far side of the southern Far West with their discussion of a WST variant along the Pacific Coast which they name the *Island Paleocoastal Tradition* (IPT). The IPT is characterized by an absence of fluted points and presence of crescents and small stemmed and tanged projectile types including Channel Islands Amol and Channel Islands Barbed points. Erlandson and colleagues explore the link between projectile points of the IPT and stemmed technologies of the Intermountain West, drawing heavily on the extensive work that they and others have conducted on the Northern Channel Islands where more than 100 sites older than 8000 cal BP have been recorded. The authors suggest common ancestry between WST and IPT and predict that future work will reveal both are linked to an early migration into the Americas along the Pacific Rim.

Conclusions

This volume and the decades of research that precede demonstrate that the technological and cultural landscapes of the late Pleistocene in North America were more complex and diverse than traditionally recognized. Authors throughout this volume intentionally focus on the technological, chronological, and spatial relationships of WST and fluted points. This focus on stone tool technology and WST's relationship to fluted points reflects historic interests. At the same time, the work here and elsewhere strongly suggests that WST and fluted point users interacted in some places but have different origins and histories. As such, moving forward we need to consider WST technology and makers on their own terms. Doing so may lead us to reconsider some long-held perceptions about Pleistocene lifeways, provoke new questions, and generally broaden archaeological perspectives surrounding the First Peoples of the Western Hemisphere.

Many exciting avenues of future research promise to expand our understanding of WST makers in the Far West. For example, work of the past two decades has demonstrated that the region has some of the most diverse dietary evidence on the continent (e.g., Blong et al. 2020; Gill et al. 2021; Hockett 2015; Hockett et al. 2017; Kennedy 2018; Louderback and Pavlik 2017; McDonough et al. 2022). These studies coupled with advancing analytical techniques show great potential for further macroscopic, microscopic, and molecular approaches to studying human nutrition, health, and seasonal mobility at both open-air and rockshelter sites.

Similarly, significant research has developed paleoecological, geologic, and hydrologic records over the last century (e.g., Goebel et al. 2021; McLaren et al. 2019). These studies highlight the importance of refining local landscape histories and leave abundant opportunities for further environmental reconstructions throughout the Far West. Such work is critical for interpreting archaeological records, informing theoretical models, and developing predictive models to identify new sites. On the cutting edge are biomolecular studies, such as genetics, proteomics, and lipid analyses, that are providing powerful new tools for identifying residues and reconstructing natural and cultural histories (e.g., Hendy 2021; Shillito et al. 2020). Complete genome research has and will continue to change the way we understand group interactions and the timing of early migrations (see Raff 2022; Willerslev and Meltzer 2021).

In addition to diversifying our methods, we need to diversify the field. A holistic view of Pleistocene lifeways will not be achieved through a homogenous lens, and if we seek to understand and actualize the First Peoples of the Americas, we should be talking with, listening to, and involving their relatives who are here today. We acknowledge and regret that Indigenous voices are not represented in this volume, and that this absence reflects the broader lack of Indigenous representation in North American Pleistocene archaeology (Pitblado 2022; Steeves 2021). Indigenous ontologies, oral histories, and traditional knowledge are indispensable ways of knowing, yet are infrequently included in research programs. Considering Indigenous perspectives and research interests at the onset of research projects will no doubt lead to improved understandings about the First Peoples, and cultural and social aspects of their lives that have gone unrecognized.

Much room remains for growth within Pleistocene research of the Far West, but in reviewing the history of this field it is also apparent that many of the ideas proposed by early Far Western researchers such as Elizabeth and Bill Campbell, Luther Cressman, and Alan Bryan were well reasoned based on their limited evidence relative to today. This illustrates that thinking outside of the dominant paradigm is valuable. The archaeological record is inherently incomplete, and having multiple working hypotheses is the most prudent way to investigate the past.

Our hope is that this volume also highlights the importance of making cross-regional connections. Understanding the peopling and settling-in processes of the Americas must take a similar approach and discard the superficial sociopolitical and continental boundaries for more holistic views that consider North, Central, and South America together. We do not expect that all researchers will agree with the ideas presented in this volume, nor do we feel that is necessary. Instead, we believe that differences in perspective—based on expertise, solid evidence, and thoughtful review—will result in a more complete view of the Pleistocene record within the Far West and the larger picture of the peopling of the Americas.

PART I

Stemmed Technologies

2

Western Stemmed Tradition Projectile Point Chronology in the Intermountain West

Richard L. Rosencrance, Daron Duke,
Amanda Hartman, *and* Andrew Hoskins

Deciphering chronological sequences for stylistically diagnostic projectile point forms has been a foundation of North American Paleoindian archaeology for almost a century (Holliday 2000). That foundation has largely been derived from the Great Plains and Rocky Mountains([GPRM] sensu Surovell, Chapter 10) where numerous extinct megafauna kill sites and deep stratigraphic sequences of projectile points provide a recognizable and cogent framework (Bryan 1988; Surovell, Chapter 10; Wormington 1957). The limited amount of such evidence in the Intermountain West (Great Basin and Columbia Plateau) has sidelined the region in discussions of Paleoindian projectile point chronologies with researchers assuming Western Stemmed Tradition (WST) forms, which dominate the record, coexist over millennia (Beck and Jones 1997; Willig and Aikens 1988). Similarly, because of the absence of a well-dated Clovis or fluted point site, a relative lack of fluted points in the record, and the historic dominance of the Clovis-first hypothesis, the Intermountain West Paleoindian record is often viewed as a regional development out of Clovis and Folsom in the GPRM (Fiedel and Morrow 2012; Reid et al. 2015; Surovell, Chapter 10; Willig and Aikens 1988).

Much debate exists among Intermountain West archaeologists regarding fluted and stemmed point chronologies and general acceptance that WST types do not meaningfully vary in age (Beck and Jones 1997, 2010; Brown et al. 2019; Bryan and Tuohy 1999; Davis et al. 2012; Goebel and Keene 2014). But a large-scale effort to investigate WST sites in recent decades, both in terms of new fieldwork and the revisiting of old collections, is providing fresh insight into WST issues that suffer from lack of chronometric data (Figure 2.1; Rosencrance 2019; McDonough et al., Chapter 1; Smith and Barker 2017; Smith et al. 2020). In this chapter we consolidate and evaluate the existing WST radiocarbon record in order to explore what it says about the age of different WST forms, how it compares to the GPRM record, and finally, what all of that might tell us about our broader understanding of the peopling of the Americas.

Comparisons of other regional Paleoindian projectile point chronologies to the Intermountain West and arguments about potential relationships have always been limited by a lack of refined WST chronology in the region (Beck and Jones 2010; Bryan and Tuohy 1999; Goebel and Keene 2014). Researchers established decades ago that WST points, not fluted points, are found in the basal components of sites throughout the Intermountain West (Bedwell 1970; Bryan 1980; Cressman 1942; Layton 1970; McDonough

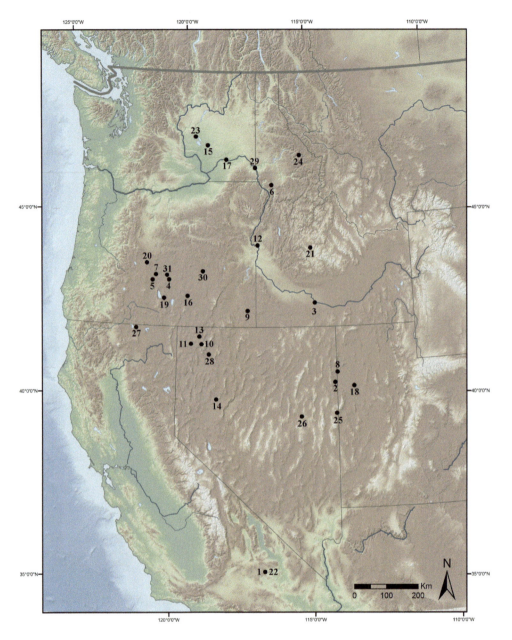

FIGURE 2.1. Map of Western Stemmed Tradition (WST) sites discussed in text: (*1*) Awl site; (*2*) Bonneville Estates Rockshelter; (*3*) Buhl burial; (*4*) Dietz site; (*5*) Connley Caves; (*6*) Cooper's Ferry; (*7*) Cougar Mountain Cave; (*8*) Danger Cave; (*9*) Dirty Shame Rockshelter; (*10*) Five Mile Flat (Parman Localities); (*11*) Hanging Rock Shelter; (*12*) Hetrick site; (*13*) Last Supper Cave; (*14*) Leonard Rockshelter; (*15*) Lind Coulee; (*16*) LSP-1 Rockshelter; (*17*) Marmes Rockshelter; (*18*) Old River Bed Delta (ORBD) and Wishbone; (*19*) Paisley Caves; (*20*) Paulina Lake; (*21*) Redfish Overhang; (*22*) Rodgers Ridge; (*23*) Sentinel Gap; (*24*) Alpha and Beta Rockshelters; (*25*) Smith Creek Cave; (*26*) Sunshine Locality; (*27*) Tule Lake Rockshelter; (*28*) Wallman Bison; (*29*) Wewukiyepuh; (*30*) 35LK2593; (*31*) 35LK1880, 35LK1881, and 35LK2095 (Bunny Pits).

et al., Chapter 1). Those researchers were acutely aware of (and in various cases, defined) the variable forms of WST projectile points but, largely unsuccessfully, grappled with making sense of what the variation meant (Amsden 1937; Bedwell 1970; Butler 1965; Daugherty 1956; Layton 1970; Leonhardy and Rice 1970; Swanson 1972; Tuohy 1969).

It has always been clear that different WST projectile point forms are technologically comparable and associated with similar ecological settings such as pluvial lakes, deltas, riverine settings, and wetlands. As a result, researchers of the twentieth century developed numerous models that broadly connected WST points and the cultural lifeways of the people who used them (Bedwell 1970; Butler 1961; Davis 1963; Layton 1970; Leonhardy and Rice 1970; Tuohy and Layton 1977; Warren 1967; Willig and Aikens 1988). Several works hypothesized relationships between Intermountain West stemmed points and those on the GPRM, although the nature of the relationship varied (Bryan 1980, 1988; Daugherty 1956; Tuohy 1969, 1974). As mentioned above, the relatively rare occurrence of stratified sequences of Paleoindian sites in the Intermountain West precluded a convincing WST projectile point chronology during those times.

Beyond a dearth of dated sites, efforts to understand WST projectile point variation are confounded by a great deal of overlap in morphology between forms (Figure 2.2). For example, the shoulder-less Haskett style is easily distinguishable from other forms when specimens are complete or mostly complete; however, small basal Haskett fragments can resemble Cougar Mountain basal fragments (Duke and Stueber, Chapter 4). Intraresearcher identification and point typing also plague our ability to form a coherent WST projectile point sequence. This issue is partially due to the fact that researchers are sometimes slow to adopt new evidence. The persistence and entanglement of the various Windust concepts developed in the early 1970s, that we discuss below (Beck and Jones 2009; Brown et al. 2019; Willig and Aikens 1988), is a prime example. But these problems of morphological overlap are not unique to the Intermountain West, as anyone engaged in the Plainview-Goshen or Midland-Folsom debates of the GPRM can attest (e.g., Holliday et al. 2017; Lassen 2015).

Difficulties aside, there is a body of research that focuses on WST projectile point stylistic variability as it might relate to chronology. A number of researchers have proposed that longer stemmed varieties such as Haskett, Cougar Mountain, and Lake Mohave are older than short-stemmed varieties such as Silver Lake and Parman. Layton (1970, 1972, 1979) argued this model using obsidian hydration measurements and the stratified sequences at Cougar Mountain Cave and Hanging Rock Shelter. He hypothesized the existence of two sequences, one from Cougar Mountain to Parman in the northern Great Basin and the other from Lake Mohave to Silver Lake in the southern Great Basin. Duke (2011; Duke and King 2014; Smith et al. 2020) has similarly argued that age is the primary driver of meaningful stylistic variability, especially if subtypes are grouped into broader morphological categories based on size and stem shape. He has contended that on the Old River Bed Delta (ORBD) larger and longer/wider-stemmed styles (e.g., Haskett, Cougar Mountain, Lake Mohave, and certain Parman forms) date earlier than shorter/narrower-stemmed styles (e.g., Silver Lake, Bonneville, and Stubby) based on the relative ages of dated stream channel deposits and spatial distribution of point types. Duke (2011) also found technological and land-use changes accompanying this trend.

While pre-1990s radiocarbon data confirmed the late Pleistocene/Early Holocene (LP/EH) antiquity of WST projectile points, the resolution of those data is coarse. The most recent attempts of ^{14}C data consolidation come from Beck and Jones (1997; Jones and Beck 1999) and Bryan and Tuohy (1999). Beck and Jones (1997:189–190, 196) specifically asked whether different point forms vary in age, stating that based on the available data "it is difficult to argue temporal differences among these types" and instead favored resharpening, breakage, or functional differences as the primary drivers of morphological variability (also see Beck and Jones 2009:216; 2015b:157). Bryan and Tuohy (1999:251) likewise eschewed a chronological explanation, contending that "projectile point hafting traditions should not be used as period markers" and more specifically asserting that the central Great Plains sequence "should not be extrapolated either west or east of the Plains." Each study concluded that stemmed point types in the Intermountain West fall between ~11,200–7100 ^{14}C BP (Beck and Jones 1997) or ~11,000–8500 ^{14}C BP (Bryan and Tuohy 1999). As often-cited review articles, these studies have resonated with regional archaeologists, and over two decades later, the positions remain largely unchanged or presumed among many researchers.

Refinements in radiocarbon dating and the discovery of more reliably dated WST sites over the past 20 years allow for a reassessment of the age-variation hypothesis. To further address the possibility of change over time, this chapter provides three main contributions. We: (1) compile and critically evaluate the current radiocarbon record associated with widely recognized WST projectile point forms; (2) present new images and descriptions of WST points; and (3) provide new radiocarbon dates and interpretations associated with WST points. From these data, we are able to consider a more refined view of the WST projectile point chronology across time and space and how that compares to the well-established GPRM record.

Methods and Materials
Projectile Points

We examine nine WST projectile point types in this study (see Figure 2.2; Table 2.1). We do not discuss their primary definitions and literature in detail (except for Windust, Table 2.1) but recommend Beck and Jones 2009, 2015b; Duke 2011; Smith and colleagues 2020; and Rosencrance 2019 for recent considerations. We recognize the overlapping and variable nature of WST point morphology and the comparative limitations this imposes. Table 2.1 provides the identification scheme we employ here. It is developed from the primary literature and some of our own work (Duke 2011; Hartman 2019; Rosencrance 2019).

We examined every projectile point that we assigned a type, either through firsthand analysis or the use of published images. We do not always type projectile points the same way as the original authors. Our assignments are firmly grounded in the scheme outlined in Table 2.1 in an attempt to minimize ad hoc classifications. Some points do not fit neatly into an idealized form definition, but our approach accounts for this by focusing on broader patterns of stem shape and length, as well as the prominence, shape, and design of shoulders. The scheme also considers technological attributes such as flaking, manufacture, and retouch strategies (see Table 2.1).

Technological research on WST technology generally confirms the utility of the types in Table 2.1 (Beck and Jones 2009, 2015b; Davis et al. 2012; Davis et al. 2014; Davis et al. 2017; Duke 2011; Duke and Stueber, Chapter 4; Graf 2001; Hartman 2019; Knell and Sutton, Chapter 5; Smith 2007; Pratt et al. 2020). Still, modes of projectile point manufacture, maintenance, and discard are critical to consider in arguments of cultural and chronological affiliation of types. Multiple researchers have stressed that assuming a particular projectile point type is a cultural or chronological marker is not always valid, and specifically, that one type may change to another by maintenance and breakage during its use life (Flenniken and Raymond 1986; Shott 1996).

Beck and Jones (1993, 2009) proposed and tested these concerns (i.e., a resharpening continuum) regarding WST point forms, finding that breakage patterns (probably linked to design, e.g., Davis et al. 2017; Musil 1988) dictate how and where resharpening can occur. The consistency in neck width of all types in their sample precludes the chance that a large basal stem element (from a Haskett or Cougar Mountain) can be reworked into the blade of a shorter form (e.g., Parman or Silver Lake). A resharpening continuum would also require resharpening to primarily occur on bases, considering those are the most common fragments found that could be interpreted as different types. Rather, Beck and Jones (2009) find resharpening almost always occurred on blades—largely invalidating the resharpening continuum hypothesis. Thus, we assume here that WST knappers designed specific templates of forms and that resharpening plays a minor role in determining the widely held types outlined in Table 2.1.

Beck and Jones (2009) and Lafayette and Smith (2012) also assessed whether functional differences explain WST point variability. Both studies suggest that WST points likely served a variety of functions throughout their use lives, including use as knives, thrusting spears, and projectiles. Those studies are limited in scope compared to the broader WST record, so future use wear studies could provide new functional insights. Regardless, we assume here that all WST points were designed and intended to be used as projectiles first. A number of studies have observed hallmarks of projectile use such as basal edge grinding and impact and burination fractures (Fischer et al. 1984) on WST points that support our assumption (Beck and Jones 2009, 2015b; Duke 2011, 2015; Duke and Stueber, Chapter 4; Lafayette and Smith 2012; Lynch et al., Chapter 6; Rosencrance et al. 2022).

The last consideration is that basal morphology of projectile points is the most reliable way to distinguish between types because bases are not typically subject to resharpening like blade elements are—something established through traditional morphometric analysis and more recent geometric morphometric approaches (Beck and Jones 2009; Hartman 2019; Lohse and Moser 2014; Musil 1988; Smith and Goebel 2018; Thomas 1981; Thulman 2012). Our typological scheme considers total length, the length of stems relative to total length, and in some cases shoulder morphology, because of the significant overlap in basal morphologies of most WST point types. For instance, blade shape and shoulder configuration are sometimes the only way to distinguish between a Haskett and a Cougar Mountain point. Hartman (2019) shows that shoulder configuration can be a discriminating attribute with at least some WST types.

Indeed, our type assignments consider basal shape and technology first, leaving less reliable attributes such as total length to make more refined calls when possible. This conundrum exemplifies the longstanding problem with WST typology. A more ambitious consideration of WST point variability such as a geometric morphometric approach (e.g., Davis et al. 2017) is beyond the scope of this study, and we are working under the assumption that widely held typologies have practical value for assessing chronological trends.

Clarifying Windust

Because "Windust" refers to a specific projectile point form, a regional phase, and a projectile point series, it may be one of the most ambiguous terms practitioners use to describe WST points (Table 2.2). The aforementioned concepts are derived from one another and researchers often confuse them or use them inconsistently. To achieve future clarity and consistency, we provide a brief history of each application, followed by a discussion of why it is necessary to apply them explicitly and correctly.

All Windust concepts derive their name from the Windust Caves, a series of nine caves located along the north bank of the Lower Snake River in southeastern Washington state. Harvey Rice (1965) excavated the caves between 1959 and 1961 and observed what he called two lithic traditions in the lowest deposits of Windust Cave (originally Windust Cave C). Tradition 1 points are lanceolate in shape with broad, shallow transverse or collateral flake scars with very little retouching and are thin in relation to their width. His Windust "Type" is within Tradition 1 and differs from the tradition's other two point forms by having more distinct shoulders, a broader stem in relation to the blade, and a

FIGURE 2.2. Type specimens for WST projectile point types: (*a–b*) Haskett points, Haskett site; (*c*) Cougar Mountain, Cougar Mountain Cave; (*d–f*) Lind Coulee Types 1, 2, 3, Lind Coulee site; (*g*) Windust/square, Granite Point; (*h*) Windust, Marmes Rockshelter; (*i*) Parman, Parman Localities; (*j*) Lake Mohave, Lake Mojave; (*k*) Silver Lake, Lake Mojave; (*l*) Bonneville, Old River Bed Delta; (*m*) Stubby, Old River Bed Delta. Note that different Haskett and Lind Coulee types are consolidated into single types now. Images (*j*) and (*k*) are courtesy of Ed Knell, and (*l*) and (*m*) are courtesy of Daron Duke.

TABLE 2.1. Western Stemmed Tradition Type Definitions.

Type (Reference)	Stem (Base)	Shoulders	Cross Section	Flaking	Stem Margin	Stem Length	Region(s)	Other Notes
Haskett (Butler 1965; Duke 2015)	tapers to a rounded base that can exhibit variability; heavy grinding	none	lenticular or diamond	broad collateral followed by fine pressure	tapering	longer than width	GB and CP	grinding can extend ⅔ of length
Cougar Mountain (Layton 1970)	tapers to rounded base; heavy grinding	sloping	lenticular or diamond	broad collateral followed by fine pressure	tapering	longer than width	GB	base similar to Haskett
Lind Coulee (Daugherty 1956)	usually short but sometimes ~⅓ length; rounded with light grinding	pronounced	plano-convex to lenticular	moderate-sized collateral followed by fine pressure	parallel or tapering	shorter than width	CP	few dated sites
Parman (Layton 1970)	short, rounded or tongued; basal grinding present	pronounced	plano-convex to lenticular	collateral and irregular, followed by fine pressure	parallel or tapering	longer or shorter than width	GB	varies between EGB and NWGB
Windust (Lohse 1994; Rice 1965)	parallel margins and concave base; grinding on margins and concavity	squared	lenticular	broad, shallow transverse to collateral, little retouching	parallel	shorter than width	CP and GB	bases are distinct from other WST
Windust/square (Rice 1965; Rice 1972; this study)	parallel margins with square base; grinding present on basal margins	squared	lenticular	precise collateral to transverse percussion and pressure	parallel	shorter than width	CP and GB	very similar to Alberta/Cody
Lake Mohave (Amsden 1937)	rounded, takes up at least ½ of point size. grinding present	sloping	plano-convex to lenticular	moderate-sized collateral and irregular	tapering	longer than width	GB	blades often heavily reworked
Silver Lake (Amsden 1937)	very short, expanding, and rounded	pronounced	plano-convex to lenticular	irregular	parallel or tapering	less than or equal to width	GB	flared, half-circle base is diagnostic
Bonneville (Duke 2011)	very short (<⅓ of length), informal, vary widely	crude, constricted	plano-convex	irregular, crude, minimal	any	less than or equal to width	EGB	overall crude and expedient
Dugway Stubby (Schmitt et al. 2007)	square, round, or flat.	square to sloping	plano-convex	irregular	contracting to parallel	irregular	EGB	blades heavily reworked

Note: GB = Great Basin; CP = Columbia Plateau; EGB = Eastern Great Basin; NWGB = Northwest Great Basin.

TABLE 2.2. A Summary of Windust Concepts by Researcher.

Concept	Type	Phase	Series
Author	H. Rice 1965	Leonhardy and D. Rice 1970; D. Rice 1972	Lohse 1995; Lohse and Schou 2008
Examples and assumed ages	Windust "Type" 10,200 cal BP Tradition 1	11,500–10,200 cal BP Early subphase 10,200–8900 cal BP Late subphase	Windust A, B, and C/Farrington Base-notched (H. Rice 1965)
	10,200–8300 cal BP Tradition 2		
Description	The Windust "Type" point has a lanceolate blade, broad shallow flake scars, and is thin relative to width.	Constituents of an assemblage that suggests evolutionary ties to earlier Lind Coulee and later Cascade assemblages.	A series of projectile points that includes stemmed and unstemmed lanceolate forms with straight and indented bases.
Interpretive significance	The point type was recovered from the basal layers of the type site and represents an early lithic tradition.	Suggests an Early Archaic riverine adaptation of an in situ population.	Early Holocene projectile points.

Note: Age ranges are those assigned by original works, not the ages evaluated in this chapter.

concave base (Figure 2.2h). Tradition 2 points are thicker than those in Tradition 1 and exhibit random flake scars, retouching, and edge grinding along the stem. Tradition 2 also includes points that have parallel stems and straight bases (e.g., Figure 2.2g).

Leonhardy and (David) Rice (1970:2) proposed the Windust phase conceptually as a "synchronic stylistic macrostructure which articulates a polythetic set of similar components found within a region" or in other words, a "regional cultural type." To formulate this regional cultural type, they used the earliest cultural assemblages from Marmes Rockshelter, Granite Point, and Windust Caves, all located on the Lower Snake River. As such, their definition of the Windust Phase encompasses a suite of projectile point forms (including those defined by H. Rice from Windust Caves), flake tools, other cultural remains, and riverine settlement/subsistence strategies from time-transgressive archaeological deposits. It is important to note that: (1) they only had radiocarbon dates (mostly on unreliable freshwater shell) from Marmes Rockshelter to estimate the age of the Windust phase at that time; and (2) we now know they were combining materials from occupations spanning a thousand years as a singular regional cultural type.

D. Rice (1972)—again using materials from Windust Caves, Granite Point, and Marmes Rockshelter—proposed a model in which the Windust phase represents a time when Columbia Plateau groups moved into the Lower Snake River drainage system and pursued a lifeway that exploited riverine resources. He also proposed the Windust phase as part of a larger somewhat homogenous cultural complex, similar to how we view the WST today. Of the tools in those assemblages, D. Rice (1972) identified seven main projectile point forms that he believed to be contemporaneous and continuous at Marmes, Granite Point, and Windust Caves. Some, but not all of projectile point forms within the Windust Phase are congruent with H. Rice's (1965) Tradition 1 and 2 at Windust Cave. D. Rice's Windust Phase suffers from the same two interpretive limitations to that of Leonhardy and Rice (1970) listed above.

Finally, Lohse (1994) suggested that Paleoindian projectile points on the Columbia Plateau can be described as lanceolate or shouldered lanceolate. He applied discriminant function to a sample of both and identified a clear separation between shouldered lanceolate forms he calls Windust A (one of the types in H. Rice's Tradition 2) which are shouldered with a straight base, and Windust B which are shouldered with a concave base (H. Rice's Windust type).

Considerable overlap, as well as disconnect, is evident among the Windust concepts outlined above (see Table 2.2). Each includes points that have defined shoulders, slightly contracting to slightly expanding stems with either straight or concave bases, and lenticular cross sections. However, an important interpretive difference remains in how these concepts should be employed. The Windust Phase (Leonhardy and Rice 1970; Rice 1972) is intended to refer to the sets of cultural assemblages in the earliest deposits at the type sites, and more broadly the Lower Snake River (i.e., the regional cultural type): not a projectile point type per se. Both D. Rice's (1972) and Leonhardy and Rice's (1970) assemblage groupings are biased by imprecise knowledge of artifact vertical distribution and 1970s radiocarbon dating. They are simply grouping too many artifacts from too long of a time span to be of much use in projectile point sequences today. We posit that WST as a moniker for the broad technological tradition that D. Rice (1972) envisioned is more appropriate than Windust phase, especially considering the complexity of using the name "Windust" as we have reviewed here.

We think Windust as a projectile point type name should refer to points congruent with the Windust type as described by H. Rice (1965) and Lohse's (1994) Windust B—specifically those with a concave base. Square-based points (Lohse's Windust A) in the Intermountain West do not appear to be associated with

TABLE 2.3. Chronological ^{14}C Hygiene Scoring System Employed to Evaluate the Existing WST ^{14}C Record.

A. Sample type
1. Bulk carbon, bone without reporting of dated fraction, freshwater shell date, or marine shell without isotope values
2. Unidentified dispersed charcoal, collagen from bone, or dispersed marine shell with isotopes
3. Unidentified, dispersed charcoal, or collagen from bone associated with non-hearth cultural features (i.e. activity area, living floor) or single occupational site.
4. Unidentified hearth charcoal or bone collagen from close association of hearth, identified dispersed charcoal, identified hearth charcoal with "old wood" possible.
5. Identified hearth charcoal with "old wood" not ruled out or dispersed bone with specific amino acids identified.
6. Identified hearth charcoal with "old wood" ruled out, cut-marked bone with specific amino acids identified, or direct date on artifact.

B. Sample measurement and lab reporting
1. Conventional bone without pretreatment reported or not on collagen, any freshwater shell date.
2. Conventional organic, collagen bone date, or marine shell with reported isotopes.
3. AMS bone date on collagen or amino acid without reporting isotopes.
4. AMS organic, single amino acid bone date, or marine shell with reported isotope values.

C. Positive association of sample and archaeology [a]
1. Association unlikely (i.e. paleontological setting).
2. Association possible due to presence of archaeology; however, materials diffusely distributed.
3. Association likely due to numbers and spatial patterning of cultural remains.
4. Association highly likely due to demonstrated functional relationship.
5. Full certainty of association due to direct assay on anthropogenic item or feature.

D. Relevance of dating sample to a specific diagnostic archaeological phenomenon
1. No artifacts associated with sample.
2. Dispersed charcoal <10 cm above or below diagnostic archaeological material.
3. Dates cultural feature but relationship with diagnostic artifacts is ambiguous.
4. Association highly likely because radiocarbon sample is on hearth feature stratigraphically associated with diagnostic archaeological material.

E. Quantity and character of age estimates[a]
1. Only determination for given cultural layer or one of several that falls outside of a 2 σ range.
2. Determination is one of only two for given cultural layer and overlaps at 2 σ range.
3. Determination is one of three in a given cultural layer that overlap at 2 σ range.
4. Determination is one of four in a given cultural layer that overlap at 2 σ range.
5. Determination is one of five in a given cultural layer that overlap at 2 σ range.

F. Standard deviation
1. >500
2. 500–200
3. 199–100
4. 99–50
5. <50

G. Stratigraphic context and age of sample[b]
1. No obvious correlation between age and stratigraphic context or stratigraphic context unknown.
2. Age determination does not fit stratigraphic context but overlaps at 2 σ with one or more other determinations in stratum or cultural layer
3. Age determination is only date and fits stratigraphic context or does not overlap with other determinations at 2 σ.
4. Age determination fits stratigraphic context and overlaps at 2 σ with at least one other determination.
5. Age determination fits stratigraphic context and overlaps at 2 σ with at least two other determinations.

[a] From Pettit et al. 2003.
[b] From Graf 2009.

a specific environmental context, assemblage, or adaptive strategy. Rather, these points may represent transmontane interaction during the Early Holocene (Amick 2013; Hartman 2019). The Windust Phase should be applied to an Early Holocene riverine adaptive strategy described by Leonhardy and Rice (1970) and should not be used as a stand-in for all stemmed projectile points on the Plateau (e.g., Brown et al. 2019). We propose that moving forward there be two type names: (1) Windust, that describes shouldered concave base points of H. Rice's (1965) "Windust type" and Lohse's (1994) Windust B (Figure 2.2h); and (2) Windust/square, that describes square-based points in H. Rice's (1965) Tradition 2, and Lohse's (1994) Windust A (Figure 2.2g). Windust/square points resemble Alberta/Cody points from the GPRM (Hartman 2019; Knell and Muñiz 2013). We use this nomenclature herein.

Radiocarbon Dataset Evaluation

Critically evaluating radiocarbon datasets is paramount to establishing precise chronological models. Objective evaluation criteria, sometimes referred to as chronological hygiene methods, provide equitable and transparent ways to evaluate radiocarbon datasets. Before engaging in specific evaluation criteria, it was necessary for us to cull sites worth evaluating. First, for us to consider a site, it must contain a WST projectile point and have reported, relevant stratigraphic information. For example, sites like Fort Rock Cave and Elephant Mountain Cave contained WST projectile points and have reliable radiocarbon dates from textile artifacts, but the relationships of dates to specific points and the nature of the stratigraphy is extremely limited due to imprecise excavation methods or looting. Such sites are not included in this review.

Table 2.3 displays the evaluation criteria we used to assess the reliability of the WST radiocarbon record. These criteria are largely developed from Graf (2009) and Pettit and colleagues (2003) but with some of our own modifications. It evaluates the methodological, archaeological, and stratigraphic contexts of any date(s) associated with a WST point and results in nominal scores between 0–27. We use 13 as a pass-fail value, assuming that any combination of these criteria that equals more than 13 can be considered relatively reliable—the higher the score, the more reliable the date. We choose to do a pass/fail system instead of a three-tiered system (sensu Graf 2009; Pettit et al. 2003) for simplicity. Nonetheless, this explicit criterion provides transparent justification for accepting and rejecting dates while allowing for refinements with new parameters and information in future iterations. We still discuss some sites without ideal dates or contexts, as in some cases they provide tentative evidence that agrees with the reliable evidence that can be confirmed or rejected with future work.

We chose not to analyze the reliable WST radiocarbon record using Bayesian statistics beyond calibration (Bronk Ramsey 2009), again, for the sake of simplicity. We are fully aware and acknowledge we could constrain the start and end intervals of forms with more formal models. Instead, we view the calibrated 95.4% probability distribution ranges of the oldest and youngest reliable dates as endpoints for a particular point type.

Throughout the chapter, we use both radiocarbon dates (^{14}C BP) and their calibrated 95.4% probability distribution ranges (cal BP) when discussing specific dates or components. We also use approximate radiocarbon years (e.g., ~9800 ^{14}C BP) when discussing general trends across the region because one calibrated age is not necessarily correct or representative of the timing we discuss in those contexts. These considerations are particularly salient in the Discussion section. All dates are calibrated with the IntCal20 curve (Reimer et al. 2020) using OxCal v4.4 (Bronk Ramsey 2009) and rounded following the conventions of Stuiver and Polach (1977).

New WST Projectile Point Data

This chapter provides new information on seven WST sites: (1) the Connley Caves; (2) Tule Lake Rockshelter; (3) Paulina Lake; (4) three sites from the Bunny Pits complex;

and (5) Danger Cave (see Figure 2.1). Relevant background information and details about samples submitted for radiocarbon dating are provided below.

The Connley Caves (35LK50) are a string of eight shallow rockshelters located in Oregon's Fort Rock Basin in the far northwestern Great Basin (Figure 2.1). Bedwell (1970, 1973) reported a large number of stemmed projectile points and LP/EH radiocarbon dates from the site. His expedient excavations and the stratigraphic inversion of some radiocarbon dates have prompted researchers to question the reliability of the site's stemmed point chronology (Goebel et al. 2011; Goebel and Keene 2014; Rosencrance et al. 2022). The University of Oregon (UO) Archaeological Field School recently completed its tenth year of ongoing reinvestigations at the site (Jenkins et al. 2017; McDonough et al. 2022). Here, we address the types of complete WST projectile points from Connley Caves 4 and 5 and their spatial relationships to radiocarbon-dated cultural features. We submitted three isolated charcoals from Cave 5 and two isolated charcoal samples from Cave 4, all recovered by recent UO investigations.

Tule Lake Rockshelter (CASIS218A) is in northern California just south of present-day Klamath Lake. Radiocarbon ages indicate that eyed bone needles and three "edge ground stemmed points" date to the Younger Dryas (Erlandson et al. 2014:778). We recently revisited the collection at the University of California, Davis to examine and photograph the points to assign types.

The Paulina Lake site was excavated by the UO Museum of Natural and Cultural History between 1990 and 1992 as part of a highway widening and realignment project (Connolly 1999). Containing both Windust and Windust/square points inside a house, it has long served as a very important early site at the borderlands of the southern Columbia Plateau and northern Great Basin. While relatively well dated, existing radiocarbon dates from the central hearth and house posts have standard deviations between 80 and 100 years. We submitted a charcoal sample from Feature 7 (central hearth) and Feature 8 (house post) to improve chronological precision of the house and its timing of use (Connolly and Jenkins 1999).

The Bunny Pits are a series of open-air sites located in the Buffalo Flats area of the Christmas Valley sub-basin in the Fort Rock Basin, Oregon (see Figure 2.1). Heritage Research Associates, Inc. conducted a large cultural resource management survey and excavation project at Buffalo Flats in the late 1980s that identified many surface sites and several sites shallowly buried in sand dunes (Oetting 1994). They are referred to as the Bunny Pits because they contained large combustion features consisting almost exclusively of leproid bones—one (35LK1880) with more than 14,000 elements—providing evidence for early communal rabbit hunting (Aikens et al. 2011). All four of the sites produced WST point fragments (Windust/square and WST bases) and LP/EH-aged radiocarbon dates, though some of the standard deviations are more than 150 years. We submitted charcoal samples from combustion features at 35LK1880, 35LK1881, and 35LK2095 to increase the precision of existing age estimates.

Danger Cave (42TO13) is located in the Bonneville Basin of Utah. While radiocarbon dates from Jennings' (1957) excavations and subsequent works (Harper and Alder 1972; Hoskins 2016; Madsen and Rhode 1990; Rhode et al. 2006; Tamers et al. 1964) establish Danger Cave as an important LP/EH site in the Great Basin, we currently have a poor understanding of stemmed points from the site. This is largely because: (1) Jennings (1957) employed a sequenced, descriptively based W-type (Wendover type) series; (2) Aikens (1970) reclassified Danger Cave points using binomial Berkeley types that lacked stemmed types as we know them today; and (3) pictures of Danger Cave points from those aforementioned monographs are limited and of low quality. Using photographs obtained by Erick Martin between 2015 and 2016, and our typological scheme, we reassess the probable typologies of stemmed points from Danger Cave.

Results
The Connley Caves

Some radiocarbon dates and projectile point proveniences are reported in Jenkins and colleagues (2017) and Rosencrance and colleagues (2022) for Cave 4 and McDonough and colleagues (2022) for Cave 5. All published and new radiocarbon dates associated with WST points at the site are listed in Table 2.4. The earliest complete projectile point from Connley Cave 4 (Figure 2.3g), found at an elevation of 1354.95 m above sea level (masl), does not fit neatly into any of the widely used morphological types. It is similar to Haskett points in that it is shoulderless; however, considering it was found below a large Haskett assemblage, it is more gracile in size and cross section than typical Haskett points but has similar flaking techniques, suggesting it could represent a Haskett antecedent. This point is associated with two new dates of 10,545 ± 35 ^{14}C BP (12,680–12,480 cal BP) and 10,410 ± 40 ^{14}C BP (12,590–12,055 cal BP) from 1354.91 and 1354.90 masl, respectively. None of those dates unequivocally come from a hearth feature, but the older date is stratigraphically below younger combustion features (see below). Future research at the Connley Caves aims to evaluate different techno-typological assignments for this point and other fragments in the component.

Between ~1355.00 and 1355.45 masl in both Connley Cave 4 and 5 is a large Haskett assemblage (Figure 2.3h–j) with at least five stratified features dating between ~10,450 ^{14}C BP and 10,150 ^{14}C BP (McDonough et al. 2022; Rosencrance et al. 2022). The three isolated charcoals we submitted for dating provide confirmation of the ages of the stratified features and the lateral extent of those deposits across the Cave 5 block (see Table 2.4). The first, found at an elevation of 1355.37 masl in Unit 26, returned an age of 10,145 ± 30 ^{14}C BP (11,935–11,410 cal BP). This point is just below and older than Feature 4 (25-HF-2) found in the adjacent unit. The second charcoal returned a date of 10,095 ± 35 ^{14}C BP (11,825–11,400 cal BP) from over 3 m to the south in Unit 29 at an elevation of 1355.32 masl. Considering the dip of the stratigraphy (see McDonough et al. 2022), this new date is consistent with the feature sequence. The third charcoal, also from Unit 29 but at an elevation of 1355.17 masl, returned a date of 10,135 ± 35 ^{14}C BP (11,935–11,410 cal BP) which is consistent with the new date from Unit 29 listed above and the stratigraphic position of Feature 2 (15B-HF-1).

Higher in the profile of Cave 5, Feature 4 (25-HF-2) found between 1355.45 and 1355.38 masl dates to ~10,000 ^{14}C BP (see Table 2.4). Directly associated with this hearth is a sloping shoulder point that most closely resembles a small Cougar Mountain point (Figure 2.3l). Next up in stratigraphic order is a large leaf-shaped biface (Figure 2.3p) from 1355.60 masl in the 2-×-2m unit (4B) north of 4A. This point is associated with feature 4A-30-F1 found between ~1355.65 and 1355.59 masl and dated to 9155 ± 30 ^{14}C BP (10,480–10,235 cal BP). The point could be classified as a Cougar Mountain point, though it is unclear whether it is finished or in its latest stages of production. Recent UO excavations also recovered two edge-ground WST bases at 1355.67 and 1355.51 masl (Figure 2.3r, q) less than 2 m southeast of Bedwell's feature. The first specimen (Figure 2.3r) has a slight inflection at the break with both points being overall more gracile, thicker, and flaked differently than Haskett points found below them. These may represent Parman or Cougar Mountain point bases, but almost certainly do not represent Haskett points.

Other Early Holocene examples from similar elevations at the Connley Caves include the basal midsection of a possible Windust/square found by Bedwell in Level 27 (1355.99–1355.89 masl) of unit 4B (see Thatcher 2001:

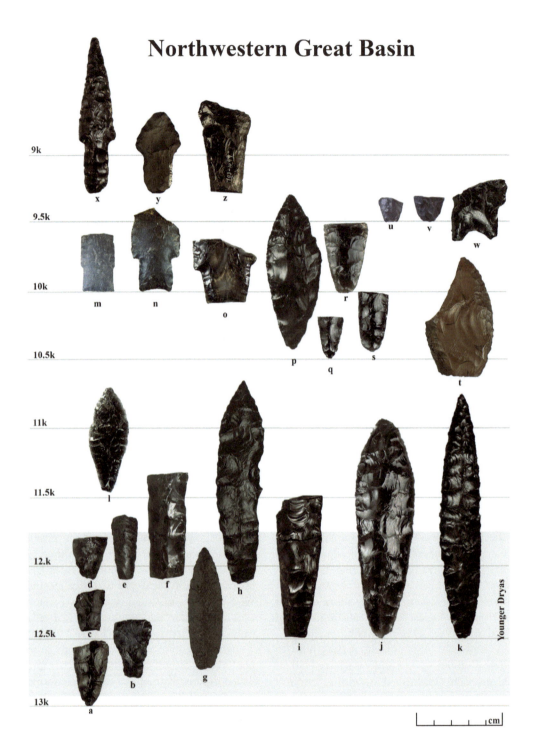

FIGURE 2.3. WST projectile points from the northwestern Great Basin with reliably associated radiocarbon ages: *early WST* from Paisley Caves (*a–c*) and Connley Caves (*g*); *Haskett* from Tule Lake Rockshelter (*d–f*), Connley Caves (*h–j*), and Cougar Mountain Cave (*k*); *Cougar Mountain* from Connley Caves (*l, p*), Dirty Shame Rockshelter (DSR, *t*), and Hanging Rock Shelter (*z*); *Windust and Windust/square* from Paulina Lake (*m–n*), 35LK2096 (Bunny Pits, o), and DSR (*w*); *Parman* from Connley Caves (*q–s*), LSP-1 Rockshelter (*x*), Hanging Rock Shelter (*y*), WST 35LK1180 (*u*), and 35LK1881 (*v*).

276), the debated "fluted" point from Level 29 in Cave 5 (5A; 1355.59–1355.49 masl; Beck et al. 2004:284) that we classify here as a Windust point, and finally a thick, well-flaked, edge-ground base from 1355.63 masl in Cave 6 (Figure 2.3s) that is likely a Parman or Cougar Mountain point. Based on their stratigraphic positions relative to dated features, these points date somewhere between ~10,200 cal BP and ~9000 cal BP (see Saper et al. 2019 for 9000 cal BP feature details).

In sum, at the Connley Caves Haskett is firmly and unequivocally dated to at least ~10,450 ^{14}C BP, with another WST occupation dating to ~10,600 ^{14}C BP and possibly earlier. A shift to Cougar Mountain points occurs around the Pleistocene–Holocene transition followed by a use of probable shouldered forms during the late Early Holocene. Ongoing UO work in Caves 4, 5, and 6 will provide updated perspective in the future.

Tule Lake Rockshelter

The stemmed projectile points from Tule Lake Rockshelter (Figure 2.3) fit most closely with the Haskett type (see Table 2.1). The points came from Levels 20 (Catalog #451-293: Figure 2.3f; Catalog #451-294: Figure 2.3e) and 23 (Catalog #451-312: Figure 2.3d), which corresponds well with the provenience of the radiocarbon-dated samples and eyed bone needles (see Table 2.4).

Paulina Lake Site

The charcoal sample from the central house hearth feature (Feature 7) returned a date of 9190 ± 30 ^{14}C BP (10,490–10,430 cal BP), and the charcoal from the house post (Feature 8) returned a date of 8565 ± 30 (9555–9485 cal BP). Both samples were *Pinus contorta* (not for trying to find other taxa in the collections), and thus we cannot rule out old wood as an issue. Indeed, as Connolly and Jenkins (1999) point out, the central hearth dates are significantly older (~1000 calibrated years) than the dates obtained on the house posts. Our new dates have replicated this issue.

We think the two likeliest scenarios that would cause this are: (1) occupants used very old pine blocks for fuel in the central hearth feature and young pine trees for house posts; or (2) various occupants reused the house and central feature over and over through time, depositing various ages of wood in the hearth, but replacing the house posts through time. Nevertheless, we can confidently say Windust and Windust/square points date to between ~10,400 and 9500 cal BP at the Paulina Lake site.

The Bunny Pits

All three of our submitted charcoals returned similiar ages to existing dates, but much more precise ages for features at 35LK1180, 35LK1881, and 35LK2076. The sample from 35LK1180 returned a date of 8525 ± 30 ^{14}C BP (9540–9485 cal BP), while the sample from 35LK1881 returned a date of 8490 ± 30 ^{14}C BP (9535–9470 cal BP). The sample from 35LK2076 returned a date of 8855 ± 35 ^{14}C BP (10,160–9780 cal BP). The WST points from 35LK1180 and 35LK1881 are small contracting basal fragments, likely from Parman points; however, we cannot know for sure (Figure 2.3u–v). The point from 35LK2076 is undoubtedly the base of a Windust/square point (Figure 2.3o).

Danger Cave

Hoskins (2016) and Goebel and colleagues (2007) provide recent analyses of Danger Cave's geochronology that assess the reliability of individual dates and stratigraphic integrity (Harper and Alder 1972; Jennings 1957; Madsen and Rhode 1990; Rhode et al. 2006; Tamers et al. 1964). Both studies make it clear that there is either considerable mixing of the deposits or coarsely recorded items from the early excavations. For example, coprolites that supposedly came from stratum DII that should have dated to the Early Holocene, returned Late Holocene radiocarbon dates (Rhode et al. 2006). Still, recent work demonstrates that stratum DI is likely late Pleistocene in age, while DII is Early Holocene in age (Goebel et al. 2007; Rhode et al. 2006).

The apparent mixing of deposits complicates our ability to unequivocally tie specific

FIGURE 2.4. WST projectile points from Danger Cave. Types include Bonneville (*a–k*), Silver Lake (*n–p*), Lake Mohave (*q–s*), and Windust (*l–m*). All original photos by Erik Martin and used with permission.

points to specific strata. However, as mentioned, what types of WST points might be present at Danger Cave are largely unknown to most researchers. Moreover, Jennings (1957) reports very few projectile points in DI and that stemmed projectile points do not persist into the Middle Holocene in the Bonneville Basin. Therefore, any diagnostic stemmed points more than likely come from DII and date to the Early Holocene.

Our analysis identifies the presence of Windust, Lake Mohave, Silver Lake, and Bonneville types at Danger Cave (Figure 2.4a–s). The chronology for specific point types at Danger Cave is much coarser than is ideal but serves the purpose here of clarifying the record from the eastern Great Basin. Our review indicates some meaningful information can be garnished from this record because some of the point types (e.g., Bonneville, Lake Mohave, and Silver Lake) have very few other dated occurrences from a stratified site. As we cannot connect specific dates to the points at Danger Cave, the sequence is listed separately in Table 2.4. The Danger Cave WST profile suggests an Early Holocene emphasis like that seen at the nearby ORBD (Duke 2011; Madsen, Oviatt, et al. 2015) versus the predominately late Pleistocene signatures at the prominent Bonneville basin outcrop cavity sites, Bonneville Estates Rockshelter (Goebel et al. 2007; Goebel and Keene 2014) and Smith Creek Cave (Bryan 1979, 1988; Lynch et al., Chapter 6).

Dataset Summary

Most reliable dates in our sample are on charcoal or organic artifacts; however, dates on bone require specific discussion. We recognize the only way to be absolutely certain a radiocarbon date from bone collagen is accurate is by dating specific amino acids (Devièse et al. 2018) and that having stable isotope information ensures confidence via demonstrating good collagen preservation (Van Klinken 1999). For this dataset, Paisley Caves (UCIAMS dates only), the Wallman Bison, and Hetrick site have radiocarbon dates on specific amino acids. Only Hetrick has measured stable isotope information (that we present here for the first time; see Table 2.4). Other bone dates from Lind Coulee, non-UCIAMS dates from Paisley, and Marmes Rockshelter Floodplain thus could be excluded in a more stringent consideration (e.g., Waters, Stafford, and Carlson 2020). Nonetheless, all of the ultrafiltration collagen dates are internally consistent and fit broader patterns observed of other dates at each site. As such, we consider the nonamino acid bone dates in Table 2.4 as part of our chronology, but it is important to keep in mind the possibility that all contaminants were not removed during pretreatment.

After critical evaluation and the incorporation of our new data, the reliable WST radiocarbon dataset totals 166 dates from 35 sites and 47 components. To us, such a sample goes against the notion that the WST record is poorly dated (sensu Fiedel and Morrow 2012; Reid et al. 2015; Pratt et al. 2020) and that WST styles exhibit no meaningful age-related variation (sensu Beck and Jones 1997, 2009; Bryan and Tuohy 1999). There is indeed variation of forms with age, especially separated by the Younger Dryas and Early Holocene. We discuss the variation in more detail below.

Discussion

Our evaluation and review of radiocarbon dates associated with WST projectile points in the Intermountain West shows that morphological variability does fluctuate with age, although work still remains. To better organize the following discussion, we scale the WST archaeological record to three major time periods based on widely accepted climatic chronozones: the (1) Bølling-Allerød (14,700–12,900 cal BP); (2) Younger Dryas (12,900–11,700 cal BP); and (3) Early Holocene (11,700–8200 cal BP). These chronozones correspond to important climatic shifts that may have caused technological adaptations by people living in the region.

Bølling-Allerød

The only WST projectile points unequivocally dated to the Bølling-Allerød are at Cooper's Ferry (Davis, Chapter 7; Davis et al. 2019) and Paisley Cave 5 (Jenkins et al. 2012). Both date to the latter half of the chronozone and are older (Cooper's Ferry) as well as coeval (Paisley Caves) with Clovis (Miller et al. 2013; Surovell, Chapter 10; Waters, Stafford, and Carlson 2020). Points from both of those sites do not fit neatly within later WST point classifications. Points 73-60685, 73-62464, and 73-42800 from LU3 at Cooper's Ferry are unlike any WST points found in the Intermountain West yet. Davis and colleagues (2019) compare them both morphologically and technologically with Tachikawa points from Japan that date to around the same time, suggesting they have a shared technological ancestry (also see Davis and Madsen 2020; McDonough et al., Chapter 1). Davis (Chapter 7) proposes the earliest of these, 73-60685, be referred to as the *Cooper's Ferry type*. We find the points from PFA2 to resemble the Lind Coulee type with their short bases and well-defined shoulders. We and Davis and colleagues (2019) hesitate to call them "Lind Coulee" because the point type is found infrequently and in few dated contexts that leave many viable alternative hypotheses, but their design is undoubtedly similar and perhaps represents an antecedent. The points from PFA2 and LU3 are currently the earliest versions of the small shouldered design that dominates the Columbia Plateau for the next several thousand years.

The earliest WST point from Paisley Cave 5, 1895-PC-5/16A-24, resembles either a Haskett base or perhaps, as Davis (Chapter 7) suggests, a Cooper's Ferry type base (see Figure 2.4a). Our extensive experience

TABLE 2.4. Reliable Radiocarbon Dates from Western Stemmed Tradition Sites.

Site Name	^{14}C Date	95.4% prob.	Lab #	Material	Reference	Score	Notes[a]
Early WST							
Cooper's Ferry (10IH73)	11,370±70	13,410–13,115	Beta-114949	charcoal	Davis et al. 2019	15	In PFA2, 410.88 masl, Cooper's Ferry type/Lind Coulee
	11,410±130	13,375–13,090	TO-7349	charcoal	Davis et al. 2019	14	Surface of LU3, 411.90 masl, Cooper's Ferry type
	11,630±80	13,735–13,310	OxA-X-2792-45	bone collagen	Davis et al. 2019	15	LU2, below WST base 73-60685 and above WST base 73-42800
Paisley Cave 5 (35LK3400)[f]	11,340±30	13,305–13,165	UCIAMS-90581	human coprolite, macroflora sample	Jenkins et al. 2012	26	1365.88 masl, lower bracket for 5/16A-24, Haskett or Cooper's Ferry
	11,070±25	13,090–13,165	UCIAMS-80378	unburnt twig (Artemisia)	Jenkins et al. 2012	26	1365.97 masl, upper bracket for 5/16A-24, Haskett or Cooper's Ferry
	10,855±30	12,830–12,735	UCIAMS-98932	macerated plant material	Jenkins et al. 2012	26	1366.06–1366.01 masl, upper bracket for 5/16A-23-6A, Haskett or Cooper's Ferry

Early WST Sites: 2
Total Dates: 6
Total Components: 2

Haskett							
Paisley Cave 2 (35LK3400)[f]	10,585±35	12,705–12,490	UCIAMS-102112	*Homo sapiens* hair	Jenkins et al. 2013	26	Botanical Lens
	10,390±40	12,485–12,000	Beta-429639	cut bone—unidentified artiodactyl	Jenkins et al. 2013	26	Botanical Lens

Site	Date	Cal range	Lab ID	Material	Reference	#	Notes
	10,370±40	12,475–12,000	Beta-429641	cut bone—unidentified artiodactyl	Jenkins et al. 2013	26	Botanical Lens
	10,365±30	12,470–12,000	UCIAMS-79680	knotted bark (*Artemisia*)	Jenkins et al. 2013	26	Botanical Lens, same artifact as D-AMS-1217-411
	10,355±45	12,470–11,970	D-AMS-1217-411	knotted bark (*Artemisia*)	Jenkins et al. 2013	26	Botanical Lens, same artifact as UCIAMS-79680
	10,350±40	12,470–12,950	Beta-429640	cut bone—unidentified artiodactyl	Jenkins et al. 2013	26	Botanical Lens
	10,330±30	12460–12,456	UCIAMS-98933	hair (*Antilocapra americana*)	Jenkins et al. 2013	26	Botanical Lens
	10,320±60	12,475–11,880	AA-96490	braided cordage (*Artemisia*)	Jenkins et al. 2013	26	Botanical Lens
	10,300±45	12,460–11,830	D-AMS-012789	wooden peg (*Betula*)	Jenkins et al. 2013	26	Botanical Lens
	10,290±40	12,450–11,830	Beta-195908	braided cordage (*Artemisia*)	Jenkins et al. 2013	26	Botanical Lens
	10,290±30	12,445–11,830	UGAMS-A26415	human coprolite, bone	Jenkins et al. 2013	26	Botanical Lens
	10,260±60	12,460–11,750	Beta-239083	cut bone—unidentified artiodactyl	Jenkins et al. 2013	25	Botanical Lens
	10,210±30	11,970–11,755	UGAMS-A26420	human coprolite, bone	Jenkins et al. 2013	26	Botanical Lens
	10,160±60	12,000–11,400	Beta-182920	processed edible tissue	Jenkins et al. 2013	26	Botanical Lens
Connley Cave 4 (35LK50)	10,545±35	12,680–12,480	PSUAMS#6721	isolated charcoal (Rosaceae)	this study	20	1354.91 masl, early Haskett?
	10,410±40	12,590–12,055	PSUAMS#6720	isolated charcoal (*Artemisia*)	this study	20	1354.90 masl, early Haskett?

TABLE 2.4. (cont'd.) Reliable Radiocarbon Dates from Western Stemmed Tradition Sites.

Site Name	14C Date	95.4% prob.	Lab #	Material	Reference	Score	Notes[a]
	10,445±40	12,615–12,100	D-AMS 12793	feature charcoal (*Artemisia*)	Jenkins et al. 2017	26	Feature 3/5-HF-1, 1355.03 masl
	10,455±40	12,615–12,100	D-AMS 12797	feature charcoal (*Artemisia*)	Jenkins et al. 2017	26	Feature 3/5-HF-1, 1355.05 masl
	10,400±45	12,590–12,000	D-AMS 12799	isolated charcoal (*Artemisia*)	Jenkins et al. 2017	20	1354.72 masl, moved downward by boulder
	10,260±40	12,435–11,765	PSUAMS#6724	feature charcoal (*Artemisia*)	Rosencrance et al. 2022	23	Feature 4A-32/34-F1, 1355.18 masl
	10,270±35	12,435–11,820	PSUAMS#6725	feature charcoal (*Artemisia*)	Rosencrance et al. 2022	23	Feature 4A-32/34-F1, 1355.34–.29 masl
Connley Cave 5 (35LK50)	10,560±35	12,690–12,480	PSUAMS#6716	feature charcoal (*Artemisia*)	McDonough et al. 2022	24	hearth, Feature 1, 1355.03 masl
	10,490±35	12,630–12,190	PSUAMS#6714	feature charcoal (*Artemisia*)	McDonough et al. 2022	24	hearth, Feature 1, 1355.05 masl
	10,420±35	12,600–12,090	PSUAMS#6715	feature charcoal (*Artemisia*)	McDonough et al. 2022	24	hearth, Feature 1, 1355.02 masl
	10,275±35	12,435–11,820	PSUAMS#6712	feature charcoal (*Artemisia*)	McDonough et al. 2022	25	combustion area, Feature 2, 1355.21 masl
	10,150±40	11,940–11,505	PSUAMS#7103	feature charcoal (*Artemisia*)	McDonough et al. 2022	25	combustion area, Feature 2, 1355.22 masl
	10,290±35	12,450–11,830	PSUAMS#7104	feature charcoal (*Artemisia*)	McDonough et al. 2022	24	combustion area, Feature 2, 1355.24 masl
	10,030±95	11,875–11,245	D-AMS 30298	feature charcoal (*Artemisia*)	McDonough et al. 2022	24	combustion area, Feature 2, 1355.26 masl
	10,145±30	11,935–11,410	PSUAMS#5005	isolated charcoal (*Artemisia*)	this study	23	Unit 26, 1355.37 masl

Site	14C age BP	cal BP range	Lab #	Material	Reference		Provenience
	10,135±35	11,935–11,410	PSUAMS#5004	isolated charcoal (*Artemisia*)	this study	23	Unit 29, 1355.17 masl
	10,190±35	11,970–11,735	PSUAMS#5009	hearth charcoal (*Artemisia*)	McDonough et al. 2022	23	hearth area, Feature 3, 1355.27 masl
	10,120±35	11,930–11,405	PSUAMS#5008	hearth charcoal (*Artemisia*)	McDonough et al. 2022	23	hearth area, Feature 3, 1355.20 masl
	10,115±50	11,935–11,400	D-AMS 030299	hearth charcoal (*Artemisia*)	McDonough et al. 2022	23	hearth area, Feature 3, 1355.20 masl
	10,095±35	11,825–11,400	PSUAMS#5003	isolated charcoal (*Artemisia*)	this study	23	Unit 29, 1355.32 masl
Bonneville Estates Rockshelter, West Block (26EK3682)	10,970±60	13,070–12,760	Beta-200874	hearth charcoal (*Pinus*)	Goebel et al. 2021		Stratum 18b, F05.06/06.02
	10,800±60	12,840–12,690	AA-58594	hearth charcoal	Goebel et al. 2021	20	Stratum 18b, F013.15a
	10,760±60	12,825–12,670	AA-58592	hearth charcoal	Goebel et al. 2021	20	Stratum 18b, F013.15a
	10,690±70	12,760–12,490	AA-58590	hearth charcoal	Goebel et al. 2021	21	Stratum 18b, F03.16/04.13
	10,540±60	12,720–12,190	Beta-274455	hearth charcoal	Goebel et al. 2021	21	Stratum 18b, F03.16/04.13
	10,640±60	12,740–12,490	Beta-200875	hearth charcoal	Goebel et al. 2021	20	Stratum 18b, F03.17
	10,540±40	12,680–12,480	Beta-195047	hearth charcoal	Goebel et al. 2021	21	Stratum 18b, F03.14
	10,560±50	12,700–12,480	Beta-182931	hearth charcoal (*Artemisia*)	Goebel et al. 2021	20	Stratum 18b, F04.15
	10,405±50	12,595–12,000	AA-58593	hearth charcoal	Goebel et al. 2021	21	Stratum 18b, F03.14
Smith Creek Cave (26WP46)	10,740±130	13,070–12,465	Birm-702	hearth charcoal	Bryan 1979	20	TP-8 hearth 4
	10,660±220	13,090–11,885	Gak-5442	hearth charcoal	Bryan 1979	19	TP-8 hearth 2
	10,630±190	12,995–11,935	Gak-5443	hearth charcoal	Bryan 1979	20	TP-8 hearth 3
	10,570±160	12,820–11,935	Gak5445	hearth charcoal	Bryan 1979	20	TP-8 hearth 3

TABLE 2.4. (cont'd.) Reliable Radiocarbon Dates from Western Stemmed Tradition Sites.

Site Name	¹⁴C Date	95.4% prob.	Lab #	Material	Reference	Score	Notes[a]
	10,460±260	12,885–11,350	Gak-5444b	hearth charcoal	Bryan 1979	19	TP-8 hearth 4
	10,420±100	12,670–11,935	TO-1173	S-twist cordage	Bryan 1988	25	gray ash and silt stratum
	10,330±190	12,700–11,400	Tx-1638	hearth charcoal	Bryan 1979	16	TP-6 hearth 12
	9940±160	12,040–10,800	Tx-1420	hearth charcoal	Bryan 1979	14	TP-6 hearth 9
Cougar Mountain Cave (35LK55)	10,490±40	12,670–12,190	ICA-18C/0385	isolated charcoal (*Artemisia*)	Rosencrance et al. 2019	18	Unit S14, 60–68 in.
	10,450±40	12,615–12,100	ICA-18O/387	braided cordage (*Artemisia*)	Rosencrance et al. 2019	19	same cordage as UGAMS#35050
	10,430±40	12,610–12,095	ICA-18C/0384	isolated charcoal (*Artemisia*)	Rosencrance et al. 2019	18	Unit S14, 60–68 in.
	10,250±30	12,095–11,820	UGAMS-#35050	braided cordage (*Artemisia*)	Rosencrance et al. 2019	19	same cordage as ICA-18O/387
Tule Lake Rockshelter (CASIS218A)	10,425±25	12,590–12,100	UCIAMS-79297	carbonized twig	Erlandson et al. 2014	21	Unit OS1, Level 21
	10,310±25	12,445–11,935	UCIAMS-80836	carbonized twig	Erlandson et al. 2014	21	Unit OS1, Level 24
	10,285±25	12,435–11,830	UCIAMS-79293	carbonized twig	Erlandson et al. 2014	21	Unit OS1, Level 21
	10,280±40	12,445–11,825	UCIAMS-80839	carbonized twig	Erlandson et al. 2014	21	Unit OS1, Level 24
Wishbone site (42TO6384)	10,430±40	12,610–12,095	Beta-428729	hearth charcoal (*Salix*)	Duke et al. 2022	25	single occupation, one hearth
	10,370±40	12,475–12,000	Beta-428730	hearth charcoal (*Salix*)	Duke et al. 2022	25	single occupation, one hearth
	10,370±30	12,485–12,000	Beta-428728	hearth charcoal (*Salix*)	Duke et al. 2022	25	single occupation, one hearth
Wewukiyepuh (10NP336)	10,390±40	12,485–12,000	Beta-124447	dispersed charcoal	Sappington and Schuknecht-McDaniel 2001	16	single occupation

Site	Age (BP)	Cal BP	Lab #	Material	Reference		Provenience
	10,270±50	12,455–11,815	Beta-124446	hearth charcoal	Sappington and Schuknecht-McDaniel 2001	20	Unit 4, Feature 1, single occupation
Sentinel Gap (45KT1362)	10,010±60	11,745–11,265	Beta-133664	charcoal from flake concentration	Galm and Gough 2000	22	Feature 99.6
	10,130±60	11,940–11,400	Beta-133665	hearth charcoal	Galm and Gough 2000	24	Feature 99.3, burn
	10,160±60	12,000–11,400	Beta-133663	hearth charcoal	Galm and Gough 2000	24	Feature 99.1, burn
	10,180±40	11,950–11,645	Beta-124167	oxidized staining	Galm and Gough 2000	24	oxidized stain and artifacts
Lind Coulee (45GR97)	10,250±40	12,430–11,760	CAMS-94857	bone collagen (*Cervus/B. bison*)	Craven 2004	14	0.20–0.25 m below datum
	10,060±45	11,815–11,345	CAMS-94856	bone collagen (*Cervus/B. bison*)	Craven 2004	14	0.29–0.39 m below datum

Total Haskett Sites: 10
Total Dates: 70
Total Components: 11

Lind Coulee

Site	Age (BP)	Cal BP	Lab #	Material	Reference		Provenience
Marmes Rock-shelter floodplain (45FR50)	10,130±300	12,725–10,815	W-2218	charcoal	Hicks 2004	12	Stratum I, Harrison Horizon
	9840±300	12,470–10,500	W-2212	charcoal	Hicks 2004	12	Stratum I, Harrison Horizon
Lind Coulee (45GR97)	9810±40	11,275–11,175	CAMS-95524	bone collagen (*Cervus/B. bison*)	Craven 2004	14	0.30–0.40 m above datum

Total Lind Coulee Sites: 2
Total Dates: 3
Total Components: 2

TABLE 2.4. (cont'd.) Reliable Radiocarbon Dates from Western Stemmed Tradition Sites.

Site Name	¹⁴C Date	95.4% prob.	Lab #	Material	Reference	Score	Notes[a]
Cougar Mountain							
Paisley Cave 5 (35LK3400)[f]	10,200±35	11,970–11,745	UCIAMS-79676	twig (*Artemisia* sp.)	Jenkins et al. 2012	24	1365.09 masl, upper limiting for 5/28a-10-1, Cougar Mountain? Haskett?
Connley Cave 5 (35LK50)	10,010±50	11,735–11,275	D-AMS 030300	hearth charcoal (*Artemisia*)	McDonough et al. 2022	26	hearth, Feature 4, 1355.43 masl
	9985±35	11,690–11,265	PSUAMS#5007	hearth charcoal (*Artemisia*)	McDonough et al. 2022	26	hearth, Feature 4, 1355.44 masl
Redfish Overhang (10CR201)	10,015±35	11,730–11,315	PSUAMS#5010	isolated charcoal (Rosaceae)	Rosencrance 2019	20	sand pedestal around cache
	9930±30	11,605–11,240	PSUAMS#5243	hearth Charcoal (conifer)	Rosencrance 2019	25	hearth behind cache
	9910±35	11,500–11,230	PSUAMS#5244	hearth Charcoal (conifer)	Rosencrance 2019	25	hearth behind cache
	9810±35	11,265–11,185	PSUAMS#5245	hearth Charcoal (conifer)	Rosencrance 2019	25	hearth behind cache
Dirty Shame Rockshelter (35MI65)	9500±95	11,165–10,520	SI-1774	isolated charcoal	Aikens et al. 1977	15	terminus ante quem. Zone V
Connley Cave 4 (35LK50)	9155±30	10,480–10,235	PSUAMS#6726	feature charcoal (*Artemisia*)	Rosencrance et al. 2022	23	Feature 4A-30-F1, hearth, 1355.65–.59 masl
Leonard Rockshelter (26PE14)	9835±45	11,390–11,185	D-AMS 030013	isolated charcoal	Smith et al. 2022	15	Area B, Stratum 8, terminus post quem
	8410±45	9530–9300	D-AMS 031970	*Amaranthaceae* wood	Smith et al. 2022	—	Area B, Stratum 6, terminus ante quem, not included in total

Site	Date	Range	Lab #	Material	Reference	Component	Notes
Last Supper Cave (26HU102)	8190±50	9275–9000	Beta-242510	hearth charcoal	Ollivier et al. 2017	17	listed in Parman, Upper Shell
	8260±90	9455–9020	WSU-1706[b]	hearth charcoal	G. Smith, Felling, Taylor, et al. 2015	17	listed in Parman, Lower Shell
	8920±50	10,220–9820	Beta-242511[b]	hearth charcoal	G. Smith, Felling, Taylor, et al. 2015	23	listed in Parman, Lower Shell
	8925±40	10,200–9905	D-AMS 012575	Fort Rock sandal	Ollivier et al. 2017	26	listed in Parman, Lower Shell
	8960±190	10,510–9545	Tx-2541[b]	hearth charcoal	G. Smith, Felling, Taylor, et al. 2015	19	listed in Parman, Lower Shell,
Hanging Rock Shelter (26WA1502)	8210±35	9290–9025	PSUAMS#4994	hearth charcoal (*Artemisia*)	Rosencrance and McDonough 2020	23	listed in Parman, Feature 24
	8270±35	9420–9125	PSUAMS#4469	hearth charcoal (*Artemisia*)	Rosencrance and McDonough 2020	23	listed in Parman, Feature 24
	8345±35	9475–9155	PSUAMS#4995	hearth charcoal (*Artemisia*)	Rosencrance and McDonough 2020	23	listed in Parman, Feature 24

Total Cougar Mountain Sites: 8
Total Dates: 18
Total Components: 8

Parman

Site	Date	Range	Lab #	Material	Reference	Component	Notes
Sunshine Locality	9800±60	11,395–11,095	Beta-69782	charred material	Beck and Jones 2009	14	1993 excavation, Stratum B/C contact
Five Mile Flat (26HU5105)	9720±40	11,240–10,875	Beta-304833	charcoal	Hildebrandt et al. 2016	20	Locus A, CU1, 30–50 cm
Five Mile Flat (26HU4943)	9660±50	11,205–10,780	Beta-304847	charcoal	Hildebrandt et al. 2016	20	Lower, CU2 79–93 cm
Bonneville Estates Rockshelter, East Block (26EK3682)	9440±80	11,080–10,430	AA-58599	hearth charcoal	Goebel et al. 2021	23	Stratum 10; E6-10-C10
	9520±60	11,100–10,585	Beta-161891	hearth charcoal	Goebel et al. 2021	23	Stratum 10; E6-10C10
	9570±40	11,110–10,720	Beta-195044	hearth charcoal	Goebel et al. 2021	24	Stratum 10; E4-10C3/ E5-9-C5b

TABLE 2.4. (cont'd.) Reliable Radiocarbon Dates from Western Stemmed Tradition Sites.

Site Name	¹⁴C Date	95.4% prob.	Lab #	Material	Reference	Score	Notes[a]
	9580±40	11,145–10,735	Beta-195042	hearth charcoal	Goebel et al. 2021	24	Stratum 10; E4-10-C3/ E5-10-C7
35HA3293	9080±35	10,295–10,185	D-AMS013827	hearth charcoal	Gilmour et al. 2015	18	Feature 1, EU-17, 65 cmbs
Last Supper Cave (26HU102)	8190±50	9275–9000	Beta-242510	hearth charcoal	Ollivier et al. 2017	17	listed in Cougar Mtn; Upper Shell
	8260±90	9455–9020	WSU-1706[b]	hearth charcoal	G. Smith, Felling, Taylor, et al. 2015	17	listed in Cougar Mtn; Lower Shell
	8920±50	10,220–9820	Beta-242511[b]	hearth charcoal	G. Smith, Felling, Taylor, et al. 2015	23	listed in Cougar Mtn; Lower Shell
	8925±40	10,200–9905	D-AMS 012575	Fort Rock sandal	Ollivier et al. 2017	26	listed in Cougar Mtn; Lower Shell
	8960±190	10,510–9545	Tx-2541[b]	hearth charcoal	G. Smith, Felling, Taylor, et al. 2015	19	listed in Cougar Mtn; Lower Shell
LSP-1 Rockshelter (35HA3735)	8265±40	9420–9030	D-AMS 10594	isolated charcoal (Artemisia)	Kennedy and Smith 2016	20	N105E99, 101–106 cmbs
	8290±40	9430–9130	Beta-282809	isolated charcoal	Kennedy and Smith 2016	19	N105E99, 120 cmbs
	8300±20	9425–9140	UGA-15594	isolated charcoal (cf. Rhus)	Kennedy and Smith 2016	20	N105E99, 106 cmbs
	8340±40	9480–9145	Beta-287251	isolated charcoal	Kennedy and Smith 2016	19	N105E99, 103 cmbs
	8340±30	9465–9275	PRI-14-069	isolated charcoal (Artemisia)	Kennedy and Smith 2016	20	N107E99, 124 cmbs
	8350±30	9465–9285	UGA-14916	isolated charcoal (Artemisia)	Kennedy and Smith 2016	20	N103E101, 86 cmbs

Site	14C BP	cal BP	Lab #	Material	Reference	#	Provenience
	8400±50		Beta-297186	isolated charcoal (Artemisia)	Kennedy and Smith 2016	20	N105E99, 131 cmbs
	8630±20		UGA-21829	Olivella bead[c,e,g]	Smith et al. 2016	25	N102E102, 121–126 cmbs
	8670±40		Beta-306419	isolated charcoal	Kennedy and Smith 2016	18	N102E99, 97 cmbs
	8700±30		UGA-15142	hearth charcoal (Artemisia)	Kennedy and Smith 2016	25	F.13-01, N103E100, 125 cmbs
	8870±30		UGA-21825	Olivella bead[e,g]	Smith et al. 2016	24	N105E100, 111–116 cmbs
	8930±15		UGA-21826	Olivella bead[d,e,g]	Smith et al. 2016	24	N104E101, 107 cmbs
	9200±30		UGA-21828	Olivella bead[e,g]	Smith et al. 2016	22	N102E102, 121–126 cmbs
Hanging Rock Shelter (26WA1502)	8210±35	9290–9025	PSUAMS#4994	hearth 24 charcoal (Artemisia)	Rosencrance and McDonough 2020	23	listed in Cougar Mountain; Hearth 24
	8270±35	9420–9125	PSUAMS#4469	hearth 24 charcoal (Artemisia)	Rosencrance and McDonough 2020	23	listed in Cougar Mountain; Hearth 24
	8345±35	9475–9155	PSUAMS#4995	hearth 24 charcoal (Artemisia)	Rosencrance and McDonough 2020	23	listed in Cougar Mountain; Hearth 24

Total Parman Sites: 9
Total Dates: 31
Total Components: 9

Windust and Windust/square

Site	14C BP	cal BP	Lab #	Material	Reference	#	Provenience
Hetrick (10WN469)	9835±35	11,315–11,190	UCIAMS-87908	bone collagen (medium mammal)	Manning 2011	25	30N15W, IIId, 250–260 cmbs, Feature E, Windust, XAD[h]
	9850±110	11,750–10,815	Beta-78880	bone collagen	Rudolph 1995	23	30N15W, IIIc, 200–210 cmbs, Feature F, Windust
	9730±60	11,255–10,800	Beta-78722	bone collagen	Rudolph 1995	24	30N15W, IIId, 210–220 cmbs, Feature E, Windust
	9830±30	11,275–11,195	UCIAMS-87907	bone collagen (medium mammal)	Manning 2011	25	30N15W, IIIc, 220–230 cmbs, Feature F, Windust, XAD[i]

TABLE 2.4. (cont'd.) Reliable Radiocarbon Dates from Western Stemmed Tradition Sites.

Site Name	^{14}C Date	95.4% prob.	Lab #	Material	Reference	Score	Notes[a]
Marmes Rock-shelter floodplain (45FR50)	9870±50	11,465–11,190	Beta-120802	bone	Hicks 2004	16	63.7 ftbs, Stratum I, Marmes Horizon, Windust
	9710±40	11,235–10,870	Beta-156699	bone	Hicks 2004	15	62.7 ftbs, Stratum III, Marmes Horizon, Windust
Wallman Bison (26HU58)	9770±50	11,270–10,895	UCR-3782	bone collagen (*B. bison*)	Dansie and Jerrems 2005	18	Windust/square, XAD
Bonneville Estates Rockshelter (West Block; (26EK3682)	9580±40	11,145–10,735	Beta-207010	hearth charcoal	Goebel et al. 2021	24	Stratum 18a/17b contact, F05.02, Windust/square
	9440±50	11,065–10,510	AA-58589	hearth charcoal	Goebel et al. 2021	23	Stratum 17b, F03.13, Windust/square
	9430±50	11,060–10,505	AA-58588	hearth charcoal	Goebel et al. 2021	23	Stratum 17b, F03.13, Windust/square
Marmes Rockshelter (45FR50)	9430±40	10,990–10,515	Beta-120803	charcoal	Hicks 2004	17	84ftbs, Stratum II/I, Windust
	9360±60	10,750–10,380	Beta-156696	charcoal	Hicks 2004	16	82ftbs, Stratum II/I, Windust
	9200±110	10,680–10,185	Y-2482	charcoal	Hicks 2004	15	Stratum II/I, Windust
Paulina Lake (35DS34)	9060±80	10,490–9910	Beta-56725	hearth charcoal (*P. ponderosa*)	Connolly and Jenkins 1999	24	Feature 7, Unit YB12/3-F7, 40 cmbs, Windust/square
	8880±110	10,235–9560	Beta-60883	hearth charcoal	Connolly and Jenkins 1999	22	Feature 7, Unit XC-8/3-C2, 35 cmbs, Windust/square
	9190±30	10,490–10,430	PSUAMS#6039	hearth charcoal	this study	22	Feature 7, Unit 7/A-6 II, Windust/square
	8980±190	10,560–9545	Beta-60884	isolated charcoal	Connolly and Jenkins 1999	20	Unit EEA-9/3-A1, 34 cmbs, Windust/square

Site	Date BP	Lab #	Material	Reference	#	Provenience
	8680±70	Beta-56723	feature charcoal	Connolly and Jenkins 1999	23	Charcoal feature, OA-10/3-A2, 33 cmbs, Windust/square
	8670±110	Beta-57733	post charcoal (*P. contorta*)	Connolly and Jenkins 1999	23	YC-7/3C1, 21 cmbs, Windust/square
	8540±90	Beta-59316	post charcoal (*P. contorta*)	Connolly and Jenkins 1999	24	Feature 8, ZA-6/3-A1, 24cmbs, Windust/square
	8565±30	PSUAMS#6039	post charcoal (*P. contorta*)	this study	24	Feature 8, ZA-6/3-III, 24cmbs, Windust/square
	8460±110	Beta-59315	post charcoal (*P. contorta*)	Connolly and Jenkins 1999	23	UD-7/3-D2, 24 cmbs, Windust/square
	8210±60	Beta-24298	isolated charcoal	Connolly and Jenkins 1999	17	~20 cmbs, Windust/square
(Bunny Pits) 35LK2095	9130±130	Beta-23593	scattered charcoal	Oetting 1994	14	TP-1, 20–30 cmbs, Windust/square
(Bunny Pits) 35LK2076	8870±200	Beta-26026	hearth charcoal	Oetting 1994	17	TP-6, Q.B, 60–70 cmbs, Windust/square
	8855±35	PSUAMS#5255	hearth charcoal (*Artemisia*)	this study	25	TP-6, Q.A, 50–60 cmbs, Windust/square
	8780±120	Beta-22580	hearth charcoal	Oetting 1994	18	TP-4, Q.D, 50–60 cmbs, Windust/square
Dirty Shame Rockshelter (35MI65)	8905±75	SI-1775	isolated charcoal	Aikens et al. 1977	15	Zone VI, Windust
	8865±95	SI-2265	isolated charcoal	Aikens et al. 1977	15	Zone VI, Windust
	8850±75	SI-2268	uncharred twigs	Aikens et al. 1977	21	Zone VI, Windust
Beta Rockshelter (10LH63)	8175±230	WSU-402	charcoal	Swanson and Sneed 1966	13	Block S-4, layer 6D, Windust

Total Windust, Windust/square Sites: 10
Total Dates: 31
Total Components: 11

TABLE 2.4. (cont'd.) Reliable Radiocarbon Dates from Western Stemmed Tradition Sites.

Site Name	^{14}C Date	95.4% prob.	Lab #	Material	Reference	Score	Notes[a]
Silver Lake							
The Awl Site (CASBR4562)	9410±115	11,100–10,295	Beta-16100	charcoal	Basgall and Hall 1993	15	Locus A, Area 5, Unit S50/W65, 80–90 cmbs
	9470±115	11,805–10,875	Beta-16313	hearth charcoal	Basgall and Hall 1993	17	Locus A, Area 5, Unit S44/W64, 80–90 cmbs
Bonneville Estates Rockshelter (East Block; 26EK3682)	8830±60	10,180–9675	Beta-203507	hearth charcoal	Goebel et al. 2021	18	Stratum 10, A4-9-C1
Total Silver Lake Sites: 2							
Total Dates = 3							
Total Components: 2							
Lake Mohave							
The Awl Site (CASBR4562)	9410±115	11,100–10,295	Beta-16100	Charcoal	Basgall and Hall 1993	15	also listed in Silver Lake
	9470±115	11,805–10,875	Beta-16313	hearth charcoal	Basgall and Hall 1993	17	also listed in Silver Lake
Rodgers Ridge (CASBR5250)	8180±150	9480–8645	Beta-13463	feature charcoal	Jenkins 1987	15	Spring Locus, Feature 4, 60–70 cmbs
	8410±140	9670–9020	Beta-12840	hearth charcoal	Jenkins 1987	19	Spring Locus, Feature 3 50–65 cmbs
	8410±210	10,120–8775	Beta-12840	hearth charcoal	Jenkins 1987	18	Southern Locus, Feature 2, 20–30 cmbs
Total Lake Mohave Sites: 2							
Total Dates = 5							
Total Components: 2							

Site	Date	Range	Lab #	Material	Reference	Page	Notes
Danger Cave (42TO13)	10310±40	12,465–11,885	Beta-168656	hearth charcoal	Rhode et al. 2006	24	Stratum DI, Feature F111/112, Haskett? Nothing?
	10270±50	12,455–11,815	Beta-158549	hearth charcoal	Rhode et al. 2006	24	Stratum DI, Feature F111/112, Haskett? Nothing?
Danger Cave (42TO13)	8570±40	9660–9475	Beta-193123	pickleweed chaff (*Allenrolfea occidentalis*)	Rhode et al. 2006	18	Stratum 04-11, Middle DII, Lake Mohave, Silver Lake, Windust, Bonneville
	8440±50	9540–9315	Beta-190887	not reported	Rhode et al. 2006	18	Stratum 6, Middle DII, probably charcoal, see above types
	8410±50	9535–9295	NSRL-11436	not reported	Rhode et al. 2006	18	Stratum 8, Upper DII, probably charcoal, see above types
	8380±60	9535–9145	Beta-193124	pickleweed chaff (*Allenrolfea occidentalis*)	Rhode et al. 2006	18	Stratum 04-10, Middle DII, see above types
	8380±40	9490–9285	Beta-187449	human coprolite	Rhode et al. 2006	23	DII, see above types
	8300±40	9440–9010	Beta-187450	human coprolite	Rhode et al. 2006	27	DII, see above types
	8270±40	9425–9035	Beta-168857	charcoal, F119	Rhode et al. 2006	22	Upper DII, see above types
	8200±50	8400–9010	Beta-190866	not reported	Rhode et al. 2006	17	Stratum 7, Middle/Upper DII, see above types
	8190±50	9295–9005	Beta-187448	human coprolite	Rhode et al. 2006	23	DII, see above types
	8160±40	9270–9005	Beta-189084	human coprolite	Rhode et al. 2006	26	DII, see above types
	8130±50	9275–8985	Beta-187447	human coprolite	Rhode et al. 2006	26	DII, see above types
	8100±40	9265–8785	Beta-187453	human coprolite	Rhode et al. 2006	26	DII, see above types
	8100±40	9265–8785	Beta-187454	human coprolite	Rhode et al. 2006	26	DII, see above types
35LK1180 (Bunny Pits)	8525±30	9545–9480	PSUAMS#5253	hearth charcoal (*Artemisia*)	this study	21	TP-2, 90–100 cm

TABLE 2.4. (cont'd.) Reliable Radiocarbon Dates from Western Stemmed Tradition Sites.

Site Name	^{14}C Date	95.4% prob.	Lab #	Material	Reference	Score	Notes[a]
35LK1881 (Bunny Pits)	8710±140	10,175–9490	Beta-34209	dispersed charcoal	Oetting 1994	18	TP-S3/W1, 80–90 cm
	8880±120	10,235–9555	Beta-30340	feature charcoal	Oetting 1994	22	TP-MA2, 70–80 cm
	8950±120	10,375–9605	Beta-30342	feature charcoal	Oetting 1994	21	TP N1/E1, 30–35 cm
	9120±120	10,645–9905	Beta-30341	feature charcoal	Oetting 1994	21	TP-S1, 35–40 cm
	8680±40	9755–9540	D-AMS 11251	filtered leporid bone gelatin	Chatters et al. 2017	25	Feature 1. Followed Stafford et al. 1991 gelatin extraction methods.
	8490±30	9540–9465	PSUAMS#5254	hearth charcoal (*Sarcobatus*)	this study	27	TP-MA2, 70–80 cm, WST convex base

[a] Some sites contain more than one WST projectile point type in the same component. Dates in these components are summed under each projectile point type summation, but only included once in the total number of dates associated with WST sites in the text. Final category without type designations is not included in final counts.
[b] Layton originally split charcoal samples and sent them to two different labs for dating (WSU-1706 and Tx-2541); this same sample was then dated a third time (Beta-242511).
[c] Average of two dates.
[d] Average of four dates.
[e] Calibrated using the reservoir age of 240±40 developed by Moss and Erlandson (1995) for the Oregon coast.
[f] UCIAMS dates on faunal remains from the Paisley Caves were all processed using XAD resins by Tom Stafford following the methods in Waters and Stafford (2007a).
[g] *Olivella* beads from LSP-1 Rockshelter were sampled across growth rings and sometimes dated multiple times to ensure an accurate radiocarbon age. See Smith and colleagues (2016) for details.
[h] Stable isotope values provided by Cassandra Manning and Brenden Culleton, δ^{15}N (‰) = 5.6; δ^{13}C (‰) = −19.4; %N = 8.5; %C = 23.1; C/N = 3.17.
[i] Stable isotope values provided by Cassandra Manning and Brenden Culleton, δ^{15}N (‰) = 6.1; δ^{13}C (‰) = −20.0; %N = 7.5; %C = 20.7; C/N = 3.21.

with Haskett assemblages from Oregon and Utah suggests to us the former: the size, ground stem margins, lenticular to almost diamond cross section, and remnant break/platform at the base are common Haskett attributes that are even more discriminating when found together (Duke and Stueber, Chapter 4). By either interpretation, the artifact establishes the advent of WST technology in the Great Basin to Clovis times. The second earliest point from Paisley Caves is 1294-PC-5/6D-47-1 and dates to the end of the Bølling-Allerød or the earliest Younger Dryas (Jenkins et al. 2012; see Figure 2.4b). That point is at the end of its use life and is heavily reworked on all sides precluding a confident type assignment (our examination of this point indicates it is not shouldered). It is certainly WST technology based on its cross section, collateral flaking, retouch, and design.

Both Bonneville Estates Rockshelter and Smith Creek Cave contain possible evidence of Haskett points dating to between ~13,000–12,700 cal BP (Goebel et al. 2021; Lynch et al., Chapter 6). At Bonneville Estates in Stratum 18b of the west block, excavations uncovered a complex of five combustion features within a roughly 2-x-2 m area ranging from 10,970 ± 60 ^{14}C BP (13,070–12,760) to 10,405 ± 50 ^{14}C BP (12,600–12,000 cal BP; Goebel 2007; Goebel et al. 2021). A Haskett base was found ~2 m south of this complex, and it is unclear which of the five combustion features it is specifically associated with (Ted Goebel, personal communication 2021).

Bryan's (1979, 1988) hearth feature dates from Smith Creek Cave suggest a terminal Bølling-Allerød age for the Haskett fragments around the features, though the dates have relatively large standard deviations that limit precision. Lynch and colleagues (Chapter 6) present more evidence of 13,000 cal BP deposits but determine the association with cultural occupations is still equivocal.

The number of projectile points that date to this early period in the Intermountain West is small but nonetheless provocative. At both Cooper's Ferry and the Paisley Caves, the earliest projectile point technologies are very similar (but not typical) in form to the more widespread record that appears after 12,600 cal BP. The apparent dichotomy of shouldered forms in the earliest Columbia Plateau site and shoulderless forms in the earliest Great Basin site might indicate important regional differences in shared technological knowledge and trajectory very early on.

Younger Dryas

Western Stemmed Tradition projectile point technology expands during the Younger Dryas into a widespread technological tradition. Haskett is the most securely dated WST type, with 70 dates from 10 sites and 11 components in both the subregions (see Table 2.4; excluding the earliest dates at the Paisley Caves). For context, Surovell (Chapter 10) considers 39 dates from 11 sites and 37 dates from 10 sites as reliable age estimates for Clovis and Folsom in the GPRM, respectively. Similarly, Buchanan and colleagues (2021) consider 37 dates from 11 sites and 14 components reliable estimates for Folsom. Most Haskett sites date to the middle and late Younger Dryas between ~12,600 and 11,800 cal BP. Pre-12,600 cal BP Haskett evidence is possible at the Connley Caves, Bonneville Estates Rockshelter, Smith Creek Cave, and the Paisley Caves (see above).

The current sample of dated sites suggests the inception of Haskett is older in the Great Basin (~13,000 or 12,600 cal BP) than in the Columbia Plateau (~12,400 cal BP), although the sample size for the Plateau is small (two sites). Points from Wewukiyepuh are slightly variable from typical Haskett technology, but date to near the end of the interval perhaps when the use of Haskett technology began to wane. Smith (2008) reports a radiocarbon date of 10,280 ± 40 (12,445–11,925 cal BP; Beta-231717) obtained on charcoal from a hearth-like feature in the lowest cultural stratum of Last Supper Cave (LSC), Nevada. While promising, more work with the collection and field notes is needed to determine what WST points, if any, are associated with this feature.

Lind Coulee points appear in the Marmes Rockshelter Floodplain deposits sometime during the Younger Dryas. The charcoal dates from the Harrison horizon are reliable in terms of context and measurement, but the 300-year standard deviations only indicate a Younger Dryas age. This finding supports the early appearance of shouldered forms in the Columbia Plateau as indicated by Cooper's Ferry. Until more Lind Coulee points are found in reliably dated contexts, the precise age and span of the Lind Coulee type will remain tenuous. Overall though, there is continuity in projectile form during the Younger Dryas throughout the Intermountain West: Haskett in both the Great Basin and Columbia Plateau and Lind Coulee on the Plateau. These types are the only two that date to the Younger Dryas in the Intermountain West as of now.

The Buhl burial contained a shouldered biface referred to by the primary authors as Windust (Green et al. 1998). Their use of Windust followed its use as a catchall for stemmed points in the Plateau as we discussed earlier. Based on its design, this biface was not intended to be a projectile point. Morphologically speaking, it is most similar to Parman points in the ORBD (Beck and Jones 2015b; Duke 2011). This would be the oldest Parman point by nearly 700 ^{14}C years, although few dates for Parman have been identified in the eastern Great Basin and our current sample may not be representative. The Buhl date is probably unreliable because of poor collagen preservation (Devièse et al. 2018; Jazwa et al. 2021). Jazwa and others (2021) argue that even if we assume the date is reliable (stable isotope information indicates it is not) the Buhl burial likely dates towards the end of Younger Dryas if not later. In any case, because of the questionable reliability of the radiocarbon date we do not include the WST biface from Buhl in this review.

Early Holocene

The onset of the Early Holocene brings about a profound diversification of WST projectile point forms. At the Younger Dryas–Early Holocene transition (~10,000 ^{14}C BP), shouldered WST point forms proliferate and diversify in the Great Basin *and* Columbia Plateau. Specimen 1961-PC-5/18a-10-1 at the Paisley Caves dates to the late Younger Dryas and has slight shouldering that indicates it may be a Cougar Mountain point (Jenkins et al. 2012; Figure 2.4c).

Authors Rosencrance and Duke, along with Dan Stueber, recently reexamined the technology of WST points and preforms at Redfish Overhang. The technology in that cache is consistent with Cougar Mountain technology, but not Haskett, based on small preforms and shouldering; however, two projectile point midsections from stratigraphically below the cache are technologically consistent with Haskett (Stueber and Rosencrance 2021). The dates of ~9800 ^{14}C BP from the feature serve as *terminus ante quem* estimates for the Haskett points at Redfish Overhang. Considered together with the Connley Caves data (McDonough et al. 2022), Cougar Mountain technology appears to have been in use in the northern Intermountain West at those two sites by ~9900 ^{14}C BP, or slightly earlier.

Parman and Cougar Mountain points were in use in the eastern Great Basin at the Sunshine Locality and Bonneville Estates Rockshelter by ~9800 ^{14}C BP (see Table 2.4). Windust type points appear at ~9850 ^{14}C BP at the Hetrick site (Manning 2011; Rudolph 1995). Two house pits with Parman points in the surface assemblage date to ~9700 ^{14}C BP at Five Mile Flats (i.e., Parman Localities) in northwestern Nevada (Hildebrandt et al. 2016). A Cougar Mountain blade came from below a charcoal sample dated to ~9500 ^{14}C BP at Dirty Shame Rockshelter (Hanes 1977, 1988). At the Lind Coulee site, Lind Coulee points appear to date between ~10,250 ^{14}C BP and 9800 ^{14}C BP although much is left to understand about the chronology at the site (Craven 2004). In sum, between ~9900 and 9500 ^{14}C BP, broad-bladed, shouldered forms (Cougar Mountain, Parman, Windust types) appear throughout the Intermountain West with an absence of Haskett points. There is a clear transition out of shoulderless Haskett forms (and possibly sinuously shouldered Cougar Mountain forms) in the Great Basin and increased hard-shouldered morphological diversification in the Columbia Plateau.

Over the next 1000 to 1500 calendar years, Parman, Windust, Windust/square, and Cougar Mountain types continue to be used concurrently. Cougar Mountain points may not persist into the latter Early Holocene in the eastern Great Basin, like they do in the northwest (Last Supper Cave and Hanging Rock Shelter) as suggested by the ORBD dated channels and the few stratified rockshelter records (Duke 2011; Goebel et al. 2011; Madsen, Oviatt, et al. 2015). Bonneville, Stubby, Lake Mohave, and Silver Lake point types appear to date to the latter part of the Early Holocene as well, based on the records at Bonneville Estates Rockshelter, Danger Cave, Rogers Ridge, and the Awl site. This sequence is also supported by work with the ORBD channels (Duke 2011; Madsen, Oviatt, et al. 2015). The persistence of Cougar Mountain, Parman, and Windust throughout the entire Early Holocene (~2500 years) seems extreme. More light will hopefully be shed on this remaining ambiguity with future research on discriminating between and among these types at smaller regional scales, whether using 2D metrics (Beck and Jones 2009; Knell and Sutton, Chapter 5) or geometric morphometrics (Davis et al. 2015; Hartman 2019; Keyes, Chapter 11; Thulman 2012).

Based on the morphological diversity in Early Holocene assemblages and the fact that multiple point types appear to be used concurrently, future research should consider regional records at smaller scales than we do here. By ~9000 cal BP most knappers no longer made WST points, although there seems to be a persistence and overlap of Stubby, Silver Lake, and Bonneville with Pinto on the ORBD between ~9000 and 8000 cal BP (Duke 2011; Madsen, Oviatt, et al. 2015). Our data provide strong support for Layton's (1970, 1972, 1979) and Duke's (2011; Duke and King 2014) arguments that longer stemmed varieties are older than short stemmed varieties in the Great Basin. This is more difficult to assert on the Columbia Plateau.

Stemmed and Fluted Points in the Intermountain West, Great Plains, and Rocky Mountains

We are left with one of the main questions of this volume: how do stemmed and fluted forms relate in time? This chapter does not add new data on the fluted point chronology of the Intermountain West, but it does provide a fresh look at the WST point chronology that we can better compare to the chronologies east of the Rocky Mountains that have historically dominated Paleoindian research. Figure 2.5 shows projectile point chronologies for the Great Basin, Columbia Plateau, and GPRM. The GPRM chronology is derived from published literature (Buchanan et al. 2021; Knell and Muñiz 2013; Lee et al. 2011; Miller et al. 2013; Waters and Stafford 2014; Waters, Stafford, and Carlson 2020). As such, the methods for evaluating and determining the age of GPRM technocomplexes vary slightly, but most are determined through some form of stringent criteria and are reliable for the purpose of Figure 2.5.

The first thing we identify when comparing these chronologies is that the WST sequence is similar to the GPRM with regard to timing of technocomplex change and patterns of diversification. While there is good reason to consider WST on its own terms (McDonough et al., Chapter 1) the data strongly indicate that broadly paralleling patterns through time between the Intermountain West and GPRM might illuminate connections of the technologies and peoples

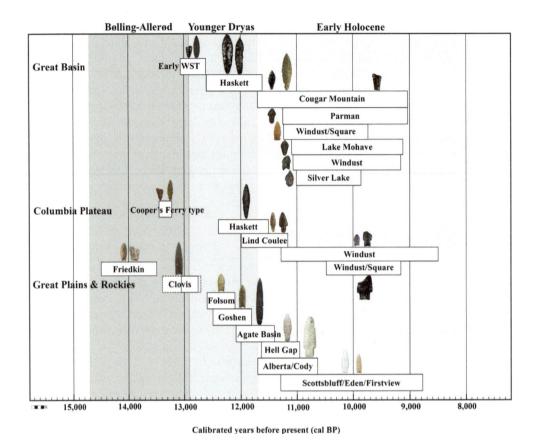

FIGURE 2.5. Paleoindian projectile point chronologies of the Intermountain West and Great Plains and Rocky Mountains (GPRM). The dotted box for Clovis represents Miller and colleagues' (2013) chronology and the solid box represents Waters, Stafford, and Carlson, (2020) chronology.

(also see Galm and Gough 2008; Martin et al. 2018; Pitblado 2003).

Prior to ~13,200 cal BP, the Cooper's Ferry type was in use in the Columbia Plateau (Cooper's Ferry; Davis, Chapter 7) and other small to medium stemmed points were in use in the southern GPRM (Gault and Debra L. Friedken sites; Williams et al. 2018; Waters et al. 2018). After 13,200 cal BP, Clovis became established in the GPRM and probably west of the Rocky Mountains, albeit in low numbers. Stemmed points remained in use in the Great Basin and Plateau as seen at Cooper's Ferry, Paisley Caves, and perhaps Bonneville Estates and Smith Creek Cave. By at least 12,800 cal BP and perhaps a few centuries earlier, the distinct types of Haskett and Folsom were established west and east of the Rockies, respectively. Haskett remained the primary technology in use throughout the Younger Dryas in the Great Basin, while people employed Lind Coulee points in the Plateau. As the Younger Dryas progressed in the GPRM, Plainview/Goshen and Agate Basin followed Folsom, then Agate Basin points seem to have transitioned into Hell Gap points at the beginning of the Early Holocene. As the Early Holocene progressed, all regions experienced a proliferation of technologies and styles, with stemmed points of various forms eventually being used across the GPRM and Intermountain West (e.g.,

Holliday 2000; Knell and Muñiz, eds. 2013; Pitblado 2003). Together the chronologies and point forms show a common trajectory of change through time that could benefit our resolution if not studied in regional vacuums.

Stepping back to the Bolling Allerød–Younger Dryas transition and the earliest period of the above-described sequences, we find the earliest forms of fluted (Clovis) and stemmed points (Cooper's Ferry and Haskett) to be highly divergent from one another (see also Bradley 2010). We believe this argues against the idea that the WST developed from Clovis/fluted technology (sensu Fiedel and Morrow 2012; Surovell, Chapter 10; Reid et al. 2015; Willig and Aikens 1988). Numerous studies, best exemplified by work at the Dietz site (Fagan 1988; Pinson 2011; Willig 1988), provide strong evidence for such a technological divergence between Intermountain West Clovis and WST assemblages. The age of Clovis/fluted points in the Intermountain West remains ambiguous, and our inquiry about fluted-stemmed relationships in the region will remain limited until someone finds a buried fluted point site (Jones and Beck, Chapter 8; Smith et al. 2020).

In sum, our data lead us to propose the following model of distinct lithic technology trajectories in the Intermountain West and the GPRM beginning prior to 13,200 cal BP. Both apparently started with variable small-stemmed points. As populations grew, people invented fluting east of the Rockies (Smith and Goebel 2018; Waters et al. 2018), and WST users west of the Rockies continued to make and develop new stemmed point technologies as the Pleistocene came to an end. In the first few centuries of the Early Holocene, stemmed point technologies dominated both regions possibly via centuries of technological drift or inevitable change, and/or group interaction and technological sharing. Such a model could explain why stemmed points typically appear stratigraphically above fluted points in the GPRM and fluted points never appear below stemmed points in the Intermountain West. The causes for these shifts across time and space are hypotheses to be tested, as well as many other questions that show a bright future for research on Intermountain West projectile point chronologies.

Conclusion

This chapter provides a reformed view on the age of different WST projectile point types, finding that there *is* change over time. The oldest WST projectile point forms are at Cooper's Ferry and Paisley Caves and date to between ~13,500 and 12,800 cal BP. Haskett points appear throughout the Intermountain West by at least ~12,600 cal BP (or 13,000 cal BP) and persist through much of the Younger Dryas. Lind Coulee points also date to the Younger Dryas but with a small sample size and are only found in the Columbia Plateau. Cougar Mountain, Parman, Windust, Windust/square, and Lake Mohave types appear in the first half of the Early Holocene and continue until about 9500 cal BP while Silver Lake, Stubby, and Bonneville types begin later in the Early Holocene and continue after ~9500 cal BP.

We urge archaeologists to carefully consider their conceptual use of Windust and to adopt the terminology suggested herein. Understanding Windust is one of the larger questions moving forward in WST research. Ultimately, it is tied to a large suite of questions, including technological and cultural interaction, transmission, and change. Our reasoning for focusing on Windust early in this chapter is to clarify Windust's meaning in light of what we know now so researchers can begin to move past models developed in the 1970s.

The WST projectile point chronology established by our review raises important questions about the spread of stemmed technology from the Intermountain West into the Plains, as well as reciprocal relationships of lithic technological knowledge between both regions throughout the Paleoindian period. It also suggests that it would be prudent to examine the Columbia Plateau chronology separately from the Great Basin when more chronological data become available. Nonetheless, lithic technology appears to display differences across the Pleistocene-Holocene boundary in the Intermountain West, and we would wager many other differences are yet to be explored.

While not all chronological problems are solved, this chapter is a positive step forward in refining and understanding the LP/EH cultural chronology of the Intermountain West. The proposed time-sensitive nature of WST projectile point forms can now be leveraged to investigate the abundant surface record and a large suite of new questions regarding WST technological development and variance. It should be apparent that the WST is not monolithic but instead a complex, changing set of lithic technologies that share a common ancestry (Bryan 1980). With this new chronological framework, we can begin to ask more nuanced questions about the WST and make more informed regional comparisons to the diverse cultural landscape of North America during the late Pleistocene and Early Holocene.

Acknowledgments

A big thank you to Chelsea Karthauser for creating Figure 2.1. Research at the Connley Caves receives generous and ongoing support from the University of Oregon Museum of Natural and Cultural History (MNCH) Paleoindian Research Fund. Thank you to MNCH, the Nevada State Museum, Idaho Museum of Natural History, the University of California, Davis, Natural History Museum of Utah, Lakeview BLM, Loren Davis, Ed Knell, and Joshua Tree National Park for providing access to collections and photographs of projectile points. We appreciate Cassie Manning sharing and allowing us to present the stable isotope information from dates at the Hetrick Site. Lastly, thanks to Katelyn McDonough and Derek Reaux for comments on an early version of this chapter and to the editors and anonymous reviewers whose comments improved this manuscript.

3

Western Stemmed Tradition Toolstone Conveyance and Its Role in Understanding How Early Populations Settled into the Northwestern Great Basin

Geoffrey M. Smith, Dennis L. Jenkins, Derek J. Reaux, Sophia Jamaldin, Richard L. Rosencrance, *and* Katelyn N. McDonough

Our understanding of the Western Stemmed Tradition (WST) has improved substantially in recent years. Researchers have established and/or refined the ages of important sites (Davis et al. 2019; Graf 2007; Jenkins et al. 2012), the overall duration of the WST and the respective ages of the projectile points that it encompasses (Brown et al. 2019; Rosencrance 2019; Rosencrance et al., Chapter 2), and major technological and subsistence trends (Beck and Jones 2009; Duke 2011; Goebel 2007; Hockett 2007; Hockett et al. 2017; Pratt et al. 2020). Despite this progress, substantial challenges remain. Foremost is the fact that many WST sites are open-air lithic scatters that lack datable materials and food residues. Thus researchers are forced to lean on the records from undated surface assemblages to understand technology and land-use, and, at the same time, utilize caves and rockshelters to understand subsistence and chronology. Neither site type can provide a complete picture of past lifeways, and to best understand the WST, information both from open and closed sites should be used together.

In this chapter, we discuss one element of the WST that most late Pleistocene and Early Holocene (LP/EH) sites in the northwestern Great Basin possess: tools and waste flakes made from obsidian or other fine-grained volcanic (FGV) toolstone. These artifacts can tell us a great deal about how groups used individual sites and, when considered together, how and where people moved across the landscape. We focus on 14 assemblages from WST sites, components, or locales (i.e., groups of related sites) that together provide the largest collection of published LP/EH sourcing data for the northwestern Great Basin if not the entire Intermountain West.

The Western Stemmed Tradition

The WST refers to a constellation of artifact types dating to the LP/EH found in the Intermountain West. Lithic artifacts include long- and short-stemmed projectile points, unfluted concave-base points, and crescents (Smith and Barker 2017). Most WST sites probably date to between ~12,500 and ~9000 cal BP (Rosencrance 2019), but two sites—the Paisley Caves (Jenkins et al. 2012) and Cooper's Ferry (Davis et al. 2019)—have produced Clovis-aged and/or older-than-Clovis dates (before ~13,500 cal BP) in good association with stemmed points. Fluted points are sometimes found with stemmed points in surface contexts; however, their role in the initial peopling of the region is debated (Beck and Jones 2010; Davis et al. 2012; Davis et al. 2019; Fiedel and Morrow 2012; Jenkins et al. 2012; Jones and Beck, Chapter 8). Because of the Clovis-aged and/or older-than-Clovis WST occupations at the Paisley Caves and Cooper's Ferry, we do not think that fluted points mark the first visitors to the region and may instead reflect the spread of a novel technology or groups from east of the Rocky Mountains into an already populated region (sensu Beck and Jones 2010; Davis et al. 2012; Jones and Beck, Chapter 8).

Stemmed points, crescents, and other WST tools are mostly found around relict pluvial lakes and wetlands (Sanchez et al. 2017; Smith 2007; G. Smith, Felling, Wriston, et al. 2015), but they have also been found along delta channels (Beck and Jones 2009; Elston et al. 2014; Madsen, Oviatt, et al. 2015; Reaux 2020, 2021; Reaux et al. 2018), in mid-elevation caves and rockshelters (Goebel 2007), and deep in upland canyons (Bryan 1979; Felling 2015; Hanes 1988; Layton 1970; Lynch et al., Chapter 6; G. Smith, Felling, Taylor, et al. 2015). Some of those caves and shelters also contain textiles including sandals, mats, bags, baskets, and cordage dated to the LP/EH (Connolly et al. 2016). Food residues include most of the resources consumed ethnographically except seeds processed using milling stones (Hockett 2007; Hockett et al. 2017; Kennedy 2018). WST groups also produced rock art (Middleton et al. 2014) and traded for marine shell beads with Paleocoastal groups (Smith et al. 2016).

Our understanding of the WST is imperfect and incomplete; however, in most regards WST lifeways appear to have been similar to those documented for later groups. This has prompted some researchers to adopt terms like *Paleoarchaic* (Willig 1989) or *Prearchaic* (Elston et al. 2014) to emphasize continuity between early and later lifeways. We also recognize this relative continuity but focus here on one aspect of the WST that was fundamentally different from later cultures: toolstone conveyance. WST groups used a wider range of obsidian and FGV sources and conveyed those materials greater distances via residential and/or logistical movements, or trade, than later groups (King 2016; McGuire 2002; Reaux 2020; Smith 2010, 2022). We suspect that this difference had something to do with how WST groups initially explored and later settled into the region.

In this chapter, we bring together samples of sourced WST artifacts from 14 assemblages recovered from surface sites, caves, and rockshelters in the northwestern Great Basin—a region that features one of the richest lithic terrains and WST records in the Intermountain West. We focus on two topics: (1) the earliest recognizable conveyance patterns in the region; and (2) possible diachronic shifts in WST toolstone conveyance.

Materials and Methods

Source provenance data collected for WST points and other artifacts form the basis of our study.

The Sites

The artifacts analyzed in this study come from excavated and surface-collected sites in three parts of the northwestern Great Basin: (1) the Fort Rock and Chewaucan basins; (2) southeastern Oregon's lake basins; and (3) Nevada's High Rock Country (Figure 3.1). Fort Rock and Chewaucan basin sites include the Connley Caves, Paisley Caves, and Fort Rock Cave. Southeastern Oregon sites include North Warner Valley, Guano Valley, and Hawksy Walksy Valley. High Rock Country sites include the four Parman Localities, Hanging Rock Shelter, and Last Supper Cave.

The Connley Caves

The Connley Caves are eight wave-cut shelters situated at the north end of Paulina Marsh in the Fort Rock Basin. The caves contain deposits reaching depths of 3.0–3.5 m. Stephen Bedwell (1970, 1973) excavated there in the late 1960s and reported rich WST assemblages together with LP/EH radiocarbon dates, but the hasty pace of his work left important questions unanswered. The Univer-

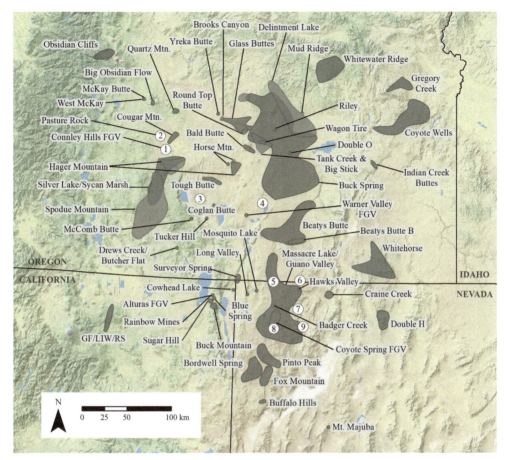

FIGURE 3.1. Map of Western Stemmed Tradition sites and toolstone sources discussed in the text: (*1*) the Connley Caves; (*2*) Fort Rock Cave; (*3*) the Paisley Caves; (*4*) North Warner Valley; (*5*) Catnip Creek Delta Locality (Guano Valley); (*6*) Hawksy Walksy Valley; (*7*) Last Supper Cave; (*8*) Hanging Rock Shelter; and (*9*) the Parman Localities. Map courtesy of Erica Bradley.

sity of Oregon (UO) field school renewed investigations in 2000 and 2001 in caves 3, 5, and 6. Following the conclusion of excavations at the Paisley Caves (described below), the field school returned in 2014 to focus on caves 4 and 5. These excavations produced hundreds of additional tools from dense cultural deposits, and fieldwork is ongoing.

The site has now yielded more than 50 cultural late Pleistocene and six Early Holocene-aged radiocarbon dates (Jenkins et al. 2017; McDonough et al. 2022; Rosencrance et al. 2022). The caves were most frequently occupied during the late Pleistocene, with repeated visits taking place between ~12,700 and 11,600 cal BP. We are still evaluating possible evidence for a pre-12,700 cal BP component. Site use declined during the Early Holocene, but two hearth features date between ~10,500–10,100 cal BP. Here, we present X-ray fluorescence (XRF) data for artifacts from the caves' LP/EH components, most of which are new and some of which were previously presented by Jamaldin (2018) and Thatcher (2001).

The Paisley Caves

The Paisley Caves lie ~80 km southeast of the Connley Caves in the Summer Lake subbasin of the Chewaucan Basin. The seven caves and shelters containing evidence of human occupation were wave-cut by pluvial Lake Chewaucan at elevations between 1,367 to 1,378 m asl. They contain deep WST deposits that reach depths of 2.5–3.0 m. Luther Cressman (1942; Cressman et al. 1940) excavated in caves 1–3 between 1938 and 1940. In Cave 1, he recovered WST points, bifaces, flake tools, and braided cordage from Younger Dryas and older deposits. In Cave 3, he recovered horse, camel, bison, and waterfowl bones on and around a small U-shaped boulder-lined house/living floor. Some bones were charred and appeared to have been broken for marrow extraction, convincing Cressman that people processed and consumed the animals in the cave. Others argued that Cressman failed to adequately demonstrate a Pleistocene occupation (Heizer and Baumhoff 1970; Krieger 1944).

The UO field school investigated the site in 2002, 2003, 2007, and 2009–2011 to determine if human occupations were contemporaneous with extinct megafauna by dating cultural materials and megafauna bone. Currently, the three caves have provided 155 late Pleistocene and 35 Early Holocene radiocarbon dates. Human occupations are dated to between ~14,400 and 11,600 cal BP for the former and between ~11,600 and 9000 cal BP for the latter (Jenkins et al. 2013). Coprolites containing human DNA and fecal biomarkers date occupations as early as ~14,200 cal BP (Gilbert et al. 2008; Shillito et al. 2020), and cut-marked bone has been dated to ~13,800 cal BP (Jenkins et al. 2013) and ~14,400 cal BP (Hockett and Jenkins 2013). Accepted dates for camel, horse, and mammoth remains range between 14,500 and 13,200 cal BP (Jenkins et al. 2013), overlapping with human occupations by a millennium or more. Stemmed points are the oldest diagnostic artifacts at the Paisley Caves, dated to ~13,000 cal BP (Jenkins et al. 2012). The pre-13,000 cal BP occupations contain copious debitage, retouched flakes, and scrapers. Here, we present sourcing data for tools and flakes from the caves' late Pleistocene and Early Holocene components, most of which have never been published.

Fort Rock Cave
Fort Rock Cave was excavated several times during the twentieth century (Bedwell 1970; Cressman 1938). This work produced dozens of Fort Rock sandals that we now know date to the Early Holocene (Connolly and Barker 2004; Smith and Barker 2017), along with numerous WST points and other tools. Unfortunately, scant field notes and poor excavation standards have made understanding the site's history difficult. Based on excavations conducted in 2015 and 2016, Connolly and colleagues (2017) concluded that: (1) the contexts from which most artifacts were recovered are probably unknowable; and (2) a conservative estimate of when groups first occupied the site is ~11,000 cal BP, with a heavy period of use ~10,500–9200 cal BP. The sourcing data we present here come from Jamaldin's (2018) thesis.

North Warner Valley
Between 2011 and 2013, the University of Nevada, Reno (UNR) conducted survey and backhoe trenching to reconstruct the natural and cultural history of North Warner Valley. As the Pleistocene ended, pluvial Lake Warner receded southward, pausing at ~1,390 m asl sometime between ~14,500 and 12,400 cal BP (Wriston and Smith 2017). Smith and colleagues (2015b) reported WST points from mostly along but also above and below the 1,390 m asl shoreline. They argued that WST sites along the shoreline probably date to around the onset of the Younger Dryas. Here, we only include artifacts from those presumptive Younger Dryas-aged sites.

Guano Valley (The Catnip Creek Delta Locality)
Guano Valley is one of the smallest lake basins in the region. It receives much of its water from drainages emanating from Nevada's High Rock Country, located to the south. During wet periods, Guano Lake would have filled to a depth of ~2–4 m before overflowing into Guano Slough at the valley's north end. Derek Reaux and colleagues (Reaux 2020, 2021; Reaux et al. 2018) discovered a

rich WST record along a channel system at the valley's south end that they refer to as the Catnip Creek Delta (CCD) Locality. The CCD was likely occupied when a productive delta characterized the area. The locality remains undated, but it contained a large number of short-stemmed points. Similar points have been dated to the Early Holocene at several nearby WST sites (e.g., Last Supper Cave, Hanging Rock Shelter, Little Steamboat Point-1 Rockshelter [Rosencrance 2019 and references therein]), suggesting that the CCD also dates to that general period. Reaux and colleagues (2018) published preliminary XRF data for the CCD. Here, we present the results of Reaux's (2020, 2021) more comprehensive sourcing study.

Hawksy Walksy Valley

UNR visited Hawksy Walksy Valley in the 1990s and collected WST points from sites ringing the basin (Christian 1997). In 2018 and 2019, UNR returned to Hawksy Walksy Valley to more fully document the sites and reconstruct the basin's hydrographic history. Our analysis and reporting of those records are in their infancy; however, we know that a shallow marsh covered the valley floor ~9000 cal BP (Bradley et al. 2020). Most WST sites sit just above what was likely the marsh's edge. The largest site, 35HA840, stretches ~2.5 km along a low ridge that extends into the basin's center. The dated marsh deposits and abundant short-stemmed points at 35HA840 and other sites suggest that most WST activity in Hawsky Walksy Valley occurred during the Early Holocene. Christian (1997) originally sourced some of the WST points, but given improvements in both XRF analysis and our understanding of Oregon's lithic landscape since then, we reanalyzed all of the WST points in his sample.

Last Supper Cave

Last Supper Cave is located above Hell Creek deep in Nevada's High Rock Country. Tom Layton excavated most of the cave's deposits in 1973 and 1974 (Layton and Davis 1978). Since then, work with the collection has proceeded in a piecemeal fashion, and discussions of site chronology (Felling 2015; G. Smith, Felling, Taylor, et al. 2015), textiles (Camp 2017; Ollivier et al. 2017), and fauna (Grayson 1988) are available. Layton recovered stemmed points and other artifacts from deposits dated between ~10,400 and 9200 cal BP (Felling 2015; Layton and Davis 1978; G. Smith, Felling, Taylor, et al. 2015). Smith (2008, 2009) published sourcing data for the stemmed points and a sample of debitage. More recently, Felling (2015) presented sourcing data for some additional artifacts.

Hanging Rock Shelter

Hanging Rock Shelter is located in Hanging Rock Canyon ~35 km southwest of Last Supper Cave. Layton (1970) excavated there a few years before Last Supper Cave and recovered WST points from the site's Yellow and Suborganic strata. Grayson (1988) analyzed the Hanging Rock Shelter fauna. Until recently, the site remained largely undated, but Rosencrance (2019) has presented new radiocarbon dates from a hearth feature that show the WST occupations occurred ~9400–9300 cal BP, roughly around the same time as Last Supper Cave's WST occupations. Smith and colleagues (2011) published sourcing data for WST points from the site.

The Parman Localities

The Parman Localities are four open-air sites located along the margins of Five Mile Flat, a subbasin of the larger Summit Lake basin. Layton (1979) briefly visited the sites during the same period as he excavated Last Supper Cave and Hanging Rock Shelter. Smith (2006, 2007) returned to the localities three decades later and surface collected numerous WST points and other artifacts. Because the sites sit just above the basin floor, Layton (1979) suggested that they represent lakeside camps occupied during the same general but unknown period. A few years ago, the Far Western Anthropological Research Group excavated a portion of Locality 3 and another nearby WST site and obtained radiocarbon dates of ~11,200 cal BP (Hildebrandt et al. 2016), suggesting that groups occupied the Parman Localities during the initial Early Holocene. Smith (2006, 2007) originally presented sourcing data for localities 1 and 3. Here, we also present data from localities 2 and 4 for the first time.

The Artifacts

Our sample of sourced WST points ($n = 1{,}248$), other tools including bifaces, crescents, cores, and flake tools ($n = 2{,}514$), and debitage ($n = 894$) is derived from these sites. The sites occur in a range of settings, were investigated in various ways, and reported in different levels of detail. Some sites, such as the Paisley and Connley caves, have been recently excavated using high-precision methods; therefore, most artifacts come from well-dated contexts. Other sites (e.g., Last Supper Cave, Hanging Rock Shelter) were carefully excavated, but our understanding of their stratigraphy and chronology remains imperfect. Yet others (e.g., Fort Rock Cave) were excavated hastily and without careful note-taking. Finally, our most sizeable WST assemblages come from surface sites that are loosely dated by associations with landforms of known ages (e.g., the Parman Localities, Hawksy Walksy Valley, North Warner Valley) and/or typological cross-dating (e.g., the CCD). All sites have obsidian or FGV sources located less than 20 km from them, and all sites occur more broadly within a rich lithic landscape, which offers some degree of control over the effects of raw-material availability on technological organization and toolstone conveyance (Andrefsky 1994; Smith and Harvey 2018).

Table 3.1 lists the sites included in our study and the age estimates for the deposits/landforms from which the artifacts were recovered. It also lists the publications in which the source provenance data first appeared. For the sites listed in Table 3.1, we indicate the method(s) used to characterize the artifacts. Many artifacts were sourced by staff at the Northwest Research Obsidian Studies Laboratory (NWROSL).[1] Others—in particular those presented in recent publications by UNR researchers—were sourced using an Olympus portable X-ray fluorescence (pXRF) unit.[2] Trace-element data from NWROSL projects may be directly compared to those generated by other commercial laboratories, but data from UNR's pXRF studies cannot. We excluded any characterized obsidian and FGV artifacts that could not be assigned to known source locations. We also excluded artifacts made of cryptocrystalline silicates (CCS), which comprise less than 10% of the artifacts in each assemblage.

The variability of our sample reflects the nature of the broader WST record: it is derived from work conducted using various methods over nearly a century. Conclusions drawn from it must necessarily be broad, and any recognizable patterns will likely be coarse-grained. With these issues in mind, we now turn our attention to toolstone conveyance in the northwestern Great Basin and what it can tell us about WST landscape use and if and how it changed over time.

Results

Tables 3.2–3.6 list the source assignments for projectile points, other tools, and debitage from 14 sites, components, or locales. More than 50 obsidian and FGV types are present. Sources of these materials occur mostly in southeastern Oregon, northeastern California east of the Cascade Range, and northwestern Nevada north of the Lahontan Basin (see Figure 3.1). One WST point made of obsidian from Utah's Wildhorse Canyon was found in North Warner Valley. At 745 km from the source of material on which it is made, the point is a clear outlier. The rest of the artifacts are made of materials found 1–267 km from the sites where they were discarded. Tables 3.2–3.6 also list the numbers of projectile points, other tools, and debitage made of unknown obsidian and FGV types for each assemblage. Again, we did not include these in our analysis but present them to demon-

TABLE 3.1. Western Stemmed Tradition Sites from Oregon and Nevada Included in This Study.

Study Area and Site	Period[a]	Dating Method[b]	Sourcing Method[c]	Publications Containing Sourcing Data
Fort Rock and Chewaucan Basins				
Paisley Caves 1, 2, and 5	LP	^{14}C, OH	CL	this study; Jenkins et al. (2016)
Paisley Caves 1, 2, and 5	EH	^{14}C, OH	CL	this study
Connley Caves 4, 5, and 6	LP	^{14}C, OH	CL, pXRF	this study; Jamaldin (2018); Thatcher (2001)
Connley Caves 4, 5, and 6	EH	^{14}C, OH	CL, pXRF	this study; Jamaldin (2018); Thatcher (2001)
Fort Rock Cave	EH	^{14}C	pXRF	Jamaldin (2018)
Southeastern Oregon lake basins				
North Warner Valley	LP	AL	CL	G. Smith, Felling, Taylor, et al. (2015)
Catnip Creek Delta Locality	EH	TCD	CL, pXRF	Reaux (2020)
Hawksy Walksy Valley	EH	AL	pXRF	this study
Nevada's High Rock Country				
Last Supper Cave	EH	^{14}C	CL	Felling (2015); Smith (2008, 2009, 2010)
Hanging Rock Shelter	EH	^{14}C	CL	Smith et al. (2011)
Parman Locality 1	EH	AL, TCD	CL	Smith (2006)
Parman Locality 2	EH	AL, TCD	CL	this study
Parman Locality 3	EH	^{14}C, AL, TCD	CL	Smith (2006)
Parman Locality 4	EH	AL, TCD	pXRF	this study

[a] LP = late Pleistocene; EH = Early Holocene.
[b] ^{14}C = radiocarbon dating; OH = obsidian hydration; AL = associated dated landform; TCD = typological cross-dating.
[c] CL = commercial laboratory; pXRF = portable x-ray fluorescence unit.

strate that they comprise a very small part of each sample.

General Patterns

A common trend at the WST sites in our sample is a reliance on local (≤20 km) raw materials (Table 3.7). This trend contrasts with long-distance toolstone procurement patterns at WST sites in the eastern Great Basin, some of which are presented elsewhere in this volume (Duke and Stueber, Chapter 4; Lynch et al., Chapter 6). This difference may reflect regional variation in groups' degrees of planning depth and/or risk sensitivity (Brantingham 2006) or, perhaps more likely, toolstone availability (Jones et al. 2012; Smith and Harvey 2018). A preponderance of local raw materials at WST sites in the northwestern Great Basin is reflected not only in the high proportion of projectile points (37%) made of local sources but especially other tools (76%) and flakes (63%), the latter of which mostly reflect onsite tool production or maintenance. At the Connley Caves,

TABLE 3.2. Source Assignments for Western Stemmed Tradition Artifacts from Fort Rock and Chewaucan Basin Sites.

Geochemical Type	Connley Caves No. 4–6 Late Pleistocene				Connley Caves No. 4 and 5 Early Holocene				Paisley Caves 1, 2, and 5 Late Pleistocene			
	Points	Other Tools	Flakes	km	Points	Other Tools	Flakes	km	Points	Other Tools	Flakes	km
Badger Creek	—	—	—	—	—	—	—	—	—	—	2	133
Bald Butte	2	4	3	22	—	—	—	—	—	—	—	—
Beatys Butte[a]	1	—	2	140	1	—	—	140	—	—	1	105
Big Stick	3	—	—	97	2	1	—	97	—	—	—	—
Blue Spring	—	—	1	170	—	—	—	—	—	—	—	—
Buck Mountain	3	—	—	170	2	—	—	170	—	—	—	—
Coglan Buttes	6	2	1	74	1	—	—	—	—	2	—	18
Connley Hills FGV	13	289	—	1	2	2	—	1	—	—	—	—
Cougar Mountain	15	63	119	22	5	12	20	22	—	—	10	75
Cowhead Lake	3	4	—	155	—	—	—	—	—	—	1	100
Drews Creek/Butcher Flat	—	—	2	113	—	—	—	—	—	—	—	—
Glass Buttes (all varieties)	15	10	18	77	2	3	4	77	—	3	2	92
GF/LIW/RS[b]	—	1	—	160	—	—	—	—	—	—	—	—
Hager Mountain	1	4	6	8	2	—	—	8	—	—	—	—
Hawks Valley	1	—	—	205	—	—	—	—	—	—	—	—
Horse Mountain[c]	6	9	6	66	1	3	2	66	1	—	8	55
Massacre Lake/Guano Valley	—	—	—	—	—	—	—	—	1	—	—	178
McComb Butte	—	—	—	—	—	—	—	—	—	—	3	20
McKay Butte	—	—	1	64	1	—	—	64	—	—	—	—
Pasture Rock	—	—	—	—	—	1	—	16	—	—	—	—

Source												
Quartz Mountain	7	7	12	44	5	1	1	44	1	—	1	81
Silver Lake/Sycan Marsh	10	13	31	5	3	3	—	5	—	—	5	50
Spodue Mountain	8	2	5	24	2	—	1	24	—	—	3	50
Sugar Hill	7	1	—	164	—	1	—	164	—	—	—	—
Surveyor Spring	—	—	—	—	—	—	—	—	—	—	1	95
Tough Butte	—	—	—	—	—	—	—	—	—	—	1	25
Tucker Hill	3	7	5	81	3	2	1	81	4	5	125	20
Variety 5	1	3	—	26	2	—	—	26	—	—	3	39
Venator[d]	2	—	—	230	—	—	—	—	—	—	—	—
Wagontire	1	1	—	100	—	—	—	—	—	—	—	—
Yreka Butte	3	—	—	68	1	1	—	68	—	—	—	—
Unknown obsidian/FGV[e]	1	1	2	—	1	3	—	—	—	—	—	—
Total	111	420	212		35	30	29		7	10	166	
Mean distance (km)	61	13	31		52	42	35		56	41	31	

Note: FGV = fine-grained volcanic materials
[a] Includes Beatys Butte B obsidian.
[b] GF/LIW/RS = Grasshopper Flat/Lost Iron Well/Red Switchback.
[c] Includes Horse Mountain B obsidian.
[d] Includes both obsidian and FGV.
[e] Not included in total artifact counts.

TABLE 3.3. Source Assignments for Western Stemmed Tradition Artifacts from Additional Fort Rock and Chewaucan Basin Sites.

	Paisley Caves 1, 2, and 5 Early Holocene				Fort Rock Cave Early Holocene			
Geochemical Type	Points	Other Tools	Flakes	km	Points	Other Tools	Flakes	km
Alturas FGV	—	—	2	135	—	—	—	—
Badger Creek	—	—	2	133	—	—	—	—
Bald Butte	—	1	—	80	3	—	—	93
Big Obsidian Flow	—	—	—	—	3	—	1	35
Big Stick	—	—	—	—	—	—	1	107
Blue Spring	—	—	1	92	—	—	—	—
Buck Mountain	—	—	1	92	1	—	—	191
Coglan Buttes	—	3	—	18	—	—	—	—
Cougar Mountain	—	—	2	75	27	6	91	16
Cowhead Lake	—	—	—	—	4	—	—	177
Double O[a]	—	—	—	—	1	—	—	143
Glass Buttes (all varieties)	—	2	3	92	12	—	6	79
Hager Mountain	—	—	—	—	5	1	1	28
Hawks Valley	—	—	—	—	1	—	—	233
Horse Mountain[b]	—	4	5	55	—	1	1	82
Massacre Lake/Guano Valley	—	—	—	—	1	—	—	178
McComb Butte	—	—	2	20	—	—	—	—
McKay Butte	—	—	—	—	8	2	1	42
Obsidian Cliffs	—	—	—	—	1	—	—	105
Quartz Mountain	—	—	1	81	17	—	29	28
Round Top Butte	—	—	—	—	1	—	—	95
Silver Lake/Sycan Marsh	1	—	1	50	23	—	1	27
Spodue Mountain	—	—	2	50	9	—	—	40
Tank Creek	—	—	1	80	—	—	2	102
Tough Butte	—	—	—	—	—	—	—	—
Tucker Hill	—	7	127	20	1	—	—	103
Whitewater Ridge	—	—	—	—	1	—	—	44
Yreka Butte	—	—	1	95	4	—	1	67
Unknown obsidian/FGV[c]	—	—	1		6	1	—	
Total	1	17	151		123	10	135	
Mean distance (km)	50	40	29		47	29	25	

Note: FGV = fine–grained volcanic materials
[a]Includes both obsidian and FGV.
[b]Includes Horse Mountain B obsidian.
[c]Not included in total artifact counts.

knappers primarily used Connley Hills FGV to manufacture scrapers and retouched flakes, but rarely bifaces or WST points (Donham et al. 2020). At the Paisley Caves, people used Tucker Hill, Coglan Buttes, and Bald Butte obsidian to make both bifaces and flake tools. Finally, at the CCD and the Parman Localities, people used Massacre Lake/Guano Valley obsidian to manufacture hundreds of bifaces.

North Warner Valley is an exception to this trend. While cobbles of Buck Spring obsidian naturally occur there, people did not use them to any great extent. Instead, the more distant Beatys Butte source was the "go-to" source, perhaps because it offered larger or higher-quality cobbles (Reaux 2020). At each location, the high proportions of artifacts made of local materials could either reflect the last sources that people visited before they arrived (either intentionally as part of a gearing-up strategy [Binford 1978] or during chance encounters [Brantingham 2003]) or the sources that they traveled to while living there.

Artifacts made of nonlocal toolstone occur in different frequencies: 63% of WST points, 24% of other tools, and 37% of flakes are made of exotic raw materials (see Table 3.7). These proportions differ significantly from those present in the local artifact sample (χ^2 = 525.79, df = 2, p < 0.001), and WST points are made of nonlocal sources more often than expected by chance while other tools are made of nonlocal sources less often than expected by chance. This difference is not surprising given that people seem to have curated stemmed points to a greater extent than other tool types (Smith and Harvey 2018). That said, projectile points were not the only tools that people carried between sites. Other transported tools include broken bifaces (some of which are probably stemmed point fragments), scrapers, retouched flakes, and cores. Unmodified flakes of materials originating 100+ km away also occur at several of the sites, though generally in low frequencies. Some sites contain nontrivial numbers of scrapers made of nonlocal materials (e.g., 24 from the CCD and 42 from the Connley Caves' late Pleistocene sample), suggesting that people sometimes carried flake blanks or finished flake tools as they traveled.

Change Across Time

In regards to how people first explored and settled into new regions, one reasonable expectation is that the first generations would know less about the landscape than later generations. In terms of sites' source profiles, this progressive knowledge might be reflected several ways. First, earlier assemblages might contain fewer toolstone types. Second, earlier assemblages might contain higher proportions of artifacts made of toolstone from more visible or recognizable sources (e.g, Glass Buttes or Beatys Butte, both of which are associated with prominent volcanic landforms; Stueber and Skinner 2015). Third, earlier assemblages might contain higher proportions of artifacts made of toolstone from more spatially extensive sources (e.g., Massacre Lake/Guano Valley obsidian, which covers ~2,600 km² in Oregon and Nevada) because people would have had a greater chance of encountering them than more localized sources. Finally, earlier assemblages might exhibit higher average artifact transport distances if groups moved unencumbered through a sparsely populated landscape and/or later WST groups increasingly relied on local sources as residential mobility decreased and/or territorial circumscription increased (Jones et al. 2003).

With only three late Pleistocene components in our sample (one of which, North Warner Valley, includes only projectile points and lacks a corresponding Early Holocene component), it is difficult to assess whether any of these trends are evident. First, in terms of toolstone richness, when adjusted for sample size the WST point sample from the late Pleistocene component of the Connley Caves is not significantly richer than the Early Holocene WST point sample (p = 0.999).[3] This is also the case for the LP/EH WST point

TABLE 3.4. Source Assignments for Western Stemmed Tradition Artifacts from Southeastern Oregon Lake Basins.

Geochemical Type	North Warner Valley Late Pleistocene				Catnip Creek Delta Locality Early Holocene				Hawksy Walksy Valley Early Holocene			
	Points	Other Tools	Flakes	km	Points	Other Tools	Flakes	km	Points	Other Tools	Flakes	Km
Alturas FGV	—	—	—	—	6	12	—	105	—	—	—	—
Badger Creek	1	—	—	119	34	50	2	24	7	—	—	39
Bald Butte	1	—	—	50	—	—	—	—	—	—	—	—
Beatys Butte[a]	9	—	—	37	85	94	4	46	27	—	—	44
Big Stick	3	—	—	48	—	—	—	—	—	—	—	—
Blue Spring	1	—	—	126	4	2	—	68	—	—	—	—
BS/PP/FM[b]	—	—	—	—	7	11	2	72	4	—	—	83
Buck Mountain	—	—	—	—	26	22	1	62	6	—	—	100
Buck Spring	1	—	—	1	—	3	—	82	—	—	—	—
Cowhead Lake	—	—	—	—	44	43	4	45	6	—	—	75
Coyote Springs FGV	—	—	—	—	13	47	3	44	7	—	—	43
Coyote Wells	—	—	—	—	1	—	—	222	1	—	—	220
Craine Creek	—	—	—	—	—	4	—	61	2	—	—	51
Double H/Whitehorse	—	—	—	—	9	4	—	121	9	—	—	102
Double O[c]	1	—	—	54	2	—	—	139	3	—	—	142
Drews Creek/Butcher Flat	—	—	—	—	1	—	—	111	—	—	—	—
Glass Buttes (all varieties)	3	—	—	76	5	4	—	181	—	—	—	—
GF/LIW/RS[d]	—	—	—	—	2	—	—	191	—	—	—	—
Gregory Creek	2	—	—	177	—	—	—	—	—	—	—	—
Hawks Valley	—	—	—	—	18	23	—	30	52	—	—	5
Horse Mountain[e]	12	—	—	57	7	4	—	137	—	—	—	—
Indian Creek Buttes	1	—	—	121	1	1	—	170	2	—	—	150
Long Valley	1	—	—	104	11	17	—	21	1	—	—	50

Source	C1	C2	C3	C4	C5	C6	C7	C8	C9	C10	C11	C12	C13	C14	C15	C16	C17	C18	C19
Massacre Lake/Guano Valley	5	—	—	—	—	—	—	64	196	1292	175	1	50	—	—	—	—	—	13
McKay Butte	—	—	—	—	—	—	—	—	—	—	—	—	—	—	—	—	—	—	—
Mosquito Lake	1	—	—	—	—	—	—	110	29	35	—	32	5	—	—	—	—	—	61
Mount Majuba	—	—	—	—	—	—	—	—	—	—	—	—	1	—	—	—	—	—	163
Mud Ridge	1	—	—	—	—	—	—	99	—	—	—	—	—	—	—	—	—	—	—
Quartz Mountain	—	—	—	—	—	—	—	—	1	1	1	191	—	—	—	—	—	—	—
Rainbow Mines	—	—	—	—	—	—	—	—	5	5	—	68	—	—	—	—	—	—	—
Riley	—	—	—	—	—	—	—	—	2	—	—	165	—	—	—	—	—	—	—
Silver Lake/Sycan Marsh	1	—	—	—	—	—	—	98	—	—	—	—	—	—	—	—	—	—	—
Spodue Mountain	—	—	—	—	—	—	—	—	1	1	—	140	—	—	—	—	—	—	—
Sugar Hill	1	—	—	—	—	—	—	128	4	2	1	71	1	—	—	—	—	—	104
Surveyor Spring	—	—	—	—	—	—	—	—	6	4	—	39	—	—	—	—	—	—	—
Tank Creek	2	—	—	—	—	—	—	50	1	3	—	161	—	—	—	—	—	—	—
Tough Butte	—	—	—	—	—	—	—	—	—	—	—	—	—	—	—	—	—	—	—
Tucker Hill	2	—	—	—	—	—	—	115	—	—	—	—	1	—	—	—	—	—	144
Variety 5	—	—	—	—	—	—	—	—	—	—	—	—	—	—	—	—	—	—	—
Venator[f]	—	—	—	—	—	—	—	—	1	2	—	236	4	—	—	—	—	—	200
Wagontire	2	—	—	—	—	—	—	58	2	—	—	152	—	—	—	—	—	—	—
Warner Valley FGV	—	—	—	—	—	—	—	—	1	1	—	89	—	—	—	—	—	—	—
Whitewater Ridge	—	—	—	—	—	—	—	—	1	—	—	250	—	—	—	—	—	—	—
Wildhorse Canyon	1	—	—	—	—	—	—	745	—	—	—	—	—	—	—	—	—	—	—
Yreka Butte	2	—	—	—	—	—	—	106	—	—	—	—	—	—	—	—	—	—	—
Unknown obsidian/FGV[g]	1	—	—	—	—	—	—	—	30	96	14	—	—	—	—	—	—	—	—
Total	54	—	—	—	—	—	—	526	1687	193		189	—	—	—	—	—	—	—
Mean distance (km)	83	—	—	—	—	—	—	36	12	6		40	—	—	—	—	—	—	—

Note: FGV = fine-grained volcanic materials.
[a] Includes Beatys Butte B obsidian.
[b] BS/PP/FM = Bordwell Spring/Pinto Peak/Fox Mountain.
[c] Includes both obsidian and FGV.
[d] GF/LIW/RS = Grasshopper Flat/Lost Iron Well/Red Switchback.
[e] Includes Horse Mountain B obsidian.
[f] Includes both obsidian and FGV.
[g] Not included in total artifact counts.

TABLE 3.5. Source Assignments for Western Stemmed Tradition Artifacts from High Rock Country Sites.

	Hanging Rock Shelter Early Holocene				Parman Locality 1 Early Holocene				Parman Locality 2 Early Holocene			
Geochemical Type	Points	Other Tools	Flakes	km	Points	Other Tools	Flakes	km	Points	Other Tools	Flakes	km
Badger Creek	1	—	—	27	2	3	—	37	1	1	—	37
Beatys Butte[a]	—	—	—	—	4	—	—	94	—	—	—	—
BS/PP/FM[b]	7	—	—	23	2	1	—	50	2	1	—	50
Buck Mountain	2	—	—	70	1	—	—	98	—	—	—	—
Buffalo Hills	1	—	—	78	—	—	—	—	1	—	—	90
Cowhead Lake	2	—	—	64	1	—	—	87	1	1	—	87
Coyote Springs FGV	2	—	—	7	1	6	—	28	2	2	—	28
Craine Creek	—	—	—	—	2	2	—	17	2	1	—	17
Double H/Whitehorse	—	—	—	—	1	3	—	86	1	—	—	86
Hawks Valley	1	—	—	51	—	—	—	—	2	1	—	40
Indian Creek Buttes	—	—	—	—	1	—	—	191	—	—	—	—
Long Valley	—	—	—	—	2	—	—	63	—	—	—	—
Massacre Lake/Guano Valley	11	—	—	17	11	64	2	3	13	26	—	3
Mount Majuba	—	—	—	—	—	1	—	113	—	—	—	—
Surveyor Spring	1	—	—	68	1	—	—	89	—	—	—	—
Venator[c]	1	—	—	244	—	—	—	—	—	—	—	—
Whitewater Ridge	1	—	—	267	—	—	—	—	—	—	—	—
Unknown obsidian/FGV	1	—	—		1	—	—		—	1	—	
Total	30	—	—		29	80	2		25	33	—	
Mean distance (km)	46	—	—		46	12	3		24	11	—	

Note: FGV = fine-grained volcanic materials.
[a] Includes Beatys Butte B obsidian.
[b] BS/PP/FM = Bordwell Spring/Pinto Peak/Fox Mountain.
[c] Includes both obsidian and FGV.

TABLE 3.6. Source Assignments for Western Stemmed Tradition Artifacts from Additional High Rock Country Sites.

Geochemical Type	Parman Locality 3 Early Holocene				Parman Locality 4 Early Holocene				Last Supper Cave Early Holocene			
	Points	Other Tools	Flakes	km	Points	Other Tools	Flakes	km	Points	Other Tools	Flakes	km
Badger Creek	2	5	—	37	1	3	—	37	1	10	2	26
Beatys Butte[a]	1	—	—	94	—	—	—	—	4	—	—	76
Big Stick	—	—	—	—	1	—	—	194	—	—	—	—
BS/PP/FM[b]	4	—	—	50	—	1	—	50	2	—	—	56
Buck Mountain	1	—	—	98	—	1	—	98	1	—	—	90
Cowhead Lake	2	1	—	87	—	—	—	—	—	—	—	—
Coyote Springs FGV	2	10	—	28	4	4	—	28	1	1	—	22
Craine Creek	3	4	—	17	1	1	—	17	1	—	—	29
Double H/Whitehorse	8	2	—	86	3	1	—	86	1	—	—	91
Hawks Valley	6	1	—	40	2	1	—	40	2	5	1	21
Long Valley	1	—	—	63	—	—	—	—	—	—	—	—
Massacre Lake/Guano Valley	24	76	—	3	14	52	—	3	22	47	3	1
Mount Majuba	—	—	—	—	—	1	—	113	—	—	—	—
Venator[c]	1	—	—	229	1	—	—	229	—	—	—	—
Unknown obsidian/FGV[d]	1	—	—		2	2	—		—	—	—	
Total	55	99	—		27	65	—		35	63	6	
Mean distance (km)	37	11	—		36	11	—		21	7	13	

Note: FGV = fine-grained volcanic materials.
[a] Includes Beatys Butte B obsidian.
[b] BS/PP/FM = Bordwell Spring/Pinto Peak/Fox Mountain.
[c] Includes both obsidian and FGV.
[d] Not included in total artifact counts.

TABLE 3.7. Frequencies of Local and Nonlocal Toolstone.

Site	Period	Local (≤20 km)				Nonlocal (>20 km)			
		Points	Other Tools	Flakes	Total	Points	Other Tools	Flakes	Total
Fort Rock and Chewaucan Basins									
Paisley Caves 1, 2, and 5	LP	4	7	128	139	3	3	38	44
Paisley Caves 1, 2, and 5	EH	—	10	129	139	1	7	22	30
Connley Caves No. 4–6	LP	24	306	37	367	87	114	175	376
Connley Caves No. 4–6	EH	7	6	—	13	28	24	29	81
Fort Rock Cave	EH	27	6	91	124	96	4	44	144
Subtotal		62	335	385	782	215	152	308	675
Southeastern Oregon Lake Basins									
North Warner Valley	LP	1	—	—	1	54	—	—	54
Catnip Creek Delta Locality	EH	196	1292	175	1663	330	395	18	743
Hawksy Walksy Valley	EH	102	—	—	102	87	—	—	87
Subtotal		299	1292	175	1766	471	395	18	884
Nevada's High Rock Country									
Last Supper Cave	EH	22	47	3	72	13	16	3	32
Hanging Rock Shelter	EH	11	—	—	11	19	—	—	19
Parman Locality 1	EH	13	66	2	81	16	14	—	30
Parman Locality 2	EH	15	27	—	42	10	6	—	16
Parman Locality 3	EH	27	80	—	107	28	19	—	47
Parman Locality 4	EH	15	53	—	68	12	12	—	24
Subtotal		103	273	5	381	98	67	3	168
Total		464	1900	565	2929	784	614	329	1728

Note: LP = Late Pleistocene; EH = Early Holocene.

samples at the Paisley Caves ($p = 0.592$). Second, in terms of changing proportions of Beatys Butte, Glass Buttes, and Massacre Lake/Guano Valley obsidian (obsidian types associated with prominent landforms or distributed across wide areas), while those material types do occur in low frequencies in the late Pleistocene samples from the Connley and/or Paisley Caves, so too do numerous materials from localized obsidian sources, many of which are not associated with prominent landforms. Furthermore, the combined contributions of these sources to the LP/EH samples from the Connley Caves and Paisley Caves do not differ substantially (6% vs. 11% for the Connley Caves and 4% vs. 3% for the Paisley Caves). These trends suggest that early groups developed a knowledge of the northwestern Great Basin's lithic landscape fairly quickly.

Finally, in terms of artifact transport distances, the mean distances for stemmed points from the late Pleistocene assemblages (56 km for the Paisley Caves, 61 km for the Connley Caves, and 83 km for North Warner Valley) are each higher than those for the 11

Early Holocene assemblages, which range from a low of 21 km (Last Supper Cave) to a high of 52 km (the Connley Caves). As a group, the late Pleistocene mean distances are significantly greater than the Early Holocene mean distances ($U = 33.0$, $Z = 2.497$, $p = 0.013$). This difference may reflect a decrease in residential mobility and a concomitant increase in occupation span across the Pleistocene–Holocene boundary, though our sample is very small. It is worth noting that Duke and Stueber (Chapter 4) also note a similar reduction in residential mobility between LP/EH sites in Utah's Old River Bed Delta (ORBD). Additionally, at the two sites that offer sourcing data for both late Pleistocene and Early Holocene occupations, no consistent directional trends in transport distances have been found. At the Connley Caves, the mean transport distance for stemmed points decreases over time but increases for other tools and flakes. At the Paisley Caves, the mean transport distances for points, other tools, and flakes remain essentially unchanged.

In sum, a lack of clear diachronic differences in our sample may indicate that people established their seasonal, annual, or longer-term rounds fairly early in time and did not alter them dramatically until the onset of the Middle Holocene (Reaux 2020). The establishment of these patterns may have featured a rapid accumulation of knowledge about the distribution and quality of toolstone sources in the northwestern Great Basin, perhaps within just a few generations—an interval that is probably impossible to detect archaeologically.

Movement Between Areas

Almost every site contains artifacts made of materials found well beyond the one-way distances of ethnographically documented daily foraging ranges and/or multiday logistical forays (Kelly 2011). This pattern is common in most WST assemblages in the Great Basin (Duke and Stueber, Chapter 7; Jones et al. 2003; Jones et al. 2012; King 2016; Lynch et al., Chapter 6; Page and Duke 2015; Smith 2010). While it is difficult to know with certainty how groups conveyed these artifacts (e.g., residential or logistical movements, trade), patterning in the conveyance of exotic materials can at least provide some hints about the interconnectedness of places, if not the people living in those places. Two patterns warrant brief discussion.

First, obsidian and FGV from the Warner Mountains (Alturas FGV and Blue Spring, Buck Mountain, Rainbow Mine, and Sugar Hill obsidian) occur in each assemblage despite the fact that they are found more than ~60 km from the closest site in our sample. While the previously documented sources of these materials occur along the mountains' piedmonts and higher elevations, Reaux (2020) recently discovered cobbles of these materials in the drainages that descend from the Warner Mountains' western slope and debouche into Goose Lake. These raw materials are not appreciably better in terms of their quality, size, or areal extent than any number of closer obsidian types (Reaux 2020), so it seems unlikely that people specifically sought them out. Instead, we believe that if any toolstone types in our sample reflect cyclical movements through the northwestern Great Basin (sensu Jones et al. 2003), it is likely these Warner Mountain sources.

While the presence of Warner Mountain sources at WST sites located both to the north (Oregon's Fort Rock and Chewaucan basins) and south (Nevada's High Rock Country) suggests that groups from both areas visited Goose Lake and/or the adjacent mountains, it is not clear that people ranged throughout an area extending from northwestern Nevada in the south to the Fort Rock Basin in the north. Rather, dissimilarities in the source profiles of assemblages from the different areas suggest that the Warner Mountains may have been along a boundary between the two regions. Most notably, Horse Mountain and Glass Buttes obsidian occur regularly in assemblages from both the Fort Rock and Chewaucan basins, even though those sources are located no closer than ~55 km to any of the sites. In contrast, they are absent in assemblages from Nevada's High Rock Country. Similarly, High Rock Country sources are virtually absent in assemblages from the Fort Rock and Chewaucan basins.

Recognizing these differences, Reaux (2020) conducted a social network analysis (SNA) of WST assemblages from the northwestern Great Basin, including the ones on which we have focused here. He found that sites in the Fort Rock and Chewaucan basins were most closely connected with each other. Sites in the High Rock Country were likewise most closely connected with each other. The CCD possessed the strongest connections of any site in the SNA and was linked to sites in both of those areas. Reaux (2020, 2021) suggested that people moving between the Fort Rock/Chewaucan basins in the north and the High Rock Country in the south repeatedly stopped at the CCD to replenish their lithic tool inventories, which would account for the presence of both northern and southern sources in that assemblage (see Table 3.4). Another possibility is that southern Guano Valley, where the CCD is located, was, like Goose Lake and the Warner Mountains, visited by groups originating from both the north and south. While we currently do not know which of these possibilities is more likely, it is interesting to note that southern Guano Valley and Goose Lake share the same latitude (essentially today's border between Oregon and California/Nevada). As such, it is possible that together they mark an area where smaller northern and southern home ranges overlapped, much like Jones and others (2003) initially envisioned for the northwestern Great Basin.

Regardless of whether the sites included in our study were visited by people ranging through a single large range (sensu Reaux 2020) or smaller northern and southern ranges (sensu Jones et al. 2003), a final notable pattern is that none of the 14 assemblages in our sample contain obsidian or FGV from sources located across the Cascade Range to the west. Similarly, with just one exception (the WST point from North Warner Valley made of obsidian from Utah's Wildhorse Canyon), none of them contain obsidian from Idaho or Utah sources.[4] Similarly, northwestern Great Basin obsidian and FGV sources are generally absent at sites on the Snake River Plain and eastern Great Basin (Duke and Stueber, Chapter 4; Lynch et al., Chapter 6; Page and Duke 2015). Thus, while we know that WST groups lived in northeastern California (Erlandson et al. 2014), the Snake River Plain (Green et al. 1998; Jazwa et al. 2021), and the eastern Great Basin (Goebel 2007; Graf 2007; Madsen, Oviatt, et al. 2015) during the LP/EH, little evidence suggests that they frequented Nevada's High Rock Country, southeastern Oregon's lake basins, or the Fort Rock and Chewaucan basins, or traded toolstone with people who did.

Discussion and Conclusion

Due to its rich WST record and well-documented lithic landscape, the northwestern Great Basin is one of the best places to study Paleoindian mobility and land use in the Intermountain West. Based on the data we have presented, early populations quickly accumulated knowledge about the region's lithic landscape. They may have initially encountered geographically extensive sources or found sources associated with prominent volcanic landforms, but they quickly discovered and frequently returned to many other more localized sources.

In addition to the locations of the sites themselves, the presence of certain obsidian and FGV types in the assemblages indicates that people not only spent time around the region's pluvial lakes but also places somewhat removed from littoral environments. They collected toolstone during their travels, but food resources likely dictated when and where they moved and, in turn, how they selected raw materials (Reaux 2020). Sites positioned in ecotones (transitions between two or more biological communities) that also happened to offer high-quality toolstone—such as the CCD, the Connley Caves, the Parman Localities, and Hawksy Walksy Valley—may have seen people replace worn-out tools in a systematic fashion, while also hunting and gathering in those places. However, we think that most of the time WST groups—at least those traveling between sites—resupplied themselves with toolstone encountered opportunistically.

Similarities in the WST source profiles from the Fort Rock and Chewaucan basins, southeastern Oregon's lake basins, and Nevada's High Rock Country suggest that if the same groups did not visit all of those places at least occasionally, they experienced, at a minimum, periodic interactions between the different groups living there. Moving forward, it may be productive to model the attractiveness of the different areas to try and tease these possibilities apart; for example, would the lower-elevation Fort Rock Basin have been a better place to spend the winter than the higher-elevation High Rock Country or Hawksy Walksy Valley? Did populations move north and south with the changing seasons? Do food residues from WST sites support such scenarios? Coupled with analyses of the faunal, macrobotanical, and pollen records from caves and shelters, paleoenvironmental reconstruction can help to generate predictions about when during the year groups occupied certain places. Source provenance studies may help us to understand the sequence in which groups visited those places.

Acknowledgments

We thank the Northern Paiute and Klamath Tribes (Klamath, Modoc, and Yahooskin), whose traditional lands encompass the area on which we have focused here, for facilitating our ongoing research. Today, most of those lands are administered by the Bureau of Land Management or U.S. Fish and Wildlife Service. Those agencies have provided critical logistical and financial support for archaeological research throughout our respective careers and Bill Cannon, Kathy Stewardson, and Anan Raymond have been especially strong supporters. The UO Museum of Natural and Cultural History's Paleoindian Research Fund provides significant and ongoing financial support to our research at the Paisley and Connley Caves. The Artemisia Archaeological Research Fund provides ongoing support for UNR's work in the northwestern Great Basin. Countless graduate and undergraduate students have participated in the field and lab work on which our study is based. Craig Skinner and Alex Nyers characterized many of the artifacts in our sample but also helped UNR faculty and staff understand how to generate and interpret trace element data collected with our pXRF unit. We thank the editors and peer reviewers for their feedback on this manuscript. Any errors remain our own.

Notes

1. NWROSL staff used a Spectrace 5000 energy dispersive XRF spectrometer to characterize most artifacts. They determined the trace element compositions (Ti, Mn, Fe_2O, Zn, Ga, Rb, Sr, Y, Zr, Nb, Ba, and assorted peak ratios) and compared them to geochemical profiles collected from geologic source samples.

2. The Olympus Delta DP-6000 pXRF uses a 40 kV Rhodium (Rh) anode x-ray tube and Olympus Innov-X Systems software. We employed the fundamental parameters calibration provided by the Innov-X software and ran the device using the two-beam (40 and 10 kV) GeoChem mode at 60 seconds per beam. To build our comparative collection, we initially characterized almost 1,000 previously sourced artifacts analyzed by the NWROSL from 2004 to 2013. Over 60 obsidian/FGV types from the northwestern Great Basin are represented in that sample. Additionally, during the past five years we visited obsidian and FGV sources in the northwestern Great Basin to collect geologic samples to build a robust comparative collection. Our comparative collection currently contains over 90 geochemically distinct obsidian/FGV types from the region. To make

source assignments, we initially analyzed ratios (in ppm) of the mid-Z elements (Sr, Zr, Nb, Y, and Rb) using bivariate scatterplots with R software. With the growth of our comparative collection, we now make all source assignments using discriminant function analysis in the FORDISC program (Pilloud et al. 2017). To assess the accuracy of our in-house assignments using these methods, we submitted 42 previously uncharacterized artifacts from the Parman Localities to the NWROSL for geochemical characterization. Our source assignments of those artifacts included 11 different material types and matched the NWROSL's source assignments in 41 of 42 cases (98%), indicating that our assignments are accurate.

3. To compare toolstone richness among WST points from the LP/EH components at the Paisley and Connley caves, we bootstrapped the larger samples. We drew 1,000 samples of n from the larger of the assemblages, where n is equal to the number of WST points in the smaller of the two components being compared. We also used a bootstrapping technique to generate the p values.

4. The comparative collection that we used to make source assignments with the pXRF unit does not include Idaho or Utah sources; therefore, it is possible that some of the unknown artifacts characterized using the pXRF unit are made of materials from those states. We do not believe that this prospect poses a major problem for two reasons. First, commercial laboratories with more extensive comparative collections that include Idaho and Utah sources have characterized thousands of WST artifacts from southeastern Oregon and northwestern Nevada (our study area) over the past few decades. To our knowledge, *very* few of those artifacts are made of material from Idaho or Utah sources. Second, regardless of whether they were characterized by a commercial lab or our pXRF unit, the artifacts made of unknown obsidian and FGV types represent a very small percentage of each assemblage (see Tables 3.2–3.6). As such, the *potential* presence of a few artifacts made of exotic material types does not weaken our arguments about the robust patterns of WST toolstone use and conveyance that we discuss here.

4

Haskett and Its Clovis Parallels

DARON DUKE *and* DANIEL STUEBER

*Someday the question of Clovis origins will be resolved,
but meanwhile archaeologists should not ignore evidence that indicates
there were parallel developments of other bifacially flaked-stone
projectile-point traditions elsewhere in the Americas.*

—Alan Bryan (1991)

Haskett is a lanceolate projectile point style of the Western Stemmed technological tradition (WST; Figure 4.1).[1] As will be described in this study, it exhibits large size, skilled manufacture, and engineering much like that of the Clovis fluted tradition, despite obvious morphological differences. Clovis points were used to dispatch extinct megafaunal herbivores, notably proboscideans, albeit not exclusively. There is no such evidence for Haskett points, but their timing overlaps the latest directly dated evidence for megafauna in the Great Basin[2] (Grayson 2016), which comes in the form of a ca. 12,2000-year-old human-made ivory point from near Pyramid Lake in western Nevada (Dansie and Jerrems 2004, 2005; Grayson 2016:180; Jerrems et al. 2013) and similarly dated camelid remains in south-central Oregon's Fossil Lake area (Grayson 2016:93; Minor and Spencer 1977).

These are scant data, to be sure, but combined with the technological patterning, they beg the question: Were there two megafauna-caliber projectile point technologies in late Pleistocene North America? Regardless of the timing and preservation imperfections of the archaeological record, circumstantial evidence is sufficient to scale out and consider why Haskett should not be considered with Clovis as a continental interior-wide[3] hunting strategy aimed at megafaunal species during exactly the 500–1,000-year period when they were waning and expiring. If people had a hand in megafaunal extinctions, then their behavior and biogeography should complement the fossil and environmental records.

Last appearance dates frame the question, but technological evidence drives this study. Our analysis centers on data from the Old River Bed Delta (ORBD), an ancient wetland in what is now western Utah's Great Salt Lake Desert. As will be detailed, there is an unambiguous Haskett occupation during the Younger Dryas distinct from the Early Holocene WST record that otherwise dominates the ORBD and early marsh settings across much of the Great Basin (Beck and Jones 1997; Grayson 2011; Madsen, Oviatt, et al. 2015). What are we to do with these outsized WST points, consistent in many ways with a wider North American pattern, against a complete lack of kill sites, megafaunal or otherwise? Poor fossil preservation would seem a poor reason to cordon off the region and discount a conspicuous amalgam of technology and behavior at such an important time in the human experience of the Americas. Our perspective is necessarily broad, emphasizing technological rules over the exceptions to them that, while possible, tend not to be

FIGURE 4.1. Complete Haskett points from the Old River Bed Delta: (*a*) Isolated Find, FS #57; (*b*) 42TO5138, FS #43; (*c*) Isolated Find, FS #71; (*d*) Isolated Find, FS #520; (*e*) 42TO5138, FS #1; (*f*) 42TO6384 (Wishbone site), FS #220; (*g*) Isolated Find, FS #443.

parsimonious. These issues will be discussed as appropriate, but we very simply need a forward hypothesis to account for Haskett, and for a host of reasons that will be explored, we think Clovis on its average provides the best basis for comparison, interpretation, and pushing a stagnant discourse forward.

In this chapter, we present a case for Haskett and Clovis representing two stylistically distinct but technologically similar solutions to the same problem—the hunting of megafaunal herbivores at the largest size scale available in North America. These animals potentially include mammoths, camels, horses, and extinct bison species, but we make no estimation of human preference within this list. Based on Clovis, there is also no reason to limit prey options to megafauna, as we know that modern large game ungulates, such as deer, wapiti, pronghorn, or similar-sized genera were hunted. Our examination emphasizes the technological engineering that governs both point types, and we suggest for current purposes that the largest body sizes are driving maximum point size. We thus also assume that both Haskett and Clovis represent hunting weapons foremost. As will be discussed, clear evidence supports that both styles were also used as knives and other tools, but we view this as part of a subsidiary tier of practical and economizing functions within an overall *chaîne opératoire*. Finally, our theoretical perspective is that technology solves social as well as functional problems, so this approach implies nothing to us about the caloric place of large game in the overall diet.

If Haskett is best compared to Clovis, then potential alternatives should deviate from Haskett where Clovis shows parallels. We use Agate Basin technology as our alternative case. We argue that Agate Basin represents a descendent form of Haskett, akin to the credible descendent relationship of Folsom to Clovis, and represents a specialized shift in focus to smaller bodied prey at the top end, such as the transition between Clovis and Folsom from proboscideans to bison.

Technological Perspective

Technology is an expansive concept that almost eludes definition for practical purposes (e.g., Bettinger et al. 2006; Bijker 1995; Bright et al. 2002; Ingold 1997; Klein and Kleinman 2002; Schiffer 2001, 2011; Ugan et al. 2003). At its broadest, technology can be defined simply as a material solution to a problem. Useful definitions specify the material and the problem for the analytical task at hand. Implicit to this is that the problem in need of solving arises from a base of working knowledge through an evolving set of cultural priorities and pursuant individual incentives.

Put another way, a technology is the ma-

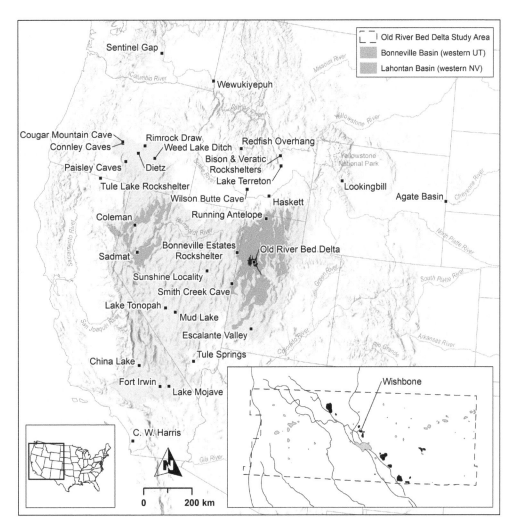

FIGURE 4.2. Map of sites discussed in text and the Old River Bed Delta study area. In inset, black-filled sites are Haskett, and gray-filled are post-Haskett Western Stemmed Tradition (WST).

terial result of all its component parts to ensure success within some socioeconomically determined set of requirements and tolerances. This definition serves to distinguish technology from the purely *technical*. The technical strategies and design parameters that define a technology must be examined against functional variability, which clarifies the fluid decision-making that drives usage and change through time. This approach also reduces the potential for any biased portrayals on our part. To examine technology in this way, context is needed to help narrow influencing factors (Schiffer 2011).

Below, we develop technological contexts for Haskett and Clovis. We begin with Clovis, which is already well-known and requires only pertinent elaboration (see also Jones and Beck, Chapter 8). For Haskett, we present its defining technical features, chronology, geography, and environmental context, the latter focusing on the potential for persistence of megafauna in the Great Basin. Figure 4.2 shows the key sites and locales discussed.

Clovis Technological Context

Perhaps no artifacts in the North American record elicit the fascination and mystery that Clovis projectile points do. They evoke a peerless innovation by the earliest Americans to, in rapid order, settle two continents during an Ice Age via the largest terrestrial mammals on Earth. This is the romantic narrative anyway, enriched by archaeologists and widely believed by the interested public, but it is not true. Archaeological finds over the past half century now show that people were in the Americas several thousand years prior to Clovis (Davis et al. 2019; Jenkins et al. 2012, Shillito et al. 2020; Waters 2019). Whether people were everywhere on the continents and how densely distributed remains unknown, but they nevertheless would have intersected with extinct Pleistocene fauna at numbers exceeding those in Clovis times. Likewise widely accepted radiocarbon evidence confirms that several megafaunal species in the Intermountain West persisted after Clovis until the mid-Younger Dryas (Broughton and Weitzel 2018; Faith and Surovell 2009; Grayson 2016; Grayson and Meltzer 2015; Grayson et al. 2021; Stewart et al. 2021; Wolfe and Broughton 2020, 2021).

The consensus on Clovis timing is that it emerged prior to the Younger Dryas as a relatively short-lived cultural phenomenon spanning ca. 13,050–12,750 cal BP (Waters, Stafford, and Carlson 2020; see also Waters and Stafford 2007a, 2007b). Others have advocated for Clovis extending further back to 13,400 (Miller et al. 2013) or 13,500 cal BP (G. Haynes 2015), but a terminal date of ca. 12,750 cal BP is well-established and generally agreed-upon.

Clovis has a nine-decades-long history of research, with prominent volumes written specifically about its technological complex (e.g., Boldurian and Cotter 1999; Bonnichsen and Turnmire 1991; Bradley et al. 2010; Callahan 1979; Collins 1999; Huckell and Kilby 2014; Jones and Beck, Chapter 8; Smallwood and Jennings 2015; Waters, Pevny, and Carlson 2011; also see Ellis 2013), along with innumerable papers, theses and dissertations, and book chapters. The Clovis lens has not only highlighted the technology as sophisticated but has in many regards driven broader research in flaked stone analysis, especially biface reduction and its economic underpinnings (e.g., Bamforth 2003; Bradley 1982, 1991; Callahan 1979; Goodyear 1989; Huckell 2007; Kay 1996, 2018; Kelly and Todd 1988; Prasciunus 2007; Smallwood 2012; Wilke et al. 1991). Recent efforts in experimental and digital archaeology are rapidly and impressively expanding our understanding of the defining attributes of Clovis projectile points and their variability (e.g., Buchanan and Hamilton 2020; Buchanan et al. 2011; Buchanan, Kilby, et al. 2012; Buchanan et al. 2014; Buchanan, Andrews, et al. 2018; Eren, Buchanan, and O'Brien 2015; Eren et al. 2020; Eren, Meltzer, Story, et al. 2021; Eren, Bebber, et al. 2022; Eren, Meltzer, et al. 2022; O'Brien 2019; O'Brien and Buchanan 2017; O'Brien et al. 2014; O'Brien et al. 2016; Sholts et al. 2012; Smith and Goebel 2018; H. Smith et al. 2015; Story et al. 2019; Thomas et al. 2017; Werner et al. 2018).

The apparent investments in Clovis technology are often argued to be beyond necessity, entailing social processes for its creation, use, and proliferation. Some argue that evolutionary models in costly signaling and prestige hunting hold a promising explanation (Amick 2017; Speth et al. 2013), although the religio-magical has also been suggested (Bradley and Collins 2013). Costly signals are in play when elaborate displays entail costs beyond utilitarian benefits to aid reproductive success (e.g., Bliege Bird et al. 2001; Martin 2019; Stibbard-Hawkes 2019). As yet, no formal models have been developed for Clovis although there is precedent for such work with other time periods (e.g., Hildebrandt and McGuire 2002; Martin 2019). Speth and colleagues (2013) have been the most vocal on the subject, suggesting that costly signaling would explain a problematic discrepancy between conventional notions of specialized big game hunting and archaeologically demonstrated realities of Clovis diet breadth and mobility, among other factors. There would thus be no necessary relationship between the investment in Clovis points and the dietary contribution of the fauna hunted; the largest fauna, elephants especially, may not be worth the effort to hunt for purely consumptive purposes (Lupo and Schmitt 2016).

The use of stone follows in the same vein as a defining aspect of Clovis technology. Experimental studies show that stone tips are not necessary for hunting success at any prey size; wooden or osseous alternatives also are suitable (e.g., Smith 2003; Speth 2018; Waguespack et al. 2009; Wilkins et al. 2014). By the technological perspective in the current study, people must also have known toolstone sources before building a lithic economy on them (G. Haynes 2015; Meltzer 2009; Waters 2019). Evidence for a low-stone invested technology precursor is scant and contested, but Waters and colleagues (2015) argue that early kill sites without direct Clovis associations, such as Wally's Beach (*Camelops, Equus*), Manis (*Mammut*), and Page-Ladson (*Mammut*) represent exactly that.

Clovis projectile points are sometimes associated with proboscideans—at least 16 sites and perhaps more (Mackie and Hass 2021; Mackie et al. 2020)—but other large mammals were hunted as well (Cannon and Meltzer 2004, 2008; G. Haynes 2002; G. Haynes and Hutson 2013; Waguespack and Surovell 2003). Variability in Clovis point size may reflect different prey sizes to some extent, although we know that small Clovis points are found in proboscidean kills, the Colby site in northern Wyoming being a good example (Frison and Todd 1986). Reworking upon breakage is also common (Shott et al. 2021), as is secondary, nonprojectile point use. There is debate as to the extent to which Clovis size variability represents raw projectile performance needs versus tolerances accommodating its full functional profile (see Eren, Meltzer, Story, et al. 2021; Eren, Bebber, et al. 2022; Eren, Meltzer, Story, et al. 2022; Kilby et al. 2022).

The distribution of Clovis puts the emphasis of its use east of the Rocky Mountains and in the deep Southwest into Mexico (Ballenger 2015; G. Haynes 2002; C. V. Haynes and Huckell 2007; Pearson 2017; Sánchez 2016; Sánchez et al. 2014; Shott 2021). They are not so common in the Intermountain West, although morphologically and technologically "classic" Clovis points are present (Beck and Jones 2010; Beck, Jones, and Taylor 2019; Jones and Beck, Chapter 8; Reid et al. 2015; Rondeau 2015a, 2022; Willig et al. 1988). Clovis points fit into a generally consistent morphological template across their range relative to later types but do display regional variability (e.g., Eren et al. 2015; O'Brien and Buchanan 2017; Morrow and Morrow 1999; H. Smith et al. 2015). More broadly, Clovis and descendant fluted forms are well-documented across the Americas, although the first fluted styles in Alaska are thought to be late or post-Clovis, having originated somewhere in the North American interior south of the ice sheets (Morrow and Morrow 1999; Smith and Goebel 2018). Fluted points in South America are less obviously related to Clovis points and appear by approximately 13,000–12,800 cal BP (Nami and Capcha 2020; Prates and Ivan Perez 2021; Suárez 2017).

Haskett Technological Context

Haskett was first defined by Butler (1965; also see 1964, 1967) and recently described by Duke (2015). The intervening half century has not yielded the sorts of key sites and chronological resolution that have been crucial to our understanding of Clovis. Haskett also lacks the conspicuously diagnostic fluted styling of Clovis, which limits friendly field identification, and archaeologists unfamiliar with the technical nuances can mistake Haskett stems for other stemmed points or nondescript biface fragments.

What Is It?

Haskett projectile points possess discernable technical attributes (Figure 4.1; Butler 1964, 1965; Galm and Gough 2008; Swanson 1972:90; Warren and Ranere 1968). In outline, they are unshouldered lanceolates that possess tapering stems and rounded bases. Square, indented, and triangular bases also occur but are less common. Small platform remnants or reworked breaks are sometimes retained at the base. None of the variations alter the overall engineering of Haskett points but rather look to be regional affectations or accommodations for flintknapping and damage vagaries (e.g., manufacturing mishaps, breakage repair, adjustments to facilitate hafting, etc.). The stems usually represent half to three-quarters of the total point length with the position of maximum width being forward. Some are almost bi-pointed, but the blade and stem are readily distinguishable. Stems can possess a distinct lobate and sequential broad collateral flaking style that reaches the middle of the stem faces to produce a medial ridge and a diamond- or oval-shaped cross section. Long overface flaking can be observed on some specimens alongside a thinner lenticular cross section. Intensive grinding of the stem margins is usually applied. These attributes are not so distinctive individually, but they are diagnostic in combination.

Postimpact reworking of Haskett points is common and often shows a substantial drop-off in the symmetry and detail applied during initial production. Rework flaking sometimes invades the stem beneath the original position of maximum width. Reworked blades often become less pointed. Specimen *e* in Figure 4.1 exhibits these attributes over a substantial impact finial. These points may reflect a functional transition to knives (see also Galm and Gough 2008; Lafayette and Smith 2012), and the overall shortening and blunting of the blade lend leverage to the stem for a cutting motion. Some items are refurbished to retain sharp tips. Specimen *d* in Figure 4.1 is one such example where a pointed tip was remade after impact (evidenced by a large finial) but tapered above preserved portions of the original blade. This process creates a staggered outline on each side, but the blade line connecting the two regions is maintained. We surmise this strategy maintained an effective projectile tip, retained heft, and probably managed further breakage, but some experimenting would be needed to know more definitively.

Early descriptions of Haskett technology must be understood with reference to Don Crabtree, who both Robert Butler and Earl Swanson, colleagues at Idaho State University, state that they were consulting with on their respective finds from the Haskett site (also known as the Lake Channel locality), and two rockshelters (Veratic and Bison) along Birch Creek. The importance of Crabtree's insights was widely known to archaeologists at the time and is infused in their work (Max Pavesic, personal communication 2022). The technological and temporal relationships among point types across the greater Snake River Plain in Idaho were considered complex, as they remain today, and a priority research problem.

Butler (1965) identified similarities among Haskett points, the lanceolate points from Cougar Mountain Cave in south-central Oregon (Cowles 1960; Rosencrance et al. 2019), and the Birch Creek points recovered by Swanson at Veratic Rockshelter, Idaho (Swanson et al. 1964; see also Swanson 1972). His discussion of Haskett reduction technology references replication experiments by Crabtree to assert the use of pressure flaking to create the hallmark broad collateral flaking pattern (Butler 1964). Butler (1965) distinguished two Haskett variants, Type I and Type II, with the former being shorter with a broader, thicker blade and the latter being larger overall with a longer blade relative to the stem. Duke (2015) argues that these subtype distinctions are typologically meaningless, Type I being the product of reworking after breakage. Here, we would extend this strategy to the manufacturing process itself when flintknapping choices, necessitated or planned, dictate variations in length and form.

Regarding comparisons, Butler (1965) stated that "Swanson...believes that the Haskett type is probably a later version of the Birch Creek type," although Swanson (1972: 91) later noted the similarity with Haskett among some points in his assemblage. Our own physical viewing of the Birch Creek artifacts confirms that many would rightfully be called Haskett based on technique. Swanson (1972:90) states:

> All of the Birch Creek points have in common…a distinctive pattern of flake scars. [These] are broad collateral pressure flaking scars which feather at the midline on both faces so that the point has a smooth lenticular cross section lacking a median ridge altogether. The collateral flake scars can be replicated with either a sharply pointed or a more broadly beveled pressure flaker. If the pointed fabricator is used, it is necessary to remove small flakes along the edge to isolate a platform which is set between two ridges rather than in line with a ridge. This allows the flake to expand rapidly and leaves a small hollow in the edge. A blunt fabricator takes more of the edge. In either case, the flake is removed by a sudden snapping of downward force which is greater than inward force.

Swanson (1972:90–91) notes that adherence to these techniques declines through time with three Birch Creek type variants, transitioning from the patterned broad collateral flaking to the more irregular removal of narrow, parallel scars. Age control in the early strata of Veratic Rockshelter is problematic (see Keene 2018), so Swanson's subdivisions must be viewed cautiously, but we now know that the flaking patterns observed on Birch Creek points, especially those he thought were the earliest (Birch Creek A and B), are broadly defining of Haskett throughout the Intermountain West, as are several of the attributes with Agate Basin. Both styles are present in eastern Idaho (see also Butler 1978). Swanson's subdivisions were less technological than morphological in the sense that he put some emphasis on basal shape (which may simply represent unresolved spatiotemporal variability or abovementioned flintknapping incidences), so the earlier defined "Haskett" is the preferable term.

Warren and Ranere (1968) cite personal communication with Crabtree as part of their consideration of "Haskett-like" material in the western United States. They present the following seven attributes:
1. "straight lateral margins"
2. collateral flaking at right angle to the margin
3. diffuse bulb of force resulting in shallow flake scars
4. flakes terminate without margins, that is, they feather out at midsection of blade
5. point of pressure not applied directly in line with a ridge, therefore flakes expand
6. first step in manufacture appears to have been done initially by well-controlled direct percussion, then pressure flaking with ridge at margin of bulbar scars removed by very delicate pressure flaking
7. thin lenticular cross section

These attributes are consistent with those already presented, although we would highlight the last item, "thin lenticular cross section," as limiting and indicative of the diverse typological conversation at the time. Thin lenticular cross sections occur and are present at the Haskett site (Butler 1965), but thicker and rounder versions, such as those described in the early levels at Veratic Rockshelter (Swanson 1972:90), are not uncommon. Another often-used term is "diamond-shaped" (also see Duke 2015; Galm and Gough 2008), which is where the faces possess a pronounced midline or crest that lends this shape to the stem in cross section. All these shapes are present in Haskett, but the thicker ones are the most defining.

Butler (1965) showed the Haskett site assemblage to Marie Wormington and Cynthia Irwin-Williams for their experience with the Agate Basin points from Wyoming. In his words, they "remarked that the Agate Basin appeared to have been made by a different flaking technique. That is, the Haskett point fell within the range of variation in form of the Agate Basin points; however, the flake scars on the latter were neither as broad nor as neatly spaced as they were on the Haskett point" (Butler 1965:7). Frison (1978:33; 1983) likewise saw marked differences between Haskett and Agate Basin points. Our own observation is that the most defining Haskett points exhibit a flower petal style of collateral flaking along the stem compared to the often narrow, ribbony style of Agate Basin, although there is substantial overlap. The differences are nonetheless important, as they show willful and discerning commitments by toolmakers to the defining techniques of their regional traditions.

The Intermountain West's Cougar Mountain style exhibits stem tapering much like Haskett, but with outwardly flaring shoulders (see Beck and Jones 2009; Layton 1970, 1972). These shoulders are soft, expanding from the stem before curving back to the blade. Both Haskett and Cougar Mountain stems are edge ground, although there is more standardization and investment apparent with the former. Haskett also shows greater reliance on one or more series of short, narrow, and sequential pressure flakes, which confine and finish the stem. Cougar Mountain appears to immediately postdate Haskett (Rosencrance et al., Chapter 2) with an age and form relationship like that between Agate Basin-Hell Gap on the High Plains (Pitblado 2003). Technologically, both Cougar Mountain and Hell Gap points represent a shift in emphasis from full to partial tang within the haft, a tradeoff that reduces weight and length, and possibly haft longevity, while reducing raw material commitments. Their comparably wide blades reflect reduced attention to projectile penetration (Eren, Bebber, et al. 2022) and may represent a lean toward secondary uses.

On a stem-by-stem basis, Haskett and Cougar Mountain are virtually indistinguishable, but assemblages from which complete specimens are wholly or nearly restricted to one type provide some comparative value, such as the ORBD for Haskett and the Sunshine Locality for Cougar Mountain (Beck and Jones 2009). Data from these assemblages (Duke et al. 2018) suggest that Haskett stem fragments are longer on average, but only specimens at the largest widths, when combined with quintessential flaking and grinding, might cautiously be classified as Haskett.

In 1980, Alan Bryan hypothesized that stemmed points were "hafted into socketed shafts." He contrasted this attribute with fluted points, which he argued were hafted "onto a split stick or beveled shaft," as is now well supported (Callahan 1994; Frison 1986; Lahren and Bonnichsen 1974). Bryan's idea was widely accepted, and it was elaborated on by Musil (1988; see also Willig 1989). The possibility has also been entertained for stemmed points on the High Plains (Bradley 1974; Frison 1978:161, 1991:294–295; Kornfeld et al. 2010), but Frison (2004:110) would later state that he preferred the simplicity of a split haft based on his own experiments. No extant archaeological evidence supports the socketed haft hypothesis, and we contend Haskett points were hafted using a split method. Archaeological support comes from the "clothespin" foreshaft found in association with Haskett points at the Sentinel Gap site (Galm and Gough 2008; Gough and Galm 2002). In an atlatl dart or spear weapon system, a hafted foreshaft possessing a round and pointed proximal end would be inserted into a hole drilled into the distal end of the main shaft. But a round socketed hole, created by the labor-intensive drilling process at the distal end of a foreshaft, is a complex element for inserting the biconvex or planoconvex shaped stem of a Haskett point. These shapes would require additional filler material, such as pitch, around the gap to create a solid haft, adding more production effort. The split or clothespin type haft element is less labor intensive to make than a drilled socket and enables a solid hafting foundation that would be less susceptible to failure by component parts.

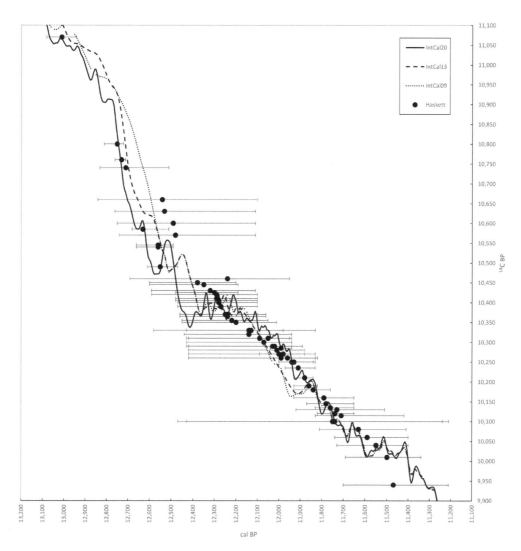

FIGURE 4.3. Display of calibrated Haskett-associated radiocarbon dates and ranges from Rosencrance and colleagues (Chapter 2).

When Is It?

The maximum age range of Haskett technology can be argued to begin within or alongside the Clovis era and end a few hundred years into the Early Holocene, a total of some 1,600 years between ca. 13,100 and 11,500 cal BP. A more defensible range based on the data is post-Clovis between ca. 12,600 and 11,700 cal BP (see also Rosencrance 2019), but radiocarbon calibration during the Younger Dryas is problematic. A detailed radiocarbon record for Haskett is presented by Rosencrance and colleagues (Chapter 2), but for practical discussion the dates are provided again here with the 68% probability ranges and rounded to the nearest 10 years (Table 4.1, Figure 4.3). The average 68% probability range for these is about 400 years (Table 4.1, Figure 4.3).

A single stem fragment from Paisley Cave 5 in southeastern Oregon represents the best case for Haskett within the Clovis era (Jenkins

TABLE 4.1. Haskett-Associated Radiocarbon Dates.

Site Name	Lab No.	Conventional Radiocarbon Age (^{14}C BP)	Median Probability (cal BP)	Calibrated Range (68% Probability)
Paisley Cave 5[a]	UCIAMS-80378	11,070 ± 25	13,010	13,080–12,940
Paisley Cave 2	UCIAMS-102112	10,585 ± 35	12,630	12,680–12,510
Paisley Cave 2	Beta-429639	10,390 ± 40	12,270	12,470–12,100
Paisley Cave 2	Beta-429641	10,370 ± 40	12,240	12,460–12,060
Paisley Cave 2	UCIAMS-79680	10,365 ± 30	12,240	12,460–12,060
Paisley Cave 2	D-AMS-1217-411	10,355 ± 45	12,220	12,450–12,050
Paisley Cave 2	Beta-429640	10,350 ± 40	12,200	12,450–12,010
Paisley Cave 2	UCIAMS-98933	10,330 ± 30	12,140	12,430–11,980
Paisley Cave 2	AA-96490	10,320 ± 60	12,140	12,440–11,940
Paisley Cave 2	D-AMS-012789	10,300 ± 45	12,070	12,430–11,940
Paisley Cave 2	Beta-195908	10,290 ± 40	12,030	12,430–11,890
Paisley Cave 2	UGAMS-A26415	10,290 ± 30	12,020	12,420–11,940
Paisley Cave 2	Beta-239083	10,260 ± 60	11,990	12,420–11,820
Paisley Cave 2	UGAMS-A26420	10,210 ± 30	11,880	11,930–11,840
Paisley Cave 2	Beta-182920	10,160 ± 60	11,790	11,930–11,650
Connley Cave 4	Gak-2143	10,600 ± 190	12,490	12,750–12,110
Connley Cave 4	PSUAMS#6721	10,545 ± 35	12,560	12,660–12,490
Connley Cave 4	PSUAMS#6720	10,410 ± 40	12,290	12,480–12,100
Connley Cave 4	D-AMS 12793	10,445 ± 40	12,350	12,600–12,190
Connley Cave 4	D-AMS 12797	10,455 ± 40	12,440	12,610–12,200
Connley Cave 4	D-AMS 12799	10,400 ± 45	12,280	12,470–12,100
Connley Cave 4	PSUAMS#6724	10,260 ± 40	11,960	12,040–11,830
Connley Cave 4	PSUAMS#6725	10,270 ± 35	11,980	12,090–11,880
Connley Cave 4	Gak-1742	10,100 ± 400	11,740	12,470–11,210
Connley Cave 5	PSUAMS#5002	10,310 ± 40	12,090	12,430–11,940
Connley Cave 5	PSUAMS#5009	10,190 ± 35	11,860	11,930–11,820
Connley Cave 5	PSUAMS#5005	10,145 ± 30	11,780	11,870–11,650
Connley Cave 5	PSUAMS#5004	10,135 ± 35	11,760	11,830–11,650
Connley Cave 5	PSUAMS#5008	10,120 ± 35	11,740	11,820–11,650
Connley Cave 5	D-AMS 30299	10,115 ± 50	11,710	11,830–11,420
Bonneville Estates Rockshelter	AA-58594	10,800 ± 60	12,750	12,810–12,720
Bonneville Estates Rockshelter	AA-58592	10,760 ± 60	12,730	12,760–12,710
Bonneville Estates Rockshelter	Beta-195047	10,540 ± 40	12,560	12,660–12,490
Bonneville Estates Rockshelter	AA-58593	10,405 ± 50	12,280	12,480–12,100

TABLE 4.1. (cont'd.) Haskett-Associated Radiocarbon Dates.

Site Name	Lab No.	Conventional Radiocarbon Age (^{14}C BP)	Median Probability (cal BP)	Calibrated Range (68% Probability)
Bonneville Estates Rockshelter	Beta-170443	10,040 ± 70	11,550	11,730–11,400
Bonneville Estates Rockshelter	Beta-164229	10,080 ± 50	11,630	11,810–11,410
Bonneville Estates Rockshelter	Beta-170444	10,130 ± 60	11,730	11,920–11,510
Smith Creek Cave	Birm-702	10,740 ± 130	12,710	12,830–12,510
Smith Creek Cave	Gak-5442	10,660 ± 220	12,540	12,840–12,100
Smith Creek Cave	Gak-5443	10,630 ± 190	12,530	12,760–12,110
Smith Creek Cave	Gak5445	10,570 ± 160	12,480	12,740–12,110
Smith Creek Cave	Gak-5444b	10,460 ± 260	12,240	12,690–11,950
Smith Creek Cave	TO-1173	10,420 ± 100	12,290	12,590–12,100
Smith Creek Cave	Tx-1638	10,330 ± 190	12,130	12,580–11,830
Smith Creek Cave	Tx-1420	9940 ± 160	11,470	11,700–11,210
Cougar Mountain Cave	ICA-18C/0385	10,490 ± 40	12,550	12,610–12,470
Cougar Mountain Cave	ICA-18O/387	10,450 ± 40	12,380	12,600–12,200
Cougar Mountain Cave	ICA-18C/0384	10,430 ± 40	12,320	12,590–12,110
Cougar Mountain Cave	UGAMS-#35050	10,250 ± 30	11,930	12,000–11,840
Tule Lake Rockshelter	UCIAMS-79297	10,425 ± 25	12,300	12,480–12,190
Tule Lake Rockshelter	UCIAMS-80836	10,310 ± 25	12,050	12,420–11,950
Tule Lake Rockshelter	UCIAMS-79293	10,285 ± 25	11,990	12,040–11,940
Tule Lake Rockshelter	UCIAMS-80839	10,280 ± 40	12,010	12,420–11,880
Wishbone	Beta-428729	10,430 ± 40	12,320	12,590–12,110
Wishbone	Beta-428730	10,370 ± 40	12,240	12,460–12,060
Wishbone	Beta-428728	10,370 ± 30	12,250	12,460–12,100
Wewukiyepuh	Beta-124447	10,390 ± 40	12,270	12,470–12,100
Wewukiyepuh	Beta-124446	10,270 ± 50	12,000	12,420–11,830
Sentinel Gap	Beta-133664	10,010 ± 60	11,500	11,690–11,340
Sentinel Gap	Beta-133665	10,130 ± 60	11,730	11,920–11,510
Sentinel Gap	Beta-133663	10,160 ± 60	11,790	11,930–11,650
Sentinel Gap	Beta-124167	10,180 ± 40	11,840	11,930–11,760
Lind Coulee	CAMS-94857	10,250 ± 40	11,940	12,000–11,830
Lind Coulee	CAMS-94856	10,060 ± 45	11,590	11,740–11,400
Redfish Overhang	WSU-1396	10,100 ± 300	11,750	12,430–11,240

Note: See also Rosencrance and colleagues, Chapter 2.
[a] Not included as Haskett-associated by Rosencrance and colleagues (Chapter 2); the remaining dates are presented in the same order as their Table 2.4.

et al. 2012; also see Waters, Stafford, and Carlson 2020). This specimen (1895-PC-5/16A-24) is reported to have a late-limiting radiocarbon age of 11,070 ± 25 ^{14}C BP (13,080–12,940 cal BP) based on its stratigraphic position relative to dated materials. Jenkins and colleagues (2012) do not refer to the artifact as Haskett but only generically as Western Stemmed. It is cautiously interpreted as a possible Haskett by Rosencrance and colleagues (Chapter 2), but we think it qualifies as a Haskett basal stem fragment based on our own physical viewing, and it is consistent by every attribute. This specimen possesses a ground and tapering stem, too wide for Cougar Mountain in most cases, as well as the characteristic broad collateral and overface flaking. It also retains a small remnant break/platform at the base, which is not uncommon for Haskett. Two other artifacts reported by Jenkins and colleagues (2012:Table 1) with early date associations are not stylistically distinctive. The fourth, 1961-PC-5/18a-10-1, is a probable shouldered Cougar Mountain style with a late-limiting age of 10,200 ± 35 ^{14}C BP (11,930–11,820 cal BP).

Post-Clovis chronometric timing of Haskett is abundant. In the Bonneville basin, where our study sample is located, dated combustion features at Bonneville Estates Rockshelter (Goebel et al. 2021; Goebel and Keene 2014; Graf 2007) and Smith Creek Cave (Bryan 1979; Goebel and Keene 2014) show human occupation closely associated with Haskett use beginning at nearly the same time, ca. 12,900–12,700 cal BP. Goebel and Keene (2014) scrutinize the record at both sites and argue no clear evidence supports an association before ca. 12,600 cal BP. They interpret that the lone pre-Clovis hearth at Smith Creek Cave suffers from an old wood dating bias, and that three features at Bonneville Estates Rockshelter with acceptable dates prior to 12,700 cal BP cannot be confidently associated with projectile points.

If they are correct, we see three behavioral possibilities for the early occupations: (1) they represent an earlier Haskett record with no clear diagnostic lithic association; (2) they represent an earlier Clovis record with no clear diagnostic lithic association; or (3) the occupants (not Haskett, not Clovis) did not yet prioritize stone projectile points (i.e., relied on wooden/osseous implements). The presence of debitage assemblages near these features with similar raw material and flake type profiles to that of the Haskett-associated features (Goebel 2007) suggests the first scenario is the most likely (see also Madsen, Schmitt, and Page 2015:13–15), but we do not know.

Both shelters exhibit clear evidence for Haskett immediately after 12,600 cal BP. Goebel and Keene (2014) associate a feature dating to 10,540 ± 40 ^{14}C BP (ca. 12,660–12,490 cal BP) with Haskett at Bonneville Estates Rockshelter, and a series of Haskett-consistent stem fragments from Smith Creek Cave (Bryan 1979; Lynch et al., Chapter 6) align with Goebel and Keene's (2014) accepted six early dates from the site from four features and a piece of cordage. The latter are from samples that were collected in the 1970s–80s (Bryan 1979; 1988) and have large error ranges, but taken together the strongest statistical probabilities suggest a Haskett occupation between ca. 12,600–12,100 cal BP.

This timing corresponds well with recently excavated Haskett levels at the Connley Caves in Oregon. As described by Rosencrance and colleagues (Chapter 2; also see Jenkins et al. 2017), age estimates of 10,545 ± 35 and 10,410 ± 40 ^{14}C BP from Cave 4 are close in age to Bedwell's (1973) previously published date of 10,600 ± 190 ^{14}C BP. The new dates are from isolated charcoal stratigraphically beneath hearth charcoal ages of 10,455 ± 40 and 10,445 ± 40 ^{14}C BP and an isolated charcoal specimen from the hearth stratum dating 10,400 ± 45 ^{14}C BP (Rosencrance et al. 2022). Minimally, these ages place the early Haskett occupations in Cave 4 to be between approximately 12,600–12,300 cal BP. Rosencrance and colleagues (Chapter 2; Rosencrance et al. 2022) further associate with Haskett two hearth charcoal dates of 10,270 ± 35 and 10,260 ± 40 ^{14}C BP from stratigraphically overlying contexts that would extend the occupation to ca. 11,900 cal BP. In Cave 5, Rosencrance and others (Chapter 2) and McDonough and others (2022) associate a mostly later stratified series of 13 dates with Haskett starting with three dates on one feature (1) of 10,560 ± 35, 10,490 ± 35, and 10,420 ± 35 ^{14}C BP, stratigraphically overlain by three dates from another feature area (2) of 10,275 ± 35, 10,150 ± 40, and 10,290 ± 35 ^{14}C BP. Yet another feature (3) overlies Feature 2, with dates of 10,190 ± 35; 10,120 ± 35, and 10,115 ± 50 ^{14}C BP. Rosencrance and colleagues (Chapter 2) report two new isolated charcoal dates of 10,135 ± 35 and 10,145 ± 30 ^{14}C BP similar in elevation to Feature 3, although the Haskett versus Cougar Mountain projectile point association among Feature 3 and these later dates is debatable due to limited and fragmentary associated points.

Additional Haskett-associated dates summarized by Rosencrance and colleagues (Chapter 2) from Cougar Mountain Cave, Tule Lake Rockshelter, Wewukiyepuh, and the ORBD's Wishbone site represent a similar time range. The Wishbone site is on the ORBD (Duke et al. 2022). Three statistically overlapping dates on willow wood charcoal samples from the site's hearth provide a combined radiocarbon age estimate of 10,390 ± 20 ^{14}C BP, with a calibrated median probability of 12,270 cal BP and a 68% probability range of 12,470 to 12,100 cal BP. Sentinel Gap represents the most definitive late Haskett site, with a strong association between complete points and burned features (Galm and Gough 2000, 2008). Three radiocarbon age estimates from cultural features—10,180 ± 40; 10,160 ± 60; and 10,130 ± 60 ^{14}C BP—are bookended by more aberrant dates and probably represent the defining occupation of the site to be ca. 11,800 cal BP. At Redfish Overhang in central Idaho (Sargeant 1973; Rosencrance 2019; Rosencrance et al., Chapter 2), a Cougar Mountain preform cache (previously considered to represent Haskett [see Stueber and Rosencrance 2021]) with a series of upper limiting dates suggests this style was in use shortly thereafter, ca. 11,700 cal BP (~9900 ^{14}C BP), but, again, the calibration uncertainty at this time is a problem. Haskett point fragments are found stratigraphically below the cache and associated hearth feature (Rosencrance 2019).

Haskett emerges earlier than Agate Basin. Surovell (Chapter 10) places Agate Basin on the Plains at ca. 12,200 cal BP, immediately postdating Folsom (see also Buchanan et al. 2021). He further notes that, dates aside, this sequence is clearly supported stratigraphically. Thus, while Folsom was preferred on the Plains prior to 12,200 cal BP, Haskett was the prevailing technological choice in the Intermountain West by 12,600 cal BP at the latest. Use of Haskett and Agate Basin appears to have ceased about the same time, however. The transition from Agate Basin to Hell Gap points on the Plains is similar, both in timing and form, to the Haskett-Cougar Mountain transition out west. Both transitions occur by the end of the Younger Dryas (ca. 11,700 cal BP). The Cody complex is well established as emerging at the Pleistocene-Holocene transition in the Great Plains (Knell and Muñiz 2013), and so, too, do the various shorter and narrower stemmed styles of the Western Stemmed series (Rosencrance et al., Chapter 2).

Where Is It?

Butler (1965) considered the core geography of Haskett to be from the Columbia Plateau's high lava plains and northern Great Basin of east-central Oregon west through Idaho's Snake River Plain to the Yellowstone area. His view was anchored by Cougar Mountain Cave and the Haskett type site. As discussed above, Swanson's (1972) Veratic Rockshelter in eastern Idaho's Birch Creek valley can also be considered a key site, and there is now a well-documented Haskett record in its vicinity where Birch Creek empties onto the Snake River Plain into the sink of pluvial Lake Terreton (Marler 2004, 2009).

Frison (1983; also see Kornfeld et al. 2001) identified Haskett in the lowest stratigraphic levels of the Helen Lookingbill site on the Wyoming side of Yellowstone and noted similar surface finds in the area. Yellowstone was a convenient mountainous boundary to Butler, but it can be considered the optimal passageway through the Rocky Mountains between the High Plains of Wyoming into the high desert of Idaho. Haskett, Agate Basin, Folsom, and other early point types are all present in the latter and paint a complex picture of human use (Hartman 2019; Henrikson et al. 2017; Marler 2004; Titmus and Woods 1991a).

Back west, Cougar Mountain Cave is in the northern Great Basin, where Haskett is widely distributed and common in the lowest cultural levels of the regional caves and dry shelters (see Rosencrance et al., Chapter 2). Paisley Caves and Connley Caves combine with Cougar Mountain Cave to represent three key such sites situated near the east flank of the Cascade Range, each in hills overlooking the well-watered catchments of the Fort Rock and Summer Lake basins. This context inspired Bedwell's (1970:231) concept of the Western Pluvial Lakes Tradition, which he defined as "extending from Fort Rock (as the northernmost point), south along the Cascade-Sierra Nevada uplift in western Nevada and part of northeastern California (in the region of Lake Lahontan) and finally south into the desert areas of southeastern California and pluvial Lake Mohave[sic]." The material culture of this tradition begins with Haskett—what Bedwell (1970:224) referred to as the "P2" point type—which he described as "the typical artifact of this assemblage" (Bedwell 1970:232). He considered a radiocarbon date of 10,600 ± 190 ^{14}C BP (ca. 12,600 cal BP) at Connley Cave 4 to represent the earliest estimated age of the type.

Haskett points are found on the ground surface throughout southeastern Oregon and south into Nevada, although they are not always recognized as such. Key open-air sites in Oregon include Weed Lake Ditch (Smith et al. 2020; Wriston 2003), Dietz (Fagan 1988; Willig 1988, 1989), and the Rimrock Draw vicinity (O'Grady et al. 2019), but stem fragments consistent with Haskett are found throughout various basins where there was wetland habitat and at toolstone sources (Bradley et al. 2022; Christian 1997; Pettigrew 1984; G. Smith, Felling, Wriston, et al. 2015; Stueber and Skinner 2015). The Dietz site is widely recognized as Clovis-associated, but illustrations of Haskett-consistent stem fragments are also present and in places, abundant (Fagan 1988; Willig 1988). The Lahontan Basin of western Nevada, the Sadmat site (Graf 2001; Tuohy 1968, 1988; Warren and Ranere 1968; Warren 1967), and Coleman site (Graf 2001; Tuohy 1970) contain long stem fragments and have for some time been part of the conversation about an early Haskett/Cougar Mountain record in the Great Basin. Other more recently examined sites from the area, such as Overlook (Rice 2015), Fire Creek (Cunnar et al. 2016), and several in Grass Valley (Elston and Kuypers 2018) can be considered similarly.

Pluvial lake-margin sites and distributary wetland localities such as Lake Tonopah (Pendleton 1979; Tuohy 1988), Mud Lake (Fenner 2011), and Tule Springs (Duke et al. 2019; Susia 1964; Wormington and Ellis 1967) extend the pattern south into the Mojave Desert. As with Dietz, the Lake Tonopah assemblage is better known for its fluted point component, but it also possesses a rich stemmed point record consistent with Haskett.

Tule Springs, much maligned for the pre-Clovis claims that led to hyperbolized excavations in 1962–63, possesses a surface archaeological record that agrees well with its late Pleistocene wetland deposits (Springer et al. 2018). Susia (1964) conducted a surface survey alongside the 1960s excavations that yielded at least one Haskett/Cougar Mountain base—what she referred to as "a point similar to an Agate Basin point" (Figure 4.4a) and several similar leaf-shaped items. A recent survey of the area by Duke and colleagues (2019) yielded a Haskett basal fragment (Figure 4.4b). Recently reported lithostratigraphic, geochronological, and

FIGURE 4.4. Haskett points from Tule Springs: (*a*) photo taken at Nevada State Museum of Artifact XI-19 (Susia 1964:10, Plate 4p); (*b*) Artifact 10 from Duke and colleagues (2019:Figure 13). Used with permission.

paleontological work at Tule Springs provides a faunal pairing for the Haskett time frame. Springer and colleagues (2018:41; also see Scott et al. 2017) state that vertebrate fossils from a stratigraphic unit they refer to as Bed E_{2a} contain the remains of extinct megafauna, although they do not specify the genera. Based on four radiocarbon ages from charcoal, organic sediment, and *Succineidae* shells, they place the timing of this unit between ca. 12,900 and 12,350 cal BP.

In southern California, Haskett artifacts can be found in the interconnected pluvial systems of Lake Mojave,[4] Death Valley, Owen's Valley, and Searles Lake catchments and neighboring lowlands. These are often referred to typologically as Lake Mohave out of regional convention for any tapering-stemmed early point (cf. Campbell et al. 1937; Sutton et al. 2007; Warren 1984; Warren and Crabtree 1986). The term has also been applied to represent the Mohave expression of Great Basin stemmed points more broadly (e.g., Campbell et al. 1937; Tuohy 1968). In the most recent regional overview, Sutton and colleagues (2007) state "the only cultural complex dating to the Pleistocene is Clovis." The reality is that Clovis is rare in the Mojave but readily identifiable (e.g., Basgall and Hall 1991; Byerly and Roberson 2015; Rondeau 2015a), while Haskett is never called out but can be identified in report illustrations. One good example, shown in Figure 4.5, comes from a cultural resource management survey on Fort Irwin (Wohlgemuth 2006). This

FIGURE 4.5. Haskett point classified as a Lake Mohave point from Fort Irwin.

specimen was identified as a Lake Mohave point and has been geochemically sourced as Coso (West Sugarloaf) obsidian, an important obsidian source in the Mojave Desert.

Elizabeth Campbell and colleagues initiated WST studies in the 1930s at Lake Mohave (Campbell et al. 1937). Amsden (1937; also see Campbell 1936) distinguishes the Lake Mohave type, with its long tapering stem and hard shoulders, from the Silver Lake type, with its short and usually expanding stem (also see Knell and Sutton, Chapter 5), but defines what we would now refer to as Haskett points as "leaf-like[*sic*] blades" (Amsden 1937:78). This seems a great understatement in retrospect, but Amsden's description deserves repeating here. While judging Lake Mohave flaked stone technology in general as "good enough for an emergency use, but not up to a decent standard of workmanship" (Amsden 1937:53), his take on leaflike blades, aided by the replicative flintknapping of Joseph Barbieri, was markedly different:

> In shape they suggest a projectile point, but the size of many seems rather large unless we assume the use of a lance or hand-spear. However, some of the implements found…in the Clovis region, apparently used in elephant hunting, run to comparable lengths, one measuring just under 10 cm, while the longest of ours…measures 11 cm. With its maximum thickness of only 9 mm, it is remarkably light for its size and probably could have been used successfully with the dart-thrower or atlatl…The group as a whole testifies to high skill at percussion work [Amsden 1937:78–80].

Warren (1966, 1967; also see Warren and Ranere 1968) noticed similarities between the Lake Mohave bifaces and those from the C. W. Harris site in coastal San Diego (Knell and Becker 2017; Rogers 1939; Warren and Ore 2011; Warren and True 1961). He connected the industry northward through the Intermountain West to sites such as Haskett, Cougar Mountain, Sadmat, and Veratic Rockshelter to argue that it represented an early stemmed point component not restricted to a desert adaptation. This observation entails a broader argument about pan-Western industry. Davis and colleagues (1969; also see Davis 1963, 1967, 1975) called this the Western Lithic Co-tradition based on their work in the Mojave, and like Warren, considered it evidence of a big game hunting tradition much as represented elsewhere by what she termed the Fluted Point Co-tradition.

In the eastern Great Basin, Haskett is widely distributed in the Bonneville basin of western Utah and extreme eastern Nevada. The ORBD represents the distinguishing open-air locality in what is now the southern Great Salt Lake Desert, with numerous sites set within what would have been the biggest marshland complex in the region (Madsen, Schmitt, and Page 2015b). The Wishbone site is the signature ORBD Haskett site, representing a single hearth-side occupation (Duke et al. 2022). Other noteworthy open-air sites of the Bonneville basin, albeit undated, include the Running Antelope site north of the Great Salt Lake (Russell 1993, 2004) and the Escalante Valley locality in the basin's southern arm (Keller and Hunt 1967). Bonneville Estates Rockshelter (Goebel 2007) and Smith Creek Cave (Bryan 1979; Lynch et al., Chapter 6), already discussed, are the key dry-shelter sites. Both are situated near the western margin of the basin at the Nevada-Utah border.

We delimit Haskett geography to the Intermountain West, but the basic template and technology by other names can be found from Alaska to South America (Borrero 2009; Bryan 1965, 1969, 1991; Waters 2019; Waters et al. 2018). Early on, Bryan (1965:62) argued this for what he called the Willow Leaf Bipoint Tradition extending "along the mountainous backbone of both American continents." He later abandoned this label but maintained the central idea that a regionally varied set of stemmed points defined a bifacial tradition that "developed at least as early as the Fluted Point Tradition" (Bryan 1980:102; also see Bryan 1988, 1991; Bryan and Tuohy 1999; McDonough et al., Chapter 1).

In Alaska, Sluiceway and Mesa points represent much the same technology as Haskett, especially the former, and they are solidly dated to the Younger Dryas (Bever 2001; Kunz and Reanier 1994; Kunz et al. 2003; Rasic 2011; H. Smith et al. 2013). Fedje and colleagues (2008) report similarly scaled bifacial technology with edge grinding by the early Younger Dryas at Haida Gwaii off the coast of British Columbia, immediately south of Alaska. South of the United States southern border, similar forms, such as El Jobo or Lerma, are found at Santa Maria Iztapan in central Mexico (Gonzalez et al. 2015; Sánchez and Carpenter 2016, 2021), at Taima-Taima in Venezuela (Bryan 1978; Dillehay 2013; Gruhn 1988) and Monte Verde in Chile (Dillehay 1997, 2013; Dillehay et al. 2008). These points have been found in Pleistocene contexts and in proximity to late Pleistocene-dating megafauna fossils. The associations are case-by-case dubious, but at scale repeat with early lanceolate forms being found in contexts where any later-period types would be suspect.

One can go farther afield and find Upper Paleolithic lanceolate precursors along the Pacific Rim (see Davis, Chapter 7; Pratt et al. 2020), but the resemblances are generic and may be better figured as a bifacial template for both Haskett and Clovis. With some 2,000 or more years of human presence prior to Clovis in coastal and near-coastal regions of North America, cultures far removed from one another would have had ample time to create their own technological traditions. Waters and colleagues (2018; also see Waters 2019) have argued as much based on the presence of stemmed and lanceolate forms found beneath the Clovis levels in strata dating between 15,500–13,500 years ago at the Friedkin site in central Texas.

Environment, Extinctions, and Preservation

Given our proposition that Haskett points were functional at megafauna scale, our environmental context centers on the potential for megafauna to have endured in the Great Basin until the mid-Younger Dryas. A few last appearance dates suggesting this have already been presented, but here we consider if these dates are broadly supported by the regional paleoenvironment. The subject of extinctions is widely debated, often contentiously so, with most researchers still framing the problem within the question of whether climate change or human predation (usually referred to as "overkill") was the ultimate cause (Grayson 2016; Grayson et al. 2021; G. Haynes 2013; Meltzer 2020; Perrotti et al. 2022; Stewart et al. 2021; Surovell, Pelton, et al. 2016; Ugan and Byers 2007; Waguespack 2013; Wolfe and Broughton 2020, 2021).

The most definitive treatment of megafaunal extinctions in the Great Basin is by Grayson (2016). He accepts the Younger Dryas last appearance dates for mammoth and camelid in the region already mentioned, and that they overlap human settlement for more than a thousand years, but he argues against human predation factoring into their extinction based on the lack of direct evidence (Grayson 2016:242–243).

The Great Basin, and much of the Intermountain West, tends to be biotically heterogeneous with the main contrast being the presence or absence of surface water (see Grayson 2011; Hershler et al. 2002; Madsen 2007). The Snake River Plain of Idaho is a vast dryland zone split by its namesake river. The Great Basin is well known to be structured by alternating basin and range topography with valley catchments maintaining lakeside and distributary marshes well into the Early Holocene; a few persist today. Altitudinal and latitudinal differences in temperature and precipitation structure much of the remaining variability. Paleoenvironmental data suggest more of a mixed mosaic habitat characterized for the region in the late Pleistocene, as in much of North America, which would have reduced the moisture dichotomy and benefited large herbivores. Post-Last Glacial Maximum (LGM) disintegration of this mosaic prior to the Younger Dryas is thought to be a driver of extinctions, and researchers emphasize the need to study individual species' histories and their interrelationships with others and the biome at large to better understand this process (see discussions by Grayson 2016; G. Haynes 2002, 2013; Scott 2010).

Grayson (2016) argues the Great Basin was never an optimal setting for megafaunal herbivores based on a lack of other plant and animal species defining to their evolution and argues that extinctions were climate-induced and not caused or hastened by human hunters (Grayson 2016:280; also see Grayson and Meltzer 2015; Grayson et al. 2021). He states: "it seems likely that large, now extinct mammals were never common in the floristic Great Basin and that they were particularly uncommon toward the very end of the Ice Age" (Grayson 2016:272). His discussions include little about water, even suggesting too much could be a constraint when elevated pluvial lake levels combined with low-elevation coniferous zones to narrow the strip of optimal forage (Grayson 2016:270). Nevertheless, Grayson (2016) summarizes data showing that megafaunal herbivores ate plants from all these zones, including saltbush, sedges, and subalpine conifers.

G. Haynes (2002:200–208; also see G. Haynes 2013) argues that forage would have been secondary to water as a cause of herbivore stress, stating "water would have been the primary factor in the daily lives of big-game animals." Proboscideans cannot live more than a few days without access to moisture either in their food or from water sources, but they can survive longer without quality food or nutritive content. Contra Grayson, G. Haynes (2002, 2013) advocates for human behavior as the decisive factor in megafaunal extinctions. In G. Haynes' model, which centers on proboscideans, the food problem in the late Pleistocene was shorter growing seasons and loss of the mixed mosaic habitats that supplied diverse and seasonally successive forage. Fragmentation of these habitats would have driven proboscideans to refugia (G. Haynes 2002:201; G. Haynes 2013) that retained productivity and were anchored by abundant water. In the Great Basin, this would especially be the case for mammoths, followed by horse then camel (*Camelops*), the latter of which was the most drought tolerant and amenable to consuming halophytic shrubs (see G. Haynes 1991:276; Vetter 2007).

Water in the post-LGM Great Basin peaked between about 18,000 and 15,000 cal BP, with many closed-basin pluvial lakes reaching high stands within this period (Lyle et al. 2012; McGee et al. 2018; Munroe and Laabs 2013). Pronounced warming and drying began with the onset of the Bølling-Allerød interstadial at 14,600 cal BP, and lake levels declined substantially. (Benson et al. 2013; Garcia and Stokes 2006; Lyle et al. 2012; Munroe and Laabs 2013). Lake Bonneville retreated to about the average elevation of the modern Great Salt Lake by 13,000 cal BP (Godsey et al. 2011; Oviatt 2015). Vegetation structure followed, with the upland retreat of tree species and the expansion of halophytic scrub (Kirby et al. 2018; Rhode and Adams 2016; Wigand and Rhode 2002). These trends reversed with the Younger Dryas beginning ca. 12,900 cal BP, albeit variably and asynchronously. Colder temperatures brought reduced surface evaporation (Ibarra et al. 2014), and north–south shifting precipitation regimes further contributed to increased surface water levels (Hudson et al. 2019; Lyle et al. 2012).

This climate change may have reprieved stressed and dwindling megafauna populations. In addition to lengthened growing seasons for preferred forage, pluvial lakes resuscitated from their Bølling-Allerød desiccation would have brought new wetland habitat. This habitat would be maximized in a "Goldilocks" zone where expansive shallows (<~1.5 m deep) and low-gradient distributary networks support emergent plants such as

Typha, Carex, Phragmites, and *Scirpus* (Duke and King 2014; Smith and Monte 1975; Young 1998). If lake level is too low or too high (the latter happening with rise above the inflection of a basin's upland margins), wetland potential significantly decreases (Duke and King 2014). Younger Dryas–Early Holocene conditions appear to have provided these optimal parameters in many basins (Benson et al. 2011; Benson et al. 2013; Duke and King 2014; Goebel et al. 2011; Lachniet et al. 2014; Madsen 2002; Oviatt et al. 2005; Pigati et al. 2019; Rhode and Adams 2016; Wigand and Rhode 2002).

Even with megafaunal herbivores at low numbers, people could have easily mapped onto their movements across the repeating landscape along regularly used game trails. Mammoths, leaving substantial evidence of their travels, would have been easy to locate, then taken when needed if people tracked alongside them as a priority (cf. G. Haynes 2006, 2013). Contrast this with the Great Plains, where these times were also cold and dry, but without the patchwork of watery sinks. Frison (1978:2) characterizes the Plains distribution of water sources as "relief to an otherwise monotonous and rather drab scene." Meltzer and Holliday (2010) summarize the paleoenvironmental and geomorphic data to argue that the Plains was a place of expanding grasslands, reduced streamflow, and eolian accumulation during the Younger Dryas—good for bison but not so much for competing herbivores requiring abundant water.

Thus, even if the Great Basin was a modest place for megafauna on the whole of the Pleistocene, the data suggest it provided persistent refugia during the Younger Dryas. The most well-watered areas of the Great Basin, the Lahontan and Bonneville basins, dominate the hydrology of its western and eastern regions, respectively (see Figure 4.2). This physiography complements the distribution of Haskett in Nevada and Utah, and much the same applies in southeastern Oregon off the Cascades.

Extinct bison species would seem a likely option for Haskett hunters, but no direct evidence indicates that they were a priority target over any other megafauna. Scott (2010) argues that bison outcompeted other herbivores in western North America at the end of the Pleistocene by tolerance to increasing proportions of warm-season grasses and otherwise variable forage. This finding is consistent with the Great Plains record, but the archaeology of the desert west provides no widespread gain resonating with human hunters at the Pleistocene–Holocene transition. Technologically, post-Haskett investment in Western Stemmed projectile points, and hunting overall, drops (Duke 2011; Pitblado 2003). The opposite is true on the Plains, where a series of Cody complex styles are demonstrated to be very directly aimed at bison, moving through both the extinct to extant species (see Knell and Muñiz 2013; Pitblado 2003). The clearest early evidence of bison hunting in the Great Basin is at the Wallman site in northwestern Nevada, dated ca. 11,200 cal BP, and this, too, is a Cody complex site (Amick 2013; Dansie et al. 1988; see also Hartman 2019), although Grayson (1979) identifies bison remains in the deposits of Connley Caves now known (Rosencrance et al. 2022) to date to the Younger Dryas. Amick (2013) suggests the Wallman bison kill occurred at a time of increased summer moisture and concomitant expanded grassland that drew Cody hunters southward.

The fossil record overwhelmingly places megafaunal herbivores in the Pleistocene wetlands of the Great Basin. Mammoth, camel, and horse dominate the extinct fauna throughout the region (Grayson 2016:250). Their remains are usually found in eroded exposures of the lacustrine and spring-fed sediment deposits representing pluvial marshes. Well-known localities such as Tule Springs (Nevada), China Lake (California), Rye Patch Reservoir (Nevada), and Fossil Lake (Oregon) exemplify this context. The sediment profiles at each exhibit an inverse preservation relationship (cf. Surovell et al.

2009) whereby the youngest fossils are less-often preserved than older ones because they were at or near the erosional interface when the wetlands desiccated in the Pleistocene or Early Holocene.

This finding is well-documented at Tule Springs, in southern Nevada, in new work by Springer and colleagues (2018; see also Pigati et al. 2019; Scott et al. 2017). The Younger Dryas-aged sediments of interest to archaeologists are largely eroded and uncommon, while the older underlying sediments remain protected en masse. Springer and colleagues (2018:41) describe their Younger Dryas-dated geologic stratum (Bed E_{2a}) as scarce "because the lack of resistant capping material...left it particularly vulnerable to erosion." This bed is nevertheless fossiliferous. Springer and others (2018:41; see also Scott et al. 2017) state that this unit represents "the last vestiges of Pleistocene megafauna in the Las Vegas Valley prior to the terminal Pleistocene extinction" (although they do not qualify this with a list of genera or any further description of the remains). As already discussed, Haskett points are found on the ground surface at Tule Springs.

Similar processes are at work at Fossil Lake in central Oregon. Here, Minor and Spencer (1977) report what they interpret to be a camelid kill site with similar context but better association. Bone from the site was radiocarbon-dated to 10,275 ± 95 ^{14}C BP (ca. 12,600–11,700 cal BP). The site boundaries for land management purposes include surface artifacts deposited throughout prehistory, lagging down by erosion to the currently exposed ground surface. Grayson (2016:192–193) dismisses it as a kill site for this reason, but he accepts the date as "the youngest well-dated member of the camel family known from North America." However, the bone bed and related artifacts are confined to a 10-×-10 m area with strong context. Minor and Spencer (1977) describe three artifacts as being in direct association with the bones—a projectile point recovered in three refit fragments, an indeterminate projectile point/biface fragment with edge grinding, and a small flake.

The fragmented projectile point from Fossil Lake is compelling (Figure 4.6). Two of the fragments were found among the bones, and one nearby at the erosional interface with the primary sediments. They were interpreted as blade fragments broken by impact, and Minor and Spencer (1977:26–27) provided detailed supporting analysis. We concur with Minor and Spencer's interpretation based on our own examination of the fragments. The three conjoining fragments broke on impact as evidenced by a series of attributes: a complex bending break across the distal region; an impact burin that travels down through the center of the point, hinging and exiting at a lateral edge; a second small burin initiated from the proximal end along a lateral edge (superficially resembling a slight shoulder in Figure 4.6); and a second bending break across the proximal end. These traits and their context are consistent with a kill and otherwise difficult to explain as coincidental lag. Although stemless and having a reworked blade, the point's size and flaking history are consistent with the only projectile point that should be predicted for the time in the Great Basin—Haskett. Although the site does not meet the most conservative standards for a kill (see Grayson and Meltzer 2015 and Rosencrance et al., Chapter 2), it begs review as a strong coincidental association in the manner recently discussed for some proboscidean sites with possible Clovis associations (Mackie and Hass 2021).

Materials and Methods

Our examination of parallels centers on four aspects: size, design, skill, and toolstone conveyance. The Haskett sample consists of 95 specimens, 19 complete and 76 Haskett-consistent fragments, from the ORBD distributary wetland. This total includes two specimens found in direct association with the Wishbone site hearth, dated ca. 12,270

FIGURE 4.6. Fragmented projectile point blade from Fossil Lake site. Photos by Richard L. Rosencrance and courtesy of the University of Oregon Museum of Natural and Cultural History, Eugene.

cal BP. The study area is a roughly rectangular 9,200-acre block defined by the boundaries of five contiguous cultural resource management surveys conducted between 2001 and 2017 (Byerly et al. 2018; Duke 2003; Duke et al. 2016; Duke, Rice, et al. 2018; Duke, Young, et al. 2018; Figure 4.2). The data also include 339 post-Western Stemmed point types that are used to aid in comparing Haskett-specific patterning. X-ray fluorescence (XRF) sourcing was conducted by the Far Western XRF Lab. For Clovis and Agate Basin, we rely on published data as needed.

Results

In this section we discuss the size, design, skill, and toolstone conveyance patterns of Haskett projectile points and how those patterns compare to widely employed ideas of the nature regarding Clovis.

Size

The size metrics on Haskett put it at Clovis scale. We are referring to functional projectile point size, not that of the unfinished or differently purposed forms found in Clovis caches (see Gramly 1993; Huckell and Kilby 2014; Morrow 1995). As shown in Figure 4.1, specimen A is the longest artifact, although its stem sits modestly within the statistical range of the rest of the assemblage. Specimen E illustrates this well. It has been resharpened into the stem following an impact break, and by proportionate measure it could have easily exceeded the size of specimen A along every dimension. But length alone is a poor measure of function given variable effects of production nuances and reworked breaks (e.g., Figure 4.1c and 4.1d). Thickness is also incomparable owing to the different design approaches of Haskett and Clovis. Maximum

TABLE 4.2. Descriptive Statistics for Kill Site-Associated Clovis and Folsom Points, Haskett Points, and Agate Basin Points.

Mammoth kill-associated (Clovis)	N	Mean	SD	Min	Max	Haskett (ORBD)	N	Mean	SD	Min	Max
Length	36	72.5	25.4	26.6	117.2	Length	19	98.0	35.2	65.0	226.0
Width	36	26.7	5.5	16.0	36.6	Width	24	26.2	3.4	20.1	33.6
Thickness	36	7.5	1.4	4.2	9.8	Thickness	30	8.3	1.3	4.9	10.3
Bison kill-associated (Folsom and Clovis)						Agate Basin (type site)					
Length	38	43.2	14.4	20.8	83.1	Length	41	79.2	20.7	42.0	139.0
Width	38	21.5	4.2	15.3	34.6	Width	41	21.3	3.3	15.0	27.0
Thickness	32	4.9	2.0	3.0	11.1	Thickness	41	7.1	1.0	5.4	9.0

Note: Clovis and Folsom points are from Buchanan and colleagues (2011). Haskett points are from the Old River Bed Delta (ORBD), and Agate Basin points are from the Agate Basin site. SD = standard deviation. All measurements are in mm.

width, however, tends to correspond at a less variable scale and rarely changes through manufacture, use, and discard. For Haskett, maximum width and maximum stem width are the same owing to the tapering of the stem.

In a 2011 paper, Buchanan and colleagues (2011) argue for a correlation between projectile point and prey size based on comparing Clovis and Folsom points against mammoth and bison body sizes. By their metrics for Clovis, Haskett was calibrated similarly for a maximum prey size consistent with mammoth. The summarized data are presented in Table 4.2, and a visual comparison is provided in Figure 4.7. In Buchanan and colleagues' (2011) sample, 36 complete Clovis points from mammoth kill sites average 26.7 mm wide. Our average for Haskett points with complete widths from the ORBD is nearly the same at 26.2 mm. The ORBD Hasketts possess a tighter range of widths than Clovis, but both assemblages exhibit smaller items that could accommodate the smaller prey body sizes we know supplemented human diet in the Pleistocene. Nuances aside, the overall data agreement between two technological traditions lends to the hypothesis examined by Buchanan and colleagues (2011) supporting a projectile point and prey size correspondence, one that was driven at the largest scale by proboscideans.

Further support comes from the points-prey association with bison (Table 4.2). In the Buchanan and colleagues (2011) sample, 38 fluted points from bison kill sites—including some Clovis but mostly Folsom—average 21.5 mm in width, a 20% size reduction. Folsom points alone average 20.0 mm. Both measures are shown to be statistically significantly different from the mammoth-associated Clovis points. To provide an analogous comparison with Haskett, we used the measurements from 41 complete Agate Basin specimens from the type site (Frison and Stanford 1982), which, like Folsom, are directly associated with now-extinct species of bison and appear to arrive on the High Plains late in the Younger Dryas. These average 21.3 mm wide. Comparing just Haskett and Agate Basin points, we see an 18% size reduction, much like that between the mammoth and bison kill points. The differences are statistically significant at a less than 5% significance level ($t = -5.65$, $df = 47$, $p < 0.001$) and support the hypothesis of a point-prey association in the Younger Dryas being

FIGURE 4.7. Haskett and Clovis artifact silhouettes. The Haskett group includes all artifacts possessing the stem base. The Clovis groups are complete specimens from proboscidean kill sites examined by Buchanan and colleagues (2011).

expressed in two technological traditions at paralleling size scales.

Design

Haskett and Clovis both have lanceolate shapes that, while stylistically distinct, are designed for hunting. Each is strongly edge abraded along the stem, an application that provides several safeguards including protection from breakage, protection of the haft, and adhesion in the haft (see Titmus and Woods 1991b; Werner et al. 2018). They both commonly exhibit postimpact reworking. Reworking over previous impact fractures is evident on Haskett specimens d and e in Figure 4.1. Clovis is well-demonstrated to be reworked, sometimes moving functionally from projectile point to knife and even back again (Kay 2018; Smallwood 2015). Use wear and experimental analysis by Lafayette and Smith (2012) indicate much the same for Haskett.

Unfortunately, we have a problem on the ORBD with artifact weathering having destroyed use wear evidence in most cases, but changes in blade shape, the reworking of blades into other tool forms, and remnant facial bending finials support the design of Haskett as a projectile point first (see Duke 2011:203–206). As blade tips get resharpened, they become thicker, more obtuse, and less effective as a point, but simultaneously add leverage for use as a knife. There is a corresponding lack of attention to tip sharpness, blade symmetry, and edge angle. This attribute may signal the subordinate need for the detail invested in first production and use or transition to a knife. Both possibilities are consistent with Clovis.

From a ballistics standpoint, the long stem—that is, the hafted and thus covered region of the point—serves by weight to add penetrative power and offset propulsive force (Hughes 1998; Hutchings 2015). This design has two main benefits: impaling the prey with force, then sending any rebound force through the projectile in a manner that reduces critical breakage. Impact fractures, evidenced either by finial flakes extending from the break or burination, are present on 45% of the broken specimens in the ORB assemblage (n = 34 of 75). The remainder are common bending breaks on the stems, a predictable result of "end shock" whereby the tool mass cannot absorb the force of impact (Purdy 1975). Haskett points on the ORBD are rarely broken at their point of maximum width. In our assemblage, only three of the 95 items show clear breaks across this region. Toolmakers appear to have buffered this fatal breakage risk by guiding shock down the long and tapering edge-ground stems.

Haskett and Clovis stem/base treatments differ conspicuously, but the data suggest they represent superficial overlays on an otherwise functionally identical lanceolate template. Haskett points tend to be weight-forward with convex stem cross sections, while Clovis points are weight-backward with concave stem cross sections; however, both approaches provide weight within the haft. The differences could be cultural affectations that were functionally within tolerances, but how tolerances are expressed from the engineered baseplate that defines the design's functional reliability is not well understood. Clovis technology has been extensively studied, but whether Clovis points were used on throwing and/or thrusting spears or with the leverage of throwing sticks (or all three as appropriate) is not known.

Recent experimental studies seek insights from Clovis blade geometry and its effect on penetrative power (Eren, Meltzer, Story, et al. 2021; Eren, Bebber, et al. 2022; Eren, Meltzer, Story, et al. 2022; Kilby et al. 2022). This research advances the work of Hughes (1998; see also Sisk and Shea 2009; Sitton et al. 2020) mentioned above. Eren and colleagues (2021c, 2022b) argue that the primary function for Clovis bifaces as projectile points has been overestimated, as they would not be especially effective at fatally penetrating proboscideans. At issue are two of Hughes' (1998) measures of penetrative capability—tip cross-sectional area (TCSA) and tip cross-sectional perimeter (TCSP). Both represent the cross-sectional region that opens the hole through which a projectile will travel. Extrapolated from maximum width and thickness, the former represents the surface area of the cross section (maximized by thick and narrow tips) and the latter the perimeter length (maximized by thin and wide tips) (Hughes 1998:382). All things being equal, especially velocity in the experiments, lower TCSA and TCSP values are better for penetration. Eren and colleagues (2021c, 2022b) find Clovis points to have the high TCSA and TCSP values relative to most Paleoindian projectile points and argue that this attribute reflects a low priority of proboscidean hunting, even hunting at all, versus other functions.

For ORBD Haskett points, 22 specimens with complete widths and thicknesses yield a mean TCSA of 107.99 cm^2 (SD = 22.49, median = 107.44) and a mean TCSP of 54.39 cm (SD = 6.23, median = 55.67). These scores are relatively high by the reckoning of Eren and colleagues (2022a, 2022b), closer to Clovis (TCSA = 137.79, TCSP = 71.71) than late Paleoindian styles. That said, Eren and others' (2022b) Clovis sample consists of 46 specimens, 40 of which are from caches. We question these as functionally representative. Using the width and thickness of Clovis points associated with dead mammoths (killed or scavenged) seems more appropriate. The means reported in Buchanan and others' (2011) study of size variability discussed above provides smaller TCSA (100.22) and TCSP (55.45).

By extension, this finding does not make the Haskett points of the ORBD, which are associated with no kill sites, necessarily more representative, but they are superficially comparable by these values. Buchanan and others (2011) argue that their data support a direct point size-prey size correlation. Consistent with this, Eren and others (2021c) argue that lower TCSA and TCSP values for Folsom represent further specialization to bison hunting. Agate Basin points, also closely associated with bison, likewise have lower TCSA (79.57) and TCSP (47.53) values.

Much about why these points look the way they do needs scrutiny from both behavioral and morphological standpoints (e.g., Kilby et al. 2022), but if we are to advance from the data points produced in these published studies, then we must again assign a parallel between Haskett and Clovis. They share a system of repair, long use life, and multipurpose functional trajectory that has some quantifiable measure of similarity. As to their functional priority, nothing presented by Eren and colleagues (2021c, 2022b) addresses why the heavy skill and training invested in Clovis points is more proportionate to primary use as a multitool of reworked longevity than as a priority projectile point.

Skill

Haskett and Clovis reduction strategies require extensive skill and training arguably exceeding functional requirements. The possibility, discussed in the context section but not well understood, is that these investments are purely social signals with only tangential relationships to performance.

Like Clovis (Bradley et al. 2010; Wilke et al. 1991), Haskett points were made using a system that started with large bifacial preforms, but Haskett knappers on the ORBD primarily used fine-grained volcanic (FGV) rock—60% (n = 56 of 94) in our sample—which is challenging for controlled flaking compared to the cherts preferred by Clovis knappers. This finding is especially noteworthy because obsidian of adequate package size for Haskett is both available and preferred throughout post-Haskett prehistory in the eastern Great Basin. Among the other, later-dating, WST points in the ORBD study area, obsidian is preferred almost three to one over FGV (73%, n = 230 of 313); the preference varies by subtype but holds easily throughout the series. The Haskett disregard for chert is practical in the Intermountain West where volcanic rocks are abundant, but may have a cultural component too, as Clovis in the west maintains a chert (and obsidian) preference with a seeming disregard for FGV.

Haskett biface reduction can be assessed using the phases of reduction usually applied to Clovis (see Bradley et al. 2010:7; Callahan 1979; see also Aubry et al. 2008), and this analysis is supported by our own ongoing replicative work. The steps are as follows: early phase material acquisition, testing, and initial edging; middle phase shaping and thinning; and late phase finishing. The early phase begins with a core of sufficient size to remove a flake (also referred to as spall or blank) that is large enough to produce a finished biface of the desired size. This approach may result in the production of several finished bifaces. In circumstances where a flake-to-biface sequence is not possible, a second approach is core-to-biface whereby reduction begins with a nodule of material only large enough to enable the production of a single finished biface of the desired size. Agate Basin exhibits a similar approach but with ribbony flaking, different position of maximum width, and less pronounced convexity in the stem cross section.

Both approaches may be used depending on the natural form of the raw material. This technique is known for Clovis, and it is likewise evident for Haskett. In the ORBD assemblage, we see the first approach, early phase biface production beginning with large flake spalls. This method is to be expected given the large, cobble size of both FGV and obsidian sources in the region. The second approach is evidenced at Sentinel Gap in central Washington, with early phase production beginning with nodules (Galm and Gough 2008:218). At both localities, overface/overshot flaking was used during the reduction process, including middle phase shaping and thinning, as shown by Galm and Gough (2008:Figure 3) for Sentinel Gap and in Figure 4.8[5] for the ORBD; this technique is often considered diagnostic of Clovis, although there is some discussion as to whether this is necessarily so (Eren et al. 2013, Eren, Patten, et al. 2014; Huckell 2014; Lohse et al. 2014).

The final phase of Haskett production consisted of driving off a series of short collateral percussion and pressure flakes, enabling knappers to create a long, narrow outline while maintaining a robust bi-convex cross section. Haskett final-phase reduction was technically sophisticated and risky; as the biface gets narrower, the chance of fracture mistakes gets higher. Fracturing includes both the twisting and bending fractures directly associated with mis-hits and indirect breaks by end shock. Based on our flintknapping experience, all are interrelated as the preform narrows and room for error diminishes (also see Galm and Gough 2008:214–216). When successful, finished points were long, skillfully made, and needlelike. Thus, we consider

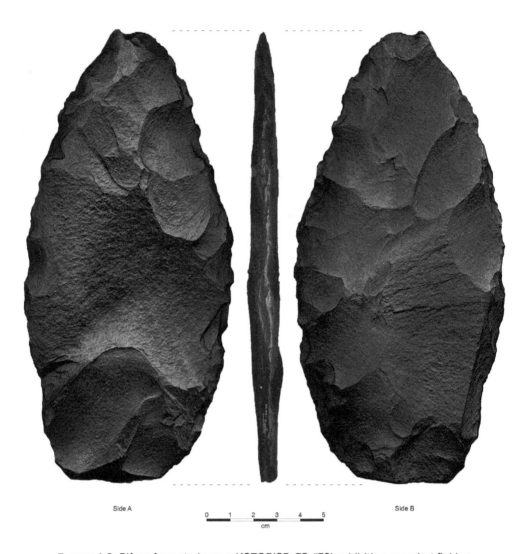

FIGURE 4.8. Biface from study area (42TO5135, FS #79) exhibiting overshot flaking.

the technical challenges and risks entailed in Haskett production to be a rough parallel with Clovis, although we cannot assert to what extent. The data imply separate cultural traditions, supporting an argument Beck and Jones (Chapter 12) make, presuming these technologies truly overlap in time.

To attain the skill displayed in either knapping tradition requires long-term and culturally fostered learning and sustained practice. Lohse and colleagues (2014; also see Apel and Knutsson 2006) have discussed this aspect at length for Clovis as a sign of hunting specialization, and the connection naturally extends to Haskett. Stueber is a highly skilled traditional flintknapper who, like most modern knappers, was trained on a Clovis model. Subsequently, his Haskett replication efforts for this study require continued stepping back in the process to get to a Haskett form that is true to specifications. Haskett requires a subtle but meaningful twist on the Clovis reduction model by its deviation of priority from pure thinning to managing stem cross-section shape during the late production stages. Thus, while Haskett and Clovis have aesthetic differences, we see a parallel in skilled and trained production investment.

Toolstone Conveyance

Much has been made of Western Stemmed obsidian conveyance, with Jones and colleagues (2003) arguing it ranged some 400 kilometers north–south in the eastern Great Basin. Debate since has focused on shrinking this distance, as exotic obsidians tend to account for a small percentage of the source profile and therefore may not represent group-level residential mobility (Jones et al. 2012; Madsen 2007; Madsen, Schmitt, and Page 2015b; Page and Duke 2015; Smith 2010; Smith et al., Chapter 3). An important limitation to this research has been difficulty in distinguishing the various stemmed point styles chronologically. Each could contribute to the overall conveyance pattern differently based on several abundance factors changing through time, such as mobility, hunting priority, or manufacturing investment (see Duke and Young 2007).

In the ORBD case, we know that the Early Holocene record overwhelms that of the Pleistocene. This assessment is evident from both the geoarchaeological associations of Western Stemmed styles with radiocarbon dated distributary channels (Duke 2011; Beck and Jones 2015b; Madsen, Oviatt, et al. 2015) and the now better-understood sequence of types through time from dated contexts across the Intermountain West (Rosencrance et al., Chapter 2). The 95 Haskett points in our study represent 22% of the 434 Western Stemmed points collected from the study block, but this locality is unique, and perhaps more telling is that Haskett represents less than 5% of the almost 2,000 points reported in prior publications about the ORBD, inclusive of some 82,000 surveyed acres (see Beck and Jones 2015b; Duke 2011; Madsen, Schmitt, and Page 2015a; Page and Duke 2015).[6] We also know that residential mobility on the ORBD diminished through time based on toolstone selection and associated shifts in tool reduction strategies (Duke 2011).

The chronological implication for current purposes is that Haskett represents a less visible Pleistocene component of the eastern Great Basin record than do later Early Holocene stemmed points, and the pattern likely extends outside the region. If Haskett hunters were indeed among the earliest in the Great Basin, then they should exhibit the high mobility known with Clovis. The data support this prediction (Table 4.3, Figure 4.9). Eight obsidian sources are represented by 33 Haskett points. The majority (55%, $n = 18$ of 33) cover a total geography of about 650 km (Figure 4.9). Among the 227 post-Haskett stemmed points, 12 sources are represented but seven of these account for less than 1% each, and three others just 2% to 7%. This post-Haskett profile is dominated by Browns Bench[7] and Topaz Mountain obsidians, the two nearest sources, representing 84% in similar proportions. These sources are within 200 km of the study area.

No obsidian is local to the study area by the usual metrics applied, typically presented as a foraging roundtrip or day trip distance of 10–20 km (see discussion in Surovell 2009: 78). Browns Bench is at least 180 km to the northwest and Topaz Mountain is 75 km to the south. Such distance suggests that obsidian was either brought into the ORBD en route by people moving through briefly using short-term camps or was directly procured as needed from longer-stay ORBD residences. Researchers have a few ideas about what this means for explaining the ORBD lithic record in general (Beck and Jones 2015b; Duke 2011; Page and Duke 2015; Madsen, Schmitt, and Page 2015b), but these two sources always dominate the previously studied ORBD record. We can now see under a blanket of intensive Early Holocene occupation that the pattern is reversed with Haskett.

Haskett conveyance resembles that of Clovis at its maximum (Holen 2014; Kilby 2014), which has for years anchored long-distance settlement-subsistence interpretations and colonization models (e.g., Ellis 2011; Goodyear 1989; G. Haynes 2002; Kelly 1999;

TABLE 4.3. Obsidian Source Profile for Western Stemmed Points from Old River Bed Delta Study Area.

Obsidian Source	Source Distance (km) from Wishbone	Haskett	Cougar Mountain	Ovate[a]	Parman	Lake Mohave	Windust	Silver Lake	Bonneville	Stubby	Total
Browns Bench Group	180	9	—	2	5	10	—	22	31	28	107
Bear Gulch	465	2	—	—	—	—	—	—	—	—	2
Black Rock Area	190	7	4	—	1	—	—	3	3	4	22
Big Southern Butte	340	—	—	—	—	—	—	1	—	—	1
Double H	410	1	—	—	—	—	—	—	—	2	3
Malad	245	3	—	—	—	1	1	1	2	—	8
Modena	290	—	—	—	—	—	—	1	—	1	2
Paradise Valley	365	1	—	—	—	—	—	—	1	1	1
Timber Butte	470	1	—	—	—	—	—	—	1	—	2
Topaz Mountain	75	6	—	2	5	5	—	13	39	28	98
Unknown	—	—	—	—	—	1	—	—	—	—	1
Venator	510	—	—	—	—	—	—	—	—	1	1
Wildhorse Canyon	215	4	—	—	—	—	—	4	4	—	12
Totals		33	4	4	11	17	1	45	80	65	260

[a] As defined by Beck and Jones 2009.

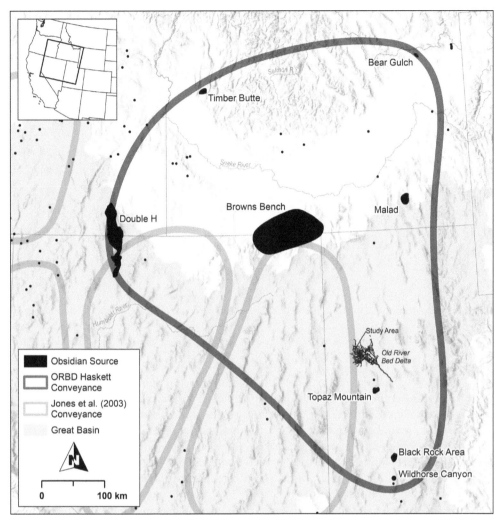

FIGURE 4.9. Obsidian sources (labeled with geographic extents) represented among Haskett projectile points in the study area. Unlabeled dots represent centroid locations for other obsidian sources.

Kelly and Todd 1988; Meltzer 2002). Clovis caches contain material from great distances at times, often over 300 km (Kilby 2014). But discarded Haskett projectile points are not best compared to these caches, which consist of items that still possess the potential for future use and were placed for undetermined reasons (Kilby 2014). Comparable behavioral context is needed. While the ORBD sites are largely surficial and subject to the abovementioned downward lag of post-Haskett artifacts, people's emphasis shifted through time alongside changing distributary landforms to produce a horizontal stratigraphy that yields some spatial separation among sites.

Of the total 55 sites within our study area, 14 contain either only or overwhelmingly Haskett projectile points in their assemblages; the remainder are defined by post-Haskett WST styles. Using this simple distinction to define the component, a strong association with one of the arterial paleochannels of the area is revealed. The channel most closely associated with Haskett on the ORBD has

TABLE 4.4. Obsidian Sources Represented by Count and Weight for Nonprojectile Point Tools in Haskett and Post-Haskett Western Stemmed Tradition (WST) Sites in the Study Area.

Obsidian Source	Count			Weight (g)		
	Haskett	Post-Haskett WST	Total	Haskett	Post-Haskett WST	Total
American Falls	1		1	6.9		6.9
Browns Bench Group	9	64	73	163.3	303.9	467.2
Bear Gulch	1		1	24.4		24.4
Black Rock Area	9	5	14	59.9	21.2	81.1
Big Southern Butte	1		1	37.7		37.7
Ferguson Wash		2	2		13.4	13.4
Malad	11	4	15	120.5	18.1	138.6
Modena	1		1	4.1		4.1
Topaz Mountain	18	80	98	171.6	430.9	602.5
Unknown	1		1	19.2		19.2
Wildhorse Canyon	8	6	14	78.9	24.7	103.6
Totals	60	161	221	686.5	812.2	1498.7

been radiocarbon-dated to ca. 12,100 cal BP (Madsen, Oviatt, et al. 2015), generally consistent with that of the Wishbone site, although we do not know when the channel initiated or how long it endured. The sites separate on several predictable fronts. Haskett sites have the heaviest tools (11.4 to 5.0 g/tool), inclusive of the large scrapers, biface fragments, and multipurpose tools typical of hunting-based toolkits throughout late Pleistocene-Early Holocene North America. They also exhibit the least weathering with 38% showing light/moderate weathering to 19% among post-Haskett points, the latter having more recently been exposed by erosion to the ground surface.

Obsidian source data from nonprojectile point tools tighten these converging patterns to further support long-distance toolstone conveyance and high residential mobility for Haskett. Madsen (2007; Madsen, Schmitt, and Page 2015b) argues that projectile points may represent the long-distance movements and interactions of hunters but not necessarily their most closely affiliated residential base. By this logic, toolstone diversity should be high among projectile points and low for nonprojectile point tools. Also, the overall proportion of distant toolstone should be low, as already discussed, indicative of its ephemeral relationship to overall group movement. As shown in Table 4.4, 10 sources are represented among the 60 tools in 13 Haskett sites compared to only six sources among 161 tools in 41 post-Haskett stemmed sites. By percentage weight contribution of the obsidian, Haskett site tools exhibit a nearly 50% split, a difference with statistical similarity to the Haskett point assemblage. Post-Haskett sites show only 10% of total weight contributed by nonlocal obsidian sources. In sum, Haskett points and tools support a case for high, whole-group residential mobility, and post-Haskett stemmed point assemblages do not.

We thus interpret Haskett toolstone conveyance as a Clovis parallel. Great distance on the order of hundreds of kilometers is the empirical evidence of this, but this high mobility also represents further facets of behavior strongly tied to Clovis. Haskett groups moved through the landscape swiftly enough to rotate diverse obsidian sources through their entire toolkit (e.g., Brantingham 2003; Duke and Young 2007). They represent a small archaeological signature that is the initiative of the WST pattern of wetland use, with later-dating stemmed point components on the ORBD exhibiting longer residential stays.

Discussion

The results of this study show parallels between Haskett and Clovis in size, design, skill, and toolstone conveyance that suggest two independent technological traditions made for the same purpose in late Pleistocene North America—the hunting of now-extinct and extant Pleistocene mammals. The two styles combine to cover the North American continent with a singular adaptive technological response, converging on the interior during a unique period when an expanding human populace intersected with a pivotal decline in megafaunal herbivores.

We interpret that the lack of direct archaeological or paleontological evidence of megafaunal prey is more parsimoniously explained by a lack of bone preservation than by an alternative interpretation of Haskett points. To the latter, legitimate Clovis points also occur in the Great Basin, so, notwithstanding other prey options (e.g., wapiti, bison), we would be left with providing an alternative interpretation for their function if no megafauna were in the region.

The technology can be used to better examine the spatiotemporal nuances of megafaunal die-offs. Grayson (2016) makes a strong case that the Great Basin was not an optimal environment for megafauna, but what is true at long time scales in the Pleistocene may not be so for short-term episodes like the Younger Dryas. On the High Plains, the cold and dry conditions of the Younger Dryas would have presented a constraint on megafaunal populations, especially proboscideans in need of huge amounts of daily water intake. By contrast, water increased in the Great Basin during this period, as the cooler temperatures depressed evaporation rates and facilitated the rising of pluvial lakes and accompanying lakeside and distributary marshlands. Some of these could be vast, such as the ORBD, and closely associated with others in mountain-fed catchments off the Sierra Nevada, Wasatch, Cascades, and northern Rockies.

Such context also agrees well with a conservative view of the projectile point chronologies. While published data suggest that Haskett may overlap with Clovis, extending as far back as ca. 13,000 cal BP, the peak time for Haskett is beginning to resolve as immediately postdating Clovis for a period between approximately 12,600 and 11,800 cal BP. Haskett thus encompasses Folsom[8] and most, if not all, of Agate Basin times on the High Plains. Surovell (Chapter 10) argues that the radiocarbon record on the High Plains demarcates Folsom from Agate Basin transition at ca. 12,200 cal BP, Agate Basin persisting and overlapping with Hell Gap to the end of the Younger Dryas. This distinction is an important temporal one for Haskett as a western precursor to Agate Basin, the latter a bison-centric descendent technology with Plains technical signatures.

The people who created Haskett and Clovis technology must have done so with a working knowledge of the interior landscape and its prey options. People must also have been sparsely distributed, as has been surmised by others, and we argue that the technologies represent the material signature of a unique inflection point in the past whereby declining megafaunal populations met with a threshold push of human population from the margins of the continent. Alternatively, the stone weaponry we see may represent a simple transition from osseous and/or wood-focused industries, but this explanation lacks a cultural catalyst. If costly signaling extends to the use of stone, then the arrival of Haskett and Clovis would best be interpreted as responses to dwindling megafauna populations, as predicted by evolutionary theory, which we know declined substantially at about the time of Haskett and Clovis innovation. This interpretation does not preclude this lithic record from having value to questions of the settlement of interior North America, only that it is best viewed as an effect, not a cause.

On Extinctions

Our findings are inextricably tied to ongoing debate on whether the extinction of the megafaunal herbivores at the end of the Pleistocene was caused by humans or climate change. If Haskett points were used to hunt megafauna, as we contend, then these points are proxy evidence for persistence of some species, and the killing of them. Mammoth, camel, and horse were the three most abundant megafaunal herbivores in the desert west in pre–Younger Dryas (and pre-Clovis) times. We have made the case that Haskett engineering parallels Clovis at a size calibration adequate to encapsulate proboscideans; smaller species, extinct and extant, would also have been hunted, as was the case for Clovis. The last appearance dates for mammoth and camel support this assertion. Whatever animals drove Haskett technology during the Pleistocene were apparently gone immediately thereafter. Great Basin technological evidence shows a reduction in projectile point size, frequency, and investment by the Early Holocene even while persistent bison-specialized weaponry was being used on the High Plains.

As to the debate itself, now 50 years running, it occurs to us that neither side thus far benefits from the persistence of megafauna after Clovis. A short-run extinction "event" is analytically convenient, but last appearance dates in North America give up to a 1,500-year timeline during which some 50 human generations were witnesses. More anthropological examinations of people's relationship with the animals they hunted could be explored to enhance the discourse. After centuries of settlement and learning about the whereabouts and behavior of the largest prey animals in the interior, how did humans respond to their changing distributions as the environment transitioned? If we consider Clovis potentially together with Haskett as a purely technological event, what was the catalyst? Formal modeling in human behavioral ecology suggests that scarcity of large game drives escalation of prestige hunting (Martin 2019), which could explain the investments, or costly signals, we see in these technologies. This possibility would implicate humans in megafaunal extinctions, but in useful contrast to regional environmental conditions. For the purposes of this study, we do not know, but our interests are sociocultural. The fossils themselves cannot provide any such insight, so it may be these enduring stone tools that lead us to a better understanding of what happened.

Conclusion

We have made a case for considering Haskett with Clovis as same-calibrated hunting technologies in North America's late Pleistocene. Although the attributes they share are not all specific to these types, the combined and proportionate occurrences of these within an engineered whole that captures both types are distinguishing. Haskett and Clovis are based on effectively the same lanceolate template. But for a flute or a taper, their differences are likely based on culturally distinct technical strategies and the advanced training required to perfect them. Although they had secondary functional roles, their foremost purpose—the purpose that explains their investment and stylings—is argued here to serve as projectile points. Haskett and Clovis represent a singular approach to stone projectile point technology that emerged at an inflection point in megafaunal extinctions between at least 13,000 and 12,500 years ago. At this scale, the matter of which came first is not so relevant compared to why both arrived at this approximate time, in variable geography, after people entered the Americas and had familiarity with its resident fauna.

Several aspects of Haskett and its technological context deserve further attention and could be more powerfully applied with targeted questions. We can put these in three broad categories: the prey-oriented, the sociocultural, and the technical. On the prey side, if megafauna were present in the Great Basin during the Younger Dryas, then we should find paleoenvironmental data to line up with a stable, tolerable, or even improved foraging situation for them during this time. This patterning can be understood through comparisons with neighboring areas and patterns of change through times immediately before and after the Younger Dryas. These comparisons might yield more insight into critical vegetation shifts, species responses, and trophic effects on the biome at large. Seeking proxy data, such as coprophilous spore abundance in Younger Dryas sediments (e.g., Perrotti et al. 2022), and developing a fuller human subsistence profile through the examination of macrofloral contents in association with western hearths (e.g., McDonough et al. 2022) would help situate technological patterns within adaptive priorities.

This methodology lends to understanding Haskett as a technological response. To say Haskett or Clovis are engineered to hunt megafauna is one thing, but to suggest they are manufactured to send an additional human message is another. There is wide agreement that Clovis projectile points are crafted beyond functional necessity, and we argue the same for Haskett. This clue is revealing for social incentives beyond basic consumption. In general, reducing people to gastric and utilitarian motives defies obvious human behavior, and evolutionary theory has now sufficiently developed from such baselines to formally model risk-taking behavior. If costly signaling was a driving incentive, then we should expect deviations from straight subsistence payoff. Better engagement with Native American tribes and tribal groups about Indigenous hunting practices could be informative along these lines (Pitblado 2022).

To the technical, we issue a straight challenge to pit Haskett against Clovis with replicative, experimental, and digital analyses. Clovis point studies could use a counterpoint. For example, Thomas and colleagues (2017) argue "that the fluted-point base acts as a 'shock absorber,' increasing point robustness and ability to withstand physical stress via stress redistribution and damage location." This suggestion is intriguing but difficult to confirm without a competing alternative. Thomas and colleagues (2017) make brief reference to Frison's (2004) personal experience with Agate Basin to suggest that this style, by contrast, was designed to "break upon impact in order to cause maximum damage to prey," but Frison (2004:110) also says that Agate Basin's "tapering base and sinew wrapping *absorb the shock* [emphasis added] of impact, and transverse breaks usually result in sections that can be retrieved and easily reworked for further use." We expect overall for Haskett and Clovis to possess similar performance tolerances, following from our prediction that their separate stylings are not functionally meaningful within the engineered whole.

That said, we predict that no matter how similar the tolerances, one must show some performance gain over the other if put to the test. While Clovis won the early battle for our attention, Haskett and subsequent stemmed forms won the war in prehistory, originating during the late Pleistocene in the Intermountain West, supplanting fluted points on the High Plains and emanating in use across much of the continent in the Early Holocene. To understand why, questions with physically addressable predictions are needed to fully integrate the technical nuances into a richer technological, ultimately sociocultural, context. We wager that Haskett will win this head-to-head, performing better as measured by fewer fatal breaks, more reworking potential, and greater overall performance. We mean this playfully, of course, as we are as curious as anyone.

Acknowledgments

We would foremost like to thank the U.S. Air Force, and Hill Air Force Base, for its continued care and management of the ORBD record. Jaynie Hirschi deserves special credit for her long-time stewardship and support of this research. Anya Kitterman has likewise been very supportive. Jenni DeGraffenried and Nate Nelson have been key collaborators, sharing their thoughts and access to collections from the ORBD on Dugway Proving Ground. More people than can be listed from Far Western Anthropological Research Group have been valuable to the project work and reporting yielding the data. D. Craig Young and Sarah Rice are longtime and important colleagues in this regard. Several people have been generous with access to collections. These include Amy Commendador with the Idaho Museum of Natural History for the Haskett site, Suzann Henrikson with the Idaho National Laboratory for Lake Terreton and Veratic Rockshelter, and Rick Minor for Fossil Lake. Dennis Jenkins and Patrick O'Grady, both with the University of Oregon Museum of Natural and Cultural History, let us see collections from Paisley Caves, Connley Caves, and Rimrock Draw Rockshelter. Loren Davis, Oregon State University, showed us artifacts from Cooper's Ferry. Richie Rosencrance facilitated much of the above access.

We would also like to thank: Max Pavesic for his friendship and inspiration and for the loan of many issues of *Tebiwa* and other volumes for this research; Nancy Stueber for her constant support and keen editorial eye; to the editors of this volume, Katelyn McDonough, Richie Rosencrance, and Jordan Pratt for their patience, editorial comments, and help in bringing this to completion. Gary Haynes, Ruth Gruhn, and David Madsen provided valuable feedback. Any errors, omissions, or wayward thoughts are our own.

Notes

1. We are referring to the whole technology as represented by associated projectile point styles. Haskett is one of several styles commonly attributed to the Western Stemmed Tradition (Bryan 1980; Layton 1970; Tuohy and Layton 1977; Willig and Aikens 1988), much as Clovis is to the fluted point tradition.
2. Haskett is described herein as a phenomenon of the Intermountain West, but our study pertains most specifically to the Great Basin. This location is where our primary data are from and where the history of research and paleoenvironmental considerations are most relevant. This area is also pertinent to stemmed point chronology insofar as Haskett has no demonstrated predecessor but there may be exceptions elsewhere (cf. Davis, Chapter 7; Rosencrance et al., Chapter 1; Smith et al. 2020).
3. Our question is framed as one of the interior, which we consider distinct from coastal regions in terms of the nature and timing of human occupation. To the latter, we refer the reader to Erlandson and colleagues' Chapter 13 in this volume.
4. We use the common California spelling of Lake Mojave, consistent with the soft-j Spanish spelling, instead of the alternate "Lake Mohave." The latter remains in formal use for many place names and is often used to refer to the Mohave people of the lower Colorado River and for the projectile point type.
5. Images of this biface have been published twice in discussions by Beck and Jones (2015b) and Schmitt and colleagues (2007) about the lithic record of the ORBD. Beck and Jones' (2015b:163) interpretation, perhaps from photos, is that the overshot flake scar is actually remnant evidence of the flake interior, but this assessment is clearly not true upon physical examination, and the opposing face possesses the remnant bulb of the blank. Originally collected and provenienced by U.S. Air Force personnel in the early 2000s, the item's provenience had no further archaeological association until formal archaeological survey in 2012 (Duke, Rice, et al. 2018).
6. Studies by Madsen and colleagues (2015a) and Duke (2011) represent the primary summaries and discussions of the ORBD record to date, although CRM projects continue to record stemmed points at a rapid pace. Duke (2011:Table 10) uses Cougar Mountain as a catchall inclusive of Haskett. In Madsen and colleagues (eds., 2015), Beck and Jones (2015b) distinguish between the types for diagnostic specimens and combine them for the indeterminate fragments.
7. Browns Bench represents three geochemically separable but similar sources that can be grouped as distinct from other sources. Their known spatial distribution on the ground overlaps to the extent shown in Figure 4.9 (Page and Bacon 2016:Figure 13).
8. Folsom also occurs sparsely in the eastern Great Basin (Copeland and Fike 1988) and Snake River Plain (Butler 1973; Henrickson et al. 2017; Titmus and Woods 1991a) alongside otherwise named and presumably post-Clovis fluted point forms (Beck et al. 2019; Jones and Beck, Chapter 8).

5

Regional Morphological Homogeneity among Mojave Desert Terminal Pleistocene/Early Holocene Projectile Points

EDWARD J. KNELL *and* MARK Q. SUTTON

The Mojave Desert, like many regions of the Great Basin, has a substantial terminal Pleistocene/Early Holocene (TP/EH) archaeological record. But, unlike some areas of the Great Basin, the Mojave Desert has few buried (much less stratified) TP/EH deposits that significantly contribute to refining fluted (Clovis) and Western Stemmed Tradition (WST) point chronologies. Rather than dwell on the limited chronological evidence, here we use univariate statistics to assess whether and how the Mojave Desert's primary TP/EH projectile point types—Great Basin Concave Base (GBCB; including Clovis, Western Fluted, and other basally thinned lanceolate points) and WST (Lake Mohave and Silver Lake)—morphologically vary. We specifically assess whether and to what degree morphologic homogeneity exists among and between GBCB and WST points within three regions of the Mojave Desert. Comparisons are then drawn between the Mojave Desert record and two study areas in the central and eastern Great Basin to provide a broader regional assessment of the patterns. Because this study represents a first attempt at assessing morphologic homogeneity from multiple areas of the Mojave Desert and beyond, the goal is to document patterns and propose initial interpretations rather than test the identified patterns.

Morphologic homogeneity, as conceived here, is met for a projectile point type if no or few (<30%) statistically significant differences occur among seven metric, one ratio, and three angle variables across or, in cases, within the different Mojave Desert and Great Basin spatial units. Conversely, morphologic heterogeneity results if most variables (>70%) significantly differ. A univariate statistics-based approach is necessary since we nearly entirely relied on other researchers' reported point type identifications and measurements (some made 30+ years ago). More sophisticated approaches are possible but would require us to physically access and analyze large numbers of points and/or have enough scanned images of the points for geometric morphometric analyses, neither of which is currently feasible.

The 499 GBCB and WST projectile points that comprise the Mojave Desert database are from academic and unpublished cultural resource management reports affiliated with four military bases and two research hotspots (pluvial Lake Mohave and the Borden site; Figure 5.1). Limiting our search for projectile point data to these study areas

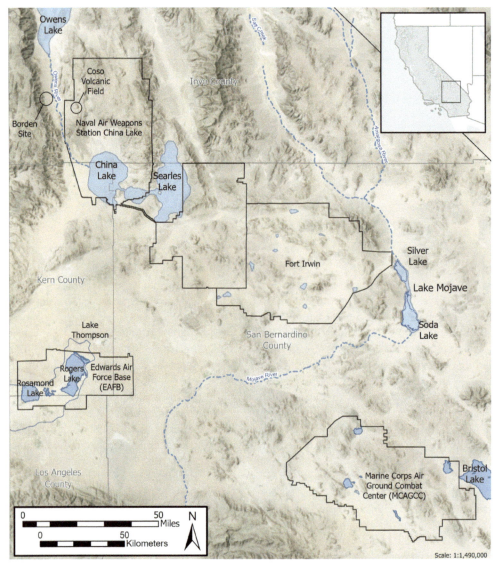

FIGURE 5.1. Map depicting the location of Mojave Desert study areas. Map created by Albert Garcia, and used with permission.

was a necessary time saver, but also a calculated effort since these areas have or were thought to have a substantial number of measured TP/EH projectile points. Moreover, these study areas cover three large, spatially discrete regions of the Mojave Desert. These "regions"—western Mojave (Edwards Air Force Base), north-central Mojave (Naval Air Weapons Station China Lake, Fort Irwin National Training Center, Borden site, and pluvial Lake Mojave), and south-central Mojave (Marine Corps Air Ground Combat Center, Twentynine Palms)—represent spatially discrete clusters of study areas rather than established physiographic regions. To broaden the research implications, we compare the Mojave Desert database to comparably measured clusters of TP/EH points in the central Great Basin (Sunshine Locality and Eastern Nevada Comparative Collection [Beck and Jones 2009]) and eastern Great Basin (Old River Bed Delta [Madsen et al., eds. 2015]).

Three primary research questions establish if and to what degree GBCB and WST points in the Mojave Desert are morphologically homogenous, and how the Mojave Desert pattern compares to other regions of the Great Basin. The first question considers whether the Mojave Desert database is valid in the sense that GBCB, Lake Mohave, and Silver Lake points represent statistically separate populations amenable to univariate statistical analyses. Second, we assess whether GBCB, Lake Mohave, and Silver Lake points from the respective Mojave Desert regions are morphologically homogenous, and third, whether morphological homogeneity exists across the Mojave Desert, central, and eastern regions of the Great Basin.

Projectile Point Chronology and Technology

Before addressing these questions, background is provided on the respective projectile point types and Mojave Desert study areas. Answers to the questions form the basis of the discussion section.

Fluted Points

Clovis was long thought to be the earliest formal projectile point type in North America, and until recently, most any fluted point found in western North America was called "Clovis." Recent analyses of fluted points from Tulare Lake in central California reveal, however, that relatively few are firmly identifiable as Clovis (Rondeau 2015a:47). These and other studies suggest that some fluted points traditionally called "Clovis" actually represent a separate fluted/basally thinned point technology, now generally called Great Basin Concave Base (e.g., Beck and Jones 1997; Pendleton 1979; Rondeau 2015a; Rondeau and Hopkins 2008) or "Western Fluted" (Miller et al. 2013:215; Willig and Aikens 1988). Distinguishing between these technologies is difficult and applied unevenly across the Mojave Desert/Great Basin, especially in older reports. Therefore, given the difficulty of knowing whether points reported as Clovis are actually Clovis, a fluted point variant, or concave base point, we lump all "fluted" points into the broader GBCB category.

The temporal placement of Clovis remains unclear. A "short" chronology (ca. 13,050–12,750 cal BP; Waters, Stafford, and Carlson 2020) and "long" chronology (ca. 13,500–12,900 cal BP; Haynes 2005; also Miller et al. 2013:215 and Beck, Jones, and Taylor 2019) are proposed, though the current sample of dated Clovis sites may be too small to accurately define its time range (Prasciunas and Surovell 2015). Further confusing the issue is the date range for the Clovis or Clovis-derived concave-base lanceolate points from the Borden site that obsidian hydration dating indicates are 13,800–11,300 years old (calendar years before AD 2000; Moratto et al. 2018). The early end of this date range places these GBCB points as slightly older than Clovis. The individual obsidian hydration dates used to create this range have standard deviations that are thousands of years old at just 1-sigma (Moratto et al. 2018:Table 4), however, and thus do not provide definitive evidence of a Clovis or pre-Clovis age.

Other Mojave Desert fluted point sites likewise do not substantially contribute to the chronology. The Lakebed Locality (CA-KER-2143) and Charlie Range Basalt Ridge (CA-INY-5825) sites at China Lake have fluted points generally associated with Rancholabrean fauna, though reanalysis of both sites questions any specific relationship (Basgall 2003, 2007a). The Henwood site on Fort Irwin has a fluted point found 10 cm below an approximate 9500 cal BP radiocarbon date, making its actual age uncertain (Warren 1991). None of the Mojave Desert sites thus has definitive evidence that establishes or contributes to the fluted point chronology.

Western Stemmed Tradition

The Western Stemmed Tradition refers to several cultural complexes across the Intermountain West that have stemmed, shouldered, and lanceolate points, as well as crescents (Willig and Aikens 1988:3; see also Pratt et al. 2020 and Smith et al. 2020). WST points take many

FIGURE 5.2. Images of Lake Mohave (*bottom*) and Silver Lake (*top*) projectile points from the north-central Mojave Desert, particularly pluvial Lake Mojave. Points photographed or scanned by Edward J. Knell.

forms (e.g., Smith et al. 2020), with the Lake Mohave and Silver Lake types most common in the Mojave Desert (Knell et al. 2021; Figure 5.2). Amsden (1937:80–84) first described the Lake Mohave and Silver Lake projectile point types using the specimens collected by Elizabeth Campbell and associates in the 1930s from pluvial Lake Mojave (Campbell et al. 1937), with other researchers having since expanded on Amsden's definitions (e.g., Beck and Jones 2009, 2015b; Gilreath et al. 1987; Justice 2002; Knell et al. 2021; Rogers 1939; Warren 2002). The Lake Mohave and Silver Lake projectile point descriptions provided below are condensed versions of those in Knell et al. (2021).

The temporal placement and association of WST projectile points with other TP/EH point types remains a topic of debate. Until recently, most researchers thought that Clovis preceded the WST; however, new research suggests the WST may be earlier or at least contemporaneous with Clovis (e.g., Becerra-Valdivia and Higham 2020; Beck, Jones, and Taylor 2019; Davis et al. 2019; Rosencrance 2019; Rosencrance et al., Chapter 2; Shillito et al. 2020; Smith et al. 2020). Also debated is the association between WST and fluted/GBCB points. Willig and Aikens (1988:28–30) view the WST as including fluted and stemmed points since they often co-occur around wetland systems. Others view them as an overlapping historical and/or technological continuum, or as distinct cultural complexes (e.g., Basgall 2003, 2007a, 2007b; Basgall and Hall 1991:63; Moratto 1984:103; Rosenthal et al. 2001; Sutton 2018b, 2019; but see Beck and Jones 2010; Beck, Jones, and Taylor 2019) based on varying raw material profiles, obsidian hydration dates (Basgall 1988; Garfinkel et al. 2008; Gilreath and Hildebrandt 1997), manufacturing techniques (e.g., Basgall and Hall 1991), and discrete clusters of WST and GBCB points at some large sites (Basgall 2003, 2007a, 2007b; Sutton et al. 2007:234). It has also been suggested that "Clovis" might reflect a ritual system associated with WST groups and not a separate cultural entity (Sutton 2021).

Lake Mohave Points

> "The Lake Mohave type is characterized by a long, tapering stem, produced by shouldering the point (usually very slightly), just below the center of its vertical axis. This results in a generally diamond-shape form, with more shoulder than blade. The form is not highly standardized" [Amsden 1937:80].

Building on Amsden's description, Justice (2002:86) describes Lake Mohave points as a "highly variable stemmed-lanceolate projectile point type with an elongated and slender design, weak shoulders, and heavy lateral grinding with lenticular to biconvex cross section," and contracting stem (Justice 2002:90). Because Lake Mohave points are often broken and heavily reworked, they usually have a short blade segment, a long stem that comprises half or more of the entire length (i.e., high stem length to total length [STL/TTL] ratio), and beveled edges (Beck and Jones 2009; Knell et al. 2021). They are made by percussion followed by some pressure flaking. Knell and colleagues (2021) found, using principal components analysis, the key distinguishing characteristics of Lake Mohave points to be a long, narrow stem, high STL/TTL ratio, and high distal shoulder angle and notch opening index when compared to Silver Lake points. Beck and Jones (1997:196) suggest Lake Mohave points date between 13,200 and 8600 cal BP, with more recent interpretations suggesting they are an Early Holocene point type (Rosencrance 2019:126; Rosencrance et al., Chapter 2).

Silver Lake Points

> "[T]he [Silver Lake type has] more definition of shoulder and less basal taper than the Lake Mohave type. The base comprises never more than half the whole length, usually about a third. It is always somewhat rounded at the butt.... The better specimens show good pressure retouch, the poorer ones...percussion only" [Amsden 1937:84].

Justice (2002:98) describes the Silver Lake type as "characteristically short with a wider, bulbous haft element and shoulders that are clearly demarcated...[often with] weak side notch indentations at the shoulder/haft juncture and below this the haft element expands before constricting to the [convex] base." Beck and Jones (2009) characterize Silver Lake points as heavily reworked, with a short stem but long blade segment that is usually one-third to just under half of the entire point (i.e., low STL/TTL ratio), and proximal shoulder angle greater than 91°. This conforms to the principal components analysis results of Knell et al. (2021) that Silver Lake points have short, broad stems, low STL/TTL ratio, and high proximal shoulder angle compared to Lake Mohave points. The age of Silver Lake points is less well known than Lake Mohave points, but likewise probably date to the Early Holocene (Rosencrance 2019:126; Rosencrance et al., Chapter 2).

Mojave Desert Study Areas

The Mojave Desert occupies much of southeastern California and extends into portions of Arizona and Nevada. It is a warm temperature desert, with the Joshua tree (*Yucca brevifolia*) being the standard vegetative marker in higher elevations (Rowlands et al. 1982). Creosote (*Larrea tridentata*) is ubiquitous, and mesquite (*Prosopis* spp.) occurs in many basins. The Mojave Desert is for our purposes divided into three "regions" (see Figure 5.1).

The western region is represented by Edwards Air Force Base (EAFB) in the Antelope Valley. The Rogers-Buckhorn-Rosamond Lake (playa) system, a remnant of Pleistocene Lake Thompson (Orme 2004), covers much of the military base. Extensive stands of mesquite surround the playas, with creosote dominant away from the playas. TP/EH sites occur along the lake margins, with a major cluster having many measured points located at Rosamond Dry Lake (Basgall and Overly 2004).

The north-central region includes four study areas: the Borden site, China Lake, Fort Irwin, and pluvial Lake Mojave. The Borden site and China Lake are located as far west as EAFB but being substantially farther north create a useful spatial unit when combined with Fort Irwin and Lake Mojave. The surface collection from the Borden (or Rose Valley) site (CA-INY-1799), which represents the westernmost extent of the north-central region, is comprised of some 3,700 artifacts (Borden 1971), including 14 GBCB points (Moratto et al. 2018; Rondeau 2009a) and 29 Lake Mohave and Silver Lake points (Stephens and Yohe 2012).

The Owens River flowed south through Rose Valley into Lake China during the

TP/EH. Located on Naval Air Weapons Station China Lake, pluvial Lake China is a hotspot for GBCB and WST points, with 150 in our database (e.g., Andrews 2018; Basgall 2007a, 2007b; Giambastiani 2008; Giambastiani and Bullard 2007; Rosenthal et al. 2001). Within the China Lake military base is the Coso Range, which has substantial outcrops of obsidian that collectively are known as the Coso Volcanic Field (CVF) and was used by hunter-gatherers since the TP/EH (e.g., Gilreath and Hildebrandt 2011).

Located east-southeast of China Lake, Fort Irwin is dominated by creosote scrub, low mountain ranges flanked by alluvial piedmonts, bajadas, pediments, and several valleys with remnants of lakes. TP/EH foragers left a substantial record that includes surface scatters and larger sites, some with buried deposits (e.g., Basgall and Hall 1993; Warren 1991). This record is robust and well-documented, and our largest source for measured GBCB and WST points (n = 242; e.g., Basgall 1993; Basgall and Hall 1993; Gilreath et al. 1987; Ruby et al. 2010).

Pluvial Lake Mojave represents the far eastern extent of the north-central study area. It formed when water from the Mojave River, with its headwaters in the San Bernardino Mountains, filled today's Soda and Silver Lake playas (e.g., Kirby et al. 2015; Wells et al. 2003). At its Pleistocene maximum, this 35 km long lake covered 300 km^2 and held more than 7 km^3 of water (Wells et al. 2003). The current vegetation around the lake includes creosote scrub, saltbush, grasses, and some mesquite.

Pluvial Lake Mojave has a long history of archaeological investigations focused on its TP/EH record (e.g., Brainerd 1953; Campbell et al. 1937; Knell 2014; Knell et al. 2014; Warren and Ore 2004a, 2004b). The projectile point sample (n = 30) from Lake Mojave includes points from the Campbell collection at Joshua Tree National Park, the Brainerd (1953) collection, and those reported from recent excavations and surveys around the lake (Knell 2014; Knell et al. 2014; Knell et al. 2021; Warren and Ore 2004a).

The south-central region includes the Marine Corps Air Ground Combat Center (MCAGCC) at Twentynine Palms, which encompasses much of this creosote scrub-dominated region. The northwest–southeast trending Bullion Mountains crosscut the region, forming ranges separated by small valleys. Interspersed among these ranges are lava flows with knappable rhyolite and small obsidian cobbles, and 14 now dry pluvial lakes (the six largest are Ames, Deadman, Lavic, Emerson, Quackenbush, and Dry). Other than three isolated surface finds of fluted (Clovis) points (Byerly and Roberson 2015; Roberson and Gingerich 2015; Rondeau 2014), there are no known Clovis sites on the base (Byerly and Roberson 2015:197). The early record consists almost entirely of WST materials, mainly sites with one or two diagnostic points. Despite the many pluvial lakes, relatively few GBCB and WST points have been found at MCAGCC.

Methods

The Mojave Desert projectile point database includes 499 GBCB and WST points generated from publications and cultural resource management (CRM) reports from sites within the six study areas (Table 5.1). We had to rely on a limited number of CRM reports due to the restricted distribution of military base CRM reports, the lack of reported measurements in some reports (particularly from Edwards Air Force Base), and the paucity of up-to-date catalogs with point measurements. Despite these limitations, we believe this database to be the largest and most spatially diverse of its kind thus far published.

The metric and angle variables selected for analysis follow Beck and Jones (2009), though we analyzed fewer variables given our limitation of gathering data from extant reports that often contain a limited number of measured attributes compared to what is obtainable via direct analysis. Data ultimately were collected for seven linear, one ratio, and three angle variables. The linear measurements include maximum length (mm), stem length (mm), neck width (mm), width (mm), basal width (mm), thickness (mm), and

TABLE 5.1. Frequency of Point Types by Region and Mojave Desert Study Area.

Region	Study Area	Point Type				Total
		Great Basin Concave Base	Lake Mohave	Silver Lake	Nondiagnostic Western Stemmed	
North-central	Borden site	14	19	10		43
	China Lake	12	86	44	8	150
	Fort Irwin	13	101	97	31	242
	Lake Mojave	3	15	7	5	30
South-central	MCAGCC	2	10	3	3	18
West	Edwards Air Force Base	7	7	2		16
Total		51	238	163	47	499

Note: MCAGCC = Marine Corps Air Ground Combat Center.

mass (g). The stem length to total length ratio (STL/TTL ratio) is a derived measure from two of the linear variables. The three angle variables are distal shoulder angle (DSA), proximal shoulder angle (PSA), and notch opening index (NOI). Not every report contained information for each variable, and because we included incomplete or broken specimens, not all attributes were present on every point. Only attributes deemed complete (i.e., reflect the maximum extent of that attribute) by the original analyst are in the database. Mass was included in the database for complete or unbroken specimens only. Lithic raw material type was also recorded.

The projectile point type designations adhere to the original report the data were obtained from (i.e., we made no attempt to reclassify the points). Depending on the author, points designated GBCB in the original report may be fluted or basally thinned concave-base points; since the actual type is unknown, all fluted points (including those identified as Clovis) are included in the GBCB category. Lake Mohave and Silver Lake points are recorded as such, but points identified only as WST or wide stem are in the nondiagnostic WST category.

SigmaPlot version 14 was used to calculate the statistics. Preference was given to parametric statistics (one-way ANOVA or t-test), with nonparametric statistics (Mann-Whitney U [U] or Kruskal-Wallis one-way ANOVA on ranks [H]) substituted when the data could not be transformed to a normal distribution. The angle degree variables were transformed into radians to treat them as linear measurements.

Results

The 499 projectile points are not evenly distributed among the Mojave Desert regions (Table 5.1). The sample is heavily biased towards the north-central region ($n = 465$ or 93.2% of the entire sample), which includes the Borden site ($n = 43$), China Lake ($n = 150$), Fort Irwin ($n = 242$), and Lake Mojave ($n = 30$). Though this bias results from lumping four study areas into the north-central region compared to one study area in the other regions, China Lake and Fort Irwin also arguably have more substantial and completely studied TP/EH archaeological records than the (roughly) similarly sized EAFB and MCAGCC. The south-central region (MCAGCC) has 18 projectile points (3.6% of the entire sample): 2 GBCB points (including the Clovis point reported by Byerly and Roberson [2015]) and 16 WST points (a 30.8% sample of known WST points as per a 2016 database compiled by Ryan Byerly, personal communication 2019). The western region or

TABLE 5.2. Summary Data for Projectile Points from All Mojave Desert Study Areas.

Variable	Statistic	Point Type			
		GBCB (n = 51)	Lake Mohave (n = 238)	Silver Lake (n = 163)	Western Stemmed (n = 448)
Total length (mm)	N	14	114	104	231
	Range	36.1–68.9	29.6–89.3	20.5–62.8	18.3–89.3
	Mean	51.69	47.48	40.39	43.87
	SD	9.83	10.83	9.32	11.16
	SE	2.63	1.02	0.91	0.73
Stem length (mm)	N	—	124	127	273
	Range	—	7.7–42.6	4.8–28.4	4.7–42.6
	Mean	—	22.62	13.55	17.64
	SD	—	6.87	4.01	7.25
	SE	—	0.62	0.36	0.44
Neck width (mm)	N	—	109	135	267
	Range	—	12.6–28.2	10.4–26.7	7.6–33.5
	Mean	—	20.37	17.53	18.79
	SD	—	3.37	2.81	3.58
	SE	—	0.32	0.24	0.22
Maximum width (mm)	N	37	170	137	339
	Range	13.61–43.5	7.5–38.3	12.4–36.6	7.5–42.3
	Mean	26.29	23.91	23.95	23.71
	SD	5.84	4.66	3.79	4.55
	SE	0.96	0.36	0.32	0.25
Basal width (mm)	N	37	161	132	328
	Range	9.53–37.3	3.55–25.0	5.6–30.4	3.55–30.4
	Mean	22.25	12.15	16.29	14.0
	SD	5.3	4.2	4.05	4.63
	SE	0.87	0.33	0.35	0.26

EAFB sample is smallest with 16 points (3.2% of the entire sample): a sample we know is underrepresented since most of the points are from a single report (Basgall and Overly 2004) and the undercount that resulted from the lack of measurement data in some reports.

Discussion

Here we address the three primary research questions established at the beginning of this chapter: if the database is statistically valid, whether morphologic homogeneity exists among TP/EH projectile point types in the Mojave Desert, and whether these same point types are morphologically homogenous across the Great Basin. Morphologic homogeneity is recognized if <30% of the analyzed variables significantly differ, morphologic heterogeneity if >70% of the variables significantly differ, and a mixed or indeterminate pattern between these thresholds. Table 5.2 provides summary statistics for the

TABLE 5.2. (cont'd.) Summary Data for Projectile Points from All Mojave Desert Study Areas.

Variable	Statistic	Point Type			
		GBCB (n = 51)	Lake Mohave (n = 238)	Silver Lake (n = 163)	Western Stemmed (n = 448)
Thickness (mm)	N	42	200	154	390
	Range	4.1–9.9	4.2–12.0	4.2–17.6	4.2–17.6
	Mean	6.48	7.01	7.14	7.07
	SD	1.27	1.37	1.53	1.44
	SE	0.20	0.10	0.12	0.07
Stem length:total length (mm)	N	—	83	89	183
	Range	—	0.09–0.078	0.15–0.84	0.09–0.84
	Mean	—	0.47	0.36	0.41
	SD	—	0.13	0.11	0.13
	SE	—	0.01	0.01	0.01
Mass (g)	N	8	93	89	192
	Range	4.4–18.9	3.2–32.4	1.8–18.3	1.6–41.1
	Mean	10.33	8.25	7.0	7.71
	SD	5.03	4.22	2.9	4.38
	SE	1.78	0.44	0.31	0.32
Distal shoulder angle (°)	N	—	75	122	213
	Range	—	144–277	162–260	144–277
	Mean	—	227.95	215.95	220.37
	SD	—	20.49	18.76	21.13
	SE	—	2.37	1.7	1.45
Proximal shoulder angle (°)	N	—	75	112	204
	Range	—	65–112	64–140	64–140
	Mean	—	84.84	98.35	92.55
	SD	—	8.81	12.72	13.08
	SE	—	1.02	1.2	0.92
Notch opening index (°)	N	—	49	101	159
	Range	—	80–180	53–180	53–180
	Mean	—	143.45	117.44	125.81
	SD	—	19.38	24.13	25.91
	SE	—	2.77	2.4	2.06

Note: WST points include all Lake Mohave, Silver Lake, and nondiagnostic WST points. SD = standard deviation; SE = standard error.

11 analyzed variables and follows the format of Beck and Jones (2009:171) for comparability to other Great Basin projectile point studies.

Is the Database Valid?

Validating the database is crucial to establishing that the database itself and univariate statistical approach are viable analytical tools. We consider the database valid if, respectively, GBCB and WST and Lake Mohave and Silver Lake points are statistically distinguishable (i.e., represent different point type populations). We acknowledge, following Knell et al. (2021) for Lake Mohave and Silver Lake points, that identifying individual points to type using univariate statistics alone is not possible because univariate statistics compare differences in central tendency only. That is, the mean (or median depending on the test) may differ significantly, but substantial overlaps among the linear, ratio, and/or angle measurements make it difficult to adequately separate individual points into a type (see Knell et al. 2021:Figure 6 for this issue with Lake Mohave and Silver Lake points). To overcome this challenge, Knell et al. (2021) used multivariate statistics (principal components and linear discriminant function analysis) to separate Lake Mohave from Silver Lake points with an approximate 80% success rate; the other 20% still had too many overlapping measurements to classify correctly. This success rate indicates the Lake Mohave and Silver Lake point types are valid and usually distinguishable by archaeologists. No attempt is made here to classify individual Lake Mohave and Silver Lake points to type; instead, univariate statistics are used only to examine broad patterns between populations of points within and across spatial units. This method, of course, assumes that the respective populations of points are statistically distinguishable, which the univariate statistical analyses (below) indicate is the case.

The 51 GBCB and 448 WST (all types) points represent separate populations given that all four statistical analyses differ significantly. GBCB points are significantly longer than WST points ($t = 2.6$, $df = 243$, $p = 0.01$), wider in maximum dimension ($U = 4527$, $p = 0.005$), and have wider bases ($t = 10.17$, $df = 363$, $p = <0.001$), whereas WST points are significantly thicker ($U = 6000$, $p = 0.004$). This finding suggests, not surprisingly, that our sample of GBCB and WST points is drawn from significantly different populations and validates the database for subsequent comparative statistical analyses between these types.

Lake Mohave ($n = 238$) and Silver Lake ($n = 163$) points also represent separate populations since all but two (maximum width and thickness) of the 11 analyzed variables differ significantly. Lake Mohave points have a significantly longer maximum length ($t = 5.27$, $df = 216$, $p = <0.001$) and stem length ($t = 13.04$, $df = 249$, $p = <0.001$), higher STL/TTL ratio (MW-U, $df = 1631.5$, $p = <0.001$), wider neck ($t = 7.18$, $df = 242$, $p = <0.001$), greater mass ($t = 2.55$, $df = 180$, $p = 0.012$), and wider DSA ($t = 4.37$, $df = 195$, $p = <0.001$) and NOI ($t = 7.1$, $df = 115.9$, $p = <0.001$) than Silver Lake points. Silver Lake points have a significantly wider base ($t = 8.53$, $df = 291$, $p = <0.001$) and higher PSA ($t = 8.14$, $df = 185$, $p = <0.001$). Lake Mohave points thus have a long, narrow stem, high STL/TTL ratio, and higher DSA and NOI values than Silver Lake points, which have short, broad stems, a low STL/TTL ratio, and high PSA. This pattern matches the one identified by Knell et al. (2021), which is unsurprising since we use the same sample of Lake Mohave and Silver Lake points with the minor caveat that the current sample includes one additional Lake Mohave point from Fort Irwin. More importantly for this study, Lake Mohave and Silver Lake points were drawn from significantly different populations, which validates the database for subsequent comparative statistical analyses.

Mojave Desert Region Morphologic Homogeneity?

The projectile point database was built with the intent to statistically compare the three Mojave Desert regions (see Figure 5.1); however, the small number of GBCB,

Lake Mohave, and Silver Lake points from the south-central and western regions (each ≤10) prevented such analysis (Table 5.1). The sample of points from the four study areas that comprise the north-central Mojave Desert region (Borden, China Lake, Fort Irwin, and Lake Mojave) is much larger with 221 Lake Mohave and 158 Silver Lake points, so our analysis focuses on this region; the frequency of GBCB points was too small (each ≤14) for statistical analysis, however.

Statistical analysis of the Lake Mohave points focused on eight variables: length, stem length, neck width, width, thickness, basal width, STL/TTL ratio, and mass. Three variables differ significantly, with the significant pairwise comparisons indicating that Lake Mohave points from Fort Irwin are wider ($H = 24.78$, $df = 3$, $p = <0.001$) and thicker ($F = 6.1$, $df = 3$, $p = <0.001$) than those from China Lake, and those from Borden thicker than those from China Lake. The basal width of Lake Mohave points from China Lake, Fort Irwin, and Lake Mojave differs significantly from each other ($H = 25.89$, $df = 2$, $p = <0.001$). With just 37.5% of the variables differing significantly, Lake Mohave points from the north-central Mojave Desert tend towards morphologic homogeneity but fall outside the established threshold (<30%) for this pattern.

It is beyond the scope of this chapter to fully explain this pattern, but two lithic raw material-based factors are examined for their influence on north-central Mojave Desert Lake Mohave point morphology—regional availability and physical properties. The 221 points are manufactured primarily from fine-grained volcanic (FGV) stones such as dacite and rhyolite ($n = 104$), followed closely by obsidian (OB; $n = 89$), but with a lower frequency of cryptocrystalline silica-based raw materials (CCS) like chert, jasper, and chalcedony ($n = 26$); two points made from other raw materials are excluded from this analysis. The proportion of OB and FGV Lake Mohave points (excluding CCS due to small sample size for some study areas) differs significantly ($\chi^2 = 102.9$, $df = 3$, $p = <0.001$), with the adjusted residuals revealing that Borden and China Lake are significantly overrepresented by OB and Fort Irwin and Lake Mojave by FGV (also see Figure 5.3a). This distribution is explained by the closer proximity of China Lake and the Borden site to the Coso Volcanic Field than Fort Irwin and Lake Mojave (Figure 5.1), which have immediately available and substantial outcrops of FGV and CCS. Proximity to lithic raw material source thus underlies the selection of lithic materials used to manufacture north-central Mojave Desert Lake Mohave points.

Proximity to source influences the proportion of raw materials used to make Lake Mohave points in the different study areas, but does this explain some of the morphologic heterogeneity evident in the Lake Mohave point sample? We anticipate that different physical properties of the three lithic material types will influence point morphology (e.g., Brantingham et al. 2000:257; Loendorf et al. 2018; but see Eren, Roos, et al. 2014) given that OB is a glassy, isotropic, homogenous stone that flakes nicely and has sharp edges, but dulls quicker than more brittle, less homogenous (granular), and harder to flake FGV stones (e.g., Duke 2013; Reid 2014). CCS typically falls between these extremes.

Statistical analysis of the Lake Mohave points by raw material type was possible for six variables: length, width, thickness, stem length, basal width, and mass. Three variables differ significantly: width ($H = 12.35$, $df = 2$, $p = 0.002$), basal width ($H = 15.72$, $df = 2$, $p = <0.001$), and mass ($F = 3.64$, $df = 2$, $p = 0.031$; see Figure 5.4). One significant pairwise comparison reveals basal width to be wider among FGV and OB points than CCS points. Others indicate FGV Lake Mohave points are significantly wider and heavier than those made from OB, which could result if knappers preferred larger initial FGV blanks to accommodate for the difficulty of controlling flake removals from this brittle, granular stone compared to the easier to flake OB (Duke 2013). If correct, this finding implies

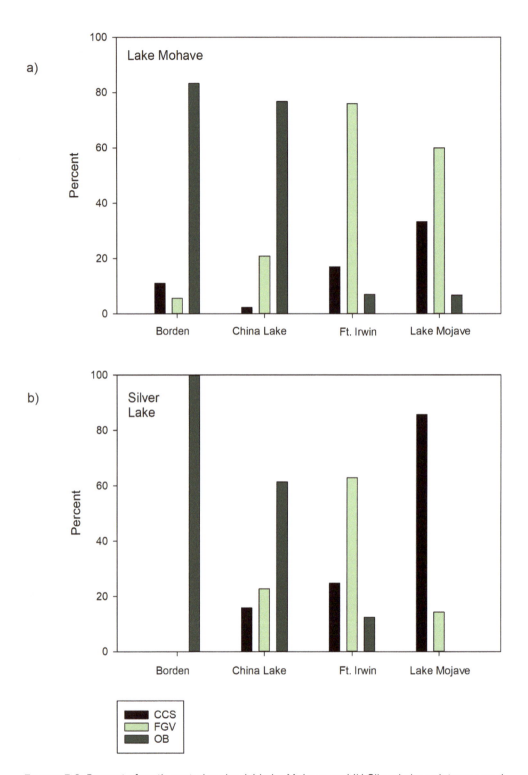

FIGURE 5.3. Percent of north-central region (*a*) Lake Mohave and (*b*) Silver Lake points grouped by raw material type (CCS = cryptocrystalline silica-based raw materials; FGV = fine-grained volcanics; and OB = obsidian).

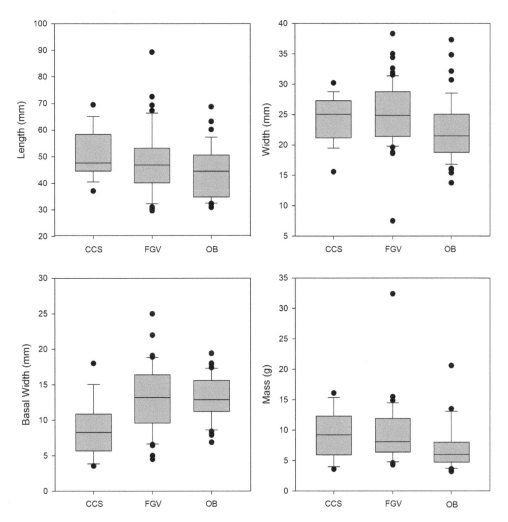

FIGURE 5.4. Box plots depicting the length, width, basal width, and mass of north-central region Lake Mohave points grouped by raw material type (CCS = cryptocrystalline silica-based raw materials; FGV = fine-grained volcanics; and OB = obsidian).

that toolmakers who opted to use FGV rather than OB sacrificed a degree of precision during manufacture, and presumably some utility, for savings in the time and trouble involved to procure better, but more distant, toolstone. Given that just half of the statistically analyzed variables differ significantly, it remains uncertain how much raw material type, or the inherent properties of those raw materials, accounts for morphologic heterogeneity among Lake Mohave points.

The distribution of the 158 north-central region Silver Lake points is highly skewed, with China Lake ($n = 44$) and Fort Irwin ($n = 97$) accounting for 89.2% (n = 141) of the total sample (Table 5.1). Consequently, statistical analyses are limited to these study areas. Five of the 11 analyzed variables differ significantly: Silver Lake points from China Lake have longer stems ($t = 2.54$, $df = 90.7$, $p = 0.013$), and higher DSA ($t = 2.03$, $df = 112$, $p = 0.045$) and NOI ($t = 3.16$, $df = 92$, $p = 0.002$) compared to those from Fort Irwin, which have wider necks ($t = 2.06$, $df = 124$, $p = 0.042$) and higher PSA ($t = 2.26$, $df = 105$, $p = 0.026$). With 45.5% of the variables differing significantly, a strong pattern does not emerge for homogeneity or heterogeneity among the Silver Lake points.

The 141 Silver Lake points from China Lake and Fort Irwin are manufactured primarily from FGV ($n = 71$), OB ($n = 39$), and CCS ($n = 31$; Figure 5.3b), with the proportion of raw material types differing significantly by study area ($\chi^2 = 37.04$, $df = 2$, $p = <0.001$). Adjusted residuals indicate China Lake is overrepresented by obsidian and Fort Irwin by FGV, which, like Lake Mohave points, implies that proximity to source influenced the selection of raw materials used to make Silver Lake points. Physical properties of the raw materials are not a major influence on Silver Lake point morphology, however. When excluding CCS points due to small sample size, none of the 11 t-tests comparing FGV and OB Silver Lake points differed significantly. Reasons for these findings are unclear and beyond the scope of this chapter to assess, but possibly relate to the overall lack of evidence for morphologic homogeneity or heterogeneity among Silver Lake points.

Great Basin Morphologic Homogeneity?

Here we consider whether morphological homogeneity exists among TP/EH projectile points across the Great Basin. We address this using statistical comparisons between the entire Mojave Desert (MOJ) dataset (GBCB and WST from all regions) and datasets from the Sunshine Locality/Eastern Nevada Comparative Collection in the central Great Basin and the Old River Bed Delta (ORBD) in the eastern Great Basin (Figure 5.5).

The ORBD, in the Bonneville Basin of Utah, supported TP/EH foragers for more than 3,000 years (Madsen et al., eds. 2015). A north-flowing river connected the Sevier Basin to the ORBD, forming a large (2,000+ km²) distributary wetland system in the ORBD. These wetlands created a large, relatively uniform ecosystem or resource megapatch (Madsen, Schmitt, and Page 2015b:247) that enabled TP/EH foragers to tether their movements to the ORBD for considerable lengths of time. Lacking from this megapatch, however, are lithic raw material sources—the closest being some 60 to 80 km away. Beck and Jones (2015b:Table 5.11 and 5.14) provide comparable summary data for nine unfluted/GBCB, 29 Lake Mohave, and 108 Silver Lake points.

The Sunshine Locality (SUN) is in southern Long Valley, Nevada, and the Eastern Nevada Comparative Collection (ENCC) is a collection of WST points from sites in Butte, Long, and Jakes Valleys (Beck and Jones 2009). Artifacts from these sites come from repeatedly occupied basin and wash settings. Beck and Jones (2009:Table 6.6 and 6.8) provide summary data for 72 unfluted lanceolate or GBCB points from SUN, and 30 Lake Mohave and 71 Silver Lake points from the ENCC.

GBCB points from the MOJ and SUN study areas are statistically analyzed for four variables; the ORBD sample is too small for statistical analysis with a maximum of seven measurements on these same variables. Compared to those from SUN, GBCB points from the MOJ are significantly longer ($t = 2.8$, $df = 27$, $p = 0.009$), wider ($t = 2.44$, $df = 66$, $p = 0.017$), and thicker ($t = 5.47$, $df = 112$, $p = <0.001$), and have wider bases ($t = 2.49$, $df = 100$, $p = 0.014$). GBCB points from the MOJ are thus larger than those from SUN in all respects, fitting a pattern of morphological heterogeneity among Great Basin GBCB points. This result may be more apparent than real, however, because the methodologies used to create the GBCB databases differ since Beck and Jones (2009) separated fluted from unfluted lanceolate points (we used their unfluted data), but Mojave Desert CRM reports usually conflate fluted and unfluted lanceolate points into the GBCB point type (e.g., Basgall and Hall 1993; Basgall and Overly 2003). Another possible explanation relates to raw material type, with GBCB points from SUN disproportionately made from CCS and those from MOJ nearly evenly made from CCS and OB (Figure 5.6a). Fewer such comparability issues exist for WST points.

Lake Mohave points from the three Great Basin study areas are statistically analyzed

Homogeneity among Terminal Pleistocene/Early Holocene Projectile Points

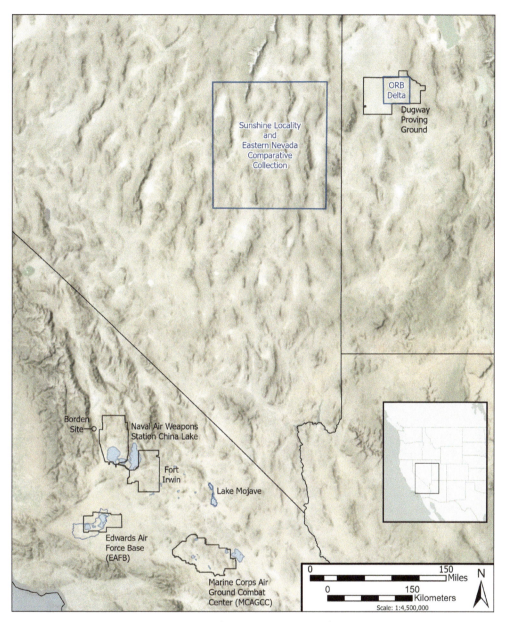

FIGURE 5.5. Map depicting the location of Mojave Desert and Great Basin study areas. Map created by Albert Garcia, and used with permission.

for eight variables: length, stem length, neck width, width, thickness, basal width, DSA and PSA. All but PSA vary significantly. ENCC and MOJ points, compared to those from ORBD, are significantly longer ($F = 4.41$, $df = 2$, $p = 0.014$) and have longer stems ($F = 5.9$, $df = 2$, $p = 0.003$), are wider ($F = 6.81$, $df = 2$, $p = 0.001$), have wider necks ($F = 23.87$, $df =$

2, $p = <0.001$), and are thicker ($F = 18.41$, $df = 2$, $p = <0.001$). Five of seven (71.4%) variables thus indicate ORBD Lake Mohave points are, in some way, significantly shorter, narrower, and thinner than those from the other study areas. The other two significant variables indicate Lake Mohave bases from ENCC are wider than those from MOJ ($F = 7.15$, $df = 2$,

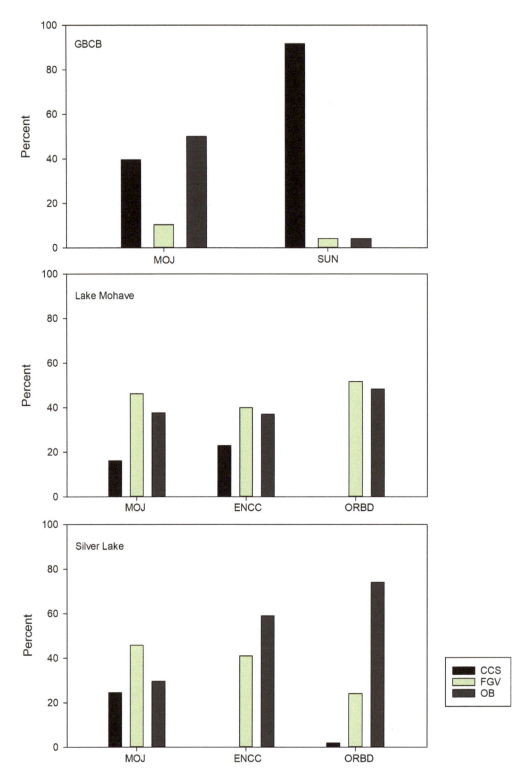

FIGURE 5.6. Percent of: (*a*) Great Basin Concave Base (GBCB), (*b*) Lake Mohave, and (*c*) Silver Lake points when grouped by Great Basin study area (MOJ = Mojave Desert; SUN = Sunshine Locality; ENCC = Eastern Nevada Comparative Collection; ORBD = Old River Bed Delta) and raw material type (CCS = cryptocrystalline silica-based raw materials; FGV = fine-grained volcanics; and OB = obsidian).

$p = 0.001$), and DSA higher from ENCC and ORBD than MOJ ($F = 7.73$, $df = 2$, $p = <0.001$). The paucity of significant differences between MOJ and ENCC Lake Mohave points indicates they are morphologically homogenous, but morphologically different (i.e., heterogeneous) from those in the ORBD. Lithic raw material type (Figure 5.6b) does not significantly ($\chi^2 \, p > 0.05$) influence this pattern.

Silver Lake points share the same basic pattern, but not as strongly. Statistical analyses of the same eight variables reveal significant differences, except for basal width. Compared to ORBD, ENCC and MOJ Silver Lake points are significantly longer ($F = 33.81$, $df = 2$, $p = <0.001$), have longer stems ($F = 34.04$, $df = 2$, $p = <0.001$) and wider necks ($F = 41.47$, $df = 2$, $p = <0.001$). Silver Lake points from MOJ are also significantly wider ($F = 7.52$, $df = 2$, $p = <0.001$) and thicker ($F = 14.29$, $df = 2$, $p = <0.001$) than those from ORBD. Together then, Silver Lake points from ORBD are shorter, narrower, and thinner than those from the other study areas. DSA ($F = 8.23$, $df = 2$, $p = <0.001$) and PSA ($F = 6.22$, $df = 2$, $p = <0.001$) are significantly higher, however, in the ORBD than MOJ sample. ORBD is thus a morphological outlier compared to the more morphologically homogenous ENCC and MOJ Silver Lake points. Lithic raw material type may influence the patterning given the visually (Figure 5.6c) and significantly ($\chi^2 = 80.32$, $df = 4$, $p = <0.001$) different raw material profiles.

It lies beyond the scope of this chapter to fully explain the regional variations in point morphology, but we suggest that differences in resource structure hold important clues. Hunter-gatherers faced with small, comparatively low productivity resource patches theoretically moved more frequently across the landscape than those occupying large, highly productive resource patches where they could tether their movements for longer periods of time (e.g., Madsen 2007; see also Elston et al. 2014; Knell 2007; G. Smith et al. 2013). Both situations should result in reworked and resharpened projectile points, but foragers tethered to resource patches without nearby raw material sources are expected to more extensively resharpen and rework projectile points than mobile groups who moved more freely across the landscape and benefitted from the flexibility to regularly refresh toolkits (assuming toolstone is regionally available). The effects of point reworking and resharpening are extremely complex (e.g., Azevedo et al. 2014; Beck and Jones 2009; Buchanan 2006; Flenniken and Raymond 1986) and not something adequately addressed here. Despite the complexity, extensive reworking and resharpening generally should result in shorter, and perhaps narrower and thinner projectile points than those from less heavily reworked assemblages. This statement oversimplifies the effects of resharpening but provides testable predictions.

The ENCC and MOJ include basin, riverine, and shoreline settings with nearby sources of lithic material. In contrast, the ORBD is a resource megapatch where TP/EH foragers tethered their movements for sustained periods of time, relied on somewhat distant raw materials (60–80 km or more), and extensively resharpened their tools (oftentimes to stubs; Duke and Young 2007; Madsen et al., eds. 2015). These characterizations of the study areas and technological expectations possibly explain the morphological heterogeneity between the points from ORBD and other study areas: Lake Mohave and Silver Lake points from the ORBD are significantly shorter, narrower, and thinner than those from ENCC and MOJ due to extensive resharpening by foragers tethered to this productive resource patch but without immediately available raw materials to replace exhausted projectile points. If correct, this implicates resource structure as an influence on projectile point morphology.

Conclusion

The primary goal of this univariate statistics-based pattern recognition study was to establish whether morphologic homogeneity exists among and between GBCB and WST (Lake Mohave and Silver Lake) projectile points within the Mojave Desert, and secondarily, to assess if the Mojave Desert pattern extends to other parts of the Great Basin. Causative explanations were provided that relate to lithic raw material type and proximity to source, resharpening, and occupation span.

Before undertaking the pattern recognition study, it was necessary to establish the validity of the Mojave Desert projectile point database, which contains 499 GBCB, Lake Mohave, and Silver Lake projectile points. The database was deemed valid or to represent separate statistical populations of GBCB and WST and Lake Mohave and Silver Lake points, respectively, given the high number of statistically significant differences among 11 analyzed variables. Though classifying each point to type was not possible given limitations of the univariate statistics (see above), each population of points (roughly GBCB, Lake Mohave, Silver Lake) has its own underlying morphology or design properties that separate it from the others. Whether these design properties relate to performance, function, and/or style, among other possibilities, is beyond the scope of this research to establish.

Sample size issues limited our attempt to establish whether GBCB, Lake Mohave, and Silver Lake points are morphologically homogenous across the Mojave Desert. Consequently, we focused on the north-central region because it has a large enough sample of Lake Mohave and Silver Lake points for statistical analysis. These analyses revealed a moderate number of significant differences—37.5% for Lake Mohave and 45.5% for Silver Lake points—which, according to the parameters established for this chapter, does not clearly indicate a pattern of morphologic homogeneity or heterogeneity but rather a mixed or indeterminate pattern. To explain this, we considered whether lithic raw material type (CCS, FGV, OB), proximity, and their physical properties influenced point morphology. Borden and China Lake have a significant overrepresentation of CVF obsidian points because this material outcrops locally, whereas Fort Irwin and Lake Mohave are overrepresented by FGV since this material, unlike obsidian, outcrops nearby. While proximity to source appears to underlie the patterning (see Knell 2022 for a similar pattern among north-central Mojave Desert unifacial flake tools), statistical analyses comparing the 11 variables by raw material type revealed few significant differences, which suggests inherent physical properties of the raw material types had little effect on the morphology of Lake Mohave and Silver Lake points. Thus, while the economics of procuring toolstone from nearby sources was important, other factors—like performance, function, resharpening, and/or style—appear to have exerted more influence on Mojave Desert, Lake Mohave and Silver Lake point morphology.

Additional patterns emerge when comparing the Mojave Desert (MOJ) dataset to the central (SUN/ENCC) and eastern (ORBD) Great Basin datasets. Statistical analyses reveal that Lake Mohave and Silver Lake points from ORBD are significantly smaller (e.g., shorter, narrower, and thinner) than those from ENCC and MOJ. Smaller ORBD points likely result from extensive resharpening by foragers who tethered their movements to this raw material poor but biotic rich resource megapatch for considerable lengths of time. Conversely, in lower quality biotic resource patches with nearby lithic sources (like ENCC and MOJ), the optimal solution for hunter-gatherers was to employ a mobility strategy that facilitated more regular access to raw material so they could replenish weaponry as needed. By comparison to ORBD, this approach should result in somewhat less resharpened or larger size projectile points. If these predictions are correct, occupation span, lithic raw material availability, biotic resource structure, and resharpening influenced point morphology.

To conclude, the lack of morphological homogeneity among Lake Mohave and Silver Lake points (i.e., mixed pattern) from the Mojave Desert, as well as morphological differences between the ENCC/MOJ and

ORBD Lake Mohave and Silver Lake points from the Great Basin wide study, suggests that overall these point types are morphologically heterogeneous. Causes of this heterogeneity seemingly occur, however, for predictable reasons like proximity to raw material source, occupation span, resharpening, and biotic resource structure. The Lake Mohave and Silver Lake point types thus each seemingly exhibit an underlying logic that persists within and across the Mojave Desert/Great Basin, but with differential use related primarily to local-scale situational factors, morphological heterogeneity gradually developed over time.

The main contribution of this study was to assemble a sizeable database of GBCB and WST (Lake Mohave and Silver Lake) projectile points from a large swath of the Mojave Desert (the largest such published database we are aware of and one that is generated primarily from CRM reports) and to characterize, using univariate statistics, the morphology and morphological variability of each type. Despite its large size, the 499 points that comprise the database still proved too small to be entirely effective, requiring the exclusion of certain statistical analyses, running some analyses with small samples, and limiting certain statements regarding point morphology (especially GBCB points). We recognize this approach is not ideal and intend to continue building the database, particularly the western (Edwards Air Force Base) and south-central (MCAGCC) study areas. The patterns described here thus represent a first attempt at assessing morphologic homogeneity rather than the final word on this subject—more work is certainly needed to flesh these ideas out. Moreover, because this is a pattern recognition study, the causative explanations are *post hoc* and best considered propositions for further testing. Caveats aside, we hope readers view this study as a step towards better understanding broad issues of TP/EH projectile point morphology within and across the Mojave Desert and Great Basin.

Acknowledgments

Creating the Mojave Desert database was a team effort, and we thank many people for their assistance: Mark Basgall, Mark Becker, Ryan Byerly, Daron Duke, Mark Giambastiani, and Janelle Harrison. We also thank the 2019 Kelso Conference attendees for comments on the initial presentation of this paper, and Jan Taylor for assisting with the data collection. EJK also wishes to thank David Nichols of the Mojave National Preserve and Jim Shearer of the Barstow, California, Bureau of Land Management for their ongoing support of his research around pluvial Lake Mojave. Comments on a prior draft of this manuscript by David Madsen, two anonymous reviewers, and the editors improved its quality and coherence. We, of course, absolve all these individuals of blame for any misinterpretations of the data.

6

The Younger Dryas-Aged Stemmed Points from Smith Creek Cave, Nevada

Joshua J. Lynch, Caitlin Doherty, Ted Goebel, *and* Pat Barker

Recently much attention has been drawn toward the Paleoindian record of the Intermountain West of North America, where new pre-Clovis discoveries have been made (Davis et al. 2019; Gilbert et al. 2008), and ancient autosomal DNA has been retrieved from the remains of two Early Holocene humans (Hockett and Palus 2018; Rasmussen et al. 2015). Furthermore, archaeologists have begun to seriously consider whether Western Stemmed points west of the Rocky Mountains are as old as Clovis east of the mountains, thereby indicating the presence of two contemporaneous Paleoindian traditions in North America prior to 12,700 calendar years ago (cal BP), each potentially the result of separate late-glacial dispersals out of Beringia or a much earlier, pre-Clovis migration along the Pacific Coast (e.g., Beck and Jones 2010; Braje et al. 2020; Pratt et al. 2020). Recent evidence for early stemmed points comes chiefly from three sites. Jenkins and colleagues (2012) have argued that at least two stemmed points came from contexts predating 13,000 cal BP at Paisley Cave 5 (eastern Oregon), and Davis and colleagues (2019; see also Davis, Chapter 7) have similarly reported the discovery of Western Stemmed points in association with organic samples dated as early as ~13,500 cal BP at Cooper's Ferry (Idaho). Bonneville Estates Rockshelter (northeast Nevada) has also yielded stemmed points in the same stratum as fire-hearth features radiocarbon-dated to Clovis times, as early as 12,950 cal BP, but not before (Goebel 2018; Goebel et al. 2011; Graf 2007).

The proposal that Western Stemmed points may have been coeval with Clovis, however, is not new, but one that Alan Bryan developed four decades ago, citing the discovery at Smith Creek Cave (eastern Nevada) of Western Stemmed points around hearth features radiocarbon-dated to as early as 13,500 cal BP and possibly earlier (Bryan 1979, 1988). Yet inconsistencies in radiocarbon dates have led to questions about site-formation processes and associations of individual artifacts and dated organic materials (Thompson 1985; see also Goebel et al. 2007; Smith et al. 2020:30–31), and when originally reported, the early Western Stemmed points from Smith Creek Cave were at odds with the Clovis-first paradigm that governed interpretations of the peopling of the Americas (e.g., Haynes 1964, 1980). As a result, the potential significance of Smith Creek Cave was never fully realized by the American archaeological community.

Now, given renewed interest in nailing down the precise timing of the emergence of Western Stemmed points in the Far West of North America, sites like Smith Creek Cave that were excavated decades ago are being reconsidered. The site and its assemblage offer a rare glimpse of the Western Stemmed technocomplex from a stratified deposit associated

FIGURE 6.1. Map of the western United States, showing location of Smith Creek Cave in east-central Nevada and locations of other archaeological sites mentioned in the text.

with radiocarbon-dated materials and other well-preserved ecofacts. In this chapter, we report the first results of a new study of the cave's evidence, particularly presenting novel information on the site's geochronology and the stemmed points recovered during Bryan's early excavations.

Smith Creek Cave

Smith Creek Cave is located along the eastern slope of the Snake Range, in eastern White Pine County, Nevada, 5 km west of the Utah state line (Figure 6.1). It is positioned on a steep southeast-facing slope about 200 m above the floor of Smith Creek canyon, at an elevation of ~1950 m. The cave was carved into limestone bedrock; its opening is about 50 m wide and 18 m tall, and the cavity itself extends about 30 m into the hillside (Bryan 1979). Alan Bryan led field investigations at Smith Creek Cave for three years in 1968, 1971, and 1974, focusing excavations on a 28 m² area near the front-western area of the cave, just inside the drip line (Figure 6.2; Bryan 1979). In this area, he found Western Stemmed points in a stratified context, which he labeled the Mount Moriah occupation zone.

Paleoindian artifacts came from two successive stratigraphic layers, a "gray ash and silt" layer mantled by a "dung, rubble, and silt" layer, with numerous archaeological

FIGURE 6.2. View of Smith Creek Cave in 2019. The remains of Alan Bryan's excavation at the front of the cave are shown in the foreground. Photo by Caitlin Doherty and used with permission.

materials occurring in both (Bryan 1979). Bryan found five features he interpreted to represent fire hearths (Figure 6.3). Stratigraphically the tops of these features were within the upper dung and rubble zone, but they protruded downward into the lower ash zone. Seven of nine conventional radiocarbon ages on charcoal from these hearths (two ages were obviously discordant and dismissed) provided chronological control on the upper dung and rubble zone, with Bryan (1979) concluding that it and its contents (i.e., the late Mount Moriah occupation zone) spanned from 11,140 ± 120 to 9940 ± 160 radiocarbon years ago (^{14}C BP). An eighth conventional radiocarbon age of 10,660 ± 220 ^{14}C BP on dispersed charcoal from the dung and rubble zone fits with this assessment.

To determine the age of the lower ash layer (i.e., the early Mount Moriah occupation zone), however, Bryan (1979) relied on potentially noncultural materials, specifically a wooden twig, a sample of dispersed charcoal, and a sample of cellulose from another piece of wood. These yielded conventional radiocarbon ages of 12,150 ± 120, 11,680 ± 160, and 10,700 ± 180 ^{14}C BP, respectively. Later, Bryan (1988) reported four accelerator mass spectrometry (AMS) radiocarbon ages on materials from the lower ash layer, including 14,220 ± 650 ^{14}C BP on a strand of artiodactyl hair, 12,060 ± 450 ^{14}C BP on a strand of camelid hair, 10,840 ± 250 ^{14}C BP on a strand of bovid hair, and 10,420 ± 100 ^{14}C BP on a piece of twisted-fiber cordage. The first of these, he reasoned, was aberrantly old, because AMS ages on well-preserved plant macrofossils from a lower-lying deposit were as young as 12,600 ^{14}C BP (Bryan 1988:67).

Bryan (1979, 1988) presumed a primary context for the Western Stemmed points, interpreting that the full suite of accepted radio-

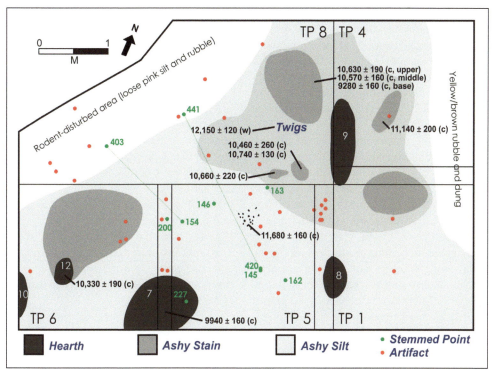

FIGURE 6.3. Map of Bryan's 1968–1974 excavation at Smith Creek Cave, showing provenience of hearths, dated samples, some of the Western Stemmed bifacial points (*green*), and other artifacts (*red*). For radiocarbon ages, "c" refers to charcoal, "w" refers to uncharred wood.

carbon ages from the dung and rubble zone and gray ash zone represented their age range at the site, and that the accumulation of the uncharred plant and animal remains within the gray ash zone could have resulted from a very slow depositional rate. He also reasoned, however, that "unburned wood and other perishables could have been deposited in the white ash *only after* fires had been locally extinguished" (Bryan 1988:65; italics added). In other words, the artifacts of the lower Mount Moriah occupation zone could have been intrusive, perhaps from later human trampling, thus explaining the association of the 10,840, 10,700, and 10,420 ^{14}C BP dates with the 12,150, 12,060, and 11,680 ^{14}C BP dates. It is also possible that the ash layer formed long before humans entered and used the cave. If the ash layer was still partially exposed at the beginning of the Western Stemmed occupation, cultural remains may have been quickly mixed into the older ash deposit (Goebel et al. 2007; Thompson 1985).

From this perspective, it is reasonable to argue that the radiocarbon ages on cultural hearths and artifacts, especially those from the upper dung and rubble zone, are most important for inferring the age of the Mount Moriah occupation zone. These dates range from 11,140 ± 200 to 9940 ± 160 ^{14}C BP, therefore indicating that makers of Western Stemmed points may have occupied Smith Creek Cave as early as 13,372–12,698 cal BP. This interval overlaps with the age of Clovis elsewhere in North America. Goebel and others (2007) and Goebel and Keene (2014), however, conservatively suggested that the oldest date (11,140 ^{14}C BP) is disputable, because it was produced using non-AMS methods and has not been replicated, a potential problem given that dating of multiple samples from other hearths led to discordant results and the possibility that Paleoindians burned old wood in their fires (Bryan 1979, 1988). Needless to say, AMS dating of additional samples from the oldest hearth features is needed to confirm their synchronicity with Clovis and to learn precisely when humans first deposited Western Stemmed points at the cave.

The lithic artifact assemblage attributed to the Mount Moriah occupation zone included more than 2000 small pieces of debitage and 238 artifacts assumed to represent tools (Bryan 1979). Among them were 22 fragments of bifaces that, once assembled, represented 18 bifaces. "About half" of these were classifiable as bifacial points (Bryan 1979, 1988), while the other half were too fragmentary to determine their stage of production (i.e., whether they represent finished points or bifaces that broke during manufacture). All of the recognized bifacial-point fragments represented Western Stemmed forms with contracting to square stems and variable degrees of edge grinding, although some were recycled as scrapers, gravers, or burins (Bryan 1979:203–204). Besides the bifacially worked tools, Bryan (1979) described ten unifacial scrapers, five core/scrapers, three large flakes with retouch, and 199 small flakes with retouch, or "microtools" (Bryan 1979:207). In addition to these, 10 bone fragments were interpreted to represent perforators (awls or needles), and 13 bone fragments had evidence of surface modifications (grooving, scraping, flaking, or cutting, Bryan 1979:219–222). Perishable artifacts included five short segments of fiber cordage, an untwisted piece of plant fiber, a wad of shredded and crimped juniper bark that Bryan (1979:224) interpreted as moccasin padding, and several possibly chewed yucca leaves.

Most of the faunal remains came from the dung and rubble zone, representing the upper Mount Moriah occupation (Bryan 1979:185). Among the taxonomically identifiable specimens were bones of mountain sheep (*Ovis canadensis*), mountain lion (*Felis concolor*), jackrabbit (*Lepus* sp.), cottontail (*Sylvilagus* sp.), marmot (*Marmota* sp.), and unidentified fish and birds, as well as hair attributed to bison (*Bison* sp.) and *Hemiauchenia* sp. (Bryan 1979).

Dating the Western Stemmed Occupation Zone

As the review above indicates, lingering questions remain regarding the age of the Mount Moriah occupation at Smith Creek Cave. In the early 2000s, G. T. Jones and colleagues returned to the cave to address these questions, conducting a geoarchaeological test excavation alongside Bryan's early block (David Madsen, personal communication, 2022). This work may very well have produced material that could confirm Bryan's radiocarbon chronology, and we look forward to learning of their results.

Another way to address the problem is to work with curated collections from Bryan's excavation. Hence, Goebel recently approached the Nevada State Museum about redating some of the features from the cave, prompting Barker to search through the existing collection from Bryan's excavation for any charcoal remaining from the earliest, Clovis-aged hearth. His search failed to produce any more of the hearth sample; moreover, he found only one small sample of charcoal left in the entire assemblage, one that we agreed with museum staff needed to be conserved. However, Barker did find an uncharred wooden twig from area TP5 of Bryan's original excavation, the same area that produced the original scattered charcoal date of 11,680 ± 160 ^{14}C BP, as well as six of the original Western Stemmed point fragments recovered from the Mount Moriah occupation zone.

Using low-power microscopy, Heather Thakar at Texas A&M University identified the twig as belonging to the genus *Pinus* (pine), but a more precise species designation (e.g., *P. flexilis*, *P. longaeva*, or *P. monophylla*) could not be made. We then submitted a portion of the twig to the University of Georgia's Center for Applied Isotope Studies, for AMS radiocarbon analysis. This resulted in an age of 10,900 ± 30 ^{14}C BP (UGAMS-33916). Using the CALIB Radiocarbon Calibration program (calib.org/calib/, accessed 30 December 2020), this new radiocarbon age represents a range of 12,751–12,883 cal BP (2 σ), with a median probability of 12,800 cal BP.

This result confirms that the pine twig found in close proximity to the Western Stemmed points from TP5 dates to the last century of the Clovis era in North America, 12,850–12,750 cal BP (see Waters, Stafford, and Carlson 2020). Unfortunately, however, we cannot prove that this sample was of cultural origin, so it still does not provide unequivocal proof that the associated Western Stemmed points from Smith Creek Cave temporally overlap with Clovis. Additional AMS dates on curated animal bone, especially those with obvious signs of butchery, could help solve the problem, as could the dating of materials recovered by Jones and colleagues in their recent test excavations.

The Western Stemmed Points

We examined 14 bifacial-point/biface fragments from the Mount Moriah occupation zone. These included artifact numbers 144, 145 (three articulating pieces), 146, 162, 163, 200, 399, 403 (two articulating pieces), 414, 415, 516, 517, 523, and 535 (Figure 6.4). Provenience information for some of these artifacts is shown in Figure 6.3, and details about each point are presented in Table 6.1. All are fragments (seven proximal, three midsection, three distal, and one unidentifiable). Eight are definitely classifiable as fragments of Western Stemmed points, while five are undiagnostic bifacial-point fragments, and one is too small to distinguish as a previously hafted or unhafted biface.

Raw-material Procurement

Of the 14 fragments, 12 were made on obsidian and two on cryptocrystalline chert (CCS). None bears cortex. We subjected the 12 obsidian artifacts to X-ray fluorescence (XRF) analysis, using the portable Bruker Tracer III SD at the Center for the Study of the First Americans (CSFA), Texas A&M University. This instrument was equipped with a 10-mm 2X Flash SDD Peltier-cooled detector capable of 145 eV at 100,000 cps. Doherty scanned each sample for 180 deadtime-corrected seconds with a 12-mil Al, 1-mil Ti, and 6-mil Cu filter, correcting the results using the current GL1 calibration (following Ferguson 2012).

Along with the artifacts, Doherty also analyzed the CSFA's growing collection of natural obsidian samples from known sources in the greater Bonneville Basin region (e.g., Browns Bench, Malad, Ferguson Wash, Topaz Mountain, Black Rock Area, Wildhorse Canyon/Mineral Mountain, and Modena/Panaca). Using GAUSS (available at http://archaeometry.missouri.edu/data sets/GAUSS_download.html), trace-element ppm values of mid-Z elements Iron (Fe), and Niobium (Nb), Rubidium (Rb), Strontium (Sr), Yttrium (Y), and Zirconium (Zr) of the artifacts and the geologic samples were calculated and plotted two-dimensionally, with source assignments for the artifacts being made according to correspondence with source clusters and their 90% confidence intervals. One obsidian artifact (516) did not unequivocally match any of the source profiles in our database, because of its small size and probably because original conservators coated it with thin white paint that ran into fissures and caused inaccurate measurements. In an attempt to overcome this problem, we submitted the artifact to the Northwest Research Obsidian Studies Laboratory in Corvallis, Oregon, for further analysis.

We documented five obsidian sources among the Western Stemmed points from Smith Creek Cave (Figure 6.5). Two artifacts came from the Wildhorse Canyon/Mineral Mountain source area, located about 150 km southeast of Smith Creek Cave (a straight-line distance). These include a proximal fragment of a Western Stemmed point (162) and one midsection fragment of an untypeable bifacial point (517). Three artifacts probably came from the Modena/Panaca source, located approximately 170 km south of the

TABLE 6.1. Details on the Western Stemmed Points in the Smith Creek Cave Assemblage.

Artifact No.	Type	Raw Material	Condition	Length (mm)	Width (mm)
144	bifacial point tip	obsidian (Topaz Mountain)	tip fragment	(22.13)	(23.53)
145	Western Stemmed point	obsidian (Modena/Panaca)	basal fragment	(33.76)	18.60
146	bifacial point tip	obsidian (Browns Bench)	tip fragment	(25.36)	(27.29)
162	Western Stemmed point	obsidian (Wildhorse Canyon)	basal fragment	(26.73)	(21.72)
163	Western Stemmed point	chalcedony	midsection fragment	(10.18)	(20.58)
200	Western Stemmed point	obsidian (Browns Bench)	basal fragment	(28.73)	(20.56)
399	Western Stemmed point	obsidian (Browns Bench)	basal fragment	(23.29)	(21.40)
403	Western Stemmed point	obsidian (Browns Bench)	basal fragment	(51.54)	(25.54)
414	Western Stemmed point	obsidian (Modena/Panaca)	basal fragment	(23.07)	(28.18)
415	Western Stemmed point	obsidian (Modena/Panaca)	basal fragment	(26.68)	(17.28)
516	biface fragment	obsidian (Topaz Mountain)	biface fragment	—	—
517	bifacial point fragment	obsidian (Wildhorse Canyon)	midsection fragment	(8.99)	(13.37)
523	possible point tip	chert	tip fragment	(12.44)	(12.83)
535	bifacial point fragment	obsidian (black rock)	midsection fragment	(12.29)	(22.95)

Note: Parentheses represent partial measurements or indefinite calculations/observations. Wildhorse Canyon designation includes Black Mountain and Pumice Hole Mine.

cave.[1] These artifacts are proximal fragments of Western Stemmed points (145, 414, and 415). Four artifacts came from the Browns Bench source area, located about 300 km north of the cave, including three proximal fragments of Western Stemmed points (200, 399, 403) and one tip fragment of an untypeable bifacial point (146). Two artifacts originated from the Topaz Mountain source area, located 100 km northeast of the cave, including a distal fragment of an untypeable bifacial point (144) and a midsection fragment of an untypeable bifacial point (517). The latter artifact was characterized by the Northwest Obsidian Research Laboratory. Lastly, a midsection fragment of a bifacial point (535) originated from the Black Rock Area source, located 125 km east-southeast of Smith Creek Cave. The mean transport distance from source to site is 190.8 km.

Morphometrics and Technology

Goebel and Lynch carried out morphometric and technological analyses of the 14 point fragments. Variable scores are presented in Table 6.1. Metric variables were difficult to

TABLE 6.1. (cont'd.) Details on the Western Stemmed Points in the Smith Creek Cave Assemblage.

Thickness (mm)	Width: thickness ratio	Reduction ratio	Plan View	Edge Sinuosity	Flake-Removal Technique	Flake-scar Morphology	Flaking Pattern
7.69	(3.060)	0.889	—	moderate	soft-hammer percussion	scaly, to midline	lateral
7.17	2.594	1.093	lanceolate	weak	pressure	scaly, to midline	lateral
6.31	(3.217)	0.940	—	weak	soft-hammer percussion	scaly, to midline	lateral
6.81	(3.189)	1.132	lanceolate	straight	pressure	scaly, overface	lateral
5.94	(3.465)	0.885	lanceolate	weak	pressure	scaly, to midline	lateral
6.03	(3.410)	1.046	lanceolate	weak	pressure	scaly, overface	lateral and end
7.73	(2.768)	1.093	lanceolate	weak	pressure	scaly, to midline	lateral and end
8.97	(2.847)	1.095	lanceolate	weak	pressure	scaly, to midline	lateral and end
8.76	(3.217)	0.742	lanceolate	weak	hard-hammer percussion	scaly, to midline	lateral and end
6.42	(2.692)	1.092	lanceolate	moderate	pressure	scaly, overface	lateral
—	—	—	—	—	—	—	—
(3.56)	(3.756)	(0.691)	-	(straight)	soft-hammer percussion	scaly, to midline	lateral
(6.03)	—	—	—	straight	pressure	scaly	lateral
(22.95)	(2.844)	0.992	—	straight	soft-hammer percussion	scaly, to midline	lateral

measure, given the fragmentary nature of the points. Width and thickness measures, however, could be taken on most of the point fragments, bearing in mind that they often do not reflect maximum widths or thicknesses of previously intact tools. Conditional width-to-thickness ratios were calculated for all but two artifacts, which were then used to assign a stage of manufacture following Callahan (1979; see also Andrefsky 1998:181). We also calculated a reduction ratio for each point fragment, following Miller and Smallwood (2012), counting the number of secondary-reduction flake scars evident along the preserved margins of the points, and dividing the sum by the total length (in mm) of preserved biface edge(s). Accordingly, a low value represents an early-stage biface that was minimally worked with relatively large-sized flake scars, while a high value represents a finished or late-stage biface that was extensively worked, with relatively small-sized flake scars.

Width-to-thickness ratios range from 2.594 to 3.756 (Table 6.1), all within the range of early- to mid-stage bifaces, not finished

FIGURE 6.4. The Western Stemmed bifacial-point fragments from Smith Creek Cave analyzed in this study: (a) 144; (b) 145; (c) 146; (d) 162; (e) 163; (f) 200; (g) 399; (h) 403; (i) 414; (j) 415; (k) 516; (l) 523; (m) 517; (n) 535.

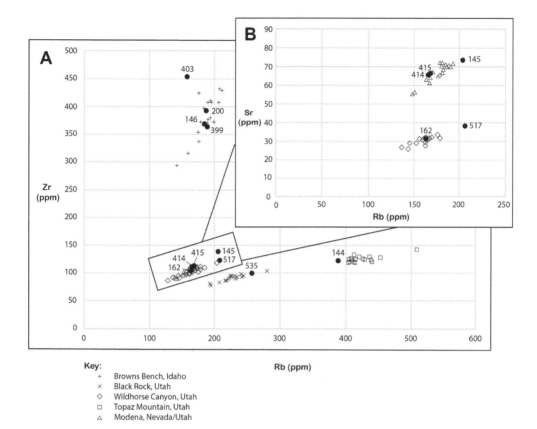

FIGURE 6.5. (*a*) Biplot of rubidium (Rb) and zirconium (Zr) measures for obsidian artifacts (by catalog number) and relevant sources in the western Bonneville Basin; (*b*) biplot of rubidium (Rb) and strontium (Sr) measures, differentiating Wildhorse Canyon and Modena source clusters. Corresponding artifact values are indicated by catalog number.

bifaces. Reduction ratios, however, are from 0.742 to 1.132, all within the range of finished points in Miller and Smallwood's (2012) Clovis biface sample. We interpret this result to mean that the Smith Creek Cave bifaces were all finished and used, but that they were technologically designed to retain thicker-than-normal cross sections (in contrast to Callahan's [1979] models of generalized-biface and Clovis-biface reduction, where the goal was to create a flattened cross section). This practice at Smith Creek Cave of producing finished points that were thick relative to their width could have facilitated hafting into large-aperture (probably open or split) sockets (see Duke and Stueber, Chapter 4; Galm and Gough 2008; Musil 1988:379), and their use as dart tips (Lynch 2020; discussed further below).

Morphologically, plan-view shapes of the definable point fragments are all lanceolate, and cross sections are all bi-convex. Six of the bases are contracting, or "tongue-shaped" (Figure 6.4d, f–j), while another has a sharply cornered, "square" stem (Figure 6.4b). None of the fragments have distinct shoulders; however, one of the tongue-shaped bases (403; Figure 6.4h) appears to have broken above the haft and preserves only slight waisting, suggesting it represents a Haskett form (e.g., Butler 1965; Duke and Stueber, Chapter 4; Rosencrance et al., Chapter 2). Another (200; Figure 6.4f) broke just below the haft, but also appears to have been only slightly waisted, so it may also represent a Haskett point. The other three tongue-shaped basal fragments are too undiagnostic to define a type. One of the square-based points (145; Figure 6.4b) has a much longer stem (30.6 mm) than is typical of "square stem" Windust points from the nearby Old River Bed Delta, which range from 4.5 to 18.4 mm (n = 36; Beck and Jones 2015b:127). Given that it contracts slightly toward the base, it more likely represents a long-stemmed Haskett point than a Windust point. Such square-based Haskett points are known from other locations in the Great Basin, including Connley Caves, Cougar Mountain Cave, and the Old River Bed Delta (Beck and Jones 2015b; Jenkins et al. 2017; Rosencrance et al. 2019).

Technologically, few signs of blank selection are preserved on the points. None bears cortex, and initial blank type (e.g., cortical spall, core-reduction flake, cobble) could not be specifically determined for any of them. Two points (162, 415; Figure 6.4d, j), however, preserve at their base a small platform surface, indicating they were produced on some form of a detached piece (i.e., a flake). Another point (414; Figure 6.4i) is longitudinally curved, and its proximal end is relatively thick and appears to represent the platform/bulbar remnant of an original flake blank. This orientation suggests these points were produced on long, narrow flakes (e.g., Pendleton 1979; Duke and Steuber, Chapter 4), not on short, wide (i.e., side-struck) flakes (e.g., Beck and Jones 2015b).

In terms of early-stage biface reduction, flake-scar morphologies are chiefly scaly and collateral, covering entire faces of the points, typically to the midline. Three points, however, display overface flake scars that extend beyond the midline. A single point tip (146; Figure 6.4c) bears opposing burinations that resemble an intentional "squared-off chisel-tip" (e.g., Tuohy 1969:139).

Regarding late-stage biface reduction and point finishing, edge sinuosity varies minimally, with almost all points having weakly sinuous or straight edges. Eight points appear to have been finished through pressure flaking, four through soft-hammer percussion, and one through hard-hammer percussion. Edge grinding occurs on all seven basal fragments and one of three midsection fragments. Combined, these characteristics of the Smith Creek Cave projectile-point assemblage with a few ambiguities and exceptions are broadly consistent with Haskett-point technology found elsewhere in the Great Basin, including the nearby Old River Bed Delta (Beck and Jones 2009, 2015b; Duke 2015; Duke and Steuber, Chapter 4; Jones et al. 2003).

Use Wear

Lynch analyzed the Smith Creek Cave points at CSFA's microscopy lab. Full lengths of the edges of each biface, as well as both faces, were examined macroscopically and microscopically at 0×, 8×, 10×, and 20× magnification. All notable features and identifiable attributes indicative of use wear, impact, and hafting were documented and photographed. Terms used to describe attributes, features, flake scarring, and fracture patterns indicative of use followed standard North American use-wear studies (e.g., Beck and Jones 2009; Bradley 1982; Bradley and Frison 1987; Collins 1993; Crabtree 1972; Fischer et al. 1984; Frison 1974; Frison and Bradley 1980; Ho Ho Committee 1979; Iovita et al. 2013; Johnson 1979; Lafayette and Smith 2012; Lazuén 2012; Odell and Cowan 1986; Villa, Boscato, et al. 2009; Villa, Soressi, et al. 2009; Villa and Lenoir 2006, 2009; Wilkins et al. 2012). Further, diagnostic indicators of impact and other damage were documented following Dockall (1997), Ho Ho Committee (1979), Fischer et al. (1984), Odell (1981), Odell and Cowan (1986), and Rots and Plisson (2014), acknowledging the complexity of identifying fragmentation and breakage patterns from impact (i.e., Rots and Plisson 2014). We have not yet subjected the points to high-power microscopy, so micro-scratching and polishing have not been documented. Nonetheless, given the complex and variable nature of the use-wear traces identified on the points, we present each one individually below.

Artifact 414 is a basal fragment of a finished Western Stemmed (likely Haskett) point produced on obsidian (Figure 6.4i). Although fragmented below the point's shoulders, it appears slightly waisted, continuing to gradually expand past the distal break. Along the lateral margins of the biface are multiple stacked, step-terminating flake removals that likely represent multiple, repetitive attempts to thin the base of the biface. The margins are weakly ground, most obviously around the base. The broken face of the biface is a unifacial rolling fracture suggestive of breakage caused by impact. Although the rolling fracture was painted over for curative purposes, there is clear evidence of microflaking and damage along the edge of the break, on the face of the fracture, suggesting use of the fragment following failure as a projectile point.

Artifact 403 is composed of two biface fragments that were refitted and glued together during curation (Figure 6.4h). Together they represent a basal fragment of a finished Western Stemmed (likely Haskett) point. The artifact's lateral margins expand distally but are slightly waisted about three-fourths up both margins, suggesting that the distal break occurred above the hafted portion of the point. Weak edge grinding was observed along both lateral margins, starting at the area of slight waisting and becoming stronger closer to the base of the point. The surface of the distal transverse break was thickly painted over during labeling and curation, and the surfaces of the more proximal transverse break are not visible because of gluing. Nonetheless, both breaks appear to have been the result of impact damage, especially at the proximal break where a large rolling-hinge fracture extends far onto the point's face (see Lafayette and Smith 2012). The distal break occurs at the point of a phenocryst about 2.8 mm in diameter. There is no evidence of reworking on this biface; instead it seems to have been discarded following impact-related failure of the point.

Artifact 145 is a basal fragment of a Western Stemmed (possibly Haskett) point produced on obsidian (Figure 6.4b). It consists of three fragments that were refitted and glued together during curation. Both lateral margins are heavily edge ground. Although two fracture surfaces are not observable, both ends of the point fragment exhibit evidence of impact fracture. First, the basal margin is partially damaged by a large unifacial-spin-off fracture, while the distal break is a rolling-hinge fracture with a burin facet originating from the distal end of the point. These are clear indications of breakage resulting from high-energy impact (Fischer et al. 1984; Lafayette and Smith 2012). None of the three pieces exhibit evidence of reworking or reshaping following breakage of the projectile.

Artifact 399 is the basal fragment of a Western Stemmed point (type unidentifiable) produced on obsidian (Figure 6.4g). Its stem expands significantly from the base and continues to expand through the fragment's distal break. Weak edge grinding is present around the base of the point, extending along both lateral margins about halfway to the break. However, at the base of the point, several small flake scars terminate in deep distal hinges that might represent impact damage resulting from contact with the hafting element. The distal break is a rolling-hinge fracture, diagnostic of impact damage. This break has been painted over, but some microflaking is still visible on the face of the break, suggesting that the fragment may have been used after breakage. Further, a unifacial notch along one lateral margin was created after the point was removed from its hafting.

Artifact 200 is the basal fragment of a Western Stemmed point (type unidentifiable) produced on obsidian (Figure 6.4f). It exhibits very strong edge grinding along nearly the entire length of one lateral margin, the distal third of the opposing lateral margin, and on about half of the basal margin. Where the grinding is absent it has been obscured by more recent retouching along the tool's margins. The distal break is a step-terminating unifacial spin-off fracture, indicative of impact damage. The face of this fracture was completely painted over for labeling during curation, but "silhouettes" of some microflake scars on the fracture surface can be observed through the paint. The base of the fragment exhibits lateral waisting, although this waisting appears to have been created after breakage and removal from the hafting element. Two deep notches were also flaked into one of the edge-ground lateral margins. These likely represent reshaping of the biface after the point broke, either in an attempt to resharpen and rehaft the point, or to recycle the fragment for some other purpose.

Artifact 415 is the basal fragment of a Western Stemmed point (type unidentifiable), which broke below the top of its stem (Figure 6.4j). The base of the point is relatively blunt, caused by the preservation of the original flake blank's platform. The base also exhibits evidence of crushing potentially resulting from contact with a hafting element during the point's use. One lateral margin of the biface is dominated by a series of stacked step fractures due to failed attempts to thin the biface. This margin is lightly ground around the basal corner. The opposing lateral margin has been reshaped with some large flake removals that obliterated the original finished edge of the biface. These removals likely represent reshaping of the base after failure of the original hafted point. The fragment's distal break is a rolling-hinge fracture, indicative of impact while being used as a hafted projectile. This fracture was painted over during labeling and curation, but no obvious microflaking occurs on its face or around its perimeter.

Artifact 162 is the "tongue-shaped" basal fragment of a Western Stemmed point (type unidentifiable) produced on obsidian (Figure 6.4d). Its bifacially worked perimeter has been heavily edge ground, but, as mentioned above, the base still preserves a small platform surface from the biface's original flake blank. The distal break was heavily painted over during curation, preventing a detailed analysis of the fracture surface. Although it appears to represent a step-down break, without a clearer view of the surface we could not determine whether it is attributable to impact damage.

Artifact 146 is the distal fragment of a hafted point (type unidentifiable) produced on obsidian (Figure 6.4c). Retouch along one lateral margin is irregular and rough, leading to a weakly serrated margin. The proximal break is a unifacial spin-off fracture potentially indicative of impact-related breakage. The distal end of the fragment exhibits three possible impact scars (two on one face and one on the reverse) originating from the removed tip of the point, a possible sign that this artifact broke while in use as a projectile point. However, as noted above, these features more likely relate to the intentional creation of a "chisel-bit" tip during the point's manufacture (see Tuohy 1969). Although no obvious attempt to reshape the artifact after breakage was apparent, a notch and deliberate retouch (some within the notch) near the distal tip's lateral margin suggest recycling.

Artifact 144 is the distal fragment of a hafted point (type unidentifiable) on obsidian (Figure 6.4a). Retouching is rough, stepped, and irregular, and no signs of edge grinding are evident. Finer trimming occurs along both lateral margins just above the transverse break, suggesting that the biface broke just above the shoulders of a Western Stemmed point. The break is covered by paint from cataloging; however, it appears to represent a rolling fracture from impact (Fischer et al. 1984).

Artifact 163 is a midsection of a Western Stemmed point (type unidentifiable) produced on tan-gray chalcedony (Figure 6.4e). Both lateral margins exhibit weak-to-moderate edge grinding. They show no sign of having been reworked, which is not surprising given the short length of this fragment. Neither the proximal nor the distal fractures present clear signs of what caused the point to fail.

Artifact 517 is a possible basal fragment

of a Western Stemmed point (type unidentifiable) produced on obsidian (Figure 6.4m). Being less than 9 mm long and having its entire fracture surface painted for numbering, not much can be determined about this artifact, except that both faces appear to have been worked, and that the break appears to represent a rolling-step fracture, potentially indicative of impact while in use as a hafted weapon tip.

Artifact 535 is a midsection fragment of a biface (type unidentifiable) produced on a black and orange obsidian (Figure 6.4n). Very little of one lateral margin is preserved, but a lack of edge grinding suggests that it may represent a portion of the blade element of a biface. Both the proximal and distal breaks appear to be rolling fractures, indicative of impact damage. One of the breaks displays stepped retouching along both opposing faces, suggesting an attempt to rework the biface after breakage.

Artifact 523 is a possible tip fragment of a biface (type unidentifiable) on tan-red chert. One of its faces is entirely painted over from curation and labeling (Figure 6.4l). This alteration and its small size preclude it from being analyzed in any more detail.

Artifact 516 is a tiny fragment of a biface on obsidian, too small for detailed analysis (Figure 6.4k). It may represent the tip or a corner of a hafted point.

Discussion

Our results provide novel information regarding toolstone use and procurement, as well as the morphology, reduction technology, and function of the projectile points. We discuss these topics in detail below.

Toolstone Procurement and Conveyance

Analysis of raw-material procurement and selection in Paleoindian assemblages has contributed greatly to our current understanding of early mobility and technological organization in the Great Basin (e.g., Graf 2001; Jones et al. 2003; Kelly 2001; Smith 2010). Such studies must start with a characterization of the local and regional lithic landscapes. In 2019, we initiated a comprehensive local toolstone survey of the northern Snake Range. Although we have not identified any knappable stones naturally occurring within Smith Creek Canyon, we have found knappable quartzites and cherts elsewhere in the Snake Range, and thus both could constitute locally-procured components of the artifact assemblage. Farther afield, in the greater Bonneville Basin, an area of 134,900 km^2, geochemically-traceable toolstone sources are sparse and patchily distributed. Obsidians are known from only nine isolated locations, and none of these are located within 100 km of Smith Creek Cave. Fine-grained volcanics (FGV) are also patchily distributed, and so far they are not known to be closer than ~70 km west (e.g., Jones et al. 1997) and ~100 km north of the cave (Page and Duke 2015).

Although analysis of the full Smith Creek Cave assemblage is pending, our study of the assemblage's bifacial points reveals a clear pattern of raw-material selection that heavily favors the use of obsidian (86%) over other materials (i.e., chert, FGV, quartzite, etc.). Geochemical characterizations of the obsidian point fragments have delineated an extensive zone within which the Paleoindian occupants of the cave procured this toolstone. This area extends nearly 500 km north to south and 100 km east to west (Figure 6.6). The northern extent of obsidian conveyance is 300 km from the cave, at Browns Bench near the juncture of the Idaho, Nevada, and Utah borders, just beyond the northwestern fringe of the Bonneville Basin, and accounts for 33% of the obsidian represented in the analyzed assemblage. The southern extent of obsidian conveyance is likely the Modena/Panaca source, located approximately 170 km to the south along the Nevada/Utah border. Within this far-reaching conveyance zone is the Topaz Mountain source, 100 km east-northeast of the cave, represented by 17% of the bifacial points, and the Wildhorse Canyon and Black Rock source areas, located

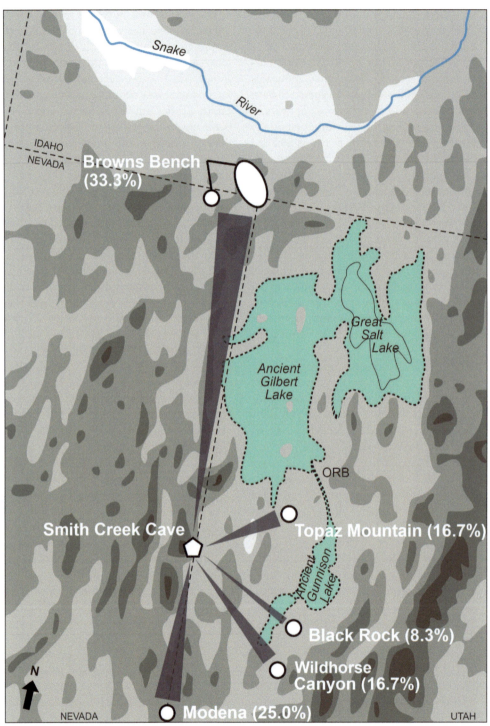

FIGURE 6.6. Map of eastern Great Basin showing geographic distribution of obsidians so far identified in the Smith Creek Cave Paleoindian assemblage. Blue-shaded area represents extent of shallow Younger Dryas-aged lakes in the western Bonneville Basin.

150 and 125 km, respectively, to the southeast and collectively representing 25% of the bifacial points.

This obsidian conveyance zone is consistent in scale and orientation with the elongated north–south zones described in other Nevada Paleoindian studies (Graf 2001; Jones et al. 2003), and it reinforces Jones and colleagues' (2012) observation that most raw materials appear to have been transported in a north–south pattern but not necessarily in an east–west pattern between the eastern and central Great Basin (although this hypothesis needs to be further tested with a geochemical analysis of fine-grained volcanics in Smith Creek Cave's assemblage of unhafted bifaces, unifaces, and debitage). Considering just bifacial points, the average distance between Smith Creek Cave and its known obsidian sources is 190.8 km, indicating that its Paleoindian occupants routinely traveled great distances across this range. This average is similar to what Goebel and coauthors (2018) found for Bonneville Estates Rockshelter's Paleoindian obsidian bifacial points and unhafted bifaces—180.0 km. Surface assemblages of Western Stemmed points from the Old River Bed Delta (also located in the western Bonneville Basin) have lower average source distances—131.8 km for its proximal area and 148.8 km for its distal area—a trend that reflects reliance on that area's nearby Topaz Mountain source as well as more local fine-grained volcanics (Page and Duke 2015).

Given the vagaries of using average transport distance alone to characterize procurement (see King 2016), we calculated an "obsidian-procurement premium" statistic for Smith Creek Cave's bifacial-point assemblage and compared it to previously reported obsidian premiums from Paleoindian bifacial-point assemblages in northern/northwestern Nevada (King 2016), as well as new premiums calculated here for other Western Stemmed bifacial-point assemblages in the eastern Great Basin using published data (Table 6.2; Goebel et al. 2018; Page and Duke 2015). This statistic is calculated by subtracting the shortest procurement distance (in the case of Smith Creek Cave, Topaz Mountain) from that of all sourced specimens and taking the resulting average. Smith Creek Cave's premium statistic is 92.9, similar to premium values calculated for the distal and proximal Old River Bed Delta assemblages of 94.8 and 82.8, respectively (based on data from Page and Duke 2015:SOM, Tables 1 and 5). These three eastern Great Basin premiums, however, are still far lower than that for Bonneville Estates Rockshelter (170; Table 6.2), where all obsidian bifacial points came from a sole source, Browns Bench.

Together, and in agreement with interpretations by investigators working in the Old River Bed Delta (Duke and Stueber, Chapter 4), these four premium statistics—calculated on the basis of obsidian projectile points alone—from the eastern Great Basin suggest a broad pattern of higher mobility in this region than across northern/northwestern Nevada, where the average premium equals only 26.8 (King 2016:Table 83). It should be noted, however, that when data on additional artifact classes and raw materials are available for these and other Western Stemmed assemblages, average procurement distances drop significantly (Duke and Stueber, Chapter 4; Newlander 2018; Page and Duke 2015; Smith and Harvey 2018), and we expect procurement premiums would drop as well. Likely this pattern will also happen as we expand our analysis of the Smith Creek Cave assemblage to include additional artifact and raw material classes. Moreover, as we learn more about the provenance of other raw materials represented in the assemblage and are able to make more specific comparisons with other Paleoindian assemblages in the region, we are hopeful that distance-decay analyses can be conducted (e.g., Ambrose 2012).

The analysis of obsidian projectile points from Smith Creek Cave reported here reveals an interesting pattern of raw-material procurement potentially operating at a smaller scale than the eastern Great Basin as a whole. Importantly, the obsidian-source distribution

TABLE 6.2. Obsidian-Procurement Statistics for Paleoindian Projectile Point Assemblages in the Eastern Great Basin.

Obsidian Source	Smith Creek Cave			Bonneville Estates Rockshelter			Old River Bed Delta Proximal			Old River Bed Delta Distal		
	Distance to Source (km)	N	Prem	Distance to Source (km)	N	Prem	Distance to Source (km)	N	Prem	Distance to Source (km)	N	Prem
BBID	300	4	210	180	5	170	240	15	187	211	78	157
BBIDA	—	—	—	—	—	—	240	2	187	211	2	157
BRUT	125	1	35	—	—	—	159	6	106	187	13	133
BVIDA	—	—	—	—	—	—	347	—	—	318	8	264
FWUT	—	—	—	10[a]	—	—	69	1	16	54[a]	3	0
KSNV	—	—	—	—	—	—	368	1	315	389	—	—
MAID	—	—	—	—	—	—	256	2	203	235	5	181
MOUT	170	3	80	—	—	—	314	—	—	338	3	284
OWID	—	—	—	—	—	—	406	1	353	378	—	—
PVNV	—	—	—	—	—	—	389	1	336	367	4	313
TMUT	90[a]	2	0	—	—	—	53*	41	0	82	133	28
WHUT	150	2	60	—	—	—	200	4	147	228	6	174
Unknown	—	—	—	—	—	—	—	1	—	—	5	—
Total (Average)	—	12	(92.9)	—	5	(170)	—	75	(82.8)	—	260	(94.8)

Note: Data from Old River Bed Delta proximal and distal assemblages from Page and Duke 2015, Tables 1 and 5. Prem = premium statistic. Source abbreviations: BBID = Browns Bench, Idaho; BBIDA = Browns Bench A, Idaho; BRUT = Black Rock Area, Utah; BVIDA = Butte Valley A, Idaho; FWUT = Ferguson Wash, Utah; KSNV = Kane Springs, Nevada; MAID = Malad, Idaho; MOUT = Modena, Utah; OWID = Owyhee, Idaho; PVNV = Paradise Valley, Nevada; TMUT = Topaz Mountain, Utah; WHUT = Wildhorse Canyon, Utah.
[a] Indicates the least-distance source for each assemblage.

highlights a majority of southern Bonneville Basin sources (e.g., Modena, Wildhorse Canyon, Topaz Mountain, and Black Rock Area). In fact, 67% of the bifaces originated from these southern sources, similar to the proximal and distal Old River Bed Delta assemblages (71% and 61%, respectively; Page and Duke 2015). Such a "subregional" focus of procurement is not rare among Western Stemmed assemblages in the Great Basin. At the more northerly Bonneville Estates Rockshelter, 100% of the obsidian bifaces and 88% of the total obsidian assemblage thus far reported originated from northern Bonneville Basin sources (i.e., Browns Bench and Malad; Goebel 2007; Goebel et al. 2018). To the west in central Nevada, however, patterns of shared use between these and other northern and southern sources have been shown in Jakes, Butte, and Long valleys (Jones et al. 2003), but reevaluation of procurement patterns in these central valleys (Estes 2009; Jones et al. 2012) suggests the Western Stemmed sites represent marginal, shared locations along the "frontier" of discrete northern and southern zones, particularly in light of the exclusion of northern sources in Western Stemmed assemblages in the more southerly Coal Valley (Jones et al. 2012). The Sadmat site, located in western Nevada, contains artifacts from some very far-flung sources to the north and south as well (Graf 2002); it too could represent a location shared by northern and southern groups.

Smith and colleagues (Chapter 3) have reported a similar pattern of preferential procurement within potentially discrete northern and southern zones in the northwestern Great Basin. There, northern assemblages from the Fort Rock and Chewaucan basins share the ubiquitous Warner Mountain sources with southern Nevada High Rock Country assemblages, perhaps suggesting that this intermediate territory served as a point of intersection or collective aggregation between zones—a possibility potentially supported by recent social-network analyses (Reaux 2020; Smith et al., Chapter 3). Consequently, in light of this evidence, Smith Creek Cave could likewise lie in an intermediate location between two subregional conveyance zones, though whether this reflects a pattern of alternate occupation by southern and northern groups, with more frequent visits by southern groups, or of collective aggregation by groups from both directions, is difficult to discern given current evidence. Again, further analysis of the raw-material distribution in the Smith Creek Cave unhafted biface, uniface, and debitage assemblages will facilitate testing of this hypothesis and undoubtedly uncover additional patterns of procurement.

Morphology and Reduction Technology

Nearly all of the points represent basal fragments, so any attribution to a specific stemmed-point form has to remain uncertain. However, at least two tongue-shaped basal fragments appear to represent unshouldered lanceolate points, probably Haskett forms (403 and 414). Square-stemmed points also occur in the Smith Creek Cave assemblage, and one of these is extraordinarily long relative to the Windust average and may again represent a Haskett form (145). The presence of Haskett points at Smith Creek Cave adds to a growing body of cases (the Wishbone site and Bonneville Estates Rockshelter) suggesting that Younger Dryas-aged inhabitants of the Bonneville Basin regularly produced these lanceolate-shaped, unshouldered biface forms (Duke 2015; Goebel 2018; Smith et al. 2020).

The points and bifaces in the Smith Creek Cave assemblage also document important features of Western Stemmed technology. At least three appear to have been produced on elongate flakes, a blank-selection strategy documented elsewhere by Beck and Jones (2010) and Pendleton (1979). Most display collateral, "to-the-midline" bifacial flaking, a diagnostic bifacial-reduction strategy of Western Stemmed, generally, and Haskett and Cougar Mountain forms, specifically (Amick 2004:132; Beck and Jones 2015b; Duke 2015; Duke and Steuber, Chapter 4; Pratt et al. 2020:9), and one tip fragment displays a possible squared-off chisel-tip, a peculiar manner of preparing a stemmed-point tip previously documented at the McNine Cache, Sunshine, Buhl burial, and Sadmat sites (Amick 2004:127; Beck and Jones 2009: Figure 6.27; Graf 2001; Green et al. 1998; Tuohy 1969:139). At Smith Creek Cave, where the bifacial points are very beat up, resharpened, and recycled, we would anticipate that the chisel-tipping could be a product of either high-velocity impact damage or retouching, but given the occurrence of this feature on complete, potentially unused points from a cache and burial, we hypothesize instead it is a component of production and not resharpening or recycling. An actualistic study coupled with a comprehensive use-wear analysis of such points is needed to test this idea.

Final preparation of the Smith Creek Cave points employed a variety of techniques, including soft-hammer percussion and pressure flaking, and all preserved stems show evidence of edge grinding. These technical strategies, too, are recurrent among Western Stemmed bifacial industries. A surprising feature, however, is the occurrence of overface flaking ($n = 3$; 21.4% of the points), which has also been identified among the McNine Cache's points from northwestern Nevada (Amick 2004), an indication that not all Western Stemmed points were flaked strictly following the "to-the-midline" technique. Obvious and intentional overshot flaking—a technological marker of Clovis in North America (e.g., Goebel 2015; Smallwood 2010a; see also Eren and Desjardine 2015)—has not been identified in the Smith Creek Cave assemblage.

An important methodological concern relates to the application of metric attributes to define bifacial stages of production in Western Stemmed contexts. In our analysis, standard width-to-thickness ratios do not seem to reflect the stage of reduction among the Smith Creek Cave points, probably because of the Paleoindians' intentional production of thick points with lenticular to diamond-shaped cross sections. Instead, we found the use of Miller and Smallwood's (2012) reduction ratio to be a better gauge for metrically defining stage (or degree) of reduction. However, we caution that in our study only fragments of finished bifaces have been measured, so that this variable needs to be considered in other Western Stemmed contexts where a full range of bifacial reduction is evident, and complete points are available so that variation along the full length of the stemmed points can be measured.

Function

Functional assessments of Western Stemmed points are essential to understanding the morphological variability of stemmed-point forms within the tradition, and the relationship of these points to potentially contemporaneous Paleoindian lithic traditions in western North America (e.g., Clovis; Beck and Jones 2010; Bryan 1979: Goebel 2018; Jenkins et al. 2012). Although our analysis included a sample of only 14 fragments, it still contributes to the larger regional effort to interpret the functional role(s) of Western Stemmed points (Beck and Jones 1993, 1997; Duke 2015; Galm and Gough 2008; Lafayette and Smith 2012). Generally, Smith Creek Cave's assemblage is best characterized as the result of the discard of hafted projectile points, broken during impact, with significant degrees of retouch, recycling, and reuse.

Although four of the 14 artifacts (29%) are very small and so fragmented that we could not interpret what led to their failure or what function they may have performed prior to breakage and discard, 10 (71%) exhibit diagnostic attributes of impact-related breakage (following Fischer et al. 1984; Lafayette and Smith 2012), including burin damage (as previously observed by Bryan [1980]). As noted above, the morphologies of three of the fragments suggest the assemblage partially represents a set of Haskett points, which, when coupled with the impact damage recorded on these fragments, supports the interpretation of Beck and Jones (2009) and Duke (2015) that Haskett points were an important component of Western Stemmed *projectile* technology. Moreover, the classic, often dramatic, markers of impact damage we have documented on the Smith Creek Cave points are likely the product of using these points as tips of atlatl darts launched at high velocities, not as low-velocity, hand-held thrusting spears. Our actualistic studies (Lynch 2020) testing the effectiveness of large lanceolate points have repeatedly shown that when used to arm atlatl darts, they cause massive incised wounds that gape open and bleed profusely (e.g., Farjo and Miclau 1997). Further, these same experiments show that large lanceolate points like Hasketts are prone to failure when impacting hard tissue, a finding that corresponds to the complete and dramatic fragmentation of the Smith Creek Cave points.

Five of the biface fragments (36%) bear signs of post-breakage reworking, most commonly notching ($n = 3$) and edge modification of breakage facets with small, noninvasive flake removals perpendicular to the long axis of the points ($n = 2$). Not surprisingly, the highest incidences of resharpening and recycling are on points made of obsidian from the two farthest sources, Wildhorse Canyon (150 km) and Browns Bench (300 km). This recycling behavior signals the importance of raw-material conservation at the cave, >100 km from the nearest natural source of obsidian. Continued studies of the complete assemblage will more comprehensively assess the effects of raw-material quality and distance on other components of the lithic assemblage, including unfinished bifaces, unifaces, cores, and debitage, and whether the broken and recycled points were being actively replaced with new tools manufactured on more local raw materials at the cave.

In a general sense, these findings support the characterization of Western Stemmed points as important components of a highly curated toolkit made up of a narrow range of forms (e.g., Beck and Jones 1997; Duke 2011). They also complement the interpretations of Lafayette and Smith (2012: Table 7), who found a high incidence of nonprojectile knife use among Western Stemmed points in their archaeologically derived study sample from the northwestern Great Basin. More specifically, however, if we are correct in our assessment of three of the extravagantly broken point fragments being of the Haskett form, our findings (and those of Duke 2015) contradict previous interpretations of Haskett points serving primarily as knives (Galm and Gough 2008; Lafayette and Smith 2012). Experimentally, Lafayette and Smith (2012:147, 156) found that Haskett points did not perform well as projectile tips, but they hand-threw their replicated points and did not test them as atlatl-dart tips, and they appear not to have modified their "attack" angle to avoid the hard-to-penetrate rib cage, a behavioral adaptation suggested by Wood and Fitzhugh (2018) to increase the effectiveness of the weaponry. In the eastern Great Basin, evidence continues to emerge that Haskett points served as projectiles, not exclusively as knives. Actualistic tests specifically employing Haskett points as high-velocity projectiles obviously need to be accomplished and reported.

Conclusions

Based on the analyses presented here, we offer the following conclusions regarding the 14 bifacial-point and biface fragments from the Western Stemmed occupation at Smith Creek Cave:

1. The points were mostly manufactured on obsidian and were transported significant distances before arriving at Smith Creek Cave, the majority from sources in the Sevier and Escalante deserts to the south and southeast (125–170 km) and the minority from the much-more-distant Browns Bench area (300 km north of the cave).

2. The point fragments are difficult to categorize morphologically, but at least three display signs suggesting they represent unshouldered Haskett points.

3. The points were manufactured following characteristic technology of the Western Stemmed Tradition, being produced on long, slender flake blanks, shaped with distinctive collateral flaking along lateral margins, typically to the midline but

sometimes past it, with final forms produced through soft-hammer percussion and pressure-flaking, with edge grinding of stem margins.
4. The points undeniably served as weapon tips, possibly as high-velocity projectiles thrown from atlatls.
5. Smith Creek Cave's stemmed points were components of an extravagantly curated toolkit (sensu Odell 1996), with fragments being removed from hafts and often recycled into processing tools used in butchery or other expedient tasks.

Overall, these interpretations suggest that the occupants of Smith Creek Cave represented a group (or groups) of highly mobile hunters who made use of a large territory, centered on the southern Bonneville Basin but possibly extending as far north as the Idaho-Utah/Nevada border; however, we also need to consider that the site could lie in a "frontier" zone between southern and northern Paleoindian groups inhabiting the Bonneville Basin. Much of the assemblage represents an occupation during the Younger Dryas, and perhaps even earlier, coeval with other early Western Stemmed occupations known from the western Bonneville Basin, for example, Bonneville Estates Rockshelter and the Wishbone site along the Old River Bed Delta, and possibly other undated, surficial Old River Bed Delta sites (Duke 2015; Goebel et al. 2011; Madsen, Oviatt, et al. 2015; Rhode et al. 2005; Smith et al. 2020).

Together the evidence from these sites reveals a rich fabric of technological and subsistence organization, from short-term special-task camps at upland-situated Smith Creek Cave and mid-elevation Bonneville Estates Rockshelter to longer-term base camps anchored by productive lowland marshes like the Old River Bed. As our analyses of the Smith Creek Cave materials continue, we hope to provide a more detailed portrayal of the Paleoindian experience at this location, building on our understanding of the early-human settlement of the eastern Great Basin. By continuing our work with the Paleoindian collection from Smith Creek Cave, we will expand our analysis to include unifaces, cores, and debitage originally recovered by Alan Bryan, and to apply high-power microscopy to further investigate the functions of the bifaces and unifaces in the assemblage. Redating of the Paleoindian occupation and analyses of hearth contents to fully characterize diet and subsistence will require additional work with curated faunal and floral assemblages, and possibly new excavations.

Acknowledgments

We gratefully acknowledge the hard work of Rachel Delovio and Gene Hattori at the Nevada State Museum, for administering the loan of the Smith Creek Cave stemmed points and wood sample. Thanks also to Heather Thakar at Texas A&M University for taxonomically identifying the dated wood fragment, and to Alex Nyers at the Northwest Research Obsidian Studies Laboratory for providing an analysis of one of the obsidian fragments. Likewise, we deeply appreciate the efforts of federal cultural-resource managers who helped facilitate permits for our raw-material survey and sample collection, including Lisa Gilbert, Bryan Hockett, Stephanie Jeffries, Nicole Lohman, Courtney Mackay, Scott Shaley, Michael Sheehan, Michael Terlep, Nate Thomas, and Wesley Willoughby. Deanna Flores and Peyton Harrison assisted in raw-material survey around Smith Creek Cave during summer 2019.

Notes

1. Other analyses in which we are currently engaged suggest that the Wildhorse Canyon source contains geochemical variability which may be indistinguishable from Modena/Panaca using pXRF. At this time, our Modena/Panaca attributions are provisional.

7

The Western Stemmed Tradition Predates Clovis in the Columbia River Plateau

Archaeological Evidence from the Cooper's Ferry Site

Loren G. Davis

In the decades following the initial discovery of fluted projectile points at the Folsom and Clovis sites, archaeologists sought to find evidence of a Paleoindian cultural pattern in the southern Columbia River Plateau of the interior Pacific Northwest region of the United States (Figure 7.1). These excavation efforts consistently found unfluted stemmed and lanceolate projectile points at the base of sites, but no fluted points (Daugherty 1956; Leonhardy and Rice 1970). Later in the 1980s, excavations at the East Wenatchee site produced the largest examples of Clovis fluted points in an intact buried context (Gramly 1993; Mehringer 1988); however, this site lacked chronometric ages and other diagnostic projectile points that would help to clarify the place of fluted points in the archaeological record of the Plateau. In time, archaeologists began to question whether stemmed points, not fluted points, might be truly foundational in the Plateau culture history sequence, representing a Western Stemmed Tradition (WST) that was contemporaneous with the Clovis Paleoindian Tradition (CPT) (Bryan 1980).

Alan Bryan's (1979) excavations at Smith Creek Cave led to the discovery of stemmed points and a hearth feature dated to 13,200–12,900 cal BP, providing the first radiocarbon evidence that stemmed points probably overlapped in time with the CPT. The discovery of a stemmed point base at Paisley Caves in good stratigraphic context dated to 11,070 ^{14}C BP (12,950 cal BP)[1] confirmed the contemporaneity of stemmed points with the CPT in the Great Basin (Jenkins et al. 2012). The pattern of WST-CPT contemporaneity was not confirmed in the Plateau until stemmed points were discovered at the Cooper's Ferry site in a pit cache associated with radiocarbon ages of 11,410 ^{14}C BP and 11,370 ^{14}C BP (13,260 and 13,210 cal BP; Davis et al. 2015; Davis et al. 2019; Davis and Schweger 2004; Davis and Sisson 1998). More recent archaeological excavation at the Cooper's Ferry site produced evidence that WST artifacts precede the CPT (Davis et al. 2019), which is discussed here at greater length.

Columbia River Plateau WST

The WST is defined from several excavated sites throughout western North America where radiocarbon dating shows it to appear in the late Pleistocene and end during the Early Holocene period (Beck and Jones 2010; Bryan 1980; Davis et al. 2012; Smith et al. 2020). Late Pleistocene–aged archaeological components (i.e., diagnostic WST projectile points in associative context with samples chronometrically dated in excess of 10,000

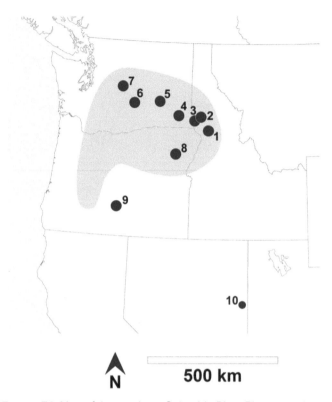

FIGURE 7.1. Map of the southern Columbia River Plateau region (*shaded area*) and noted Great Basin sites. Site locations (*black dots*) include: (*1*) Cooper's Ferry; (*2*) Hatwai; (*3*) Wewukiyepuh; (*4*) Marmes Rockshelter; (*5*) Lind Coulee; (*6*) Sentinel Gap; (*7*) East Wenatchee Clovis; (*8*) Pilcher Creek; (*9*) Paisley Caves; (*10*) Smith Creek Cave.

^{14}C BP or ~11,500 cal BP) are known from a relatively small number of sites in the Plateau region, including Lind Coulee (Daugherty 1956; Irwin and Moody 1978), Marmes Rockshelter (Hicks 2004), Hatwai (Ames et al. 1981; Sanders 1982), Sentinel Gap (Galm and Gough 2008), Wewukiyepuh (Sappington and Schuknecht-McDaniel 2001), and Cooper's Ferry (Davis and Schweger 2004; Davis et al. 2014; Davis et al. 2017; Davis et al. 2019; Figure 7.1).

Plateau WST sites contain various forms of shouldered and lanceolate stemmed projectile points (Lohse and Moser 2014), including the Lind Coulee (Daugherty 1956), Windust (Leonhardy and Rice 1970; Rice 1972), and Haskett types (Butler 1967; Galm and Gough 2008; Figure 7.2); crescents (Davis et al. 2012; Daugherty 1956; Irwin and Moody 1978); unidirectional, multidirectional, centripetal, and Levallois-like cores (Davis and Willis 2018; Muto 1976); blade cores; and end and side scrapers (Davis et al. 2012). Lithic raw material use is diverse and typically focused on local sources of varying quality. Many Plateau WST points are made on linear macroflakes (Davis et al. 2017), whereas direct, multistage reduction of large bifacial preforms to smaller finished biface forms is present in some instances, most notably reported from the Sentinel Gap site (Galm and Gough 2008). Like the Great Basin, Plateau WST sites show a subsistence focus on hunting and appear to lack evidence of intensive plant processing (e.g., hopper mortars, metates) that appear later in the region. Ames (1988) and Davis

(2001) argue that WST peoples pursued specialized resource extraction activities similar to Binford's (1980) collector pattern.

Evidence of the Clovis Paleoindian Tradition in the Columbia River Plateau

Clovis fluted projectile points have been identified from all Far Western states, Alaska, many Canadian provinces, and northwestern Mexico (Anderson et al. 2010; Des Lauriers 2008; Willig 1991). The evidence for the timing of the CPT comes from sites excavated in the Great Plains and Southwest regions where researchers describe "long" and "short" CPT chronologies. The "short" Clovis chronology is argued to have occurred during a 300-calendar year period between 13,050–12,750 cal BP (Waters, Stafford, and Carlson 2020). The "long" Clovis chronology spans a 480-year period between 13,350–12,870 cal BP (Haynes 1980, 1982, 1987; Haynes et al. 1984). For some, the long chronology can be extended by the addition of ages from two more controversial sites. Radiocarbon ages on dispersed organic materials from the Clovis-gomphothere kill site of El Fin de Mundo potentially extend the timing of the CPT to ~11,550 ^{14}C BP (~13,390 cal BP); however, Waters and colleagues (2020b) question if the dated material is actually cultural in origin and whether its age was affected by local groundwater. Ferring (2001) reports two radiocarbon ages on charcoal from the Aubrey site Clovis component that average 11,570 ^{14}C BP (~13,490–13,335 cal BP); however, Waters and colleagues (2020b) argue that the ages may come from fossil charcoal that predates the Clovis occupation.

Although fluted projectile points have been found in surface contexts at many Far Western sites, and only rarely in buried context, archaeologists have not yet been able to independently demonstrate the chronometric age of the CPT from sites in the Far Western regions of the Great Basin, Pacific Northwest, Alta California, British Columbia, or the Baja California peninsula. Moreover, the relative temporal relationship between fluted projectile points and WST projectile points is not known from primary buried stratigraphic contexts.

Fluted points have been found in several parts of the Plateau as surface finds (e.g., Galm et al. 1981; Hollenbeck 1987), indicating a regional presence for the CPT. The in situ discovery of fluted points in the Plateau within buried context, however, is currently limited to the East Wenatchee Clovis site of eastern Washington (Gramly 1993; Mehringer 1988), which contained fluted points, preforms and other lithic tools, and carved bone rods. Glass shards of Glacier Peak tephra—which was initially thought to have erupted at ~11,200 ^{14}C BP (~13,120 cal BP; Mehringer et al. 1984) but has been more recently redated to ~11,600 ^{14}C BP (~13,440 cal BP; Kuehn et al. 2009)—were found adhering to the bottom of at least one fluted point. This association between fluted points and Glacier Peak tephra can only provide a maximum age estimate, not an absolute chronometric age.

The absence of chronometric ages for Clovis archaeological components in the Plateau means that we also lack empirical validation that the age of the Plains/Southwest Clovis cultural tradition will be the same farther west. We also lack a clear understanding about whether fluted points found in the Plateau are technologically and culturally the same as fluted points found at CPT sites in the Plains/Southwest. Whereas the term "Western Fluted" has been applied to morphometrically different fluted points found in the Great Basin (e.g., Beck and Jones 2010), this term is not commonly used in the Plateau region, where fluted points are nearly always assumed to reflect the CPT. In the absence of evidence to the contrary, I will, for the purposes of this discussion, simply assume that the East Wenatchee Clovis assemblage and other ex situ and surficial discoveries of Clovis probably reflect an expression of the CPT in the Plateau at or very near the same time that the CPT is dated in the Plains/Southwest region.

FIGURE 7.2. Stemmed projectile points and fragments excavated in situ within LU3 at Cooper's Ferry: (*a*) stemmed point base (73-60685; RN 56938); (*b*) stemmed point base (73-42800; RN 50948); (*c*) projectile point blade (73-62464; RN 59067); (*d–g*) stemmed projectile points found within Pit Feature A2 (PFA2).

Early WST Occupation at Cooper's Ferry

Davis and others (2019) report evidence of repeated cultural occupation in an aeolian loess deposit (called lithostratigraphic unit 3 [LU3]) that accumulated before 13,070 ^{14}C BP up to 11,370 ^{14}C BP (before ~15,660 until ~13,210 cal BP); Bayesian modeling predicts cultural occupation contained in LU3 deposits that lie stratigraphically below the position of the 15,660 cal BP age may have started as early as 16,560 cal BP. Excavation of this early deposit revealed multiple cultural features, including a hearth feature (Feature 129) that produced three charcoal fragments that dated to 12,348 ± 71 ^{14}C BP (14,785 to 14,075 cal BP), 12,472 ± 61 ^{14}C BP (15,030 to 14,250 cal BP), and 12,598 ± 54 ^{14}C BP (15,195 to 14,670 cal BP), and charcoal found ~2.5 m away at the same elevation returned an AMS age of 12,363 ± 49 ^{14}C BP (14,725 to 14,120 cal BP). Artifacts found within LU3 include two WST projectile point bases and a projectile point blade fragment, biface fragments, modified flake tools, and a burin.

The earliest stemmed point at Cooper's Ferry (Figure 7.2a) is stratigraphically positioned beneath an AMS age of 11,630 ^{14}C BP (~13,460 cal BP) and above the AMS charcoal ages associated with the F129 hearth and adjacent surface that span 12,600–12,350 ^{14}C BP (~14,960–14,380 cal BP). The next oldest point from LU3 (Figure 7.2b) is bracketed between ages of 11,630 ^{14}C BP and 11,410 ^{14}C BP (~13,460 and 13,260 cal BP). The four stemmed points (Figure 7.2c–f), recovered from the PFA2 cache pit, were associated with AMS ages of 11,410 ^{14}C BP and 11,370 ^{14}C BP (~13,260 and 13,210 cal BP). Taken together, the spatial distribution of these stemmed point specimens and radiocarbon ages present a clear chronostratigraphic sequence for the presence of WST projectile points at Cooper's Ferry (Figure 7.3).

The Western Stemmed Tradition Predates Clovis in the Columbia River Plateau 157

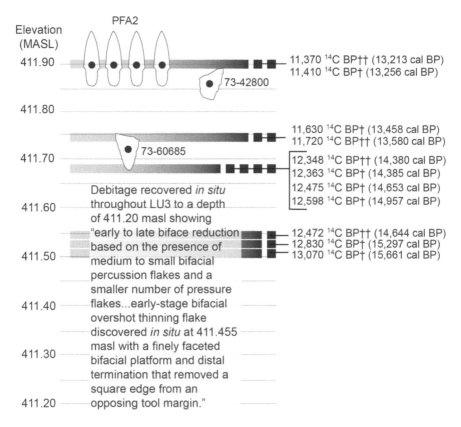

FIGURE 7.3. Chronostratigraphic context of WST projectile point technology and evidence of bifacial reduction debitage at Cooper's Ferry within LU3 in relation to elevation (meters above sea level [masl]) and stratigraphically associated AMS radiocarbon ages. Black squares show stratigraphic positions of specific radiocarbon-dated samples († = charcoal age, †† = bone collagen age). Shaded horizontal bars show chronostratigraphic markers at elevations relative to the positions of stemmed projectile points found in LU3. Black dots show vertical position of associated stemmed point specimens. Text describing the distribution and types of debitage is from Davis and colleagues (2019:894).

Comparison of WST and CPT Timing in the Plateau

Stemmed projectile point technology dates to before 13,460 cal BP but after ~14,380 cal BP at the Cooper's Ferry site. Based on these ages, the WST predates Clovis by either 530 or 240 years, depending on whether a long or short radiocarbon chronology is used. These findings show that the WST was present in the Plateau for a time that, at a minimum, was even greater than the 300-year duration of the "short" Clovis period (Waters, Stafford, and Carlson 2020). Even if the redated maximum age estimate of 11,600 ^{14}C BP (~13,440 cal BP; Kuehn et al. 2009) for the Glacier Peak tephra is used and assuming the tephra layer was a primary airfall unit dating immediately after the eruption (which is not known)—making the East Wenatchee Clovis site the oldest known instance of fluted projectile point technology in the world—the earliest WST projectile point at Cooper's Ferry is still older than the appearance of the CPT. Of course, if the maximum tephra age for East Wenatchee Clovis points is used, then the reported association of stemmed points with Glacier Peak (or older) tephra at the Pilcher Creek site in northeastern Oregon (Brauner 1985;

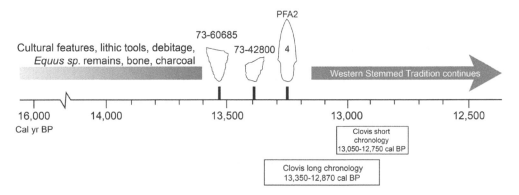

FIGURE 7.4. Archaeological timeline showing the initial radiocarbon-dated appearance of cultural occupation in the bottom portion of LU3, diagnostic WST artifacts (artifacts 73-60685, 73-42800, and four WST points excavated from Pit Feature A2 [PFA2]) at the Cooper's Ferry site, compared to the timing of the long and short Clovis radiocarbon chronologies.

Figure 7.1) must also be accepted, adding even more confirmatory evidence about the antiquity of the WST.[2] The discovery of early WST components at the Cooper's Ferry site clearly demonstrates that stemmed point technologies unequivocally predate and overlap with the CPT as radiocarbon-dated elsewhere in North America.

Evolutionary Relationships

Archaeologists have hypothesized that the WST is a technological descendent from the CPT (Willig and Aikens 1988), much in the way that the Llano-Plano relationship appears elsewhere in North America where stemmed projectile point forms (e.g., Eden, Hell Gap, Scottsbluff) are manufactured after Clovis and Folsom fluted point types disappear from the archaeological record. The recent discovery that WST projectile point technology at Cooper's Ferry predates the CPT (Davis et al. 2019) allows the rejection of such a Llano-Plano type hypothesis for WST origins in the Plateau region, at least (see also Bryan 1988). Given this situation, one might ask: did the CPT lithic technology evolve from a WST cultural ancestor? That the WST precedes, overlaps with, and succeeds the CPT in the Plateau (and in the Great Basin, for that matter) strongly suggests that they do not share a direct ancestor-descendent relationship (Figure 7.4). The kind of evidence needed to directly address the issue of evolutionary relationships would need to come from an archaeological sequence with a robust WST lithic tool and debitage assemblage found beneath an equally revealing CPT archaeological component, like that reported in Texas from the Gault (Williams et al. 2018) and Friedkin sites (Waters et al. 2018).

In what ways these "older than Clovis" stemmed points relate to the WST is not clear at this time; however, the projectile points found beneath the Clovis components at Gault and Friedkin directly demonstrate that smaller, short-stemmed forms predate fluting technologies in North America. Most likely, the WST and the CPT both share ancestral origins among the earlier unfluted lanceolate and stemmed projectile point technologies that appear in upper Paleolithic sites in northeastern Asia (Davis and Madsen 2020; Davis et al. 2019; Madsen 2004, 2015; Madsen and Williams 2019; Pratt et al. 2020). The traditional technological knowledge of upper Paleolithic style biface and blade production that accompanied the initial human migrants to the Americas probably gave rise to the WST and other early stemmed point forms in North America and is likely also foundational to other early technological traditions that followed, including the CPT (Madsen

2015; Waters 2019; Waters et al. 2018; Williams et al. 2018).

Analysis of debitage from the lower half of LU3 at Cooper's Ferry—which radiocarbon-dated samples and Bayesian modeling predict (with 95.4% confidence) should date between ~16,560–14,650 cal BP—confirms that bifaces were among the earliest lithic tools manufactured in the Plateau. The site's initial occupants performed bifacial thinning, including the production of an overshot flake that removed an opposing square edge, and the removal of smaller retouch flakes to finish or maintain bifacial tools (Davis et al. 2019). Exactly what forms of bifaces were being made at this earliest period is not clear at this time; however, it is probably safe to assume that the lithic tools associated with the initial settlement of North America should be similar to pre-Bølling-Allerød period tool forms produced in northeast Asia, which notably include an array of lanceolate and stemmed projectile point types (Davis et al. 2019; Graf and Buvit 2017; Pratt et al. 2020).

Antiquity of Stemmed Projectile Point Forms

The contracting base stemmed point (Figure 7.2a) is not only the earliest typological artifact at Cooper's Ferry, but also represents a new form of stemmed projectile point that is the earliest point type in western North America. This new stemmed point form (Figure 7.2a), which I provisionally call the *Cooper's Ferry type*, possesses contracting, slightly convex haft margins that terminate at a narrow, rounded base. The haft margins expand distally toward the blade element and retain slight shoulders at the haft to blade transition. The second oldest stemmed point fragment (Figure 7.2b) bears contracting (toward the distal end of the haft base) haft margins that terminate at a narrowed, roughly flattened base. The four stemmed points found in the bottom of Pit Feature A2 (Davis and Schweger 2004; Davis et al. 2014) retain different haft forms: parallel-sided with roughly squared base (Figure 7.2d); slightly expanded convex haft margins that contract to a rounded base (Figure 7.2e); and relatively straight-sided haft margins that contract to a rounded base (Figure 7.2f).

If these point forms had not been found as contemporaries in the same cultural pit feature, but instead as surface isolates, it might be tempting to define them as different temporally diagnostic types based on their haft morphologies. Multiple longer stemmed and shoulderless lanceolate projectile points, similar in form to the Haskett type (Butler 1967; Galm and Gough 2008) have been found in situ at Cooper's Ferry, but so far only in deposits that postdate 12,500 cal BP. What is perhaps most important to highlight here is that projectile points with short stems and shouldered hafting elements are not only earliest at Cooper's Ferry but represent the oldest radiocarbon-dated stemmed projectile point forms in North America.[3] Indeed, the short-stemmed and shouldered point forms (i.e., Figure 7.2) associated with LU3 at Cooper's Ferry are the very oldest WST projectile point types.

Conclusion

The discovery that WST projectile points at the Cooper's Ferry site are dated 530 to 240 years before the appearance of the CPT in the Americas confirms that short-stemmed point forms predate fluted projectile points in the Columbia River Plateau as they do elsewhere in North America. The evolutionary relationship between the WST and the CPT remains unclear and will require new discoveries of buried archaeological components in regional sites that clarify the Far Western fluted point production sequence. Research is underway to explore the links between late Pleistocene-aged northeast Asian and the earliest WST lithic technologies (Davis et al. 2019), and pursuing this particular line of research should generate insights about the technological commonalities shared among early peoples who practiced late Pleistocene-aged lithic traditions of the northern Pacific Rim region.

Acknowledgments

The archaeological excavations that led to the discovery of the early WST artifacts at the Cooper's Ferry site were funded through challenge cost share agreements between the Bureau of Land Management's Cottonwood Field Office and the University of Alberta (1997; agreement 1422-D-065-A-96-0007) and with Oregon State University (2009 to 2019; assistance agreements L09AC15147 and L14AC00232), by the Bernice Peltier Huber Charitable Trust, the Keystone Archaeological Research Fund, and Oregon State University.

Notes

1. Unless otherwise provided by the cited author, radiocarbon ages were calibrated with Calib (Stuiver et al. 2020).
2. Brauner (1985) reports the discovery of WST points in direct contact with a layer of tephra that he describes as Glacier Peak (layer B or G), based on analyses conducted by geoarchaeologist Bruce Cochran at Washington State University; however, no lab report with elemental data was included in the site report. Because of this, Reid (2017) argues that the WST points found during excavation at the Pilcher Creek site were probably associated with Mazama O tephra (6850 ^{14}C BP; 7680 cal BP) and not with Glacier Peak tephra. It is worth noting that there are two tephra layers in the Pilcher Creek site stratigraphy and that stemmed points were found in direct association with the lowermost layer. If the uppermost layer is not Mazama O, then it could be Mount St. Helens Set Ye, which erupted between 3510–2920 ^{14}C BP (~3770–3060 cal BP) and has a reported distribution into northeastern Oregon (Mullineaux 1986). Even this seems unlikely since large stemmed projectile points, like those recovered from the lower deposits at Pilcher Creek, do not appear in the Middle to Late Holocene culture history pattern of this area (e.g., Leonhardy and Rice 1970). Although Reid (2017) suggests Mazama O tephra was perhaps redeposited twice at Pilcher Creek, this hypothesis is questionable as a paleosol was recorded in the stratigraphic sequence between the two tephra layers, indicating the passage of considerable time. Another viable hypothesis is that the uppermost tephra layer is Mazama O and the lower tephra layer is the next oldest Cascade Range volcanic eruptive event. There are several probable candidates to choose from here. If the lowermost tephra is not Glacier Peak B or G, then the next probable tephra would be Mount St. Helens Set J, which has been dated between 10,980 ± 250–10,740 ± 250 ^{14}C BP (median ages of ~12,880–12,610 cal BP; Mullineaux 1996), and the next oldest tephra is Mount St. Helens Set S, which dates between 12,910 ± 160–12,120 ± 100 ^{14}C BP (median ages of ~15,436–13,983 cal BP; Crandell et al. 1981). Respectively, these tephras would indicate that the Pilcher Creek WST artifacts are either younger or older than the relative tephrochronological age estimate applied to the East Wenatchee Clovis site. Ultimately, this situation can only be resolved by sampling a stratigraphic sequence from the site and performing direct geochemical characterizations on the two tephra layers.
3. The stemmed point bases found in Cave 5 during excavations at Paisley Caves (Jenkins et al. 2012:Figures 1b and 1c) represent some of the earliest WST projectile point specimens yet discovered. Point base 1895-PC-5/16A-24 is a convex-sided contracting base hafting element found in a thin silt layer that contained a sagebrush twig AMS dated to 11,070 ^{14}C BP, which was underlain by charcoal dated to 11,340 ^{14}C BP. Point base 1294-PC-5/6D-47-1 was found ex situ during excavations of a deposit that was bracketed by ages of 11,135 to 11,600 ^{14}C BP. Arguably, point base 1895-PC-5/16A-24 does not bear the straight-sided margins seen on long-stemmed point types such as Haskett and Cougar Mountain and could just as easily have been associated with a different point form, such as the Cooper's Ferry type. Point base 1294-PC-5/6D-47-1 is clearly shouldered with a short stem, and if it was indeed primarily associated with the deposits it was excavated from, it provides another line of evidence that long-stemmed, shoulderless WST projectile point types are not the earliest form in western North America.

PART II

Fluted Technologies

8

The Clovis Record in the Far West

GEORGE T. JONES *and* CHARLOTTE BECK

During the summer of 1933, Luther Cressman began an ambitious archaeological field project in eastern Oregon. His main goal was to record locations of petroglyph sites and other sites containing artifacts with rich stylistic content (e.g., textiles). Cressman hoped these data would prove useful to evaluate the prehistoric movements of different cultural groups in this desert region.

On the lookout for unusual cultural features, Cressman made a brief stop at Big Spring west of Denio, Nevada, where he discovered a distinctive set of stone tools. Among the artifacts he collected were several crescent-shaped objects and long-stemmed projectile points, as well as the basal segment of a fluted projectile point. Being familiar with studies like the one completed a few years earlier at the Folsom site (Cook 1927; Figgins 1927), Cressman suspected the Big Spring fluted point was quite old (Cressman 1936).

Seeking counsel from an authority on "early man," Cressman contacted Edgar B. Howard, who just then was excavating at Blackwater Draw near Clovis, New Mexico. Soon to become famous as the Clovis site, Blackwater Draw not only contained a distinctive assemblage of artifacts but it also possessed an association between fluted points and extinct large mammals including mammoth. The makeup of this fauna suggested it was probably older than that at Folsom.

The fluted projectile point at the Clovis site was larger and less "refined" than the Folsom point and in his reply to Cressman, Howard emphasized this, referring to the point as "Folsom-like" or "Folsomoid" (Howard 1936).

Cressman was disappointed that Howard had not provided a more definitive attribution for the Big Spring point. He knew it did not exhibit Folsom point morphology. Instead, it was more robust and had other distinctive morphological traits. And like other fluted points with this morphology, it waited another 15 years before the archaeological community recognized it as a distinct typological entity (Sellards 1952).

Cressman went on to conduct many field studies (Cressman 1942) in the northern Great Basin at sites like Fort Rock Cave, Catlow Cave, and the Paisley Caves. These sites contained an abundance of "early man" evidence. At the Paisley Caves, for example, bones of extinct horse and camel rested in a stratigraphic relationship with artifacts that convinced Cressman of the site's great antiquity. In his view, the site likely dated to the end of the last pluvial, perhaps 15,000 years ago, when lakes covered most of the valley floors of the Great Basin. This evidence was not sufficiently compelling, however, to convince other archaeologists that the artifacts and Pleistocene fauna found at the Paisley Caves were of comparable age. That would require a battery of new techniques and new evidence (see Gilbert et al. 2008; Jenkins et al. 2012).

The greatest success of Cressman's efforts to build a cultural chronology of south-central Oregon came with his use of a new dating technique, radiocarbon dating. Its application to fiber sandals from Fort Rock Cave demonstrated that human occupation of the cave was more than 10,000 cal yr BP. With evidence of deep antiquity, the discovery of fluted points in buried contexts surely would be forthcoming. On that score, however, Cressman's work, as well as that of future archaeologists in the Far West (FW),[1] was a disappointment; they found no fluted points in buried contexts.

More often, however, the absence of fluted points coincided with the presence of diagnostic elements of another early tool tradition, the Western Stemmed Tradition (WST). For years the WST record was thought to postdate Clovis in the FW. However, discoveries in the last two decades have demonstrated instead that the two tool traditions either were contemporaneous or, at the least, overlapped in age. In fact, some cultural sequences, like the one developed for the Paisley Caves, place the WST in an earlier chronological position than Clovis by at least several centuries (Jenkins et al. 2012). Although fluted points occur in many artifact assemblages in the FW (Beck, Jones, and Taylor 2019), they nearly always are found on the surface, not in secure stratigraphic contexts containing remains suitable for radiocarbon dating.

To summarize then, the fluted point record of the FW, though not insubstantial, often rests on the surface and lacks evidence that would make it possible to deduce its age. Thus, chronological inferences for the age of Clovis in the FW commonly come up short, forcing archaeologists to rely on Clovis chronologies developed in distant North America (NA) culture areas.

Over the years, an interpretive rift has developed concerning the ages of early FW cultural traditions in which two positions are most prominent. One is the view, expressed by Jennings (1986) and Willig and Aikens (1988), that Clovis is the basal stratum of a 13,000-year-long cultural sequence in the FW (see also: Fiedel and Morrow 2012; Morrow 2019; Reid et al. 2015) that was followed chronologically by the WST in most parts of the FW and contiguous regions. This argument, a regional variant of the Clovis-First hypothesis, faces contravening evidence at several FW sites consisting of WST artifact debris that predates what would be the expected ages of Clovis by several centuries (e.g., Jenkins et al. 2012; Davis et al. 2019). It also includes a substantial record of fluted projectile points that exhibit "derived" features, in addition to generally less robustness, that distinguish them from "classic Clovis" (Beck, Jones, and Taylor 2019). How is this morphological signal interpreted? Whether morphologic variation represents functional or stylistic variation, aspects of either might prove useful as chronological indices. Or they might represent morphological diversification attributable to isolation or ecological processes working at the local demic level. We touch on these matters below.

Finally, what about Cressman's Big Spring fluted point? Is it Clovis or not Clovis? Like so many FW examples, the Big Spring point is missing a good deal of its former morphology, making attribution difficult. Nevertheless, it is more gracile than a classic Clovis point although it leans toward the robust end of the Clovis–post-Clovis morphocline. Its base morphology, especially its deep basal concavity, clearly is like that of a post-Clovis fluted point.

In sum, Clovis research is predominantly culture historical and comparative. Building chronologies, a prerequisite for other sorts of inference, is complex as Clovis research amply illustrates. In the remainder of this chapter, we review chronological matters along with other research themes that engaged professional and avocational archaeologists working on the Clovis complex in the FW.

The Clovis Record in the Far West

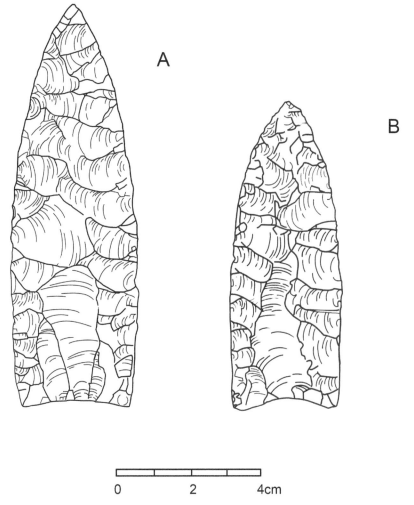

FIGURE 8.1. Fluted points exhibiting classic Clovis morphology: (*a*) Blackwater Draw site, New Mexico (drawn from Denver Museum of Natural History cast); (*b*) #553-319 "Ester Green," Dietz site, Oregon (drawn from photograph).

But First, What Is Clovis?

For students who have spent a little time in an archaeology laboratory or a seminar devoted to North American prehistory, "What is Clovis?" should not be a difficult question. For starters, Clovis refers to a type of projectile point. In her classic treatise, *Ancient Man in North America*, Wormington (1957:263) describes several distinctive features of Clovis point morphology. They include the following: the point's lanceolate shape, parallel or slightly divergent stem margins, length of three inches or greater, flute channels present on both sides of the point, flute channels most often composed of multiple flake scars, and an abraded, concave base.

Figure 8.1 shows two examples of Clovis points. The first specimen, which was recovered at Blackwater Draw, is quite long but in all other respects typifies classic Clovis point morphology. The second projectile point illustrated in Figure 8.1 was collected at the Dietz site in southern Oregon. Although shorter than the Blackwater Draw specimen, it also exhibits classic Clovis morphology, as described by Wormington (1957).

More broadly, Clovis refers to a tool technology, the Clovis technocomplex (Bradley et al. 2010), which includes not only the Clovis projectile point, but other diagnostic tools such as large prismatic blades and bone and ivory rods.

Technology embodies more than a set of objects, of course. It also includes knowledge shared among members of a social group for the production and maintenance of sets of tools. Minimally, then, the Clovis technocomplex is a set of percussive techniques that, applied according to a template of operations (conventions), enables the manufacture of tools of specific morphologies. This knowledge system also may encompass predispositions as to the kinds of stone that were best for these purposes and where to find them.

Clovis also refers to a period during which this diagnostic technology was used, as well as to a characteristic adaptation(s) encompassing, for example, the hunting of extinct late Pleistocene mammals (although there is debate as to the economic importance to Clovis groups of taxa like mammoth and mastodon [e.g., Cannon and Meltzer 2004; Haynes and Hutson 2013; Kelly and Todd 1988; Surovell and Waguespack 2008, 2009]).

The length of the Clovis era is also subject to some debate. One model claims it encompasses the late Pleistocene, between ca. 11,600 and 10,800 ^{14}C BP (ca. 13,700–12,800 cal years BP [Taylor et al. 1996]), a period of warming temperatures and significant reduction in the size of the continental ice sheets, as well as geographic adjustments of plants and animals. This era ended in the abrupt return of cool temperatures and greater moisture during the Younger Dryas (YD). An alternative model of Clovis chronology is offered by Waters and Stafford (2007a), who discount ^{14}C ages from the Aubrey site in Texas (Ferring 2001), arguing they cannot with certainty be associated with cultural remains. Consequently, their model suggests a shorter duration for the Clovis era, between ca. 11,100 and 10,800 ^{14}C BP (ca. 13,200–12,900 cal years BP). Not every specialist, however, is willing to dismiss the Aubrey site dates (e.g., Haynes et al. 2007; see also discussion in Miller et al. 2013), and thus the length of time represented by the Clovis era remains a point of contention.

Clovis is believed by many archaeologists to represent a colonizing population associated with small residential groups that moved rapidly across large tracts of land to secure sustenance (but see Bamforth 2014; Kilby 2014). In the process, Clovis people and their descendants are believed to have colonized much of North America south of the retreating continental ice sheets and, late in the colonization process, made their way northward through an ice-free corridor (IFC) into Arctic latitudes (Smith and Goebel 2018).

Clovis, of course, also is a small city in eastern New Mexico where, in 1932 at nearby Blackwater Draw, gravel mining uncovered spear points intermingled with mammoth bones. As often is the case in archaeology, a new discovery like this one is named for its geographic locale. Hence, the projectile point form found with the mammoth bones was named "Clovis." We discuss each of these aspects in more detail below, focusing on how generalizations developed concerning Clovis in the better-known parts of its range in North America may or may not apply to the Clovis record in the FW.

The Clovis Projectile Point

When asked, most archaeologists probably would identify the bifacially flaked, fluted projectile point as the most distinctive element of the Clovis technocomplex. Attached at the tip of a javelin, thrusting spear, or dart, the Clovis point was the weapon of choice for dispatching large prey animals, including an occasional mammoth or bison. Use-wear scars on Clovis points indicate they also served as cutting tools, needed for the efficient conversion of flesh to food and hide and bone to shelter, clothing and other tools.

Subsequent to Wormington's (1957) effort, there have been several attempts to isolate which morphological features best exemplify the Clovis fluted point (e.g., Beck, Jones, and Taylor 2019; Buchanan and Collard 2007; Buchanan et al. 2014; Howard 1990; Morrow and Morrow 1999). But assemblages of these points, even those that appear to represent a narrow band of time and are confined to a small geographic area, commonly exhibit considerable morphological variation (Huckell 2007). The task of identifying diagnostic morphological criteria, of course, is complicated because fluting persisted after the Clovis era. Also, while Clovis points may have been made to approximate a morphological standard, breakage during use often necessitated retipping or rebasing, altering point morphology and producing an annoyance for the analyst.

Perhaps, then, we should not be surprised that Clovis points exhibit morphological variation. After all, they represent part of an evolving technological lineage and thus were subject to processes of transmission and selection. Consequently, Clovis point morphology is likely to exhibit distinctive geographic patterns relating to vectors of population movement, as well as effects of isolation and variation in environmental contexts. Despite these factors, Clovis fluted points exhibit morphological uniformities that reflect the fact that they were part of a knowledge system inherited by populations over a large portion of North America. What is regarded as classic Clovis point morphology persisted across a large area of development, essentially coincident with the Great Plains to the eastern seaboard on an east–west axis and north–south from southern Alberta to the southeastern U.S.

Are There Clovis Points in the Far West?

Fluted points bearing an attribute set shared with classic Clovis points are present throughout the FW (Beck, Jones, and Taylor 2019), although they are concentrated primarily within the area encompassing Oregon, central California, and northern and central Nevada (Beck and Jones, Chapter 12). Two Clovis caches, East Wenatchee (Gramly 1993; Mehringer and Foit 1990) and Simon (Butler 1963), are also present, respectively in central Washington State and the Snake River Plain of Idaho. A third, the Fenn Cache (Frison and Bradley 1999), is believed to have been located near where the state boundaries of Idaho, Utah, and Wyoming meet. Judging from the distribution of isolates, sites, and caches, it seems likely that groups with a Clovis technology entered the FW from the northern Plains (Beck and Jones 2010, 2013, Chapter 12; Speer et al. 2019), probably via the Green River Basin, a corridor that presented the fewest obstacles to movement. A southern route of entry cannot be ruled out however and, indeed, might account for the presence of Clovis points along the southern coast and Mojave Desert of California.

If, as assumed here, this dispersal event took place during the Clovis era (ca. 13,500–12,700 cal BP[2]), it should be marked archaeologically by fluted points of classic Clovis morphology. Again, though, what is classic Clovis point morphology? The problem for archaeologists working in many places across North America is that Clovis is closely followed by other fluted projectile forms, technological descendants with slightly different morphological traits. These points, for example, tend to be more gracile, exhibit deeper basal concavities (like Folsom points from the Plains and Vail and Debert points in the northeastern U.S.), have longer flute scars relative to their lengths, or have a slight constriction of the stem just above the base (like Cumberland points from the southeastern U.S.).

To evaluate whether FW fluted points, or a subset of these points, match Clovis morphology, it is first necessary to establish which morphological attributes of classic Clovis are best for comparison. Ideally, examples of classic Clovis points will share similar values of key morphological attributes that set them apart from post-Clovis morphologies. To a degree, this exercise is an arbitrary one, since what sets the standard for any morphological feature is who first called attention to it and identified its modal character.

To illustrate how to differentiate Clovis points from other point types, Beck and colleagues (2019b) compared two sets of fluted points. One set represented 96 classic Clovis points from the Northwest, Great Plains and Southwest. The other set consisted of 462 fluted points from throughout the Far West compiled in the Far Western Fluted Point Database, an expansion of the database developed by Taylor (2002, 2005). Our purpose was to determine if FW fluted points strictly conform to classic Clovis morphology or if a subset(s) of points from this sample exhibit other morphologic modalities.

Variables used to characterize Clovis point morphology were drawn from a set of 14 developed by Howard (1990). As most specimens in the Western Fluted Point Database are fragmentary, only a subset of Howard's variables could be measured on all points. Basal width and basal depth, which are important for distinguishing point types (see Miller et al. 2013), could be measured on all specimens (see Beck, Jones, and Taylor 2019 for details of the analytic protocol).

Comparisons of the distributions of selected variables were made between classic Clovis and FW fluted points using simple statistical tests and graphical techniques. For example, comparisons were made using the depth of the basal concavity and basal width. Classic Clovis points typically have a shallow basal concavity and are comparatively wider at the base than post-Clovis points from other regions in North America. When these variables are used to compute a ratio (basal concavity depth:basal width), 95% of classic Clovis points lie within a range of values between 0.05 and 0.2 (mean = 0.132). Among FW fluted points, about one-third of the specimens lie within this range, while two-thirds have higher values and lie outside the classic Clovis range, indicating the latter specimens exhibit both deeper basal concavities and narrower bases. The results of a fuller treatment of the point sample reveal that 46.9% of the points in the database are consistent with Clovis criteria while 48.7% are not. The name Sunshine Fluted was applied to points in the latter group (Beck, Hughes, and LaPierre 2019).

Analyses like these can be refined using more sensitive evaluative techniques like geometric morphometrics and multivariate statistics (e.g., Buchanan et al. 2014; H. Smith et al. 2015). The test results also would be more persuasive if a simultaneous evaluation of age or stratigraphic relationship was performed. Still, the analyses presented by Beck and colleagues (2019b) strongly indicate that, just as in other parts of North America, Clovis represents the basal member of the FW fluted point series. This continuum appears also to contain more gracile specimens that are likely to have evolved from a classic fluted form. The continuum may conclude with an unfluted concave base form (e.g., Black Rock Concave Base; Rondeau et al. 2017) that persisted through the Younger Dryas and an early phase of the Holocene.

Point Descent in the Far West?

Just as in other parts of North America, the FW contains fluted points that match the features of classic Clovis points. Other examples also appear to differ from this classic form with respect to one or more of those morphological features. Such morphologic gradations have been argued as representing evidence of descent within intellectual lineages (O'Brien and Lyman 2003). Morphological gradations probably reflect the effects of one or more evolutionary processes, including transmission (e.g., Beck and Jones, Chapter 12; Bettinger and Eerkens 1999; Boyd and Richerson 1985), technological selection (e.g., for efficiency of manufacture), functional selection (e.g., for ballistic performance relating to prey types), social selection (e.g., for signaling functions), and the evolution of neutral traits (e.g., drift or stylistic change [see Eren et al. 2013 and O'Brien et al. 2015]). More work will be necessary to determine which of these processes shaped the evolution of fluted point morphology in the FW. Still, such processes are likely to have caused changes in projectile point morphology in this region just as they apparently did in other parts of North America.

In recent years, studies of technological phylogenesis have been put on firmer methodological footing with the application of cladistic analysis (e.g., O'Brien et al. 2001; O'Brien and Lyman 2003). Briefly, cladistic analysis is a method that uses homologous similarity among related taxa to posit lines of descent. Like other clustering algorithms, cladistic analysis weighs the similarity between entities like the bones of organisms or components of technological systems to identify which kinds (i.e., "taxa") are most similar, and thus most closely related (alike by virtue of descent from a common ancestral form).

Application of a cladistic approach to a set of 87 classic Clovis points and 137 fluted points from the FW (Beck and Jones 2007) found fluted point descent was organized in several branching episodes. Each was marked by change in fluted point morphology, such as size reductions and shifts in the shape of the base.

To test this phylogenetic hypothesis, future analyses would benefit from a larger point sample, composed of complete points for which a larger set of morphological variables could be measured. Recovery of fluted points from secure, well-dated stratigraphic contexts also would aid such a test. Still, the fact that Beck and Jones' (2007) results exhibit geographic consistency (e.g., the deepest ancestry is in the Great Plains; the shallowest ancestry is in the southern Great Basin) suggests the approach has introduced realistic answers to two questions: (1) "from what geographic source did FW Clovis originate," and (2) "do other fluted point morphologies derive from FW Clovis?"

Results of conventional morphologic comparison of fluted points from the FW, aided by efforts using cladistics, support the inference that the Far Western fluted point record is composed both of points that share classic Clovis morphology and of divergent forms that most likely represent technological descendants and postdate the Clovis era, if by just a century or two. The latter bear morphological similarities to point types like Folsom and Gainey and may have arisen as a response to similar selective pressures, e.g., changes in prey type. Chronological control is too imprecise, however, to establish how much time these morphological changes represent or when fluted points stopped being used. Still, if these aberrant forms postdate use of classic Clovis morphologies, and they almost certainly do, this conclusion will help to explain why most of the radiocarbon dates associated with FW fluted points fall in the post-Clovis era (see below).

In sum, until recently all fluted points in the FW were thought to be Clovis points. Over the last two decades, however, an increasing number of archaeologists have come to recognize a good deal of variation among these points and that not all of them match classic Clovis morphology. Reminiscent of debates following the Folsom discovery, FW researchers have used such terms as "Clovis-like" and "Western Fluted" to refer to fluted points that differ from the "classic Clovis" fluted form. These terms are poorly defined, however, or not defined at all, and thus fail to clearly differentiate between FW Clovis and alternative fluted varieties. Use of the name "Sunshine Fluted" by Beck and colleagues (2019a), for example, is an attempt to recognize one morphological modality—a gracile one—among FW fluted points that is clearly different from classic Clovis.

Other Diagnostic Features of Clovis Technology

Although Clovis fluted projectile points have received the greatest attention among specialists, other artifact classes and associated processes of tool manufacture also are distinctive. Collins (1999), for example, states that diagnostic Clovis artifacts represent not one but two lithic reductive strategies.

One was for producing bifacial projectile points and similar tools. The other was for producing prismatic blades. We begin this section by reviewing diagnostic products of biface preparation, then turn our attention to Clovis blades.

Biface Technology: Thinning and Overshot Flaking

There are several stages in the production sequence of fluted points in which distinctive morphological attributes of bifaces and corresponding manufacture byproducts (i.e., flake debris) are produced. One of these stages, biface thinning, is a critical step in shaping a biface for use as a projectile point. Thinning reduces mass and, combined with shaping the edge and point of a projectile preform, improves the resulting point for flight and penetration. To thin a biface to a uniform thickness, flakes are detached from the lateral edges. These flakes must travel across the midline of the biface (called overface flaking). Flaking that fails to do this produces a thick, narrow biface, one that is not well suited to projectile function.

Clovis biface thinning is distinctive for incorporating an extreme type of overface flaking. Referred to as overshot flaking, this technique achieves thinning by detaching a flake that travels across the face of the biface and removes part of the opposing edge (Bradley et al. 2010). Overshot flaking is rare in many biface reduction industries since it may decrease a biface's width precipitously and create overly thin, weakened margins. But as Bradley and colleagues (2010) argue, Clovis knappers developed considerable control of the overshot technique and frequently used it to thin production bifaces and simultaneously to correct awkward edge morphology like square edges on opposing margins.[3]

Overshot flaking is quite apparent as it produces flakes of distinctive shape. Similarly, the flake scar topography of bifaces flaked in this manner is distinctive. As can be seen in the illustration of a Clovis bifacial preform from the Fenn Cache (Figure 8.2), overshot flakes are typically of such a large size that they were used "as-is" or modified into other tools. Most often overshot flaking was used by Clovis knappers in the middle phases of reduction, after a general degree of plan symmetry was achieved by trimming the biface edges and clearing the faces of topographic irregularities.

Clovis artifact assemblages containing bifaces and flakes illustrating use of overshot flaking are not common in the FW. This absence may relate to a thin distribution of Clovis populations, but as likely reflects a discovery bias relating to a failure to identify quarry and workshop sites of Clovis affiliation (but see Reid et al. 2015). Such biases may reflect the fact that fluted point production typically was staged across a sizable territory, not exclusively at a raw material source. For example, in his report on the lithic assemblage from the Dietz Clovis site in south-central Oregon, Fagan (1988) observes that fluted projectile points are represented by obsidians from distant sources as well as from the nearby Horse Mountain source, which lies about 2 km from the Dietz site. The Dietz site Clovis assemblage also contains a large component of lithic debris consistent with an emphasis on tool-manufacture at the site. Still, observing that cortical and large flakes are uncommon in the assemblage, Fagan (1988) concludes that a large share of biface preparation had been conducted off-site. Although the Horse Mountain obsidian source lay nearby, Dietz toolmakers appear to have staged only the initial reduction phases at the material source and finished fluted point manufacture at the Dietz site. As a result, little evidence for use of overshot flaking is found at this site. Instead, the assemblage appears to be derived from later phases of biface shaping and flute removal, which erased evidence of the use of overshot flaking.

Circumstances occur, however—like caches of unfinished bifaces—where evidence of overshot flaking is well-represented. For example, the Fenn Cache (Frison and Bradley 1999) contains a sizable number of bifaces

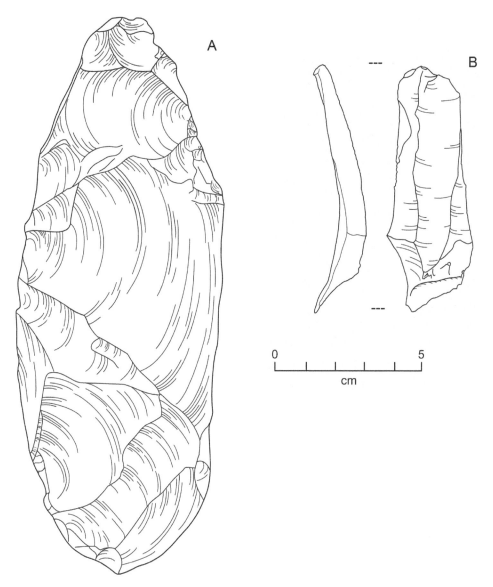

FIGURE 8.2. (*a*) Biface (#104) from the Fenn Cache illustrating use of overshot flaking (drawn by George T. Jones from photograph [Frison and Bradley 1999:Plate 51]); (*b*) Clovis blade from the Sunshine Locality, Nevada, illustrating longitudinal curvature.

that exhibit overshot flake scars (Figure 8.2). Similarly, the East Wenatchee Clovis Cache (Gramly 1993) contains unfinished fluted bifaces that also display use of this thinning technique. Another workshop site, Sage Hen Gap, near Burns, Oregon, lies within an obsidian source. In contrast to the Dietz site, Sage Hen Gap includes the full series of biface stages and production debris, including overshot and fluting flakes (O'Grady et al. 2008). Sites like Sage Hen Gap, where raw materials were shaped into tools on-site or nearby, appear to be rare in the FW. But again, the paucity of workshop sites may be more apparent than real and reflect the difficulty of isolating Clovis manufacture debris amidst other artifacts produced over a 13,000-year span of use following Clovis occupation.

Biface Fluting

As it pertains to shaping Clovis bifaces, fluting refers to the removal of longitudinally oriented flake(s) from a platform constructed at the basal edge. The resulting flake removal produces a central channel on the face of the biface preform. In addition to thinning the biface, fluting levels the hafting surface, which may have aided in binding the point to a foreshaft. Although sometimes executed early in the thinning process, fluting Clovis points generally began during the middle phases of manufacture. This step was followed by additional shaping (Morrow 1995, 2015), such as removing flakes to straighten the stem margin. This results in flake scars that intruded into the flute facet at 90 degrees. In contrast, post-Clovis fluted point types, like Folsom, were fluted later in the reduction process, after the point had been shaped and thinned (Morrow 2015).

According to Bradley and colleagues (2010), the point at which Clovis knappers began fluting is of less diagnostic value than the technique used to detach flute flakes. They identify two approaches for flute removal. In both methods platforms were constructed on the basal edge of the preform to produce a strengthened area that was less likely to fail (shatter) under the load produced by percussion flaking. These platforms, however, were aligned differently with respect to the medial plane (or center plane, see Morrow 2015). On Clovis points, the fluting platform was positioned at the medial plane of the biface, whereas post-Clovis fluted points had platforms that lay closer to the face from which the flute flake was detached (the platform lies below the medial plane [Bradley et al. 2010: 100–101]). In the former case the ventral plane of the flute flake scar has a diagonal orientation in relation to the medial plane of the preform and tends to run for a short distance, perhaps one-fourth to one-third of the length of the point preform. In the latter case, the flute scar has an orientation that parallels the medial plane, and typically runs for a greater distance down the face of the preform. Precisely how fluting was carried out is debated, but some specialists believe that Clovis fluting was achieved by direct percussion (Morrow 2015), while the fluting of post-Clovis points employed some form of indirect percussion or pressure technique.

Flute flakes also exhibit distinctive morphology. They tend to be quite thin and roughly rectangular (blade-like) if removed from a preform with a relatively flat surface. Conversely, a flute flake detached from an undulating surface may have a ragged plan or be snapped transversely into smaller segments.

Clovis Blade Technology

Another distinctive aspect of the Clovis technocomplex is the manufacture of prismatic blades. As the term is conventionally used, a blade is a flake having: (1) a length that is at least twice its width, (2) nearly parallel margins, and (3) one or two longitudinal ridges running the length of the dorsal surface, giving it a triangular or trapezoidal cross section. Clovis blades have additional diagnostic features (Figure 8.2). They tend to be quite long, between 50 and 160 mm in length, and have "small platforms, flat bulbs, smooth interiors and marked curvature" (Collins and Lohse 2004:176). A Clovis blade recovered at the Sunshine Locality appears as Figure 8.2b.

Clovis blades that were struck from conical or wedge-shaped cores tend to exhibit "robust" cross sections, and possess steep lateral edges that are both sharp and strong (Bradley et al. 2010). A variety of tools were made from blade blanks, as well as from rectangular segments produced by transversely snapping the blade.

The geographic distribution of Clovis blades is strongly patterned (Beck and Jones 2010; see also Figure 12.4). From a North American perspective, Clovis blades are most common in the southern Plains and mid-South. In both regions, assemblages with blades and blade cores often are associated with geologic outcrops of cherts and other microcrystalline rocks. Blades are also well-represented in Clovis caches in the southern Plains (Collins 1999). Moving northward along the Rocky Mountain Front (western

Great Plains), the contents of caches change. Blades become less common while the numbers of bifaces and other tools increase, along with an increase in cache size. With few exceptions, caches in the northern Great Plains contain abundant bifaces and fluted points but have few blades and no blade cores.

Although Clovis blades and blade cores are certainly present in the FW (e.g., Rhode et al. 2022), they are rare (Beck and Jones 2010:Figure 7). Huckell (2007) reports that blades also are uncommon at sites in the San Pedro Valley of southeastern Arizona. He observes that blades "seem to form a relatively less important facet of the lithic technological repertoire" and goes on to suggest "that with the Clovis industry we are seeing the last vestiges of blade manufacture and use, the passing of a technology no longer central to the industry as a whole" (Huckell 2007:212).

We reached a similar conclusion based on the geographic distribution of blades in the Great Plains (Beck and Jones 2015a). The drop in blade frequency in northern caches, we suggested, may have been a response to the costs of maintaining technological alternatives (e.g., Bettinger et al. 2006; Ugan et al. 2003). Moving northward from the southern Plains where sources of high-quality cherts were common, dispersing Clovis groups encountered fewer closely spaced lithic sources. While maintaining their biface technology, which was critical for projectile point manufacture, Clovis knappers may have substituted large flakes derived from biface manufacture for blades. While these substitutes may not have been as effective as their blade-tool counterparts, transport efficiency was gained by reducing the proportion of a transport load made up of blades and tools made from blades.

The Age of Clovis in the Far West

Estimating the age of Clovis occupation in the FW is difficult because of the dearth of radiocarbon-dated deposits containing Clovis diagnostics. In all, just six FW sites have dated buried deposits containing fluted points.[4] These sites are described below.

Table 8.1 shows radiocarbon dates associated with fluted points in the FW. More than just their rarity, these dates suggest an unusual facet of this record; except for the date from Heil Pond (and perhaps the East Wenatchee Clovis Cache), each is much younger than Clovis dates from sites in the Great Plains and Southwest from which the Clovis chronology is derived. Some of these dates, like those from the Sunshine Locality, fall in the middle of the Younger Dryas interval. The Connley Cave and Henwood site dates appear to be even younger. Based on their gracile morphologies, the Sunshine and Connley Cave points probably should be attributed to the "Sunshine Fluted" type, as both almost certainly are post-Clovis in age (Beck, Jones, and Taylor 2019).

This set of dates also suffers from other problems, not the least being questionable associations between the points and dates. The most reliable date is from the Sunshine Locality, where a radiocarbon date of 10,320 ± 50 ^{14}C BP (ca. 12,100 cal yr BP) was obtained from detrital charcoal in a thick bed of sandy alluvium. The charcoal rested about 13 cm above a Sunshine Fluted point, a Clovis blade, and a crescent fragment. Seven other ^{14}C dates of detrital charcoal were acquired from this stratigraphic unit in other exposures at the site. Most of the dates come from above an unconformity that divides the alluvium into upper and lower units and suggests a likely age of less than 10,600 BP based on ages that are distributed evenly across a 1000-year interval (between ca. 10,950 and 9850 ^{14}C BP [Holmes and Huckleberry 2009]).

The East Wenatchee Clovis Cache is buried in terraces along the east side of the Columbia River, near Wenatchee, Washington. The cache is underlain by sandy colluvium and loess that contains particles of volcanic ash. Based on its major and trace element chemistry, the ash most closely resembles Glacier Peak G tephra. The tephra originally was thought to date to ca. 11,250 ^{14}C BP (Mehringer and Foit 1990). More recently, Kuehn and colleagues (2009) evaluated a large sample of ^{14}C assays associated

TABLE 8.1. Radiocarbon Dates Reported to Be Associated with Fluted Points in the Intermountain West.

Site	¹⁴C Date (Lab #)	2σ cal BP	Material Dated	Reference
East Wenatchee Clovis Cache, WA	<11,600 BP		tephra estimate	Kuehn et al. 2009
Danger Cave, UT	10,310 ± 40 (Beta-168656)	12,465–11,885	feature charcoal	Rhode et al. 2006
	10,270 ± 50 (Beta-158549)	12,455–11,815	feature charcoal	
Sunshine Locality, NV	>10,320 ± 50 (Beta-86205)	12,470–11,885	charcoal	Beck and Jones 2009
Henwood site, CA Component 1	8470 ± 370 (AA-648)	10,485–8545	charcoal	Douglas et al. 1988
Connley Cave 5, OR	9540 ± 260 (Gak-1744)	11,705–10,215	charcoal	Bedwell 1973
	7430 ± 140 (Gak-2135)	8455–7970	charcoal	
Heil Pond, ID	10,880 ± 260 (Beta-10069)	13,325–12,055	humates	Reid et al. 2015
Sylwester (Twain Harte), CA	9240 ± 40 (OS-93325)	10,555–10,250	wood charcoal	Moratto et al. 2017
	9510 ± 35 (OS-93301)	11,075–10,600	wood charcoal	
	9640 ± 40 (Beta-321935)	11,190–10,780	organic sediment	
	9970 ± 45 (OS-93302)	11,690–11,250	wood charcoal	
	10,200 ± 69 (OS-95438)	12,440–11,405	wood charcoal	

Note: Dates calibrated with OxCal version 4.4 (Bronk Ramsey 2009), using the IntCal20 curve (Reimer et al. 2020).

with the tephra in geological exposures across the Pacific Northwest. They estimate Glacier Peak G tephra dates to ca. 11,600 ^{14}C BP (approximately 13,700 to 13,400 cal BP). A siliceous crust produced by the dissolution of tephra particles is reported to coat the underside of some of the stone artifacts in the cache (Mehringer and Foit 1990). The chronological relationships between the deposition of the tephra, the manufacture of the cache, and the deposition of the siliceous crust are unclear; the tephra does not appear to be in a primary context but has been redeposited. While the East Wenatchee Clovis Cache was emplaced following the deposition of the tephra, and thus postdates the tephra, it is uncertain how much younger the cache is.

Douglas and colleagues (1988) state that the younger date from Component 1 at the Henwood site is questionable because it is out of line stratigraphically with other dates, which include 7400 ± 280 ^{14}C BP and 7150 ± 290 ^{14}C BP for Component 2.

The projectile point recovered by Bedwell at Connley Cave No. 5, Oregon, is a base fragment (Bedwell 1973). Analysts disagree as to whether this projectile point is fluted (Beck et al. 2004) or if it is a basally thinned Windust stemmed point (Musil 2004; Rosencrance et al., Chapter 2). A radiocarbon date suggests the latter interpretation is correct, but the "flute" and base morphology of the point favor the former interpretation.

The Heil Pond site (Reid et al. 2015), a workshop/occupation locale near the Browns Bench obsidian source in southwestern Idaho, contained two fluted points, a fluted preform, and several other Clovis diagnostics. The site was uncovered during expansion of a stock pond, and samples for radiocarbon dating were collected from the contents of a basin-shaped charcoal feature that was thought to be a hearth (although its carbon content—0.02%—is quite low). A fluted point was discovered near the charcoal feature by one of the developers of the stock pond, but its precise stratigraphic relationship with the feature is uncertain. As Reid and colleagues (2015) discuss, intact deposits may remain at Heil Pond and further investigation will be necessary to increase certainty as to the age of the Clovis assemblage at the site.

The Sylwester point was found in 1969 eroding from a clay-rich matrix in the floor of a streambed near Twain Harte, California. Moratto and colleagues (2017) investigated the stratigraphic context of the discovery in 2011 and reported on the geoarchaeology and dating of several alluvial strata preserved at the site. The stratigraphic position of the point could not be reestablished with certainty, but Moratto and colleagues (2017:263–264) argue that the likely source was one of the two oldest levels of clay loam exposed in the modern stream cut. A radiocarbon age of 10,200 ± 60 ^{14}C BP (ca. 11,900 cal yr BP) was acquired from the deepest level, while several dates that range between 9970 ± 45 ^{14}C BP and 9240 ± 40 ^{14}C BP (ca. 11,400 cal BP) were acquired from the younger level. The association of the Sylwester specimen and the radiocarbon dates cannot be established with certainty. The Sylwester point exhibits a predominantly Clovis morphology and not that of a Sunshine (post-Clovis) fluted point. The radiocarbon ages, thus, appear to underestimate the age of the point.

The FW fluted point chronology is far from satisfactory. To begin with, there are few radiocarbon dates, and many are conventional dates with broad error ranges. Few of them have been replicated using datable samples from the same depositional contexts. At face value, then, these dates suggest that Clovis points continued to be used well into the YD in the FW. But it is more likely, given the high frequency of gracile morphologies among many of these fluted points, that they are of post-Clovis age.

Clovis on the Move

The westerly dispersal of Clovis migrants into the FW may have been accomplished along several routes. Migration may have been initiated from a jumping off point in either the southern or the northern Great

Plains, depending upon the model favored. The best-known dispersal model, the Clovis-first hypothesis, argues that Clovis groups were derived from Arctic hunting groups who moved southward from eastern Beringia along a route that bordered the southwestern edge of the Laurentide Ice Sheet (LIS). Although a significant barrier to travel, the LIS may have retreated sufficiently at times during the late Glacial to permit humans and other biota to move southward through an IFC. Potter and colleagues (2018a), for example, estimate one of these times occurred ca. 15,000 cal yr BP.

The timing of ice retreat and the opening of the IFC remain controversial, however. Recent work by Norris and colleagues (2022) reports ^{10}Be, radiocarbon, and optically stimulated luminescence dating, which help to isolate when sections of the IFC were available to southward-traveling pedestrian migrants. Their results indicate the IFC was blocked by the LIS much more recently than the estimate provided by Potter and colleagues (2018a). Norris and colleagues estimate the IFC opened between 13,500 and 13,000 cal yr BP, some 2,000 to 1,500 years after Potter and colleagues estimate it to have opened, and too recently to have played a significant role in the timing of the Clovis spread from a northern population source into the northern Great Plains.

Other archaeologists consider it more likely that a geographic source of Clovis migrants occupied the Gulf Coast of the southern and southeastern U.S. Presumably, their antecedents reached the Gulf Coast and adjacent interior regions by way of a Pacific coastal corridor. In this model, a "push"—perhaps initiated by sea level change in the Gulf of Mexico—or by deepening disruptions of Clovis subsistence produced by Younger Dryas climate change—induced some Clovis migrants to explore interior dispersal routes, including ones along the eastern front of the Rocky Mountains (Beck and Jones 2010, 2013).

Perhaps slowed by high mountains, narrow passes, short growing seasons, or small herd populations (but see Pitblado 2017), Clovis migrants who followed these migration corridors would have sought breaks in the mountain barrier to their west. One of these, the Green River Basin in southwestern Wyoming, lay close to the Snake River Plain and formed a natural conduit for humans crossing the northeastern edge of the FW. This route would have presented migrants with relatively benign landscapes containing large expanses of grassy steppe and supporting herd animals like bison, in addition to several megafaunal taxa that would be lost to extinction by the end of the YD (Jennings 2015). The continuity of biotic patches in this area would have enabled Clovis groups to pursue traditional subsistence practices, including hunting large mammals, and sustained further dispersal into the heart of the FW.

A Foothold in the Far West

Occurrences of Clovis fluted points provide evidence of Clovis dispersal in the Snake River Plain. Additional evidence is provided by the Clovis cache record which contains exotic toolstone transported from sources 200–300 km to the south and southeast of their find spots in the FW. This geographic pattern suggests northwesterly conveyance of toolstone (Beck and Jones 2010, 2013; Speer et al. 2019). The Simon Clovis Cache, for example, contains lithic artifacts sourced to the Big Horn Mountains in north-central Wyoming (Kilby 2014). While the provenance of the cache artifacts does not confirm the actual routes taken by Clovis groups to cross the NE part of the FW, it demonstrates that Clovis migrants were familiar with lands further to the east.

At the time Clovis migrants began moving in a westerly direction following the Snake River, other groups were apparently moving from the northern Plains in an easterly direction. The respective chronologies are poorly resolved, but these movements may have been synchronous and well underway during the earlier stages of the Younger Dryas.

In addition to questions about the timing of dispersal and the circumstances of Clovis arrival in the FW, a related set of questions acknowledges the social complexity that may have arisen from the presence in that region of another Indigenous population, the people of the Western Stemmed Tradition. It seems likely that Clovis and WST migrants encountered each other. The dynamics of such encounters may not have been entirely negative for members of these groups. Indeed, as Meltzer (2009) and others point out, contacts between members of these demes may have gone a long way toward solving a problem faced by small groups of highly mobile people: how to remain biologically viable.

These and other unanswered questions relate to when and from what geographic centers Clovis migrants dispersed. The routes of dispersal were evidently numerous, but was this process also essentially simultaneous and can it be attributed to a single cause? The answer to these questions may be as simple as pointing out that Clovis and other Paleoindian migratory events occurred at the end of the last glacial period, at approximately the same time as climatic perturbations associated with the Younger Dryas event. Shifts to use of larger subsistence ranges, expansions of prey lists, and changes in subsistence practices all may have been responses to diminished food resources. To take one example, Kelly and Todd (1988) describe climate change to be responsible for drawing down the density of prey and causing animal species to organize in zonal distributions rather than in patches. A reasonable supposition is that a nearly contemporaneous event transpired in the northern Great Plains and the Great Lakes region, and that all three migratory events were tied to onset of environmental changes associated with the YD climate event.

Possible Interactions between Clovis and the WST

Specialists represent Clovis and post-Clovis dispersal from the mid-continent as rapid and unhindered, reflecting the relative emptiness of the landscapes being crossed. Dispersal relied on a mode of organization that helped to accomplish several purposes. Long-distance mobility, for example, accomplished the goal of placing hunter-foragers near large mammal prey and other subsistence objectives in a timely fashion. But it was also part of a strategy for increasing landscape recognition. Another goal was to complete exploratory travel by which members of migrant groups scheduled periodic meetings and shared information for other social purposes (e.g., Barton et al. 2004; Hamilton and Buchanan 2007; Kelly and Todd 1988; Martin 1973 [but see Meltzer 2009 for discussion of colonization models]).

Among the uncertainties created by this mobility strategy was the maintenance of demographic viability. A constant tug likely was present between a need to expand the area exploited for subsistence and other exploitive purposes and the risk that in the process of increasing the sizes of foraging ranges, demes would become isolated from other similar reproductive units.

Along with Paleoindian research more specifically, archaeological studies in the Great Basin have been the beneficiary of ecological frameworks for many decades. By the end of the last century, those theoretical perspectives had matured with the inclusion of a foraging theory perspective. Put simply, this framework assumes that foraging decisions, such as where to search for dietary resources and what subsistence prey to take, are made according to the relative costs each incurs. Those costs primarily reflect time or energy outlays to locate and capture prey. Thus, an optimal diet will be one that maximizes the recovery of energy while minimizing the time devoted to accumulating that energy. An optimal diet, then, will typically encompass large mammal prey, providing they are common members of the local biota. As those animals diminish in concentration, foragers will shift to lower-ranked prey, commonly animals with smaller body sizes. Foragers will, however, always be ready to realign hunting priorities should more highly ranked prey become available.

Along with prey choice (diet breadth) models, another common framework for modeling subsistence choice asks how long a forager should remain in a foraging patch before moving to another one where resource content assures a higher return. If the productivity of an exploited patch continues to decrease, at what point does a forager abandon that patch to seek another one that continues to possess available food energy[4] (see Charnov's [1976] discussion of the marginal value theorem)?

An ecological approach is not limited to these two models, although ecological studies of subsistence will predominantly use one or the other. Another ecological process, one that appears to be germane to the success of Clovis demes in the FW is a topic we close this section with. Besides the search for food and other resources, the Clovis occupants of the FW faced other ecological constraints.

At the arrival of Clovis, Indigenous WST groups at the Paisley Caves had already been in the FW for several centuries, and perhaps much longer. We can reasonably imagine that the earliest of these WST colonists made their way into the FW following riverine corridors from the Pacific Coast. In the span during which the WST colonists adapted to the relatively well-watered NW Great Basin, they developed a subsistence pattern drawing from a diverse suite of small prey types. These included an array of waterfowl and shorebirds, fish, mollusks, and small and medium-sized mammals, e.g., rabbit, and antelope (Jenkins et al. 2016). These taxa and other environmental evidence indicate the presence of wetlands, including marshes and streams in the vicinity of the Paisley Caves during its YD occupation (Jenkins et al. 2016).

Judging from the occupation chronologies of the Cooper's Ferry site (Davis et al. 2019) and the Paisley Caves (Jenkins et al. 2016), these WST occupants arrived in the FW at least several centuries and perhaps as much as 2,000 years before Clovis. YD cultural deposits are well-developed at the Paisley Caves. Along with a wide variety of biotic remains, lithic artifacts, bone, fiber, hair and other classes of environmental evidence, the assemblage contains a broad suite of plant and animal food remains that could only be described as diverse. The biotic remains reflect the presence of marshes and other wetlands in the vicinity of the Paisley Caves, settings that were foci of WST subsistence. The sites also contain a small number of stemmed projectile points.

Seasonality evidence suggests the Paisley Caves were not occupied on a year-round basis, but seasonally, when each cave provided optimal thermal comfort. The YD may have disturbed natural systems to such an extent that it reduced human subsistence opportunities, forcing changes in the distribution of animal prey. These changes in prey distribution may have been responsible ultimately for the initiation of Clovis movement into the FW. We begin with the assumption that this phase of dispersal coincided with the movement of other Clovis groups from starting points in the High Plains, moving in an easterly direction.

An Ecological Framework

For our final discussion, we consider one of the richest bases of inference or conjecture about Clovis, that being the ecological paradigm embodied in foraging theory. The logical structure of argument is that for a set of options or choices, some will produce better results. Here, "better" is not meant in some absolute sense but is more correctly identified as the "least" or "more" costly option. Thus, a decision rule for a foraging question is what options are available? That is, among a set of behavioral options, some will produce better results (are less costly). Arguments are contrasted based on the assumption (or rule) that behavioral options are developed in an ecological framework. For example, returning to Kelly and Todd's (1988) study of Paleoindian subsistence and mobility, their study was one of the earliest to make explicit use of a logical structure based on foraging theory (Stephens and Krebs 1986). Kelly and Todd (1988) argued that higher faunal biomass at the close of the last glacial would have favored human diets rich in large and moderate-size mammalian prey, but that periodic declines among prey species would have altered cost/benefit relationships and cast animal prey in a less favorable light.

During the Younger Dryas, environmental changes were instrumental in altering the relationship between humans and their prey. What had been patchy prey distributions changed to zonal distributions corresponding to latitude and elevation. During this period of environmental perturbations, Clovis foragers faced increasingly unpredictable prey numbers to which they responded by developing a familiarity with the foraging ranges of their prey, as well as a capacity for rapid deployment across resource spaces.

In contrast, WST foragers emphasized a wider set of subsistence resources, including many that were abundant, but which demanded considerable effort by foragers to secure. Many of these resources came from wetlands, including lakes, adjoining marshes, and streams. Like that of Clovis groups, the WST lithic industry was generalized, consisting mainly of a small set of flake-based tools such as unifacial scrapers, gravers, notched tools, and other simply modified forms. These tools are so much like Clovis tools that they appear to have developed from a common industrial progenitor. Only the projectile point components of each industry reveal different design choices, with the WST favoring stemmed hafting and Clovis employing fluting. These hafting distinctions suggest different subsistence emphases during the lead-up to the arrival of each tradition in the FW.

But WST foraging wasn't more clearly a generalized foraging pattern; it was a seasonal pattern for extracting a wide range of resources, whereas Clovis subsistence relied on a narrower set of large and intermediate size prey.

The proximity of wetlands and streams to the rockshelters occupied by WST colonists ensured access to a variety of plant and animal foods. The success of this generalized pattern of resource use by WST groups is evidenced by the persistence of this adaptation, reaching forward from the late Pleistocene, across the YD, and ending following a period of substantial warming in a new adaptation during the Early Holocene known as the Desert Archaic.

In contrast, Kelly and Todd's (1988) model of Paleoindian dispersal attributes adaptive success to a subsistence focus on large and intermediate-size terrestrial mammals and a flexible hunting technology, which permitted Clovis and later Paleoindians to adjust to subsistence opportunities by rapidly shifting the distribution of logistic hunting teams. Declines in prey may have been met with adjustments to the size of Clovis foraging ranges along the lines predicted by patch choice models like the marginal-value theorem (see Stephens and Krebs 1986). A consistent feature of these models is their logical connection to behavioral optimality. Thus, we expect to see success in foraging to be a result of the balance sought among costly behavioral alternatives involving which subsistence resources to choose; when and how far to travel to find those resources; search time, which influences the size of foraging ranges; and so forth. Together, these subsistence features would tend to limit the extent of resource diversification and to, instead, seek greater resource returns through behavioral and industrial efficiency.

Despite the behavioral distinctions drawn between Clovis and WST foraging, occurrences of sites in the FW containing mixtures of WST and Clovis technology may indicate that members of these traditions, at least periodically, used the same resource patches.

But does this evidence reflect episodes of common use involving face-to-face interaction? If so, would such episodes of common use occasion competitive behavior? We might be led to this expectation knowing that competitive relations may be governed by the principle of competitive exclusion—the likelihood that among competitors, those with an adaptive advantage will displace a competing individual or group. Here, the success of WST technology relative to fluted point technology is suggested by changes in the Clovis lithic tool industry, specifically simplification of inventory, including the loss of blade tools and changes in the morphology of fluted projectile points with classic Clovis forms being replaced by more gracile morphologies.

Among FW foraging groups, competitive actions might move from the ecologic sphere into those of economic and social actions. Were kinds of competition active components of WST-Clovis economic and social worlds? Did either WST or Clovis display such adaptive advantages (e.g., a more effective technology, a better schedule of labor deployment) that any single or combination of features was sufficient to displace a competing group? Just one simple piece of evidence suggests that this was not the case: fluted and stemmed projectile points are regularly found together in spatial associations at sites attributed either to Clovis or WST (though it should be remembered that some fluted points may represent a post-Clovis cohort rather than an earlier one). Moreover, circumstances that might encourage competition may have been mediated socially, for example, by practices to directly or indirectly meet demographic needs or to acquire environmental information.

Just as Clovis people are known, from our point of view, by their distinctive lithic technology, the same can be said of the people of the Western Stemmed Tradition. WST folk differed in many ways from Clovis people. Might the ways they interacted with the natural environment—in subsistence and settlement practices, for example—have precluded competition? This hypothesis seems unlikely; after all, WST occupation was quite successful, lasting until after the Younger Dryas and long after evidence of the Clovis technocomplex in the FW had disappeared.

If the dispersal of Clovis groups into the FW was like the movement of other Clovis groups throughout the North American interior, it was likely a rapid event, completed within a span of as little as several hundred years. Details of the process are uncertain, but Kelly and Todd (1988; see also Meltzer 2009) attribute rapid colonization to the capacity of Clovis foragers to rapidly advance over unoccupied territory, as well as the fact that they frequently changed foraging ranges. Their greatest success in acquiring foods came from a focus on high-return resources, predominantly large mammals. They did not remain in any one place long enough to significantly expand diet breadth as preferred alternatives were depleted. Foraging theory explains that the abandonment of a foraging range should occur when returns from favored resource patches drop to the average return of all patches within the foraging range. Had Clovis groups instead operated as subsistence generalists using a wide range of food items, the pace of their dispersal across new foraging ranges would have been slower. A generalist adaptation also may have incurred risks in the face of biotic subsistence reorganization taking place during this period. Although regular movement may have required adjustments to new types of prey, Clovis hunting technology was easily accommodated to these prey taxa and did not require the level of labor investment and time that a finer-grained pattern of resource use would entail.

There are alternatives to the "Clovis as colonists" model. Cannon and Meltzer (2004), for example, have surveyed Clovis subsistence evidence and found that in some parts of the Clovis range, these groups pursued a wide range of food resources, including small animals. One answer to these apparently contradictory ecological models is that the first one may apply to a short period of rapid dispersal—the exploratory phase along the colonization front—while the other applies to the succeeding phase in which Clovis people brought up from the rear "settled in" along the existing colonization front. The specialist/generalist distinction, then, may apply to different cohorts of Clovis settlers, some who traveled rapidly over large foraging territories, simultaneously exploring new country for technology and subsistence resources while keeping track of other Clovis migrants whose foraging was more intensive and, thus, required longer occupation times.

An alternative view of Clovis dispersal attributes the spread of Clovis technology to exchange among members of a thinly distributed population of pre-Clovis people in the Great Plains and adjacent provinces. Several expectations follow from this model. First, of course, there should be evidence of pre-Clovis peoples in these areas. This supposition appears to be supported by a handful of sites that lie south of the Laurentide ice sheet, e.g., Schaefer and Hebior, Wisconsin (Joyce 2013), and further south, e.g., Page-Ladson, Florida (Dunbar 2006) and Friedkin-Gault, Texas (Waters et al. 2018; Williams et al. 2018; see Waters 2019 for recent review). In the FW, this expectation is confirmed by discoveries at pre-WST sites at the Paisley Caves, Oregon, and the Cooper's Ferry site, Idaho. Second, Clovis technology itself may have undergone changes in tool morphology, reduction techniques, and choice of lithic materials/lithologies reflecting interactions with Indigenous groups. An absence of evidence that fulfills these expectations lends credence to the model of demic spread.

Prospects for Clovis Research in the Far West

Our review of the Far West Clovis record has been organized by several topics. Among these, the age of Clovis occupation is one that has not lent itself to an easy solution. Archaeologists also have looked to refine descriptions of the Clovis technocomplex to delineate which of these were in situ developments or, more accurately, were later innovations that arose within groups identified as the Western Stemmed Tradition, whose members probably descended from colonists who moved into the FW from the Pacific Coast around 15,000–14,000 cal BP.

We have suggested that WST land-use was a generalist subsistence strategy aimed at procurement of plant and animal resources predominantly in valley wetlands (Elston et al. 2014). In contrast, Kelly and Todd (1988) characterize Clovis land-use as encompassing substantial mobility with regular movements across large foraging territories to acquire a narrow set of prey species.

As the sample of Clovis and other fluted projectile points expands in the FW, opportunities will emerge to enhance descriptions of morphological variation among fluted points. These advances, in turn, will enable typological refinements and improve tests of phylogenetic hypotheses. With larger samples we should come to understand if the fluted points that postdate the Clovis occupation were derived directly from the FW Clovis form or if they had another progenitor (e.g., a form contemporaneous with the Folsom point). Most will continue to be surface finds, and their chronometric assessment will remain challenging. Increasingly sophisticated geoarchaeological modeling and field investigation, however, will increase the chances of discovery of stratified deposits containing datable Clovis materials.

Unlike many other parts of North America where Clovis colonizers appear to be the first occupants, the FW Clovis migrants likely encountered human occupants who had colonized the FW several centuries before their own arrival (Davis et al. 2012; Davis et al. 2019; Jenkins et al. 2012; Pinson 2011). These early occupants in the northern FW can be traced back to nearly 14,500 cal BP (ca. 12,400 ^{14}C BP) at Paisley Caves (Jenkins et al. 2012) and to at least 15,000 cal BP at Cooper's Ferry (Davis et al. 2019). Both sites contain strata and associated artifact assemblages that have been radiocarbon-dated to the Clovis era. These Indigenous foragers probably descended from colonists who entered the Intermountain West by way of riverine corridors originating on the Pacific Coast. The artifact assemblages left by these colonists, however, do not contain fluted points but are associated with assemblages that contain stemmed projectile points. At Cooper's Ferry those points bear a morphologic resemblance to WST types like the Lind Coulee form; the stemmed points from Paisley Caves do not exhibit a clear affiliation to a particular WST type but have quite different morphologies from fluted forms.

How Clovis people adapted to FW landscapes probably depended a good deal on the land-use practices of their WST contemporaries. Did these groups engage in active competition or were social practices arranged so members of the groups could reconcile social and economic differences? For FW Clovis and WST foragers to practice similar patterns of resource use, especially if those resources were easily depleted, appears to violate the ecological principle of competitive exclusion—that an individual or group displaying an adaptive advantage should displace a competing group. But perhaps WST and Clovis populations were quite small as H. Smith and colleagues (2015) have argued, reducing the likelihood that the foraging ranges of these groups overlapped. Moreover, circumstances that might often have encouraged arrangements could, alternatively, have been mediated by social rules.

On these points several studies (e.g., O'Grady et al. 2012; Pinson 2011; G. Smith, Felling, Wriston, et al. 2015) have used obsidian source records to compare Clovis and WST organizational patterns in the northern FW. The results of these studies indicate that lithic provenance samples from Clovis and WST assemblages exhibit several differences. First, although all assemblages have diverse source profiles, Clovis assemblages are represented by fewer obsidian sources than WST assemblages. Second, the obsidian sources in Clovis assemblages lie nearer to source outcrops than do those in the WST assemblages. Third, within the geographic area defined by source locales, only about half of the potential sources are represented in the Clovis assemblages.

The meaning of these patterns is open to several interpretations. While source representation surely is related to the expanse of territory in which both Clovis and WST foragers operated, the specific processes responsible for occurrences of distant source materials may be traced to foraging group mobility, mobility among specific cohorts within residential groups (e.g., logistic teams), or exchange for economic or social purposes. None of these processes leave unambiguous signatures, and distinguishing their roles has proven vexing, not just for archaeologists working in the FW (e.g., papers in Hughes 2011; Madsen 2007; Newlander 2018; Smith and Harvey 2018), but for archaeologists working in this time frame across North America (Meltzer 1989).

Possibly, Maybe, Perhaps

The Far Western fluted point record is not a thing of substantial size or long persistence. Nor is it a record of particularly distinctive character. Still, we have learned from its study over the last couple of decades that this record has an important role to play in discerning whether coeval cultural traditions persisted in the late Pleistocene FW. Methodological complexities are attached to questions regarding the Clovis and WST traditions, and perhaps the pre-Clovis and post-Clovis phenomena. One of these traditions—the Western Stemmed Tradition—is characterized by manufacture of stemmed projectile points and persisted long after the disappearance of Clovis. But apart from identifying the presence of the Clovis tradition in parts of the FW, archaeological studies have failed to provide much clarity regarding its age, the content of its associated technocomplex in the FW, if it remained largely independent of influences from the WST, or if it and Clovis industries quickly blended. Were post-Clovis fluted points the last vestige of that encounter, or did Clovis make more extensive contributions to the long-lived Western Stemmed Tradition? Addressing these questions will remind archaeologists how difficult even the "easy" questions are to answer.

Notes

1. Several terms have been used to refer to parts or all the desert region of the western U.S., including physiographic provinces like the Great Basin and Colorado Plateau. As used herein, the "Far West" describes a geographic area bordered on the east by the Wasatch Range and Rocky Mountains and on the west by the Sierra Nevada and Cascade ranges. The northern border crosses the southern portion of the Columbia Plateau and includes the Snake River Plain, while the southern section includes mountain and basin sections of western Arizona, southern California and Nevada. It differs from the Great Basin, which is the western desert region that is internally drained and lies within the Intermountain West. The "Far West" includes the Central Valley of California and the coastal regions of California, Oregon, and Washington state.
2. Radiocarbon dates and calibrated ages are taken from published sources and rounded to the nearest decade or century. Hence, no error values are reported in this chapter. Readers should consult original publications for actual dates. Depending on when the ^{14}C dates were acquired, different curves will have been used to derive calibrated ages.
3. Eren and colleagues (2013) dispute the contention that Clovis toolmakers made intentional use of overshot flaking in the production of bifaces. They make two arguments. First, they show through experimental results that overshot flaking is no more efficient than overface flaking for thinning a bifacial blank. Second, they point out that archaeological evidence indicates the frequency of overshot flakes in Clovis workshop assemblages is lower than would be expected if the technique was an integral part of the Clovis technocomplex. Davis and colleagues (2012) point out that overshot flaking is not restricted to Clovis lithic assemblages, but also is found in WST biface assemblages, albeit in low frequencies.
4. Some of these sites contain fluted points with morphologies like those of classic Clovis, e.g., East Wenatchee Clovis Cache, Sylwester. Fluted points from other sites, e.g., Sunshine Well, Connley Cave No. 5, bear greater similarity to post-Clovis points.

9

Geographic Variability of Far West Fluted Points

Michael F. Rondeau,
Nicole D. George, *and* John W. Dougherty

In a previous study Rondeau and colleagues (2007) found that two samples of fluted points from adjacent Long Valley and Jakes Valley in Nevada exhibited systematic differences in size, form, and technology. The data from two studies, that of Jakes Valley (Rondeau 2006a) and the Sunshine Well Locality (Rondeau 2006b), revealed that the Jakes Valley (JV) points are generally wider and thicker, as well as tend to have wider flute scars, more pronounced margin grinding on lateral and basal edges, less refined lateral margin retouch, and generally more shallow concave bases than the Sunshine Well Locality (SWL) specimens. In addition, the JV artifacts lack all evidence of fluting nipple remnants inset in concave bases and lack the "multi-flute" technique, both of which are found on some SWL points. This multi-flute technique of basal flaking (Figure 9.1) is discussed below.

The JV specimens appear to be more Clovis-like in technology and morphology (Rondeau et al. 2007). The features of the SWL points may argue for a fluted point variant from typical Clovis points. Some SWL features are somewhat similar to Folsom points occurring further east. These features might include refined lateral edge pressure flaking (Bement 1999; Hofman 1999a; Wilmsen and Roberts 1978) and less commonly the retention of fluting nipple remnants (e.g., Frison and Bradley 1980; T. Morrow and J. Morrow 1999). The proposed SWL divergence from Clovis features has led to the argument that they may represent a post-Clovis fluted point type (sensu Beck et al. 2004; Beck and Jones 2010, 2012b).

The potential for post-Clovis fluted point types in the Far West may be a blind spot in regional Paleoindian research. Several other archaeological regions of North America tend to have post-Clovis fluted points although they appear to lack Clovis. One is Alaska with such sites as Serpentine Hot Springs and Raven Bluff (Goebel et al. 2013; Smith et al. 2013). Another is northeastern North America which includes such sites as Debert (MacDonald 1968) and Vail (Gramly 1982). However, the state of Sonora in northern Mexico has Clovis artifacts as well as the proboscidean kill site of El Fin del Mundo (Sánchez 2016), but so far no post-Clovis fluted points have been found.

Largely unexplained variability in Far West fluted points has repeatedly been reported (e.g., Grayson 1993; Rondeau 2006c, 2009b, 2015a; Thomas and O'Grady 2006; Tuohy 1988; Warren and Phagan 1988). Beyond the efforts of Beck and Jones (2010, 2012b), however, there has been little systematic characterization of this variability (but see Thomas and O'Grady 2006). The reasons for such variability vary with some aspects possibly being time transgressive.

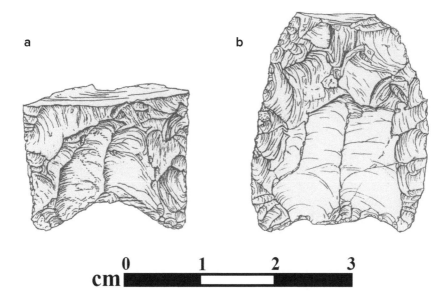

FIGURE 9.1. Multi-flute points from Sunshine Well Locality: (a) 2122; (b) 1905 (after Rondeau 2009a).

Here we explore Far West fluted point variations as they occur among four geographically separate clusters. The four subregional clusters include the SWL points from Nevada (Beck and Jones 2009; Beck et al. 2004), the Dietz site sample from Oregon (Fagan 1988; Willig 1988), the combined Lake Tonopah (Campbell 1949; Campbell and Campbell 1940; Pendleton 1979) and Mud Lake (Haynes 1964; Tuohy 1968) collections (T/M) from western Nevada, and the Milford Flat Locality (MFL) collection from Utah (Mullins and Herzog 2008; Mullins et al. 2009).

Methods

In the initial comparison of JV and SWL specimens analyzed by Rondeau and colleagues (2007), the JV sample is very small ($n = 6$). Limitations of this small sample size do not allow a comparison to the samples analyzed below. The trends suggested below of chert verses obsidian fluted points do not pertain to JV as four (66.7%) are chert and two obsidian (33.3%). Likewise, the JV sample size does not provide a reliable comparison to the size trend findings below. While the JV points trended larger than SWL, specimen 7721-143 (16.7%) is notably smaller (Rondeau 2006a). We use larger sample sizes from a greater geographic area across the Far West to explore potential Far West fluted point variability more thoroughly.

Here we utilize a sample of 172 fluted points. The points were recovered from the four geographic clusters. These include (1) the Sunshine Well Locality (SWL), Nevada, (2) the Dietz site, Oregon, (3) the Lake Tonopah and Mud Lake basins (T/M), Nevada, and (4) the Milford Flat Locality (MFL), Utah. The SWL points ($n = 19$) are at the Nevada State Museum, Carson City (Rondeau 2006b). The Dietz site specimens ($n = 65$) are from the collections at the University of Oregon Museum of Natural and Cultural History, Eugene, and the Lakeview District Office, Bureau of Land Management, Lakeview, Oregon (Rondeau 2008a, 2009c, 2009d, 2013). The T/M sample ($n = 56$) is from Joshua Tree National Park, Twentynine Palms and several private collections (Rondeau 2008b,

2010; Rondeau and Coffman 2007). The final geographic cluster, MFL, provides 32 fluted points curated at Logan Simpson Design, Salt Lake City, Utah, at the time of analysis (Rondeau and Nelson 2013a, 2013b, 2013c).

We are aware of important limitations imposed on this study by the nature of the clusters evaluated here. These collections do not represent areas of comparable size. The Dietz site cluster is the only single site sample of the four. In contrast, the other samples represent larger landscape areas that contain several sites and artifact isolates. The areal extent of some collections is unknown. Further, collection methods are certainly not comparable in all cases, adding an additional bias to these samples. Even so, these four clusters provide some representation of diverse geographic areas in the Far West, and robust patterns are anticipated.

An additional limitation on this study is the sample numbers. These samples represent a moderate number of points at best, but lesser numbers in each cluster are often relevant to the evaluation of selected attributes (Tables 9.1–9.9). Such limited numbers impose statistical limitations. Therefore, any significance attributed to these preliminary findings should remain circumspect without further support from additional studies. Nonetheless, these fluted point differences reflect past prehistoric differences in fluted point manufacture and use.

This cluster selection allowed an examination of two predominantly obsidian clusters, the Dietz site and MFL, and two predominantly chert collections, SWL and T/M. The variability among these clusters is explored in terms of basal flake scar types beyond channel scars (e.g., guide scars, ridge removal scars, platform isolation scars), morphology, and artifact size. Collection of the data for these comparisons was made by direct observation and measurements of the specimens as part of the California Fluted/Lanceolate Uniform Testing and Evaluation Database (CalFLUTED) laboratory studies. Relevant attributes, measurements, and comparisons are described below.

Technological Comparisons

We begin our comparison by focusing on three aspects of flaking technology. First, we examine the presence of fluting platform variations along the basal margin (Table 9.1) that may suggest differences in channel flake removal. Second, we evaluate basal flaking strategies revealed by pre-fluting, fluting, and post-fluting flake scar variations (Tables 9.2 and 9.3). Finally, we examine the orientation of the flute scars on opposite faces as they relate to the form of the original preforms (Table 9.4).

Four *basal margin elements* are tabulated in Table 9.1. They are the presence of a basal notch in the concave basal margin (BNt), the presence of the inverted "V" basal margin (IVM) variant of the concave base, the evidence of a fluting nipple at the apex of the basal concavity (FNiE), and beveled basal margins (BMB). These basal element identifications are generally confirmed by observations of diagnostically associated flake scars. To increase this count, morphologically similar basal elements are also included when weathering has obscured the associated flake scars.

The first three of these basal elements are thought to be related. The fluting nipple platform appears to have broken off during the fluting event creating the basal margin notch in some cases. Several other examples suggest basal impact damage focused by an unremoved fluting nipple remnant. This damage shows less symmetrical basal notches. The inverted "V" basal margin appears to be the result of pressure retouch that removed the notch during final shaping of the proximal edge.

For the comparison of six basal attributes from the four clusters (Table 9.1), 123 fluted points proved relevant. Of the relevant artifacts, 13 (32.5%) from the Dietz site, 13 (44.8%) from MFL, 24 (68.6%) from T/M, and 13 (68.4%) from SWL provided useful data. With over two-thirds of both samples providing relevant attributes, the similarity between the chert-dominated clusters is striking and could suggest a somewhat different approach to fluting techniques for chert than for the obsidian clusters. This difference may or not be toolstone-based.

Beveled basal edges are not common on finished fluted points. Their presence usually argues for placement in the unfinished biface category. For example, in the Dietz site assemblage there are seven unfinished fluted bifaces that exhibit beveled bases that appear to be a form of platform preparation for fluting. Still, rare exceptions exist such as RA-33-1 from Nevada (Davis and Shutler 1969:Figure 4g; Rondeau 2006d:Figure 1a). This point has a beveled proximal edge due to the flaking of a transverse break surface into a new biface edge. This new beveled edge runs at a relatively steep angle from one face to the other.

Flute scar configurations are divided into four categories. The single flute category represents those points with a single fluted face and a single flute or that have a single flute on both faces. The other three categories are those with a double flute scar on at least one face, those with three flute scars on at least one face, and those with a multi-flute on at least one face. Some examples bear single flute scars on one face and a different flute scar configuration on the other. No additional flute scar combinations are present in these collections.

The multi-flute does not exhibit the typical fluting approach. It has two pressure scars that usually do not overlap, sitting side by side, and each is smaller than a typical flute scar (Figure 9.1). They nonetheless create a hafting groove commensurate with the groove produced by a single, typically larger flute scar (Rondeau 2015a). The multi-flute scar form is not the same flute configuration as a "multiple flute." The multiple flute scar configuration shows more than one of the typical, larger flute scars on a single face. In this case they commonly overlap with the earlier scar, either extending further to distal or offset to one side of the later channel scar.

When the distribution of flute scar forms is examined by collection group (Table 9.2), SWL stands out as having the lowest frequency of single flute scars (52.6%), the highest frequency of multi-flute flute scars (47.4%) and lacks double and triple flute examples. The notable SWL difference from the other three clusters might be influenced by the smaller sample size ($n = 19$). The Dietz site and T/M have nearly identical single flute face frequencies at 73.2% and 73.7% respectively. MFL is somewhat divergent from the other clusters with the highest single flute occurrence (90.3%) and lacks both triple flute and multi-flute specimens.

Flute scars are often accompanied by other basal flake scars (Table 9.3), usually produced by pressure flaking before or after the fluting event. These scars are notably smaller than the flute or channel scars. Although the use of these descriptive names for the flake scars is reasonably standardized in the literature (e.g., basal end thinning, platform isolation scars, basal edge retouch), several require additional explanation.

Pre-fluting guide scars originate on the basal margin and are thought to have helped to "channel" or guide the removal of the channel flake. For our purposes, the term is used for basal pressure scars that are partially overlapped by the flute scar even though not all such scars can be shown to have actually guided the channel flake removal.

The ridge removal scar is often confused with guide scars due to their similarities in position, form, and size. These are post-fluting scars that removed the thicker basal cross-section segments left at the margins of some channel scars (Figure 9.2). They served to further thin the base and sometimes to expand the width of the hafting groove. In some cases, a single ridge removal scar helped center the hafting groove on the point face (e.g., Rondeau and George 2017).

The two obsidian clusters clearly exhibit the highest frequencies of non-flute scar basal flaking (e.g., end thinning, guide scars, ridge removal scars). Considerably fewer specimens of chert have these basal flake scars. Platform isolation flake scars (similar to guide scars only shorter in length) proved rare and appear to have seldom survived both fluting and subsequent basal margin flaking. Basal

TABLE 9.1. Basal Margin Elements.

Cluster	Total	BNt N	BNt %	WNtF N	WNtF %	IVM N	IVM %	WIVF N	WIVF %	FNiE N	FNiE %	WNiF N	WNiF %	BMB N	BMB %	WBMF N	WBMF %
Dietz site	40	4	10	1	2.5	3	7.5	0	0	2	5	3	7.5	4	10	2	5
Milford Flat Locality	29	5	17.2	1	3.4	2	6.9	2	6.9	2	6.9	1	3.4	0	0	0	0
Lake Tonopah/Mud Lake	35	8	22.9	7	20	0	0	4	11.4	2	5.7	1	2.9	0	0	0	0
Sunshine Well Locality	19	4	21.1	1	5.3	0	0	0	0	5	26.3	1	5.3	1	5.3	0	0
Total	123	21	17.1	10	8.1	5	4.1	6	4.9	11	8.9	6	4.9	5	4.1	2	1.6

Note: BNt = basal notch; WNtF = width of notch to flute; IVM = inverted "V"; WIVF = width of inverted "V" in flute; FNiE = fluting nipples; WNiF = width of nipple in flute; BMB = beveled margin; WBMF = width of beveled margin.

edge retouch appears to have been practiced at the Dietz site as a margin finishing technique. Despite this, the Dietz assemblage also retained the largest sample of platform isolation scars. This would seem contradictory except that the number of platform isolation scars remains small ($n = 5$).

Flute scar relationships refers to the long-section orientation of flute scars on opposing point faces of a point in relation to each other. Whether the flute scars are aligned to the same longitudinal plane or not can inform upon the original relationship of the opposing preform surfaces prior to fluting. Channel scars can only follow the pre-fluting surfaces. In the case of many Folsom points, flute scars run parallel to each other because the preform surfaces they followed are also parallel. For most Far West fluted points, the flute scars and the preceding preform surfaces diverged further apart in the distal direction.

Among the four samples, flute scar relationships are similar as indicated by the range of 73.7% to 92.3% for flute scars diverging further apart as they move towards the distal end (Table 9.4). This attribute resulted from Far West fluted point preforms being thicker at the distal end, while Folsom preforms usually have the same thickness from one end to the other (Michael Rondeau, personal observation). The SWL point sample did not show a Folsom-like trend of flute scar parallelism.

Morphological Comparisons

Two attributes are used to describe morphologic differences among the bases of points in the four collections. These attributes include the basal relationship of the lateral margins (Table 9.5) and the shape of the basal cross section (Table 9.6).

The lateral margins examined here do not include incurvate edges sometimes referred to as a fish tail configuration (Table 9.5). That form is not present in these clusters and is largely indicative of fluted point forms further east in North America (J. Morrow and T. Morrow 1999). Those with lateral margins converging towards the distal end are thought

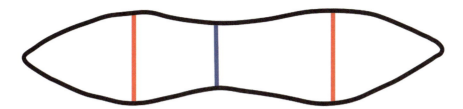

FIGURE 9.2. Bi-concave basal cross section.

TABLE 9.2. Flute Scar Configurations.

Cluster	Total	Single		Double Flute		Triple Flute		Multi-Flute	
		N	%	N	%	N	%	N	%
Dietz site	56	41	73.2	10	17.9	1	1.8	4	7.1
Milford Flat Locality	31	28	90.3	3	9.7	0	0	0	0
Lake Tonopah/Mud Lake	38	28	73.7	5	13.2	1	2.6	4	10.5
Sunshine Well Locality	19	10	52.6	0	0	0	0	9	47.4
Total	144	107	74.3	18	13	2	1.4	17	11.8

TABLE 9.3. Other Basal Scars Associated with Flutes.

Cluster	Total	ET		GS		RRS		PIS		BER	
		N	%	N	%	N	%	N	%	N	%
Dietz site	56	23	41.1	25	44.6	23	41.1	5	8.9	21	37.5
Milford Flat Locality	31	13	41.9	8	25.8	11	35.4	2	6.5	4	12.9
Lake Tonopah/Mud Lake	38	8	21.1	5	13.2	8	21.1	0	0	2	5.3
Sunshine Well Locality	19	5	26.3	2	10.5	4	21.1	1	5.3	3	15.8
Total	144	49	34	40	27.8	46	32.9	8	5.6	30	20.8

Note: ET = end thinning; GS = guide scars; RRS = ridge removal scars; PIS = platform isolation scars; BER = basal edge retouch.

TABLE 9.4. Flute Scar Relationships.

Cluster	Total	Diverge		Converge		Parallel		Mixed	
		N	%	N	%	N	%	N	%
Dietz site	38	28	73.7	1	2.6	4	10.5	5	13.2
Milford Flat Locality	26	22	84.6	0	0	0	0	4	15.4
Lake Tonopah/Mud Lake	26	24	92.3	0	0	0	0	2	7.7
Sunshine Well Locality	11	10	91	0	0	1	9.1	0	0
Total	101	84	83.3	1	0.9	5	4.9	11	10.9

TABLE 9.5. Base Lateral Margin Relationships.

Cluster	Total	Distal N	Distal %	LMC N	LMC %	Parallel N	Parallel %	LME N	LME %	LMI N	LMI %	LMM N	LMM %
Dietz site	13	7	53.8	0	0	3	23.1	1	7.7	2	15.4	0	0
Milford Flat Locality	20	10	50.0	2	10	6	30	2	10	0	0	0	0
Lake Tonopah/Mud Lake	21	17	81	1	4.8	10	47.6	2	9.5	1	4.8	0	0
Sunshine Well Locality	17	14	82.4	0	0	1	5.9	2	11.8	0	0	0	0
Total	71	48	67.6	3	4.2	20	28.2	7	9.9	3	4.2	0	0

Note: LMC = lateral margin convergence; LME = lateral margin excurvate; LMI = lateral margin irregular; LMM = lateral margin mixed.

TABLE 9.6. Basal Cross Sections.

Cluster	Total	Bi-convex N	Bi-convex %	Lenticular N	Lenticular %	CVC N	CVC %	PCX N	PCX %	PCV N	PCV %	Irregular N	Irregular %
Dietz site	37	34	91.9	1	2.7	0	0	1	2.7	0	0	1	2.7
Milford Flat Locality	31	27	87.1	1	3.2	2	6.5	0	0	0	0	1	3.2
Lake Tonopah/Mud Lake	36	28	77.8	0	0	3	8.3	3	8.3	1	2.8	1	2.8
Sunshine Well Locality	19	14	73.7	0	0	2	10.5	0	0	0	0	3	15.8
Total	123	103	83.7	2	1.6	7	5.7	4	3.3	1	0.8	6	4.9

Note: CVC = concave-convex; PCX = plano-convex; PCV = plano-concave.

not to have their original bases, but rather to have resulted from the rebasing of longer blade fragments.

Fluted points showing a divergence of lateral margins in the distal direction ranged between 50% and 60% for three clusters. Here SWL is the exception with a more substantial diverging margin trend (82%). Moreover, the T/M exhibited a frequency of parallel-sided bases (32.3%) that is more like MFL (30%) and Dietz (23.2%). The higher percentage of diverging margins in the SWL sample coincides with its near lack of parallel margins.

A look at the general morphology of basal cross sections (Table 9.6) sought to confirm the idea that fluted points from all four clusters would mainly exhibit bi-concave basal cross sections (Figure 9.2) regardless of the fluting method employed. "Fluting method," as used here, refers to the entire suite of flaking techniques used to create basal grooves running vertically on point faces (Tables 9.1 and 9.2). We expected the basal cross sections to mainly exhibit a bi-concave shape.

Three fluting techniques may be defined by the forms of their fluting platforms. These include the use of an inset nipple, a larger and usually not-inset nob, or a beveled edge as the fluting platform. A fourth is the pressure based multi-flute technique (Figure 9.1). Further, pressure flaking of pre-fluting guide scars and post-fluting ridge removal scars also contributed to the central concavities of some basal cross sections. Neither pressure

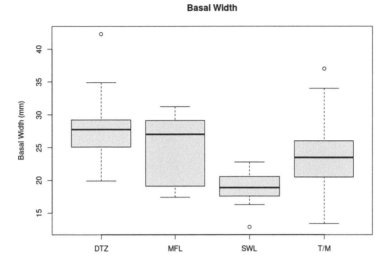

FIGURE 9.3. Basal width comparisons: DTZ = Dietz site; MFL = Milford Flat Locality; SWL = Sunshine Well Locality; TML = Lake Tonopah/Mud Lake Locality.

end thinning of the bases nor pressure edge retouch to shape concave proximal margins contributed to the formation of the grooves.

Table 9.6 shows the dominance of the biconcave cross-section type among the clusters with a range of 73.7% to 91.9% regardless of fluting technique. All other cross-section forms only occur in minor frequencies. The production of these grooves apparently adheres to an established mental template designed for functionality. Such likely functions include a more secure haft by placing the shaft within the groove and helping to control the location of basal breakage (sensu Thomas et al. 2017).

Size Comparisons

Basal point segments from both fragmentary and complete specimens provide the most reliable and largest datasets from which to draw comparisons. Here we look at basal measurements of terminal basal width, concave basal depth, and a size ratio of width and depth.

Basal width provides one measure of point size. SWL point bases are clearly the narrowest, having the smallest median and interquartile range (Figure 9.3). That range does not overlap with the other clusters. The Dietz site has the largest median width and interquartile range with MFL also trending larger than either chert-based cluster, but its second quartile range subsumes all of the T/M interquartile range. T/M shows the second narrowest median width, but the greatest overall range (Figure 9.3, Table 9.7) of any cluster.

The comparison of *basal depth* measurements shows less variability than expected from casual observation (Figure 9.4, Table 9.8). Obsidian and chert clusters do not display significant differences. The interesting aspect here is the T/M cluster showing the shallowest median, shallowest first quartile range, and the shallowest segment of overall range. SWL, on the other hand, has the deepest median and range segment. The medians of the two obsidian clusters fall between the two for chert.

A basal ratio of measurements is used here to metrically characterize the form of fluted point bases (Table 9.9). This *basal index* (BI) ratio is determined by dividing the basal depth (Table 9.8) by basal width (Table 9.7). Basal depth is determined by subtracting

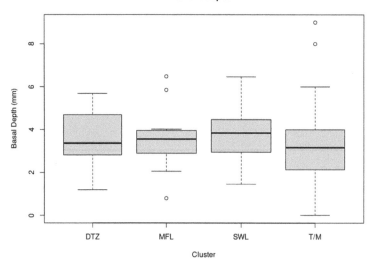

FIGURE 9.4. Basal depth comparisons: DTZ = Dietz site; MFL = Milford Flat Locality; SWL = Sunshine Well Locality; TML = Lake Tonopah/Mud Lake Locality.

TABLE 9.7. Basal Width.

Cluster	N	Mean	SD	Median	Minimum	Maximum	Range	SE
Dietz site	14	28.123	5.452	27.755	19.910	42.280	22.370	1.457
Milford Flat Locality	10	25.394	5.310	27.005	17.450	31.250	13.800	1.679
Lake Tonopah/ Mud Lake	48	23.786	5.098	23.475	13.410	37.000	23.590	0.736
Sunshine Well Locality	10	18.640	2.749	18.900	12.900	22.800	9.900	0.869

Note: SD = standard deviation; SE = standard error.

TABLE 9.8. Basal Depth.

Cluster	N	Mean	SD	Median	Minimum	Maximum	Range	SE
Dietz site	32	3.586	1.265	3.370	1.190	5.690	4.500	0.224
Milford Flat Locality	12	3.601	1.507	3.560	0.800	6.480	5.680	0.435
Lake Tonopah/ Mud Lake	53	3.491	1.699	3.170	0.010	9.000	8.990	0.233
Sunshine Well Locality	18	3.792	1.296	3.845	1.460	6.460	5.000	0.306

Note: SD = standard deviation; SE = standard error.

Geographic Variability of Far West Fluted Points

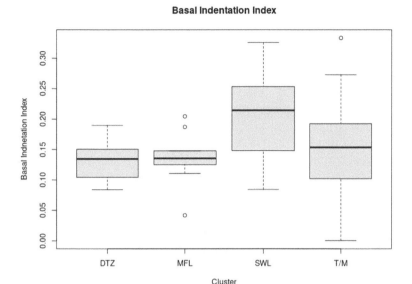

FIGURE 9.5. Basal indentation index comparisons: DTZ = Dietz site; MFL = Milford Flat Locality; SWL = Sunshine Well Locality; TML = Lake Tonopah/Mud Lake Locality.

TABLE 9.9. Basal Index (Basal Depth/Basal Width).

Cluster	N	Mean	SD	Median	Minimum	Maximum	Range	SE
Dietz site	14	0.133	0.031	0.134	0.084	0.190	0.106	0.008
Milford Flat Locality	10	0.136	0.044	0.135	0.042	0.205	0.163	0.014
Lake Tonopah/ Mud Lake	48	0.151	0.065	0.153	0.000	0.333	0.333	0.009
Sunshine Well Locality	10	0.201	0.072	0.214	0.084	0.326	0.241	0.023

Note: SD = standard deviation; SE = standard error.

the axial length from total length. This measurement should not be confused with the basal indentation ratio (BIR) which divides axial length by the total length (Thomas 1981). While BIR is a measure of basal depth relative to length, BI is a measure of basal size and morphology.

The basal index indicates that the Dietz site and MFL bases are quite similar in measurable form (Figure 9.5). SWL is again the most divergent as expected since it has already been shown to have the deepest and narrowest bases (Tables 9.7 and 9.8). SWL basal size is clearly different from the other clusters. T/M has an interquartile range that overlaps that of the other three clusters, but its median falls below the second quartile for SWL, but still above the two obsidian medians. If these differences are hypothesized to be time transgressive, this straddling of ranges of the other three clusters by the T/M points might suggest a transition from the two larger-sized obsidian clusters towards the SWL specimens. Alternatively, the T/M collection may represent a mix of several fluted point variants of differing size.

Evaluation of Basal Flaking Characteristics

We note several apparent differences in fluting techniques between the two chert and two obsidian clusters (Table 9.1). The two chert groups have over two-thirds of their fluted points showing or suggesting basal notches, remnant fluting nipples, or inverted "V" basal margins. Less than one-third of the points in the two obsidian clusters have these attributes. These differences could suggest an age, toolstone flaking characteristics, or preform size influence on fluting techniques.

A temporal influence on the choice of fluting technique might be somewhat analogous to the different fluting processes between Clovis and Folsom (e.g., Bradley et al. 2010; Clark and Collins 2002). Typical differences between the toolstones include chert being more resistant to flaking and retaining greater tensile strength, while obsidian flakes with greater ease but is more brittle. Such differences can influence the form of striking platforms, how force is applied, and therefore how fluting might have been accomplished.

Concerning size, a smaller initial package for the chert is suggested, leading to smaller flake blanks and subsequent preforms that restricted the available flaking techniques that could be applied. In contrast, the basal flaking of obsidian points are not as restricted by preform size. Greater size allowed for more potential fluting techniques beyond pressure such as force application by either direct or indirect percussion and differing platform configurations.

In general, the fluting evidence (Table 9.2) showed that individual fluted point faces commonly showed only a single flute scar (73.3%). However, the two chert clusters diverge here, with single flute scar faces in the T/M collection at 73.7%, which is similar to the Dietz site (73.2%), while SWL has fewer at 52.6%. Further, the rest of the SWL specimens (47.4%) show a different approach to manufacturing hafting grooves with the multi-flute approach. This scar form is the second most common in the T/M cluster (10.5%), but all of these numbers are very small. Nonetheless, a notable difference in fluting techniques, at least for the SWL cluster, is suggested.

A final look at basal flaking characteristics compared other flake scar types associated with fluting (Table 9.3). Again, there seems to be a split in similarities between the two obsidian and two chert clusters. Higher frequencies of basal end thinning, guide scars, and ridge removal scars are generally present in the obsidian clusters. A greater need for additional basal flaking before and after fluting may simply be due to the larger size of the obsidian specimens. In the case of the SWL cluster, the notable presence of an alternative fluting technique may have reduced the need for additional forms of pressure flaking. Regardless, a difference is apparent in the basal treatments between the obsidian and chert clusters.

A final look at flute scar forms (Table 9.4) sought to compare evidence of preform variations that might also signal fluting differences. However, 83.3% of the specimens showed an increasing point width between the flute scars on opposite faces as they diverge towards distal. This divergence means that the point thickness between the flutes increases towards the distal tip. While the two chert clusters showed the greatest percentages in this diverging category, the limited numbers do not suggest a significant difference from the obsidian collections. Parallel flute scars have a very limited to nonexistent presence among the clusters, unlike a sample of Folsom points ($n = 234$) where nearly all (98.7%) showed flute scar parallelism (Rondeau 2016).

Evaluation of Morphological Characteristics

Table 9.5 presents a tabulation of lateral margin forms for fluted point bases. Again, the T/M cluster is more like the two obsidian clusters in which half or slightly more of the specimens have lateral margins that diverge in the distal direction. In contrast, more than 82.4% of the SWL cluster points exhibit diverging margins. Likewise, the three other clusters have nearly a quarter to almost a third of their specimens showing parallel lateral margins. Only one specimen from the SWL sample has parallel margins. Such parallel edges do occur on Folsom points, but more SWL specimens diverge to distal (e.g., Rondeau 2016:Figures 15, 16).

Sample size may play some role in the comparative differences among the clusters. This time, the Dietz site cluster, for example, is quite small ($n = 13$) due to a lack of specimens with two sufficiently intact lateral margins. These missing or minimally surviving edge remnants are one of the results of the "broken up" nature of numerous Dietz site specimens, a unique characteristic itself among fluted point clusters in the Far West. The condition of this collection resulted largely from reusing fragments as practice pieces by novice flintknappers and several possibly used as wedges (Fagan 1988). A few may have also been reused as cores to produce smaller flake tools.

Table 9.6 reports on basal cross sections in a search for additional evidence of differing basal treatments among the clusters. Notable differences are not found due to the dominance of the bi-concave cross section in all clusters. However, the efficacy of the multi-flute technique as an alternative approach to creating hafting grooves is supported.

Evaluation of Size Characteristics

Fluted points in the two obsidian clusters have wider bases (Table 9.7, Figure 9.3). The SWL cluster is clearly different in having the smallest basal widths. Again, the SWL points retain a unique characteristic among the clusters.

The considerable overlap between the MFL and T/M clusters raise a different consideration. T/M also has the second narrowest basal width median and the greatest overall width range of any cluster (Figure 9.3). Given these width characteristics, especially having the greatest variability in size, it raises the question of whether a mix of more than one fluted point variant could be included in this cluster.

Basal depth (Table 9.8) shows a relative consistency among three clusters with the T/M displaying a significant divergence towards the shallow end of the scale (Figure 9.4). Two possibilities may be entertained regarding the T/M cluster. First, do the shallower bases suggest a more Clovis-like fluted point form? Further analysis of these shallow specimens needs to consider if other attributes may also distinguish them as more Clovis-like and different from fluted points in the other clusters. Second, because two separate drainage basins are subsumed in this cluster, a reevaluation of basal depth by basin may be warranted. Might one basin be more in line with the rest of the clusters and the other trending towards shallower bases? If so, the fluted point set with shallower bases might be expected to show other divergent attributes.

Finally, the BI (Table 9.9) shows that the relationship between depth and width varies across space, and while it is tempting to suggest that this difference is also temporal, that has not been documented. The SWL points have smaller bases with proportionately deeper indentations. The actual cause for these smaller points has not been determined, although a smaller initial size of available toolstone is suspected. T/M has the greatest basal size variability, but its mean is closer to the Dietz site and MFL than the SWL cluster, despite the fact that its range overlaps with all three. Multiple factors may have contributed to the T/M BI range.

Evaluation of Efficacy

In the search for characteristics defining fluted point variants, we review the utility of the studied attributes. Three result categories are indicated by the data. These are (1) those attributes that signal that SWL points are a distinctive fluted point variant, (2) those that argue for differences between the obsidian and chert fluted points, and (3) those that did not prove useful in this exploratory study.

Nearly half (47.4%) of the SWL fluted points exhibit a multi-flute configuration (Table 9.2). The multi-flute scar configuration might be a starting point for assigning other specimens to an SWL variant, but this scar configuration is not limited to the SWL cluster. Additional characteristics are needed to convincingly argue for a "Sunshine Well" type and the assignment of points from elsewhere to that type.

Table 9.5 argues that such points should also have bases with divergent lateral edges. Only one specimen did not, but the other three clusters show that half or slightly more of their specimens have this same margin divergence. Therefore, this attribute, by itself, is also insufficient to attribute a specimen to the Sunshine Well variant.

The basal widths of the SWL points are notably narrower (Table 9.7) and, in conjunction with the proportionately deepest basal depths (Table 9.8), produce a significantly higher BI ratio (Table 9.9) than the other clusters. Thus, additional fluted specimens elsewhere in the Great Basin that show the multi-flute on at least one side may also be expected to have lateral margins diverging to distal, a commensurately small basal width, and high BI. If so, a Sunshine Well variant might be suggested. The presence of a fluting nipple remnant (Table 9.1) might lend further support to such a placement except that they are expected to be numerically rare.

However, such specimens would only be a variant, not a type as some SWL points lack multi-flutes. Because 52.6% of the SWL fluted faces show only a typical single flute scar (Table 9.2), only the multi-flute version of the Sunshine Well fluted point type would be provisionally defined by the attributes listed above. A fully robust Sunshine Well type description has not been established here. Further testing is needed to determine if these diagnostic attributes, minus the multi-flute configuration, are sufficient to confidently address the full variability of a potential Sunshine Well point type.

The second data trend is separations between the obsidian and chert clusters. The obsidian clusters consistently show more non-fluting scar forms (e.g., guide, ridge removal, end thinning, and platform isolation) than the chert clusters. This difference appears to suggest that a more complex set of basal flaking behaviors addressed the manufacture of obsidian fluted points. However, the smaller size of chert bases may have worked against the survival of pre-fluting guide and platform isolation scars, especially if the scars are commensurately smaller than on the obsidian points.

However, specimens with basal notches cluster in the two chert units, while the inverted V basal form is found in the obsidian clusters (Table 9.1). The two attributes are thought to be sequentially related with the inverted V form resulting from the flaking away of the notch. This finding suggests some difference in the finishing of basal margins, but whether it is due to differences in toolstone, preform size, or an intentional difference in proximal margin treatment remains to be determined.

The percentages of bi-concave cross sections (Table 9.6) and basal width percentages find the chert clusters on one end of the spectrum and the obsidian on the other. Table 9.9 shows the BI for the obsidian clusters has similar central tendencies while the BI for the chert pair has a greater range of ratios. The smallness of the chert bases argues for an overall smaller size of the points relative to the obsidian specimens. Leading hypotheses to explain the size differences are (1) the presence of a later, smaller fluted variant, or (2) the available chert is generally in smaller initial package size than the obsidian.

Finally, attributes of questionable utility are also noted. Increasing inter-flute thickness in the distal direction is so common in the sample (Table 9.4) that it did not usefully discriminate between the four clusters. Basal depth differences are not sufficiently pronounced by themselves to distinguish one cluster from another (Table 9.9) and could not be counted on, especially with isolated specimens, to suggest a fluted point variant.

Fluted Point Clusters in the Far West

This preliminary study found that more work is needed to evaluate the comparability of the clusters as analytical units. How much of the variability portrayed above might be a function of differences in the geographic clusters rather than the points themselves? Clearly some variability is due to differences in the points studied. Candidate causes of inter-cluster point variability may have resulted from prehistoric circumstances such as toolstone quality including initial nodule size, toolstone availability within seasonal movements potentially affecting curation and repair rates as well as available hafting materials, temporal drift among clusters, and mixing of temporal variants within clusters.

Other differences in these analytical units, such as collection methods and their geographic extent, need to be evaluated as part of follow-up studies to this exploratory effort. The T/M cluster is used below as an example of selected issues of cluster comparability.

While the similarity between T/M and SWL is noted above in comparing the chert clusters and obsidian clusters, some specific elements of T/M fluted points align more with the obsidian clusters than SWL. The T/M chert cluster has a similar percentage of single flute faces to the Dietz site (Table 9.2). T/M also shows the highest percentage of parallel-sided bases. This attribute is most like MFL rather than the Dietz site. Its percentage of lateral margins diverging distally is also similar to the two obsidian clusters rather than SWL (Table 9.5).

For basal width (Table 9.7), T/M has the greatest range of any cluster and has considerable overlap with MFL even though it has the second narrowest median after SWL. T/M diverges with the shallowest basal depth median, while the other three clusters are somewhat like each other (Table 9.9). The T/M BI mean is more like the Dietz site and MFL rather than SWL, and shows the greatest size variability of the four clusters (Table 9.9).

In various ways the T/M cluster seems to straddle differences between SWL and the obsidian clusters. Do the T/M results suggest a mixing of several fluted point variants? One test for this possibility would be a reanalysis treating the Lake Tonopah and Mud Lake basins as two separate clusters. If both still show the distributed results of the combined cluster, the question of variant mixing may not be answered one way or the other. However, if both show narrower distributions for selected attributes, then spatial variants might be suggested. Such an expectation could allow predictions, one of which would be finding that one chert cluster is more like the obsidian clusters. Given the T/M results, one cluster might be more like SWL points, but would still show differences such as the lack of multi-flutes.

The leading question at this point is not to ask why these different clusters vary as they do, but why there is so much overlap in characteristics. Does this suggest a single point type that varies due to local circumstances? Before more complex answers may be proposed, the differences in such basic influences as initial package size of available toolstone and point curation/repair rates need to be adequately addressed for their influence on fluted point variability.

Additionally, the analyses and findings detailed above only consider the variability of selected fluted point collections from the Far West and do not involve a comparative study of Clovis points from other areas. At this time there is simply no Clovis database comparable to that of the Far West CalFLUTED study. A detailing of the variability of more eastern Clovis points in size, form, and technology (e.g., basal flaking strategies), as well as their indicated causes, is needed to avoid creating a false dichotomy between one dataset that, by construction, shows the extent of variability and others that are more normalized by design.

What this study does suggest is that it is premature to argue that fluted points in the Far West are significantly different from Clovis point variability elsewhere in size, form, and technology. It is argued here that no studies thus far have sufficiently demonstrated that Far West fluted point variability is significantly different from the range of Clovis points elsewhere. Therefore, it can be hypothesized that an adequate review of Clovis variability will show not just that Far West fluted points are Clovis, but that Clovis variability indicates a projectile point series rather than a single type.

Conclusion

This preliminary exploration of variability for Far West fluted points found expected and unexpected differences and similarities among the four clusters. Future comparative analysis of such clusters is needed to refine our understanding of the nature and extent of Far Western fluted point variability. As an example, the fluted point component of the Borax Lake collection (Harrington 1948) has been likened to that of the Dietz site (Fagan 1988:391). An actual comparison could provide informative similarities and contrasts. The preliminary nature of the foregoing study has left other Far West clusters, their potential subregional fluted point trends, and additional point attributes unexplored.

In a similar vein, the highly variable forms of Western Stemmed Tradition (WST) points have not been characterized on the level produced by this study. Much received wisdom regarding the differences between the two point traditions, fluted and stemmed, has yet to be tested in the Far West. An example is illustrated below by a series of questions asking for detailed data that can support observation-based conclusions.

How often are WST basal elements, the stems, generally narrower and proportionally thicker than fluted points? In what ways and to what extent is WST flaking technology different from Western fluted points (e.g., Beck and Jones 2010)? Specifically, are Windust (see Rosencrance et al., Chapter 2) stems broader relative to thickness than other Far Western WST types? Are their basal-width-to-thickness ratios more in line with fluted points? Does this attribute suggest that their hafting technology is more like that for fluted points than narrower WST points (e.g., Musil 1988)? Appearances can be deceiving (Musil 2004), but metrical data to answer these questions has yet to be compiled and analyzed.

Some Windust points have square basal corners unlike most Far Western WST convex bases (Amick 2013; Hartman 2019). Finally, the basal thinning of the proximal margins of some of these square bases from the general Dietz subregion are much like pressure flake scar sequences on some fluted points in this study. Does this aspect suggest technological convergence? This seeming difference may be explained by the interpretation that Windust points are a westward extension of the Cody complex (Amick 2013). A recent comparative analysis of Cody and Windust points supports the likelihood that Windust specimens have a Cody origin (Hartman 2019). However, the later age of Cody and Windust points (Hartman 2019; Knell 2007; Rosencrance et al., Chapter 2) precludes a temporal connection to fluted points.

The WST concept is sometimes used as a broad catchall. Detailed scrutiny of its types is needed to refine perceptions of this tradition. The means are available, and we argue that it is time for a greater examination of both fluted and WST point trends and variability in the Far West. A comparative analysis between the two point traditions might then be pursued with more clarity.

10

The Ages of Stemmed and Fluted Points in the Great Plains and Rocky Mountains

Todd A. Surovell

In this chapter, I review evidence for the absolute and relative ages of fluted and stemmed points in the western Great Plains and Rocky Mountains (GPRM) to provide context for areas to the west. At the outset, I note that little of what I have to contribute is new, as the basic facts of culture history are well-known and have been since before my career began (e.g., Bryan 1988; Frison 1978; Irwin 1968; Irwin-Williams et al. 1973). If I have anything new to contribute to the focus of this volume, it is to update and summarize the radiocarbon and stratigraphic evidence from the study area including new data and improved radiocarbon calibration (Reimer et al. 2020). As is usually the case with sampling, new and larger samples of dates and sites—with few and maybe no exceptions—have reinforced what we already knew.

In the Far West, questions of the relative and absolute ages of stemmed and fluted points remain a matter of much debate and speculation (Beck and Jones 1997, 2010; Brown et al. 2019; Davis et al. 2019; Goebel and Keene 2014; Jenkins et al. 2012; McDonough et al., Chapter 1; Rosencrance 2019; Rosencrance et al., Chapter 2; G. Smith, Felling, Wriston, et al. 2015; Smith and Barker 2017). In the GPRM, however, there is little debate—stemmed points are younger than fluted points (cf., Waters et al. 2018; Williams et al. 2018). To demonstrate that conclusion, I begin with some historical context by briefly recounting a similar but resolved problem in the culture history of the GPRM. I then summarize what we know about the ages of fluted and stemmed points in the study area with a simple analysis of the radiocarbon and stratigraphic evidence for the ages of fluted and stemmed point complexes. Finally, I discuss what those conclusions might mean for the culture history of the Far West. My study area includes a region spanning more than 2.4 million km², stretching from Alberta to Texas (Figure 10.1).

The Yuma Problem

From the late 1930s through the 1950s, Plains archaeologists were enmeshed in a similar problem to the one that inspired this volume, the so-called "Yuma Problem." The Yuma type, much like "Western Stemmed," was a catch-all category that included a wide variety of Paleoindian point forms (Fischel 1939; Howard 1939, 1943; Roberts 1937; Sellet 2011; Wormington 1939, 1948), including a series of unfluted projectile point varieties (e.g., Agate Basin, Eden, Scottsbluff, Alberta, and Jimmy Allen), some stemmed and some not, that were first recognized in the Andersen family collection in Yuma County in northeastern Colorado (see Wormington 1948). A few quotations from the first edition of Wormington's (1939) *Ancient Man in North America* succinctly summarize the state of knowledge a decade after the Folsom excavations:

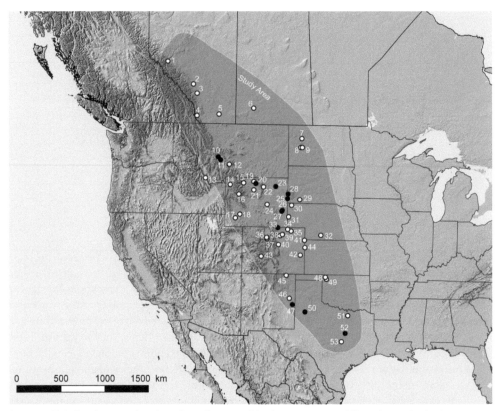

FIGURE 10.1. Study area showing sites discussed in the text or providing chronological data (white dots show sites where only radiocarbon data are available, and black dots are those where stemmed and fluted points are stratigraphically superimposed): (*1*) Swan Landing; (*2*) EkPu-8; (*3*) EgPn-480; (*4*) DjPm-16; (*5*) Fletcher; (*6*) Heron Eden; (*7*) Beacon Island; (*8*) Bobtail Wolf; (*9*) Benz; (*10*) MacHaffie; (*11*) Indian Creek; (*12*) Anzick; (*13*) Mammoth Meadow; (*14*) Osprey Beach; (*15*) Horner; (*16*) Helen Lookingbill; (*17*) Blue Point; (*18*) Finley; (*19*) Hanson; (*20*) Two Moon Shelter; (*21*) Colby; (*22*) Sister's Hill; (*23*) Carter/Kerr-McGee; (*24*) Casper; (*25*) Agate Basin; (*26*) Hell Gap; (*27*) Powars II; (*28*) Jim Pitts; (*29*) Lange/Ferguson; (*30*) Hudson-Meng; (*31*) Scottsbluff; (*32*) Allen; (*33*) Lindenmeier; (*34*) Nelson; (*35*) Frasca; (*36*) Jerry Craig; (*37*) Barger Gulch, Locality B; (*38*) Dent; (*39*) Frazier and Jurgens; (*40*) Lamb Spring; (*41*) Jones-Miller; (*42*) Olsen-Chubbuck; (*43*) Mountaineer; (*44*) Kanorado; (*45*) Folsom; (*46*) San Jon; (*47*) Blackwater Draw, Locality I; (*48*) Waugh; (*49*) Cooper, Badger Hole, and Jake Bluff; (*50*) Lubbock Lake; (*51*) Aubrey; (*52*) Horn Shelter; (*53*) Gault and Debra L. Friedkin.

Owing to the frequent discovery under the same conditions of Folsom and points of another type, to which the name Yuma has been applied, and because of certain typological similarities between them, they have often been linked.... Yumas are often found associated with Folsoms on the surface. At the type locality, Yuma County, Colorado, the two are consistently found together in blowouts.... As to the relationship between Folsoms and Yumas, there is little agreement [Wormington, 1939: 22, 28, 31].

One could easily substitute a few words in those quotations to describe our understanding of the temporal relationship between fluted and stemmed points in the Far West today (Beck and Jones 1997, 2009; G. Smith, Felling, Wriston, et al. 2015; Tuohy 1974; Willig 1988). Fluted and stemmed points, for example, are sometimes found close to one another on the surface in the Great Basin in similar contexts, and as to their relationship, there is little agreement (McDonough et al., Chapter 1). Interestingly, while some Great Basin archaeologists emphasize technological differences between stemmed and fluted points (Beck and Jones 2010; Bryan 1991; Campbell 1949; Davis et al. 2012; Erlandson and Braje 2015), Wormington and other early GPRM archaeologists saw them as fundamentally similar. After all, unlike the vast majority of later projectile points, fluted and stemmed points share a few important attributes. They tend to be large, well-made, basally ground, and not notched.

If it is any solace to Far Western archaeologists, the Yuma problem is nothing more than a curious footnote in the history of Plains archaeology because it is no longer a problem. Prophetically, Marie Wormington wrote in 1939 that current evidence suggested that Folsom and Yuma points were "roughly contemporaneous. Beyond that it is impossible to go…" (Wormington 1939:32). She went on: "until clear stratigraphical [sic] evidence is available it will probably be impossible to come to any definite conclusions as to their relationship." Writing after the Great Depression and before World War II, Wormington probably could not have predicted the radiocarbon revolution that would soon follow. However, while radiocarbon dating provided some evidence regarding the relative ages of stemmed and fluted points in the GPRM, stratigraphic superposition was what unambiguously solved the Yuma problem. I turn to those lines of evidence now.

The Ages of Stemmed and Fluted Points in the GPRM

Although many stemmed projectile point types are recognized in the Great Plains (Frison 1998; Hofman and Graham 1998; Kooyman 2000; Kornfeld et al. 2010), I only discuss those from the Middle Paleoindian period (sensu Kornfeld et al. 2010): Agate Basin, Hell Gap, and the Cody complex. I am particularly concerned with Middle Paleoindian varieties because my focus is on the relative ages of fluted and stemmed points as well as the date of the transition from one to the other. Regarding fluted points, two varieties, Clovis and Folsom, are recognized to be in the study area. Although these types display some morphological overlap, they are, in my opinion, generally distinctive. I am intentionally omitting GPRM basally indented unfluted varieties—like Goshen, Plainview, and Midland (Haynes and Hill 2017; Holliday et al. 2017)—from all analyses herein because they are neither fluted nor stemmed.

To answer the question of age, I present data from two dating methods, radiocarbon and stratigraphic superposition. While radiocarbon is the prevailing geochronological method of most North American archaeology, this technique brings inevitable noise to questions of chronology, particularly when sample sizes are small. Achieving sub-century precision in radiocarbon dating remains challenging, particularly in the Pleistocene due to measurement error, association and context issues, reservoir effects, old wood, contamination, vertical mixing, and other problems, often in combination. In that light, stratigraphy, though old-fashioned, probably remains the best dating method we have for answering questions of the type "Is A older than B?" or "Are A and B the same age?" In the GPRM, unlike the Far West, stratigraphic data on the question at hand are not in short supply.

Beginning with the radiocarbon record, I turned to four scholarly works whose authors had already done the difficult task of filtering out problematic dates and isolating those they considered reliable. For Clovis, I used the Great Plains radiocarbon dates compiled by Waters and Stafford (2007a). Folsom dates came from my recent compilation (Surovell, Boyd, et al. 2016). Dates for the Agate Basin and Hell Gap complexes were taken from an unpublished Paleoindian context written for the Wyoming State Historic Preservation Office (Grund 2020). Cody complex

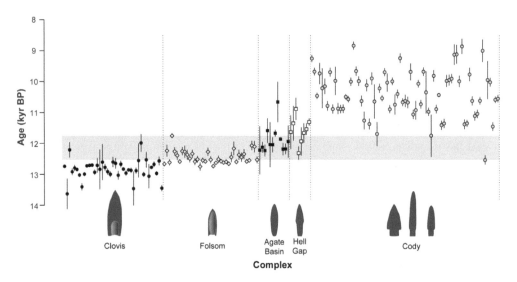

FIGURE 10.2. Calibrated continuous 1-sigma radiocarbon dates from fluted (Clovis and Folsom) and stemmed (Agate Basin, Hell Gap, and Cody) point components from the GPRM. Gray rectangle shows period of overlap defined by the youngest fluted and oldest stemmed mean calibrated ages.

dates were taken from a recent compilation by Knell and Muñiz (2013). In sum, this dataset includes 169 ^{14}C dates from 68 archaeological components (Table 10.1). There are 76 dates on fluted point components and 93 from stemmed point contexts. All dates were calibrated using the Bchron package version 4.7.3 (Haslett and Parnell 2008) for R version 4.0.3 (R Core Team 2020) using the IntCal20 calibration curve (Reimer et al. 2020). For ease of date averaging, I used continuous calibrated age ranges so that each calibrated age is reduced to only a mean age with a continuous 1-sigma error value.

It is clear from the radiocarbon database that fluted points are generally older than stemmed points (Figure 10.2). The total range of mean calibrated ages on fluted points spans the period from 13,632 to 11,759 cal BP. Dates from stemmed components range from 12,539 to 8842 cal BP. Notably, the youngest date on a fluted point component is from the Agate Basin Area 2 Folsom component (11,759 ± 70 cal BP, UCIAMS-122571) where the Folsom (fluted) component is stratigraphically beneath an Agate Basin (stemmed) component (Frison and Stanford 1982). The oldest date on a stemmed point component is from the Cody (stemmed) component of Hell Gap Locality I (12,539 ± 143 cal BP, AA-20545) where it is stratigraphically above the Folsom (fluted) component (Irwin-Williams et al. 1973; Larson et al. 2009). Taken at face value, this analysis suggests 709 years of overlap between fluted and stemmed points in the study area. In reality, however, the overlap was much smaller, and it is extremely unlikely that there was any overlap at all temporally between the Folsom and Cody complexes. The appearance of overlap is due to dating errors. The oldest stemmed points in the GPRM are those of the Agate Basin complex.

A simple way to reduce error is to average multiple radiocarbon dates from sites or components (Table 10.2). Averaging is best justified when dates are from single features or stratigraphically distinct components. To average dates, after calibration, I used the Long and Rippeteau (1974) method. When this dataset is reduced by averaging, a total of 23 well-dated fluted point components in the Plains and Rocky Mountains are identified

TABLE 10.1. Radiocarbon Dates from Plains and Rocky Mountain Fluted (Clovis and Folsom) and Stemmed (Agate Basin, Hell Gap, and Cody) Archaeological Components.

Complex	Components	Lab No.	Age±σ (^{14}C BP)	Cal. Age±σ (BP)
Clovis	Lange/Ferguson, SD	UCIAMS-11345	11,140±140	13,033±134
Clovis	Lange/Ferguson, SD	UCIAMS-11344	10,710±130	12,650±165
Clovis	Lange/Ferguson, SD	AA-905	11,110±40	13,024±57
Clovis	Anzick, MT	AA-2978	10,240±120	11,991±281
Clovis	Anzick, MT	AA-2979	10,820±100	12,796±91
Clovis	Anzick, MT	AA-2980	10,710±100	12,673±102
Clovis	Anzick, MT	AA-2981	10,940±90	12,886±93
Clovis	Anzick, MT	AA-2982	10,370±130	12,210±244
Clovis	Anzick, MT	CAMS-80538	10,705±35	12,712±21
Clovis	Anzick, MT	Beta-163832	11,040±60	12,964±76
Clovis	Anzick, MT	Beta-168967	11,040±40	12,973±65
Clovis	Dent, CO	I-622	10,980±90	12,915±94
Clovis	Dent, CO	AA-2941	10,660±170	12,534±246
Clovis	Dent, CO	AA-2942	10,800±110	12,778±105
Clovis	Dent, CO	AA-2943	10,600±90	12,572±135
Clovis	Dent, CO	AA-2945	10,710±90	12,679±83
Clovis	Dent, CO	AA-2946	10,670±120	12,606±159
Clovis	Dent, CO	AA-2947	11,065±35	12,995±57
Clovis	Dent, CO	UCIAMS-11339	10,940±30	12,833±45
Clovis	Dent, CO	UCIAMS-11340	11,480±450	13,462±543
Clovis	Domebo, OK	AA-825	10,860±450	12,608±570
Clovis	Domebo, OK	AA-811	10,810±420	12,559±540
Clovis	Domebo, OK	AA-805	10,960±30	12,859±52
Clovis	Colby, WY	UCIAMS-11342	10,790±30	12,742±11
Clovis	Colby, WY	UCIAMS-11343	10,950±30	12,845±49
Clovis	Jake Bluff, OK	CAMS-79940	10,750±40	12,729±16
Clovis	Jake Bluff, OK	CAMS-90968	10,840±45	12,777±34
Clovis	Jake Bluff, OK	CAMS-90969	10,700±45	12,703±33
Clovis	Indian Creek, MT	Beta-4619	10,980±110	12,918±101
Clovis	Lubbock Lake, TX	SMU-548	11,100±60	13,005±70
Clovis	Lubbock Lake, TX	SMU-263	11,100±80	12,999±85
Clovis	Kanorado, KS	CAMS-112741	10,950±60	12,874±80
Clovis	Kanorado, KS	CAMS-112742	11,005±50	12,934±78
Clovis	Blackwater Draw, NM	A-481	11,170±360	13,063±381
Clovis	Blackwater Draw, NM	A-490	11,040±500	12,841±634
Clovis	Blackwater Draw, NM	A-491	11,630±40	13,632±490

TABLE 10.1. (cont'd.) Radiocarbon Dates from Plains and Rocky Mountain.

Complex	Components	Lab No.	Age±σ (^{14}C BP)	Cal. Age±σ (BP)
Clovis	Blackwater Draw, NM	SMU-1880	10,780±180	12,714±229
Clovis	Aubrey, TX	AA-5271	11,540±110	13,404±108
Clovis	Aubrey, TX	AA-5274	11,590±90	13,449±94
Folsom	Agate Basin, WY	UCIAMS-122570	10,430±25	12,341±125
Folsom	Agate Basin, WY	UCIAMS-122571	10,135±25	11,759±70
Folsom	Agate Basin, WY	SI-3733	10,780±120	12,753±125
Folsom	Badger Hole, OK	UCIAMS-98369	10,300±25	12,074±140
Folsom	Badger Hole, OK	PSU-5144/ UCIAMS-111184	10,395±35	12,278±126
Folsom	Badger Hole, OK	PSU-5457/ UCIAMS-122579	10,370±25	12,256±128
Folsom	Barger Gulch, Loc. B, CO	Beta-173385	10,770±70	12,739±50
Folsom	Barger Gulch, Loc. B, CO	Beta-173381	10,470±40	12,450±141
Folsom	Carter/Kerr-McGee, WY	UCIAMS-122573	10,600±25	12,633±54
Folsom	Carter/Kerr-McGee, WY	UCIAMS-122572	10,520±25	12,552±50
Folsom	Cooper Lower, OK	CAMS-94850	10,600±40	12,624±64
Folsom	Cooper Lower, OK	PSU-6077/ UCIAMS 140849	10,560±30	12,582±64
Folsom	Cooper Lower, OK	PSU-6078/ UCIAMS-140520	10,570±30	12,593±65
Folsom	Cooper Lower, OK	PSU-6079/ UCIAMS-140581	10,630±30	12,661±44
Folsom	Cooper Middle, OK	CAMS-82407	10,530±45	12,554±82
Folsom	Cooper Middle, OK	PSU-6075/ UCIAMS-140847	10,565±30	12,587±65
Folsom	Cooper Middle, OK	PSU-6076/ UCIAMS-140848	10,575±30	12,600±65
Folsom	Cooper Upper, OK	CAMS-94849	10,505±45	12,519±109
Folsom	Cooper Upper, OK	PSU-6073/ UCIAMS-140845	10,565±30	12,587±65
Folsom	Cooper Upper, OK	PSU-6074/ UCIAMS-140846	10,575±30	12,600±65
Folsom	Folsom, NM	CAMS-74656	10,450±50	12,372±157
Folsom	Folsom, NM	CAMS-74658	10,450±50	12,372±157
Folsom	Folsom, NM	CAMS-96034	10,475±30	12,497±114
Folsom	Folsom, NM	CAMS-74657	10,500±40	12,522±101
Folsom	Folsom, NM	CAMS-74659	10,520±50	12,534±105
Folsom	Folsom, NM	CAMS-74655	10,520±50	12,534±105
Folsom	Hanson, WY	AA-106384	10,626±77	12,619±92
Folsom	Hanson, WY	AA-106385	10,600±77	12,594±107

TABLE 10.1. (cont'd.) Radiocarbon Dates from Plains and Rocky Mountain.

Complex	Components	Lab No.	Age±σ (^{14}C BP)	Cal. Age±σ (BP)
Folsom	Hanson, WY	AA-106386	10,688±77	12,669±70
Folsom	Hell Gap, WY	AA-77592UF	10,490±62	12,447±160
Folsom	Mountaineer, CO	CAMS105764	10,440±50	12,349±155
Folsom	Mountaineer, CO	CAMS105765	10,295±50	12,110±172
Folsom	Mountaineer, CO	UCIAMS-11240	10,380±30	12,264±126
Folsom	Mountaineer, CO	UCIAMS-11241	10,445±25	12,396±138
Folsom	Mountaineer, CO	AA-98753	10,328±100	12,170±215
Folsom	Waugh, OK	NZA-3602	10,379±85	12,244±184
Folsom	Waugh, OK	NZA-3603	10,404±87	12,274±186
Agate Basin	Frazier, CO	CURL-11668	10,200±30	11,866±52
Agate Basin	Frazier, CO	CURL-11671	10,100±30	11,674±105
Agate Basin	Beacon Island, ND	CAMS-90966/ SR-6231	10,330±45	12,183±160
Agate Basin	Beacon Island, ND	CAMS-90967/ SR-6232	10,305±45	12,129±167
Agate Basin	Beacon Island, ND	ETH-26779	10,338±82	12,191±188
Agate Basin	Beacon Island, ND	ETH-26780	10,371±80	12,235±180
Agate Basin	Agate Basin, WY	RL-557	10,430±570	12,043±723
Agate Basin	Agate Basin, WY	M-1131	9990±225	11,590±391
Agate Basin	Agate Basin, WY	O-1252	9350±450	10,664±644
Agate Basin	Hell Gap, WY	AA-16608/ AA16108	10,260±95	12,045±236
Agate Basin	Allen, NE	TX-6594	10,600±620	12,222±773
Agate Basin	Allen, NE	TX-6595	10,270±360	11,945±511
Hell Gap	Agate Basin, WY	SI-4430	10,445±110	12,317±208
Hell Gap	Casper, WY	RL-208	10,060±170	11,668±309
Hell Gap	Casper, WY	RL-125	9830±350	11,352±555
Hell Gap	Indian Creek, MT	Beta-5118	10,010±110	11,540±183
Hell Gap	Indian Creek, MT	Beta-5119	9860±70	11,310±109
Hell Gap	Sister's Hill, WY	I-221	9560±250	10,887±351
Hell Gap	Jones-Miller, CO	SI-1989	10,020±350	11,637±541
Hell Gap	Hell Gap, WY	A-500	10,240±300	11,938±453
Cody	Benz, ND	UCR-3466	9540±50	10,893±128
Cody	Benz, ND	SMU-1271	8910±70	10,009±127
Cody	Benz, ND	SMU-1282	8700±70	9702±122
Cody	Blackwater Draw, NM	SMU-1672	8970±70	10,072±116
Cody	Blackwater Draw, NM	Y-2488	8830±60	9908±145
Cody	Blackwater Draw, NM	SMU-1671	8690±160	9773±210

TABLE 10.1. (cont'd.) Radiocarbon Dates from Plains and Rocky Mountain.

Complex	Components	Lab No.	Age±σ (^{14}C BP)	Cal. Age±σ (BP)
Cody	Blue Point, WY	Beta-133208	9540±40	10,895±123
Cody	DjPm-16, AB	AECV-746C	9600±210	10,926±295
Cody	DjPm-16, AB	BIS-17	9450±230	10,746±315
Cody	EgPn-480, AB	Beta-127235	9540±70	10,889±143
Cody	EkPu-8, AB	TO-2999	9750±80	11,112±144
Cody	Finley, WY	SMU-250	9026±118	10,127±188
Cody	Finley, WY	RL-574	8950±220	10,036±288
Cody	Fletcher, AB	CAMS-42980	9540±110	10,876±175
Cody	Fletcher, AB	TO-1097	9380±110	10,629±195
Cody	Frasca, CO	SI-4848	8910±90	9990±148
Cody	Hell Gap I, WY	AA-20545	10,560±80	12,539±143
Cody	Hell Gap I, WY	AA-28774	9410±95	10,677±181
Cody	Hell Gap I, WY	AA-27675	9120±490	10,351±675
Cody	Hell Gap V, WY	A-753C3	9050±160	10,158±241
Cody	Hell Gap V, WY	A-753A	8890±110	9956±170
Cody	Hell Gap V, WY	A-35655	8685±70	9684±114
Cody	Heron Eden, SK	S-3308	9210±110	10,404±132
Cody	Heron Eden, SK	S-3114	8930±120	9993±178
Cody	Heron Eden, SK	S-3309	8920±130	9980±188
Cody	Horner I, WY	SI-4851	9390±75	10,626±138
Cody	Horner I, WY	UCLA-697A	8750±120	9817±180
Cody	Horner I, WY	UCLA-697B	8840±140	9904±192
Cody	Horner II, WY	I-10900	10,060±220	11,700±385
Cody	Horner II, WY	SI-4851A	9875±85	11,353±142
Cody	Hudson-Meng, NE	Beta-64318	9890±90	11,381±151
Cody	Hudson-Meng, NE	Beta-64320	9920±80	11,410±140
Cody	Hudson-Meng, NE	Beta-65276	9970±60	11,452±130
Cody	Hudson-Meng, NE	Beta-65277	9900±60	11,350±108
Cody	Hudson-Meng, NE	SMU-224	9820±160	11,262±280
Cody	Hudson-Meng, NE	CAMS-10364	9630±60	10,974±128
Cody	Hudson-Meng, NE	CAMS-12841	9720±80	11,064±144
Cody	Hudson-Meng, NE	NZA-29717	9539±55	10,891±132
Cody	Jerry Craig, CO	Beta-109467	9310±50	10,498±85
Cody	Jim Pitts, SD	AA-23779	9390±65	10,621±114
Cody	Jurgens, CO	SI-3726	9070±90	10,226±143
Cody	Lamb Spring, CO	M-1463	8870±350	9981±447
Cody	Lindenmeier, CO	TO-339	9880±100	11,373±169

TABLE 10.1. (cont'd.) Radiocarbon Dates from Plains and Rocky Mountain.

Complex	Components	Lab No.	Age±σ (^{14}C BP)	Cal. Age±σ (BP)
Cody	Lindenmeier, CO	TO-341	9690±60	11,045±132
Cody	Lubbock Lake, TX	SI-4177	8655±90	9683±132
Cody	Lubbock Lake, TX	SMU-830	8210±240	9119±299
Cody	Lubbock Lake, TX	SMU-827	7980±180	8862±236
Cody	MacHaffie, MT	GX-15152	8620±200	9689±266
Cody	MacHaffie, MT	GX-15153-G	8280±120	9246±150
Cody	MacHaffie, MT	L-578A	8100±300	9004±356
Cody	Malin Creek Fishing Hole, MT		8880±50	9997±115
Cody	Malin Creek Fishing Hole, MT	Beta-196111	9530±50	10,880±133
Cody	Mammoth Meadow, MT	TO-1976	9390±90	10,635±168
Cody	Medicine Lodge Creek, WY	RL-150	9360±380	10,650±544
Cody	Medicine Lodge Creek, WY	RI-439	9030±470	10,220±634
Cody	Medicine Lodge Creek, WY	RL-446	8830±470	9951±610
Cody	Nelson, CO	UCIAMS-26939	9260±20	10,436±58
Cody	Nelson, CO	SI-4898	7995±80	8842±123
Cody	Olsen-Chubbuck, CO	A-744	10,150±500	11,751±677
Cody	Olsen-Chubbuck, CO	NSRL-2801/CAMS-31812	9290±60	10,465±96
Cody	Olsen-Chubbuck, CO	NSRL-2797/CAMS-31813	9340±60	10,542±97
Cody	Olsen-Chubbuck, CO	NSRL-2797/CAMS-32682	9350±70	10,556±115
Cody	Olsen-Chubbuck, CO	NSRL-2799/CAMS-32683	9370±60	10,589±98
Cody	Olsen-Chubbuck, CO	NSRL-2798/CAMS-24968	9420±60	10,668±119
Cody	Olsen-Chubbuck, CO	NSRL-2801/CAMS-32684	9460±50	10,733±132
Cody	Olsen-Chubbuck, CO	NSRL-2799/CAMS-31814	9480±60	10,790±151
Cody	Osprey Beach, WY	Beta-148567	9360±60	10,573±97
Cody	Red Rock Canyon, AB	GX-1435	8220±260	9130±324
Cody	San Jon, NM	A-7438.1	8275±65	9258±108
Cody	Scottsbluff, NE	AA-67443	8939±85	10,024±137
Cody	Scottsbluff, NE	AA-67442	8680±85	9703±134
Cody	Swan Landing, AL	S-2178	8675±270	9744±339
Cody	Swan Landing, AL	AEVC-10cx	8630±100	9667±141

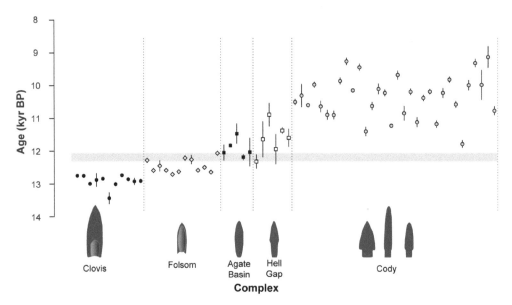

FIGURE 10.3. Calibrated continuous 1-sigma radiocarbon dates averaged by component from fluted (Clovis and Folsom) and stemmed (Agate Basin, Hell Gap, and Cody) point components from the GPRM. Gray rectangle shows period of overlap defined by the youngest fluted and oldest stemmed calibrated mean averaged ages.

to go along with 43 stemmed components. With averaging, the appearance of overlap is reduced dramatically (Figure 10.3). Fluted points date between 13,430 and 12,063 cal BP, while stemmed points were produced in the Middle Paleoindian period from ca. 12,317 to 9130 cal BP. If accurate, this analysis would suggest a period of overlap of approximately 250 years, and the transition from fluted to stemmed points occurred between ca. 12,320 and 12,060 cal BP.

Two important points can be taken from this analysis of averaged radiocarbon dates, neither of which is particularly surprising: (1) when averaging of dates is possible, error is reduced, as is the appearance of contemporaneity; (2) even after averaging, dating error likely remains. Put another way, radiocarbon dating is an error-prone method, and until error can be reduced dramatically, it is difficult to know for certain if the appearance of temporal overlap is real or an artifact of imprecision in the dating method. One way to eliminate radiocarbon dating error is to not use it at all, a statement that highlights the value of a more reliable, less expensive, and often underappreciated dating technique—stratigraphic superposition.

In the best case, across a series of stratified sites, we would find regular patterns of superposition between fluted and stemmed points. If these point styles were contemporaneous or the transition from fluted to stemmed was prolonged, we might expect to see some intercalation of fluted and stemmed components. Although cultural stratigraphy is not infallible as a dating method due to the possibility of vertical mixing (Brantingham et al. 2007; Hofman 1986; Perreault 2019; Surovell et al. 2022; Villa 1982), confidence is gained in relative dating by superposition with large sample sizes and repeated patterns. In order for fluted and stemmed points to occur in stratigraphic superposition requires a few conditions to be met in a site—early and repeated occupation by humans (locations with a high probability of use), relatively rapid rates of deposition with little to no erosion afterward, and the discard of both types of diagnostic artifacts.

After a literature search and consulting several colleagues who work across the study area, I identified 12 sites that have fluted and

TABLE 10.2. Component-Averaged Radiocarbon Dates from Plains and Rocky Mountain Fluted (Clovis and Folsom) and Stemmed (Agate Basin, Hell Gap, and Cody) Archaeological Components.

Complex	Locality	N Dates	Cal. Age±σ (BP)
Clovis	Lange/Ferguson, SD	3	12,991±50
Clovis	Anzick, MT	8	12,750±18
Clovis	Dent, CO	9	12,837±28
Clovis	Domebo, OK	3	12,854±52
Clovis	Colby, WY	2	12,747±11
Clovis	Jake Bluff, OK	3	12,732±13
Clovis	Indian Creek, MT	1	12,918±101
Clovis	Lubbock Lake, TX	2	13,003±54
Clovis	Kanorado, KS	2	12,905±56
Clovis	Blackwater Draw, NM	4	12,875±197
Clovis	Aubrey, TX	2	13,430±170
Folsom	Agate Basin, WY	3	12,063±55
Folsom	Badger Hole, OK	3	12,211±76
Folsom	Barger Gulch, Loc. B, CO	2	12,707±47
Folsom	Carter/Kerr-McGee, WY	2	12,589±37
Folsom	Cooper Lower, OK	4	12,625±28
Folsom	Cooper Middle, OK	3	12,584±40
Folsom	Cooper Upper, OK	3	12,582±42
Folsom	Hanson, WY	3	12,639±49
Folsom	Folsom, NM	6	12,495±48
Folsom	Hell Gap, WY	1	12,447±160
Folsom	Mountaineer, CO	5	12,279±69
Folsom	Waugh, OK	2	12,259±131
Agate Basin	Frazier, CO	2	11,828±47
Agate Basin	Beacon Island, ND	4	12,182±86
Agate Basin	Agate Basin, WY	3	11,464±303
Agate Basin	Hell Gap, WY	1	12,045±236
Agate Basin	Allen, NE	2	12,029±426
Hell Gap	Agate Basin, WY	1	12,317±208
Hell Gap	Casper, WY	2	11,593±270
Hell Gap	Indian Creek, MT	2	11,370±94
Hell Gap	Sister's Hill, WY	1	10,887±351
Hell Gap	Jones-Miller, CO	1	11,637±541
Hell Gap	Hell Gap, WY	1	11,938±453

TABLE 10.2. (cont'd.) Component-Averaged Radiocarbon Dates from Plains and Rocky Mountain Fluted (Clovis and Folsom) and Stemmed (Agate Basin, Hell Gap, and Cody) Archaeological Components.

Complex	Locality	N Dates	Cal. Age±σ (BP)
Cody	Benz, ND	3	10,184±73
Cody	Blackwater Draw, NM	3	9971±83
Cody	Blue Point, WY	1	10,895±123
Cody	DjPm-16, AB	2	10,842±215
Cody	EgPn-480, AB	1	10,889±143
Cody	EkPu-8, AB	1	11,112±144
Cody	Finley, WY	2	10,100±157
Cody	Fletcher, AB	2	10,766±130
Cody	Frasca, CO	1	9990±148
Cody	Hell Gap, Loc. I, WY	3	11,783±111
Cody	Hell Gap, Loc. V, WY	3	9821±88
Cody	Heron Eden, SK	3	10,191±92
Cody	Horner I, WY	3	10,222±95
Cody	Horner II, WY	2	11,395±133
Cody	Hudson Meng, NE	8	11,222±49
Cody	Jerry Craig, CO	1	10,498±85
Cody	Jim Pitts, SD	1	10,621±114
Cody	Jurgens, CO	1	10,226±143
Cody	Lamb Spring, CO	1	9981±447
Cody	Lindenmeier, CO	2	11,169±104
Cody	Lubbock Lake, TX	3	9439±108
Cody	MacHaffie, MT	3	9312±123
Cody	Malin Creek Fishing Hole, MT	2	10,375±87
Cody	Mammoth Meadow, MT	1	10,635±168
Cody	Medicine Lodge Creek, WY	3	10,305±342
Cody	Nelson, CO	2	10,145±52
Cody	Olsen-Chubbuck, CO	8	10,597±42
Cody	Osprey Beach, WY	1	10,573±97
Cody	Red Rock Canyon, AB	1	9130±324
Cody	San Jon, NM	1	9258±108
Cody	Scottsbluff, NE	2	9860±96
Cody	Swan Landing, AB	2	9678±130

stemmed points in stratigraphic superposition. Several other sites contain both but not clearly superposed, such as Water Canyon (Dello-Russo 2015; Holliday et al. 2020), Casper (Frison 1974), San Jon (Roberts 1942), Bobtail Wolf (Root 2000), Barger Gulch, Locality A (Kornfeld 2013), Beacon Island (Mandel et al. 2014), and Claypool (Dick and Mountain 1960; Stanford and Albanese 1975). Stratified fluted and stemmed sites cluster into two groups, one in the north and another in the south (Figure 10.1). The northern group is centered on Wyoming where five sites occur, and two sites are just outside of Wyoming, literally within a few miles of its border. The most famous Wyoming site for stratified Paleoindian occupations is Hell Gap in Goshen County (Irwin-Williams et al. 1973; Larson et al. 2009; Pelton et al. 2017) because it has one of the most complete Paleoindian sequences for the Northern Plains preserved at Locality I, except that no buried Clovis component has yet been discovered there. At Locality I, a Folsom component is overlain by Agate Basin, Hell Gap, and multiple Cody complex layers. This basic pattern of stemmed occupations overlying fluted is repeated across the GPRM.

In the Northern Plains, Hell Gap was not the first site to show this pattern. That was Lindenmeier (Wilmsen and Roberts 1984) in northern Colorado where a Cody component overlies Folsom. The same sequence was discovered at MacHaffie in Montana in the late 1940s and early 1950s (Forbis 1955; Forbis and Sperry 1952). In addition to these early discoveries, six other sites show the same stratigraphic sequence, whether complete or partial. In Montana, Indian Creek has a Folsom component underlying Agate Basin, which underlies Hell Gap (Davis and Greiser 1992). In Wyoming, four sites in addition to Hell Gap provide evidence: Two Moon Shelter (Finley et al. 2005; Marcel Kornfeld, personal communication 2019), Agate Basin (Frison and Stanford 1982), Powars II (Frison et al. 2018; Pelton et al. 2022), and Carter/Kerr-McGee (Frison 1984), the last of which contains the most complete sequence in the study area. The Jim Pitts site in South Dakota rounds out the Northern Plains sample (Sellet et al. 2009). These sites show clear and repeated patterns of superposition that in combination produce a well-known and unambiguous sequence from oldest to youngest: Clovis, Folsom, Agate Basin, Hell Gap, and finally Cody (Figure 10.4). The switch from flutes to stems occurs between Folsom and Agate Basin.

Although only three sites in the Southern Plains contribute to the dataset, they show the same pattern. Those are Blackwater Draw, New Mexico (Hester 1972), Lubbock Lake, Texas (Johnson 1987), and Horn Shelter, Texas (Redder 1985). In the Southern Plains, Agate Basin only occurs at one of these, Blackwater Draw, and Hell Gap is not present at all. This finding suggests that the transition from fluted to stemmed projectile points generally occurred earlier in the Northern Plains than in the South, although the spatiotemporal dynamics of that transition are murky outside of the Northern Plains. Indeed, all of the radiocarbon-dated Agate Basin and Hell Gap components in this study occur in the Northern Plains.

Notably the Southern Plains contain the only possible stratigraphic exceptions to the pattern of stemmed over fluted—the Debra L. Friedkin (Waters et al. 2018) and Gault sites (Williams et al. 2018), separated by only 400 m, where questions of stratigraphic integrity remain (Morrow et al. 2012; Surovell et al. 2022). Until these finds are independently replicated elsewhere, they will remain anomalous.[1] Whatever the bifaces from Friedkin and Gault represent, it seems unlikely that they are related to the stemmed point traditions that appear in Texas some 2,000 to 4,000 years later.

The stratigraphic evidence in combination with radiocarbon data in the GPRM presents a clear pattern. Fluted points are older than stemmed points. The degree to which fluted and stemmed points appear to overlap in time is proportional to the amount of error

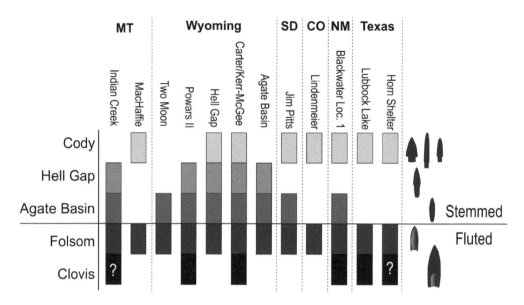

FIGURE 10.4. Localities with stratified fluted and point components from the GPRM shown in order of superposition. Colored rectangles indicate presence of a component. No rectangle indicates absence of a component. Question mark indicates uncertainty.

inherent to each dating technique. Raw radiocarbon dates from fluted and stemmed components suggest about 710 years of overlap, even after applying methods of chronological hygiene to the entire sample of radiocarbon dates. Once dates are averaged by component, a shorter period of overlap of 180 years is suggested. Stratigraphic evidence shows no overlap whatsoever. While some temporal overlap must have occurred, increasingly reliable methods of identifying it show less evidence of it. This finding suggests that the transition from fluted to stemmed was likely rapid. These results should be of interest to archaeologists in the Far West—not only the specifics of culture history, but also the lessons gleaned from these three approaches to dating stemmed and fluted points.

Discussion

In the GPRM, archaeologists were able to solve the Yuma problem through the discovery of more than a dozen sites showing clear and repeated patterns of stratigraphic superposition. Radiocarbon dating confirmed those age relationships and allowed us to assign absolute ages to them, but it is important to keep in mind that raw radiocarbon ages suggest considerable overlap in time, overlap that has no support in stratigraphy. In addition to the presence of many stratified open-air sites in the GPRM, certain aspects of culture history made this possible. Fluted points were used for at least 1,000 years, meaning that there were many opportunities for them to be deposited in stratified sites. Stemmed points were used for much longer, at least 3,000 years. Additionally, this region is replete with large mammal (mammoth and bison) kill sites that have generated large samples of projectile points made during short windows of time. These sites have been invaluable for refining our typology of chronologically distinctive projectile point forms. Such sites are rare west of the Rocky Mountains.

In stark contrast to the GPRM, Smith and colleagues (2015b:360) noted that the question of the ages of stemmed and fluted points in the Great Basin "could be resolved with radiocarbon dates associated with WST [Western Stemmed Tradition] and Clovis points or their respective stratigraphic positions at sites. Unfortunately neither source of information is available." Certainly many dates are associated with stemmed point components in the Great Basin (Rosencrance 2019; Rosencrance et al., Chapter 2; Smith and Barker 2017), but no reliable dates are associated with fluted points (Jones and Beck, Chapter 8). Also, stemmed and fluted points have never been found in stratigraphic superposition in the region. Thus, it is difficult to say anything about the relative ages of these points in the Far West without appealing to Clovis dates elsewhere and assuming the geologic stratigraphic principle of lateral continuity can be applied to cultural stratigraphy.

Furthermore, averaging of radiocarbon dates is complicated by culturally continuous rockshelter records where discrete dateable components or events, from which a series of dates can be logically averaged, are difficult to identify. Instead, to determine the age relationships between stemmed and fluted points in the Far West requires comparing raw radiocarbon dates from the region—after applying some method of selecting which ones should be included in an analysis—to Clovis dates from other places (e.g., Brown et al. 2019). Given the results of my analysis above, there are reasons to believe that such approaches could overestimate the actual time span during which stemmed points were in use.

I suspect a Great Basin archaeologist might look at the open-air record in the GRPM with stratigraphy envy and rightly so. Nonetheless, I want to make the argument that the records of the GRPM and Basin are not very different. If we were only to change two things about the archaeological record and culture history of the GPRM, I would argue we can make the record in the study area look very similar to that of the Far West:

Thing 1: *If the transition from fluted to stemmed projectile points had occurred at least 600 years earlier*, at or before the start of the Younger Dryas, those stratified sites with fluted point components only represented by Folsom would not give us any insight into the chronological question because they would have stemmed points in those horizons. That would remove seven sites from the stratigraphic sample shown in Figure 10.4.

Thing 2: *If we did not have deeply stratified open-air sites*, all but one site would be removed from the stratified sample. We would be left only with Horn Shelter in Texas, which probably does not have a Clovis component (Redder 1985).

With only these two changes, we would be left with a record that looks just like that of the Far West where there are no sites with fluted and stemmed points in stratigraphic superposition. Following from that idea, then, with only two propositions, one related to culture history and one to geomorphology, we can show that these two records might be congruent.

In that light, I propose a working hypothesis of technological and chronological relationships across the western United States. If the western U.S. was a single archaeological site stretching from central Nebraska to the Pacific and we were to dig a trench through that site, cutting right through the Rockies and the Great Basin, what would the cultural stratigraphy look like? From the evidence presented herein, we know what the stratigraphy on the eastern side of that trench would look like. West of the Rocky Mountains, however, the early part of that sequence remains somewhat unclear.

We know that fluted points, though morphologically variable, were used across this entire space, including fluted points that overlap morphologically with the points from classic Clovis sites (Jones and Beck, Chapter 8; Rondeau et al., Chapter 9). Such points are even found within spitting distance of the Pacific Ocean and on Pacific coastal islands

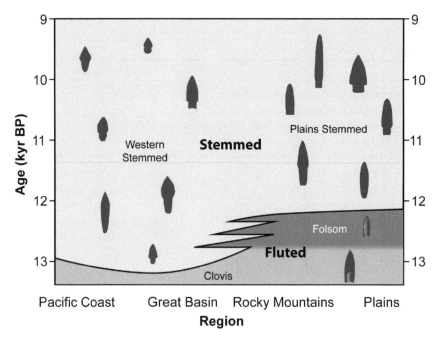

FIGURE 10.5. Hypothesized cultural time-space relationships between fluted and stemmed points across the western United States. X-axis shows a hypothetical transect from west (*left*) to east (*right*) from the Pacific Coast through the Great Basin and Rocky Mountains to the western Great Plains. Time is shown on the y-axis.

(Des Laurier 2008; Erlandson et al. 1987; Fitzgerald and Rondeau 2012; LeTourneau 2010; Mills et al. 2005; Simons et al. 1985). While I recognize that we do not have good dates on Clovis fluted points from the Great Basin or areas further west, we know that east, south, and north of the Great Basin, Clovis points date to a very narrow and consistent range (Becerra-Valdivia et al. 2018; Mehringer 1988; Mehringer and Foit 1990; Sánchez et al. 2014; Waters, Stafford, and Carlson 2020; Waters and Stafford 2007a). If we assume that they date to approximately the same time in the Great Basin,[2] when is the transition from fluted to stemmed in that region? If the transition to stemmed points in the Great Basin happened much earlier than we see in the GPRM, say at the start of the Younger Dryas (~12,850 cal BP) or earlier (Figure 10.5), then the record would look much like it does today.

I want to end this section with one additional idea. Leaving aside the question of pre-Clovis,[3] if fluted points were used before stemmed in the Far West and were only used for a very short period of time (200 to 300 years), they would be expected to be very rare in stratified contexts, which they clearly are. That simple difference in culture history could be the reason why the question of their age remains in the Far West today but was solved more than 50 years ago in the GPRM where they were used for about a millennium.

Conclusion

Archaeologists working in the GPRM in the early days of Paleoindian archaeology also struggled with the relative ages of stemmed and fluted points. That struggle came to an end after the discovery of a dozen sites showing repeated stratigraphic relationships that leave no doubt that fluted points are older than their stemmed counterparts. The transition from flutes to stems occurred in the Northern Plains around 12,200 years ago when the last of the Folsom points were fluted and the first of the Agate Basin points were lashed to the tips of spears. The transition may have been later in the Southern Plains. These basic facts have been known for five decades, although the exact timing of the transition is now better known thanks to improvements in radiocarbon calibration.

How the culture history of the GPRM relates to that of the Great Basin, Columbia Plateau, and the west coast of the United States remains unclear. While it is tempting to correlate cultural variation across this vast space, it may be problematic to do so. The GPRM, in contrast to the Far West, benefits from several open-air stratified sites showing repeated superposition of point forms. It may be that the cultural historical relationships between fluted and stemmed points west of the Rocky Mountains may remain an open question until a similar record is found there.

Acknowledgments

Despite my hesitance to accept their invitation, I am grateful to Jordan Pratt, Katelyn McDonough, and Richie Rosencrance for asking me to participate and for organizing this volume and the symposium from which it derived. Many people helped me to compile the database of stratified sites from the study area and/or to better understand the Great Basin record including Jason LaBelle, David Kilby, Marcel Kornfeld, Bob Kelly, Geoff Smith, Frédéric Sellet, Spencer Pelton, and Robert Dello-Russo. I appreciate Dave Madsen's efforts as a reviewer to check some of my biases. A big thanks to C. Vance Haynes Jr., who instilled in me a love of and appreciation for stratigraphy.

Notes

1. Given questions of stratigraphic integrity, it is unclear if the stemmed points from Gault are in situ or have moved down from overlying components. This remains a serious question to be addressed because as Williams and colleagues (2018:2) note, "superficially, they [Gault stemmed points] resemble point types within the Early Archaic." The presumed stemmed points from the nearby Debra L. Friedkin site are not clearly projectile points, not clearly in situ, and look little like those from Gault. For these reasons and because they are likely part of the same contiguous scatter of chipped stone, I do not consider these sites to be cases of independent replication. Finding similar forms at additional localities would go a long way to support the hypothesis that some stemmed points predate fluted points in the GPRM. Furthermore, refitting studies at both localities (Waters, Pevny, and Carlson 2011) would help to determine to what extent artifacts are moving vertically.

2. I acknowledge the possibility that some fluted points in the Far West might postdate the well-defined Clovis age range (Beck and Jones 2009, Chapter 12; Jones and Beck, Chapter 8) with Folsom points in the eastern Great Basin being the clearest example. But until fluted points are found in securely dated contexts, speculation about their age is just that. I will note that *not one* in situ fluted point, of the hundreds recovered from excavated contexts across the continent, has been found in Holocene deposits. Finally, my statement here is not a declaration of age; it is an assumption and nothing more.

3. If stemmed points predate fluted points in the Far West and parts of the Southern Plains (Davis et al. 2019; Waters et al. 2018; Williams et al. 2018), it is interesting to consider how fluted points fit in this cultural sequence west of the Rockies. One hypothesis would be that claims of pre-Clovis stemmed points are false, but it is also worth considering the possibility that stemmed and fluted points were used simultaneously across the region for multiple centuries.

PART III

Broader Interactions

11

Stemmed Points in the Southwest

CASSANDRA L. KEYES

Recent research into the Archaic period in the Southwest has expanded our knowledge of the preceramic period, yet stemmed points of the Early Archaic remain enigmatic across the region (see Vierra 2018). This, in large part, has to do with vague definitions, small sample sizes, insufficient evidence, and a paucity of sites from which secure dates have been obtained that correspond to the Early Archaic period (~7500–6800 cal BP; Chapin 2017; Huckell 1996; Pitblado 2003; Turnbow 1997; Vierra 2018). As a result, we are left with obscure chronologies and confounding technological relationships.

Early interpretations of the Early Archaic period were not based on secure dates or solid evidence but rather on projectile point morphology and relative stratigraphic relationships (see Chapin 2017). Researchers have long noted similarities between the large tapering stemmed points of the Southwest—Jay points of the Oshara Tradition (Irwin-Williams 1973) in particular—and points of the Western Stemmed Tradition (WST) of the Great Basin, as well as Hell Gap points from the Plains. This resemblance has led to uncertainties about the origins of stemmed technology in the Southwest.

Much debate in the Southwest has surrounded whether this style of point represents groups adopting a subsistence economy focused on a big game hunting strategy more closely tied to late Paleoindian groups of the Plains as proposed by Kenneth Honea (1969). The alternate perspective hypothesizes that these points represent the earliest manifestation of a "broad-spectrum" Archaic adaptation in the region with affiliations to the WST as proposed by Cynthia Irwin-Williams (1973; Irwin-Williams and Haynes 1970).

Both Honea (1969) and Irwin-Williams (1973) based their arguments on similar morphology of large tapering stemmed points. But what is the degree of similarity or dissimilarity between tapering stemmed points of the Southwest and these other technocomplexes? In this study, I assess the relationship between a collection of tapering stemmed points from southern New Mexico and similar point types from the Great Basin, the Plains, and northern New Mexico (Figure 11.1) by using a series of statistical tests to quantitatively evaluate and compare attribute measurements. By bringing morphological relationships into focus, this study provides a starting point for elucidating connections between those regions during the Paleoindian-Archaic interface. It also highlights the need for more research and suggests directions such research might take.

The basis for this chapter comes from the Cycyk collection, named after the late collector Maurice Cycyk. The Cycyk collection was donated to the University of New Mexico in 2017 and contains thousands of artifacts collected from the Tularosa Basin in southern

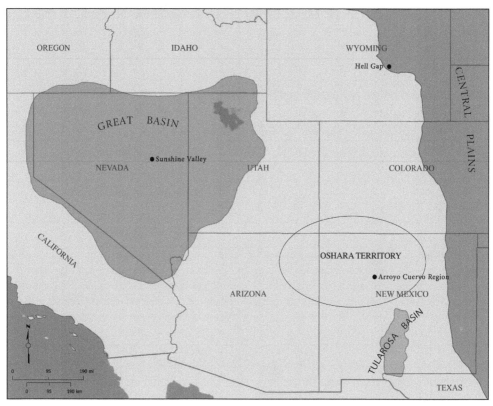

FIGURE 11.1. Map of the geographic regions and site locations discussed in the text. Map by Cassandra L. Keyes.

New Mexico. Artifacts in the collection range in time from the Paleoindian to the Historic period, though only stemmed points were considered for analysis. Among the thousands of projectile points donated, over 100 exhibit tapering stems with a straight-to-convex base and weakly defined shoulders. This collection greatly expands the sample size of large tapering stemmed points in the Southwest and provides ample opportunity to broaden our understanding of stemmed point technology. Although some researchers use the term "contracting stemmed," I have chosen to refer to these points as tapering stemmed forms to emphasize that the stems are long and taper gently from the top of the stem to the base.

This style of point is not unique to this region of the Southwest, and these attributes also typify point types found within surrounding geographic regions that represent distinct temporal-cultural traditions. On the Plains, for example, this style of point resembles Hell Gap (dated to ~10,000 ^{14}C BP; see Surovell, Chapter 10); in the Great Basin several stemmed point types display these characteristics (~11,400–8100 ^{14}C BP; Rosencrance et al., Chapter 2); and in the Southwest there is Jay (~7500–6800 cal BP; Chapin 2017). So, to which of these technocomplexes might the points in the Cycyk collection most closely compare?

My first objective with this chapter is to classify the points in the Cycyk collection. I use a series of statistical tests to quantitatively examine how the points in the Cycyk collection relate to Jay points of the Oshara Tradition, to points of the WST, and to points of the Hell Gap complex. My second objective is to use the sample of Jay points to address observations that Jay points, Hell Gap points, and some WST types are morphologically similar. In doing so, I hope to broaden our collective understanding of stemmed points in the Southwest and the Jay phase as it relates to regional typologies and chronologies. The purpose of this study is to establish a framework of comparative morphology that may inform future and more focused research.

Tapering Stemmed Point Classification and Chronology in the Southwest

When Cynthia Irwin-Williams proposed the Oshara Tradition in the 1960s, she created a typology and chronology for Archaic period projectile points in the northern Southwest based on morphological, technological, and functional differences (Irwin-Williams 1973). Irwin-Williams' work in northwestern New Mexico was initiated in an effort to understand the development of Pueblo society and was coined the Anasazi Origins Project (AOP). Though three other Archaic cultural traditions are recognized for the Southwest— the Western or San Dieguito-Pinto Tradition, the Southern or Cochise Tradition, and the Southeastern or Chihuahua Tradition (Irwin-Williams 1979; see Huckell 1996)—the Oshara Tradition has been widely used as the framework for Archaic period culture history in the northern Southwest (Chapin 2017).

As part of the AOP, Irwin-Williams and other researchers from Eastern New Mexico University carried out investigations in the Arroyo Cuervo region, an area that covers about 500 km² between the Rio Puerco and Jemez River drainages (Hicks 1982). Occupation in the Arroyo Cuervo region spans the Paleoindian period (11,000–7500 cal BP) to the Pueblo I phase (1250–1100 cal BP; Irwin-Williams 1973). The Paleoindian occupation included evidence of Clovis, Folsom, and Cody traditions. Irwin-Williams considered the materials associated with the subsequent Early Archaic occupation to be the earliest evidence of the Pueblo culture's development; she observed that the Early Archaic tool assemblage differed so greatly from those of the preceding Paleoindian period that there was "evidently no generic connection between them" (Irwin-Williams 1973:5). However, some researchers have pointed out that the differences she saw were based on "general temporal trends" in point morphology, rather than on attribute measurements (Chapin 2017:77). As a result, the Oshara typology is considered highly subjective and has limited interpretive power (Chapin 2017).

The Oshara Tradition divides the Archaic period (~7500–1450 cal BP) into Early, Middle, and Late phases, and assigns Jay and Bajada to the Early Archaic (~7500–5200 cal BP), though the date range for Jay (7500–6800 cal BP; Irwin-Williams 1973) is not clear. The Jay phase is thought to represent the earliest manifestation of an Early Archaic occupation at Arroyo Cuervo and the northern Southwest (Irwin-Williams 1973). Though stemmed points resembling the Jay type were recognized throughout the Southwest for decades before Irwin-Williams devised the Oshara Tradition (Renaud 1942), it was only after she did so that the point style became attached to a specific name: "Jay." Since then, "Jay" has become a catchall category for projectile points found in New Mexico and surrounding regions that have a tapering stem, convex base, and weak shoulders (Turnbow 1997).

For Irwin-Williams, the Jay phase was representative of an Early Archaic adaptation which came from the west (Irwin-Williams 1979; Irwin-Williams and Haynes 1970). She believed that the region was abandoned by Paleoindian groups following a period of decreased effective moisture around 8,000 years ago and was subsequently re-occupied by Early Archaic groups beginning around 7500 years ago (Chapin 2017; Irwin-Williams and Haynes 1970). While the transition from the Paleoindian period to the Archaic is generally marked by a shift from Plains-based big game hunting to a more broad-spectrum subsistence strategy, Irwin-Williams argued that ground stone seed-milling equipment was absent from the Jay and subsequent Bajada phases. Ground stone technologies are usually seen to be a defining characteristic of the Archaic period in other parts of the Southwest (Huckell 1996; Sayles and Antevs 1941). Rather, Irwin-Williams observed that the Jay point type bore a resemblance to other stemmed points from the Great Basin, specifically the Lake Mohave type, where the occurrence of ground stone indicates that subsistence economies had already broadened by at least ca. 8500 ^{14}C BP (Madsen 2007; Rhode and Louderback 2007; Smith and Barker 2017).

Contrary to Irwin-Williams, Honea (1969) proposed a Plains-based origin for what he referred to as the "Rio Grande Complex" in the Southwest (see also Chapin 2017: 31). Honea (1969) mentioned the similarities between Hell Gap points and the "Rio Grande" points (Renaud 1942) and posited that the various lanceolate-shaped points found in the greater Southwest must have developed from Agate Basin, as Hell Gap did, implying a localized development for stemmed points in the Southwest. Both Agate Basin and Hell Gap sites are abundant on the Plains, but point types that date chronologically between Agate Basin and Cody, including Hell Gap, are curiously absent from the record in New Mexico (Bruce Huckell, personal communication 2018; Stuart and Gauthier 1996). Huckell and Judge (2006:166) point out, though, that while no Hell Gap sites are reported from the Southern Plains or the Southwest, the morphologically similar Jay form occurs during the Early Archaic of the Southwest. More recent research on the Archaic period in the Southwest has indicated that Honea's proposed "Rio Grande Complex" fits within the Oshara Tradition typology for Jay, Bajada, and San Jose points (Boyer and Moore 2001).

What we are left with are two contrasting arguments for the origins of stemmed artifacts in the region. Honea postulates that it is conceivable that the similarities between Agate Basin, Hell Gap, and Jay point types could:

[b]e due to diffusion of a culturally determined projectile point tradition, which, on somewhat different, successive, time levels and in different regions, underwent distinct evolutionary changes giving rise to a series of local types [Honea 1969:65].

This interpretation differs from Irwin-Williams' assumption that the Southwest area was occupied by groups of the Lake Mohave tradition moving eastward from southern California (Irwin-Williams 1973; Irwin-Williams and Haynes 1970). These differences in interpretation have led to debates regarding population replacement and continuity, and at what point in time subsistence economies shifted from game specialization to broad-spectrum resource use (Chapin 2005, 2017).

Chronology

Dating of the Jay type has been complicated by the present radiocarbon record and the fact that datable sites continue to be elusive. As a result, dates for the Jay phase are widely debated with many researchers suggesting a possible Paleoindian age (Chapin 2017; Judge 1973; Matson 1991; Pitblado 2003; Vierra 2012). Arguments for an earlier occurrence are based partly on observations that the Jay type bears a resemblance to stemmed points from surrounding regions that date much earlier than the range assigned to the Early Archaic by Irwin-Williams (Chapin 2017; Justice 2002). My discussion of Early Archaic chronology here largely follows Chapin (2005, 2017) and consists primarily of data from New Mexico (see Vierra 2018 for information on other regions in the Southwest).

Evidence of the Early Archaic age comes from Irwin-Williams's excavations at Dunas Altas (LA59157), Collier Dune (LA59156), Ojito Dune (LA9348), and La Bajada (LA9500; Chapin 2005) in northwestern New Mexico. The Dunas Altas site was the only site excavated by Irwin-Williams believed to contain in situ Jay artifacts, and she based her description of the Jay phase on excavations from this site (Chapin 2005). However, a recent examination of the evidence by Chapin (2005) suggests that not only is there no clear association between the cultural deposits and the soil horizon from which Irwin-Williams obtained her dates, but the projectile points she considered to be representative of the Jay phase are nondiagnostic. For example, the end date Irwin-Williams proposed for the Jay phase is based on a single radiocarbon date of 6780 ± 250 ^{14}C BP (8170–7160 cal BP; I-3205) which was obtained from the dune deposit prior to excavations (Chapin 2005:76). This date is from a radiocarbon sample associated with a soil horizon within the dune and is not necessarily associated with any particular point type. Chapin (2005:76) notes that two other dates, 9980 ± 105 ^{14}C BP (11,820–11,215 cal BP; Beta-26302) and 10,075 ± 100 ^{14}C BP (11,945–11,265 cal BP; Beta-26301), were obtained more recently from cultural features in the paleosol underlying the Archaic period dune. This finding suggests some of the Jay phase artifacts may be associated with an earlier Paleoindian occupation (Chapin 2005:76). Overall, Chapin's (2017:89) review of Early Archaic radiocarbon dates suggests that the Jay type is more likely to date to around the same time as similar stemmed points from the Great Basin (11,400–8100 ^{14}C BP; see also Pitblado 2003).

In other regions of New Mexico, dated occurrences of Jay points are also lacking. Several radiocarbon dates, for example, have been reported for the San Juan Basin that indicate a human presence in the region by at least ~10,000 ^{14}C BP (Kearns 2018), with a handful dating to around the Early Archaic period. However, in many of these dated cases the lithic technology is non-diagnostic (Kearns 2018). Vierra and colleagues (2018) report that within the northern Rio Grande Valley no dated Early Archaic sites contain diagnostic points consistent with the Jay type. Pedestrian survey has identified Early Archaic surface sites in the Tularosa Basin (Carmichael 1986; Holliday et al. 2018; Kurota et al. 2018)—where the Cycyk collection comes from—but few have been excavated and dated (Carmichael 1986; MacNeish 1993; Miller 2018; Miller and Graves 2019).

The Tularosa Basin

The Tularosa Basin (Figure 11.2) is located in southern New Mexico along the eastern margin of the Rio Grande Rift and is part of a series of basins that make up the Basin and Range geographic province (Holliday et al. 2018; Zeigler 2018). It is flanked by the San Andres, Organ, and Franklin mountains to the west, and the Sacramento and Hueco mountains, the Sierra Blanca, and Otero Mesa to the east. The perennial Rio Grande river is located to the west of the San Andres Mountains and flows near the southern boundary of the basin along the Texas/Mexico border. Elevations in the basin range from about 12,000 ft (3,660 m) at Sierra Blanca peak to 4,000 ft (1,220 m) across the basin floor (Miller 2018). Playas and paleolakes are common features on the landscape in the Tularosa Basin and would have likely provided prehistoric foragers with important resources during the late Pleistocene and throughout the Holocene (Holliday et al. 2018).

Systematic surveys evaluating cultural resources within the Tularosa Basin are lacking, with the most intensive survey being conducted on military lands and within White Sands National Park (Holliday et al. 2018). Nonetheless, the existing evidence suggests that humans have occupied and utilized the Tularosa Basin since at least the end of the Pleistocene (Carmichael 1986; Holliday et al. 2018). However, there is a lack of reliable dates for Early Archaic sites within the basin that come from secure contexts (Miller 2018). Rather, temporal affiliation of Early Archaic sites in the Tularosa Basin is largely based on typological classifications of projectile point morphology (Carmichael 1986; Huckell 1996).

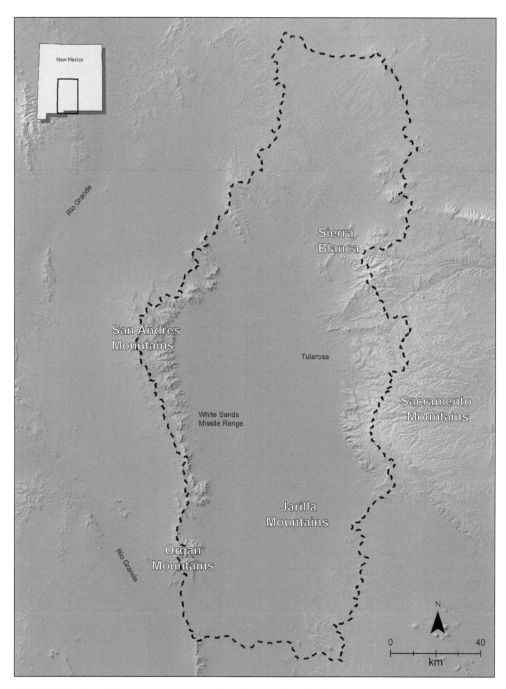

FIGURE 11.2. Map of the Tularosa Basin, New Mexico. Map by Cassandra L. Keyes.

The Cycyk Collection

The Cycyk collection, housed at the University of New Mexico Maxwell Museum, includes a sample of 125 tapering stemmed points (Figure 11.3). While this sample consists mostly of broken bases and stem fragments, at least 50 are complete points. Unfortunately, provenience data for the collection were destroyed in a house fire prior to donation. However, all of the artifacts were organized in boxes by site, and Cycyk labeled nearly all with a site number. Although there is no precise knowledge about the locations of these sites, all were in the Tularosa Basin.

I recognize that the points from the Cycyk collection that I use in this analysis have limited context. Some may question whether this fact renders them archaeologically meaningless; I disagree. We do know, with a high degree of certainty, that the points were collected exclusively from the Tularosa Basin based on conversations with individuals who knew Cycyk (Joe Ben Sanders, personal communication 2020).

Additionally, an examination of the lithic raw material used for manufacture of these points suggests a preferential use of fine-grained volcanic and altered sedimentary rocks, types that can be identified as coming from the northern Tularosa Basin (Shackley 2019; Zeigler 2018; Kate Zeigler, personal communication 2019). Points manufactured from volcanic raw material were submitted to the Geoarchaeological X-ray Fluorescence Spectrometry (XRF) Laboratory in Albuquerque, New Mexico for analysis (Shackley 2019). The XRF analysis indicates four types of volcanic materials are present: andesite, dacite, trachyandesite, and trachydacite. Unfortunately, none could be identified with known sources in New Mexico (Shackley 2011). There are, however, several igneous complexes located in the northern Tularosa Basin that could have served as potential source areas (Zeigler 2018). The Sierra Blanca volcanic field, for example, and the area around the Carrizozo volcanic field are likely sources for rhyolite, andesite, and the dacites observed in this study (Goff et al. 2014; Kelley et al. 2014; Zeigler 2018).

Other rock types—including chert, quartzite, siltstone, silicified sandstones and limestones, and "altered sedimentary" rock types—were identified visually. "Altered sedimentary" is a broad term that locally refers to a wide range of altered fine-grained sedimentary rocks and is one of the more common rock types identified in flaked stone assemblages in the basin (Carmichael 1986; Zeigler 2018). These rock types occur throughout the San Andres, Sacramento, and Jarilla mountains, as well as the northern Organ Mountains. The altered sedimentary rock types present in the Cycyk collection are consistent with raw material observed from the northern portion of the Tularosa Basin (Kate Zeigler, personal communication 2019).

I also recognize the bias inherent in using artifacts from private collections as well as metric data from multiple researchers (Beck and Jones 1989) and am aware of the effects this may have on variation in the data. However, I believe that the data I use in this study for comparison provide valuable sources of information on well-known collections that represent large samples of established point types. It is also worth noting that the Cycyk collection does not appear to be biased towards "nicer" pieces, as Mr. Cycyk collected everything from each of the sites including complete and fragmentary projectile points, bifaces, flake tools, and debitage.

The Cycyk collection is extraordinary for the number of complete stemmed points represented. Despite the limitations in provenience data, I demonstrate that an analysis of this collection helps to advance our collective understanding of tapering stemmed points in the Southwest, and consequently the Jay type, in a meaningful way.

While the Cycyk collection points lack temporal control, the collection greatly expands the sample size of tapering stem points in the Southwest. Thus, it provides several opportunities to broaden our understanding of the technological and morphological

5 cm

FIGURE 11.3. Sample of tapering stemmed points in the Cycyk collection. Photo courtesy of Maxwell Museum, University of New Mexico, Albuquerque, and used with permission.

attributes of the type as we currently understand it, as well as address questions related to the similarity, or dissimilarity, of morphological correlates. By having a greater understanding of these relationships, we can begin to address bigger questions related to population movement and interregional connections, topics which are beyond the scope of this chapter.

In terms of identifying the tapering stemmed points in the Cycyk collection, it is important to consider that it is not clear to what extent the Jay phase, as described by Irwin-Williams, extends beyond the Arroyo Cuervo region (Chapin 2017; Matson 1991). While the points in the Cycyk collection do resemble the Jay type, they were found outside what has traditionally been regarded as Oshara territory. Though this territory has not been explicitly demarcated, the location is generally considered to be northwestern New Mexico. It is therefore reasonable to question the validity of using the Jay designation to classify the Cycyk points. As discussed, assigning a typological classification is further complicated by observations that the Jay type itself is morphologically similar to points belonging to the WST as well as to those of the Hell Gap complex. With this consideration of the collection in mind, I now turn to the point types to which I compare the Cycyk tapering stemmed points.

Jay Defined

While Irwin-Williams (1973) may have been the first archaeologist to assign the Jay point to a typology, she was not the first person to identify the morphological type. Jay points ("J" points) were named after Jerry Dawson (Justice 2002:107; Stuart 2009), an anthropology graduate student at the University of New Mexico in the 1960s, who was supposedly the first person to recognize them. Earlier, however, in the upper Rio Grande Valley of New Mexico and southern Colorado, E. B. Renaud (1942:21) had identified a class of points that he referred to as Rio Grande points, which he described as being broad with a "rather long stem in regard to the relative short length of the body." Honea (1969) also described a point style from the Quemado and La Bolsa sites near Santa Fe, New Mexico, which had similar characteristics to those described by Renaud. Irwin-Williams' description of the Jay type did not further elaborate on the characteristics of the point type. To date, Chapin (2017) provides the most comprehensive definition of the Jay type, observing:

> The Jay type consists of large, contracting-stemmed points with a convex or flat base and a weakly defined shoulder. Stem length is almost always over 18 mm, and the largest examples have stems over 30 mm long. The stem width, generally over 20 mm, is greatest at the distal end of the stem and gently contracts towards the base... Relatively few examples are recovered with an intact shoulder area, either having broken below the shoulder or having been resharpened to the extent that one or both shoulders have been reduced or removed... Blade shape is usually the result of heavy resharpening [Chapin 2017:88–89].

The Jay data included in this study come from Chapin's analysis of points from the Arroyo Cuervo region and adjacent areas.

Western Stemmed Tradition

Great Basin projectile point classifications and chronologies are detailed elsewhere (also see Beck 2000; Graf and Schmitt 2007; Grayson 1993; Rosencrance et al., Chapter 2; Smith and Barker 2017). My goal here is to focus on Western Stemmed point morphology and to highlight some aspects of the adaptive strategies that characterized this time in the Great Basin, for these two things have the greatest implications for how the Jay type has been interpreted.

Of the seven various types considered to be Western Stemmed, I consider only three— Cougar Mountain (Layton 1970, 1972), Lake Mohave (Amsden 1937), and Parman (Layton 1970). I also consider the Ovate type identified by Beck and Jones (2009). The Ovate type is not traditionally included as a formal type within the WST but was added to Beck and Jones' (2009) discussion of the Great Basin Stemmed series due to its occurrence at the Sunshine Locality as well as in other early assemblages in the Great Basin. They define the Ovate type as:

> [S]imilar to points of the Cougar Mountain type in overall size and shape, except that they exhibit no definite intersection between the stem and blade but simply a widening from the base to the point of maximum width... and then a narrowing to the tip [Beck and Jones 2009:170].

Beck and Jones observe that Ovate points in some ways resemble points of the Haskett type (Butler 1965), mainly because both types display faint shouldering; however, they note that Haskett points are generally "more finely made, in that they are symmetrical" and that they exhibit a "well-defined point," but that this was not the case for the Ovate points in their sample from the Sunshine Locality (Beck and Jones 2009:170). Similarly, this was not the case for the points in the Cycyk collection.

I use data from the Eastern Nevada Comparative Collection (ENCC; Beck and Jones

2009) in my analysis, with the exception of the Silver Lake type. For the purposes of this chapter, Ovate is discussed as a constituent of the WST. The ENCC consists of 101 points identified with five WST types: Cougar Mountain ($n = 18$), Ovate ($n = 22$), Lake Mohave ($n = 30$), Silver Lake ($n = 17$), and Parman ($n = 14$). I did not attempt to identify "subtypes" within the Cycyk collection, but have chosen the Cougar Mountain, Parman, and Lake Mohave points, as well as the Ovate type, because in terms of overall morphology, these four types more closely resemble the variety of large tapering stemmed points present in the Cycyk collection and provide a logical starting point for assessing relationships.

The similarities Irwin-Williams observed between Jay points from the Arroyo Cuervo region and the Lake Mohave type prompted her to claim that the Jay phase signaled the regional beginning of a subsistence pattern that was based on "extensive mixed foraging and hunting" (Irwin-Williams 1973:17). Irwin-Williams therefore based her interpretation of the beginning of an Archaic adaptive strategy in the Southwest on similarities in stemmed point morphology between the Southwest and Great Basin rather than on specific evidence of such a mixed economy (e.g., ground stone milling equipment). This conclusion was inferred because a mixed hunting and gathering economy was already established in the Great Basin by at least 9500 years ^{14}C BP (Madsen 2007) if not earlier (Jennings 1957).

In many ways late Pleistocene/Early Holocene Great Basin research has suffered from some of the same limitations that plague the Southwest Archaic (Beck 2000; Beck and Jones 1997, Chapter 12; Roth and DeMaio 2015). That is, most early sites consist of open-air surface lithic scatters where few features are present and the preservation of organic material is lacking (Huckell 1996; Stuart and Gauthier 1996). Significantly, it is within this context that diagnostic projectile points serve as the primary indicators of temporal and cultural affiliation (Beck 2000; Huckell 1996; Keene 2018). However, the way in which projectile point stylistic variation is interpreted often complicates the situation (Huckell 1996; Lafayette and Smith 2012), and some argue that using projectile points as chronological indicators is questionable (Flenniken and Raymond 1986; Flenniken and Wilke 1989).

In the Great Basin, an increasing awareness of the diachronic and regional variability in point forms (Keene 2018; Rosencrance et al., Chapter 2) has brought attention to the fact that chronologies are not as straightforward as is often assumed. The Jay phase of the Oshara Tradition faces similar problems because we do not have accurate dates for this period, nor do we understand the range of variation with the type (Vierra 2018:253). Nonetheless, projectile points remain the best indicator that we have for a generalized temporal affiliation, particularly within surface scatter contexts (Beck 2000; Bettinger et al. 1991; Thomas 1986).

Hell Gap

The Hell Gap point type was originally identified in the Hell Gap Valley of southeastern Wyoming (Agogino 1961; Frison 1974; Stanford 2005). Agogino (1961) described the point type as being lanceolate in form, stemmed, with a straight to slightly convex base, and an oval to diamond-shaped cross section. He noted that the Hell Gap points recovered from the Hell Gap Valley were similar to "J-points" found in New Mexico. While he observed that "J-points differ from Hell Gap points by having greater body to stem width," he also noted "considerable overlap" (1961:558). Agogino (1961) also pointed out that Lake Mohave points are similar to Hell Gap points in shape but are generally more crudely flaked.

A number of important Hell Gap sites have been documented since the type was identified by Agogino. In addition to the Hell Gap site, the Sister's Hill site (Agogino and Galloway 1965), Casper (Frison 1974), Carter/Kerr-McGee (Frison 1984), and Jones-Miller sites in Colorado (Stanford 1978) have all been invaluable sources of data, especially radiocarbon dates. Available radiocarbon ages place the Hell Gap type securely at around 10,000 ^{14}C BP (Kornfeld et al. 2010; also see Surovell, Chapter 10). The Casper and the Jones-Miller sites, both bison kills, are particularly important because of the information that they provide regarding Hell Gap projectile point variation. For example, 80 Hell Gap projectile points were recovered from the Casper site, providing a generous sample from which the range of variation in length and width for Hell Gap projectile points, as well as manufacturing and repair technology, could be examined. I used data from the Casper site for this study.

Frison (1974) noted that the variation in Hell Gap points at the Casper site, indicated by differences in length and width ratios, appears in many cases to be a function of the reworking of broken specimens and the utilization of points at different stages of production. Because variation within a type is often considered to be the result of reworking and refurbishing of points as they break and are returned to service (Bradley 1974; Frison 1974), I will consider the effects this process has on point morphology as it pertains to the point types under evaluation.

Methods

I analyzed the 125 points in the Cycyk collection using attributes that characterize large, shouldered, tapering stemmed points with a convex base as defined by previous researchers (Chapin 2017; Vierra et al. 2012). Each artifact was photographed and measured. While the majority of the artifacts are fragmentary, a relatively large number of them are complete ($n = 50$). For a point to be considered complete it had to have most of the base present, no more than an estimated 3 mm missing from the distal end of the blade, and intact shoulders.

The measurement data for the Jay points were provided by Nicholas Chapin, who recently reevaluated much of the original work done by Irwin-Williams in the Arroyo Cuervo region (Chapin 2017). Data provided by Chapin include metric data for 56 points, mostly those from the Anasazi Origins Project survey and site excavations (Irwin-Williams 1973; also see Hicks 1982). Frison (1974) illustrated all of the Casper site assemblage, provided metric data for the projectile points, and included a chapter on experimental data related to patterns of breakage and reworking. I used the metric data provided by Frison for analysis. Data for the ENCC were provided by Charlotte Beck.

I consider only quantitative attributes in this study, though comparisons in qualitative attributes (e.g., flaking and use-wear patterns) would also likely produce meaningful results, especially as they relate to reworking and tool form and function.

Measurements

All points in the Cycyk collection were measured based on the set of attributes standardized by Thomas (1981; in Jones and Beck 2009) and according to the methods used by Chapin (2007, 2017). I measured the variables present in Table 11.1 with the Ruler Tool in Adobe Photoshop 20.0.6; thickness was measured using digital calipers.

Eight variables were used for statistical analysis in order to compare the four different point populations. Two additional variables (mid-stem width and shoulder height) were available for the Jay data, so 10 variables were considered when comparing the Cycyk points to the Jay type. The quantitative data for the variables are summarized in Table 11.1 and Figure 11.4.

Statistical Analysis

This study used statistical methods to evaluate the relationship between the tapering stemmed points in the Cycyk collection and Jay, Hell Gap, and WST points, as well as between Jay and the latter two. I used these tests to objectively find the best probable fit for the Cycyk points, as well as to quantitatively examine observations that Jay points are similar to Hell Gap and to points in the WST.

I used Analysis of Variance (ANOVA)/Kruskal-Wallis to assess relationships by variable between the different point types (Kruskal and Wallis 1952). ANOVA is a powerful test that uses the F-distribution to measure

TABLE 11.1. Summary of Quantitative Data for Cycyk, Jay, Western Stemmed Tradition (WST), and Hell Gap Points.

Point	Statistic	Length	Maximum Thickness	Minimum Basal Width	Distal Stem Width	Stem Length	Shoulder Width	Shoulder Height	Mid-Stem Width	Stem Length: Total Length	Width: Length
Cycyk	N	50	125	83	86	79	84	80	82	47	48
	Range	32.32–77.55	5.36–11.73	9.04–22.58	11.92–29.53	10.45–37.96	17.7–33.16	15.83–40.64	10.68–23.85	0.323–0.598	0.328–0.584
	Mean	53.53	7.89	15.15	20.29	23.79	24.58	28.63	17.59	0.439	0.45
	SD	10.16	1.19	2.66	2.86	4.99	3.49	5.09	2.24	0.066	0.068
Jay	N	16	45	49	35	30	34	29	29	16	16
	Range	29.7–81.5	5.3–13.1	9.6–22.3	14.4–32.1	9.2–41.7	19.4–33.1	9.2–42.3	13.3–26.4	0.285–0.62	0.395–0.737
	Mean	56.55	7.3	16.24	22.14	24.51	26.54	29.26	19.1	0.425	0.507
	SD	14.82	1.44	2.7	3.19	6.8	3.84	6.8	2.49	0.088	0.095
WST	N	60	80	61	65	46	83	—	—	42	60
	Range	33.4–111.7	4.9–11.4	8–20.4	11.7–29.4	13.75–48	16–36.95	—	—	0.298–0.636	0.255–0.592
	Mean	59.97	7.67	14.07	20.25	26.44	24.5	—	—	0.456	0.406
	SD	15.27	1.55	3.04	2.9	7.53	4.43	—	—	0.087	0.092
Hell Gap	N	18	52	37	43	26	43	—	—	18	18
	Range	49.9–137	5.5–9	12–20.7	18.3–34.5	29.2–63	21–39	—	—	0.346–0.653	0.241–0.521
	Mean	83.04	7.34	17.32	27	40.38	30.89	—	—	0.493	0.376
	SD	24.4	0.78	2.03	3.51	9.45	4.12	—	—	0.095	0.083

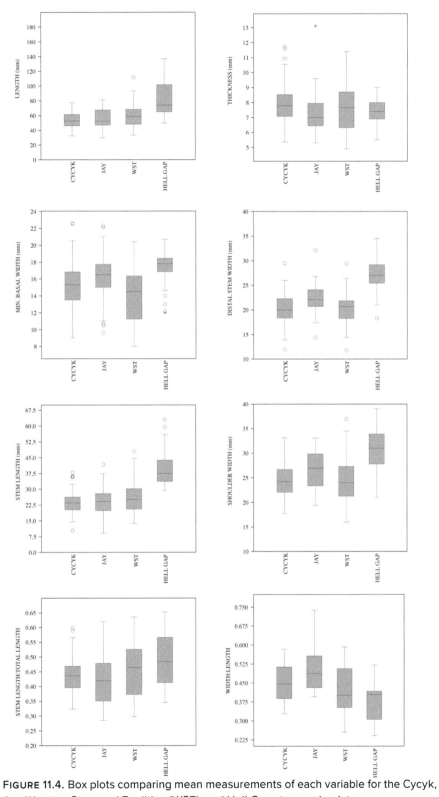

FIGURE 11.4. Box plots comparing mean measurements of each variable for the Cycyk, Jay, Western Stemmed Tradition (WST), and Hell Gap stemmed points.

the probability of a relationship between two sample variances and allows the researcher to examine sources of variation in a dataset (VanPool and Leonard 2011). I used it in this study for normally distributed data. Similarly, the Kruskal-Wallis test, a nonparametric version of ANOVA, is a ranking-based test where H reflects whether the rankings are similar between groups (VanPool and Leonard 2011), and is used for data that are not normally distributed. Tukey's pairwise (Tukey 1977), or Mann-Whitney (1947) pairwise in the case of non-normal data, were then used to understand which groups differed from one another. These post-hoc tests are used when the results of the ANOVA are significant in order to identify which pair's means are different between samples compared. For variables where the assumption of homogeneity of variance cannot be met (i.e., length) but the data are normally distributed, results for Welch's (1947, 1951) ANOVA are reported.

Because two additional variables were available for comparison between the Cycyk points and Jay points, I used t-tests or the Mann-Whitney U test to compare measures of central tendency of each variable for these two populations. A t-test is a parametric test used for the comparison of two independent samples to evaluate the probability that they have equal means (Drennan 1996; VanPool and Leonard 2011). This study used t-tests in instances where the data are normally distributed. When the assumptions of a normal distribution associated with the t-test cannot be met, the nonparametric Mann-Whitney U test is used (Mann and Whitney 1947; Nachar 2008). The null hypothesis for the t-test is that the two independent variables have equal means, and the null hypothesis for the Mann-Whitney U test stipulates that the two samples under evaluation come from the same distribution (Nachar 2008).

For the null hypothesis to be rejected for ANOVA/Kruskal-Wallis, the F/H value needs to be higher than the critical F/H value with a corresponding p-value of less than 0.05. For the null hypothesis to be rejected in the t-tests, the t statistic needs to be greater than the critical t value, with a p-value of less than 0.05. For the Mann-Whitney U test, where the sample size is greater than 20, the Z value is used rather than the value of the U statistic to evaluate the null hypothesis (Nachar 2008). In order to reject the null hypothesis, the calculated value of Z needs to be greater than or equal to the critical value of 1.96 (alpha of .05) and a corresponding p-value less than 0.05.

I used Paleontological Statistics (PAST) Software Package 3.24 (Hammer et al. 2001) to perform all statistical analyses and tests. PAST has a default alpha value of 0.05, which I chose to accept for this study.

Results

Overall, the results of the ANOVA/Kruskal-Wallis tests indicate that the tapering stemmed points in the Cycyk collection are more closely related to the sample of Western Stemmed points from the ENCC, rather than to the Jay points from northwestern New Mexico or to Hell Gap points from the Casper site. The results also suggest a probable relationship between Jay points from the AOP and the four chosen points of the WST. Hell Gap points from the Casper site are, in general, significantly different from the other point populations (Table 11.2).

That the points in the Cycyk collection are not as similar to Jay points from AOP as they are to the sample of WST from the ENCC is confirmed by the t-tests/Mann-Whitney U tests for the 10 variables measured for these two point types. I only discuss the t-test results for the two additional variables as the ANOVA provides equal results for the other eight variables (see Table 11.2). Point comparisons are illustrated using bivariate plots (Figure 11.5).

Length

Welch's ANOVA results for length indicate a significant difference in sample means between the point groups ($F = 9.229$, $df = 40.89$, $p = >0.0000$, $\omega^2 = 0.2515$). A post-hoc Tukey's pairwise comparison revealed that the mean length for Hell Gap points is significantly different than that of the other three point types

TABLE 11.2. Results of the ANOVA/Kruskal-Wallis and T-Tests Comparing Metric Attributes Between Cycyk, Jay, Western Stemmed Tradition, and Hell Gap Point Types.

Variable	Results			
Length	$F = 9.229$	$df = 40.89$	$p = 8.743\text{E-}05$	$\omega^{2*} = 0.2515$
Maximum Thickness	$H = 13.02$		$p = 0.0046$	
Minimum Basal Width	$H = 38.34$		$p = 2.395\text{E-}08$	
Distal Stem Width	$F = 54.44$	$df = 3.225$	$p = 1.703\text{E-}26$	$\omega^2 = 0.4118$
Stem Length	$H = 56.01$		$p = 4.177\text{E-}12$	
Shoulder Width	$F = 27.74$	$df = 101$	$p = 3.625\text{E-}13$	$\omega^2 = 0.2576$
Stem Length:Total Length	$F = 2.082$	$df = 41.81$	$p = 0.1172***$	$\omega^2 = 0.0379$
Width:Length	$H = 16.57$		$p = 0.0001$	
Shoulder Height**	$t = 0.456$	$df = 107$	$p = 0.6506***$	
Mid-Stem Width**	$t = 3.027$	$df = 109$	$p = 0.0031$	

* Omega squared (ω^2) provides an additional means of quantifying the relationship between point groups. It is a common measure for effect size and, essentially, indicates the degree of association between groups and the magnitude or importance of that association.
** Variables for which only the points in the Cycyk collection and Jay points were compared.
*** Nonsignificant result.

(Hell Gap/Cycyk: $Q = 10.01$, $p = 3.935\text{E-}10$; Hell Gap/Jay: $Q = 7.186$, $p = 6.982\text{E-}06$; Hell Gap/WST: $Q = 8.001$, $p = 4.985\text{E-}07$), but that there was no significant difference between Cycyk, Jay, and WST (Cycyk/Jay $Q = 0.9788$, $p = 0.9$; Cycyk/WST: $Q = 3.134$, $p = 0.1239$; Jay/WST: $Q = 1.134$, $p = 0.8535$).

Thickness

The results for the Kruskal-Wallis test for equal distribution demonstrate a significant difference in median thickness between groups ($H = 13.02$, $p = 0.0046$). A post-hoc Mann-Whitney test indicates that Cycyk points differ significantly from Jay ($U = 1922.5$, $p = 0.0017$) and Hell Gap ($U = 2350.5$, $p = 0.0038$) but not WST ($U = 4563.5$, $p = 0.2926$). Jay points also do not differ significantly from WST ($U = 1511$, $p = 0.1378$), or from Hell Gap ($U = 1021.5$, $p = 0.2834$).

Minimum Basal Width

The results of the Kruskal-Wallis test show a significant difference between group medians for minimum basal width ($H = 38.34$, $p = 2.395\text{E-}08$). An examination of the Mann-Whitney pairwise test reveals that this difference is present between all point types (Cycyk/Jay: $U = 1481$, $p = 0.0093$; Cycyk/WST: $U = 2028.5$, $p = 0.0422$; Cycyk/Hell Gap: $U = 699.5$, $p = 2.05\text{E-}06$; Jay/WST: $U = 898$, $p = 0.0003$; Jay/Hell Gap: $U = 622$, $p = 0.0132$).

Distal Stem Width

ANOVA results for distal stem width demonstrate a significant difference between the group means ($F = 54.44$, $df = 3.225$, $p = >0.0000$, $\omega^2 = .4118$). According to Tukey's pairwise comparison, however, there is no significant difference in the means between the Cycyk points and WST ($Q = 0.1013$, $p = 0.9999$). Rather, significant differences were seen between Cycyk and Jay ($Q = 4.283$, $p = 0.0145$), Cycyk and Hell Gap ($Q = 16.66$, $p = 0$), and between Jay and WST ($Q = 4.175$, $p = 0.0182$) and Jay and Hell Gap ($Q = 9.9$, $p = 1.744\text{E-}10$).

Stem Length

Results of the Kruskal-Wallis test for stem length indicate a significant difference in group medians ($H = 56.01$, $p = 4.177\text{E-}12$). The post-hoc Mann-Whitney test reveals that the median stem length for Hell Gap is significantly different from the other point types (Cycyk/Hell Gap: $U = 53$, $p = 4.92\text{E-}13$; Jay/Hell Gap: $U = 47$, $p = 1.832\text{E-}08$; WST/Hell Gap: $U = 117$, $p = 1.765\text{E-}08$) while there is no significant difference in median stem length between Cycyk, Jay, and WST (Cycyk/Jay: $U = 1106.5$, $p = 0.5967$; Cycyk/WST: $U = 1459$, $p = 0.0672$) or between Jay and WST ($U = 599$, $p = 0.3362$).

Shoulder Width

Welch's ANOVA results for shoulder width are similar to that of stem length in that there is a significant difference between group means ($F = 27.74$, $df = 101$, $p = \text{d}3.625\text{E-}13$, $\omega^2 = 0.2576$), but that the difference is largely driven by the Hell Gap points, which are significantly different from the other three groups (Cycyk/Hell Gap: $Q = 11.93$, $p = 0$; Jay/Hell Gap: $Q = 6.725$, $p = 2.023\text{E-}05$; WST/Hell Gap: $Q = 12.07$, $p = 0$). The Cycyk points do not differ significantly from Jay ($Q = 3.414$, $p = 0.0772$) or from WST ($Q = 0.1995$, $p = 0.999$). Jay points also are not significantly different from WST ($Q = 3.559$, $p = 0.0598$).

Stem Length: Total Length Ratio

The results of the Welch's ANOVA for the stem length:total length ratio demonstrate that there is no significant difference between group means ($F = 2.082$, $df = 41.81$, $p = 0.1172$, $\omega^2 = 0.0379$).

Width:Length Ratio

The Kruskal-Wallis test for the width:length ratio shows a significant difference between group medians ($H = 16.57$, $p = 0.0001$). The Mann-Whitney pairwise test indicates that this difference occurs between Cycyk and Jay ($U = 252$, $p = 0.0415$), Cycyk and Hell Gap ($U = 225$, $p = 0.0029$), Jay and WST ($U = 210$, $p = 0.0046$), and between Jay and Hell Gap ($U = 49$, $p = 0.0011$); but not between WST and Hell Gap ($U = 354$, $p = 0.1843$) or Cycyk and WST ($U = 950$, $p = 0.0762$).

T-tests

Mid-stem width and shoulder height were the two additional variables used to compare the Cycyk points to the Jay points from northwestern New Mexico. T-test results indicate that there is a significant difference between the points in the Cycyk collection and Jay points in terms of mid-stem width ($t = 3.0271$, $df = 109$, $p = 0.0031$) but not shoulder height ($t = 0.45639$, $df = 107$, $p = 0.6506$).

Discussion

Statistical analysis suggests that both the sample of large, tapering stemmed points in the Cycyk collection and the sample of Jay points from northern New Mexico are more closely related to a select sample of points in the WST than they are to Hell Gap points from the Casper site. Data in Table 11.1 and Figures 11.4 and 11.5 make it clear that there is a range of values for most variables for the Cycyk, Jay, and WST points, but there is also considerable overlap. Hell Gap differs significantly from the other three point populations. Statistically, however, there was a less than expected relationship between the Cycyk points and the Jay points as these two samples compare in terms of only half of the variables considered, despite the overlap observed in Table 11.1 and Figures 11.4 and 11.5.

Several factors may help to explain these differences and more clearly understand the variation observed. Collector bias, classification bias, and interobserver error, for example, could all be contributing to the variation among and between point types (Beck and Jones 1989). It was not feasible to appropriately correct for possible bias within the four datasets for this study, but this potential issue is something that should be addressed with more rigorous statistical analysis in future studies. Such a study may help to clarify the extent to which systematic error is influencing the data and to what extent bias may drive the variation.

Another factor worth considering is point repair and tool recycling. Beck and Jones

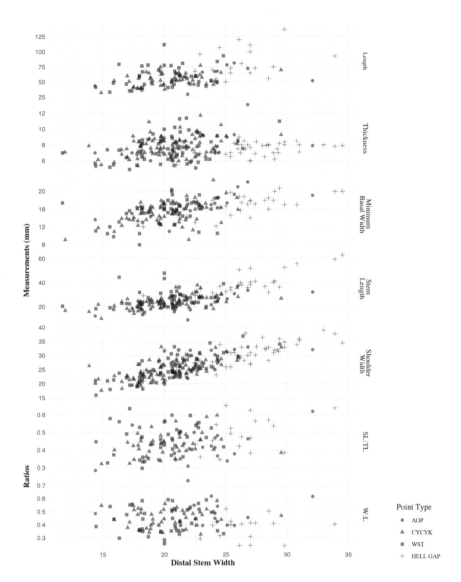

FIGURE 11.5. Bivariate plots showing the distribution of measurements by variable for the Cycyk, Jay, Western Stemmed Tradition (WST), and Hell Gap points.

(2009) recognized that resharpening could, in some ways, account for difficulties in creating reliable type definitions. Bradley (1974) and Frison (1974) also demonstrate that variation within a type is often the result of reworking and refurbishing of points as they break and are reutilized.

Data in Table 11.1 indicate that the length variable shows the greatest amount of variation for all point types. This result makes sense as the blade portion of projectile points is the most likely to be subject to breakage and reworking (Bradley 1974). The stem length: total length ratio, demonstrated by Bradley (1974) to be indicative of the amount of reworking a point has gone through, further suggests that the artifacts used in this study have undergone some degree of repair. Even though the results of the stem length:total length ratio variable suggest that the sample points have undergone modification to either the distal or proximal ends or both in their use life, Hell Gap points remain larger than the Cycyk, Jay, and WST samples in terms of overall length, with the latter three showing no significant difference.

Similarly, the width:length ratio is also a useful measure of point refurbishing (Bradley 1974) and is the second ratio with which Bradley (1974) demonstrated the amount of reworking among the Casper artifacts. Chapin (2017:88) has also noted that Jay points are heavily reworked, and Beck and Jones (2009) make the same observations for point types in the WST. Significant results for this variable might suggest that the amount of reworking that occurs at the shoulders varies more between the groups than do length variables. Among Jay points, for instance, relatively few examples have been recovered with an intact shoulder area (Chapin 2017). Chapin (2017:88) observes that this result is because the shoulders often have been reworked to the extent that they were either reduced or removed. However, no significant difference was found between the Cycyk and WST points.

Huckell (1996:326) points out that Archaic points were regularly broken and subsequently repaired, and he suggests that the morphology of a point may vary "not only as a function of the original intent of the manufacturer" but also as a result of "situational decisions made in the repair process following breakage." Data in Table 11.1 and Figure 11.4 indicate that the measurements for minimum basal width are quite variable, and Figure 11.5 shows some overlap, yet the statistical analysis indicates no similarity between the point populations. Where the break occurred along the stem would impact the minimum basal width observed once the artifact becomes part of the archaeological record, thus producing more varied measurements of this attribute. Several bases are present within the Cycyk collection ($n = 23$), and research into the significance of how these fragments broke as it relates to reworking and refurbishing of the stem is ongoing. Further analysis examining patterns of breakage of the stem may provide key insights into hafting strategies.

Raw material availability and quality can also have an impact on how stone tools are made and used (Andrefsky 1994, 2009) and are factors worth considering in terms of the variation among and between point types (Knell and Sutton, Chapter 5). Both the Cycyk and Jay samples compare with the WST sample in terms of thickness, but interestingly the Cycyk sample and Jay sample are dissimilar; the Jay sample compares closely with the Hell Gap sample. Because maximum thickness is not a dimension that is typically altered as a point breaks and is refurbished, an analysis of how raw materials influence the variation in metric attributes among and between point types would provide promising insights into variation in point morphology (see Knell and Sutton, Chapter 5). Stone tools are made with many design characteristics in mind (Bleed 1986; Nelson 1991), but the location of the raw material source, the size of the raw material nodule, and the fracture properties of the raw material are all considered to be influential factors (Andrefsky 1994, 2009). Though I do not consider lithic raw material here, investigations would be worthwhile to explore the similarities or dissimilarities in raw material choice and availability between regions and how this might be impacting the results.

Importantly, regional variability could explain the variation between the Cycyk, Jay, and WST points. Regional variation, however, is a difficult factor to measure and evaluate in the absence of reliable chronometric data and when the full range of variation among these point types is poorly understood (Beck and Jones 2009; Chapin 2017; Lafayette and Smith 2012; Vierra et al. 2012).

The Cycyk points, Jay points, and WST points were not statistically different in the stem length and shoulder width variables. The overlap among these three point populations is also clear in Figures 11.4 and 11.5. Overall, both the Jay and the Cycyk samples compare closely to the sample of WST with little similarity to the Hell Gap points. This finding lends credence to Irwin-Williams' suggestion that the tapering stemmed points of the Early Archaic may be associated with groups or technological knowledge coming into New Mexico from the west. This possibility has some interesting implications for the type as we currently understand it, as well as for our understanding of the Early Archaic occupation in the region.

As mentioned, the Archaic period in the Southwest is generally marked by a shift in subsistence that occurred at least 8,000 years ago (Chapin 2017). This transition is typically indicated by the presence of ground stone milling equipment at sites that postdate the Paleoindian period. Ground stone is often considered to be a convenient material marker indicative of the rise of more generalized Archaic economies (Huckell 1996:306) because it represents an adaptive strategy that no longer focuses on the hunting of large game but rather on broad-spectrum resource use and particularly plant seeds.

While Irwin-Williams (1973:5) stated that ground stone was absent from the Jay assemblage, ground stone seed milling equipment is now recognized as common among Early Archaic sites throughout the Southwest (Huckell 1996; Vierra 2018). Huckell (1996) points out that in some parts of the southern Southwest, economic systems that involved artifacts technologically and lithologically distinct from those of the Paleoindian period were already in place by around 9000 ^{14}C BP. Although these sites are contemporaneous with Paleoindian traditions on the Plains, their assemblages suggest an affinity with "preceramic complexes" found to the west.

Irwin-Williams had based her assumptions about subsistence not on ground stone, but on the observation that Jay points were similar to Lake Mohave points. How the points in the Cycyk collection and Jay points relate to a particular type within the WST (Lake Mohave, for example) needs evaluating. More specific analysis related to these relationships may indicate an affiliation with Lake Mohave points specifically. Additionally, further research into the relationship between stemmed points in the Southwest and the WST would be beneficial in terms of understanding the changes in subsistence economies in the Southwest.

While chronologies in the Great Basin are complicated in their own right (Beck 2000; Beck and Jones 1997; Rosencrance et al., Chapter 2), the evidence suggests that stemmed points of the WST are the primary diagnostic projectile points of the Paleoindian period (Beck 2000; Beck and Jones 1997; Rosencrance et al., Chapter 2). Until we have secure dates from Jay sites, how this plays out in the Southwest will remain unclear. If the Jay type dates to roughly the same time period as much of the WST (~11,400–8100 ^{14}C BP), as suggested by Chapin (2017), then there is some temporal overlap with the Hell Gap complex. Radiocarbon dates from Hell Gap occupations date from around 10,300 to 9600 ^{14}C BP (Kornfeld et al. 2010:86). While these point types possibly overlapped in time, the results here indicate that Jay is not a relational or a derivative form of Hell Gap as Honea (1969) suggested. This conclusion is further supported by the fact that Jay site assemblages do not resemble those of Hell Gap or other Paleoindian large mammal-focused economies of the Plains.

Rather, the Jay type does appear to relate to a sample of points in the WST in terms of some attribute measurements, as does the large sample from the Cycyk collection. The statistical difference between the Jay type from the Arroyo Cuervo region and the points in the Cycyk collection may suggest regional variation. Chapin (2017:31) submits that rather than implying a cultural connection, "general technological similarities" more likely reflect "similarities in the functional requirements of tools within similar behavioral strategies, rather than ethnic identity," and he proposes an in situ development for the Early Archaic at Arroyo Cuervo. However, the occurrence of a group of stemmed points from the Tularosa Basin that have been shown to relate to the WST is significant. Unfortunately, this debate can only be resolved through additional investigations and recovery of new assemblages from sites with high-precision temporal control.

Conclusion

Large tapering stemmed points of the Southwest have been associated with many names over the decades and not a great deal of understanding—Jay points of the Oshara Tradition, in particular, are poorly understood (Honea 1969; Irwin-Williams 1973; Renaud 1942). Debates over the classification of tapering stemmed points in the Southwest have revolved around theories of population replacement/continuity, external relationships, and the timing of shifts in subsistence economies from big-game specialization to broad-spectrum diets. It is apparent that a more complete interpretation of stemmed projectile point technologies and their place within the chronology of this early period in Southwest prehistory has important implications for understanding the Early Archaic and possibly the Paleoindian period.

My first goal in this chapter was to compare the tapering stemmed points in the Cycyk collection with recognized types that they resemble. The three types that posed the greatest likelihood for a relationship were Jay points, the type traditionally applied to this style of point in New Mexico; various WST point styles from the Great Basin; and Hell Gap points from the Plains. My second goal was to quantitatively explore the degree of similarity between those types. Understanding those interregional differences impacts not only our understanding of chronology, but also how we interpret and understand cultural change and regional cultural interactions during that time.

For example, Jay points have been presumed to date to approximately 8000–6500 cal BP, whereas their morphological counterparts in the Great Basin and on the Plains have relatively secure dates placing them in the Early Holocene if not the late Pleistocene. Because both the WST and Hell Gap technocomplexes are associated with much earlier dates than those typically assigned to the Jay phase in the Southwest, there has been much debate over the Paleoindian-Archaic transition in the Southwest region. Since Irwin-Williams did her work in the Arroyo Cuervo region, however, new evidence has suggested that the Early Archaic dates she advocated for the Oshara Tradition may not be appropriate. Possibly Jay points may, in fact, date to the same time as similar stemmed points from the Great Basin (Chapin 2017). The quantitative comparisons of this study support these notions.

Additionally, the results bolster Irwin-Williams' argument that the tapering stemmed points found in the Southwest are likely associated in some manner with groups from the Great Basin, though more evidence is necessary to determine the degree to which such similarities might reflect common cultural traditions and technological knowledge (Chapin 2017). The Southwest is a diverse region, and more data are needed before we can understand subregional variation in technology. This study has highlighted the need for a better comprehension of stemmed points in the Southwest. Research examining points from other regions, such as the western Colorado Plateau and southern Arizona, is needed to better understand the distribution of the Jay type. This analysis would also provide an opportunity to reevaluate statistical relationships between morphologically similar point types of the Southwest and Great Basin.

Acknowledgments

I would first like to thank Katelyn McDonough, Jordan Pratt, and Richie Rosencrance for their invitation to contribute to this volume and for their editorial comments. So many thanks to the two anonymous reviewers whose critical comments greatly improved this chapter. I am especially grateful to Dr. Bruce Huckell for his support, guidance and general tolerance. Dr. Huckell has been an excellent mentor and teacher and I am grateful for his insights and encouragement. I have a huge amount of gratitude for Drs. Charlotte Beck and Nicholas Chapin who generously provided me with their original data and kindly took the time to answer my emails. Many thanks to Jack Woodson and Debbie Zintak, who donated the Cycyk collection to the Maxwell Museum. I would also like to thank Kate Zeigler and Steve Shackley for helping to identify and source the raw materials present in the Cycyk collection. I am much obliged to the Archaeological Society of New Mexico and the UNM Anthropology Department for providing funding to support research related to this collection. Special thanks to Nadia Neff for her help with Figure 11.5. Last, but not least, I am indebted to my husband for assuming the role of "Mr. Mom" while I pursued my studies.

12

Cultural Transmission and the Interaction of Two Cultural Traditions in the Far West

CHARLOTTE BECK *and* GEORGE T. JONES

Much has changed since 2010 when we argued that the Western Stemmed Tradition (WST) of the Far West (FW) is at least as old as, if not older than, the Clovis complex, something Alan Bryan had maintained for years (e.g., Bryan 1980, 1988; Bryan and Tuohy 1999). Bryan's argument was disregarded because the belief in the Clovis-first hypothesis was so strong; that is, Clovis represented the first people on the continent and was ancestral to all of the traditions that followed, including the WST. By 2010, however, support for this hypothesis was beginning to decrease, and over the next 10 years new discoveries of deposits containing stemmed points in pre-Clovis contexts (e.g., Davis, Chapter 7; Davis et al. 2017; Davis et al. 2019; Jenkins et al. 2012; Jenkins et al. 2013; Waters, Forman, et al. 2011; Waters et al. 2018; Williams et al. 2018) hastened its decline. And finally, in a recent paper, Norris and colleagues (2022) argue that the ice-free corridor did not open until at least 13.5 cal ka, but more likely not until 13.2 ka. So, although a few archaeologists continue to support it (e.g., Morrow 2019; Surovell, Chapter 10), Clovis-first is all but extinct.

In 2010 we suggested that Clovis evolved along the Gulf coast of North America among people who were already living there, a scenario that the discoveries reported by Waters and colleagues (2018) tend to support (see also Williams et al. 2018). At some point, we argued, a subset of that population began moving out of this region, possibly due to the instabilities brought on by sea level changes, carrying this new technology northward on the High Plains along the Rocky Mountain Front. In 2012 and 2013 we took this argument farther. Citing the presence of the Simon Clovis Cache (Butler 1963; Woods and Titmus 1985) and the Heil Pond Clovis site (Reid et al. 2015) in southern Idaho (Figure 12.1), we suggested that some of these migrants eventually entered the FW, crossing the Rocky Mountains on to the Snake River Plain (Beck and Jones 2012, 2013). Together with small numbers of other diagnostic artifacts such as overshot flakes, bifaces exhibiting overshot flake scars, and prismatic blades (Beck and Jones 2009, 2010; O'Grady et al. 2012; Rhode et al. 2022), the hundreds of Clovis fluted points[1] found throughout the FW (Beck, Jones, and Taylor 2019) provide evidence that Clovis migrants eventually moved throughout this large region. Whether they encountered members of the Indigenous population during these travels is uncertain, but based on the co-occurrence of Clovis and WST diagnostic artifacts in the same resource areas (e.g., O'Grady et al. 2012; Rhode et al. 2022; G. Smith, Felling, Wriston, et al. 2015), it is realistic to suppose such encounters did occur. In this chapter, we investigate Clovis and WST lithic technology, arguing for the transmission of information between members of these two populations.

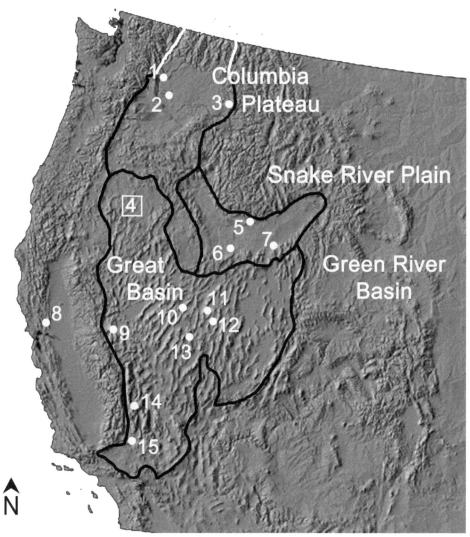

FIGURE 12.1. Map of sites and other locations mentioned in text: (*1*) East Wenatchee Clovis Cache; (*2*) Lind Coulee; (*3*) Cooper's Ferry; (*4*) concentration of 12 sites in southern Oregon: Dietz, Sage Hen Gap, Airplane Lake, Riley obsidian source, Rimrock Draw, Rimrock Lake, Sand Flat, Hat Butte, Swan Lake, Sheep Mountain, Lake on the Trail, Willow Springs; (*5*) Simon Clovis Cache; Sunshine Locality (Long Valley); (*6*) Heil Pond; (*7*) Haskett ; (*8*) Borax Lake; (*9*) Komodo; (*10*) Cowboy Rest Creek quarry (along the western edge of Grass Valley); (*11*) Sunshine Locality (Long Valley); (*12*) Butte Valley; (*13*) Little Smoky quarry (Little Smoky Valley); (*14*) Borden; (*15*) Henwood.

We examine two aspects of the archaeological record in the FW that may have been the result of such encounters. The first is the presence of two quite different lithic reduction systems in this region for the manufacture of WST projectile points. The oldest is a Levallois-like system, similar to Levallois reduction in the Old World, that was either carried by those who initially colonized North America or was developed by those occupants after they arrived on the Columbia Plateau (Davis and Willis 2018; Davis et al. 2012). This system, which was used for the production of all tools including projectile points, was also prevalent in the coastal and interior regions of Washington State (Taylor and Beck 2015) and British Columbia (Fedje et al. 2011), all areas in which available lithic material was of medium-to-low quality.

Perhaps a thousand years later, a second, quite different, biface reduction system appeared to the south in the Great Basin as well as in the central and southern parts of California, where the lithic terrain differs considerably from that of the Columbia Plateau. The toolstone available in the northern Great Basin, for example, is primarily obsidian, but to the south the most prevalent materials are fine-grained volcanics, such as dacite and andesite. In addition to good working qualities, those sources chosen for artifact manufacture are available in large packages.

Chert is also available, but with the exception of a few large quarries such as Tosawihi in north-central Nevada, these outcrops are relatively small and consist of small-to-medium-sized pebbles and cobbles. As a consequence, large stemmed points, such as Haskett and Cougar Mountain, were less often made from chert (but see Galm and Gough 2008; Lynch et al., Chapter 6; Rhode et al. 2022; Rondeau et al., Chapter 9).

As the Levallois-like system seems to have been satisfactory for at least a thousand years or more, what prompted the adoption of a new reduction system, one that differed considerably from the system that had been in place for so long? And what was the source of this new system?

The second issue is the appearance of a post-Clovis fluted point form in the FW. Until fairly recently, most archaeologists in this region assumed that any fluted point discovered in the FW represented Clovis. However, opinions have changed substantially over the last two decades as an increasing number of archaeologists have recognized the morphological variation among Far Western fluted points. Much of this variation has recently been demonstrated to be due to the fact that many of the fluted points found in the FW are actually post-Clovis in age (Beck, Hughes, and LaPierre 2019; Beck, Jones, and Taylor 2019). This dating may not seem particularly odd since Clovis is followed by later fluted forms in all other unglaciated parts of North America. But the FW is different in that Clovis was not the first and only point form in this region as was the case in most areas of the Southwest, Plains, and regions to the east.[2] Rather, stemmed point forms were being used when the Clovis point was introduced, and they had a deep history in the FW. So, why did a post-Clovis point appear in the FW, and what was its source?

We believe that the development of the WST biface reduction system and the appearance of a post-Clovis fluted point in the FW were the result of interaction between two demic groups: Clovis and WST. To frame this argument, we use the principles developed in cultural transmission theory, for which we provide a brief discussion before turning to our two empirical cases.

Cultural Transmission Theory

Cultural transmission theory (CT) comprises a set of principles that express the ways in which people convey information to one another within and across generations, a subject that has been of interest to anthropologists and archaeologists for more than a century (e.g., Boas 1904; Kroeber 1923; Sapir 1916). In other words, "[p]eople acquire beliefs and values from the people around them" (Richerson and Boyd 2005:3). In early discussions culture was the focus of study, and diffusion was regarded as the primary mechanism by which information spread from one social group to another. That is, innovations spread from person to person across space within the culture of origin, ultimately crossing physical and social boundaries within and between cultural groups.

Although it derived from diffusion theory, modern CT, which saw its beginnings during the 1970s and 1980s with the work of Cavalli-Sforza and Feldman (1973, 1976, 1981), is based explicitly on Darwinian theory, calling on the principles of natural selection

(Eerkens and Lipo 2007). The premise of CT is that individuals acquire most of their basic knowledge—about information systems, technology, morals, appropriate behavior, what foods to eat, who you can marry, and so on—through social learning (Richerson and Boyd 2005:3). In other words, individuals acquire information from other people, most often by *imitation* or *teaching* (others, such as Bettinger and Eerkins [1999], Eerkins and Lipo [2007], and O'Brien et al. [2015] use the term *copying* rather than imitation).

Social learning can occur in a number of different ways. A child learns from his or her parents through *unbiased transmission*, so described because the information transmitted by one generation to the next is the same as that transmitted to the first by the previous generation (Boyd and Richerson 1985; Richerson and Boyd 2005). As children grow older, they begin to receive information from other members of the society, such as friends, merchants, etc. They begin to make choices with respect to those they choose as close friends, whose opinions they agree with, and so forth. Once choices are involved, however, transmission is no longer unbiased.

Biased transmission results when "people preferentially adopt some cultural variants rather than others" (Richerson and Boyd 2005:79) and can be one of three types: direct, indirect, and frequency-dependent. For example, a person wants to copy a tool and is trying to decide which design, among several alternatives, to choose. To do so, she or he tests each possibility and then chooses the one that seems to work the best. This is an example of *direct bias*. *Indirect bias* refers to the situation in which the person chooses to copy the design used by the person most skilled in, or successful at, making this tool. This person often has prestige, and thus this type of bias is also referred to as *prestige bias*. Finally, a person may simply adopt the design favored by most people in the society, which is referred to as *frequency-dependent* or *conformist* bias (Richerson and Boyd 2005:120–121).

People may also acquire knowledge through *individual learning* (e.g., through trial and error), which involves experimentation with a behavior that a person has learned or copied. New innovations, which are generally modifications of existing phenomena, occur through individual learning. That is, a person adopts a particular type of tool through social learning and experiments with various changes that, in the end, may result in a new type of tool.

Boyd and Richerson put these concepts into context with the following example:

> From birth children learn from their parents through unbiased transmission, which results in the initial phenotype (receptacle of knowledge). As they age, these individuals begin to learn things from others in the society through biased transmission. As they mature, they may learn some things individually in response to their environment by experimenting with existing behaviors. Thus, the mature phenotype will consist not only of what they have learned socially (that is, through cultural transmission), but also what they have learned through experimentation (that is, individually). They then pass this body of knowledge on to the next generation. As a result of this process, variants favored by individual learning will become more common over time at the expense of those that are not favored [Boyd and Richerson 1985:95].

Boyd and Richerson (1985:95) refer to this process as *guided variation*. Guided variation and biased transmission are what Richerson and Boyd (2005:116) call *decision making forces*, although they differ in that biased transmission is a culling process while guided variation is not. "Biased transmission results from the comparison of cultural variants that are already present in the population" while in guided variation, "individuals modify their own behavior by some form of learning, and other people acquire their modified behavior by imitation" (Richerson and Boyd 2005:116).

New information can also be incorporated within a society through random forces, such as copying errors and cultural drift. For example, Hamilton and Buchanan (2007:56) note that a novice attempting to copy a projectile point may produce something quite different from the original, and even when that novice becomes an expert, the result will never be a perfect replica. As in the case of new information produced by individual learning, new information resulting from these random forces can also be transmitted to members of the next generation.

Western Stemmed Tradition Lithic Reduction Systems

For the following discussion, we frame our descriptions of two lithic reduction systems in terms of operations and physical consequences by which we hope to show how they are influenced by transmission processes. We begin with reviews of each of these systems.

Levallois-like Reduction

The oldest archaeological deposits in the Far West have been found on the Columbia Plateau at the Cooper's Ferry site in western Idaho (Figure 12.1) where stemmed points identified with the Lind Coulee type (but see Davis, Chapter 7),[3] originally defined by Daugherty (1956), were found in deposits dating to about 11,370 ± 40 ^{14}C BP (13,300–13,115 cal BP; Davis et al. 2019). These points were manufactured using what Davis and colleagues refer to as a Levallois-like reduction system (Davis et al. 2019), which is similar in many respects to Levallois reduction of the Old World. Described in 1976 by Guy Muto in his study of Cascade phase lithic technology, the end products of the Old and New World Levallois systems are identical, but "the systems which produce them *appear* [emphasis in original] to be different" (Muto 1976:32). While in the Old World "cores were prepared for specific purposes: blade cores for blades, point cores for points, and flake cores for flakes" (Muto 1976:32), in the New World "products were produced from a single core through variation within the system" (Muto 1976:32–33; Figure 12.2a). Consequently, reduction in this system was not a linear chain of operations as might be expected of a reduction system intended to yield a single product (Figure 12.2). Muto also noted that this New World system was geared toward the reduction of less tractable materials, such as coarse-grained volcanic and metamorphic rock, characteristic of the Columbia Plateau lithic terrain.

This reduction system has been discussed more recently by Loren Davis and colleagues (Davis and Willis 2018; Davis et al. 2012; Davis et al. 2019) who have found it represented in lithic assemblages from Cooper's Ferry that appear to be the oldest on the continent. According to Davis and colleagues (2012:51), the diversity of end products made on both macroflakes and blade-like flakes "may offer the best evidence for conceptualizing Paleoarchaic lithic technology as distinctly separate from Paleoindian [that is, Clovis] technology." Such diversity, they note, is well suited to the lithic terrain of the Pacific Northwest, including the coastal and interior areas of Washington state and British Columbia, which consists of a range of mostly middle-to-low quality toolstones that occur in different nodular forms.

The reduction system Davis and colleagues describe employs a range of core forms including centripetal cores that resemble those described by Muto. This core type can be used to produce both macroflakes, which were used to manufacture the Lind Coulee points from Cooper's Ferry, as well as blade-like flakes (Davis et al. 2012; Davis and Willis 2018). Although this system is limited mostly to the Pacific Northwest, it also has been found in at least one location in the Great Basin, a dacite quarry in Crescent Valley located in north-central Nevada (Cunnar et al. 2011), although the majority of debris at this quarry resulted from WST biface reduction.

As the earliest dates in the FW come from Cooper's Ferry (Davis et al. 2019), Levallois-like reduction likely predates staged biface reduction in the region. Davis and Willis

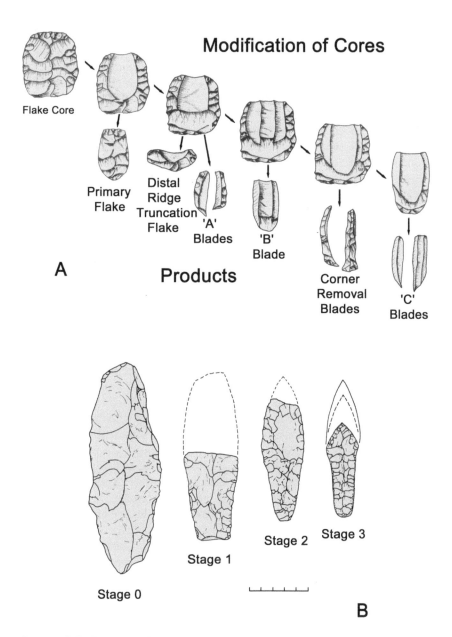

FIGURE 12.2. The two lithic reduction systems in the Far West: (*a*) the Levallois-like system (redrawn by George T. Jones from Muto 1976); (*b*) the biface reduction system (scale bar is in centimeters).

(2018) suggest that Levallois-like reduction may have been part of the technological repertoire of the first migrants to the Pacific Northwest or was independently invented there. These immigrants, they further suggest, came down the coast of Alaska and British Columbia and entered the interior of the continent along the Columbia River. Following the river upstream, early foragers would have encountered a landscape dominated by lower-quality igneous, sedimentary, and metamorphic toolstones, with only occasional occurrences of high-quality chert, quartz, or obsidian. Once they moved south and east of the Columbia River Basin, they would have found high-quality silica-rich toolstones, including obsidian, and in areas to the east of the Rocky Mountains, extensive chert and flint deposits (Davis and Willis 2018:264).

Where these high-quality raw materials occur, they state, an emphasis on staged biface reduction is present, suggesting that biface reduction proved to be more effective than Levallois-like reduction when making tools of high-quality materials like obsidian. We return to this point below.

The Biface Reduction System

The biface reduction system differs from the Levallois-like approach in a number of characteristics: the raw material used, the preparation of the core/blank, the manner in which the core/blank was reduced, and the overall size of the final product. In contrast to Levallois-like reduction, which, as noted above, can be effectively applied to a variety of medium-to-low quality materials, the raw materials reduced through biface reduction are generally of high quality. These include obsidian where available, as well as glassy examples of dacite and rhyolite (see Smith et al., Chapter 3). Although chert was sometimes used to make WST points (see, for example, Galm and Gough 2008; Rhode et al. 2022), this use appears to be a rarity.

From our observations of WST assemblages in the central and eastern Great Basin (e.g., Beck and Jones 2009, 2015b; Beck et al. 2002), when using the biface reduction system WST knappers clearly selected raw materials that would maximize the length of the tool blank, thereby making it possible to produce points of uncommon length (for example, Haskett and Cougar Mountain points can exceed 15 cm in length [see Butler 1965; Duke 2015]). Among fine-grained volcanic (FGV) sources, those containing large cobbles with glassy lithologies were preferentially selected. More often than not, these sources contained cobbles exceeding 20 cm in diameter, sometimes reaching diameters close to 100 cm.

Smaller pieces also appear to have been handled differently than large ones in the blank production stage. For example, side-struck flakes often were detached from "natural" platforms on boulder cores, while flake blanks from smaller, more rounded cobbles were made using block-on-block or anvil techniques (Table 12.1). Following removal, flake blanks were trimmed around parts or all of the edge to shape the blank into a rough oval, steepening the edge for percussion thinning. Thinning was performed to flatten the topography of the dorsal surface of the blank and to reduce thickness of the biface. The latter was achieved by driving off flakes that passed over the midline of the biface.

Occasionally these flakes carried past the midline removing a portion of the opposite edge (i.e., overshot flakes, see discussion below). In contrast to its use in Clovis assemblages, overshot flaking by WST toolmakers is believed to represent instances of knapping error (e.g., Amick 2004; Eren et al. 2013), since such an aggressive flaking technique was likely to increase the frequency of blank breakage when applied to less resilient material such as dacite. A decrease in edge sinuosity appears to reflect a change from a stone to an antler percussor. Following one or two rounds of thinning, the blank/preform increasingly exhibited co-medial flaking and shaping of the proximal segment of the biface, often by pressure flaking, into a narrow tongue-like stem.

Whether represented as a series of steps (i.e., biface reduction stages) or as a continuum, WST biface reduction shares a common form across the numerous assemblages we have studied, including quarry sites like Little Smoky quarry in Little Smoky Valley and Cowboy Rest Creek quarry in Grass Valley (Figure 12.1), both in central Nevada, as well as occupation sites in eastern Nevada (Beck et al. 2002; Kessler et al. 2009) and the Old River Bed Delta (Figure 12.1) in western Utah (Beck and Jones 2015b). In many respects, the early and middle phases of WST reduction are similar to Clovis biface reduction, resembling the process described by Calla-

TABLE 12.1. Stage Model Used in Beck and Jones Biface Analysis.

Stage	Description
0	Represents the initial interval of reduction, usually applied to a large tabular flake blank. Result is a large biface having an irregular shape and low symmetry, reflecting the initial shape of the flake blank; few very widely and/or variably spaced flake scars, typically a mix of edging and thinning flakes; flaked edge thick and irregular cross section. Segments exhibit wide edge offset (very sinuous).
1	Represents large bifaces with irregular shapes; widely and/or variably spaced flake scars, which typically encircle all or most of the biface; wide edge offset; thick and irregular cross section. The distribution of flake scars is continuous or nearly so along lateral margins, and the blank has begun to assume bilateral symmetry. Cortex and part of the striking platform of the original flake blank may still appear. Substantial reduction in preform thickness has not yet been accomplished.
2	Represents large bifaces with semi-regular and symmetrical shape; closely and/or semi-regularly spaced flake scars; edge offset is moderate; cross section is bi-convex or plano-convex. The biface has assumed a roughly symmetrical plan (an oval or bi-pointed shape), although complete bilateral symmetry has not been achieved. Flake removals travel across the midline of the biface, thinning the biface; flake scars are shallow, indicating use of soft-hammer percussion, and they are smaller, more highly concentrated and more regularly spaced.
3	Exhibits a regular, symmetrical shape; closely and/or quite regularly spaced flake scars, with fine-soft hammer percussion and pressure flaking evident; edge offset is small; cross section is thin and lenticular. Shaping may involve final edge and point preparation, and manufacture of a long, parallel or slightly divergent stem, which is accompanied by lateral edge grinding.

Note: Based on Callahan 1979.

han (1979), diverging from the Clovis system when attention turns to haft preparation (see also Duke and Stueber, Chapter 4).

Comparison of WST Biface and Clovis Reduction

In the Clovis system, which Bradley and colleagues (2010) refer to as the Clovis technocomplex, initial reduction was generalized to the extent that a number of different pathways were possible, such as flake production, blade production, and biface production. Once the core was reduced to a certain size, it became a blank that was further reduced bifacially through a number of stages into a fluted point. In this last part of Clovis reduction, we see a number of similarities with WST biface reduction.

Clovis bifaces were manufactured using a recognizable set of techniques (e.g., Bradley 1991; Bradley et al. 2010; Callahan 1979; Huckell 2007), the most distinctive feature of which is the regular and controlled use of overshot (outre passé) flaking for thinning. In this technique, a thinning flake is struck from one margin and travels across the face of the biface, removing a portion of the opposite edge. In the early stages of thinning, these flakes are large and were used to make other unifacial and bifacial tools (Bradley 1991; Bradley et al. 2010; Huckell 2007), serving to conserve raw material.

Like Clovis point manufacture, the manufacture of a WST point began with a blank that was then reduced bifacially through a set of stages. The blank, however, was not a reduced core but a large tabular flake blank or a side-struck flake. Also, in contrast to Clovis, WST biface reduction was aimed at producing a single product, a stemmed point, and as noted earlier, the debitage from the reduction was rarely used, either "as is" or as blanks for the manufacture of other tools, which was far from a conservative approach. This practice was especially the case when the point was being made from fine-grained volcanic toolstone. However, even when the raw material was chert, the reduction debris was rarely used. For example, in their discussion of Haskett manufacture at the Sentinel Gap site in eastern Washington state, Galm and Gough (2008:215) state that "one core produced a single biface and, at best, perhaps a few additional tools from ample numbers of large waste flakes. Most waste flakes were not employed in secondary lithic production."

In his analysis of the McNine Cache, however, a WST obsidian biface cache, Dan Amick (2004) found overshot flake scars on several of the bifaces. He states that the occasional use of overshot flaking to reduce bifaces in the cache was likely not a knapping error and, as such, may show some affinity with Clovis biface manufacture. The McNine Cache, one of the few WST caches found to date, was discovered by a private collector nearly 50 years ago somewhere in the Black Rock Desert of northwestern Nevada. The cache contains 18 bifaces representing all stages of reduction, from blank to finished point, and thus provides a model of at least some WST biface reduction continuum. In the beginning of the report on his analysis Amick states:

> Interestingly, several attributes of these early stemmed bifaces resemble those reported from Clovis biface caches. These include their unusually large size, the grouping of a patterned set of various stage forms that reflect the general manufacture sequence, the leaving of prepared striking platforms on the margins [that are isolated and prepared for removal but deliberately left intact (Amick 2004: 132)], evidence of abrasion on dorsal ridges that resulted from transport wear, and ochre-like mineral staining [Amick 2004:120].

Amick concludes that these similarities between the McNine and Clovis Cache bifaces are:

> suggestive and could be evidence of a Clovis-WST encounter. That is, it is possible that the WST biface system was, in part, modeled on the system used by Clovis tool makers and acquired through observation, and possibly interaction, between members of these two groups [Amick 2004:132].

It is highly likely that members of these two traditions crossed paths, perhaps a number of times, in their quest for food, raw material, and social interaction. After Clovis migrants crossed the Rocky Mountains onto the Snake River Plain, they may have found it difficult to locate sources of high-quality chert to replace broken or worn tools. They would, however, have come upon the large Browns Bench obsidian outcrop in southern Idaho and northern Nevada, as well as numerous sources in Oregon—sources that were most likely frequented by WST knappers who by this time had colonized parts of the northern Great Basin and probably areas farther south given the dates from Smith Creek Cave (see Bryan 1980). Sholts and colleagues (2012:3025) have suggested that stone outcrops were places where Clovis groups likely encountered each other, allowing "knappers to observe the tools and techniques used by other artisans, thereby facilitating the sharing of technological information." The same might be expected of encounters between Clovis and WST knappers, the latter observing the Clovis reduction system as knappers created bifaces and large flakes for the manufacture of various tools, including fluted points. We suggest that WST knappers began to experiment with biface reduction, eventually "customizing" it for the manufacture of stemmed points.

Alternatively, WST and Clovis artisans may never have actually encountered each other. Instead, WST knappers would surely have discovered the flaking debris and broken bifaces left behind at quarries by Clovis knappers. As competent toolmakers, WST knappers could have reconstructed the Clovis reduction sequence by studying this debris, applying this technological knowledge to the manufacture of WST points. In either case, technological knowledge of the biface reduction sequence appears to have been adopted through guided variation.

Although, as noted above, evidence of Levallois-like reduction is occasionally found in the Great Basin (e.g., Cunnar et al. 2011), biface reduction became the norm in this region. We have found this four-stage sequence to be standardized to the extent that it has been recognized easily at sites in the central and eastern Great Basin as well as those in the Old River Bed Delta (Figure 12.1) of western Utah. Although we have not done research in the western Great Basin, this sequence appears to be represented there as well (see, for example, Tuohy 1970). The only difference from site to site is the size of the bifaces, which is related to the package size of the raw material used for their manufacture. At Cowboy Rest Creek quarry (26LA1047) in central Nevada, for example, where dacite boulders are plentiful, biface length can be over 20 cm. Given the standardized nature of this system, it likely spread throughout the remainder of the FW through biased transmission.

Although the lithic terrain of the Columbia Plateau is composed primarily of "a range of mostly middle-to-low quality toolstones that occur in different nodular forms" (Davis et al. 2012:51), good-quality chert is also present, mainly in small quantities. This latter material, which is mostly in the form of pebbles and small cobbles, occurs on the floodplains of the Columbia and other rivers flowing through Washington state and Idaho (Reid 1997) and was the material used to manufacture the stone points from both Lind Coulee (Figure 12.3a) and Cooper's Ferry using Levallois-like reduction.

Chert, however, does occasionally occur in larger packages in this region. For example, 11 of the 12 points from Sentinel Gap were manufactured from chert; the final point was made from basalt (Galm and Gough 2008). At this site, however, the point form is Haskett, which is considerably larger than the Lind Coulee point, and biface reduction was used for their manufacture. Similarly, the points from the Haskett site (Figure 12.3c) in southern Idaho (Butler 1964, 1965) are also quite large and made using biface reduction, but the raw materials used here are mostly FGV and obsidian.

The earliest points from Paisley Cave 5 in Oregon, which are made from obsidian, also are small (Figure 12.3b), but as all three are small fragments, it is difficult to attribute them to a type (see Davis, Chapter 7; Duke and Stueber, Chapter 4; Rosencrance et al., Chapter 2).

The earliest date associated with Lind Coulee points is 11,370±40 ^{14}C BP (13,300–13,115 cal BP) from the Cooper's Ferry site (Davis et al. 2019:3). The points from Paisley Cave No. 5 date between 11,500 ± 50 ^{14}C BP (13,520–13,295) and 11,070 ± 25 ^{14}C BP (13,055–12,865; Jenkins et al. 2012). Haskett points, however, appear a good bit later, between ca. 12,600 and 11,800 cal BP (Rosencrance et al., Chapter 2).

In sum, the points found at sites with the earliest dates are located on the Columbia Plateau and in the northern Great Basin, and are small, and those from Cooper's Ferry at least were made using Levallois-like reduction. The larger points made using biface reduction come from sites on the Snake River Plain and the northern Great Basin and are younger. This finding suggests that the use of biface reduction for the manufacture of stemmed projectile points began between ca. 11,000 ^{14}C BP and 10,600 ^{14}C BP (~12,850 and 12,560 cal BP) in the vicinity of the Snake River Plain and/or the northern Great Basin. This period is roughly the same during which Clovis migrants are believed to have entered the FW (Jones and Beck, Chapter 8).

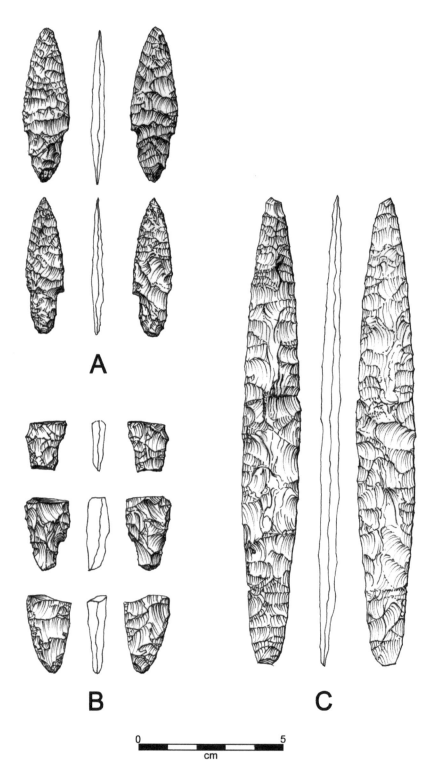

FIGURE 12.3. Comparison of the size of (*a*) Lind Coulee points from the Lind Coulee site in eastern Washington state (Daugherty 1956:246), (*b*) the earliest stemmed points from Paisley Cave 5 in south-central Oregon (Jenkins et al. 2012:500), and (*c*) a Haskett point from the Haskett site in southern Idaho (Butler 1965:47). Illustration by Tammara Norton and used with permission.

Biface Reduction, Raw Material Quality, and Point Size

As noted above, there is a good deal of difference in size between the points of the earliest known type in the Americas (Lind Coulee[3]) that appear on the Columbia Plateau by ~13,500 cal BP at Cooper's Ferry (Davis et al. 2019; Davis, Chapter 7), and the Haskett type, which was in use by at least 12,600 cal BP (but perhaps earlier) in southern Idaho and the Great Basin (e.g., Butler 1964, 1965; Galm and Gough 2008; Rosencrance et al., Chapter 2), as well as Cougar Mountain, Parman, and Lake Mohave points to the south. But why did WST points increase in size? As noted earlier, most of the raw material on the Columbia Plateau is of medium-to-low quality and occurs in small-to-medium-sized cobbles. But as we have seen, chert does occur on the plateau, mostly in small packages, and was apparently sought after for the manufacture of Lind Coulee points, both at Cooper's Ferry and the Lind Coulee site (Figure 12.1), which are fairly small. The latter's size likely was limited by the package size of the raw material being used to make them. However, the discovery of high-quality material to the south that occurred in large packages released toolmakers from the constraints that had been imposed on the Columbia Plateau.

The Post-Clovis Fluted Point in the Far West

We have suggested that the socioeconomic landscape of the FW during the late Pleistocene became more complex during the Younger Dryas with the convergence of two different populations, one that was indigenous to the region (WST) and the other whose members entered the region from the northern Plains (Clovis). Each of these populations likely knew that the other existed, even if they never came face-to-face. As a result, we believe that technological knowledge was transmitted between these groups. The relatively small number of Clovis artifacts in the FW could reflect the absorption of the Clovis population by the WST, although this argument seems to be countered by evidence of continued use of fluted point technology following Clovis. Thus, we turn our attention to the case of Clovis and post-Clovis fluting.

For many years following the discovery of the Clovis point at Blackwater Draw and the ultimate realization a decade later that it represented an entity quite different from the newly discovered Folsom point, any fluted point discovered in the FW was assumed to represent Clovis. This was still the case in 1993 when we began working at the Sunshine Locality in eastern Nevada (Figure 12.1). The district in which the Sunshine Locality is located had recently been declared a National Historic District primarily because of the number of "Clovis" fluted points that had been found there. Over the next five years we collected an additional four, three from the surface and a fourth from a buried horizon. Charcoal collected from the wall of the excavation pit ca. 11 cm above this latter point yielded a radiocarbon date of 10,320 ± 50 ^{14}C BP (12,470–11,945 cal BP), providing a minimum limiting date for the point.

These points, however, did not look like classic Clovis points (Figure 12.4b1); they were smaller, thinner, had deeper basal concavities, and showed no evidence of overshot flaking, a hallmark of Clovis point manufacture. In addition, pressure flaking was evident along the edges. A fluted preform was also collected (Figure 12.4b2). Its basal cavity contained a protrusion, or "nubbin" (see Beck, Jones, and Taylor 2019; Figure 12.1; see also Haynes and Hill 2017:268), a portion of the striking platform left following the removal of a flute flake. The nubbin indicated that the fluting process was unlike that used for Clovis points, but similar to that used to flute Folsom and other post-Clovis points.

Clovis points are believed to have been fluted by freehand percussion about halfway through the reduction process (Bradley et al. 2010; Morrow 2015), usually with multiple flutes, and then as reduction and shaping continued, flake scars impinged upon the flute scar(s). Platforms were constructed

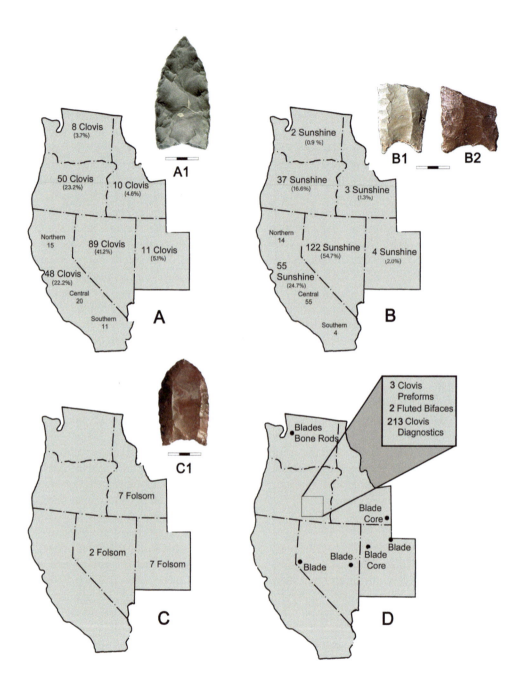

FIGURE 12.4. Numbers of (*a*) Clovis points and (*b*) Sunshine points identified in the analysis by Beck and colleagues (2019b); (*c*) Folsom points in the Far West; and (*d*) other Clovis artifacts in the Far West.

on the basal edge of the preform at the medial plane of the biface, which provided a strengthened area that was less likely to shatter when struck by the percussor (Bradley et al. 2010:100–101).

In the case of post-Clovis points, fluting didn't take place until they were almost finished. The platform was placed below the medial plane close to the face to be fluted. These points most often exhibited a single flute scar on both faces. Fluting is believed to have been accomplished using an instrument such as a punch (Bradley et al. 2010; Frison and Bradley 1980; Morrow 2015).

A systematic comparison between 17 fluted points from the Sunshine Locality and 402 classic Clovis points from the Plains and Southwest indicated that 15 of these points were, in fact, smaller, thinner, and had deeper basal concavities than Clovis points (Beck and Jones 2009). Intrigued by these results, we began to collect data on fluted points from the entire FW, adding to a database originally created by Amanda Taylor (Taylor 2002, 2005). By 2018 we had compiled data on 462 so-called "Western Fluted"[4] points. A comparison with 95 "Classic" Clovis points from the Plains and Southwest revealed that approximately half of the points in the Far Western fluted point database (FWFPD) exhibited morphologies that were different from those of Clovis points (Figure 12.4b). As we found in the Sunshine comparison, these points are, in general, smaller and thinner than Clovis points, and have deeper basal concavities. In addition, they are more often fluted only on one face and exhibit a single flute scar on at least one face. Finally, all that retained fluting platform features appear to have been fluted using a technique similar to that used to flute Folsom and other post-Clovis forms elsewhere in North America. Instead of "Western Fluted" which is problematic,[4] Beck, Jones, and Taylor (2019) have suggested the name Sunshine Fluted for this non-Clovis form, after the Sunshine Locality, as the first systematic comparison between Clovis and fluted points from the FW was done using points from this site.

Of the 462 points in the FWFPD, the majority were isolated finds. Multiple points were collected from Borax Lake, Borden, Komodo, and Henwood in California; Dietz, Sage Hen Gap, and Sheep Mountain in Oregon; and the Sunshine Locality in Nevada (Figure 12.1). All but Henwood contained both Clovis and Sunshine points; Henwood contained only Sunshine points. We note, however, that a requirement for inclusion in the database was that basal width and basal depth could be measured, and thus a number of fluted fragments were excluded.

Other Clovis artifacts are quite rare in the FW (Figure 12.4d). Twelve bone rods were recovered from the East Wenatchee Clovis Cache and at least one was left in situ (Gramly 1993). Overshot flakes, a "macroblade," and several bifaces exhibiting overshot flake scars have been collected from the Heil Pond site in southern Idaho (Reid et al. 2015:63). A large prismatic Clovis blade was recovered in the lowest level of an excavation trench at the Sunshine Locality in eastern Nevada. Two Clovis blades and a Clovis fluted point were recovered from the Nye Canyon Paleo site in western Nevada (Rhode et al. 2022). And finally, Scott Thomas (personal communication, 2020), who was the BLM archaeologist for the Burns district of Oregon but is now retired, produced a map of southeastern Oregon showing the numbers of fluted points and other Clovis artifacts from 16 sites (see list of sites in the Figure 12.1 caption). In addition to the 25 Clovis points, three Clovis preforms, two fluted bifaces, and 213 other Clovis artifacts were found, including flute flakes, overshot flakes, and prismatic blades (Figure 12.4d). These sites are near the Dietz site where a number of flute flakes were collected (Fagan 1988).

If the Snake River Plain was the entry point into the FW, as previously suggested, we might expect the majority of Clovis artifacts to be in the northern and central parts of the region, and this turns out to be the case (Figure 12.4a, d). Compared with regions to the east, however, the frequency of Clovis artifacts in the FW is quite low, which suggests that Clovis never had a large presence there, due to either a relatively late arrival in the region or the fact that once they entered the FW, the Clovis population size there remained low. The small number of Clovis artifacts could also be due to the fact that, unlike the regions to the east and south, the FW had been colonized several thousand years earlier by people utilizing a different technology, and thus Clovis migrants may have encountered some degree of resistance from the resident population when they entered the region or were eventually absorbed by that population.

Davis and colleagues (2012) have also offered an argument regarding the possibility of contact between Clovis and WST populations. They state that whether or not Clovis migrants actually entered the FW, "interaction between Paleoarchaic and Paleoindian populations undoubtedly occurred once both peoples were south of the ice" (Davis et al. 2012:58). They go on to say that if Clovis migrants "actually moved into the FW and established territorial ranges, we should expect to see sites clearly bearing Plains-style assemblages, complete with 'Clovis like' artifacts" (Davis et al. 2012:58). If, on the other hand, these migrants were unable to settle in the region, fluted points may have been introduced through interaction between the two groups at the region's margin, which is what their analysis appears to demonstrate.

As a basis for their analysis, Davis and others (2012) cite a study by Bettinger and Eerkens (1999) that focuses on the period during which bow and arrow technology was introduced into the Great Basin. In a comparison between small corner-notched points from central Nevada and eastern California, Bettinger and Eerkens found that basal width and weight were correlated in the Nevada sample, which suggested that bow and arrow technology was adopted "as a package" and thus by biased transmission. In southeastern California, however, no correlation was found among any of the attributes, suggesting that in this region bow and arrow technology was adopted one attribute at a time through guided variation.

Using Bettinger and Eerkens's (1999) argument, Davis and colleagues (2012) attempted to evaluate whether the fluted point was introduced into the Far West by Clovis migrants who actually entered and became established in that region, or if the idea of the fluted point was conveyed through interaction along the eastern margins of the region. They stated that:

> If Clovis projectiles were made by two distinct populations (one in the Great Basin, the other in the Great Plains/U.S. Southwest) and each population used a different strategy for manufacture, then we should see the signature of these strategies in the covariation of design elements (i.e., length, width, thickness, and basal indentation) from projectiles recovered from these regions [Davis et al 2012:58].

That is, if the same attributes for Clovis points from both the Plains and the Great Basin are correlated, then the points in both regions were likely made by Clovis knappers. But if different sets of attributes are correlated in the Great Basin and the Plains, then the points in these two areas were made by knappers from different traditions.

In a comparison between 87 Clovis points from the Plains and Southwest and 47 "Great Basin Clovis" points, Davis and colleagues (2012) found that for Clovis points, maximum width was correlated with basal indentation, but for Great Basin Clovis points, basal indentation was correlated with total length and maximum thickness rather than maximum width. These results led them to conclude that the Clovis and Far West Clovis points were made by members of separate populations. In other words, Clovis migrants did not enter the FW but introduced the idea of the fluted

TABLE 12.2. Results of Bivariate Analyses of the Three Classic Subgroups, Far Western Clovis, and Sunshine Fluted Points.

Operation	Point Type	Pearson's R	p value
Total length vs. basal indentation	Classic Clovis	0.443	0.000
	Far West Clovis	0.344	0.364
	Sunshine	0.347	0.018
Maximum width vs. basal indentation	Classic Clovis	0.517	0.000
	Far West Clovis	0.252	0.007
	Sunshine	0.665	0.000
Maximum thickness vs. basal indentation	Classic Clovis	0.392	0.000
	Far West Clovis	0.249	0.027
	Sunshine	0.526	0.000
Basal width vs. basal indentation	Classic Clovis	0.477	0.000
	Far West Clovis	0.585	0.000
	Sunshine	0.243	0.000

point to WST people at the margin, and thus Clovis points in the FW were not made by Clovis, but by WST knappers.

Davis and colleagues' (2012) results, however, are problematic in that their 47 "Great Basin Clovis" points include points that were identified as Clovis *as well as those identified as Sunshine* in Beck and colleagues' (2019b) analysis. A recalculation of the relationships among these variables separately for classic Clovis, Far West Clovis, and Sunshine points produced different results. Table 12.2 shows correlation and significance values for comparisons between basal indentation and total length, maximum width, maximum thickness and basal width length for each of these groups in the FWFPD. The results of all of these comparisons are significant except that between basal indentation and total length for Far West Clovis points. However, total length is the most strongly affected of these variables by breakage and thus resharpening, which is likely a factor in this comparison. Given these results Clovis migrants appear to have manufactured the Clovis points in the FW. That is, they did enter and travel across this region, which, of course, is supported by the presence of other Clovis artifacts, especially blades and blade cores. We now turn to a discussion of the Sunshine fluted point.

The Sunshine Fluted Point

The Sunshine point is a bit of a mystery, as noted in the introduction. Clovis fluted points have been found in nearly all of the lower 48 states and were believed for many years to represent the earliest human occupants of the continent. Although a number of valid pre-Clovis sites have been discovered over the last two decades, this assumption may still be the case for many regions to the east of the Rocky Mountains. The FW, however, differs from these regions in the fact that people using a completely different technology had been living in this region for perhaps several thousand years before Clovis evolved. Clovis migrants did eventually enter the FW, but probably not until relatively late in the Clovis period. The evolution of the post-Clovis fluted point makes sense in other regions such as the Plains and the Northeast as it represents a continuation of a lifeway, but in the FW, Clovis entry represents an *interruption* of a lifeway.

On the Plains, for example, Clovis subsistence depended, at least in part, on mammoths, which were replaced by bison as mammoths became extinct. Bison hunting continued during Folsom times, although it became more specialized. In the FW, however, WST subsistence was quite different from that of Clovis on the Plains. It was focused largely on shallow water resources (Grayson 2011) and continued in this vein into the Early Holocene, with some changes in particular resources. The arrival of Clovis hunters represented an intrusion of people used to a different lifeway, but as noted earlier, given the number of Clovis artifacts in this region compared with those of the WST, they did not have much impact. Yet, as was the case elsewhere in North America, there is a post-Clovis fluted point in this region. The question is, why?

Fluted and stemmed points have never been found together in a buried context anywhere in the FW, which has been extremely frustrating to archaeologists working in that region. They have, however, been repeatedly found together in surface contexts. In fact, when fluted points have not been found as isolates, as is the case for the majority of these artifacts in the FW, they have most often been found in association with WST points or in WST surface assemblages. The Sunshine Locality is a case in point. At least 20 fluted points are known to have been collected from this site, primarily by private collectors, although the total number remains unknown. By contrast, hundreds of WST artifacts have been collected there, including a large number of stemmed points (see Beck and Jones 2009). The co-occurrence of these technologies, at least on the surface, has never been answered satisfactorily. But we now have evidence from the study by Beck and colleagues (2019b) that many of these fluted points do not represent Clovis but are likely post-Clovis in age, which brings up another question: are the fluted points that have been found in association with WST assemblages Clovis points, post-Clovis points, or both?

The most distinctive feature of post-Clovis fluted points is that they were fluted using a technique different from that used to flute Clovis points. As noted earlier, while the fluting process for Clovis began about halfway through the reduction sequence (Bradley et al. 2010; Morrow 1995, 2015), post-Clovis points were fluted late in this sequence, perhaps using an instrument such as a punch. The use of this instrument allowed for more control of the fluting process and facilitated the removal of longer flute flakes (Frison and Bradley 1980; Goodyear 2010). In the case of Folsom points, flute flakes run nearly the entire length of the point, resulting in an exceptionally thin blade. The earliest radiocarbon dates associated with this new innovation are with the Folsom point: $10,780 \pm 120$ ^{14}C BP (13,065–12,490 cal BP) from Agate Basin and $10,770 \pm 70$ ^{14}C BP (12,840–12,620 cal BP) from Barger Gulch, both on the northern Plains (Buchanan et al. 2021; Surovell, Boyd, et al. 2016:84).

As new innovations do not typically spread overnight, there would have been a transitional period during which Clovis hunters were deciding whether or not to copy it. Richerson and Boyd (2005) describe the adoption rate of a new invention as sigmoidal; that is, adoption is very slow at first, because few people are familiar with it and are trying to decide whether to copy it. As the invention becomes more widely known, the adoption rate increases substantially. Once a majority of individuals are using it, the rate levels off once again.

Collard and colleagues (2010) suggest that occupation of the northern Plains was continuous during the Clovis-Folsom transition, and thus following Richerson and Boyd (2005), we might outline a scenario in which some portion of the Clovis population on the northern Plains, probably within a single social group, slowly began to copy this new point form, replacing their Clovis points with the new smaller and more stylized Folsom point (Buchanan et at. 2022). It is possible, even likely (see below), that Clovis entry into the FW took place just prior to, or during, this period. Clovis populations had been on the Plains centuries before the Folsom point first appeared, and during those years, mammoths comprised at least some portion of their subsistence (Bement and Carter 2015). Bison were hunted as well, although as Bement and Carter (2015:269) note, "Clovis sites with mammoths generally have only small numbers of bison and other game animals." As mammoths began to decrease in number, however, Clovis hunters began to take more bison. Eventually these animals became the main focus of Clovis hunters, a change that appears to have occurred sometime before the first Folsom point appeared (Bement and Carter 2015; Surovell, Boyd, et al. 2016).

This change in prey would have required a number of changes in Clovis hunting strategy. Bement and Carter (2010) describe the considerable difference between mammoth and bison migration patterns, with bison migrating over much greater distances than mammoths. Citing Hoppe (2004), they state that on the southern Plains mammoths moved along a northeast–southwest trajectory from the northeastern edge of the Texas panhandle to just beyond the eastern border of New Mexico (see Figure 2 in Bement and Carter 2010:270). Bison, on the other hand, moved on an east–west trajectory, covering an area three to four times that of mammoths.

Given that many Clovis points but very few Folsom points have been found in the FW, we suggest that Clovis migrants followed bison into that region before the Folsom point appeared. *Bison antiquus* remains have been documented as far west as San Juan Island in Washington state (Wilson et al. 2009) as well as in the Willamette Valley of Oregon (https://www.willamettevalleypleistocene.com) during the Younger Dryas, although they probably never reached the numbers that existed on the Plains. Lyman (2004), for example, notes that bison herds during this period in eastern Washington probably never included more than 10 animals.

Shortly after the appearance of Folsom points on the Plains, a number of other post-Clovis points appeared in regions to the east, such as Gainey, Cumberland, Vail/Debert, and Barnes. These point types differ from one another with respect to a number of variables, such as overall size, shape, and basal depth, but all, including the Sunshine point, are fluted using some form of the new technique.

As the Folsom point appeared on the northern Plains in close proximity to the FW, it seems logical to assume that it provided a model for the Sunshine point. However, although Sunshine and Folsom points are similar in that they are smaller than Clovis points and have deeper basal concavities and narrower basal widths (Figure 12.5a), the Sunshine point is not "the Folsom point of the Far West." A comparison between 246 Folsom and 225 Sunshine points reveals a number of important differences between these two point forms.[5] Although its morphology varies somewhat from location to location, the Folsom point is stylized in a number of ways, designed for a specific purpose: hunting bison. For instance, when fluted (see Amick 2002), Folsom points always have a single flute scar, usually on both faces, although sometimes only on one, and although 75% of Sunshine points exhibit single flutes on at least one face, 15% of these specimens exhibit multiple flutes on the other face. Folsom flute scars travel almost to the tip and cover more than half the width of the point 75% of the time, making them exceptionally thin. In contrast, while the flute scars on some Sunshine points travel past the midpoint, none of those in the FWFPD for which maximum flute length and total length could be measured have flutes that even approach the tip (Figure 12.5b). And while these flute scars can be as wide as those on some Folsom points, only 12% cover more than half the width of the face. Consequently, on average, the Sunshine points are considerably thicker than Folsom points (Figure 12.5c).

Although the Folsom point base sometimes is in the form of an arc, it more commonly is "indented" (see Haynes and Hill 2017:268; also see Folsom point in Figure 12.4c), often with a pronounced nubbin remaining in the cavity. In contrast, while Sunshine points exhibit a variety of base shapes, including indented, most are arced (Figure 12.5d). In fact, there is a significant relationship between point type and base shape (χ^2 = 432.24, df = 3, p = 0.000).

The predominance of indented bases on Folsom points may be related to the fluting process. Judge (1973) compared Clovis and

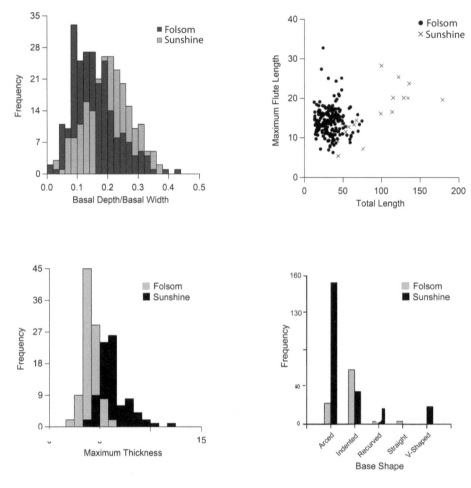

FIGURE 12.5. Histograms comparing Sunshine and Folsom points on (*a*) basal depth/basal width, (*b*) maximum flute length by total length, (*c*) maximum thickness, and (*d*) base shape.

Folsom points, finding that Folsom points are more uniform than Clovis points. He suggested that the standardization of Folsom bases facilitated replacement of a broken point with a new one using the same haft (see also, Ahler and Geib 2000; Bement and Carter 2015). Buchanan and colleagues (2018a:729) relate the standardization of Folsom bases to the fluting process, "which is believed to be integral to the process of hafting" and thus "imposed strict constraints on the form of Folsom bases" (see also Ahler and Geib 2000). The considerable variation in basal shape among Sunshine points suggests that the fluting process for these points was not as constrained as it was for Folsom points, which is probably related to the difference in subsistence strategies between the Plains and the FW. Because Folsom populations were relatively specialized in their subsistence, that is, their primary prey was bison, the Folsom point was designed specifically to hunt this animal. Sunshine points, on the other hand, were more likely used to hunt a variety of game, as bison were not as numerous in the FW as they were on the Plains.

It is more likely that the Sunshine point came about in the same manner as did other post-Clovis fluted points, all of which appeared after the innovation in fluting technique. This new technique probably originated on the Plains and quickly spread to other regions where it replaced the Clovis fluting technique. Just as the statistical analysis of Plains Clovis and Far West Clovis presented earlier showed that these two geographic samples share strongly correlated morphologic features, this is also the case for Sunshine, suggesting that it, too, was made by the Clovis migrants or their immediate descendants. As noted above, the transition period from Clovis to Folsom had begun on the Plains by ~12,600 cal BP (Surovell, Boyd, et al. 2016), and dates associated with fluted points in the FW, however, are all younger (Jones and Beck, Chapter 8). The most reliable of these is from the Sunshine Locality where a minimum limiting date of 10,320 ± 50 ^{14}C BP (12,470–11,945 cal BP) was obtained on charcoal ~11 cm above the point. However, the point was retrieved from sediments the maximum age of which is ca. 10,800 ^{14}C BP. The most we can say, however, is that this point form was probably introduced between 10,780 ± 120 ^{14}C BP (13,065–12,490 cal BP) and 10,320 ± 50 (12,470–11,945 cal BP). But given the fact that the appearance of all of the other post-Clovis fluted points occurred either during the last part of, or right after, the Clovis period, the Sunshine point most likely appeared closer to the older date.

Discussion and Conclusion

As noted at the beginning of this chapter, a lot has changed since 2010 when we suggested that Clovis evolved along the Gulf coast and migrated north along the Rocky Mountain Front. For instance, in 2011, Waters and colleagues (2011a) reported on the Buttermilk Creek deposit they discovered below the Clovis stratum at the Debra L. Friedken site in central Texas. In 2008 Gilbert and colleagues (2008) reported their finds at Paisley Cave 5 in south-central Oregon. Although these discoveries received considerable scrutiny (see McDonough et al., Chapter 1), they proved to be critical in advancing discussions about the colonization of the Americas. These publications were followed by other new discoveries, such as the stemmed points associated with dates between 11,070 ± 25 ^{14}C BP (13,055–12,865 cal BP) and 11,500 ± 50 ^{14}C BP (13,520–13,295 cal BP) at Paisley Cave 5 (Jenkins et al. 2012), and most recently, new dates from Cooper's Ferry between ~13,500 and 13,200 cal BP (Davis, Chapter 7; Davis et al. 2019). At this point, little doubt remains, at least in our minds, that the earliest colonists came from the Pacific Coast rather than the ice-free corridor (but see Morrow 2019; Surovell, Chapter 10).

In this chapter, we have attempted to build on what has been learned over the last decade, taking our original argument farther by investigating the potential impacts of the arrival of Clovis migrants on the Indigenous population of the FW. We have suggested that once Clovis migrants entered the Snake River Plain, at least some of them continued west into Oregon. The presence of archaeological sites containing Clovis artifacts in south-central Oregon attests to a northward migration through that area (see Figure 12.4a, d). During this migration Clovis toolmakers would have needed to replenish their toolkits. As they moved through Oregon, they would have encountered numerous obsidian sources, but they may also have encountered the local WST toolmakers who frequented those sources. If so, local toolmakers may have had the opportunity to observe the biface reduction system and, possibly, the manufacture of fluted points, by Clovis toolmakers. If not, they would have at least encountered the broken tools and debris Clovis knappers left behind at the quarry and could have pieced together a manufacturing sequence. Whatever the case, we have suggested that WST knappers saw an advantage in using that reduction system to manufacture stemmed points as they eventually copied it, modifying it for their own use.

While remaining members of separate ethnic groups, Clovis and WST toolmakers likely continued to visit the same quarries. The Dietz site in southern Oregon (Figure 12.1) provides an example. This site, which lies about 2 km from the Horse Mountain obsidian source, contained a large Clovis component as well as a smaller WST component.

O'Grady and colleagues (2012) present hydration values for 23 WST and 18 Clovis points manufactured from four obsidian sources. Regarding the results, they state that those who were making stemmed points were utilizing the site during a similar time range as those making fluted points, if not at the same time.

Smith and colleagues (2015b) obtained similar results around the lakebed of Pleistocene Lake Warner in Warner Valley, about 60 km south of Dietz. By 10,470 ± 70 ^{14}C BP (12,625–12,100 cal BP) the lake had retreated to a level of 1390 m. Of the 13 Clovis points collected by Smith and colleagues, 11 occurred within 9 m of elevation above the dated shoreline, between 1,366 and 1,403 m, while the 123 WST points that had been collected occurred between 1,362 and 1,411 m in elevation, both above and below the dated shoreline. Thus, the elevation interval within which Clovis points were found is completely contained within the elevation interval for WST points, which Smith and colleagues interpret to indicate that Clovis and WST points were being used about the same time. However, although Clovis and WST points appear to be associated temporally, "their horizontal distributions suggest they are not spatially associated" (G. Smith, Felling, and Wriston, et al. 2015:368). They go on to say that "Clovis points occur between 54 and 264 m from the nearest WST point, and the two types occur an average of 117 m apart" (G. Smith, Felling, and Wriston, et al. 2015:367). G. Smith, Felling, Wriston, and colleagues (2015) conclude that, initially at least, these two groups remained independent of one another while using some of the same resource areas.

The presence of Clovis points throughout the FW indicates that once Clovis migrants entered the region, they remained there for at least some period of time, at least for the remainder of the Clovis period, and likely longer given the appearance of the Sunshine point. The results of the O'Grady and others (2012) and Smith and colleagues (2015b) studies just discussed indicate that Clovis and WST knappers were both visiting particular areas during the same period of time. We continue to believe that at some point these two ethnic groups must have become one. Nearly 10 years ago we wrote:

> In sum, we suspect that the appearance of gracile fluted points in WST assemblages reflects the adoption of components of a weapon system introduced to the intermountain region by Clovis populations and the probable merging of WST and Clovis populations. Stemmed points such as Lind Coulee and possibly Haskett, which early in the sequence represented an alternative weapon technology (see Lafayette and Smith 2012), expanded in morphology and took on a wider variety of functions. These expanded functional roles seem to have paralleled increases in diet breadth and the use of a wider range of subsistence patches.
>
> At this point we are unable to discern from the predominantly surface record how long these two populations remained distinct, perhaps using similar parts of the landscape for different activities and creating palimpsests that mixed their distinct technologies. What seems clear, however, is that these two populations became one, and we believe this happened shortly after they came into contact [Beck and Jones 2012b:40].

Because the radiocarbon record for fluted points in the FW is so poor, it is impossible to say how long the Sunshine point was in use, but it may have persisted until the end of the WST. That at least some of the WST point types, such as Cougar Mountain and Parman, were used for a variety of purposes is obvious in that many are asymmetrical, overly thick, and often have blunted tips (Beck and Jones 2009, 2015b). Haskett, however, appears to have maintained its point-like form (Duke and Stueber, Chapter 4). In fact, a number of

Haskett points have been collected from the Old River Bed Delta in western Utah (Figure 12.1), one of which tested positive for mammoth blood (Duke 2015). Current evidence indicates that WST subsistence was fairly generalized, focusing primarily on shallow water resources (Blong et al. 2020; Grayson 2011; McDonough et al. 2022), but it would be interesting if it turned out that WST hunters did kill an occasional mammoth, as that could indicate interaction with Clovis hunters if the latter arrived in the FW before the extinction of these animals was complete.

Acknowledgments

We would like to thank Katelyn, Richie, and Jordan for inviting our participation in this volume. They provided many helpful comments and were very patient with the senior author who had health issues that interfered with the writing of this chapter. We would also like to thank David J. Meltzer and Robert Lassen, both of whom generously provided us with large Folsom point datasets, without which we would have been unable to write the second part of this chapter. And finally, we would like to thank Margie D'Aprix, the Interlibrary Services Coordinator at Hamilton College in Clinton, New York, who worked tirelessly to find countless articles, some pretty obscure, that we don't own but needed in order to write this chapter.

Notes

1. We were asked by our reviewer whether "the hundreds of Clovis points" that we refer to here are all actually Clovis points, meaning rather than "Western Fluted." In 2019, Beck, Jones, and Taylor (2019b) presented a comparison between 462 fluted points from the FW and 92 Classic Clovis points from the Plains and Southwest, on the basis of a set of morphological attributes. Our analysis found that approximately half of the former did not conform to Clovis criteria. Although we discuss this analysis later in the chapter, we mention it here in order to address the reviewer's concern and assure him that we do mean "hundreds of *Clovis* points."
2. Although there are a number of pre-Clovis sites to the east and southeast—such as the Buttermilk Creek complex at the Debra L. Freidkin site (Waters et al. 2018), the Gault site (Williams et al. 2018) in Texas, Page-Ladson in Florida (Halligan et al. 2016), and Cactus Hill in Virginia (Wagner and McAvoy 2004)—in the Southwest and most areas east of the Rocky Mountains, Clovis is believed to represent a colonizing population, and thus the Clovis fluted point represents the first point form in those regions.
3. In 2017 Davis and colleagues described a cache of 10 points from the Cooper's Ferry site in eastern Idaho, referring to them as Lind Coulee points as they strongly resemble points from the Lind Coulee site in eastern Washington state. We follow their lead and refer to these points, four of which are shown in Davis and colleagues (2019, Figure 12.5d), as Lind Coulee.
4. As Beck, Jones, and Taylor noted in 2019: "the term 'Western Fluted,' along with 'Great Basin Fluted,' 'Clovis-like,' and 'Folsom-like,' although useful when the variability among Far Western points was just being recognized, have now become problematic. For example, the term 'Clovis-like,' as in the case of 'Folsom-like,' implies only that a point differs morphologically from Clovis, although it is more similar to Clovis than to any other fluted form. This term says nothing about how 'Clovis-like' points relate to Clovis in time or if their makers shared cultural or biological affinities. The terms 'Western Fluted' and 'Great Basin Fluted' are even more ambiguous because in addition to suffering from the same problem as 'Clovis-like,' what they actually refer to is unclear. For instance, some may interpret them as referring only to fluted points in the Far West or Great Basin that differ morphologically from Clovis, while others might believe they refer to *all* fluted points in those regions, including Clovis. Continued use of these terms evades the question of what these points actually represent" (Beck, Jones, and Taylor 2019:10).
5. The majority of the data on Folsom points was provided by Robert Lassen and David Meltzer, to whom we are extremely grateful. Additional data were retrieved from published sources.

13

A Paleocoastal Western Stemmed Tradition Variant from the California Channel Islands

JON M. ERLANDSON, TODD J. BRAJE, KRISTINA M. GILL,
AMY E. GUSICK, *and* TORBEN C. RICK

Over the past 10 years, there has been a resurgence of scholarly interest in Western Stemmed Tradition (WST) technologies and their implications for evaluating the origins and adaptations of some of the first Americans, including in the insular Far West. Erlandson and colleagues (2011) described archaeological assemblages recovered from three stratified late Pleistocene sites on California's Northern Channel Islands (NCI). These Paleocoastal[1] assemblages, dated between about 12,200 and 11,400 cal BP, produced numerous chipped stone crescents, delicate and finely made stemmed points, and leaf-shaped bifaces—many found and mapped in situ—associated with the remains of marine shellfish, waterfowl, seabirds, fish, and marine mammals. Because of their age and the association of crescents with stemmed points, Erlandson and colleagues described these island assemblages as a unique maritime variant of the broader WST, found across most of North America's Far West.

In an accompanying story, science journalist Michael Balter (2011:1122) quoted archaeologists David Yesner and David Meltzer questioning the unique and maritime nature of these sites. Yesner suggested that the "most parsimonious interpretation is that these were seasonal forays by mobile Paleoindian groups living on the mainland." These comments might have seemed reasonable to archaeologists unfamiliar with California archaeology, but they missed the fact that no assemblages of comparable age or character were known from the adjacent California mainland coast or the Southern Channel Islands (see Erlandson et al. 2020). This is especially true of two unique Paleocoastal point types, the Channel Islands Amol (CIA) and Channel Islands Barbed (CIB) points, which have been found only in NCI sites dated earlier than 8000 cal BP (see Braje et al. 2013; Erlandson 2013; Glassow et al. 2013; Gusick 2013; Rick et al. 2013).

A decade later, more than 100 island Paleocoastal sites have now been identified, at least 31 of which have produced CIA or CIB points (Gusick and Erlandson 2019; Jazwa and Rosencrance 2019), many of them from well-dated contexts. Nonetheless, even some recent discussions of these early island sites, and the distinctive stemmed points they contain, continue to mischaracterize their antiquity or technological implications. These assessments include an assertion that "stemming is a widespread form of haft design innovated numerous times across multiple continents and is thus not an appropriate derived character on which to base a hypothesis of cultural affiliation" (Potter, Baichtal, et al. 2018:5). This statement literally misses the point, as the modification of the base area is just one among several attributes on which the definition of projectile point types is made.

In this chapter, we summarize current knowledge about the chronology, technologies, and adaptations of maritime (seafaring) Paleocoastal people who occupied the NCI for 4,000 to 5,000 years or more (~13,000–8000 cal BP). Several recent studies have focused on potential connections between Island Paleocoastal Tradition (IPT), other WST technologies, and a hypothesized coastal colonization of the Americas by northeast Asian peoples carrying seemingly similar assemblages (see Beck and Jones 2010; Davis et al. 2019; Erlandson and Braje 2011; K. Smith 2021). However, our focus here is on the distinctive projectile points associated with many IPT assemblages and their linkages with the WST.

Background: The Western Stemmed Tradition

Potter and colleagues (2018a) assert that stemmed projectile points cannot be used to determine cultural affiliation, but archaeological data from North America's Far West suggest otherwise. In fact, well-defined and broadly recognized types of stemmed projectile points (Haskett, Windust, Lake Mohave, etc.) have long been reliable markers of early human occupations in the Far West (e.g., Campbell et al. 1937; Cressman 1942; Rogers 1939; Rosencrance 2019). These and other stemmed point types are key components of broader assemblages associated with the WST or what Bedwell (1973) called the Western Pluvial Lakes Tradition (WPLT), now recognized as one subset of New World Paleoindian traditions.

These distinctive point types, along with chipped stone crescents (lunates), are most often found along the shores of relict pluvial lakes and wetlands or, more rarely, deeply buried in caves and rockshelters. Even prior to the advent of radiometric dating techniques, early twentieth century archaeologists recognized the great antiquity of these point types due to their correlation with Pleistocene and Early Holocene landforms and stratigraphic associations in deeply buried deposits. Radiocarbon dating of organic materials associated with WST points confirmed their late Pleistocene to Early Holocene age (e.g., Arnold and Libby 1951; Cressman 1951; Jennings 1957).

Until recently, however, WST points were rarely linked to the initial peopling of the Americas (see Bryan 1978, 1988 for important exceptions). For years, WST points were seen by most archaeologists as markers of late Paleoindian regionalization in the Great Basin and Intermountain West, after Clovis and the extinction of Pleistocene megafauna caused people to shift their hunting efforts to smaller terrestrial and wetland game.

By the late 1990s, with the widespread acceptance of an archaeological component at the Monte Verde II site dating to between ~14,600 and 14,000 cal BP (Dillehay et al. 2008; Erlandson et al. 2008; Meltzer et al. 1997), the foundations of the Clovis-first model began to crumble, calling into question the chronology and settlement histories of New World Paleoindian cultures. The occupations at Monte Verde placed humans in southern Chile ~1,000 years prior to the oldest Clovis sites in North America, and, perhaps, prior to or very close to the opening and viability of the ice-free corridor (IFC) route into the Americas (Dixon 1999; Froese et al. 2019; Margold et al. 2019; Munyikwa et al. 2017). More recently, the Clovis-first model collapsed as a handful of other pre-Clovis sites were described, with many now widely accepted by the archaeological community (Davis et al. 2019; Gilbert et al. 2008; Halligan et al. 2016; Jenkins et al. 2012; Waters, Forman, et al. 2011; Waters, Stafford, et al. 2011; Waters et al. 2018; Williams et al. 2018). These sites place humans in North America at least ~14,000 years ago, and a series of genetic studies suggests that they migrated from Beringia to the Americas between roughly 18,000 and 14,000 cal BP (e.g., Brandini et al. 2018; Llamas et al. 2016; Moreno-Mayar, Potter, et al. 2018; Moreno-Mayar, Vinner, et al, 2018; Raghavan et al. 2015).

From the ashes of Clovis-first, new debates have arisen about the route(s) and chronology of the initial peopling of the Americas (e.g., Braje et al. 2017; Braje et al. 2018; Potter, Baichtal, et al. 2018; Potter, Beaudoin, et al. 2018). The Pacific Coast Route (PCR) has emerged as an increasingly viable alternative or addition to terrestrial routes (Braje et al. 2020; Erlandson 2002; Madsen 2015), while others have argued for a deeper antiquity of Clovis cultures in the Americas and an early opening and viability of the IFC (see Potter, Beaudoin, et al. 2018).

A variety of new archaeological evidence also is helping redefine the geographic distribution and temporal chronology of the WST in Far Western North America (see McDonough et al., Chapter 1). Stemmed points have now been recovered from deposits dating to Clovis or pre-Clovis times at several sites, including Paisley Caves (Jenkins et al. 2012), Bonneville Estates Rockshelter (Goebel et al. 2018), the Friedkin and Gault sites in Texas (Waters et al. 2018; Williams et al. 2018), and Cooper's Ferry in Idaho (Davis, Chapter 7; Davis et al. 2019). Some archaeologists now argue that WST technology might be contemporary, or even ancestral, to Clovis in the Far West (e.g., Beck and Jones 2010; Davis et al. 2019; Smith et al. 2020), and possibly related to a late Pleistocene Pacific Rim migration into the Americas (Davis et al. 2019; Erlandson and Braje 2011; Waters et al. 2018; Williams and Madsen 2020). Late Pleistocene stemmed point types are found around the Pacific Rim in Japan, the Russian Far East, Alaska, the Pacific Northwest, the California Channel Islands, Baja California, and South America (Erlandson and Braje 2011). In many of these areas, early stemmed points are found in association with lunates and leaf-shaped (foliate) bifaces. Although possible technological and cultural links between these assemblages may be intriguing, systematic research exploring possible connections between these far-flung localities is in its infancy (Pratt et al. 2020).

Most of the research on WST and early stemmed point varieties has focused on the Great Basin and the greater California mainland. Radiocarbon dating and morphological analyses of stemmed CIA and CIB points on California's NCI, however, suggest that these point types are a distinctive maritime variant of the larger WST (Erlandson, Watts, and Jew 2014). This association seems to be confirmed by the co-occurrence of these points with chipped stone crescents—distinctive bifacial artifacts found in many WST sites across the Far West (Moss and Erlandson 2013)—especially sites located near wetlands such as lakes, marshes, and estuaries (Sanchez et al. 2017).

Island Paleocoastal Environments

Located between 20 and 44 km off the southern California coast, the NCI today consists of four islands—Anacapa, Santa Cruz, Santa Rosa, and San Miguel—separated from one another and the mainland by relatively narrow sea gaps (Figure 13.1). During the Last Glacial Maximum, however, with local sea level ~105 m lower than present (Clark et al. 2014), the NCI were connected by a series of land bridges and coalesced into a single island landmass known as Santarosae[2] (Orr 1968; Reeder-Myers et al. 2015). According to shoreline reconstruction models projecting sea level curves onto modern seafloor bathymetry, Santarosae reached its greatest extent ~20,000 cal BP, then rapidly shrunk until the islands separated between about 11,000 and 9000 cal BP (Reeder-Myers et al. 2015). Santarosae was never attached to the mainland during the Quaternary, but the water-gap between it and the mainland shrunk to ~6–8 km during the Last Glacial Maximum. Rising eustatic sea levels during the late Pleistocene and Early Holocene submerged low-lying coastal plains, inundating roughly 75% of Santarosae.

The oldest widely accepted archaeological site identified on the NCI is the Arlington Springs site (CA-SRI-173), where Phil Orr discovered the bones of Arlington Man. Orr (1960, 1968) recognized the potential

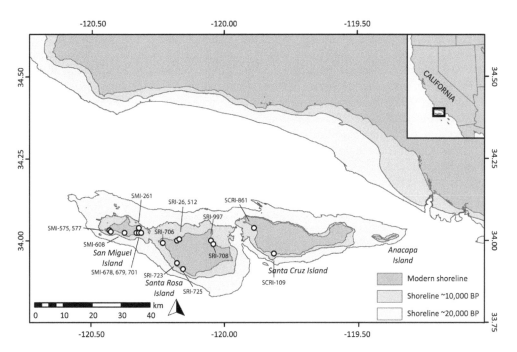

FIGURE 13.1. Reconstructed paleogeography of Santarosae Island between about 20,000 and 10,000 cal BP, including approximate locations of IPT sites listed in Table 13.1. Image by Todd J. Braje and used with permission.

antiquity of the two human femurs and one patella he found buried 11 m below the surface in the wall of an arroyo near the modern mouth of Arlington Canyon. Initial radiocarbon dating efforts supported an antiquity of at least 10,000 ^{14}C BP (Orr 1960), with more recent dating and geoarchaeological studies suggesting the site dates to ~13,000 cal BP (Johnson et al. 2002). If Arlington Man consumed some marine resources, however, the age of his skeleton may be a century or two younger.

Eleven other sites ^{14}C dated to the late Pleistocene (~11,500 cal BP or older) have been identified on the NCI, including two buried middens exposed in the coastal terraces near the mouth of Arlington Canyon (CA-SRI-26 and -512; Erlandson et al. 2011, 2020), three low-density shell middens and lithic scatters located on bluffs overlooking the southwest coast of Santa Rosa Island (CA-SRI-706, -723, and -725; Rick et al. 2013), a large site (CA-SRI-997/H) situated on the low coastal terrace near Bechers Bay on eastern Santa Rosa (Braje and Erlandson 2019; Gill et al. 2021); several small shell middens and a massive lithic scatter (CA-SMI-678, -679, -701) located near Cardwell Point on eastern San Miguel (Erlandson et al. 2011), a low-density shell midden stratum deeply buried along the dripline of the rock shelter at Daisy Cave (CA-SMI-261) on northeastern San Miguel (Erlandson et al. 1996), and a recently identified estuarine shell midden (CA-SCRI-857) on western Santa Cruz Island. Excavations at these sites demonstrate that late Pleistocene Paleocoastal people engaged in a diverse array of maritime hunting and foraging for their protein economies, including intertidal shellfish collecting (e.g., California mussel, red abalone), nearshore fishing (e.g., rockfish, Clupeidae), bird-hunting (e.g., Canada and snow goose), and marine mammal-hunting (e.g., elephant seal, harbor seal; Erlandson et al. 2011; Hofman et al. 2018). Recent archaeobotanical research also suggests that geophytes were an important food source for Paleocoastal peoples from at least 11,500 to 8000 cal BP (Gill et al. 2019; Gill et al. 2021; Reddy and Erlandson 2012).

Despite the inundation of ancient shorelines and >50% of coastal lowlands during the late Pleistocene and Early Holocene, more than 100 upland Paleocoastal sites have now been documented, all located ~2–6 km from ancient shorelines where Paleocoastal peoples probably spent most of their time. Along with highly productive coastal habitats (rocky shore, kelp forest, estuary, freshwater marsh), these maritime foragers were exploiting and occupying a variety of other resources, habitats, and landscapes on Santarosae, including freshwater springs, caves and rockshelters, outcrops of high-quality toolstone, strategic overlooks, interior wetlands, and a variety of plant communities.

Technologically, we currently know nothing about the nature of Paleocoastal watercraft. We do know, however, that Paleocoastal peoples wove sea grass for cordage and other artifacts (Connolly et al. 1995; Vellanoweth et al. 2003), used asphaltum (a.k.a. bitumen) for adhesive and waterproofing and red ochre for pigments and other purposes, made fish gorges and other bone tools, produced *Olivella* shell beads, manufactured a variety of chipped stone tools ranging from simple flake and core tools to elaborate projectile points described as examples of some of the finest flint-knapping known from North America (Heye 1921; Justice 2002; Smith et al. 2020), and occasionally used ground stone artifacts. Ground stone artifacts are very rare in WST assemblages in California and the Great Basin, as well as Island Paleocoastal assemblages. Ground stone artifacts in NCI Paleocoastal assemblages are currently limited to a single pitted stone—probably an anvil used to crack open black turban snails—from a ~12,000-year-old shell midden (CA-SMI-679) at Cardwell Bluffs (Erlandson et al. 2011), and a single grinding slab fragment from a ~10,000-year-old shell midden (CA-SMI-522) on western San Miguel Island (Watts 2013).

Among the latter are stemmed CIA and CIB points, as well as crescents that have been shown to be reliable chronological markers of Island Paleocoastal occupations dating between at least 12,200 to 8000 cal BP (Braje, Erlandson, and Rick 2005, 2013; Erlandson 2013; Erlandson et al. 2011; Glassow et al. 2008; Glassow et al. 2013; Gusick 2012; Gusick and Erlandson 2019; Rick 2008). The number of sites containing these point types has steadily grown on the NCI, suggesting that Paleocoastal islanders used Santarosae land- and seascapes intensively and extensively. The sheer number of Paleocoastal sites and evidence for sedentism going back at least 10,000 years may imply relatively large populations and a deeper human history not yet fully documented.

Morphology of Channel Island Paleocoastal Points and Crescents

Founder and director of the Museum of the American Indian George Heye (1921:68), one of the first to describe CIB points, believed they were ornamental: "Of all the chipped stone implements from San Miguel Island, the finest example...at its thickest part measures only an eighth of an inch. The object is of entirely too delicate a character to have been utilitarian." Today, the hundreds of specimens documented in old museum collections and recent field investigations make it clear that these Paleocoastal points were fully functional and that their manufacture was aided by intentional heat treatment (Jew and Erlandson 2013).

Finished CIA and CIB points generally are delicate, ultra-thin and share several readily recognizable morphological attributes, including a contracting stem, fine pressure flaking, and a biconvex to flat cross section (Erlandson 2013; Glassow et al. 2013). CIB points tend to be symmetrical and small in overall size, often within the range of bow-and-arrow points (Erlandson, Watts, and Jew 2014), with long and elaborate barbs and needle-like tips (Figure 13.2). Many examples show evidence of reworking, particularly on broken barbs, and resharpening, leaving some examples with blades less than 10 mm long.

CIA points share many morphological

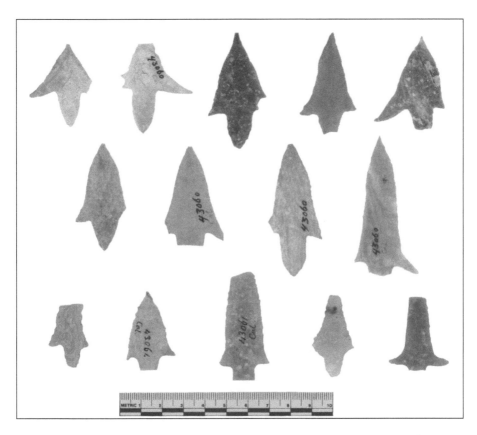

FIGURE 13.2. Channel Islands Barbed (CIB) projectile points in the collections of the Smithsonian Institution's National Museum of Natural History. Adapted and rearranged by Kristina M. Gill from an original color image by Tracy Garcia, and used with permission.

similarities to CIB points, but they are typically larger and more leaf-shaped, with wider stems relative to their size, and subtle shoulders in lieu of barbs (Figure 13.3; see Erlandson 2013). Most of the 25 or so CIA points described or illustrated have blades that are either deeply serrated or studded with a series of more irregular spurs (Erlandson 2013; Erlandson, Braje, and Gill 2019). Currently, it is unclear whether the morphological differences between CIB and CIA points are the result of their use for different functions or prey types, but they are rarely found in the same assemblages. Erlandson (2013)

FIGURE 13.3. Channel Islands Amol (CIA) point from CA-SRI-26. Adapted from original composite digital image by Keith Hamm and Jon Erlandson, and used with permission.

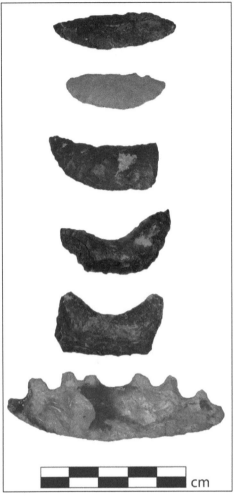

FIGURE 13.4. Various Island Paleocoastal Tradition (IPT) crescent forms from CA-SRI-512 and CA-SMI-679. Digital image by Jon Erlandson, and used with permission.

workshop sites (CA-678, -679, -680, -701) at Cardwell Bluffs, and buried occupational components at CA-SMI-261 and CA-SRI-26, -512, -708, and -997/H. At several of the latter, crescents have been found associated with numerous bird bones (waterfowl and seabirds) that support a hypothesized function primarily as transverse projectile points for hunting birds (Erlandson, Rick, et al. 2011; Erlandson et al. 2020; Moss and Erlandson 2013). Where migratory waterfowl (geese and ducks) bones are abundant, they also suggest a "winter" (late fall to early spring) occupation of the NCI by Paleocoastal people.

Crescents on the islands include several different types (see Fenenga 2010), ranging from classic half-moon "lunate" forms to deeply notched specimens (Figure 13.4). Many of the latter appear to have been manufactured on leaf-shaped bifaces notched on one side. Some unfinished or broken specimens ("crescentics") are cruder and less regular, but finished crescents tend to be finely made, bilaterally symmetrical, with thin and flat cross sections. The finer examples are ultra-thin, pressure-flaked extensively, and sometimes include serrations or notches on one edge and overshot (outre passé) flakes. Medial grinding of many crescent edges as well as fracture patterns of broken specimens seem to support a transverse point function.

Island crescents and both CIB and CIA points were constructed from a variety of medium- to high-quality cherts locally available on the NCI or along the southern California coast. Chemical analyses to reliably distinguish between mainland and island chert sources are not yet available, but given the number of new sources (i.e., Monterey, Cico, Tuqan, 'Anyapax, and Wima chert) identified on the NCI in recent years (see Erlandson, Gill, et al. 2019) they seem likely to have been fashioned primarily from local island sources (Jew et al. 2013).

The dearth of artifacts made from high-quality and distinctive Franciscan cherts or fused shales not found on the islands but abundant on the adjacent mainland suggests

hypothesized that CIA points may be earlier since the only in situ specimens found so far are from two shell middens dated to ~12,000 cal BP.

Several hundred crescents have been found on the NCI, although until recently most of these were from old museum collections lacking precise provenience information. In the last 20 years, scores of crescents have been found in sites on San Miguel, Santa Rosa, and Santa Cruz islands, ranging from surficial lithic scatters to several quarry/

that NCI Paleocoastal technological traditions were a distinctive island phenomenon. A single obsidian pressure flake recovered from a deeply buried and stratified context at CA-SRI-512—sourced to the West Sugarloaf flow in the Coso Volcanic Field in southeastern California more than 300 km distant—demonstrates that Paleocoastal people also participated in long-distance exchange networks by at least 11,700 cal BP (Erlandson et al. 2011; Gill et al. 2020).

Chronology and Distribution of NCI Crescents, CIB and CIA Points

Little more than a decade ago, CIB points were assumed to function as the tips of Late Holocene arrows and CIA points were an unrecognized type. The thin and delicate nature of CIB points and their recovery from surface contexts led Justice (2002:264)—lacking chronometric data for old museum specimens without specific provenience—to conclude that they "date roughly from ca. 1000 BC to ca. AD 1000 or later." Since no CIB or CIA points had been recovered from controlled excavations at the time, this assumption was reasonable. Then Glassow and colleagues (2008:47–50) recovered three CIB points from stratified deposits at CA-SCRI-109 dated between ~8500 and 7800 cal BP (see also Gusick 2012). Once the antiquity of CIB points was recognized, another example was soon identified in a museum collection from Daisy Cave, with field notes suggesting that it came from the very base of a shell midden which dates to ~11,700 cal BP. Subsequent surveys across the NCI have targeted landforms and features—freshwater springs, caves and rockshelters, chert sources, strategic overlooks, and potential wetlands—likely to contain late Pleistocene and Early Holocene deposits.

As noted earlier, more than 100 Paleocoastal sites have now been identified on the NCI (Gusick and Erlandson 2019), and more continue to be documented (e.g., Jazwa and Rosencrance 2019). At least 75 of these sites have been radiocarbon-dated, with the remaining cross-dated using diagnostic chipped stone artifacts (crescents and CIA and CIB points). Scores of ^{14}C dates from sites containing these distinctive and diagnostic Paleocoastal artifacts demonstrate that they date between ~12,200 and 8000 cal BP (Gusick and Erlandson 2019:Table 2). Of the 32 sites that have produced CIB and/or CIA points, 14 have associated radiocarbon dates (Table 13.1); the others have produced no datable organic remains. Of the 34 sites that have produced crescents, 13 have produced ^{14}C dates of Paleocoastal age.

Despite this robust and widely published record (e.g., Braje et al. 2013; Erlandson et al. 2005; Erlandson et al. 2011; Glassow et al. 2008; Rick et al. 2013), questions have persisted about the chronology of Paleocoastal stemmed point types on the NCI. Potter and colleagues (2018a:5) claimed "The Channel Islands sites are not associated with dated stemmed points (and stemmed points in California are not well dated)" (see also Hamilton et al. 2019:Figure 13.1). Actually, approximately half of the known archaeological sites that have produced CIB or CIA points have associated radiocarbon ages from intact and stratified midden components (see Gusick and Erlandson 2019:Figure 3.1). Of these, at least eight have produced in situ Paleocoastal points or crescents from modern, controlled excavations (see Figure 13.5 and Table 13.1). This chronology is further supported by the fact that CIA and CIB points often are found associated with crescents that are morphologically similar to those recovered at early sites throughout California, the Great Basin, and the broader Far West from Washington state to Baja California (Gusick and Erlandson 2019; Moss and Erlandson 2013).

All told, the radiocarbon chronology of Paleocoastal stemmed points and crescents on the NCI suggests an age between ~12,200 and 8000 cal BP. The chronology of the relatively rare CIA points may be restricted to the early part of this range (Erlandson 2013), but more research is needed to confirm this. The temporal continuity of CIB points on the NCI, spanning 4,000 years or more, has

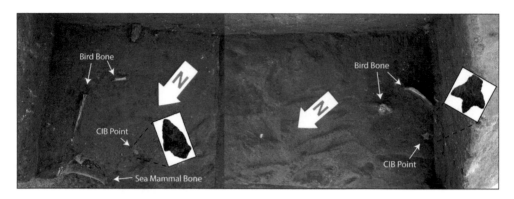

FIGURE 13.5. Paleocoastal Channel Islands Barbed (CIB) points in situ, associated with bird and marine mammal bones found in a deeply buried, ~11,700 cal BP component at CA-SRI-512. Unit photos by Torben Rick, point photos by Jon Erlandson, and figure assembled by Todd Braje. Used with permission.

been noted by several Channel Islands archaeologists as being substantial for southern California (e.g., Braje et al. 2013; Erlandson et al. 2011; Gusick and Erlandson 2019). This chronology is confirmed, however, when considering only specimens captured in controlled archaeological excavations, with CIB points recovered at CA-SRI-512 and CA-SMI-678 and -679—the oldest sites to produce such points—and CA-SCRI-109— the youngest to produce CIB points. Nearly three-quarters (8/11) of these sites that have produced CIB points, and a much larger majority of CIB points recovered from those sites, are associated with radiocarbon dates greater than 11,000 cal BP.

It is at least possible, therefore, that specimens recovered from later sites (CA-SCRI-109, CA-SMI-608, and CA-SMI-575-NE) represent heirlooms curated by later Paleocoastal people. Examples from CA-SMI-575-NE and CA-SCRI-109, for instance, are either preforms or broken and heavily resharpened—suggesting that they could have been recycled utilitarian objects intended for reuse by the site occupants. This idea may be supported by numerous Early Holocene sites investigated recently that have produced either no bifaces at all or a few sites (e.g., CA-SMI-507, CA-SRI-666) with substantial numbers of bifaces but no crescents or CIA/CIB points. A similar pattern exists for crescents found in dated NCI contexts, the vast majority of which come from earlier Paleocoastal sites or components (Braje et al. 2013).

However, the potentially long-term temporal continuity of CIB points is not unique. Several other projectile point traditions in North America's Far West persisted for 4,000 years or more, including crescents, the broader WST, Humboldt points, Mendocino concave base points, and the Pacific Coast side-notched cluster (see Hamilton et al. 2019: Figure 13.1; Justice 2002).

Future discoveries and dating efforts should help refine the chronology of crescents and CIB and CIA points on the NCI. At present, these artifact types are reasonably well-dated when compared to other Paleo-indian and Early Holocene lithic traditions in the American West (see Rosencrance et al., Chapter 2).

Early Stemmed Points on the Southern California Mainland

If chronological control of early stemmed points on the NCI is reasonably well established, their potential relationship to other WST assemblages in the Far West remains uncertain. Elsewhere in California, including the Southern Channel Islands, no CIA or CIB points have been definitively identified. Glassow and colleagues (2008:50) noted one potential CIB point from CA-SBA-52, located

TABLE 13.1. Island Paleocoastal Tradition Sites from the Northern Channel Islands with Diagnostic Technology (Stemmed Points and/or Crescents) and Clearly Associated Radiocarbon Dates.

Site No.	¹⁴C Age (cal BP)[a]	CIB Point	CIA Point	Crescent	In Situ	Reference
Santa Cruz Island						
CA-SCRI-109	8530–7890	Y	N	N	Y	Glassow et al. 2008
CA-SCRI-861	8725–8560	N	N	Y	N	Erlandson et al. 2016
Santa Rosa Island						
CA-SRI-723	12,170–11,930	N	Y	Y	N	Rick et al. 2013
CA-SRI-26	12,060–11,190	Y	Y	Y	Y	Erlandson 2013
CA-SRI-512W	12,010–11,355	Y	N	Y	Y	Erlandson et al. 2011
CA-SRI-997/H	11,610–10,560	Y	N	Y	Y	Erlandson, Braje, and Gill 2019
CA-SRI-706	11,560–11,210	N	Y	Y	N	Rick et al. 2013
CA-SRI-725	11,360–11,220	Y	N	Y	N	Rick et al. 2013
CA-SRI-708	11,190–11,120	Y	Y	Y	Y	Rick et al. 2013
San Miguel Island						
CA-SMI-679SE	12,200–11,430	Y	Y	Y	Y	Erlandson et al. 2011
CA-SMI-678	12,240–11,190	Y	Y	Y	Y	Erlandson et al. 2011
CA-SMI-701	11,540–11,410	N	Y	Y	N	Erlandson 2010
CA-SMI-261[b]	11,700–8500	Y	N	Y	N	Erlandson et al. 1996
CA-SMI-608	9860–8065	Y	N	N	N	Braje et al. 2005
CA-SMI-577	8980–8800	N	N	Y	N	Braje et al. 2005
CA-SMI-575-NE	8520–8350	Y	N	N	N	Erlandson and Braje 2007

Note: CIA = Channel Islands Amol (point); CIB = Channel Islands Barbed (point).
[a] Date ranges for the age of the archaeological assemblages provided by authors in published works or unpublished notes. See references for details.
[b] Erlandson attributes a likely age of 11,700 to 8600 cal BP based on a review of Charles Rozaire's field notes and his more recent excavations and radiocarbon dating (see Erlandson et al. 1996). A CIB point recovered by Rozaire appears to be associated with the earlier IPT occupation at Daisy Cave.

adjacent to the Goleta Slough on the Santa Barbara coast, but this finding has yet to be confirmed. Numerous Early Holocene sites along southern California's mainland coast (e.g., Drover et al. 1983; Erlandson 1994; Erlandson and Colten 1991; Glassow 1996; Jones et al. 2008; Koerper and Drover 1983) have produced stemmed points, but these do not closely resemble CIA or CIB points from the NCI.

On the other hand, dozens of crescents have been found in early sites along California's mainland coast, including at least seven examples from four sites in Santa Barbara County (Lebow et al. 2018; Sanchez et al. 2017:Table 1). On the Southern Channel Islands, 18 crescents have been found on San Nicolas Island, but just two on Santa Catalina and none on the more arid Santa Barbara and San Clemente islands (Gusick and Erlandson 2019:84).

This patterning might be best explained by dietary differences between mainland and NCI hunter-gatherers. Along the mainland coast, milling stones (manos and metates) commonly are found in Early Holocene assemblages postdating ~9000 cal BP, likely reflecting a diet heavy in plant foods such as seeds and perhaps acorns, often heavily supplemented by protein-rich shellfish from estuarine and rocky shore habitats (Erlandson 1994; Rosenthal and Hildebrandt 2019). For decades, archaeologists believed that Milling Stone (Oak Grove) Horizon sites—marked by abundant manos and metates, few projectile points, and scarce vertebrate remains—represented the first peoples along the California coast (see Olson 1930; Rogers 1929; Wallace 1955). Largely lacking a similar technological horizon on the offshore islands, most archaeologists believed the Channel Islands were not settled until the Middle Holocene (~7500–3500 cal BP).

We now know that late Pleistocene and Early Holocene islanders focused their protein diets on marine shellfish, fish, sea mammals, and birds. Together, these mostly marine and aquatic animals provided rich sources of complete proteins, fat, and essential micronutrients. These were supplemented and complemented by a wealth of carbohydrate- and calorie-rich plant foods, especially geophytes such as the *Brodiaea*-type corms (e.g., blue dicks, *Dipterostemon capitatus*; see Gill 2016; Gill and Hoppa 2016; Reddy and Erlandson 2012). Today, these geophytes are abundant on the NCI, they have relatively high return rates (~750–1,050 kCal/hr; see Gill et al. 2021) and require no milling tools to process, so their dietary importance probably explains the lack of a Milling Stone Horizon on the islands (Gill and Hoppa 2016).

Within this island adaptation, seemingly unique in California, Paleocoastal stemmed points on the NCI seem most likely to represent a specialized aquatic hunting technology for taking marine mammals (e.g., sea otters, seals) or marine fish in nearshore waters. Why CIA and CIB points are not evident along the adjacent mainland coast—where marine mammals and fish also were harvested by Early Holocene people (Erlandson 1994)—is not clear, although sites older than ~10,000–9,000 years are rare along the mainland coast.

One exception is the Sudden Flats site (CA-SBA-1547), located north of Point Conception on the northern Santa Barbara coast, which dates to ~10,700 cal BP (Lebow et al. 2015). CA-SBA-1547 is a mainland Paleocoastal shell midden that produced a faunal assemblage dominated by the remains of rocky shore marine shellfish (primarily California mussel, *Mytilus californianus*), with lesser amounts of rabbits, fish, marine mammals, cervids, canids, birds, and other animals. The artifacts recovered included abundant debitage dominated by local Monterey cherts but also obsidian artifacts from several discrete sources, several leaf-shaped bifaces, burins and burin spalls, microblades, a single notched "zoomorphic" crescent, one mano, and three spire-removed *Olivella* shell beads.

Lebow and colleagues (2015) concluded that this assemblage was unique to the Vandenberg region and distinctly different from the earlier NCI Paleocoastal assemblages—suggesting possible links to Beringian traditions such as the Denali complex. The presence of a crescent suggests a link to WST assemblages of the Far West, however, as do the interior obsidian sources (Coso Volcanic Field, Casa Diablo, Annadel, and Napa Valley) represented, and a stemmed point found eroding from the site after Lebow and colleagues' fieldwork and laboratory analyses were completed. Subsequent examination of early NCI Paleocoastal assemblages also identified small numbers of burin-like flakes or spalls and microblade-like flakes (Douglas Harro, personal communication 2016; K. Smith 2021), further suggesting that the Sudden Flats assemblage is technologically similar in many respects to early IPT assemblages.

A detailed examination of the links between these early island and coastal assemblages in California to the broader WST is beyond the scope of this chapter (but see K. Smith 2021; Beck and Jones, Chapter 12).

A large assemblage from the Witt site, located on the south margin of Tulare Lake in California's southern Central Valley, may provide an intermediate technological link between early coastal assemblages and the WST in the Great Basin. It has produced hundreds of early stemmed points and crescents, along with smaller numbers of fluted and basally thinned fluted points (Hopkins and Garfinkel 2008).

Morphologically, CIA points are also similar to early stemmed points in some assemblages from the Intermountain West (i.e., Lind Coulee in Washington and Cooper's Ferry in Idaho; see Davis et al. 2019), with their larger overall size, long stems, and slight shoulders (Pratt et al. 2020:73). On the other hand, CIB points, with their smaller size and prominent barbs, more closely resemble ~16,000 to 13,000-year-old tanged points from incipient Jomon sites in Japan (Kenji Nagai, personal communication, 2017). Detailed morphological studies of these point types are required before definitive conclusions about their relationships can be drawn.

Discussion and Conclusions

The WST persisted for ~5,000 years in western North America and includes a diverse array of points and assemblages. This endurance should be expected for a technological or cultural tradition spanning large expanses of space and time, as well as a wide range of environments and adaptations. Although some have argued that stemmed projectile points are not technologically diagnostic (Potter, Baichtal, et al. 2018), most archaeologists working in western North America have recognized a distinctive and early technological tradition that includes a variety of stemmed points, chipped stone crescents, and leaf-shaped bifaces.

On California's NCI, we have identified and defined a distinctive maritime WST variant dubbed the IPT. More than 100 sites dating between ~13,000 and 8000 cal BP have now been identified on the NCI, including the Arlington Man locality (CA-SRI-173) dated to ~13,000 cal BP that has produced no diagnostic artifacts. Numerous sites, both shell middens and lithic scatters, have produced chipped stone artifact assemblages containing lunate and notched crescents, leaf-shaped bifaces, and delicately flaked and stemmed CIA and CIB points. Where secure stratigraphy and radiocarbon dates are available with such diagnostic artifacts, these assemblages date between ~12,200 and 8000 cal BP. Crescents and Paleocoastal stemmed points are most common in IPT assemblages dated between ~12,000 and 10,000 cal BP, but it is not clear if these diagnostic Paleocoastal artifacts gradually faded out or were simply recycled by later people. The persistence of crescents and stemmed Paleocoastal points on the NCI, however, is consistent with their temporal distribution on the mainland coast, adjacent interior, and Great Basin. The disappearance of crescents in the Far West might be related to a decline in wetlands and waterfowl associated with aridification, but it is not clear why CIB points on the islands would disappear about the same time.

A handful of fluted Clovis-like points have been found along California's mainland coast, but these are undated and may well derive from a later Clovis incursion into California. Analysis of old museum collections and the investigation of Island Paleocoastal sites has cataloged more than 1,000 chipped stone bifaces on the NCI with no hint of fluted points. We once believed that evidence for a Clovis presence on the Channel Islands might someday be found, but that now seems unlikely. Instead the IPT, especially its earlier manifestations on the NCI, seems firmly linked to the WST of the American Far West. Much remains to be learned about the peopling of the Americas, but it seems increasingly probable that the WST and the IPT will one day be found to share a common ancestry derived from an initial human dispersal that followed Pacific Rim coastlines from Northeast Asia and Beringia into the Americas, probably between ~18,000 and 15,000 cal BP.

Acknowledgments

Thanks to Katelyn McDonough, Richard Rosencrance, and Jordan Pratt for inviting us to participate in their 2019 Society for American Archaeology session on the WST, as well as this edited volume. We are grateful to Katelyn McDonough, David Madsen, and two anonymous reviewers for their helpful suggestions on an earlier version of our manuscript and to Reba Rauch, Justin Bracken, and the editorial team at the University of Utah Press. Finally, we thank Kevin Smith for his technological insights, Matt Vestuto for providing a Chumash alternative to Santarosae, and Tracy Garcia for her efforts to find and photograph diagnostic IPT points housed in the collections of the Smithsonian's National Museum of Natural History.

Notes

1. The term "Paleocoastal Tradition" (or Paleo-Coastal) was coined by Emma Lou Davis (Davis et al. 1969) in a monograph exploring the similarities between early lithic assemblages from the interior and coastal areas of southern California. The concept was more fully developed by Moratto (1984:104–109), who saw "widespread technological relationships" between these assemblages—including the presence of stemmed points and chipped stone crescents, as well as a lack or dearth of milling stones—diagnostic of later assemblages along the coast. Moratto considered the Paleocoastal Tradition to be an economic variant of the Western Pluvial Lakes Tradition (a.k.a., WST), including sites with evidence for estuarine and marine foraging dated between ~11,000 and 8000 ^{14}C BP (~13,000–9000 cal BP). Although no Channel Islands assemblages of this antiquity were known in the 1960s to early 1980s, we have followed the nomenclature of Davis and Moratto and agree that the technological similarities between Paleocoastal and interior WST assemblages most likely result from a common origin and ancestry.

2. Matthew Vestuto (personal communication to Erlandson, 2021), a Chumash descendent and linguistic scholar, suggested the term "Shamalamʹa" ("it was one") as a more appropriate Chumash alternate to the Spanish-derived Santarosae.

PART IV

Moving Forward

14

Across the Continental Divide

DAVID J. MELTZER

In one of the earliest syntheses of North America's late Pleistocene archaeological record, Frank Roberts was at a loss as to how one might explain the relationship between the early artifact complexes west and east of the Rockies. The "greatest source of disagreement," as he saw it, was in regard to their relative ages (Roberts 1940:106). In those pre-radiocarbon days, estimates of the age of the Pinto Basin and Lake Mohave complexes of the Far West were based on associated pluvial events, which put their age at around 15,000 years before the present (Campbell and Campbell 1935; Campbell et al. 1937). Yet, if that were the case, these complexes would be several thousand years older than the "Clovis-Portales" sites of eastern New Mexico (e.g., Anderson Basin and Blackwater Locality 1 [Howard 1935]), which were thought to be only 12,000 to 13,000 years old (Antevs 1935). Roberts was unconvinced those Great Basin sites were older than the "Clovis-Portales" sites: he thought that at most they were all the same age (Roberts 1940:107).

How then to account for two apparently distinct cultural traditions on opposite sides of the Rockies? Compounding the problem, in the west projectile points suggestive of the "generalized type of Folsom" (i.e., Clovis points, though they were not then so-named) were occasionally found along with the Lake Mohave and Pinto Basin types (Roberts 1940:88–89, 93). In answering his own question, Roberts proposed there had been two "lines of movement" or migratory streams into the Americas (Meltzer 2015:408). One came "down the eastern slopes of the Rockies, thence out over the Plains, spreading eastward to the Mississippi River in the more southerly precincts and up its various tributary streams to leave the traces found throughout the eastern portion of the country." This was, according to Roberts, "probably the route followed by the Sandia Cave, Abilene, Folsom, and affiliated groups."[1] The other migration was apparently "down the plateau between the Rockies and the Coast Range, into the Great Basin and thence into southern California, Arizona, and on into Mexico. This was the pathway for the Lake Mohave, Pinto Basin, Cochise, and related peoples."

Assuming the latter route opened somewhat later than the one east of the Rockies suggested that the "occupation of the Basin and adjacent territory may have been slightly retarded." Given the occasional co-occurrence of the various point types, he thought "there was undoubtedly some mixing of representatives from the two main streams...as a result of contingents from one working south and from the other moving east" (Roberts 1940:108–109).

The More Things Change…

In reading the chapters in *Current Perspectives on Stemmed and Fluted Technologies in the American Far West*, it was difficult for me *not* to think of Roberts' efforts in 1940 to make sense of the variation of stemmed points found across the Far West and their possible relationship with Clovis fluted points.[2] What came immediately to mind was how much, and yet in some respects how little, has changed since Roberts pondered those issues 80 years ago, how complicated some questions and matters continue to be, and how and in what ways the late Pleistocene archaeological record differs (or doesn't) across the Continental Divide and what that might say of the earliest people on the continent.

I'll explore a number of those issues here, but let me open with an overview of where some key empirical matters stand today, as seen through the chapters in this volume and other recent publications. I will then turn to some of the broader issues raised by these chapters. This won't be a comprehensive look at all the issues and comes with the disclaimer that I am very much *not* an expert in the late Pleistocene archaeology of the Far West. Worse, the historical narrative of the archaeology that's been done there over the last eight decades (McDonough et al., Chapter 1) was a mirror to me of my own culpable neglect of the region. Beck and Jones once glumly observed that "it is always interesting to read the Paleoindian literature, which seems to focus on the Plains and the East. The Intermountain West (as well as the Pacific Coast)…is generally mentioned only in passing and then forgotten" (Beck and Jones 2010:106). Guilty as charged.

I start at the beginning, archaeologically. There's now compelling evidence of an older-than-Clovis human presence at sites in the Intermountain West, most notably Cooper's Ferry (Idaho; Davis et al. 2019; Davis, Chapter 7) and the Paisley Caves (Oregon; Jenkins et al. 2013; Smith et al., Chapter 3). The earliest levels at these sites are "pre-Clovis" in a chronological sense, though the jury is still out as to whether they are pre-Clovis in historical or ancestral terms (Davis, Chapter 7), and how far back they go in absolute years. Nonetheless, this human presence is earlier than Clovis, whether compared to a rather restrictive "short chronology" which has Clovis no older than ~13,050 cal BP (Waters et al. 2020), or against the oldest known Clovis occurrences at the Aubrey (Texas) and El Fin del Mundo (Sonora, Mexico) sites dated to ~13,400 cal BP (Miller et al. 2013; Sánchez et al. 2014).

The evidence from Cooper's Ferry and the Paisley Caves reinforces the presumption—albeit one yet to be archaeologically demonstrated—that the first Americans travelled south from eastern Beringia along the Pacific Northwest coast (Braje et al. 2017, 2020; Davis et al. 2019), and not via the ice-free corridor. The latter was not a biologically viable route for hunter-gatherers until after the earliest people were already in North and South America (Clark et al. 2022; Heintzman et al. 2016; Pedersen et al. 2016). Long reaches of the coast were ice-free after 17,000 years ago, and by ~16,000 years ago the coast was clear (Darvill et al. 2018; Darvill et al. 2022; Lesnek et al. 2018; Menounos et al. 2017). By then, we can reasonably assume the coast supported food resources necessary to human travelers who came as maritime hunters/seafarers, or foragers who exploited terrestrial and near-shore resources (Braje et al. 2020; Erlandson and Braje 2011; Erlandson et al. 2007; Erlandson et al. 2015; Mason 2020; Sutton 2017). Early peoples could have turned inland once south of the Cordilleran ice sheet and followed major river courses into the interior of the Far West (Beck and Jones 2010; Davis et al. 2019; Sutton 2017).

The northeast Asian roots of their toolkit and technology can be sketched in general terms (Pratt et al. 2020), but whether it is possible to be more specific and identify particular historical progenitors (e.g., Davis et al. 2019; Davis and Madsen 2020; Erlandson and Braje 2011; Erlandson et al., Chapter 13) is less certain. For that matter, there's the question of how the newly named "Cooper's Ferry" point type (Davis, Chapter 7) relates to stemmed points at sites east of the Rockies, such as at the Friedkin site (Texas) where the stemmed points are of comparable antiquity, or at the adjacent Gault site (Texas) where those points are reported to be much older (Waters et al. 2018; Williams et al. 2018; but see Surovell, Chapter 10).

Along with that older-than-Clovis evidence, a substantial and better dated record of sites and artifacts also now shows the presence of stemmed points in the Far West at least 12,600 years ago, and possibly as much as 13,000 years ago (Rosencrance et al., Chapter 2). At that antiquity, these overlap chronologically with Clovis on the *eastern* side of the Continental Divide (Jenkins et al. 2012; Rosencrance et al., Chapter 2; Smith et al., Chapter 3), though the duration of overlap depends on where one puts the end of the Clovis era (Surovell, Chapter 10).

Some identify 12,700 cal BP as the close of the Clovis period (Waters, Stafford, and Carlson 2020; also Duke and Stueber, Chapter 4), making the overlap with early Western Stemmed Tradition (WST) forms just a few centuries long. Yet the full chronological range of Clovis is not well established or even agreed upon; compare, for example, the lists of what are considered credibly dated Clovis sites in Becerra-Valdivia and Higham 2020, as well as Waters and colleagues 2020b. This lack of agreement occurs for many reasons. For one, there's the unfortunate reality that the vast majority of Clovis occurrences in North America are not securely dated, which means that while Clovis points "east, south, and north of the Great Basin...date to a very narrow and consistent range" (Surovell, Chapter 10:214), the sample is a very small one on which to hang a chronology (Prasciunas and Surovell 2015), let alone to assume it applies to Clovis points *in* the Great Basin. Problems also present concerning sample unevenness, representativeness, and radiocarbon uncertainties (Brown et al. 2019; Prasciunas and Surovell 2015; Surovell, Chapter 10), which can readily bias a small sample of ages. For example, five of the 10 Clovis ages Waters and colleagues (2020) deem "credible" are on mammoth bones associated with Clovis artifacts at kill/scavenging sites. However, these ages may reveal more of the window of time—and the place—when (and where) Clovis groups were preying on or scavenging these animals than the full temporal and spatial span of the Clovis period. Finally, there are debates over just what constitutes Clovis, and whether that includes sites such as Bull Brook, Debert, and Vail in northeastern North America, the ages of which are several centuries younger than 12,700 cal BP (Bradley et al. 2008; Buchanan et al. 2017; Ellis and Lothrop 2019; Miller et al. 2013; Rondeau et al., Chapter 9; Shott 2013).

Debate over the Clovis type carries over to the *western* side of the Continental Divide and, in particular, questions whether fluted points there can be considered "classic" Clovis (e.g., Duke and Stueber, Chapter 4; Jones and Beck, Chapter 8; Knell and Sutton, Chapter 5; Rondeau et al., Chapter 9). There are several reasons why that's thought to matter. None of the apparently classic Clovis points in the Far West—such as those that occur at East Wenatchee (Mehringer and Foit 1990), Fenn (Frison and Bradley 1999), and Simon (Butler 1963)—are radiocarbon-dated. Nor have any been found in a buried stratified context with stemmed points in the Far West that would make it possible to ascertain their relative age. One can readily appreciate why this is "extremely frustrating to archaeologists working in that region" (Beck and Jones, Chapter 12:256; also Brown et al. 2019; Surovell, Chapter 10). If these western occurrences could be considered classic Clovis, then "assuming the geologic stratigraphic principle of lateral continuity can be applied to cultural stratigraphy" (Surovell, Chapter 10:213), that would make them the same age as classic Clovis elsewhere (Davis, Chapter 7; Jones and Beck, Chapter 8), ignoring for the moment the complicated issue of what the age (or ages) elsewhere might be (Brown et al. 2019).

If they are classic Clovis, researchers believe that could also help clarify the typological and chronological differences with the fluted point variants that also occur in the Far West, such as the generic "Western Fluted" and "Great Basin Concave Base," and the more recently named "Sunshine Fluted" point types (Beck and Jones 2009; Beck, Jones, and Taylor 2019; Davis, Chapter 7; Jones and Beck, Chapter 8; Knell and Sutton, Chapter 5; Miller et al. 2013; Rondeau et al., Chapter 9; Willig and Aikens 1988). Specifying these point typologies might also shed light on how those variants relate historically to classic Clovis and other fluted point variants elsewhere (e.g., Smith and Goebel 2018). For others, the presence of classic Clovis points provides a warrant to assert that the types of activities Clovis groups sometimes engaged in elsewhere, such as mammoth-hunting, must have occurred in the Far West as well (Duke and Stueber, Chapter 4).

Finally, if classic Clovis points are present in the Far West, it opens the possibility of tracing the movements of people from east of the Continental Divide into the Intermountain West (Beck and Jones 2010; Beck and Jones, Chapter 12; Beck, Jones, and Taylor 2019; Davis, Chapter 7). Clarifying this matter is important, for if Clovis groups were on the same landscape at the same time as WST groups, it calls up Roberts' broader and long-unanswered question of what the relationship between the two might have been. Is the archaeological record of the Far West, as Beck and Jones and others have suggested, "a mosaic...of [separate] population migrations," possibly including from Asia (Beck and Jones 2010:106; Jenkins et al. 2012)?

That question was neglected in the decades after Roberts (1940) first raised it (McDonough et al., Chapter 1; Jones and Beck, Chapter 8), as it was long assumed WST materials were both younger than Clovis (e.g., Beck and Jones 1997; Brown et al. 2019; Goebel and Keene 2014; Grayson 1993) and derived from it (e.g., Jennings 1964; Willig and Aikens 1988). Alan Bryan had argued otherwise (e.g., Bryan 1980, 1988), though without gaining much purchase (Beck and Jones, Chapter 8; Brown et al. 2019; McDonough et al., Chapter 1).

The question of the relationship of WST and Clovis only re-emerged in a significant way with the increasing evidence that WST assemblages dated to Clovis times (Davis and Schweger 2004; Jenkins et al. 2012), and especially with Beck and Jones' provocative hypothesis that Clovis points in the Intermountain West represented the migration of Clovis groups (or the diffusion of their technology) into a region already populated by WST groups (Beck and Jones 2010). Their hypothesis sparked an ongoing archaeological debate (Beck and Jones 2012a; Davis et al. 2012; Fiedel and Morrow 2012; Morrow 2019; Waters et al. 2018; see also McDonough et al., Chapter 1; Beck and Jones, Chapter 12). The question of whether there was in-migration of a population or diffusion of a material culture is not one that can be answered by archaeology alone; fortunately, it no longer has to be, as discussed below (Moreno-Mayar, Vinner, et al. 2018; Willerslev and Meltzer 2021).

It was already apparent to Roberts in 1940 that several forms of late Pleistocene/Early Holocene stemmed points were present in the Intermountain West. Today, far more types are known, as detailed and analyzed in a number of chapters (e.g., Erlandson et al., Chapter 13; Keyes, Chapter 11; Knell and Sutton, Chapter 5; Rondeau et al., Chapter 9; Rosencrance et al., Chapter 2). Pinning down the absolute or even the relative ages of these types is challenging (Goebel and Keene 2014; Rosencrance et al., Chapter 2; Surovell, Chapter 10). This difficulty is so not least because the archaeological record of the Far West is still derived principally from open, relatively shallow surface sites (Beck and Jones 2013; Brown et al. 2019; McDonough et al., Chapter 1; Smith et al. 2020; Smith et al., Chapter 3). Assemblages of the right age have been recovered from caves, rockshelters, and other settings with the potential for sorting cultural materials stratigraphically, such as Bonneville Estates Rockshelter (Goebel et al. 2018; Goebel et al. 2021) and the Paisley Caves (Jenkins et al. 2012; Jenkins et al. 2013). Yet, none provides a clear-cut sequence of the various WST forms (Davis, Chapter 7;

Rosencrance et al., Chapter 2; Smith et al., Chapter 3).

The grass is thought to be greener on the other side of the Rockies at sites such as Blackwater Locality 1 (New Mexico) and Hell Gap (Wyoming; Haynes 1995; Holliday 2000; Pelton et al. 2017), which seemingly provide "recognizable and cogent" sequences (Rosencrance et al., Chapter 2:21; also Surovell, Chapter 10). In point of fact, the sequences at those sites are not always that cogent (Haynes 2018; Haynes and Hill 2017; Pelton et al. 2017; Pelton et al. 2018). Nevertheless, multicomponent Paleoindian sites do seem to be more numerous on the Great Plains than they are in the Far West (Holliday and Meltzer 2010; Surovell, Chapter 10). This finding could be just a matter of sampling (bad) luck or differences in the geology or hydrology of these areas; but it could also possibly reflect differences in adaptive strategies and land use between these regions, of which more is discussed below.

A larger issue is whether it will even be possible to discern a clear-cut sequence when dealing with a proliferation of types that may overlap spatially and temporally (Rosencrance et al., Chapter 2; Knell and Sutton, Chapter 5). This concern is hardly unique to the archaeology of the Far West, as a proliferation of (often undated) point types across the Pleistocene/Holocene boundary marks other areas, including the American Southwest (Keyes, Chapter 11), eastern North America (Anderson et al. 2015; Lothrop et al. 2016; Miller and Gingerich 2013a, 2013b; Morrow 2019; Newby et al. 2005; Smallwood et al. 2019; White 2013), and the Great Plains (Haynes and Hill 2017; Holliday 2000; Surovell, Chapter 10). The challenge of discerning a sequence may partly be a problem of our own devising, since we implicitly tend to think of point styles starting and stopping on chronological cue with clean lines between them (Shott 2013), essentially forming typological horizons in a layer cake of time. A more appropriate analogy, however, might be to a marble cake. I will come back to this point.

Given some apparently contemporaneous technological changes in projectile point forms between the Far West and Great Plains (Duke and Stueber, Chapter 4; Rosencrance et al., Chapter 3), it may be tempting, as Surovell (Chapter 10:215) observes, "to correlate cultural variation across this vast space." On the other hand, as he also cautions, it may be problematic to do so. Still, in a volume in response to the overarching question *"What is the chronological and morphological relationship between Western Stemmed, Western fluted, Clovis, and other Paleoindian technocomplexes throughout the continent?"* (McDonough et al., Chapter 1, emphasis in the original), this temptation is hard to avoid.

I turn now to a consideration of that and some of the other broader issues raised in this volume, once again starting from the beginning.

From Whence They Came

Edgar B. Howard had scarcely begun his excavations at the Clovis site in 1933 before he began making plans to see if he could follow the trail of fluted points up the "perfectly logical route of migration" the first people may have taken from Lake Baikal in Siberia through the Bering Sea region and down onto the Great Plains to Clovis (Meltzer 2015:386). He never was able to, but it didn't stop him from wondering.

Ever since, archaeologists have puzzled over the origins of the tools and technologies used by the first peoples to enter the Americas, with much of the initial attention naturally on lanceolate forms present in northeast Asia and Beringia that might have served as Clovis progenitors (Goebel 1999, 2002; Pitulko et al. 2004; Straus et al. 2005). That focus has changed, insofar as Clovis—or at least their fluting technology—does not have a Beringian origin, only arriving there well after the first people had passed through (Ives et al. 2019; Smith and Goebel 2018). Fluting was, as Howard came to suspect, of "purely American origin" (Meltzer 2009, 2021).

The search for a progenitor now focuses on stemmed lanceolates (Braje et al. 2020; Davis et al. 2019; Erlandson and Braje 2011;

Pratt et al. 2020; Waters et al. 2018; Williams et al. 2018). In this regard, the more interesting question is not whether it was stemmed points the first Americans carried across the Bering Land Bridge: that now appears to be the case (Pratt et al. 2020). Rather, it's why *fluting* later emerged as a technology here, persisted for roughly a millennium, but then—unlike stemmed forms—altogether disappeared. There's a corollary question as well. If the ancestral projectile point(s) were stemmed, why on the Great Plains and Rocky Mountains are fluted points *almost* always older than stemmed points (one has to hedge, given the evidence from the Friedkin and Gault sites; Rosencrance et al., Chapter 2; Surovell, Chapter 10)?

In keeping with the notion that the first Americans came via the coast, efforts have been made to trace stemmed point technologies from east and northeast Asia around the northern rim of the Pacific Ocean down to the Channel Islands of California (Braje et al. 2020; Erlandson et al., Chapter 13). It is difficult not to notice, however, the different expectations regarding what those earlier tools and technologies ought to (or do) look like, and where they (and perhaps by extension, the First Americans) might have originated. For example, some researchers have suggested that "only lithic technologies in East Asia in the Japan/PSHK [Paleo-Sakhalin-Hokkaido-Kuril] region are old enough and similar enough to be the logical progenitor(s) of the earliest stemmed projectile point traditions in the Americas" (Davis and Madsen 2020:7; also Davis et al. 2019). Yet, others anticipate different forms and technologies (Erlandson et al., Chapter 13; Erlandson and Braje 2011). Ultimately, as Braje and colleagues note, the connection around the Pacific Rim "remains tenuous" (Braje et al. 2020:10; also, Davis et al. 2021; Erlandson et al., Chapter 13; Pratt et al. 2020).

Just how tenuous is evident in a recent, detailed review by Pratt and colleagues (2020) of the late Pleistocene stemmed forms that occur from Korea and the Russian Far East to eastern Beringia (Alaska) and down the Pacific Northwest coast. Although they demonstrate that bifacial technology appears around the time of the Last Glacial Maximum, and bifacial forms often have some form of a stem, these have only broad technological affinities. In some instances, the similarities may appear closer, but then the chronologies don't fit for an archaeological ancestor-descendant relationship. Of particular relevance, they observe that the oldest potential Western Stemmed occupation at Cooper's Ferry is "synchronous, not younger than, the earliest bifacial stemmed points known in Japan" (Pratt et al. 2020:94).

At the moment, nothing in western or eastern Beringia (Gómez Coutouly and Holmes 2018) is old enough and similar enough technologically to the earliest WST forms to be an unambiguous progenitor. Moreover, technological affinities in projectile points can readily be the result of convergence, particularly when the technological elements have functional constraints, as, for example, where point types are defined by their basal attributes, which in turn have to meet certain minimal criteria for hafting purposes (Buchanan, Eren, and O'Brien 2018). Identifying emblematic styles (sensu Dunnell 1978)[3] would be more indicative of historical links, but may not be possible, given the considerable distances in time and space separating eastern and northeastern Asia from the North American Far West, as well as the cultural drift that would unfold over that span.

In the absence of being able to draw connecting lines via the archaeological record, attention has turned to ancient DNA, on the presumption that a shared genetic heritage between Native American and northeast Asian populations might shed light on a shared cultural heritage (Davis et al. 2019; Davis and Madsen 2020), and perhaps the source region, the route(s) taken (Potter, Baichtal, et al. 2018), or where a standstill may have taken place en route (Davis and Madsen 2020; Davis et al. 2021).

Although genetic and cultural ancestries

are possibly congruent, they also may not be. Groups can have had similar cultural forms without genetic relatedness (owing to convergence or borrowing, for example) and relatedness without similarity in cultural forms (owing to divergence; Johannsen et al. 2017). Even if lithic technologies in Japan/PSHK seem the only "logical progenitor(s)" of the earliest stemmed point traditions in the Americas (Davis and Madsen 2020:7), the population ancestry of the Native American peoples bearing those tools was assuredly far more complex (Willerslev and Meltzer 2021).

Cultural and genetic links can be forged, but only where ancient genomes are obtained from individuals directly associated with particular artifact forms, as with the Anzick and Upward Sun River genomes, associated with Clovis and Denali complex materials, respectively (Moreno-Mayar, Potter, et al. 2018; Rasmussen et al. 2014). As we all know, it does not follow that the population represented by a genome is only associated with a particular artifact form or technology, and vice versa (Moreno-Mayar, Vinner, et al. 2018; Willerslev and Meltzer 2021).

Inferring geographic parameters from genetics can also be problematic, particularly if the inference is based on modern populations, whose present-day location may be unrelated to where their ancestors resided in the Pleistocene (Meltzer 2009). It can be just as knotty a problem with ancient genomes, given how few have been recovered (Willerslev and Meltzer 2021). Thus, merely because "southern Siberia [is] where all ANE [e.g., Mal'ta and Afontova Gora] individuals have been located" (Potter, Baichtal, et al. 2018:2) only means exactly what it says: it does not mean southern Siberia is necessarily where gene flow between Ancient North Eurasian (ANE) and Ancestral Native Americans took place. It could have easily been elsewhere, where no ancient individual genomes have been recovered.

Thus, the question of Native American origins, biological and cultural, has yet to be settled. One significant obstacle to resolution is the lack of any older-than-Clovis genomes (Willerslev and Meltzer 2021). Still, we can perhaps say something based on the archaeological and genomic records about *who* was in the Far West in WST and Clovis times.

Clovis in the Far West, Classic and Otherwise

As earlier noted, the archaeological answer to the "who" question is thought to depend on being able to show the presence of "classic" Clovis in the Far West. Defining what's classic Clovis is both a conceptual problem and an empirical one. Regarding the former, Clovis is the material record of a population south of the continental ice sheets that developed a distinctive fluting technology, and over centuries and multiple human generations that technology spread rapidly, if unevenly, over a vast continent. I have long supposed what occurred was the dispersal of a people using that technology and not the diffusion of a technology across an existing population (Meltzer 1995), and I assume so here for the sake of discussion (see also Jones and Beck, Chapter 8).[4]

Their dispersal was time-transgressive (Meltzer 2004; Rondeau et al., Chapter 9), during which participants were subject to drift and selection, which would have had expression in their material culture (Buchanan et al. 2017; Eren and Buchanan 2016; Jones and Beck, Chapter 8; Rondeau et al., Chapter 9). What will be most important in the understanding of that dispersal process is how its products varied over time and space, whether that variation can be sorted in a meaningful way, and by what criteria those boundaries might be determined: in effect, what is the range of Clovis, and what isn't Clovis (Buchanan et al. 2017; Eren et al. 2015; Goebel 2015; Morrow 2019; Shott 2013; Rondeau et al., Chapter 9)? One can seek to categorize types within that range, such as classic Clovis, but that segments continuous variation into essentialist type, and is inevitably something of a judgement call, even when empirically derived.

Efforts to empirically define Clovis as a phenomenon are variously based on attributes of stone and bone technology, radiocarbon age(s), associated fauna, presumed adaptation(s), status as the first inhabitants of a region, or some combination of these and other measures, not all of which can be applied or are relevant in all instances (Eren and Buchanan 2016; Jones and Beck, Chapter 8; Miller et al. 2013; Morrow 2019; Shott 2013). Establishing what constitutes "classic" Clovis using those criteria—for example, what the expected age(s) and faunal associations might be—is usually based, in a somewhat circular fashion, on sites that are by some prior judgment deemed to be "classic" or "typical." Most often, that's Clovis caches and mammoth kill sites (e.g., Bradley et al. 2010; Miller et al. 2013). Yet, neither of these are typical of the Clovis archaeological record writ large, no matter how one defines it. Caches are rare and can be morphometrically atypical, and mammoth kill/scavenging sites might be considered classic, but only in the historical sense that they played an oversized (and in retrospect unduly influential) role in our initial understanding of Clovis adaptations (Meltzer 2015). Shott observes that "the farther from its time-space core the less there is to Clovis. It fades from view like the Cheshire Cat, fluted points comprising the feline grin" (Shott 2013:151). It's a fair point, but then what is the Clovis time-space core?

Given that Clovis occurrences in the Intermountain West are relatively minor (Beck, Jones, and Taylor 2019; Jones and Beck, Chapter 8; Rondeau 2015a; Rondeau et al., Chapter 9), and are neither well dated nor associated with the remains of any extinct mammals, including mammoth (Grayson 2016), defining classic Clovis in this region must depend on technological attributes of the points and tools themselves.

Unfortunately, there are no definitive or at least uniquely Clovis attributes (Eren, Bebber, et al. 2021; Eren, Meltzer, and Andrews 2021). One of the most oft-cited Clovis "hallmarks" is the occurrence of overshot/overface flakes (Beck and Jones, Chapter 12; Bradley et al. 2010; Duke and Stueber, Chapter 4; Huckell 2014; Jones and Beck, Chapter 8; Lynch et al., Chapter 6; Miller et al. 2013; Smallwood 2010a). However, these flake types are also found on post-Clovis Paleoindian projectile points (Bradley 2009; Sellet 2015), in Middle Holocene and Late Prehistoric assemblages (Eren et al. 2018; Eren, Bebber, et al. 2021; Muñiz 2014), and even on some WST point types (Davis et al. 2012; Lynch et al., Chapter 6). Such are the odds favoring convergence in the case of lithic reduction systems (Buchanan, Eren, and O'Brien 2018). Another hallmark is thought to be their distinctive blades (Bradley et al. 2010), but these occur in a limited number of Clovis sites east of the Continental Divide, and rarely in the Intermountain West (Jones and Beck, Chapter 8), vary significantly in their morphology, and do so in ways mimicked in assemblages of later age (Eren, Meltzer, and Andrews 2021).

Consequently, efforts to categorize classic Clovis are often based on comparative morphometric and technological analyses of what are identified, *a priori*, as classic forms (Beck et al. 2019; Bradley et al. 2010; Howard 1990; Miller et al. 2013). In the study of Intermountain West Clovis points reported here by Jones and Beck (Chapter 8), for example, the specimens chosen to define classic Clovis include points from four caches, and from ten mammoth kill/scavenging sites in the Great Plains and Southwest (Beck, Jones, and Taylor 2019). Yet, five of those kill/scavenging sites (Escapule, Lehner, Leikem, Murray Springs, and Naco) are from a relatively small area of the San Pedro Valley of Arizona and could represent the work of a closely related group or groups of flintknappers (Haynes and Huckell 2007).

Statistical analyses of that sample, focusing on the basal attributes of these points, suggested that "classic Clovis points typically have a shallow basal concavity and are comparatively wider at the base" (Jones and Beck, Chapter 8:168). Jones and Beck derived ratios from those measures[5] to distinguish classic from non-classic Clovis points in the Intermountain West.

The analysis, though reasonable, must be accompanied by two caveats. For one, had the analysis been conducted on a broader geographic sampling of Clovis fluted points, including the ones from the Colby mammoth site (Wyoming), with their deeply concave bases (Frison and Todd 1986), or just on a much larger sample, or even on a sample from a single, large "classic" Clovis site such as Gault, it would not necessarily produce the same central tendencies (see also the cautions offered by Knell and Sutton, Chapter 5; Morrow 2019). Sampling and analytical choices can too readily influence what constitutes the definition of classic Clovis, as opposed to variants thereof, and hence the distinctiveness of other fluted forms in the Far West such as Western Fluted and Sunshine Fluted points.

Second, there are questions as to the utility of using the point base to sort variants. The advantage to doing so, assuming the points are embedded in the haft, is that the base was less subject to breakage, reworking, and recycling, at least compared to the blade portion that extended beyond the haft and was more readily modified over the use life of the point as a projectile or cutting tool. Bases ought to better preserve the bauplan of the original manufactured form. In addition, if variants are defined by their basal attributes, the definition can be widely applied, since broken fluted point bases were more likely to be carried to a site before being discarded and, even if discarded outside a site context, can be readily identified as Clovis. Neither of those factors is likely to be true of snapped-off blades that were lost in a carcass or on the landscape, and which lack the telltale distal end of flute scars.

On the other hand, the morphometrics of fluted point bases also may not be entirely free to vary, and to a degree they were perhaps constrained by the functional and technological requirements of the haft (Ahler and Geib 2000; Bever and Meltzer 2007; Buchanan 2002; Judge 1973; Odell 1994; Sellet 2013; White 2013). In some instances, for example, points may have been made to fit the haft and not the reverse on the premise that hafts, likely made of bone or wood, were more costly to obtain or manufacture than the points themselves (Bamforth and Bleed 1997; Judge 1973; Sellet 2013). That case would especially be true in a largely treeless environment like the Intermountain West.

That said, some analyses do indicate the bases of Clovis points are no less varied in their morphometrics than the blade portions, at least when compared to complete and un-reworked points found in caches (Buchanan, O'Brien, et al. 2012). In fact, by some measures the bases are more variable than the blade portion (e.g., Buchanan, O'Brien, et al. 2012; Buchanan, Andrews, et al. 2018). Leaving aside some technical shortcomings of these studies, most especially an arbitrariness in defining the basal portion of a point,[6] they nonetheless show that certain variables of base size and shape—notably, ones related to basal width—have relatively low coefficients of variation (Buchanan, O'Brien, et al. 2012:Tables 4 and 5). This result is as one might expect if haft constraints were present. Point bases by themselves may not be entirely reliable as stylistic/historical markers: where possible, definitions should be based on whole points.

Those caveats notwithstanding, recognizing the lack of any consensus definition of what constitutes classic Clovis, and readily granting that fluted points are distinct from early WST points (even if only in their hafting technology), what might it mean that both types were present in the Intermountain West in the late Pleistocene? In this case, do different points represent different people?

Were Clovis People in the Far West?

The archaeological record is poorly equipped to identify populations in the past, let alone trace their relatedness and histories (Meltzer 2021). Nor can we assume congruency between populations (biological entities whose members were related by degrees that can be precisely measured) and archaeological cultures (classificatory labels of material culture that can vary widely over space and time and even within cultural units [Johannsen et al. 2017]). Artifacts were never a part of organic entities that had skins around them.

On the other hand, ancient genomes, at one time, did better reflect population level differences. Although only a limited number of ancient genomes are available from North America, two of them[7]—from the Anzick (Montana) and Spirit Cave (Nevada) individuals (Moreno-Mayar, Vinner, et al. 2018; Rasmussen et al. 2014)—are directly relevant and important to the question of whether distinct late Pleistocene peoples lived on opposite sides of the Continental Divide.

The Anzick individual, radiocarbon-dated to 12,800 years ago (Becerra-Valdivia et al. 2018), is situated on the Southern Native American (SNA) branch of Native Americans. Both the SNA branch and the Northern Native American (NNA) branch arrived south of the continental ice sheets as a single population, which then diverged into those two distinct branches sometime around ~15,700 years ago (95% confidence interval [CI] 17,500–14,700 years ago; Moreno-Mayar, Potter, et al. 2018; Willerslev and Meltzer 2021). Members of the NNA branch remained mostly in northern North America, moving north into Alaska and the Yukon Territory sometime after the ice sheets retreated (Moreno-Mayar, Vinner, et al. 2018; Rasmussen et al. 2014; Willerslev and Meltzer 2021).

In contrast, the descendants of the SNA branch dispersed widely, possibly in two separate pulses of movement (Nakatsuka, Luisi, et al. 2020; Posth et al. 2018), ultimately reaching the tip of South America. The small size of this population (Bergström et al. 2020; Fagundes et al. 2018; Llamas et al. 2016), the distances they and their descendants covered in their radiation throughout the hemisphere, and the rapidity of their movement (Moreno-Mayar, Vinner, et al. 2018)[8] increased the chances of isolation and divergence of groups. This pattern is evident in the repeated splitting within the SNA lineage (in both genomes and in uniparental markers) as groups made their way south (Gómez-Carballa et al. 2018; Harris et al. 2018; Moreno-Mayar, Vinner, et al. 2018; Nakatsuka, Lazaridis, et al. 2020; Pinotti et al. 2019; Reich et al. 2012), a process paralleled in divergence patterns in the mtDNA of the dogs that accompanied the people into and through the Americas (Perri et al. 2021).

Population divergence was particularly pronounced where substantial topographic barriers served to channel and/or restrict the movement of people (Meltzer 2021; Willerslev and Meltzer 2021), as seen for example in the genetic differences between groups on opposite sides of the Andes (Borda et al. 2020; Gómez-Carballa et al. 2018; Reich et al. 2012).[9] One might therefore expect that in North America, as Beck and Jones (2010) suggested, the Rocky Mountains served to separate WST and Clovis populations and kept them largely isolated from one another, leading to genomic differences. Those differences would, of course, be substantially greater were WST and Clovis groups descended from "genetically divergent, founding groups" (Jenkins et al. 2012:223) who arrived in different pulses of movement from eastern Beringia. In that case, groups on opposite sides of the Rockies should appear more or less distinct in their genomes, depending on how far back in time they were part of the same population. Evidence of admixture might also be present, marking episodes of interaction and gene flow that occurred when Clovis groups came into the Far West.

To date, neither of those expectations has been met, at least based on the window provided by the Anzick and Spirit Cave genomes (Moreno-Mayar, Vinner, et al. 2018). The Anzick individual, of course, is associated with Clovis artifacts (Becerra-Valdivia et al. 2018; Rasmussen et al. 2014). No projectile points were found directly associated with the Spirit Cave burial; two projectile fragments identified as Humboldt series points were recovered from somewhere in the cave, but their provenience is otherwise not known (Tuohy and Dansie 1997). Even so, the Spirit Cave individual dates to 10,700 years ago, and at that antiquity in the Intermountain West, his toolkit can reasonably be inferred to have been part of the WST (Grayson 2011). It is striking, then, that the Spirit Cave individual has strong genetic affinities to the Anzick individual, despite the distances in time and space separating the two (Moreno-Mayar, Vinner, et al. 2018; Willerslev and Meltzer 2021). These individuals were not descended from distinct groups whose ancestries separately trace back to Beringia or northeast Asia. Both are members of the SNA branch of ancestral Native Americans that emerged soon after people arrived south of the ice sheets.

This finding indicates that the differences between Clovis and WST groups are principally cultural (Moreno-Mayar, Vinner, et al. 2018), and they do not represent genetically divergent founding groups. Rather, the differences between them likely emerged as this population dispersed into different regions, and groups became separated, faced distinct adaptive challenges, developed new tools and technologies in response, and experienced cultural isolation and drift (Eren, Buchanan, and O'Brien 2015). Drift is particularly important, because there is too much time and space involved (not to mention topographic barriers) for drift not to have occurred as these genetically close groups spread across the landscape. The Channel Islands Amol (CIA) and Channel Islands Barbed (CIB) points on the Northern Channel Islands are a particularly striking example, for despite their distinctive forms and restricted geographic distribution, other aspects of their toolkit (notably the presence of crescents) show that these groups were "firmly linked" to the California mainland and even the more distant Great Basin WST (Erlandson et al., Chapter 13:273).[10]

The genomic evidence does not falsify the Beck and Jones (2010) model of Clovis groups moving into the Intermountain West. Rather, it indicates that the hypothesized movement involved peoples whose ancestors had spent sufficient time apart that they developed distinctive elements of their material culture and adaptation, but not so much time that significant population-level genetic differences emerged. It isn't possible to test their further supposition that there was "interaction [gene flow] between two demic groups: Clovis and WST" (Beck and Jones, Chapter 12:242), at least not without additional ancient genomes related to both (Víctor J. Moreno-Mayar, personal communication, 2022).

As to how far apart in time the Anzick and Spirit Cave groups were separated, this was more than just the difference in their radiocarbon ages (~2,100 years), but instead the time that had elapsed since both were part of the same population (Figure 14.1). For while Anzick and Spirit Cave are each on the SNA branch, their ancestors split from one another ~14,100 years ago (95% CI: 14,900–13,200 years ago; Moreno-Mayar, Vinner, et al. 2018). This division means that at the time the Spirit Cave individual was alive ~10,700 years ago, his line had been separated from that common ancestral group for ~3,400 years (95% CI: 2500–4200 years), while the Anzick child lived ~1,300 years (95% CI: 400–2,100 years) after the divergence of the respective lineages. The cultural and material culture differences between the two individuals are thus the product of the cultural evolutionary changes that took place down *each* of their respective lines, and so over a cumulative period of ~4,700 years (or longer or shorter if using the maximum [6,300 years] or minimum [2,900 years] confidence intervals).

This time span is seemingly ample for fluting technology to emerge along the Anzick line if, as earlier suggested (see also Davis, Chapter 7), the common ancestral group was equipped with unfluted stemmed points or bifaces. That much time is also in keeping with the model of lithic technology trajectories proposed by Rosencrance and colleagues (Chapter 2), though, as they rightly note, far more chronological precision—as well as evidence of processes of drift, diffusion, exchange and interaction—is needed on both sides of the Continental Divide to put their model to the test.

The *rate* at which those changes occurred would have depended on various factors,

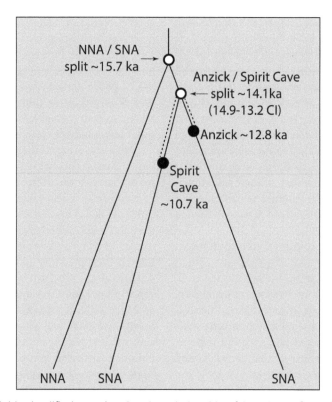

FIGURE 14.1. Highly simplified tree showing the relationship of Anzick and Spirit Cave to one another. Although these individuals were separated by ~2,100 radiocarbon years, they are on separate lineages that diverged from a common ancestral population ~14,100 years ago (95% confidence interval, 14,900–13,200 years ago). Thus, the cultural and material culture differences between them are the product of cultural changes that took place down each of their respective lines (*dashed*), and so together accumulated over a period of ~4,700 years (or longer or shorter, if using the maximum and minimum of the confidence intervals).

most especially population size and density, admixture, relative isolation and drift, and other factors affecting cultural variation and transmission (Beck and Jones, Chapter 12; Grove 2016; Jones and Beck, Chapter 8; Shennan 2001). The rate also could have varied over time and in the different regions occupied by these groups. Gaining a better understanding of these factors would help get us closer to understanding the mode and cause(s) of material culture change, as well as provide insight into the differences in patterns of cultural and genetic changes in diverging populations.

All of which, in turn, raises the question: putting the differences in WST and Clovis tools and technology aside (Beck and Jones, Chapter 12), could they nonetheless have had similar adaptations?

An Analogical Bridge Too Far

Duke and Stueber (Chapter 4) assert as much. They argue that the groups using Haskett points occupied the same adaptive niche in the Far West as did groups using Clovis points on the other side of the Continental Divide: big-game hunting. According to them, Clovis points' "calibrated function" was to hunt megafauna, and Haskett points—which they see as analogous to Clovis points in size, design, skill, and conveyance—are likewise inferred to be "megafauna-caliber" weapons (Duke and Stueber, Chapter 4:79).

However, the parallels they draw between Clovis and Haskett are nonspecific to these two types: both can be widest at the front of the haft portion, but not all such points are, and in any case that pattern is hardly unique to Clovis and Haskett. Both are lanceolate in design and were repaired and used over their use lives, but then that's true of most points from this time period (not to mention the obvious design difference that Clovis points are fluted, Haskett points are not). Knapping both types requires "skill and training," but that, too, is true of many Paleoindian point types, especially so in the case of Folsom, for example.[11] Finally, while both types were conveyed long distances, the scale of mobility can be a function of the structure of the resources and environment, not necessarily a common settlement strategy or technological organization.

Yet, even were the forms alike, does function follow form? It may, but not in the manner that it necessarily establishes a predator-prey relationship. In fact, there are ample reasons to be skeptical of the claim that Clovis points were specifically designed, used, or even effective (Eren, Meltzer, Story, et al. 2021, 2022) for the principal purpose of mammoth-killing (Duke and Stueber are hardly alone in saying so: for example, see also Fiedel and Haynes 2004; Frison and Bradley 2004; Kilby et al. 2022). Among these reasons, microwear studies indicate that Clovis points were at times used for several distinct purposes, including as weapon tips in hunting, but also in butchering and processing of animal carcasses (some quite large), and in other tasks as opportunities arose (Eren, Meltzer, Story, et al. 2021). It should not be surprising that highly mobile groups carried a limited set of tools and foraged on a vast landscape, portions of which may have been unfamiliar, or that they crafted multifunctional tools for a toolkit that overall emphasized portability, longevity and functional flexibility (Eren, Meltzer, Story, et al. 2021, 2022; see also Jones and Beck, Chapter 8). Moreover, even at presumed proboscidean kills, the great majority of these points lack impact fractures indicative of their use as projectiles (impact fractures are otherwise common on post-Clovis period kill sites of large mammals such as bison). Perhaps most important, Clovis points have the *lowest* penetration power of a range of early-to-late Paleoindian lanceolates, all else being equal (e.g., weapon systems, projectile velocity, hit target on the animal; Bebber et al. 2017; Buchanan, Andrews, et al. 2018; Eren et al. 2020; Eren, Meltzer, Story, et al. 2021, 2022; Eren, Bebber, et al. 2022; Kay 1996; Miller 2013; Smallwood 2010b, 2015; Werner et al. 2017).

What makes Clovis points less efficient at penetrating carcasses—especially the protective layers of hair and hide, and the picket fence of mammoth ribs that had to be bypassed to achieve the penetration depths needed to reach vital organs (Eren, Meltzer, Story, et al 2021)—is their broad point tip cross-sectional area (TCSA) and tip cross-sectional perimeter (TCSP; Mika et al. 2020; Sitton et al. 2020). In terms of morphometrics, these tip attributes, and not maximum point width (Duke and Stueber, Chapter 4), are the best predictors of penetration depth, and hence weaponry efficiency.

Accordingly, it does not follow that the ~6 mm difference in average width between Clovis points and Folsom points is ballistically significant and tied to the size of their prey, such that Clovis points were used to hunt mammoth, while narrower Folsom points were aimed at bison (Duke and Stueber, Chapter 4). All things considered, "6 mm" is hardly a ballistically meaningful difference if shooting at a bison as opposed to a mammoth. Pleistocene bison were "smaller" prey only if they happened to be standing next to a mammoth. For that matter, experimental work has shown that the Clovis-era replicate points that achieve the deepest penetration depths were actually the narrower Shoop points (Eren et al. 2020). And, of course, if wider points were used to bring down larger animals and narrower points smaller ones, one can scarcely imagine the prey size being pursued by Archaic foragers on the Southern Plains or Hopewell hunters, whose Calf Creek and Snyders points (respectively) are almost twice the width of Clovis points.

If a direct relationship existed between point size and prey size (Beck and Jones, Chapter 12; Boldurian and Cotter 1999; Buchanan et al. 2011; Duke and Stueber, Chapter 4; Rosencrance et al., Chapter 2), it fails to account for the presence of smaller Clovis points associated with mammoth at sites such as Blackwater Locality 1 and the Lehner site (Haury et al. 1959; Hester 1972). Nor can it account for the corollary finding: that point size and shape did not distinguish Clovis points found with mammoth from Clovis points found with bison (Buchanan et al. 2011).

Stone projectile points are not bullets, which aim to kill instantly and from far away, in which larger caliber can be more efficient against big game with tough hide, muscle, and especially, thick-boned skulls. Still, even a small-caliber bullet or stone projectile point propelled at high velocity can be lethal (Mika et al. 2020; Sitton et al. 2020). In the recent past, Plains hunters killed bison with bow-fired tiny triangular arrowheads (Frison 2004; Reher and Frison 1980).

It's not the size of the point in the kill: it's the size of the kill in the point. That's a function of Newtonian dynamics of force, mass and acceleration and, for stone projectile points, a small tip cross-sectional area and perimeter.

Back to Haskett points. Leaving aside the analogy drawn between Clovis and Haskett points and therefore their inferred function and prey, and accepting for sake of discussion the claim that Haskett points were "engineered to hunt megafauna" (Duke and Stueber, Chapter 4:111), a couple of awkward questions remain. First, if Haskett points are the Great Basin's evidence for a continent-wide pattern of megafaunal hunting, where are the Haskett mammoth kills, camel kills, horse kills, etc. (Grayson 2016; Smith and Barker 2017)?[12] Second, and in the absence of kill or scavenging sites, can the mere presence of Haskett points be used as a proxy for the "spatiotemporal nuances of megafaunal die-offs" (Duke and Stueber, Chapter 4:109)?

For Duke and Stueber, the "lack of direct archaeological or paleontological evidence of megafaunal prey is more parsimoniously explained by a lack of bone preservation than by an alternative interpretation of Haskett points" (Duke and Stueber, Chapter 4:109). There can be little doubt that the archaeological record does not always play fair, and preservation can be spotty, but nonetheless this region has no evidence of kill or scavenging sites. This absence is despite radiocarbon evidence indicating that at least seven megafaunal genera, mammoth included, were present—though admittedly not abundant—in the Great Basin until at least 10,000 years ago (Grayson 2016), and thus well into Haskett times (Duke and Stueber, Chapter 4; Rosencrance et al., Chapter 2). And it is so despite the assertion that climatic conditions for megafauna during the Younger Dryas were in some respects "optimal" and provided "persistent refugia" that human hunters could have easily mapped onto allowing them to exploit these animals (Duke and Stueber, Chapter 4:97). More importantly, there is little reason or evidence to suspect large game hunting was the dominant or even a central element of the late Pleistocene subsistence strategy in the Far West (Beck and Jones, Chapter 12; Grayson 2011, 2016; McDonough et al., Chapter 1; Smith et al., Chapter 3), just as it wasn't over much of North America (Cannon and Meltzer 2004, 2008).[13] In this adaptive regard, Haskett and Clovis probably *were* alike.

In the absence of a necessary relationship between Haskett points and megafauna (i.e., if the former is present, then the latter must be as well), let alone evidence of Haskett megafaunal associations, there are no grounds to suppose that the occurrence or frequency of Haskett points can be "proxy evidence for persistence of some [megafaunal] species," such that when the animals went extinct there was a cause-effect "reduction in [Haskett] projectile point size, frequency, and investment" (Duke and Stueber, Chapter 4:110). Point styles, size and shape, technology, forms of hafting, and the like can readily change independently of factors such as prey type. The Holocene-long record on the Great Plains of changing projectile point types aimed at the *same* prey (bison) is proof of that (Bamforth 2020).

None of this is to suggest that Haskett points did not serve as projectiles. They probably did on occasion, as is shown in the impact fractures Lynch and colleagues (Chapter 6) documented on the Smith Creek Cave specimens. But then there is no reason to think that projectile use was their sole purpose, and indeed evidence supports that, just like Clovis points, they also were used as knives (Elston et al. 2014; Lafayette and Smith 2012).

Most important, however, neither reason nor evidence indicates a binding relationship of point to prey in late Pleistocene times.

If They Weren't There for the Mammoths, What Were Clovis Groups Doing in the Far West?

Perhaps a large part of the reason why the early WST sites of the Far West initially were not considered relevant to discussions of Paleoindians was the fact that they did not look "Clovis-like" in terms of lifeways and adaptations. Or, to put it more accurately, they did not resemble the big-game hunting Clovis stereotype—and it is just a stereotype (Cannon and Meltzer 2008). As McDonough and colleagues (Chapter 1) and others note, the terms "Paleoarchaic" (Graf and Schmitt 2007; Willig 1989; Willig and Aikens 1988) and, before that, "Desert Culture" (Heizer and Baumhoff 1970; Jennings 1964), were expressly invented to distinguish the adaptive strategies practiced in the Far West from those practiced by the ostensibly highly-mobile big-game hunters of the Great Plains (McDonough et al., Chapter 1; Smith et al., Chapter 3).

McDonough and colleagues "find it unproductive to compare ~4,500 years of lifeways (Paleoarchaic) to ~7,000 years of lifeways (Archaic)" (McDonough et al., Chapter 1:8; see also Elston et al. 2014; Pinson 2007; Smith et al., Chapter 3). They're right: climates and environments shifted substantially over that time, and with those transitions came changes in resources and resource structure and human adaptations (seen especially in the intensity of seed and plant processing in later times).

For this same reason, it is unproductive to assume subsistence strategies were the same across space, especially given the very different environments of late Pleistocene North America, such as along the Pacific Coast with its rich marine and nearshore resources; the Intermountain West, a largely arid region but one dotted with lakes and marshes, and mostly dominated by sage scrub vegetation with low species richness; the Great Plains, a semiarid grassland with a highly uneven distribution of potential prey resources; and the eastern woodlands, a temperate forest with more evenness of resources and overall a richer environment (Cannon 2004; Cannon and Meltzer 2008; Erlandson et al. 2011; Grayson 2011; Grimm and Jacobson 2004; Reeder et al. 2011; Williams et al. 2004). With these differences, whether across space or through time, there were corresponding differences in the relative type, richness, and abundance of available prey species, along with differences in prey rank and especially the role played by large mammals (Byers and Ugan 2005; Cannon and Meltzer 2004, 2008, 2022; Erlandson et al., Chapter 13; Hockett et al. 2017; Jones and Beck, Chapter 8; Smith and Barker 2017; Smith et al., Chapter 3). There was no one-size-fits-all subsistence pattern.

Although a number of megafaunal species were present in the Intermountain West in the late Pleistocene, few, if any, were evidently targeted (Grayson 2016), and overall this region provided "limited subsistence opportunities" (Beck and Jones 2013:285; see also Jones and Beck, Chapter 8). This result is so, at least in the Great Basin, because megafauna were not abundant as evidenced by the fossil record and the distinctive character of the region's vegetation (Grayson 2016; Mack and Thompson 1982). Large Pleistocene mammals would have been "particularly rare here toward the very end of the Ice Age," when people were on the landscape (Grayson 2016:271). Under the circumstances, Clovis groups were unlikely to have been there for the mammoth hunting.

As to what they were doing, little is known since the very few Clovis occurrences are in the form of isolated caches, along with scattered (and sometimes clustered, as at the Dietz site) surface finds (Jones and Beck, Chapter 8). That the latter are in places associated with WST sites or found in similar habitats—such as along the edges of Pleistocene pluvial lakes, marshes, and springs—suggests similar adaptive strategies (Elston et al. 2014; Jones and Beck, Chapter 8; Madsen, Oviatt, et al. 2015, Smith et al., Chapter 3). Whatever Clovis peoples were doing, as Grayson points out, they were doing it near shallow water (Grayson 2011). If the WST sites that have yielded dietary remains can bear witness, both groups were exploiting a wide range of resources, from artiodactyls to small mammals, fish, insects, seeds, and geophytes (Elston et al. 2014; Goebel et al. 2011; Grayson 2011; Hockett 2015; Hockett et al. 2017; Jones and Beck, Chapter 8; Smith and Barker 2017).

Other common threads run between Clovis and WST adaptations in the region, principal among them a similarity in the extent and scale of residential mobility, as inferred from the distances stone was moved across the landscape. It is important to acknowledge that the straight-line distance from quarry to site takes no account of side excursions, return trips, seasonal movements, or any other archaeologically invisible aspects of travel (Meltzer 2009, 2021). Nor does the presence of stone exotic to a site necessarily indicate the inhabitants collected it themselves from the source. As Speth and colleagues (2013:120) note, "exchange or direct procurement by individuals or small task groups making long treks for the express purpose of acquiring flint become quite plausible alternatives to the widespread view of embedded procurement by entire residential groups" (see also Beck and Jones 2011; Madsen 2007; Madsen, Schmitt, and Page 2015b; Smith and Harvey 2018).

Granting that point, human populations at this time also were quite low and thinly scattered on this vast landscape (though genetic evidence indicates populations were rapidly increasing during this span: Bergström et al. 2020; Llamas et al. 2016). For groups on a still mostly empty and more or less unfamiliar landscape, as was true of Clovis and later Paleoindian groups east of the Continental Divide, and WST groups in the Intermountain West, high residential mobility had strategic and selective advantages (Cannon and Meltzer 2022; Meltzer 2004).

Based on the lithic conveyance zones in the Intermountain West, stone was moved from tens to hundreds of kilometers (Goebel et al. 2018; Jones et al. 2003; Jones et al. 2012; Lynch et al., Chapter 6; Smith et al., Chapter 3). The longer distances are comparable to the lengths stone was moved from source to site elsewhere in North America by Clovis and later Paleoindian groups. In the Intermountain West, as in those other regions, trends and patterns are apparent in the distance(s) and direction(s) stone was moved (e.g., Boulanger et al. 2015; Boulanger et al. 2021; Jones et al. 2003; Jones et al. 2012; Lynch et al., Chapter 6; Madsen, Schmitt, and Page 2015b; Meltzer 2021; Smith et al., Chapter 3). The variation in these patterns was likely dependent in large part on the structure and patchiness of lithic and food resources, which, of course, were not always spatially congruent (Elston and Zeanah 2002; Elston et al. 2014; Madsen 2007; Madsen, Schmitt, and Page 2015b; Page and Duke 2015; Smith et al. 2013, Chapter 3).

In addition, WST groups, like Clovis and

later Paleoindians, were selective in their use of exotic, high-quality (finer-grained) stone, often relying on it to fashion projectile points (Smith et al., Chapter 3), as opposed to other tools in the toolkit, which were more often expediently made of locally available and not necessarily the same high-quality stone (Amick 1996; Andrews et al. 2021; Bamforth 2009; Boulanger et al. 2015; Boulanger et al. 2021; Ellis 2011; Hofman 1999b; Lothrop and Singer 2017; Meltzer 2006).

This response, too, may be adaptive, but to the social environment rather than the natural one. Encounters among groups spread thinly on a vast landscape would have been vital to the purposes of swapping information and maintaining alliances, and they could have been marked by an exchange of emblematic gifts—like projectile points made in a style or lithic raw material distinctive of a group—to mark the occasion and the bonds forged (Meltzer 1989). This interpretation would also explain why everyday tools are not so exclusively made of high-quality stone (Amick 2017; Bamforth 2002, 2009; Madsen, Schmitt, and Page 2015b; Meltzer 1989, 2021; Speth et al. 2013). Clovis sites in eastern North America occasionally yield a distinctive point or two that may have been acquired in such a manner (Meltzer 1989). It would be interesting to ascertain whether that occurs among WST assemblages in the Intermountain West.

Yet another aspect of mobility and settlement strategies emerges as a more noticeable difference between late Pleistocene groups on opposite sides of the Continental Divide. Because all these groups had a relatively empty landscape and unfettered mobility, they rarely needed to use the same spot twice, though did return to some places on the landscape that could be counted on to provide important resources. On the Great Plains, these revisited areas included outcrops of high-quality stone for tool manufacture, and reliable freshwater springs and the plant and animal resources these supported. In a tally done a dozen years ago (the numbers have not likely changed substantially), almost 70% of Paleoindian sites on the Great Plains ($n =$ 105/152) are single component. However, a not-insignificant number of localities have two ($n = 17$) or more ($n = 30$) Paleoindian components (Holliday and Meltzer 2010). At a number of those localities the local geological and hydrological circumstances resulted in well-stratified depositional and cultural sequences.

Of course, scattered across the Intermountain West areas were places that repeatedly attracted foragers, and have multiple WST components (e.g., Elston et al. 2014; Madsen, Schmitt, and Page 2015b). However, for the most part, the depositional and erosional processes in these areas did not lend themselves to the formation of deep, well-stratified deposits (e.g., Old River Bed Delta, Utah; Madsen, Oviatt, et al. 2015) that make it possible to stratigraphically disentangle the relative ages of different WST projectile points, or those from fluted points (Beck and Jones, Chapter 12; Rosencrance et al., Chapter 2; Surovell, Chapter 10). The components at these multicomponent sites tend to be distributed horizontally, rather than vertically.

A Proliferation of Types

These previous concepts assume that the relative ages of these point styles can be disentangled. As Rosencrance and colleagues (Chapter 2) well illustrate, multiple, temporally overlapping, distinct point types are present in the Intermountain West across the Pleistocene/Holocene boundary. In some instances, the period of overlap may span as much as 1,000–1,500 years (Rosencrance et al., Chapter 2:Figure 2.5). Although the timing varies, this situation is similar to that on the Great Plains (Rosencrance et al., Chapter 2; Surovell, Chapter 10) and in eastern North America (Anderson et al. 2015; Bradley et al. 2008; Lothrop et al. 2011; Smallwood et al. 2019).

The proliferation of types around the time of the Pleistocene/Holocene boundary, even types that are presumably part of the same historical tradition, is not unexpected for several reasons. First, stone artifacts produced through reductive processes "will be inherently unstable, tending always toward variation and diversification in the absence of any stabilizing mechanism" (Schillinger et al. 2014:138). Second, by the latest Pleistocene populations had increased substantially in size, which would have led to a relaxation in the selective pressure to maintain contact with distant kin and hence common emblematic artifact forms, a steady settling-in and filling of the landscape, and a concomitant reduction in the scale of group mobility (Meltzer 2002, 2009; see also Duke and Stueber, Chapter 4; Smith et al., Chapter 3). Those two elements would have combined to increase the likelihood of isolation and drift, independent of similarities/differences in adaptation and environment, and led to the emergence of multiple point forms (Eren et al. 2015). Finally, as Beck and Jones (Chapter 12) detail, a host of other evolutionary processes were almost certainly operative, including adaptation(s) to different habitats and patches, variation in transmission processes, functional selection, social selection, convergence, and so on (see also Lycett and von Cramon-Taubadel 2015; Shott 2013). Until the effects of these forces on stone tools are unscrambled, assuming they can be, it will be impossible to say how and whether we are looking at sociohistorical markers, or to fully warrant the claim that the apparent similarities in the timing of technological changes on either side of the Rockies are necessarily historically linked (Duke and Stueber, Chapter 4; Rosencrance et al., Chapter 2).

All things considered, the chronological overlap seen in WST points may not be separable. This case will almost certainly be true if the attempt is made using only radiocarbon ages, for all the sample, technical, and taphonomic complications that Surovell (Chapter 10) identifies that limit the precision of that method for this purpose. He further argues, reasonably so, that the best approach to disentangling types chronologically is to sort them stratigraphically (where possible). Of course, this method assumes that types are temporally discrete entities that do not overlap in time and space.

That's a fair assumption on a timescale of multiple centuries or millennia (Sellet 2018; Surovell, Chapter 10). However, on a finer temporal scale—such as years, decades, or even a century or two—it is altogether likely that groups simultaneously occupying different areas of the landscape (and who were possibly even distantly related) were using typologically distinct point forms (Figure 14.2). Likewise, some real-time overlap must have occurred as types changed, no matter how rapid the transition. That is, unless that transition in point types marks a wholesale population replacement and, with it, a sweeping and universal replacement of the material culture.

In principle, this overlap could have occurred even in instances of apparent stratigraphic separation, depending on sampling and the resolution of the stratigraphic record. Consider the consequences if the projectile point styles over time appear, grow in popularity, then decline and disappear—shown on the right axis of Figure 14.2 (which, of course, is the conceptual basis of frequency seriation); and if all sites over the span of the "lifetime" of a point style had an equal chance of being occupied. The result would be a greater probability that the site stratigraphic record would capture the wider, central portion of the curves when the types are most abundant, rather than their diminishing tails. If the central portions of the different point types are different ages, then they will appear to be stratigraphically distinct, even if their chronological ranges overlap.

Thus, to determine if types are stratigraphically distinct, one continues to play the odds: if a dozen sites scattered across the Great Plains and Rocky Mountains provide consistent stratigraphic evidence that fluted points are older than their stemmed counterparts, Surovell argues (Chapter 10), it is fair to conclude that those technologies followed one another in time in that region. Nonetheless, this is not to say they do not overlap at all in time. In this regard, it is relevant to add that Surovell (Chapter 10) intentionally omitted late Pleistocene basally indented un-

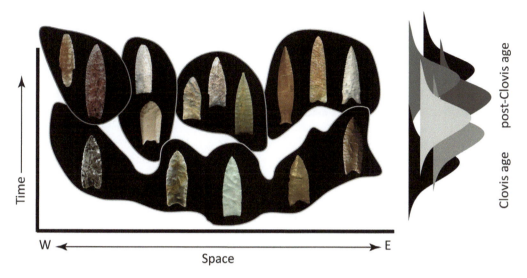

FIGURE 14.2. Cloud model of the overlapping distributions of projectile point types in space and time. The lower, west-to-east cloud represents the variation that is Clovis—there is no unanimity as to whether that variation should be treated as a continuum or segmented into distinct types, and if the latter, by what measures. The proliferation of post-Clovis forms overlaps at different temporal and spatial scales, and morphometrically as well, all of which complicates efforts to put the types into well-defined, cleanly bordered time/space boxes.

fluted varieties (e.g., Goshen, Plainview, and Midland) from his analysis because they are neither fluted nor stemmed. Had these point types been included, the cleanly separated sequence he presented would be far murkier, as these unfluted points are at least partially contemporaneous with both fluted (Folsom) and stemmed (Agate Basin) points, and also overlap in aspects of their manufacturing technology (Bradley 2009; Haynes and Hill 2017; Sellet 2015).

Although Rosencrance and colleagues (Chapter 2:57) emphasize that "fluted points never appear below stemmed points in the Intermountain West," it must be admitted this observation is accurate only because neither occurs in the same locality in a stratigraphic context where their relative ages can be determined (Smith et al. 2020; Smith et al., Chapter 3). That said, the provisionally named "Cooper's Ferry" type (Davis, Chapter 7) is, by radiocarbon evidence, substantially older than Clovis. What remains to be resolved is the chronological relationship between Clovis (and the later Sunshine) fluted points and the other WST point types (starting with Haskett, which appears to be the oldest of the other stemmed varieties; Rosencrance et al., Chapter 2).

Ultimately, clarification of the spatiotemporal patterning of late Pleistocene and Early Holocene WST forms will require not just radiocarbon and stratigraphic evidence, but also more "granular" studies on a regional and subregional geographic scale, as well-advocated and advanced in this volume (Rosencrance et al., Chapter 2; Knell and Sutton, Chapter 5; Lynch et al., Chapter 6).

Across the Continental Divide: Coda

Beck and Jones, as mentioned at the outset, lamented the neglect of the archaeology of the Far West (Beck and Jones 2010). That was a dozen years ago, and it was true. Yet, readers who have come this far in the volume know that much has changed since then—thanks in no small measure to the field and analytical efforts of many of the authors, as reported here and elsewhere. As the editors rightly observe, "irrespective of the lack of well-dated fluted points in the region, a critical review of the peopling of the Americas, or continental Paleoindian records, must include research from the Far West and of the WST" (McDonough et al., Chapter 1:13). In providing a far better and deeper sense of the evidence, issues, and challenges to understanding the chronological and morphological relationships between the various technocomplexes on both sides of the Rockies, this volume goes a fair distance toward demonstrating the validity of that observation.

Acknowledgments

I am grateful to the editors for the invitation to contribute to this volume; I gained much from the reading of it. For their comments and advice on this chapter, I would like to thank Metin I. Eren, Donald K. Grayson, David Madsen, Victor Moreno-Mayar, Dave Schmitt, and Thomaz Pinotti—none of whom can be blamed for what I have done with their wise counsel. It is also only proper that I acknowledge the work of the late Alan Bryan, who regularly sent me reprints (*paper* reprints: it was a long time ago) of his papers on the relationship of the stemmed point tradition and Clovis. They were not well appreciated by me at the time. In retrospect, it is easier to see I should have paid more attention. That I now can is owed in no small measure to work done over the decades by my good friends and graduate schoolmates Charlotte and Tom (Beck and Jones). From them, I have learned to better understand and appreciate the archaeology of the late Pleistocene Far West on its own terms, and not as some cheap Clovis knockoff.

Notes

1. Roberts can be forgiven for including Sandia: questions about Frank Hibben's claims for the antiquity of the site only first arose that same year (Bliss 1940a, 1940b).
2. Several terms are used to describe the region(s) covered in this volume. Following the editors, I generally use "Far West" as it covers the most real estate but employ other terms, such as "Intermountain West" and "Great Basin," if making a more specific geographic reference is appropriate.
3. As I understand Pratt and colleagues, this is what they mean when they speak of separating "culture versus behavior" (Pratt et al. 2020).
4. If Clovis was the diffusion of a technology, that demands a faithfulness in copying by many widely scattered groups across an entire continent; surely, were that the case, we'd see more variation than we do. Further, we ought to see that preexisting presence archaeologically and evidence of Clovis technologies being grafted on to (and replacing) the earlier "fluteless" artifact assemblages. We see neither. Diffusion seems less likely than an on-the-ground rapid movement of a people (Meltzer 2021:191; see also Jones and Beck, Chapter 8).
5. More specifically, they compute a ratio of basal concavity:basal width, and observe that in their sample 95% of classic forms have ratio values of 0.05 to 0.2. That same ratio is seen in about one-third of the Intermountain West specimens.
6. In these studies, the base is defined as an arbitrary proportion of the point length or one based on geometric morphometric landmarks. Defining the base as a proportion of length means that in these studies the base measures that prove to vary significantly are length-related ones (Buchanan, O'Brien, et al. 2012). Yet, as these measures are a function of overall length (since the definition of the base itself is), they are thus subject to changes in length that are a result of reworking and resharpening of the blades. Thus, they are not statistically independent indicators of basal morphology or haft constraints. A more archaeologically meaningful measure would be the extent of edge grinding, which represents the hafted/basal portion of a point. The edge ground extent more or less marks the area of the point not exposed to the same degree resharpening as the blade. Using that measure would make for a more meaningful analysis especially since, as the evidence shows, Clovis points were used as cutting tools, in which case grinding was critical to ensuring the base of the point stayed anchored in its haft.
7. Two genomes may not sound like much but bear in mind that a genome—unlike uniparentally-inherited mitochondrial DNA and the non-recombining portion of the Y

chromosome—harbors a mosaic of many hundreds of thousands of independent, randomly varying mutations that accumulated down innumerable lines of descent and can reveal the complexities of population ancestry, structure, and admixture (Reich 2018).

8. Just how far and how fast populations radiated is evident in the close genetic links between ancient individuals who lived at roughly the same time (~10,000 years ago) but thousands of kilometers apart in North and South America (Moreno-Mayar, Vinner, et al. 2018; Posth et al. 2018; Scheib et al. 2018).

9. The differences might have initially emerged as the first South Americans entered the continent and moved down opposite sides of the Andes; the mountain chain then served as a barrier restricting further gene flow between populations. There is some admixture, notably among the Inga of Colombia (Reich et al. 2012) who are located in northern South America, and between coastal Andean and Amazonian populations in northern Peru where a lower saddle exists in the mountain chain (Borda et al. 2020).

10. Which makes a comment by Erlandson and colleagues all the more perplexing to me. They take exception to a statement I made to *Science* journalist Michael Balter in 2011, regarding a paper they'd published on Northern Channel Islands assemblages (Erlandson et al. 2011). My comment, said to have questioned "the unique and maritime nature of these sites," was simply to wonder whether those sites "'represent a full-blown marine adaptation of a bunch of seafaring people cruising down the coast, or did they wander in' from inland areas, bringing the stemmed points and crescents with them?" It seemed to me a reasonable point to make at the time. It turns out, it still is. As Erlandson and colleagues make clear, "Radiocarbon dating and morphological analyses from stemmed CIA and CIB points on California's NCI...suggest that these point types were a distinctive maritime variant of the larger WST" (Chapter 13:264). Besides, the Balter piece was asking not about the Channel Islands sites per se, but about the larger question of whether we could at that point confirm there had been a coastal migration south from Alaska. As I replied and Balter reported, "Give me a site on the coast that is at least 15,000 years old, and I will be a happy guy." I'll stand by that statement too.

11. Duke and Stueber emphasize the "heavy skill and training" involved in Clovis and Haskett points for reasons beyond simply noting the seeming parallelism between the two. They also suggest the points are overengineered, certainly to a degree unnecessary for multifunctional tools used for quotidian purposes, but possibly even exceeding the functional requirements of weapon tips for bringing down big game. They raise the possibility, as others have (Meltzer 2009; Speth et al. 2013), that the investment in production represents costly signaling "with only tangential relationships to performance." That, in turn, leads them to surmise that the signaling arose in response to a decline in megafaunal prey. A few counterpoints to consider include, for one, the skill and training would have been learned at an early age, with that initial investment paying off over a lifetime; it did not have to be repeated each time someone made a Clovis or Haskett point. Second, one could equally argue that with a limited toolkit there was an advantage to having highly prepared multifunction tools that could be put to use in a range of anticipated and unanticipated contingencies. Finally, is costly signaling necessarily attributable to a scarcity of preferred prey? One has to be skeptical: Folsom points require a comparable (if not greater) investment in "heavy skill and training" and are overengineered (bison were killed with far less technically elaborate weapon tips), and yet their prey—bison—were abundant.

12. The oldest bison kill was found in Nevada's Black Rock Desert, dates to the Early Holocene, and was a *Bison bison* which was associated—anomalously for this place—with an Alberta-Cody point (Amick 2013; Smith and Barker 2017).

13. Nor can one justify the absence of Haskett kill sites, as Duke and Steuber do, by invoking the presence of Clovis *points* (not Clovis kills) as proof of mammoth-hunting. Doing so requires the assumption Clovis adaptive strategies focused on megafauna, which is not the case. They exploited a range of resources elsewhere in North America, and surely did in the Far West as well (Cannon and Meltzer 2004, 2008; Grayson and Meltzer 2015).

References

Agogino, George A.
1961   A New Point Type from Hell Gap Valley, Eastern Wyoming. *American Antiquity* 26(4):558–560.

Agogino, George A., and Eugene Galloway
1965   The Sister's Hill Site: A Hell Gap Site in North-Central Wyoming. *Plains Anthropologist* 10(29):190–195.

Ahler, Stanley, and Phil K. Geib
2000   Why Flute? Folsom Point Design and Adaptation. *Journal of Archaeological Science* 27(9):799–820.

Aikens, C. Melvin
1970   *Hogup Cave*. Anthropological Papers No. 93. University of Utah Press, Salt Lake City.
1978   Archaeology of the Great Basin. *Annual Review of Anthropology* 7(1):71–87.

Aikens, C. Melvin, David Cole, and Robert Stuckenrath
1977   Excavations at Dirty Shame Rockshelter Southeastern Oregon. *Tebiwa Miscellaneous Papers* 4. Idaho State Museum of Natural History, Pocatello.

Aikens, C. Melvin, Thomas J. Connolly, and Dennis L. Jenkins
2011   *Oregon Archaeology*. Oregon State University Press, Corvallis.

Ambrose, Stanley H.
2012   Obsidian Dating and Source Exploitation Studies in Africa: Implications for the Evolution of Human Behavior. In *Obsidian and Ancient Manufactured Glasses*, edited by Ioannis Liritzis and Christopher M. Stevenson, pp. 56–72. University of New Mexico Press, Albuquerque.

Ames, Kenneth M.
1988   Early Holocene Forager Mobility Strategies on the Southern Columbia Plateau. In *Early Human Occupation in Far Western North America: The Clovis–Archaic Interface*, edited by Judith A. Willig, C. Melvin Aikens, and John L. Fagan, pp. 325–360. Anthropological Papers No. 21. Nevada State Museum, Carson City.

Ames, Kenneth M., J. P. Green, and M. Pfoertner
1981   *Hatwai (10NP143): Interim Report*. Archaeological Reports 9. Boise State University, Boise, Idaho.

Amick, Daniel S.
1996   Regional Patterns of Folsom Mobility and Land Use in the American Southwest. *World Archaeology* 27(3):411–426.
1999   *Folsom Lithic Technology: Explorations in Structure and Variation*. International Monographs in Prehistory, Archaeology Series No. 12. Berghahn Books, Ann Arbor, Michigan.
2002   Manufacturing Variation in Folsom Points and Fluted Preforms. In *Folsom Technology and Lifeways*, edited by John Clark and Michael B. Collins, pp. 160–184. Lithic Technology Special Publication No. 4. University of Tulsa, Oklahoma.
2004   A Possible Ritual Cache of Great Basin Stemmed Bifaces from the Terminal Pleistocene–Early Holocene Occupation of Northwest Nevada, USA. *Lithic Technology* 29(2):119–145.
2013   Way Out West: Cody Complex Occupations from the Northwestern Great Basin. In *Paleoindian Lifeways of the Cody Complex*, edited by Edward J. Knell and Mark P. Muñiz, pp. 215–245. University of Utah Press, Salt Lake City.
2017   Evolving Views on the Pleistocene Colonization of North America. *Quaternary International* 431(B):125–151.

Amsden, Charles A.
1937   The Lake Mohave Artifacts. In *The Archaeology of Pleistocene Lake Mohave*, edited by Elizabeth W. Campbell and William H. Campbell, pp. 51–98. Southwest Museum Papers No. 11, Los Angeles.

Anderson, David G., D. Shane Miller, Stephen J. Yerka, J. Christopher Gillam, Erik N. Johanson, Derek T. Anderson, Albert C. Goodyear, and Ashley M. Smallwood
2010   PIDBA (Paleoindian Database of the Americas) 2010: Current Status and Findings. *Archaeology of Eastern North America* 38:63–90.

Anderson, David G., Ashley M. Smallwood, and D. Shane Miller
2015   Pleistocene Human Settlement in the Southeastern United States: Current Evidence and Future Directions. *Paleo-America* 1(1):7–51.

Andrefsky, William, Jr.
1994   Raw Material Availability and the Organization of Technology. *American Antiquity* 59(1):21–34.
1998   *Lithics: Macroscopic Approaches to Analysis.* Cambridge University Press, Cambridge, England.
2009   The Analysis of Stone Tool Procurement, Production, and Maintenance. *Journal of Archaeological Research* 17(1):65–103.

Andrews, Brian N., Davis J. Meltzer, and Mark Stiger (editors)
2021   *The Mountaineer Site: A Folsom Winter Camp in the Rockies.* University Press of Colorado, Boulder.

Andrews, Sherri
2018   *Section 110 Archaeological Evaluation and Eligibility Investigations on NAWS China Lake, Inyo and Kern Counties, California.* Submitted to Naval Facilities Engineering Command Southwest, San Diego, California.

Antevs, Ernst
1935   The Occurrence of Flints and Extinct Animals in Pluvial Deposits near Clovis, New Mexico, Part II: Age of the Clovis Lake Clays. *Proceedings of the Academy of Natural Sciences of Philadelphia* 87:304–12.

Apel, Jan, and Kjel Knutsson (editors)
2006   *Skilled Production and Social Reproduction: Aspects of Traditional Stone-Tool Technologies.* Societas Archaeologica Upsaliensis Stone Studies No. 2, Uppsala, Sweden.

Arnold, J. R., and W. F. Libby
1951   Radiocarbon Dates. *Science* 113(2927):111–120.

Aubry, Thierry, Bruce Bradley, Miguel Almeida, Bertrand Walter, Maria Jõo Neves, Jacques Pelegrin, Michel Lenoir, and Marc Tiffagom
2008   Solutrean Laurel Leaf Production at Maîtreaux: An Experimental Approach Guided by Techno-Economic Analysis. *World Archaeology* 40(1):48–66.

Azevedo, Soledad de, Judith Charlin, and Rolando González-José
2014   Identifying Design and Reduction Effects on Lithic Projectile Point Shapes. *Journal of Archaeological Science* 41:297–307.

Ballenger, Jesse A. M.
2015   The Densest Concentration on Earth? Quantifying Human-Mammoth Associations in the San Pedro Basin, Southeastern Arizona, USA. In *Clovis: On the Edge of a New Understanding*, edited by Ashley M. Smallwood and Thomas A. Jennings, pp. 183–204. Center for the Study of the First Americans, Texas A&M University Press, College Station.

Balter, Michael
2011   Do Island Sites Suggest a Coastal Route to the Americas? *Science* 331:1122.

Bamforth, Douglas B.
2002   High-Tech Foragers? Folsom and Later Paleoindian Technology on the Great Plains. *Journal of World Prehistory* 16(1):55–98.
2003   Rethinking the Role of Bifacial Technology in Paleoindian Adaptations on the Great Plains. In *Multiple Approaches to the Study of Bifacial Technologies*, edited by Marie Soressi and Harold Dibble, pp. 209–228. University of Pennsylvania Press, Philadelphia.
2009   Projectile Points, People, and Plains Paleoindian Perambulations. *Journal of Anthropological Archaeology* 28(2):142–57.
2014   Clovis Caches and Clovis Knowledge of the North American Landscape: The Mahaffy Cache, Colorado. In *Clovis Caches: Recent Discoveries and New Research*, edited by Bruce B. Huckell and J. David Kilby, pp. 39–59. University of New Mexico Press, Albuquerque.
2020   *The Archaeology of the North American Great Plains.* Cambridge University Press, New York.

Bamforth, Douglas B., and Peter Bleed
1997   Technology, Flaked Stone Technology, and Risk. *Archaeological Papers of the*

American Anthropological Association 7(1):109–39.

Barton, C. Michael, Steven Schmich, and Steven R. James
2004 The Ecology of Human Colonization in Pristine Landscapes. In *The Settlement of the American Continents: A Multidisciplinary Approach to Human Biogeography*, edited by C. Michael Barton, Geoffrey A. Clark, David R. Yesner, and Georges A. Pearson, pp. 138–161. University of Arizona Press, Tucson.

Basgall, Mark E.
1988 Archaeology of the Komodo Site, an Early Holocene Occupation in Central-Eastern California. In *Early Human Occupation in Far Western North America: The Clovis–Archaic Interface*, edited by Judith A. Willig, C. Melvin Aikens, and John L. Fagan, pp. 103–119. Anthropological Papers No. 21. Nevada State Museum, Carson City.
1993 *The Archaeology of Nelson Basin and Adjacent Areas, Fort Irwin, San Bernardino County, California*. Report prepared for and submitted to the US Army Corps of Engineers, Los Angeles District.
2003 *Summary Report of Archaeological Investigations at the CRBR Locality, Pleistocene Lake China, California*. Report submitted to and on file with the Naval Air Weapons Station, China Lake, California.
2007a *Prehistoric People in an Evolving Landscape: A Sample Survey of the China Lake Basin and Its Implications for Paleoindian Land Use*. Report submitted to and on file with the Naval Air Weapons Station, China Lake, California.
2007b *Another Look at the Ancient Californians: Resurvey of the Emma Lou Davis Stake Areas and Reassessment of Collections, Naval Air Weapons Station China Lake, Kern County, California*. Report submitted to and on file with the Naval Air Weapons Station, China Lake, California.

Basgall, Mark E., and M. C. Hall
1991 Relationships between Fluted and Stemmed Points in the Mojave Desert. *Current Research in the Pleistocene* 8:61–64.
1993 Archaeology of the Awl Site, CA-SBR-4562, Fort Irwin, San Bernardino County, California. Report prepared by Far Western Anthropological Research Group, Davis, California. Submitted to the US Army Corps of Engineers, Los Angeles District.

Basgall, Mark E., and S. A. Overly
2004 *Prehistoric Archaeology of the Rosamond Lake Basin, Phase II Cultural Resource Evaluations at 41 Sites in Management Region 2, Edwards Air Force Base, California*. Report submitted to and on file with Environmental Management Office, Conservation Branch, Edwards Air Force Base, California.

Bebber, Michelle R., G. Logan Miller, Matthew T. Boulanger, Brian N. Andrews, Brian G. Redmond, Donna Jackson, and Metin I. Eren
2017 Description and Microwear Analysis of Clovis Artifacts on a Glacially-Deposited Secondary Chert Source near the Hartley Mastodon Discovery, Columbiana County, Northeastern Ohio, USA. *Journal of Archaeological Science: Reports* 12:543–552.

Becerra-Valdivia, Lorena, and Thomas Higham
2020 The Timing and Effect of the Earliest Human Arrivals in North America. *Nature* 584:93–97.

Becerra-Valdivia, Lorena, Michael R. Waters, Thomas W. Stafford, Sarah L. Anzick, Daniel Comeskey, Thibaut Devièse, and Thomas Higham
2018 Reassessing the Chronology of the Archaeological Site of Anzick. *Proceedings of the National Academy of Sciences* 115(27):7000–7003.

Beck, Charlotte
2000 Dating the Archaeological Record and Modeling Technology. In *Models for the Millennium*, edited by Charlotte Beck, pp. 171–181. University of Utah Press, Salt Lake City.

Beck, Charlotte, Richard E. Hughes, and Trish LaPierre
2019 A Sunshine Point from Southern Nevada. *Journal of California and Great Basin Anthropology* 39(1):82–96.

Beck, Charlotte, and George T. Jones
1989 Bias and Archaeological Classification. *American Antiquity* 54(2):244–262.
1993 The Multipurpose Function of Great Basin Stemmed Series Points. *Current Research in the Pleistocene* 10:52–54.

1997 The Terminal Pleistocene/Early Holocene Archaeology of the Great Basin. *Journal of World Prehistory* 11(2):161–236.

2007 Early Paleoarchaic Point Morphology and Chronology. In *Paleoindian or Paleoarchaic? Great Basin Human Ecology at the Pleistocene–Holocene Transition*, edited by Kelly E. Graf and David N. Schmitt, pp. 23–41. University of Utah Press, Salt Lake City.

2009 *The Archaeology of the Eastern Nevada Paleoarchaic, Part I: The Sunshine Locality.* Anthropological Papers No. 126. University of Utah Press, Salt Lake City.

2010 Clovis and Western Stemmed: Population Migration and the Meeting of Two Technologies in the Intermountain West. *American Antiquity* 75(1):81–116.

2011 The Role of Mobility and Exchange in the Conveyance of Toolstone during the Great Basin Paleoarchaic. In *Perspectives on Prehistoric Trade and Exchange in California and the Great Basin*, edited by Richard E. Hughes, pp. 55–82. University of Utah Press, Salt Lake City.

2012a Clovis and Western Stemmed Again: Reply to Fiedel and Morrow. *American Antiquity* 77(2):386–397.

2012b The Clovis-Last Hypothesis: Investigating Early Lithic Technology in the Intermountain West. In *Meetings at the Margins: Prehistoric Cultural Interactions in the Intermountain West*, edited by David E. Rhode, pp. 23–46. University of Utah Press, Salt Lake City.

2013 Complexities of the Colonization Process: A View from the North American West. In *Paleoamerican Odyssey*, edited by Kelly E. Graf, Caroline V. Ketron, and Michael R. Waters, pp. 273–291. Center for the Study of the First Americans, Texas A&M University Press, College Station.

2015a A Case of Extinction in Paleoindian Technology. In *Lithic Technological Systems: Stone Tools, Human Behavior, and Evolution*, edited by Nathan Goodale and William Andrefsky Jr., pp. 83–99. Cambridge University Press, Cambridge, England.

2015b Lithic Analysis. In *The Paleoarchaic Occupation of the Old River Bed Delta*, edited by David B. Madsen, Dave N. Schmitt, and David Page, pp. 97–208. Anthropological Papers No. 128. University of Utah Press, Salt Lake City.

Beck, Charlotte, George T. Jones, Dennis L. Jenkins, Craig E. Skinner, and Jennifer Thatcher

2004 Fluted or Basally-Thinned? Re-Examination of a Lanceolate Point from the Connley Caves in the Fort Rock Basin. In *Early and Middle Holocene Archaeology of the Northern Great Basin*, edited by Dennis L. Jenkins, Thomas J. Connolly, and C. Melvin Aikens, pp. 281–294. Anthropological Papers No. 62. Museum of Natural and Cultural History, University of Oregon, Eugene.

Beck, Charlotte, George T. Jones, and Amanda K. Taylor

2019 What's Not Clovis? An Examination of Fluted Points in the Far West. *PaleoAmerica* 5(2):109–129.

Beck, Charlotte, Amanda Taylor, George T. Jones, Cynthia Fadem, Caitlyn Cook, and Sara Millward

2002 Rocks Are Heavy: Transport Costs and Paleoarchaic Quarry Behavior in the Great Basin. *Journal of Anthropological Archaeology* 21(4):481–507.

Bedwell, Stephen F.

1970 Prehistory and Environment of the Pluvial Fort Rock Lake Area of South Central Oregon. PhD dissertation, Department of Anthropology, University of Oregon, Eugene.

1973 *Fort Rock Basin: Prehistory and Environment.* University of Oregon Press, Eugene.

Bement, Leland C.

1999 View from a Kill: The Cooper Site Folsom Lithic Assemblages. In *Folsom Lithic Technology, Explorations in Structure and Variation*, edited by Daniel S. Amick, pp. 111–121. International Monographs in Prehistory, Archaeological Series No. 12. Berghahn Books, Ann Arbor, Michigan.

Bement, Leland C., and Brian J. Carter

2015 From Mammoth to Bison: Changing Clovis Prey Availability at the End of the Pleistocene. In *Clovis: On the Edge of Understanding*, edited by Ashley M. Smallwood and Thomas A. Jennings, pp. 263–275. Center for the Study of the First Americans, Texas A&M University Press, College Station.

Benson, Larry V., S. P. Lund, J. P. Smoot, David E. Rhode, R. J. Spencer, K. L. Verosub, Lisbeth A.

Louderback, C. A. Johnson, R. O. Rye, and R. M. Negrini
2011   The Rise and Fall of Lake Bonneville between 45 and 10.5 ka. *Quaternary International* 235:57–69.

Benson, Larry V., J. P. Smoot, S. P. Lund, S. A. Mensing, F. F. Foit Jr., and R. O. Rye
2013   Insights from a Synthesis of Old and New Climate-Proxy Data from the Pyramid and Winnemucca Lake Basins for the Period 48 to 11.5 cal ka. *Quaternary International* 310:62–82.

Bergström, Anders, Shane A. McCarthy, Ruoyun Hui, Mohamed A. Almarri, Qasim Ayub, Petr Danecek, Yuan Chen, Sabine Felkel, Pille Hallast, and Jack Kamm
2020   Insights into Human Genetic Variation and Population History from 929 Diverse Genomes. *Science* 367(6484):eaay5012.

Bettinger, Robert L., and Jelmer Eerkens
1999   Point Typologies, Cultural Transmission, and the Spread of Bow-and-Arrow Technology in the Prehistoric Great Basin. *American Antiquity* 64(2):215–230.

Bettinger, Robert L., James F. O'Connell, and David H. Thomas
1991   Projectile Points as Time Markers in the Great Basin. *American Anthropologist* 93(1):166–172.

Bettinger, Robert L., Bruce Winterhalder, and Richard McElreath
2006   A Simple Model of Technological Intensification. *Journal of Archaeological Research* 33:538–545.

Bever, Michael R.
2001   Stone Tool Technology and the Mesa Complex: Developing a Framework of Alaskan Paleoindian Prehistory. *Arctic Anthropology* 38(2):98–118.

Bever, Michael R., and David J. Meltzer
2007   Investigating Variation in the Paleoindian Life Ways: The Third Revised Edition of the Texas Clovis Fluted Point Survey. *Bulletin of the Texas Archeological Society* 78:65–99.

Bijker, Wiebe E.
1995   *Of Bicycles, Bakelites, and Bulbs: Toward a Theory of Technological Change.* MIT Press, Cambridge, Massachusetts.

Binford, Lewis R.
1978   Dimensional Analysis of Behavior and Site Structure: Learning from an Eskimo Hunting Stand. *American Antiquity* 43(3):330–361.
1980   Willow Smoke and Dogs' Tails: Hunter-Gatherer Settlement Systems and Archaeological Site Formation Processes. *American Antiquity* 45:4–20.

Bleed, Peter
1986   The Optimal Design of Hunting Weapons: Maintainability or Reliability. *American Antiquity* 51(4):737–747.

Bliege Bird, Rebecca, Eric Alden Smith, and Douglas W. Bird
2001   The Hunting Handicap: Costly Signaling in Male Foraging Strategies. *Behavioral Ecology and Sociobiology* 50:9–19.

Bliss, Wesley L.
1940a   A Chronological Problem Presented by Sandia Cave, New Mexico. *American Antiquity* 5(3):200–201.
1940b   Sandia Cave. *American Antiquity* 6(1):77–78.

Blong, John C., Martin E. Adams, Gabriel Sanchez, Dennis L. Jenkins, Ian D. Bull, and Lisa-Marie Shillito
2020   Younger Dryas and Early Holocene Subsistence in the Northern Great Basin: Multiproxy Analysis of Coprolites from the Paisley Caves, Oregon, USA. *Archaeological and Anthropological Sciences* 12(9):1–29.

Boas, Franz
1904   The History of Anthropology. *Science* 20(512):513–524.

Boldurian, A. T., and J. L. Cotter
1999   *Clovis Revisited: New Perspectives on Paleoindian Adaptation from Blackwater Draw, New Mexico.* The University Museum, University of Pennsylvania, Philadelphia.

Bonnichsen, Robson, Bradley T. Lepper, Dennis J. Stanford, and Michael R. Waters (editors)
2005   *Paleoamerican Origins: Beyond Clovis.* Center for the Study of the First Americans, Texas A&M University Press, College Station.

Bonnichsen, Robson, and Karen L. Turnmire (editors)
1991   *Clovis: Origins and Adaptations.* Center for the Study of the First Americans, Oregon State University, Corvallis.

Borda, Victor, Isabela Alvim, Marla Mendes, Carolina Silva-Carvalho, Giordano B. Soares-Souza,

Thiago P. Leal, Vinicius Furlan, Marilia O Scliar, Roxana Zamudio, and Camila Zolini
2020   The Genetic Structure and Adaptation of Andean Highlanders and Amazonians are Influenced by the Interplay Between Geography and Culture. *Proceedings of the National Academy of Sciences* 117(51):32557–32565.

Borden, Ferris W.
1971   *The Use of Surface Erosion Observations to Determine Chronological Sequence in Artifacts from a Mojave Desert Site.* Paper No. 7. Archaeological Survey Association of Southern California, Redlands, California.

Borrero, Luis Alberto
2009   The Elusive Evidence: The Archaeological Record of the South American Extinct Megafauna. In *Megafaunal Extinctions at the End of the Pleistocene*, edited by Gary Haynes, pp. 145–168. Springer, Dordrecht, The Netherlands.

Boulanger, Matthew T., Briggs Buchanan, Michael J. O'Brien, Brian G. Redmond, Michael D. Glascock, and Metin I. Eren
2015   Neutron Activation Analysis of 12,900-Year-Old Stone Artifacts Confirms 400–510+ km Clovis Tool-Stone Acquisition at Paleo Crossing (33ME274), Northeast Ohio, USA. *Journal of Archaeological Science* 53:550–558.

Boulanger, Matthew, Robert J. Patten, Brian N. Andrews, Michelle R. Bebber, Briggs Buchanan, Ian Jorgeson, G. Logan Miller, Metin I. Eren, and David J. Meltzer
2021   Antelope Springs: A Folsom Site in South Park, Colorado. *PaleoAmerica* 7(2): 114–132.

Boyd, Robert, and Peter J. Richerson
1985   *Culture and the Evolutionary Process.* University of Chicago Press, Chicago.

Boyer, Jeffrey L., and James L. Moore
2001   *Chipped Stone Material Procurement and Use: Data Recovery Investigations Along NM 522, Taos County, New Mexico.* Archaeology Notes No. 292. Museum of New Mexico Office of Archaeological Studies, Santa Fe.

Bradley, Bruce A.
1974   Comments on the Lithic Technology of the Casper Site Materials. In *The Casper Site: A Hell Gap Bison Kill Site on the High Plains*, edited by George C. Frison, pp. 191–197. Academic Press, New York.
1982   Flaked Stone Technology and Typology. In *The Agate Basin Site: A Record of the Paleoindian Occupation of the Northwestern High Plains*, edited by George C. Frison and Dennis J. Stanford, pp. 181–208. Academic Press, New York.
1991   Flaked Stone Technology in the Northern High Plains. In *Prehistoric Hunters of the High Plains*, edited by George C. Frison, pp. 369–395. Academic Press, New York.
2009   Bifacial Technology and Paleoindian Projectile Points. In *Hell Gap: A Stratified Paleoindian Campsite at the Edge of the Rockies*, edited by Mary Lou Larson, Marcel Kornfeld, and George C. Frison, pp. 259–73. University of Utah Press, Salt Lake City.
2010   Paleoindian Flake Stone Technology on the Plains and in the Rockies. In *Prehistoric Hunter-Gatherers of the High Plains and Rockies*, edited by Marcel Kornfeld, George C. Frison, and Mary Lou Larso, pp. 463–497. Left Coast Press, Walnut Creek, California.

Bradley, Bruce A., and Michael B. Collins
2013   Imagining Clovis as a Cultural Revitalization Movement. In *Paleoamerican Odyssey*, edited by Kelly E. Graf, Caroline V. Ketron, and Michael R. Waters, pp. 247–255. Center for the Study of the First Americans, Texas A&M University Press, College Station.

Bradley, Bruce A., Michael B. Collins, and Andrew Hemmings
2010   *Clovis Technology.* International Monographs in Prehistory, Archaeological Series No. 17. Berghahn Books, Ann Arbor, Michigan.

Bradley, Bruce A., and George C. Frison
1987   Projectile Points and Specialized Bifaces from the Horner Site. In *The Horner Site: The Type Site of the Cody Cultural Complex*, edited by George C. Frison and Lawrence C. Todd, pp. 199–231. Academic Press, New York.

Bradley, Erica J., Geoffrey M. Smith, and Kenneth E. Nussear
2022   Ecological Niche Modeling and Diachronic Change in Paleoindian Land Use in the Northwestern Great Basin, USA.

Journal of Archaeological Science: Reports 45:103564.

Bradley, Erica J., Geoffrey M. Smith, and Teresa A. Wriston
2020 Possible Paleoindian Geophyte Use in Hawksy Walksy Valley, Oregon. *Journal of California and Great Basin Anthropology* 40(2):129–143.

Bradley, James W., Arthur E. Spiess, Richard A. Boisvert, and Jeff Boudreau
2008 What's the Point? Modal Forms and Attributes of Paleoindian Bifaces in the New England-Maritimes Region. *Archaeology of Eastern North America* 36:119–172.

Brainerd, George W.
1953 A Re-Examination of the Dating Evidence for the Lake Mohave Artifact Assemblage. *American Antiquity* 18(3):270–271.

Braje, Todd J., Tom D. Dillehay, Jon M. Erlandson, Richard G. Klein, and Torben C. Rick
2017 Finding the First Americans. *Science* 358(6363):592–594.

Braje, Todd J., and Jon M. Erlandson
2005 Assessing Human Settlement on the South Coast of San Miguel Island, California: The Use of ^{14}C Dating as a Reconnaissance Tool. *Radiocarbon* 47(1):11–19.
2019 *From Paleoindians to Pioneers: Archaeological Investigations at CA-SRI-997/H, the Vail and Vickers Ranch House Site.* Report submitted to Channel Islands National Park, Ventura, California.

Braje, Todd J., Jon M. Erlandson, and Torben C. Rick
2005 Assessing Human Settlement on the South Coast of San Miguel Island, California: The Use of 14C Dating as a Reconnaissance Tool. *Radiocarbon* 47(1):11–19.
2013 Points in Space and Time: The Distribution of Paleocoastal Points and Crescents on California's Northern Channel Islands. In *California's Channel Islands: The Archaeology of Human-Environmental Interactions*, edited by Christopher S. Jazwa and Jennifer E. Perry, pp. 26–39. University of Utah Press, Salt Lake City.

Braje, Todd J., Jon M. Erlandson, Torben C. Rick, Loren Davis, Tom Dillehay, Daryl W. Fedje, Duane Froese, et al.
2020 Fladmark +40: What Have We Learned about a Potential Pacific Coast Peopling of the Americas. *American Antiquity* 85(1):1–21.

Braje, Todd J., Torben C. Rick, Tom D. Dillehay, Jon M. Erlandson, and Richard G. Klein
2018 Arrival Routes of First Americans Uncertain—Response. *Science* 359 (6381):1225.

Brandini, Stefania, Paola Bergamaschi, Marco F. Cerna, Francesca Gandini, Francesca Bastaroli, Emilie Bertolini, Cristina Cereda, et al.
2003 A Neutral Model of Stone Raw Material Procurement. *American Antiquity* 68(3):487–509.
2006 Measuring Forager Mobility. *Current Anthropology* 47(3):435–459.
2018 The Paleo-Indian Entry into South America According to Mitogenomes. *Molecular Biology and Evolution* 35(2):299–311.

Brantingham, P. Jeffrey, John W. Olsen, Jason A. Rech, and Andrei I. Krivoshapkin
2000 Raw Material Quality and Prepared Core Technologies in Northeast Asia. *Journal of Archaeological Science* 27:255–271.

Brantingham, P. Jeffrey, Todd A. Surovell, and Nicole M. Waguespack
2007 Modeling Post-Depositional Mixing of Archaeological Deposits. *Journal of Anthropological Archaeology* 26:517–540.

Brauner, David R.
1985 Early Human Occupation in the Uplands of the Southern Plateau: Archaeological Excavations at the Pilcher Creek Site, Union County, Oregon. Report prepared by the Department of Anthropology, Oregon State University. Submitted to the USDA Soil Conservation Service and the National Geographic Society, Washington, DC.

Bright, Jason, Andrew Ugan, and Lori Hunsaker
2002 The Effect of Handling Time on Subsistence Technology. *World Archaeology* 34:164–181.

Bronk Ramsey, Christopher
2009 Bayesian Analysis of Radiocarbon Dates. *Radiocarbon* 51(1):337–360.

Broughton, Jack M., and Elic M. Weitzel
2018 Population Reconstructions for Humans and Megafauna Suggest Mixed Causes for North American Pleistocene Extinctions. *Nature Communications* 9(1):1–12.

Brown, Thomas J., Daniel M. Gilmore, Paul S. Solimano, and Kenneth A. Ames
2019   The Radiocarbon Record of the Western Stemmed Tradition on the Southern Columbia Plateau of Western North America. *American Antiquity* 84(3):471–494.

Bryan, Alan L.
1965   *Paleo-American Prehistory*. Occasional Papers of the Museum No. 16. Idaho State University, Pocatello.
1969   Early Man in America and the Late Pleistocene Chronology of Western Canada and Alaska. *Current Anthropology* 10(4, Part 1):339–365.
1978   An Overview of Paleo-American Prehistory from a Circum-Pacific Perspective. In *Early Man in America from a Circum-Pacific Perspective*, edited by Alan L. Bryan, pp. 306–327. Occasional Papers No. 1. Department of Anthropology, University of Alberta, Archaeological Researches International, Edmonton, Canada.
1979   Smith Creek Cave. In *The Archaeology of Smith Creek Canyon*, edited by Donald R. Tuohy and Doris L. Rendall, pp. 164–251. Anthropological Papers No. 17. Nevada State Museum, Carson City.
1980   The Stemmed Point Tradition: An Early Technological Tradition in Western North America. In *Anthropological Papers in Memory of Earl H. Swanson Jr.*, edited by Lucille B. Harten, Claude N. Warren, and Donald R. Tuohy, pp. 77–107. Idaho State University Press, Pocatello.
1988   The Relationship of the Stemmed Point and Fluted Point Traditions in the Great Basin. In *Early Human Occupation in Far Western North America: The Clovis–Archaic Interface*, edited by Judith A. Willig, C. Melvin Aikens, and John L. Fagan, pp. 53–74. Anthropological Papers No. 21. Nevada State Museum, Carson City.
1991   The Fluted-Point Tradition in the Americas: One of Several Adaptations to Late Pleistocene American Environments. In *Clovis: Origins and Adaptations*, edited by Robson Bonnichsen and Karen L. Turnmire, pp. 15–33. Center for the Study of the First Americans, Oregon State University, Corvallis.

Bryan, Alan L., Rodolfo M. Casamiquela, José M. Cruxent, Ruth Gruhn, and Claudio Ochsenius
1978   An El Jobo Mastodon Kill at Taima-Taima, Venezuela. *Science* 200(4347):1275–1277.

Bryan, Alan L., and Donald R. Tuohy
1999   Prehistory of the Great Basin/Snake River Plain to about 8,500 Years Ago. In *Ice Age People of North America*, edited by Robson Bonnichsen and Karen L. Turmire, pp. 249–263. Center for the Study of the First Americans, Texas A&M University Press, College Station.

Buchanan, Briggs
2002   Folsom Lithic Procurement, Tool Use, and Replacement at the Lake Theo Site, Texas. *Plains Anthropologist* 47(181):121–46.
2006   An Analysis of Folsom Projectile Point Resharpening Using Quantitative Comparisons of Form and Allometry. *Journal of Archaeological Science* 33:185–199.

Buchanan, Briggs, Brian Andrews, Michael J. O'Brien, and Metin Eren
2018   An Assessment of Stone Weapon Tip Standardization during the Clovis–Folsom Transition in the Western United States. *American Antiquity* 83(4):721–734.

Buchanan, Briggs, Anne Chao, Chun-Huo Chiu, Robert K. Colwell, Michael J. O'Brien, Angelina Werner, and Metin I. Erin
2017   Environment-Induced Changes in Selective Constraints on Social Learning during the Peopling of the Americas. *Scientific Reports* 7(1):44431.

Buchanan, Briggs, and Mark Collard
2007   Investigating the Peopling of North America through Cladistic Analyses of Early Paleoindian Projectile Points. *Journal of Anthropological Archaeology* 26:366–393.

Buchanan, Briggs, Mark Collard, Marcus J. Hamilton, and Michael J. O'Brien
2011   Points and Prey: A Quantitative Test of the Hypothesis That Prey Size Influences Early Paleoindian Projectile Point Form. *Journal of Archaeological Science* 38(4):852–864.

Buchanan, Briggs, Metin I. Eren, and Michael J. O'Brien
2018   Assessing the Likelihood of Convergence

Among North American Projectile-Point Types. In *Convergent Evolution in Stone-Tool Technology*, edited by Michael J. O'Brien, Briggs Buchanan, and Metin I. Eren, pp. 275–287. MIT Press, Cambridge, Massachusetts.

Buchanan, Briggs, and Marcus J. Hamilton
2020 Scaling Laws of Paleoindian Projectile Point Design. *Journal of Archaeological Method and Theory* 28:580–602.

Buchanan, Briggs, J. David Kilby, Marcus J. Hamilton, Jason M. LaBelle, Kelton A. Meyer, Jacob Holland-Lulewicz, Brian Andrews et al.
2021 Bayesian Revision of the Folsom Age Range Using IntCal20. *PaleoAmerica* 7(2): 133–144.

Buchanan, Briggs, J. David Kilby, Bruce B. Huckell, Michael J. O'Brien, and Mark Collard
2012 A Morphometric Assessment of the Intended Function of Cached Clovis Points. *PLoS ONE* 7(2):e30530.

Buchanan, Briggs, J. David Kilby, Jason M. LaBelle, Todd A. Surovell, Jacob Holland-Lulewicz, and Marcus J. Hamilton
2022 Bayesian Modeling of the Clovis and Folsom Radiocarbon Records Indicates a 200-Year Multigenerational Transition. *American Antiquity* 87(3):567–580.

Buchanan, Briggs, Michael J. O'Brien, and Mark Collard
2014 Continent-Wide or Region-Specific? A Geometric-Morphometrics-Based Assessment of Variation in Clovis Point Shape. *Archaeological and Anthropological Sciences* 6:145–162.

Buchanan, Briggs, Michael J. O'Brien, J. David Kilby, Bruce B. Huckell, and Mark Collard
2012 An Assessment of the Impact of Hafting on Paleoindian Point Variability. *PLoS ONE* 7(5):e36364.

Butler, B. Robert
1961 *The Old Cordilleran Culture in the Pacific Northwest*. Occasional Papers of the Idaho State College Museum No. 9. Idaho State College Museum, Pocatello.
1963 An Early Man Site at Big Camas Prairie, South-Central Idaho. *Tebiwa* 6(1):22–33.
1964 A Recent Early Man Point Form in Southeastern Idaho. *Tebiwa* 7(1):39–40.
1965 A Report on Investigations of an Early Man Site near Lake Channel, Southern Idaho. *Tebiwa* 8(2):1–20.
1967 More Haskett Point Finds from the Type Locality. *Tebiwa* 10(1):25.
1973 Folsom and Plano Points from the Peripheries of the Upper Snake Country. *Tebiwa* 16(1):69–72.
1978 *A Guide to Understanding Idaho Archaeology: The Upper Snake and Salmon River Country*. Idaho Museum of Natural History, Pocatello.

Butler, B. Robert, and R. J. Fitzwater
1965 A Further Note on the Clovis Site at Big Camas Prairie, South-Central Idaho. *Tebiwa* 8(1):38–40.

Byerly, Ryan, Daron Duke, D. Craig Young, and Sarah K. Rice
2018 *Cultural Resources Inventory of 6,575 Acres of the West Delta of the Old River Bed, Utah Test and Training Range, Tooele County, Utah*. Report prepared by Far Western Anthropological Research Group, Henderson, Nevada. Submitted to Hill Air Force Base, Ogden, Utah.

Byerly, Ryan M., and Joanna C. Roberson
2015 Late Pleistocene to Middle Holocene Archaeology in the Mojave Desert: Recent Discoveries in Twentynine Palms, California. *PaleoAmerica* 1(2): 197–201.

Byers, David A., and Andrew Ugan
2005 Should We Expect Large Game Specialization in the Late Pleistocene? An Optimal Foraging Perspective on Early Paleoindian Prey Choice. *Journal of Archaeological Science* 32(11):1624–1640.

Callahan, Errett H.
1979 The Basics of Biface Knapping in the Eastern Fluted Point Tradition: Manual for Flint-Knappers and Lithic Analysts. *Archaeology of Eastern North America* 7:19–23.
1994 A Mammoth Undertaking. *Bulletin of Primitive Technology* 1(7):23–39.

Camp, Anna J.
2017 Catlow Twine Basketry through Time and Space: Exploring Shifting Cultural Boundaries through Prehistoric and Ethnographic Basketry Technology in the Northwestern Great Basin. PhD dissertation, Department of Anthropology, University of Nevada, Reno.

Campbell, Elizabeth W. Crozer
1936   Archaeological Problems in the Southern California Deserts. *American Antiquity* 1(4):295–300.
1949   Two Ancient Archaeological Sites in the Great Basin. *Science* 109(2831):340.

Campbell, Elizabeth W. Crozer, and William H. Campbell
1935   *The Pinto Basin Site*. Southwest Museum Papers No. 9, Los Angeles.
1940   A Folsom Complex in the Great Basin. *The Masterkey* 14(1):7–11.

Campbell, Elizabeth W. Crozer, William H. Campbell, Ernst Antevs, Charles A. Amsden, Joseph A. Barbieri, and Francis D. Bode
1937   *The Archaeology of Pleistocene Lake Mohave: A Symposium*. Southwest Museum Papers No. 11, Los Angeles.

Cannon, Michael D.
2004   Geographic Variability in North American Mammal Community Richness during the Terminal Pleistocene. *Quaternary Science Reviews* 23(9–10):1099–1123.

Cannon, Michael D., and David J. Meltzer
2004   Early Paleoindian Foraging: Examining the Faunal Evidence for Large Mammal Specialization and Regional Variability in Prey Choice. *Quaternary Science Reviews* 23(18–19):1955–1987.
2008   Explaining Variability in Early Paleoindian Foraging. *Quaternary International* 191(1):5–17.
2022   Forager Mobility, Landscape Learning, and the Peopling of the Americas. *Journal of Anthropological Archaeology* 65:101398

Carlson, Roy L.
1988   The View from the North. In *Early Human Occupation in Far Western North America: The Clovis–Archaic Interface*, edited by Judith A. Willig, C. Melvin Aikens, and John L. Fagan, pp. 319–324. Anthropological Papers No. 21. Nevada State Museum, Carson City.

Carmichael, David
1986   *Archaeological Survey in the Southern Tularosa Basin of New Mexico*. Historic and Natural Resources Report No. 3. Submitted to the Environmental Management Office, Directorate of Engineering and Housing, United States Army Air Defense Artillery Center, Fort Bliss, Texas.

Cavalli-Sforza, Luigi L., and Marcus W. Feldman
1973   Cultural versus Biological Inheritance: Phenotypic Transmission from Parents to Children (A Theory of the Effect of Parental Phenotypes on Children's Phenotypes). *American Journal of Human Genetics* 25(6):618–637.
1976   Evolution of Continuous Variation: Direct Approach through Joint Transmission of Genotypes and Phenotypes. *Proceedings of the National Academy of Sciences* 73(5):1689–1692.
1981   *Cultural Transmission and Evolution: A Quantitative Approach*. Monographs in Population Biology No. 16. Princeton University Press, Princeton, New Jersey.

Chapin, Nicholas
2005   Hunter Gatherer Technological Organization: The Archaic Period in Northern New Mexico. PhD dissertation, Department of Anthropology, University of New Mexico, Albuquerque.
2007   The Southwest Archaic Oshara Typology: The Projectile Point Collection from the Arroyo Cuervo. Poster presented at the 72nd Annual Meeting of the Society for American Archaeology, Austin, Texas.
2017   *Oshara Revisited: The Archaic Period in Northern New Mexico*. Anthropological Papers No. 10. Maxwell Museum of Anthropology, University of New Mexico, Albuquerque.

Charnov, Eric L.
1976   Optimal Foraging: The Marginal Value Theorem. *Theoretical Population Biology* 9:129–136.

Chatters, James C., James W. Brown, Steven Hackenberger, Patrick McCutcheon, and Jonathan Adler
2017   Calcined Bone as a Reliable Medium for Radiocarbon Dating: A Test Using Paired North American Samples. *American Antiquity* 82(3):593–608.

Christian, Leif J.
1997   Early Holocene Typology, Chronology, and Mobility: Evidence from the Northern Great Basin. Master's thesis, Department of Anthropology, University of Nevada, Reno.

Clark, John E., and Michael B. Collins (editors)
2002   *Folsom Technology and Lifeways*. Lithic

Technology, Special Publication No. 4. University of Tulsa, Oklahoma.

Clark, Jorie, Anders E. Carlson, Alberto V. Reyes, Elizabeth C. B. Carlson, Louise Guillaume, Glenn A. Milne, Lev Tarasov, Marc Caffee, Klaus Wilcken, and Dylan H. Rood
2022 The Age of the Opening of the Ice-Free Corridor and Implications for the Peopling of the Americas. *Proceedings of the National Academy of Sciences* 119(14):e2118558119

Clark, Jorie, Jerry X. Mitrovica, and Jay Alder
2014 Coastal Paleogeography of the California, Oregon, Washington and Bering Sea Continental Shelves during the Latest Pleistocene and Holocene: Implications for the Archaeological Record. *Journal of Archaeological Science* 52:12–23.

Clewlow, C. William, Jr.
1968 *Surface Archaeology of the Black Rock Desert, Nevada*. Archaeological Survey Reports No. 73. University of California, Berkeley.

Collard, Mark, Briggs Buchanan, Marcus J. Hamilton, and Michael J. O'Brien
2010 Spatial Dynamics of the Clovis–Folsom Transition. *Journal of Archaeological Science* 37(10):2513–2519.

Collins, Michael B.
1993 Comprehensive Lithic Studies: Context, Technology, Style, Attrition, Breakage, Use-Wear and Organic Substances. *Lithic Technology* 18(1–2):87–94
1999 *Clovis Blade Technology*. University of Texas Press, Austin.

Collins, Michael B., and Jon C. Lohse
2004 The Nature of Clovis Blades and Blade Cores. In *Entering America: Northeast Asia and Beringia before the Last Glacial Maximum*, edited by David B. Madsen, pp. 159–183. University of Utah Press, Salt Lake City.

Connolly, Thomas J. (editor)
1999 *Newberry Crater: A Ten-Thousand-Year Record of Human Occupation and Environmental Change in the Basin-Plateau Borderlands*. University of Utah Press, Salt Lake City.

Connolly, Thomas J., and Pat Barker
2004 Basketry Chronology of the Early Holocene in the Northern Great Basin. In *Early and Middle Holocene Archaeology of the Northern Great Basin*, edited by Dennis L. Jenkins, Thomas J. Connolly, and C. Melvin Aikens, pp. 241–250. Anthropological Papers No. 62. Museum of Natural and Cultural History, University of Oregon, Eugene.

Connolly, Thomas J., Pat Barker, Catherine S. Fowler, Eugene M. Hattori, Dennis L. Jenkins, and William J. Cannon
2016 Getting Beyond the Point: Textiles of the Terminal Pleistocene/Early Holocene in the Northwestern Great Basin. *American Antiquity* 81(3):490–514.

Connolly, Thomas J., Jon M. Erlandson, and Susan E. Norris
1995 Early Holocene Basketry from Daisy Cave, San Miguel Island, California. *American Antiquity* 60:309–318.

Connolly, Thomas J., Judson Byrd Finley, Geoffrey M. Smith, Dennis L. Jenkins, Pamela E. Endzweig, Brian L. O'Neill, and Paul W. Baxter
2017 Return to Fort Rock Cave: Assessing the Site's Potential to Contribute to Ongoing Debates about How and When Humans Colonized the Great Basin. *American Antiquity* 82(3):558–573.

Connolly, Thomas J., and Dennis L. Jenkins
1999 The Paulina Lake Site (35DS34). In *Newberry Crater: A Ten-Thousand-Year Record of Human Occupation and Environmental Change in the Basin-Plateau Borderlands*, edited by Thomas J. Connolly, pp. 86–127. University of Utah Press, Salt Lake City.

Cook, Harold J.
1927 New Geological and Palaeontological Evidence Bearing on the Antiquity of Mankind in America. *Natural History* 27(3):240–247.

Copeland, James M., And Richard E. Fike
1988 Fluted Projectile Points in Utah. *Utah Archaeology* 1(1):5–28.

Cowles, John
1960 *Cougar Mountain Cave in South Central Oregon*. Daily News Press, Rainier, Washington.

Crabtree, Don E.
1972 *An Introduction to Flint Knapping*. Idaho State University Occasional Paper No. 28. Idaho State University, Pocatello.

Crandell, Dwight R., Donald R. Mullineaux, Meyer Rubin, Elliot Spiker, and M. L. Kelley
1981   Radiocarbon Dates from Volcanic Deposits at Mount St. Helens, Washington. US Geological Survey Open-File Report 81-844. Washington, DC.

Craven, Sloan L.
2004   New Dates at the Lind Coulee Site (45GR97), Washington. *Current Research in the Pleistocene* 21:28–30.

Cressman, Luther S.
1936   *Archaeological Survey in the Guano Valley Region in South-Eastern Oregon*. University of Oregon Monographs, Studies in Anthropology No. 1. University of Oregon, Eugene.
1938   Original unpublished field notes from the Paisley Caves. Manuscript on file (Accession 60), University of Oregon Museum of Natural and Cultural History, Eugene.
1942   *Archaeological Researches in the Northern Great Basin*. Publication No. 538. Carnegie Institution of Washington, Washington, DC.
1951   Western Prehistory in Light of Carbon 14 Dating. *Southwestern Journal of Anthropology* 7:289–313.
1968   Early Man in Western North America: Perspectives and Prospects. In *Early Man in Western North America*, edited by Cynthia Irwin-Williams, pp. 78–87. Contributions in Anthropology Vol. 1, No. 4. Eastern New Mexico University, Portales.

Cressman, Luther S., Howel Williams, and Alex D. Krieger
1940   *Early Man in Oregon: Archaeological Studies in the Northern Great Basin*. Studies in Anthropology Monograph No. 3. University of Oregon, Eugene.

Cruxent, José M., and Irving Rouse
1956   A Lithic Industry of Paleo-Indian Type in Venezuela. *American Antiquity* 22(2): 172–179.

Cunnar, Geoffrey, William Schindler, Edward Stoner, Charles Wheeler, Mark Estes, and Tom Lennon
2011   Replication of a Paleoarchaic, Levallois-like Reduction Technique in the Great Basin: Trying to Better Understand One of America's Earliest Reduction Strategies. Poster presented at the 76th Annual Meeting of the Society for American Archaeology, Sacramento, California.

Cunnar, Geoffrey, Edward J. Stoner, and Charles W. Wheeler
2016   *The Archaeology of the Fire Creek National Register Archaeological District, Lander County, Nevada: Data Recovery at Loci AR, S, V, Y, AJ, AG, and AC*. Report prepared by Western Cultural Resource Management, Reno. Submitted to the US Bureau of Land Management. Report prepared by Geo-Marine, Inc., Las Vegas. Submitted to Hill Air Force Base, Ogden, Utah.

Dansie, Amy J., J. O. Davis, and Thomas W. Stafford Jr.
1988   The Wizard's Beach Recession: Farmdalian (25,500 yr BP) Vertebrate Fossils Co-occur with Holocene Artifacts. In *Early Human Occupation in Far Western North America: The Clovis–Archaic Interface*, edited by Judith A Willig, C. Melvin Aikens, and John L. Fagan, pp. 153–200. Anthropological Papers No. 21. Nevada State Museum, Carson City.

Dansie, Amy, and W. Jerry Jerrems
2004   Lahontan Chronology and Early Human Occupation in the Western Great Basin: A New Look at Old Collections. In *New Perspectives on the First Americans*, edited by Bradley T. Lepper and Robson Bonnichsen, pp. 55–64. Center for the Study of the First Americans, Texas A&M University Press, College Station, Texas.
2005   More Bits and Pieces: A New Look at Lahontan Chronology and Human Occupation. In *Paleoamerican Origins: Beyond Clovis*, edited by Robson Bonnichsen, Bradley T. Lepper, and Michael R. Waters, pp. 51–79. Center for the Study of the First Americans, Texas A&M University Press, College Station.

Darvill, Christopher M., Brian Menounos, Brent M. Goehring, and Alia J. Lesnek
2022   Cordilleran Ice Sheet Stability during the Last Deglaciation. *Geophysical Research Letters* 49:e2021GL097191.

Darvill, Christopher M., Brian Menounos, Brent M. Goehring, Olav B. Lian, and Marc W. Caffee
2018   Retreat of the Western Cordilleran Ice Sheet Margin during the Last Deglaciation. *Geophysical Research Letters* 45(18):9710–9720.

Daugherty, Richard D.
1956 Archaeology of the Lind Coulee Site. *Proceedings of the American Philosophical Society* 100(3):223–278.

Davis, Emma Lou
1963 The Desert Culture of the Western Great Basin: A Lifeway of Seasonal Transhumance. *American Antiquity* 29(2):202–212.
1967 Man and Water at Pleistocene Lake Mohave. *American Antiquity* 32(3):345–353.
1975 The Exposed Archaeology of China Lake, California. *American Antiquity* 40(1):39–53.

Davis, Emma Lou, Clark W. Brott, and David L. Weide
1969 *The Western Lithic Co-Tradition.* Papers No. 6. San Diego Museum of Man, San Diego, California.

Davis, Emma Lou, and Richard Shutler Jr.
1969 Recent Discoveries of Fluted Points in California and Nevada. In *Miscellaneous Papers on Nevada Archaeology 1–8*, pp. 154–169. Anthropological Papers No. 14. Nevada State Museum, Carson City.

Davis, Leslie B., and Sally T. Greiser
1992 Indian Creek Paleoindians: Early Occupation of the Elkhorn Mountains' Southeast Flank, West-Central Montana. In *Ice Age Hunters of the Rockies*, edited by Dennis J. Stanford and Jane S. Day, pp. 225–283. Denver Museum of Natural History and University Press of Colorado, Boulder.

Davis, Loren G.
2001 The Coevolution of Early Hunter-Gatherer Culture and Riparian Ecosystems in the Southern Columbia River Plateau. PhD dissertation, University of Alberta, Department of Anthropology, Edmonton.
2006 Geoarchaeological Insights from Indian Sands: A Late Pleistocene Site on the Southern Northwest Coast. *Geoarchaeology: An International Journal* 21(4):351–361.

Davis, Loren G., Daniel W. Bean, and Alexander J. Nyers
2017 Morphometric and Technological Attributes of Western Stemmed Tradition Projectile Points Revealed in a Second Artifact Cache from the Cooper's Ferry Site, Idaho. *American Antiquity* 82(3):536–557.

Davis, Loren G., Daniel W. Bean, Alexander J. Nyers, and David R. Brauner
2015 GLiMR: A GIS-Based Method for the Geometric Morphometric Analysis of Artifacts. *Lithic Technology* 40(3):199–217.

Davis, Loren G., Lorena Becerra-Valdivia, David B. Madsen, and Thomas Higham
2020 Response to Comment on "Late Upper Paleolithic Occupation at Cooper's Ferry, Idaho, USA, ~16,000 Years Ago." *Science* 368:6487.

Davis, Loren G., and David B. Madsen
2020 The Coastal Migration Theory: Formulation and Testable Hypotheses. *Quaternary Science Reviews* 249:106605.

Davis, Loren G., David B. Madsen, Lorena Becerra-Valdivia, Thomas Higham, David A. Sisson, Sarah M. Skinner, Daniel Stueber et al.
2019 Late Upper Paleolithic Occupation at Cooper's Ferry, Idaho, USA, ~16,000 Years Ago. *Science* 365(6456):891–897.

Davis, Loren G., David B. Madsen, David A. Sisson, and Masami Izuho
2021 Response to Review of "Late Upper Paleolithic Occupation at Cooper's Ferry, Idaho, USA, ~16,000 Years Ago" by Fiedel et al. *PaleoAmerica* 7(1):43–52.

Davis, Loren G., Alex J. Nyers, and Samuel C. Willis
2014 Context, Provenance, and Technology of a Western Stemmed Tradition Artifact Cache from the Cooper's Ferry Site, Idaho. *American Antiquity* 79(4):596–632.

Davis, Loren G., and Charles E. Schweger
2004 Geoarchaeological Context of Late Pleistocene and Early Holocene Occupation at the Cooper's Ferry Site, Western Idaho, USA. *Geoarchaeology: An International Journal* 19(7):685–704.

Davis, Loren G., and David A. Sisson
1998 An Early Stemmed Point Cache from the Lower Salmon River Canyon of West-Central Idaho. *Current Research in the Pleistocene* 15(1):12–14.

Davis, Loren G., and Samuel C. Willis
2018 The "Levallois-like" Technological System of the Western Stemmed Tradition: A Case of Convergent Evolution in Early North American Prehistory? In *Convergent Evolution and Stone-Tool Technology*, edited by Michael O'Brien, Metin Eren,

and Briggs Buchanan, 253–274. MIT Press, Cambridge, Massachusetts.

Davis, Loren G., Samuel C. Willis, and Shane J. Macfarlan
2012 Lithic Technology, Cultural Transmission, and the Nature of the Far Western Paleoarchaic/Paleoindian Co-Tradition. In *Meetings at the Margins: Prehistoric Cultural Interactions in the Intermountain West*, edited by David E. Rhode, pp. 47–64. University of Utah Press, Salt Lake City.

Dello-Russo, Robert D.
2015 *Archaeological Excavations at the Water Canyon Paleoindian Site (LA134761), Socorro, County, New Mexico: Interim Report for the 2012 and 2013 Field Seasons*. Office of Contract Archeology Report No. 185-1174, NMCRIS Activity No. 132823, University of New Mexico, Albuquerque.

Des Lauriers, Matthew R.
2008 A Paleoindian Fluted Point from Isla Cedros, Baja California. *Journal of Island and Coastal Archaeology* 3(2):271–276.

Des Lauriers, Matthew R., Loren G. Davis, J. Turnbull III, John R. Southon, and R. E. Taylor
2017 Earliest Shell Fishhooks from the Americas Reveal Fishing Technology of Pleistocene Maritime Foragers. *American Antiquity* 82(3):498–516.

Devièse, Thibaut, Thomas W. Stafford, Michael R. Waters, Crista Wathen, Daniel Comeskey, Lorena Becerra-Valdivia, and Thomas F. G. Higham
2018 Increasing Accuracy for the Radiocarbon Dating of Sites Occupied by the First Americans. *Quaternary Science Reviews* 198:171–180.

Dick, Herbert W., and Bert Mountain
1960 The Claypool Site: A Cody Complex Site in Northeastern Colorado. *American Antiquity* 26(2):223–235.

Dillehay, Tom D.
1997 *Monte Verde: A Late Pleistocene Settlement in Chile, Volume 2: The Archaeological Context and Interpretation*. Smithsonian Institution Press, Washington, DC.
2013 Entangled Knowledge: Old Trends and New Thoughts in First South American Studies. In *Paleoamerican Odyssey*, edited by Kelly E. Graf, Caroline V. Ketron, and Michael R. Waters, pp. 377–395. Center for the Study of the First Americans, Texas A&M University Press, College Station.

Dillehay, Tom D., C. Ramírez, M. Pino, M. B. Collins, J. Rossen, and J. D. Pino-Navarro
2008 Monte Verde: Seaweed, Food, Medicine, and the Peopling of South America. *Science* 320(5877):784–786.

Dixon, E. James
1999 *Bones, Boats, and Bison: Archaeology and the First Colonization of Western North America*. University of New Mexico Press, Albuquerque.

Dockall, John E.
1997 Wear Traces and Projectile Impact: A Review of the Experimental and Archaeological Evidence. *Journal of Field Archaeology* 24(3):321–331.

Donham, Megan, Richard Rosencrance, Katelyn McDonough, Haden Kingrey, and Dennis L. Jenkins
2020 Debitage Analysis of Younger Dryas Occupations at the Connley Caves and the Identification of a New Toolstone in the Fort Rock Basin, Oregon. *Current Archaeological Happenings in Oregon* 45(3):7–13.

Douglas, Charles L., Dennis L. Jenkins, and Claude N. Warren
1988 Spatial and Temporal Variability in Faunal Remains from Four Lake Mojave-Pinto Period Sites in the Mojave Desert. In *Early Human Occupation in Far Western North America: The Clovis–Archaic Interface*, edited by Judith A. Willig, C. Melvin Aikens, and John L. Fagan, pp. 131–144. Anthropological Papers No. 21. Nevada State Museum, Carson City.

Drennan, Robert D.
1996 *Statistics for Archaeologists: A Commonsense Approach*. Plenum Press, New York.

Drover, Christopher Elvis, Henry Carl Koerper, and Paul E. Langenwalter
1983 Early Holocene Human Adaptation on the Southern California Coast: A Summary Report of Investigations at the Irvine Site (CA-ORA-64), Newport Bay, Orange County, California. *Pacific Coast Archaeological Society Quarterly* 19:1–84.

Duke, Daron G.
2003 *Cultural Resources Inventory of the South Route to Wild Isle and TS-5, Utah Test and Training Range, Tooele County, Utah*.

Report prepared by Geo-Marine, Inc., Las Vegas. Submitted to Hill Air Force Base, Ogden, Utah.

2011 If the Desert Blooms: A Technological Perspective on Paleoindian Ecology in the Great Basin from the Old River Bed, Utah. PhD dissertation, Department of Anthropology, University of Nevada, Reno.

2013 The Exploded Fine-Grained Volcanic Sources of the Desert West and the Primacy of Tool Function in Material Selection. *North American Archaeologist* 34(4):323–354.

2015 Haskett Spear Weaponry and Protein-Residue Evidence of Proboscidean Hunting in the Great Salt Lake Desert, Utah. *PaleoAmerica* 1(1):109–112.

Duke, Daron G., and Jerome King
2014 A GIS Model for Predicting Wetland Habitat in the Great Basin at the Pleistocene–Holocene Transition and Implications for Paleoindian Archaeology. *Journal of Archaeological Science* 49:276–291.

Duke, Daron G., Kasey O'Horo, and Lindsey E. Daub
2016 *Archaeological Inventory of Five Target-Related Infrastructure Areas for Hill Air Force Basin, Utah Test and Training Range-South, Tooele County, Utah*. Report prepared by Far Western Anthropological Research Group, Henderson, Nevada. Submitted to Hill Air Force Base, Ogden, Utah.

Duke, Daron, Sarah K. Rice, and D. Craig Young
2019 *Class III Cultural Resources Inventory of Ice Age Fossils State Park, Clark County, Nevada*. IAFSP 17/19 B449, NDSP-CRR 2018-03. Report prepared by Far Western Anthropological Research Group, Henderson, Nevada. Submitted to Nevada Division of State Parks, Carson City.

Duke, Daron, Sarah K. Rice, D. Craig Young, and Ryan Byerly
2018 *The Playas Archaeological Inventory: 6,914 Acres on the Utah Test and Training Range Including Portions of the West Distal Delta of the Old River Bed and Test Excavations at the Wishbone Site (42TO6384), Tooele County, Utah*. Report prepared by Far Western Anthropological Research Group, Henderson, Nevada, for the Center for Integrated Research on the Environment, University of Montana, Missoula, and Hill Air Force Base, Ogden, Utah.

Duke, Daron, Eric Wohlgemuth, Karen R. Adams, Angela Armstrong-Ingram, Sarah K. Rice, and D. Craig Young
2022 Earliest Evidence for Human Use of Tobacco in the Pleistocene Americas. *Nature Human Behaviour* 6(2):183–192.

Duke, Daron G., and D. Craig Young
2007 Episodic Permanence in Paleoarchaic Basin Selection and Settlement. In *Paleoindian or Paleoarchaic? Great Basin Human Ecology at the Pleistocene–Holocene Transition*, edited by Kelly E. Graf and David N. Schmitt, pp. 123–138. University of Utah Press, Salt Lake City.

Duke, Daron, D. Craig Young, and Sarah K. Rice
2018 *Cultural Resources Inventory of the High-Speed Mover Test Area, a 4,548-Acre Portion of the West Delta of the Old River Bed, Utah Test and Training Range, Tooele County, Utah*. Report prepared by Far Western Anthropological Research Group, Henderson, Nevada. Submitted to and copies on file at Hill Air Force Base, Utah.

Dunbar, James S.
2006 Paleoindian Archaeology. In *First Floridians and Last Mastodons: The Page-Ladson Site in the Aucilla River*, edited by S. David Webb, pp. 403–435. Springer, Dordrecht, Netherlands.

Dunnell, Robert C.
1978 Style and Function: A Fundamental Dichotomy. *American Antiquity* 43(2):192–202.

Eerkens, Jelmer W., and Carl F. Lipo
2007 Cultural and Temporal Changes in Material Culture. *Journal of Archaeological Research* 15(3):239–274.

Egan, Joanne, Richard Staff, and Jeff Blackford
2015 A High-Precision Age Estimate of the Holocene Plinian Eruption of Mount Mazama, Oregon, USA. *Holocene* 25(7):1054–1067.

Ellis, Christopher
2011 Measuring Paleoindian Range Mobility and Land-Use in the Great Lakes/Northeast. *Journal of Anthropological Archaeology* 30(3):385–401.

2013 Clovis Lithic Technology: The Devil Is in the Details. *Reviews in Anthropology* 42(3):127–160.

Ellis, Christopher J., and Jonathan C. Lothrop
2019 Early Fluted-Biface Variation in Glaciated Northeastern North America. *PaleoAmerica* 5(2):121–131.

Elston, Robert G.
1982 Good Times, Hard Times: Prehistoric Culture Change in the Western Great Basin. In *Man and Environment in the Great Basin*, edited by David B. Madsen and James F. O'Connell, pp. 186–206. SAA Papers No. 2. Society for American Archaeology, Washington, DC.
1986 Prehistory of the Western Area. In *The Great Basin*, edited by Warren L. d'Azevedo, pp. 135–148. Handbook of North American Indians, Vol. 11, William C. Sturtevant, general editor. Smithsonian Institution, Washington, DC.

Elston, Robert G., and Martijn Kuypers
2018 Preliminary Comparison of Paleoindian Sites 26LA4434 and 26LA781 (Knudtsen Site), Grass Valley, Nevada. Poster presented at the 36th Great Basin Anthropological Conference, Salt Lake City, Utah.

Elston, Robert G., and David W. Zeanah
2002 Thinking Outside the Box: A New Perspective on Diet Breadth and Sexual Division of Labor in the Prearchaic Great Basin. *World Archaeology* 34(1):103–130.

Elston, Robert G., David W. Zeanah, and Brian F. Codding
2014 Living Outside the Box: An Updated Perspective on Diet Breadth and Sexual Division of Labor in the Prearchaic Great Basin. *Quaternary International* 352:200–211.

Eren, Metin I., Michelle R. Bebber, Edward J. Knell, Brett Story, and Briggs Buchanan
2022 Plains Paleoindian Projectile Point Penetration Potential. *Journal of Anthropological Research* 78(1):84–112.

Eren, Metin I., Michelle R. Bebber, Anna Mika, Kat Flood, Leanna Maguire, Dusty Norris, Alyssa Perrone, Damon A. Mullen, Scott Centea, and Chase Centea
2021 The Nelson Stone Tool Cache, North-Central Ohio, USA: Assessing its Cultural Affiliation. *Journal of Archaeological Science: Reports* 37:102972.

Eren, Metin I., and Briggs Buchanan
2016 Clovis Technology. In *eLS*: Citable Reviews in Life Science, 1–9, https://doi.org/10.1002/9780470015902.a0026512.

Eren, Metin I., Briggs Buchanan, and Michael J. O'Brien
2015 Social Learning and Technological Evolution during the Clovis Colonization of the New World. *Journal of Human Evolution* 80:159–170.

Eren, Metin I., and Adrienne Desjardine
2015 Overshot Flaking at the Red Wing Site, Ontario. In *Clovis: On the Edge of a New Understanding*, edited by Ashley M. Smallwood and Thomas A. Jennings, pp. 109–120. Center for the Study of the First Americans, Texas A&M University Press, College Station.

Eren, Metin I., David J. Meltzer, and Brian N. Andrews
2018 Is Clovis Technology Unique to Clovis? *PaleoAmerica* 4(3):202–218.
2021 Clovis Technology Is Not Unique to Clovis. *PaleoAmerica* 7(3):226–241.

Eren, Metin I., David J. Meltzer, Brett Story, Briggs Buchanan, Don Yeager, and Michelle R. Bebber
2021 On the Efficacy of Clovis Fluted Points for Hunting Proboscideans. *Journal of Archaeological Science: Reports* 39:103166.
2022 Not Just for Proboscidean Hunting: On the Efficacy and Functions of Clovis Fluted Points. *Journal of Archaeological Science: Reports* 45:103601.

Eren, Metin I., Robert J. Patten, Michael J. O'Brien, and David J. Metzer
2013 Refuting the Technological Cornerstone of the Ice-Age Atlantic Crossing Hypothesis. *Journal of Archaeological Science* 40:2934–2941.
2014 More on the Rumor of "Intentional Overshot Flaking" and the Purported Ice-Age Atlantic Crossing. *Lithic Technology* 39(1):55–63.

Eren, Metin I., Christopher I. Roos, Brett A. Story, Noreen von Cramon-Taubadel, and Stephen J. Lycett
2014 The Role of Raw Material Differences in Stone Tool Shape Variation: An Experimental Assessment. *Journal of Archaeological Science* 49:472–487.

Eren, Metin I., Brett Story, Alyssa Perrone,

Michelle Bebber, Marcus Hamilton, Robert Walker, and Briggs Buchanan
2020 North American Clovis Point Form and Performance: An Experimental Assessment of Penetration Depth. *Lithic Technology* 45(4):263–282.

Erlandson, Jon M.
1994 *Early Hunter-Gatherers of the California Coast.* Plenum Press, New York.
2002 Anatomically Modern Humans, Maritime Voyaging, and the Pleistocene Colonization of the Americas. In *The First Americans: The Pleistocene Colonization of the New World*, edited by Nina Jablonski, pp. 59–92. Memoirs of the California Academy of Sciences, San Francisco.
2010 CA-SMI-701: A Paleocoastal Site on San Miguel Island, California. *Current Research in the Pleistocene* 27:86–88.
2013 Channel Island Amol Points: A Stemmed Paleocoastal Type from Santarosae Island, Alta California. *California Archaeology* 5(1):105–122.

Erlandson, Jon M., and Todd J. Braje
2007 Early Maritime Technology on California's San Miguel Island: Arena Points from CA-SMI-575-NE. *Current Research in the Pleistocene* 24:85–86.
2011 From Asia to the Americas by Boat? Paleogeography, Paleoecology, and Stemmed Points of the Northwest Pacific. *Quaternary International* 239(1–2):28–37.
2015 Stemmed Points, the Coastal Migration Theory, and the Peopling of the Americas. In *Mobility and Ancient Society in Asia and the Americas*, edited by Michael David Frachetti and Robert N. Spengler III, pp. 49–58. Springer, New York.

Erlandson, Jon M., Todd J. Braje, Amira F. Ainis, Brendan J. Culleton, Kristina M. Gill, Courtney A. Hofman, Douglas J. Kennett, Leslie A. Reeder-Myers, and Torben C. Rick
2020 Maritime Paleoindian Technology, Subsistence, and Ecology at an ~11,700 Year Old Paleocoastal Site on California's Northern Channel Islands, USA. *PLoS ONE* 15(9):e0238866.

Erlandson, Jon M., Todd J. Braje, and Kristina M. Gill
2019 A Paleocoastal Site Complex from Santarosae Island, California. *PaleoAmerica* 5(3):300–305.

Erlandson, Jon M., Todd J. Braje, Kristina M. Gill, and Michael H. Graham
2015 Ecology of the Kelp Highway: Did Marine Resources Facilitate Human Dispersal from Northeast Asia to the Americas? *The Journal of Island and Coastal Archaeology* 10(3):392–411.

Erlandson, Jon M., Todd J. Braje, and Michael H. Graham
2008 How Old Is MVII? Seaweeds, Shorelines, and Chronology at Monte Verde, Chile. *Journal of Island and Coastal Archaeology* 3(2):277–281.

Erlandson, Jon M., Todd J. Braje, Torben C. Rick, and Jenna Peterson
2005 Beads, Bifaces, and Boats: An Early Maritime Adaptation on the South Coast of San Miguel Island, California. *American Anthropologist* 107(4):677–683.

Erlandson, Jon M., and Roger H. Colten (editors)
1991 *Hunter-Gatherers of Early Holocene Coastal California.* Perspectives in California Archaeology, Vol. 1. Cotsen Institute of Archaeology Press, University of California, Los Angeles.

Erlandson, Jon M., Theodore G. Cooley, and Richard Carrico
1987 A Fluted Projectile Point from the Southern California Coast: Chronology and Context at CA-SBa-1951. *Journal of California and Great Basin Anthropology* 9:120–128.

Erlandson, Jon M., Kristina M. Gill, Michael A. Glassow, and Amy E. Gusick
2016 Three Paleocoastal Lithic Sites on Santa Cruz Island, California. *PaleoAmerica* 2(1):52–55.

Erlandson, Jon M., Kristina M. Gill, Jennifer E. Perry, René L. Vellanoweth, and Andy Yatsko
2019 Mineral Resources on the Islands of Alta and Baja California. In *An Archaeology of Abundance: Re-Evaluating the Marginality of California's Islands*, edited by Kristina M. Gill, Mikael Fauvelle, and Jon M. Erlandson, pp. 171–190. University of Florida Press, Gainesville.

Erlandson, Jon M., Michael H. Graham, Bruce J. Bourque, Debra Corbett, James A. Estes, and Robert S. Steneck
2007 The Kelp Highway Hypothesis: Marine Ecology, the Coastal Migration Theory, and the Peopling of the Americas. *The*

Erlandson, Jon M., and Nicholas P. Jew
2009   An Early Maritime Biface Technology at Daisy Cave, San Miguel Island, California: Reflections on Sample Size, Site Function, and Other Issues. *North American Archaeologist* 30(2):145–165.

Erlandson, Jon M., Douglas J. Kennett, Brendan J. Culleton, Ted Goebel, Greg C. Nelson, and Craig Skinner
2014   Eyed Bone Needles from a Younger Dryas Paleoindian Component at Tule Lake Rock Shelter, Northern California. *American Antiquity* 79(4):776–781.

Erlandson, Jon M., Douglas J. Kennett, B. Lynn Ingram, Daniel A. Guthrie, Don P. Morris, Mark A. Tveskov, G. James West, and Phil L. Walker
1996   An Archaeological and Paleontological Chronology for Daisy Cave (CA-SMI 261), San Miguel Island, California. *Radiocarbon* 38(2):355–373.

Erlandson, Jon M., Madonna L. Moss, and Matthew Des Lauriers
2008   Life on the Edge: Early Maritime Cultures of the Pacific Coast of North America. *Quaternary Science Reviews* 27(23–24): 2232–2245.

Erlandson, Jon M., Torben C. Rick, Todd J. Braje, Molly Casperson, Brendan Culleton, Brian Fulfrost, Tracy Garcia et al.
2011   Paleoindian Seafaring, Maritime Technologies, and Coastal Foraging on California's Channel Islands. *Science* 331(6021):1181–1185.

Erlandson, Jon M., Jack L. Watts, and Nicholas P. Jew
2014   Darts, Arrows, and Archaeologists: Distinguishing between Dart and Arrow Points in the Archaeological Record. *American Antiquity* 79(1):162–169.

Estes, Mark B.
2009   Paleoindian Occupations in the Great Basin: A Comparative Study of Lithic Technological Organization, Mobility, and Landscape Use from Jakes Valley, Nevada. Master's thesis, Department of Anthropology, University of Nevada, Reno.

Fagan, John L.
1988   Clovis and Western Pluvial Lakes Tradition Lithic Technologies at the Dietz Site in South-Central Oregon. In *Early Human Occupation in Far Western North America: The Clovis–Archaic Interface*, edited by Judith A. Willig, C. Melvin Aikens, and John L. Fagan, pp. 389–416. Anthropological Papers No. 21. Nevada State Museum, Carson City.

Fagundes, Nelson J. R., Alice Tagliani-Ribeiro, Rohina Rubicz, Larissa Tarskaia, Michael H. Crawford, Francisco M. Salzano, and Sandro L. Bonatto
2018   How Strong Was the Bottleneck Associated to the Peopling of the Americas? New Insights from Multilocus Sequence Data. *Genetics and Molecular Biology* 41(1):206–214.

Faith, J. Tyler, and Todd A. Surovell
2009   Synchronous Extinction of North America's Pleistocene Mammals. *Proceedings of the National Academy of Sciences of the United States of America* 106(49):20641–20645.

Farjo, Laith A., and Theodore Miclau
1997   Ballistics and Mechanisms of Tissue Wounding. *Injury* 28:C12–C17.

Fedje, Daryl, Quentin Mackie, Terri Lacourse, and Duncan McLaren
2011   Younger Dryas Environments and Archaeology on the Northwest Coast of North America. *Quaternary International* 242(2):452–462.

Fedje, Daryl, Quentin Mackie, Duncan McLaren, and Tina Christensen
2008   A Projectile Point Sequence for Haida Gwaii. In *Projectile Point Sequences in Northwestern North America*, edited by Roy L. Carlson and Martin P. R. Magne, pp. 19–40. Archaeology Press, Simon Fraser University, Burnaby, British Columbia.

Felling, Danielle C.
2015   Paleoindian Settlement Strategies Across Time and Space in the Northwestern Great Basin: Lithic Technological Organization at Last Supper Cave, Nevada. Master's thesis, Department of Anthropology, University of Nevada, Reno.

Fenenga, Gerrit L.
2010   A Typological Analysis and Geographic Distribution of the Eccentric Crescent in Western North America. In *A Riddle Wrapped in Mystery Inside an Enigma:*

Three Studies of Chipped Stone Crescents from California, edited by Gerrit L. Fenenga and Jerry N. Hopkins, pp. 1–46. Contributions to Tulare Lake Archaeology. Coyote Press, Salinas, California.

Fenner, Lindsay A.
2011 Changing Landscapes during the Terminal Pleistocene/Early Holocene: The Archaeology and Paleoclimate of the Mud Lake Basin, Nye County, Nevada. Master's thesis, Department of Anthropology, University of Nevada, Reno.

Ferguson, Jeffery R.
2012 X-ray Fluorescence of Obsidian: Approaches to Calibration and the Analysis of Small Samples. In *Studies in Archaeological Sciences: Handheld XRF for Art and Archaeology*, edited by Aaron N. Shugar and Jennifer L. Mass, pp. 402–422. Leuven University Press, Leuven, Belgium.

Ferring, C. Reid
2001 *The Archaeology and Paleoecology of the Aubrey Clovis Site (41DN479), Denton County, Texas*. Center for Environmental Archaeology, Department of Geography, University of North Texas, Denton. Submitted to the US Army Corps of Engineers, Fort Worth District, Texas.

Fiedel, Stuart J.
2014 Did Pre-Clovis People Inhabit the Paisley Caves (and Why Does it Matter)? *Human Biology* 86(1):69–74.

Fiedel, Stuart J., and Gary Haynes
2004 A Premature Burial: Comments on Grayson and Meltzer's "Requiem for Overkill." *Journal of Archaeological Science* 31(1):121–131.

Fiedel, Stuart J., and Juliet E. Morrow
2012 Comment on "Clovis and Western Stemmed: Population Migration and the Meeting of Two Technologies in the Intermountain West" by Charlotte Beck and George T. Jones. *American Antiquity* 77(2):376–385.

Fiedel, Stuart J., Ben A. Potter, Juliet E. Morrow, Michael K. Faught, C. Vance Haynes Jr., and James C. Chatters.
2021 Pioneers from Northern Japan in Idaho 16,000 Years Ago? A Critical Evaluation of the Evidence from Cooper's Ferry. *PaleoAmerica* 7(1):1–15.

Figgins, Jesse Dade
1927 The Antiquity of Man in America. *Natural History* 27(3):229–239.

Finley, Judson B., Marcel Kornfeld, Brian N. Andrews, George C. Frison, Chris C. Finley, and Michael T. Bies
2005 Rockshelter Archaeology and Geoarchaeology in the Bighorn Mountains, Wyoming. *Plains Anthropologist* 50(195):227–248.

Fischel, Hans E.
1939 Folsom and Yuma Culture Finds. *American Antiquity* 4(3):232–264.

Fischer, Anders, Peter Vemming Hansen, and Peter Rasmussen
1984 Macro and Micro Wear Traces on Lithic Projectile Points. *Journal of Danish Archaeology* 3(1):19–46.

Fishel, Richard L.
1988 Preliminary Observations on the Distribution of Agate Basin Projectile Points East of the Mississippi River. *Wisconsin Archaeologist* 69(3):125–138.

Fitzgerald, Richard T., and Michael F. Rondeau
2012 A Fluted Point from Crystal Cove State Park, Orange County, Alta California. *California Archaeology* 4(2):247–256.

Fladmark, Knut R.
1979 Routes: Alternate Migration Corridors for Early Man in North America. *American Antiquity* 44(1):55–69.

Flenniken, J. Jeffrey, and Anan W. Raymond
1986 Morphological Projectile Point Typology: Replication Experimentation and Technological Analysis. *American Antiquity* 51(3):603–614.

Flenniken, J. Jeffrey, and Philip J. Wilke
1989 Typology, Technology, and Chronology of Great Basin Dart Points. *American Anthropologist* 91(1):149–158.

Forbis, Richard G.
1955 The MacHaffie Site. PhD dissertation, Department of Political Science, Columbia University, New York.

Forbis, Richard G., and John D. Sperry
1952 An Early Man Site in Montana. *American Antiquity* 18(2):127–133.

Frison, George C.
1974 *The Casper Site: A Hell Gap Bison Kill on the High Plains*. Academic Press, New York.
1978 *Prehistoric Hunters of the High Plains*. Academic Press, New York.

1983 The Lookingbill Site, Wyoming 48FR308. *Tebiwa* 20:1–16.

1984 The Carter/Kerr-McGee Paleoindian Site: Cultural Resource Management and Archaeological Research. *American Antiquity* 49(2):288–314.

1986 Mammoth Hunting and Butchering from a Perspective of African Elephant Culling. In *The Colby Mammoth Site: Taphonomy and Archaeology of a Clovis Kill in Northern Wyoming*, edited by George C. Frison and Lawrence C. Todd, pp. 115–134. University of New Mexico Press, Albuquerque.

1991 *Prehistoric Hunters of the High Plains.* 2nd ed. Academic Press, New York.

1998 The Northwestern and Northern Plains Archaic. In *Archaeology on the Great Plains*, edited by W. Raymond Wood, pp. 140–172. University of Kansas Press, Lawrence.

2004 *Survival by Hunting: Prehistoric Human Predators and Animal Prey.* University of California Press, Berkeley.

Frison, George C., and Bruce A. Bradley

1980 *Folsom Tools and Technology at the Hanson Site, Wyoming.* University of New Mexico Press, Albuquerque.

1999 *The Fenn Cache: Clovis Weapons and Tools.* One Horse Land & Cattle Company, Santa Fe, New Mexico.

Frison, George C., and Dennis J. Stanford

1982 *The Agate Basin Site: A Record of the Paleoindian Occupation of the Northwestern High Plains.* Academic Press, New York.

Frison, George C., and Lawrence C. Todd

1986 *The Colby Mammoth Site: Taphonomy and Archaeology of a Clovis Kill in Northern Wyoming.* University of New Mexico Press, Albuquerque.

Frison, George C., George M. Zeimens, Spencer R. Pelton, Danny N. Walker, Dennis J. Stanford, and Marcel Kornfeld

2018 Further Insights into Paleoindian Use of the Powers II Red Ochre Quarry (48PL330), Wyoming. *American Antiquity* 83(3):485–504.

Froese, Duane, Joseph M. Young, Sophie L. Norris, and Martin Margold

2019 Availability and Viability of the Ice-Free Corridor and Pacific Coast Routes for the Peopling of the Americas. *Society of American Archaeology Record* 19(3):27–33.

Fryxell, Roald, and Richard D. Daugherty

1962 *Interim Report: Archaeological Salvage in the Lower Monumental Reservoir, Washington.* Reports of Investigations No. 21. Washington State University Laboratory of Anthropology, Pullman.

Galm, Jerry R., and Stan Gough

2000 Site 45KT1362, ac 10,000 yr BP Occupation in Central Washington. *Current Research in the Pleistocene* 17:29–31.

2008 The Projectile Point/Knife Sample from the Sentinel Gap Site. In *Projectile Point Sequences in Northwestern North America*, edited by Roy L. Carlson and Martin P. R. Magne, pp. 209–220. Archaeology Press, Simon Fraser University, Burnaby, British Columbia, Canada.

Galm, Jerry R., Glenn D. Hartmann, Ruth A. Masten, and Garry O. Stephenson

1981 *A Cultural Resource Overview of Bonneville Power Administration's Mid-Columbia Project, Central Washington.* Archaeological and Historical Services, Reports in Archaeology and History. Eastern Washington University, Cheney.

Garcia, Antonio F., and Martin Stokes

2006 Late Pleistocene Highstand and Recession of a Small, High-Altitude Pluvial Lake, Jakes Valley, Central Great Basin, USA. *Quaternary Research* 65(1):179–186.

Garfinkel, Alan P., Jerry N. Hopkins, and Craig E. Skinner

2008 Ancient Stones of Black Glass: Tracing and Dating Paleoindian Obsidian Artifacts from China and Tulare Lakes. In *Ice-Age Stone Tools from the San Joaquin Valley*, edited by Jerry N. Hopkins and Alan P. Garfinkel, pp. 59–97. Contributions to Tulare Lake Archaeology IV. Tulare Lake Archaeological Research Group, Redondo Beach, California.

Giambastiani, Mark A.

2008 *Late Pleistocene–Early Holocene Adaptations on the Eastern Shore of China Lake: Results of the BRAC-TECH-006 Testing and Data Recovery Project.* Report submitted to Epsilon Systems Solutions, Inc., Ridgecrest, California.

Giambastiani, Mark A., and Thomas F. Bullard

2010 Terminal Pleistocene–Early Holocene Adaptations on the Eastern Shore of China Lake, California. *Pacific Coast Archaeological Society Quarterly* 43(1&2):50–70.

Gilbert, M. Thomas P., Dennis L. Jenkins, Anders Götherstrom, Nuria Naveran, Juan J. Sanchez, Michael Hofreiter, Philip Francis Thomsen, Jonas Binladen, Thomas F. G. Higham, and Robert M. Yohe

2008   DNA from Pre-Clovis Human Coprolites in Oregon, North America. *Science* 320(5877):786–789.

Gilbert, M. Thomas P., Dennis L. Jenkins, Thomas F. G. Higham, Morten Rasmussen, Helena Malmstrom, Emma Svensson, Juan J. Sanchez et al.

2009   Response to Comment by Poinar et al. on "DNA from Pre-Clovis Human Coprolites in Oregon, North America." *Science* 320(5877):786–789.

Gill, Kristina M.

2016   10,000 Years of Geophyte Use among the Island Chumash of the Northern Channel Islands. *Fremontia* 44(3):34–38.

Gill, Kristina M., Todd J. Braje, Kevin Smith, and Jon M. Erlandson

2021   Earliest Evidence for Geophyte Use in North America: 11,500-Year-Old Archaeobotanical Remains from California's Santarosae Island. *American Antiquity* 86(3):625–637.

Gill, Kristina M., Jon M. Erlandson, Richard E. Hughes, Tom Origer, Alexander K. Rogers, and René L. Vellanoweth

2020   Material Conveyance Networks of the Southern California Bight: Obsidian on Alta California's Channel Islands. *Journal of Island and Coastal Archaeology* 16(2):195–212.

Gill, Kristina M., Jon M. Erlandson, Ken Niessen, Kristin Hoppa, and Dustin Merrick

2019   Where Carbohydrates Were Key: Reassessing the Marginality of Terrestrial Plant Resources on California's Islands. In *An Archaeology of Abundance: Reevaluating the Marginality of California's Islands*, edited by Kristina M. Gill, Mikael Fauvelle, and Jon M. Erlandson, pp. 98–134. University of Florida Press, Gainesville.

Gill, Kristina M., and Kristin M. Hoppa

2016   Evidence for an Island Chumash Geophyte-Based Subsistence Economy on the Northern Channel Islands. *Journal of California and Great Basin Anthropology* 36(1):51–71.

Gilmour, Daniel M., Todd Ogle, Breanne Taylor, Charles Hodges, Jaime Kennedy, Don Shannon, and David V. Ellis

2015   *Data Recovery Excavations at Multi-Component Site 35-HA-3293, City of Burns, Harney County, Oregon.* Willamette CRA Report No. 15-29. Manuscript on file, Oregon State Historic Preservation Office, Salem, Oregon.

Gilreath, Amy J., Mark E. Basgall, and M. C. Hall

1987   *Compendium of Chronologically Indicative Data from Fort Irwin Archaeological Sites, San Bernardino County, California.* Prepared for US Army Corps of Engineers, Los Angeles District.

Gilreath, Amy J., and William R. Hildebrandt

1997   *Prehistoric Use of the Coso Volcanic Field.* Contributions of the University of California Archaeological Research Facility No. 56. University of California, Berkeley.

2011   Current Perspectives on the Production and Conveyance of Coso Obsidian. In *Perspectives on Prehistoric Exchange in California and the Great Basin*, edited by Richard E. Hughes, pp. 171–188. University of Utah Press, Salt Lake City.

Gingerich, Joseph A. M. (editor)

2013   *In the Eastern Fluted Point Tradition*, Vol. I. University of Utah Press, Salt Lake City.

2017   *In the Eastern Fluted Point Tradition*, Vol. II. University of Utah Press, Salt Lake City.

Glassow, Michael A.

1996   *Purisimeño Chumash Prehistory: Maritime Adaptations along the Southern California Coast.* Harcourt Brace College Publishers, Fort Worth, Texas.

Glassow, Michael A., Jon M. Erlandson, and Todd J. Braje

2013   A Typology of Channel Islands Barbed Points. *Journal of California and Great Basin Anthropology* 33(2):185–195.

Glassow, Michael A., Jennifer E. Perry, and Peter F. Paige

2008   *The Punta Arena Site and Early and Middle Holocene Cultural Development on Santa Cruz Island, California.* Santa Barbara Museum of Natural History, Santa Barbara, California.

Godsey, Holly S., Charles G. Oviatt, David M. Miller, and Marjorie A. Chan
2011 Stratigraphy and Chronology of Offshore to Nearshore Deposits Associated with the Provo Shoreline, Pleistocene Lake Bonneville, Utah. *Palaeogeography, Palaeoclimatology, and Palaeoecology* 310(3-4):442–450.

Goebel, Ted
1999 Pleistocene Human Colonization of Siberia and Peopling of the Americas: An Ecological Approach. *Evolutionary Anthropology: Issues, News, and Reviews* 8(6):208–227.
2002 The "Microblade Adaptation" and Re-Colonization of Siberia during the Late Upper Paleolithic. In *Thinking Small: Global Perspectives on Microlithization*, edited by Robert Elston and Steven Kuhn, pp. 117–133. American Anthropological Association, Arlington, Virginia.
2007 Pre-Archaic and Early Archaic at Bonneville Estates Rockshelter: A First Look at the Lithic Artifact Record. In *Paleoindian or Paleoarchaic? Great Basin Human Ecology at the Pleistocene Transition*, edited by Kelly E. Graf and David M. Schmitt, pp. 156–184. University of Utah Press, Salt Lake City.
2015 Clovis Culture Update. In *Clovis: On the Edge of a New Understanding*, edited by Ashley M. Smallwood and Thomas A. Jennings, pp. 325–352. Center for the Study of the First Americans, Texas A&M University Press, College Station.
2018 In Archaeology, "You Get What You Get," and Most of the Time What You Get Is Unexpected: Investigating Paleoindians in the Great Basin, Western North America. In *Engaging Archaeological Research*, edited by Stephen Silliman, pp. 159–167. John Wiley & Sons, New York.

Goebel, Ted, Kelly E. Graf, Bryan S. Hockett, and David E. Rhode
2007 The Paleoindian Occupations at Bonneville Estates Rockshelter, Danger Cave, and Smith Creek Cave (Eastern Great Basin, USA): Interpreting Their Radiocarbon Chronologies. In *On Shelter's Ledge: Histories, Theories and Methods of Rockshelter Research*, edited by Marcel Kornfeld, Sergey Vasil'ev, and Laura Miotti, pp. 147–162. BAR International Series, Archaeopress, Oxford.

Goebel, Ted, Bryan S. Hockett, David E. Rhode, and Kelly E. Graf
2011 Climate, Environment, and Humans in North America's Great Basin during the Younger Dryas, 12,900–11,600 Calendar Years Ago. *Quaternary International* 242(2):211–230.
2021 Prehistoric Human Response to Climate Change in the Bonneville Basin, Western North America: The Bonneville Estates Rockshelter Radiocarbon Chronology. *Quaternary Science Reviews* 260:106930.

Goebel, Ted, Aria Holmes, Joshua L. Keene, and Marion M. Coe
2018 Technological Change from the Terminal Pleistocene Through Early Holocene in the Eastern Great Basin, USA: The Record from Bonneville Estates Rockshelter. In *Lithic Technological Organization and Paleoenvironmental Change*, edited by Erick Robinson and Frédéric Sellet, pp. 235–261. Springer, New York.

Goebel, Ted, and Joshua L. Keene
2014 Are Great Basin Stemmed Points as Old as Clovis in the Intermountain West? A Review of the Geochronological Evidence. In *Archaeology in the Great Basin and Southwest: Papers in Honor of Don D. Fowler*, edited by Nancy J. Parezo and Joel C. Janetski, pp. 35–60. University of Utah Press, Salt Lake City.

Goebel, Ted, Heather L. Smith, Lyndsay DiPietro, Michael R. Waters, Bryan Hockett, Kelly E. Graf, Robert Gal et al.
2013 Serpentine Hot Springs, Alaska: Results of Excavations and Implications for the Age of Northern Fluted Points. *Journal of Archaeological Science* 40(12):4222–4233.

Goff, Fraser, Robert C. Roback, William McIntosh, Cathy J. Goff, and Emily C. Kluk
2014 Geochemistry and Geochronology of Intrusive and Volcanic Rocks of the Three Rivers Stock, Sierra Blanca, New Mexico. In *Geology of the Sacramento Mountains Region*, edited by Geoffrey C. Rawling, Virginia T. McLemore, Stacy Timmons, and Nelia W. Dunbar, pp. 183–196. New Mexico Geological Society 65th Annual Fall Field Conference Guidebook.

Goldberg, Paul, Francesco Berna, and Richard I. Macphail
2009   Comment on "DNA from Pre-Clovis Human Coprolites in Oregon, North America." *Science* 325(5937):148c.

Gómez-Carballa, Alberto, Jacobo Pardo-Seco, Stefania Brandini, Alessandro Achilli, Ugo A. Perego, Michael D. Coble, Toni M. Diegoli, Vanesa Álvarez-Iglesias, Federico Martinón-Torres, and Anna Olivieri
2018   The Peopling of South America and the Trans-Andean Gene Flow of the First Settlers. *Genome Research* 28(6):767–779.

Gómez Coutouly, Yan Axel, and Charles E. Holmes
2018   The Microblade Industry from Swan Point Cultural Zone 4b: Technological and Cultural Implications from the Earliest Human Occupation in Alaska. *American Antiquity* 83(4):735–752.

Gonzalez, Silvia, David Huddart, Isabel Israde-Alcántara, Gabriela Domínguez-Vásquez, James Bischoff, and Nicholas Felstead
2015   Paleoindian Sites from the Basin of Mexico: Evidence from Stratigraphy, Tephrochronology and Dating. *Quaternary International* 363:4–19.

Goodyear, Albert C.
1989   A Hypothesis for the Use of Cryptocrystalline Raw Materials among Paleoindian Groups of North America. In *Eastern Paleoindian Lithic Resource Use*, edited by Christopher J. Ellis and Jonathan C. Lothrop, pp. 1–10. Westview Press, Boulder, Colorado.
2010   Instrument Assisted Fluting as a Techno-Chronological Marker among North American Paleoindian Points. *Current Research in the Pleistocene* 27:86–88.

Gough, Stan, and Jerry R. Galm
2002   Bone Technology at the Sentinel Gap Site. *Current Research in the Pleistocene* 19:27–29.

Graf, Kelly E.
2001   Paleoindian Technological Provisioning in the Western Great Basin. Master's thesis, Department of Anthropology, University of Nevada, Las Vegas.
2002   Paleoindian Obsidian Procurement and Mobility in the Western Great Basin. *Current Research in the Pleistocene* 19:87–89.
2007   Stratigraphy and Chronology of the Pleistocene to Holocene Transition at Bonneville Estates Rockshelter, Eastern Great Basin. In *Paleoindian or Paleoarchaic? Great Basin Human Ecology at the Pleistocene–Holocene Transition*, edited by Kelly E. Graf and David N. Schmitt, pp. 82–104. University of Utah Press, Salt Lake City.
2009   "The Good, the Bad, and the Ugly": Evaluating the Radiocarbon Chronology of the Middle and Late Upper Paleolithic in the Enisei River Valley, South-Central Siberia. *Journal of Archaeological Science* 36(3):694–707.

Graf, Kelly E., and Ian Buvit
2017   Human Dispersal from Siberia to Beringia: Assessing a Beringian Standstill in Light of the Archaeological Evidence. *Current Anthropology* 58:S583–S603.

Graf, Kelly E., and David N. Schmitt (editors)
2007   *Paleoindian or Paleoarchaic? Great Basin Human Ecology at the Pleistocene/Holocene Transition*. University of Utah Press, Salt Lake City.

Gramly, Richard M.
1982   *The Vail Site: A Palaeo-Indian Encampment in Maine*. Bulletin of Buffalo Society of Natural Sciences 30. Buffalo, New York.
1993   *The Richey Clovis Cache: Earliest Americans along the Columbia River*. Persimmon Press, New York.

Grayson, Donald K.
1979   Mount Mazama, Climatic Change and Fort Rock Basin Archaeofaunas. In *Volcanic Activity and Human Ecology*, edited by Payson D. Sheets and Donald K. Grayson, pp. 427–457. Academic Press, New York.
1988   *Danger Cave, Last Supper Cave, and Hanging Rock Shelter: The Faunas*. American Museum of Natural History Anthropological Papers Vol. 66, No. 1. American Museum of Natural History, New York.
1993   *The Desert's Past: A Natural Prehistory of the Great Basin*. Smithsonian Institution Press, Washington, DC.
2011   *The Great Basin: A Natural Prehistory*. University of California Press, Berkeley.
2016   *Giant Sloths and Sabertooth Cats: Extinct Mammals and the Archaeology of the Ice Age Great Basin*. University of Utah Press, Salt Lake City.

Grayson, Donald K., and David J. Meltzer
2015   Revisiting Paleoindian Exploitation of Extinct North American Mammals. *Journal of Archaeological Science* 56:177–193.

Grayson, Donald K., David J. Meltzer, and Ryan P. Breslawski
2021   Overkill and the North American Archaeological Record—Not Guilty by Association? A Comment on Wolfe and Broughton (2020). *Journal of Archaeological Science* 128:105312.

Green, Thomas J., Bruce Cochran, Todd W. Fenton, James C. Woods, Gene L. Titmus, Larry Tieszen, Mary Anne Davis, and Susanne J. Miller
1998   The Buhl Burial: A Paleoindian Woman from Southern Idaho. *American Antiquity* 63(3):437–456.

Grimm, Eric C., and George L. Jacobson
2004   Late Quaternary Vegetation History of the Eastern United States. In *The Quaternary Period in the United States*, edited by A. Gillespie, S. C. Porter, and B. Atwater, pp. 381–402. Elsevier, New York.

Grove, Matt
2016   Population Density, Mobility, and Cultural Transmission. *Journal of Archaeological Science* 74(1):75–84.

Gruhn, Ruth
1961   The Archaeology of Wilson Butte Cave South-Central Idaho. Occasional Papers of the Idaho State University Museum No. 6. Pocatello.
1988   The Great Journey: Small Step or Giant Leap? *Mammoth Trumpet* 4(2):4–5.

Grund, Brigid
2020   Paleoindian Heartland: An Archaeological Synthesis of Wyoming's First Peoples. Submitted to the Wyoming State Historic Preservation Office, Laramie.

Gusick, Amy E.
2012   Behavioral Adaptations and Mobility of Early Holocene Hunter-Gatherers, Santa Cruz Island, California. PhD dissertation, Department of Anthropology, University of California, Santa Barbara.
2013   The Early Holocene Occupation of Santa Cruz Island. In *California's Channel Islands: The Archaeology of Human-Environment Interactions*, edited by Jennifer Perry and Christopher Jazwa, pp. 40–59. University of Utah Press, Salt Lake City.

Gusick, Amy E., and Jon M. Erlandson
2019   Paleocoastal Landscapes, Marginality, and Initial Settlement of California's Islands. In *An Archaeology of Abundance: Re-Evaluating the Marginality of California's Islands*, edited by Kristina M. Gill, Mikael Fauvelle, and Jon M. Erlandson, pp. 59–97. University of Florida Press, Gainesville.

Hall, Roberta, Loren G. Davis, Samuel C. Willis, and Matthew Fillmore
2005   Radiocarbon, Soil, and Artifact Chronologies for an Early Southern Oregon Coastal Site. *Radiocarbon* 47(3):383–394.

Halligan, Jessi J., Michael R. Waters, Angelina Perrotti, Ivy J. Owens, Joshua M. Feinberg, Mark D. Bourne, Brendan Fenerty et al.
2016   Pre-Clovis Occupation 14,550 Years Ago at the Page Ladson Site, Florida, and the Peopling of the Americas. *Science Advances* 2(5):e1600375.

Hamilton, Marcus J., and Briggs Buchanan
2007   Spatial Gradients in Clovis-Age Radiocarbon Dates across North America Suggest Rapid Colonization from the North. *Proceedings of the National Academy of Sciences* 104(4):15625–15630.

Hamilton, Marcus J., Briggs Buchanan, and Robert S. Walker
2019   Spatiotemporal Diversification of Projectile Point Types in Western North America over 13,000 Years. *Journal of Archaeological Science: Reports* 24:486–495.

Hammer, Øyvind, David A. T. Harper, and Paul D. Ryan
2001   PAST: Paleontological Statistics Software Package for Education and Data Analysis. *Palaeontologia Electronica* 4(1):9 pp.

Hanes, Richard C.
1977   Lithic Tools of the Dirty Shame Rockshelter: Typology and Distribution. In *Tebiwa Miscellaneous Papers 4*, edited by C. Melvin Aikens, David Cole, and Robert Stuckenrath, Part 6, pp. 1–24. Idaho Museum of Natural History, Idaho State University, Pocatello.
1988   *Lithic Assemblages of Dirty Shame Rockshelter: Changing Traditions in the Northern Intermontane*. Anthropological Papers No. 40. Museum of Natural and Cultural History, University of Oregon, Eugene.

Harper, K. T., and G. M. Alder
1972 Paleoclimatic Inferences Concerning the Last 10,000 Years from a Resampling of Danger Cave, Utah. In *Great Basin Cultural Ecology: A Symposium*, edited by Don D. Fowler, pp. 13–23. Publications in the Social Sciences No. 8. Desert Research Institute, Reno, Nevada.

Harrington, Mark R.
1948 *An Ancient Site at Borax Lake, California*. Southwest Museum Papers No. 16. Los Angeles.

Harris, Daniel N., Wei Song, Amol C. Shetty, Kelly S. Levano, Omar Cáceres, Carlos Padilla, Víctor Borda, David Tarazona, Omar Trujillo, and Cesar Sanchez
2018 Evolutionary Genomic Dynamics of Peruvians Before, During, and After the Inca Empire. *Proceedings of the National Academy of Sciences* 115(28):E6526–E6535.

Hartman, Amanda J.
2019 Identifying Cultural Migration in Western North America through Morphometric Analysis of Early Holocene Projectile Points. Master's thesis, Department of Anthropology, University of Nevada, Reno.

Haslett, John, and Andrew C. Parnell
2008 A Simple Monotone Process with Application to Radiocarbon-Dated Depth Chronologies. *Journal of the Royal Statistical Society: Series C (Applied Statistics)* 57(4):399–418.

Haury, Emil W., Edwin Booth Sayles, and William W. Wasley
1959 The Lehner Mammoth Site, Southeastern Arizona. *American Antiquity* 25(1):2–30.

Haynes, C. Vance, Jr.
1964 Fluted Projectile Points: Their Age and Dispersion: Stratigraphically Controlled Radiocarbon Dating Provides New Evidence on Peopling of the New World. *Science* 145(3639):1408–1413.
1980 The Clovis Culture. *Canadian Journal of Anthropology* 1(1):115–121.
1982 Were Clovis Progenitors in Beringia? In *Paleoecology of Beringia*, edited by David M. Hopkins, John V. Matthews Jr., Charles E. Schweger, and Steven V. Young, pp. 383–398. Academic Press, New York.
1987 Clovis Origin Update. *Kiva* 52(2):83–93.
1995 Geochronology of Paleoenvironmental Change, Clovis Type Site, Blackwater Draw, New Mexico. *Geoarchaeology* 10(5):317–388.
2005 Clovis, Pre-Clovis, Climate Change, and Extinction. In *Paleoamerican Origins: Beyond Clovis*, edited by Robson Bonnichsen, Bradley T. Lepper, Dennis Stanford, and Michael R. Waters, pp. 113–132. Center for the Study of the First Americans, Texas A&M University Press, College Station.
2018 A Chronostratigraphic Model for the Hell Gap Paleoindian Site and Methods for Refining Chronologies at Open Stratified Sites—Comment to the Published Paper by Pelton et al., *Quaternary Research*, 88 (2017), 234–247. *Quaternary Research* 90(1):244–247.

Haynes, C. Vance, Jr., Donald J. Donahue, Anthony T. Jull, and Theodore H. Zabel
1984 Application of Accelerator Dating to Fluted Point Paleoindian Sites. *Archaeology of Eastern North America* 12:184–191.

Haynes, C. Vance, Jr., and Matthew E. Hill Jr.
2017 Plainview-Goshen-Midland Typological Problems. In *Plainview: The Enigmatic Paleoindian Artifact Style of the Great Plains*, edited by Vance T. Holiday, Eileen Johnson, and Ruthann Knudson, pp. 249–273. University of Utah Press, Salt Lake City.

Haynes, C. Vance, Jr., and Bruce B. Huckell (editors)
2007 *Murray Springs: A Clovis Site with Multiple Activity Areas in the San Pedro Valley, Arizona*. Anthropological Papers of the University of Arizona No. 71. University of Arizona Press, Tucson.

Haynes, Gary
1991 *Mammoths, Mastodonts, and Elephants: Biology, Behavior, and the Fossil Record*. Cambridge University Press, Cambridge, England.
2002 *The Early Settlement of North America*. Cambridge University Press, Cambridge, England.
2006 Mammoth Landscapes: Good Country for Hunter-Gatherers. *Quaternary International* 142–143:20–29.
2007 Paleoindian or Paleoarchaic? In *Paleoindian or Paleoarchaic? Great Basin Human Ecology at the Pleistocene-Holocene Transition*, edited by Kelly E.

Graf and Dave N. Schmidt, pp. 251–258. University of Utah Press, Salt Lake City.
2013   Extinctions in North America's Late Glacial Landscapes. *Quaternary International* 285:89–98.
2015   The Millennium before Clovis. *PaleoAmerica* 1(2):137–162.

Haynes, Gary, David G. Anderson, C. Reid Ferring, Stuart J. Fiedel, Donald K. Grayson, C. Vance Haynes Jr., Vance T. Holliday et al.
2007   Comment on "Redefining the Age of Clovis: Implications for the Peopling of the Americas." *Science* 317(5836):320.

Haynes, Gary, and Jarod M. Hutson
2013   Clovis-Era Subsistence: Regional Variability, Continental Patterning. In *Paleoamerican Odyssey*, edited by Kelly E. Graf, Caroline V. Ketron and Michael R. Waters, pp. 293–309. Center for the Study of the First Americans, Texas A&M University Press, College Station.

Heintzman, Peter D., Duane Froese, John W. Ives, André E. R. Soares, Grant D. Zazula, Brandon Letts, Thomas D. Andrews et al.
2016   Bison Phylogeography Constrains Dispersal and Viability of the Ice Free Corridor in Western Canada. *Proceedings of the National Academy of Sciences* 113(29):8057–8063.

Heizer, Robert, and Martin A. Baumhoff
1970   Big Game Hunters in the Great Basin: A Critical Review of the Evidence. In *Papers on Anthropology of the Great Basin*, pp. 1–12. Contributions of the Archaeological Research Facility No. 7. University of California, Berkeley.

Hendy, Jessica
2021   Ancient Protein Analysis in Archaeology. *Science Advances* 7:3abb9314.

Henrikson, L. Suzann, David A. Byers, Robert M. Yohe II, Matthew M. DeCarlo, and Gene L. Titmus
2017   Folsom Mammoth Hunters? The Terminal Pleistocene Assemblage from Owl Cave (10BV30), Wasden Site, Idaho. *American Antiquity* 8(3):574–592.

Henrikson, L. Suzann, and Montana M. Long
2007   In Pursuit of Humans and Extinct Megafauna in the Northern Great Basin. In *Paleoindian or Paleoarchaic? Great Basin Human Ecology at the Pleistocene–Holocene Transition*, edited by Kelly E. Graf and Dave N. Schmidt, pp. 42–56. University of Utah Press, Salt Lake City.

Hershler, Robert, David B. Madsen, and Donald R. Curry (editors)
2002   *Great Basin Aquatic Systems History*. Smithsonian Contributions to the Earth Sciences, No. 33. Smithsonian Institution Press, Washington, DC.

Hester, James J.
1972   *Blackwater Locality No. 1: A Stratified, Early Man Site in Eastern New Mexico*. Fort Burgwin Research Center, Southern Methodist University, Rancho de Taos, New Mexico.

Heye, George G.
1921   *Certain Artifacts from San Miguel Island, California*. Museum of the American Indian, New York.

Hicks, Brent A. (editor)
2004   *Marmes Rockshelter: A Final Report on 11,000 Years of Cultural Use*. Washington State University Press, Pullman.

Hicks, Patricia A.
1982   *Archaeological Investigations at the La Bajada (LA9500) and La Bajada Annex (LA9501) Sites: 1966, 1967, and 1970*. Llano Estacado Center for Advanced Professional Studies and Research, Eastern New Mexico University, Portales.

Hildebrandt, William R., and Kelly R. McGuire
2002   The Ascendance of Hunting During the California Middle Archaic: An Evolutionary Perspective. *American Antiquity* 67(2):231–256.

Hildebrandt, William R., Kelly R. McGuire, Jerome King, Allika Ruby, and D. Craig Young (editors)
2016   *Prehistory of Nevada's Northern Tier: Archaeological Investigations along the Ruby Pipeline*. Anthropological Papers Vol. 101. American Museum of Natural History, New York.

Hockett, Bryan S.
2007   Nutritional Ecology of Late Pleistocene to Middle Holocene Subsistence in the Great Basin: Zooarchaeological Evidence from Bonneville Estates Rockshelter. In *Paleoindian or Paleoarchaic? Great Basin Human Ecology at the Pleistocene–Holocene Transition*, edited by Kelly E.

Graf and Dave N. Schmitt, pp. 204–230. University of Utah Press, Salt Lake City.
2015 The Zooarchaeology of Bonneville Estates Rockshelter: 13,000 Years of Great Basin Hunting Strategies. *Journal of Archaeological Science: Reports* 2:291–301.

Hockett, Bryan S., Martin E. Adams, Patrick M. Lubinski, Virginia L. Butler, and Dennis L. Jenkins
2017 Late Pleistocene Subsistence in the Great Basin: Younger Dryas-Aged Faunal Remains from the Botanical Lens, Paisley Cave 2, Oregon. *Journal of Archaeological Science Reports* 13:565–576.

Hockett, Bryan S., and Dennis L. Jenkins
2013 Identifying Stone Tool Cut Marks and the Pre-Clovis Occupation of the Paisley Caves. *American Antiquity* 78(4):762–778.

Hockett, Bryan S., and Emily Palus
2018 A Brief History and Perspective on Spirit Cave, Nevada. *PaleoAmerica* 4(1):1–7.

Hofman, Courtney A., Torben C. Rick, Jon M. Erlandson, Leslie Reeder-Myers, Andreanna J. Welch, and Mike Buckley
2018 Collagen Fingerprinting and the Earliest Marine Mammal Hunting in North America. *Scientific Reports* 8(1):1–6.

Hofman, Jack L.
1986 Vertical Movement of Artifacts in Alluvial and Stratified Deposits. *Current Anthropology* 27(2):163–171.
1999a Folsom Fragments, Site Types and Prehistoric Behavior. In *Folsom Lithic Technology, Explorations in Structure and Variation*, edited by Daniel S. Amick, pp. 122–143. International Monographs in Prehistory, Archaeological Series No. 12. Berghahn Books, New York.
1999b Unbounded Hunters: Folsom Bison Hunting on the Southern Plains Circa 10,500 BP, the Lithic Evidence. *Le Bison: Gibier et Moyen de Subsistence des Hommes du Paleolithique aux Paleoindiens des Grandes Plaines: Actes du Colloque International, Toulouse*, edited by Jacques Jaubert, Jean-Phillip Burgal, Francine David, and Hanes G. Enlow, pp. 383–415. Antibes, France.

Hofman, Jack L., and Russell W. Graham
1998 The Paleo-Indian Cultures of the Great Plains. In *Archaeology on the Great Plains*, edited by W. Raymond Wood, pp. 87–139. University of Kansas Press, Lawrence.

Ho Ho Committee
1979 The Ho Ho Classification and Nomenclature Committee Report. In *Lithic Use-Wear Analysis*, edited by Brian Hayden, pp. 133–135. Academic Press, New York.

Holen, Steven R.
2004 Long-Distance Movement of a Clovis Obsidian Projectile Point. *Current Research in the Pleistocene* 21:44–46.
2014 Clovis Lithic Procurement, Caching, and Mobility in the Central Great Plains of North America. In *Clovis Caches: Recent Discoveries and New Research*, edited by Bruce B. Huckell and J. David Kilby, pp. 177–200. University of New Mexico Press, Albuquerque.

Hollenbeck, Jan L.
1987 A Cultural Resource Overview: Prehistory, Ethnography and History: Mt. Baker-Snoqualmie National Forest. US Department of Agriculture, US Forest Service, Pacific Northwest Region, Portland, Oregon.

Holliday, Vance T.
2000 The Evolution of Paleoindian Geochronology and Typology on the Great Plains. *Geoarchaeology* 15(3):227–290.

Holliday, Vance T., Robert D. Dello-Russo, and Susan M. Mentzer
2020 Geoarchaeology of the Water Canyon Paleoindian Site, West-Central New Mexico. *Geoarchaeology* 35(1):112–140.

Holliday, Vance T., Allison Harvey, Matthew T. Cuba, and Aimee M. Weber
2018 Paleoindians, Paleolakes, and Paleoplayas: Landscape Geoarchaeology of the Tularosa Basin, New Mexico. *Geomorphology* 331:92–106.

Holliday, Vance T., Eileen Johnson, and Ruthann Knudson (editors)
2017 *Plainview: The Enigmatic Paleoindian Artifact Style of the Great Plains*. University of Utah Press, Salt Lake City.

Holliday, Vance T., and David J. Meltzer
2010 The 12.9-ka ET Impact Hypothesis and North American Paleoindians. *Current Anthropology* 51(5):575–607.

Holmes, Amy M., and Gary A. Huckleberry
2009 Stratigraphy and Paleoenvironment. In *The Archaeology of the Eastern Nevada Paleoarchaic, Part 1: The Sunshine Locality*, edited by Charlotte Beck and George T. Jones, pp. 67–76. Anthropological Papers No. 126. University of Utah Press, Salt Lake City.

Honea, Kenneth
1969 The Rio Grande Complex and the Northern Plains. *Plains Anthropologist* 14(43): 57–70.

Hopkins, Jerry N., and Alan P. Garfinkel (editors)
2008 *Ice-Age Stone Tools from the San Joaquin Valley*. Contributions to the Tulare Lake Archaeology IV. Tulare Lake Archaeological Research Group, Redondo Beach, California.

Hoppe, Kathryn A.
2004 Late Pleistocene Mammoth Herd Structure, Migration Patterns, and Clovis Hunting Strategies Inferred from Isotopic Analyses of Multiple Death Assemblages. *Paleobiology* 30(1):129–145.

Hoskins, Andrew J.
2016 Evaluating the Antiquity and Morphology of Corner-Notched Dart Points in the Eastern Great Basin. Master's thesis, Department of Anthropology, University of Nevada, Reno.

Howard, Calvin D.
1990 The Clovis Point: Characteristics and Type Description. *Plains Anthropologist* 35(129):255–266.

Howard, Edgar B.
1935 *Evidence of Early Man in North America*, Vol. 24 (Nos. 2–3). The Museum Journal, University of Pennsylvania Museum, Philadelphia.
1936 An Outline of the Problem of Man's Antiquity in North America. *American Anthropologist* 38(3):394–413.
1939 Folsom and Yuma Points from Saskatchewan. *American Antiquity* 4(3):277–279.
1943 Folsom and Yuma Problems. *Proceedings of the American Philosophical Society* 86(2):255–259.

Huckell, Bruce B.
1996 The Archaic Prehistory of the North American Southwest. *Journal of World Prehistory* 10(3):305–373.
2007 Clovis Lithic Technology: A View from the Upper San Pedro Valley. In *Murray Springs: A Clovis Site with Multiple Activity Areas in the San Pedro Valley, Arizona*, edited by C. Vance Haynes Jr., and Bruce B. Huckell, pp. 170–213. Anthropological Papers of the University of Arizona No. 7. University of Arizona Press, Tucson.
2014 But How Do We Know If It's Clovis? An Examination of Clovis Overshot Flaking of Bifaces and a North Dakota Cache. In *Clovis Caches: Recent Discoveries and New Research*, edited by Bruce B. Huckell and J. David Kilby, pp. 133–152. University of New Mexico, Albuquerque.

Huckell, Bruce B., and W. James Judge
2006 Paleo-Indian: Plains and Southwest. In *Environment, Origins, and Population*, edited by Douglas H. Ubelaker, pp. 148–170. Handbook of North American Indians, Vol. 3, William C. Sturtevant, general editor. Smithsonian Institution, Washington, DC.

Huckell, Bruce B., and J. David Kilby (editors)
2014 *Clovis Caches: Recent Discoveries and New Research*. University of New Mexico Press, Albuquerque.

Hudson, Adam M., Benjamin J. Hatchett, Jay Quade, Douglas P. Boyle, Scott D. Bassett, Guleed Ali, and Marie G. De los Santos
2019 North-South Dipole in Winter Hydroclimate in the Western United States during the Last Deglaciation. *Scientific Reports* 9(1):1–12.

Hughes, Richard E. (editor)
2011 *Perspectives on Prehistoric Trade and Exchange in California and the Great Basin*. University of Utah Press, Salt Lake City.

Hughes, Susan S.
1998 Getting to the Point: Evolutionary Change in Prehistoric Weaponry. *Journal of Archaeological Method and Theory* 5(4):345–408.

Hutchings, W. Karl
2015 Finding the Paleoindian Spearthrower: Quantitative Evidence for Mechanically Assisted Propulsion of Lithic Armatures during the North American Paleoindian Period. *Journal of Archaeological Science* 55:34–41.

Ibarra, Daniel E., Anne E. Egger, Karrie L. Weaver, Caroline R. Harris, and Kate Maher
2014   Rise and Fall of Late Pleistocene Pluvial Lakes in Response to Reduced Evaporation and Precipitation: Evidence from Lake Surprise, California. *Bulletin of the Geological Society of America* 126(11–12):1387–1415.

Ingold, Tim
1997   Eight Themes in the Anthropology of Technology. *Social Analysis: The International Journal of Social and Cultural Practice* 41(1):106–139.

Iovita, Radu, Holger Schönekeß, Sabine Gaudzinski-Windheuser, and Frank Jäger
2013   Projectile Impact Fractures and Launching Mechanisms: Results of a Controlled Ballistic Experiment Using Replica Levallois Points. *Journal of Archaeological Science* 48:73–83.

Irwin, Ann M., and Ula L. Moody
1978   *The Lind Coulee Site (45GR97)*. Washington Archaeological Research Center, Project Report No. 56. Washington State University, Pullman.

Irwin, Henry
1968   The Itama: Early Late-Pleistocene Inhabitants of the Plains of the United States and Canada and the American Southwest. PhD dissertation, Department of Anthropology. Harvard University, Cambridge, Massachusetts.

Irwin-Williams, Cynthia
1973   *The Oshara Tradition: Origins of Anasazi Culture*. Eastern New Mexico University Contributions in Anthropology Vol. 5, No. 1. Eastern New Mexico University, Portales.
1979   Post Pleistocene Archaeology, 7000–2000 BC. In *Southwest*, edited by Alfonzo Ortiz, pp. 31–42. Handbook of North American Indians, Vol. 9, William C. Sturtevant, general editor. Smithsonian Institution, Washington, DC.

Irwin-Williams, Cynthia, and C. Vance Haynes Jr.
1970   Climate Change and Early Population Dynamics in the Southwestern United States. *Quaternary Research* 1(1):59–71.

Irwin-Williams, Cynthia, Henry Irwin, George Agogino, and C. Vance Haynes Jr.
1973   Hell Gap: Paleo-Indian Occupation on the High Plains. *Plains Anthropologist* 18(59):40–53.

Ives, John W., Gabriel Yanicki, Kisha Supernant, and Courtney Lakevold
2019   Confluences: Fluted Points in the Ice-Free Corridor. *PaleoAmerica* 5(2):143–156.

Jamaldin, Sophia
2018   Terminal Pleistocene/Early Holocene Cave Use in Oregon's Fort Rock Basin: An Examination of Western Stemmed Tradition Projectile Point Assemblages from Fort Rock Cave, Cougar Mountain Cave, and the Connley Caves. Master's thesis, Department of Anthropology, University of Nevada, Reno.

Janetski, Joel C., Mark L. Bodily, Bradley A. Newbold, and David T. Yoder
2012   The Paleoarchaic to Early Archaic Transition on the Colorado Plateau: The Archaeology of North Creek Shelter. *American Antiquity* 77(1):125–159.

Jazwa, Christopher S., and Richard L. Rosencrance
2019   Technological Change and Interior Settlement on Western Santa Rosa Island, California. *Journal of Anthropological Archaeology* 54:235–253.

Jazwa, Christopher S., Geoffrey M. Smith, Richard L. Rosencrance, Daron G. Duke, and Dan Stueber
2021   Reassessing the Radiocarbon Date from the Buhl Burial from South-Central Idaho and Its Relevance to the Western Stemmed Tradition–Clovis Debate in the Intermountain West. *American Antiquity* 86(1):173–182.

Jenkins, Dennis L.
1987   Dating the Pinto Occupation at Rogers Ridge: A Fossil Spring Site in the Mojave Desert, California. *Journal of California and Great Basin Anthropology* 9(2):214–231.
2007   Distribution and Dating of Cultural and Paleontological Remains at the Paisley Five Mile Point Caves in the Northern Great Basin. In *Paleoindian or Paleoarchaic? Great Basin Human Ecology at the Pleistocene–Holocene Transition*, edited by Kelly E. Graf and Dave N. Schmitt, pp. 57–81. University of Utah Press, Salt Lake City.

Jenkins, Dennis L., Loren G. Davis, Thomas W. Stafford, Paula F. Campos, Thomas J. Connolly, Linda Scott Cummings, Michael Hofreiter et al.
2013   Geochronology, Archaeological Context, and DNA at the Paisley Caves. In *Paleoamerican Odyssey*, edited by Kelly E. Graf, Caroline V. Ketron, and Michael R. Water, pp. 485–510. Center for the Study of the First Americans, Texas A&M University Press, College Station.

Jenkins, Dennis L., Loren G. Davis, Thomas W. Stafford, Paula F. Campos, Bryan S. Hockett, George T. Jones, Linda Scott Cummings et al.
2012   Clovis Age Western Stemmed Projectile Points and Human Coprolites at the Paisley Caves. *Science* 337(6091):223–228.

Jenkins, Dennis L., Loren G. Davis, Thomas W. Stafford, Thomas J. Connolly, Michael F. Rondeau, Linda Scott Cummings, Bryan S. Hockett et al.
2016   Younger Dryas Archaeology and Human Experience at the Paisley Caves in the Northern Great Basin. In *Stone, Bones, and Profiles: Exploring Archaeological Context, Early American Hunter-Gatherers, and Bison*, edited by Marcel Kornfeld and Bruce B. Huckell, pp. 127–205. University Press of Colorado, Boulder.

Jenkins, Dennis L., Justin A. Holcomb, and Katelyn N. McDonough
2017   Current Research at the Connley Caves (35LK50): Late Pleistocene/Early Holocene Western Stemmed Tradition Occupations in the Fort Rock Basin, Oregon. *PaleoAmerica* 3(2):188–192.

Jennings, Jesse D.
1957   *Danger Cave*. University of Utah Anthropological Papers No. 27. University of Utah Press, Salt Lake City.
1964   The Desert West. In *Prehistoric Man in the New World*, edited by Jesse D. Jennings and Edward Norbeck, pp. 149–174. University of Chicago Press, Chicago.
1986   Prehistory: Introduction. In *Great Basin*, edited by Warren L. D'Azevedo, pp. 113–119. Handbook of North American Indians, Vol. 11, William C. Sturtevant, general editor. Smithsonian Institution, Washington, DC.

Jennings, Thomas A.
2015   Clovis Adaptations in the Great Plains. In *Clovis: On the Edge of a New Understanding*, edited by Ashley M. Smallwood and Thomas A. Jennings, pp. 277–296. Center for the Study of the First Americans, Texas A&M University Press, College Station.

Jerrems, William, John Dudgeon, and Clayton Meredith
2013   Testing the Extinction Paradigm: Evidence of Tool Manufacture from Extinct Megafauna at the End of the Younger Dryas. Paper presented at the 78th Annual Meeting of the Society for American Archaeology, Honolulu, Hawaii.

Jew, Nicholas P., and Jon M. Erlandson
2013   Paleocoastal Lithic Heat Treatment Practices on Alta California's Northern Channel Islands. *California Archaeology* 5(1):77–102.

Jew, Nicholas P., Jon M. Erlandson, and Frances White
2013   Paleocoastal Lithic Use on Western Santarosae Island, California. *North American Archaeologist* 34(1):49–69.

Johannsen, Niels N., Greger Larson, David J. Meltzer, and Marc Vander Linden
2017   A Composite Window into Human History. *Science*. 356(6343):1118–11120.

Johnson, Eileen
1987   *Lubbock Lake: Late Quaternary Studies on the Southern High Plains*. Texas A&M University Press, College Station.

Johnson, Jay K.
1979   Archaic Biface Manufacture: Production Failures, a Chronicle of the Misbegotten. *Lithic Technology* 8(2):25–35.

Johnson, John R., Thomas W. Stafford Jr., Henry O. Ajie, and Don P. Morris
2002   Arlington Springs Revisited. In *Proceedings of the Fifth California Islands Symposium*, edited by David R. Browne, Kathryn C. Mitchell, and Henry W. Chaney, pp. 541–545. Santa Barbara Museum of Natural History, Santa Barbara, California.

Jones, George T., David G. Bailey, and Charlotte Beck
1997   Source Provenance of Andesite Artifacts Using Non-destructive XRF Analysis. *Journal of Archaeological Science* 24(10): 929–943.

Jones, George T., and Charlotte Beck
1999   Paleoarchaic Archaeology in the Great

Basin. In *Models for the Millennium: Great Basin Anthropology Today*, edited by Charlotte Beck, pp. 83–95. University of Utah Press, Salt Lake City.

Jones, George T., Charlotte Beck, Eric E. Jones, and Richard E. Hughes
2003 Lithic Source Use and Paleoarchaic Foraging Territories in the Great Basin. *American Antiquity* 68(1):5–38.

Jones, George T., Lisa M. Fontes, Rachel A. Horowitz, Charlotte Beck, and David G. Bailey
2012 Reconsidering Paleoarchaic Mobility in the Central Great Basin. *American Antiquity* 77(2):351–367.

Jones, Terry L., Judith F. Porcasi, J. W. Gaeta, and Brian F. Codding
2008 The Diablo Canyon Fauna: A Coarse-Grained Record of Trans-Holocene Foraging from the Central California Mainland Coast. *American Antiquity* 73(2):289–316.

Joyce, Daniel J.
2013 Pre-Clovis Megafauna Butchery Sites in the Western Great Lakes Region, USA. In *Paleoamerican Odyssey*, edited by Kelly E. Graf, Caroline V. Ketron, and Michael R. Waters, pp. 467–483. Center for the Study of the First Americans, Texas A&M University Press, College Station.

Judge, W. James
1973 *Paleoindian Occupation in the Central Rio Grande Valley in New Mexico*. University of New Mexico Press, Albuquerque.

Justice, Noel D.
2002 *Stone Age Spear and Arrow Points of California and the Great Basin*. Indiana University Press, Bloomington.

Kay, Marvin
1996 Microwear Analysis of Some Clovis and Experimental Chipped Stone Tools. In *Stone Tools: Theoretical Insights into Human Prehistory*, edited by George H. Odell, pp. 315–344. Plenum Press, New York.
2018 Use-Wear Analysis of the Lange/Ferguson Chipped Stone Artifacts. In *Clovis Mammoth Butchery: The Lange/Ferguson Site and Associated Bone Tool Technology*, edited by L. Adrien Hannus, pp. 201–209. Texas A&M University Press, College Station.

Kearns, Timothy M.
2018 Archaic Time and Distance in the San Juan Basin. In *The Archaic Southwest: Foragers in an Arid Land*, edited by Bradley J. Vierra, pp. 215–234. University of Utah Press, Salt Lake City.

Keene, Joshua L.
2018 A Diachronic Perspective on Great Basin Projectile Point Morphology from Veratic Rockshelter, Idaho. *Quaternary International* 466:299–317.

Keller, G. N., and J. D. Hunt
1967 Lithic Materials from the Escalante Valley, Utah. *Utah Anthropological Papers* 89:15–18.

Kelley, Shari, Daniel J. Koning, Fraser Goff, Colin Cikoski, Lisa Peters, and William McIntosh
2014 Stratigraphy of the Northwestern Sierra Blanca Volcanic Field. In *Geology of the Sacramento Mountains Region*, edited by Geoffrey C. Rawling, Virginia T. McLemore, Stacy Timmons, and Nelia W. Dunbar, pp. 197–208. 65th Annual Fall Field Conference Guidebook, New Mexico Geological Society, Socorro, New Mexico.

Kelly, Robert L.
1999 Hunter-Gatherer Foraging and Colonization of the Western Hemisphere. *Anthropologie* 37(2):143–453.
2011 Obsidian in the Carson Desert: Mobility or Trade? In *Perspectives on Prehistoric Trade and Exchange in California and the Great Basin*, edited by Richard E. Hughes, pp. 189–200. University of Utah Press, Salt Lake City.

Kelly, Robert L., and Lawrence C. Todd
1988 Coming into the Country: Early Paleoindian Hunting and Mobility. *American Antiquity* 53(2):231–244.

Kennedy, Jaime L.
2018 A Paleoethnobotanical Approach to 14,000 Years of Great Basin Prehistory: Assessing Human-Environmental Interactions through the Analysis of Archaeological Plant Data at Two Oregon Rockshelters. PhD dissertation, Department of Anthropology, University of Oregon, Eugene.

Kennedy, Jaime L., and Geoffrey M. Smith
2016 Paleoethnobotany at the LSP-1 Rockshelter, South Central Oregon: Assessing

the Nutritional Diversity of Plant Foods in Holocene Diet. *Journal of Archaeological Science: Reports* 5:640–648.

Kessler, Rebecca A., Charlotte Beck, and George T. Jones
2009 Trash: The Structure of Great Basin Paleoarchaic Debitage in Western North America, In *Lithic Materials and Paleolithic Societies*, edited by Brian Adams and Brooke S. Blades, pp. 144–159. Blackwell Publishing, West Sussex, England.

Kilby, J. David
2008 An Investigation of Clovis Caches: Content, Function, and Technological Organization. PhD dissertation, Department of Anthropology, University of New Mexico.
2014 Direction and Distance in Clovis Caching: The Movement of People and Raw Materials on the Clovis-Age Landscape. In *Clovis Caches: Recent Discoveries and New Research*, edited by Bruce B. Huckell and J. David Kilby, pp. 201–216. University of New Mexico Press, Albuquerque.

Kilby, J. David, Todd A. Surovell, Bruce B. Huckell, Christopher W. Ringstaff, Marcus J. Hamilton, and C. Vance Haynes Jr.
2022 Evidence Supports the Efficacy of Clovis Points for Hunting Proboscideans. *Journal of Archaeological Science: Reports* 45:103600.

King, Jerome
2016 Obsidian Conveyance Patterns. In *Prehistory of Nevada's Northern Tier: Archaeological Investigations along the Ruby Pipeline*, edited by William Hildebrandt, Kelly McGuire, Jerome King, Allika Ruby, and D. Craig Young, pp. 303–327. Anthropological Papers Vol. 101. American Museum of Natural History, New York.

Kirby, Matthew E., Linda Heusser, Christopher A. Scholz, Reza Ramezan, M. A. Anderson, Bradley Markle, Edward Rhodes et al.
2018 A Late Wisconsin (32–10k cal a BP) History of Pluvials, Droughts and Vegetation in the Pacific South-west United States (Lake Elsinore, CA). *Journal of Quaternary Science* 33(2):238–254.

Kirby, Matthew E., Edward J. Knell, William T. Anderson, Matthew S. Lachniet, Jennifer Palermo, Holly Eeg, Ricardo Lucero et al.
2015 Evidence for Insolation and Pacific Forcing of Late Glacial through Holocene Climate in the Central Mojave Desert (Silver Lake, CA). *Quaternary Research* 84:174–186.

Klein, Hans K., and Daniel Lee Kleinman
2002 The Social Construction of Technology: Structural Considerations. *Science, Technology, and Human Values* 27(1):28–52.

Knell, Edward J.
2007 The Organization of Late Paleoindian Cody Complex Land-Use on the North American Great Plains. PhD dissertation, Department of Anthropology, Washington State University, Pullman.
2014 Terminal Pleistocene–Early Holocene Lithic Technological Organization around Lake Mojave, California. *Journal of Field Archaeology* 39(3):213–229.
2022 Allometry of Unifacial Flake Tools from Mojave Desert Terminal Pleistocene/Early Holocene Sites: Implications for Landscape Knowledge, Tool Design, and Land Use. *Journal of Archaeological Science: Reports* 41:103314.

Knell, Edward J., and Mark S. Becker
2017 Early Holocene San Dieguito Complex Lithic Technological Strategies at the C. W. Harris Site, San Diego County, California. *Journal of California and Great Basin Anthropology* 37(2):183–201.

Knell, Edward J., Matthew E. Hill Jr., and Mark Q. Sutton
2021 Assessing the Validity of Mojave Desert Lake Mohave and Silver Lake Projectile Point Types. *PaleoAmerica* 7(3):242–259.

Knell, Edward J., and Mark P. Muñiz
2013 Introducing the Cody Complex. In *Paleoindian Lifeways of the Cody Complex*, edited by Edward J. Knell and Mark P. Muñiz, pp. 1–30. University of Utah Press, Salt Lake City.

Knell, Edward J., and Mark P. Muñiz (editors)
2013 *Paleoindian Lifeways of the Cody Complex*. University of Utah Press, Salt Lake City.

Knell, Edward J., Leah C. Walden-Hurtgen, and Matthew E. Kirby
2014 Terminal Pleistocene–Early Holocene Spatio-Temporal and Settlement Patterns around Pluvial Lake Mojave, California. *Journal of California and Great Basin Anthropology* 34(1):43–60.

Koerper, Henry C., and Chris E. Drover
1983 Chronology Building for Coastal Orange

County: The Case from CA-ORA-119-A. *Pacific Coast Archaeological Society Quarterly* 19(2):1–34.

Kooyman, Brian P.
2000 *Understanding Stone Tools and Archaeological Sites.* University of Calgary Press, Calgary, Alberta.

Kornfeld, Marcel
2013 *The First Rocky Mountaineers: Coloradans Before Colorado.* University of Utah Press, Salt Lake City.

Kornfeld, Marcel, George C. Frison, and Mary Lou Larson
2010 *Prehistoric Hunter-Gatherers of the High Plains and Rockies.* Left Coast Press, Walnut Creek, California.

Kornfeld, Marcel, Mary Lou Larson, David J. Rapson, and George C. Frison
2001 10,000 years in the Rocky Mountains: The Helen Lookingbill Site. *International Journal of Phytoremediation* 21(1):307–324.

Krieger, Alex D.
1944 Review of *Archaeological Researches in the Northern Great Basin,* edited by Luther S. Cressman, Frank C. Baker, Paul S. Conger, Henry P. Hanson, and Robert F. Heizer. *American Antiquity* 9(3):351–359.

Kroeber, Alfred L.
1923 American Culture and the Northwest Coast. *American Anthropologist* 25(1):1–20.

Kruskal, William H., and W. Allen Wallis
1952 Use of Ranks in One-Criterion Variance Analysis. *Journal of the American Statistical Association* 47(260):583–621.

Kuehn, Stephen C., Duane G. Froese, Paul Carrara, Franklin Foit, Nick J. Pearce, and Peter Rotheisler
2009 Major- and Trace-Element Characterization, Expanded Distribution, and a New Chronology for the Latest Pleistocene Glacier Peak Tephras in Western North America. *Quaternary Research* 71(2):201–216.

Kunz, Michael L., Michael Robert Bever, and Constance Adkins
2003 *The Mesa Site: Paleoindians Above the Arctic Circle.* Bureau of Land Management Open File Report 86. Bureau of Land Management, Alaska State Office, Anchorage.

Kunz, Michael L., and Richard E. Reanier
1994 Paleoindians in Beringia: Evidence from Arctic Alaska. *Science* 263(5147):660–662.

Kurota, Alex, Evan Sternberg, and Robert Dello-Russo
2018 *Archaeology of the White Sands Missile Range: Evaluation of 36 Sites and Implementation of Site Protective Measures Between Highway 70 and Nike Avenue, Otero and Doña Ana Counties, New Mexico, Volume 3: Analyses and Appendices.* WSMR Report No. 913. Prepared for William Godby, Department of the Army. Copies available from the Office of Contract Archaeology, Albuquerque.

Lachniet, M. S., R. F. Denniston, Y. Asmerom, and V. J. Polyak
2014 Orbital Control of Western North America Atmospheric Circulation and Climate Over Two Glacial Cycles. *Nature Communications* 5(1):1–8.

Lafayette, Linsie M., and Geoffrey M. Smith
2012 Use-Wear Traces on Experimental (Replicated) and Prehistoric Stemmed Points from the Great Basin. *Journal of California and Great Basin Anthropology* 32(2):141–160.

Lahren, Larry, and Robson Bonnichsen
1974 Bone Foreshafts from a Clovis Burial in Southwestern Montana. *Science* 186(4159):147–150.

Larson, Mary Lou, Marcel Kornfeld, and George C. Frison
2009 *Hell Gap: A Stratified Paleoindian Campsite at the Edge of the Rockies.* University of Utah Press, Salt Lake City.

Lassen, Robert
2015 The Folsom-Midland Component of the Gault Site, Central Texas: Context, Technology, and Typology. *Plains Anthropologist* 60(234):150–171.

Layton, Thomas N.
1970 High Rock Archaeology: An Interpretation of the Prehistory of the Northwestern Great Basin. PhD dissertation, Department of Anthropology, Harvard University, Cambridge, Massachusetts.
1972 Lithic Chronology in the Fort Rock Valley, Oregon. *Tebiwa* 15(2):1–20.
1979 Archaeology and Paleo-Ecology of Pluvial Lake Parman, Northwestern Great Basin. *Journal of New World Archaeology* 3(3):41–56.

Layton, Thomas N., and Jonathan O. Davis
1978 Last Supper Cave: Early Post-Pleistocene Cultural History and Paleoecology in the High Rock Country of the Northwestern Great Basin. Manuscript on file, Department of Anthropology, University of Nevada, Reno.

Lazuén, Talia
2012 European Neanderthal Stone Hunting Weapons Reveal Complex Behaviour Long Before the Appearance of Modern Humans. *Journal of Archaeological Science* 39:2304–2311.

Lebow, Clayton G., Douglas R. Harro, Rebecca L. McKim, Charles M. Hodges, Ann M. Munns, Erin A. Enright, and Leeann G. Haslouer
2015 The Sudden Flats Site: A Pleistocene/Holocene Transition Shell Midden on Alta California's Central Coast. *California Archaeology* 7(2):265–294.

Lee, Craig M., Jennifer Borresen Lee, and Jocelyn C. Turnbull
2011 Refining the Chronology of the Agate Basin Complex: Radiocarbon Dating the Frazier Site, Northeastern Colorado. *Plains Anthropologist* 56(219):243–258.

Lenzi, Michael R.
2015 An Experimental Program to Evaluate Proposed Functions of Crescents from the Western United States. Master's thesis, Department of Anthropology, University of Nevada, Reno.

Leonhardy, Frank C., and David G. Rice
1970 A Proposed Culture Typology for the Lower Snake River Region, Southeastern Washington. *Northwest Anthropological Research Notes* 4(1):1–29.

Lesnek, Alia J., Jason P. Briner, Charlotte Lindqvist, James F. Baichtal, and Timothy H. Heaton
2018 Deglaciation of the Pacific Coastal Corridor Directly Preceded the Human Colonization of the Americas. *Science Advances* 4(5):eear5040.

LeTourneau, Phillipe D.
2010 A Clovis Point from the Pacific Northwest Coast. *Current Research in the Pleistocene* 27:115–114.

Llamas, Bastien, Lars Fehren-Schmitz, Guido Valverde, Julien Soubrier, Swapan Mallick, Nadin Rohland, Susanne Nordenfelt et al.
2016 Ancient Mitochondrial DNA Provides High-Resolution Timescale of the Peopling of the Americas. *Science Advances* 2(4):e1501385.

Loendorf, Chris, Lowell Blikre, William D. Bryce, Theodore J. Oliver, Allen Denoyer, and Greg Wermers
2018 Raw Material Impact Strength and Flaked Stone Projectile Point Performance. *Journal of Archaeological Science* 90:50–61.

Lohse, Ernest S.
1994 The Southeastern Idaho Prehistoric Sequence. *Northwest Anthropological Research Notes* 28(2):135–156.

Lohse, Ernest S., and Coral Moser
2014 The Western Stemmed Point Tradition on the Columbia Plateau. *Journal of Northwest Anthropology* 48(1):45–68.

Lohse, Ernest S., and Corey Schou
2008 The Southern Columbia Plateau Projectile Point Sequence: An Informatics-Based Approach. In *Projectile Point Sequences in Northwestern North America*, edited by Roy L. Carlson and Martin P. R. Magne, pp. 187–208. Archaeology Press, Simon Fraser University, Burnaby, British Columbia.

Lohse, Jon C., Michael B. Hemmings, C. Andrew Collins, and David M. Yelacic
2014 Putting the Specialization Back in Clovis: What Some Caches Reveal about Skill and the Organization of Production in the Terminal Pleistocene. In *Clovis Caches: Recent Discoveries and New Research*, edited by Bruce B. Huckell and J. David Kilby, pp. 153–175. University of New Mexico Press, Albuquerque.

Long, Austin, and B. Rippeteau
1974 Testing Contemporaneity and Averaging Radiocarbon Dates. *American Antiquity* 39(2):205–214.

Lothrop, Jonathan C., Darrin L. Lowery, Arthur E. Spiess, and Christopher J. Ellis
2016 Early Human Settlement of Northeastern North America. *PaleoAmerica* 2(3):192–251.

Lothrop, Jonathan C., Paige E. Newby, Arthur E. Spiess, and James W. Bradley
2011 Paleoindians and the Younger Dryas in the New England-Maritimes Region. *Quaternary International* 242(2):546–569.

Lothrop, Jonathan C., and Zachary L. F. Singer
2017 Paleoindian Peoples and Landscapes of

Northeastern North America: An Introduction. *PaleoAmerica* 3(4):283–287.

Louderback, Lisbeth A., and Bruce M. Pavlik
2017 Starch Granule Evidence for the Earliest Potato Use in North America. *Proceedings of the National Academy of Sciences* 114(29):7606–7610.

Lupo, Karen D., and Dave N. Schmitt
2016 When Bigger Is Not Better: The Economics of Hunting Megafauna and Its Implications for Plio-Pleistocene Hunter-Gatherers. *Journal of Anthropological Archaeology* 44(B):185–197.

Lycett, Stephen J., and Noreen von Cramon-Taubadel
2015 Toward a "Quantitative Genetic" Approach to Lithic Variation. *Journal of Archaeological Method and Theory* 22(2):646–675.

Lyle, Mitchell, Linda Heusser, Christina Ravelo, Masanobu Yamamoto, John Barron, Noah S. Diffenbaugh, Timothy Herbert, and Dyke Andreasen
2012 Out of the Tropics: The Pacific, Great Basin Lakes, and Late Pleistocene Water Cycle in the Western United States. *Science* 337(6102):1629–1633.

Lyman, R. Lee
2004 Late Quaternary Diminution and Abundance of Prehistoric Bison (*Bison* sp.) in Eastern Washington, USA. *Quaternary Research* 62(1):76–85.

Lynch, Joshua J.
2020 Exploring the Function and Adaptive Context of Paleo-Arctic Projectile Points. PhD dissertation, Department of Anthropology, Texas A&M University, College Station.

MacDonald, George F.
1968 *Debert: A Paleo-Indian Site in Central Nova Scotia*. Anthropology Papers, National Museum of Canada, Ottawa.

Mack, Richard N., and John N. Thompson
1982 Evolution in Steppe with Few Large, Hooved Mammals. *The American Naturalist* 119(6):757–773

Mackie, Madeline E., and Randall Haas
2021 Estimating the Frequency of Coincidental Spatial Associations between Clovis Artifacts and Proboscidean Remains in North America. *Quaternary Research* 103:182–192.

Mackie, Madeline E., Todd A. Surovell, Matthew O'Brien, Robert L. Kelly, Spencer Pelton, C. Vance Haynes Jr., George C. Frison et al.
2020 Confirming a Cultural Association at the La Prele Mammoth Site (48CO1401), Converse County, Wyoming. *American Antiquity* 85(3):554–572.

Mackie, Quentin, Loren G. Davis, Daryl W. Fedje, Duncan McLaren, and Amy E. Gusick
2013 Locating Pleistocene-Age Submerged Archaeological Sites on the Northwest Coast: Current Status of Research and Future Directions. In *Paleoamerican Odyssey*, edited by Kelly E. Graf, Caroline V. Ketron, and Michael R. Waters, pp. 133–147. Center for the Study of the First Americans, Texas A&M University Press, College Station.

Mackie, Quentin, Daryl Fedje, and Duncan McLaren
2018 Archaeology and Sea Level Change on the British Columbia Coast. *Canadian Journal of Archaeology* 42(1):74–91.

MacNeish, Richard S. (editor)
1993 *Preliminary Investigations of the Archaic in the Region of Las Cruces, New Mexico*. Historic and Natural Resources Report No. 9. Submitted to Cultural Resources Management Branch, Directorate of Environment, United States Army Air Defense Artillery Center, Fort Bliss, Texas.

Madsen, David B.
2002 Great Basin Peoples and Late Quaternary Aquatic History. In *Great Basin Aquatic Systems History*, edited by Robert Hershler, David B. Madsen, and Donald R. Currey, pp. 387–405. Smithsonian Contributions to the Earth Sciences, No. 33. Smithsonian Institution Press, Washington, DC.

2004 *Entering America: Northeast Asia and Beringia before the Last Glacial Maximum*. University of Utah Press, Salt Lake City.

2007 The Paleoarchaic to Archaic Transition in the Great Basin. In *Paleoindian or Paleoarchaic? Great Basin Human Ecology at the Pleistocene–Holocene Transition*, edited by Kelly E. Graf and Dave N. Schmitt, pp. 3–20. University of Utah Press, Salt Lake City.

2015 A Framework for the Initial Occupation of the Americas. *PaleoAmerica* 1(3):217–250.

Madsen, David B., Charles G. Oviatt, D. Craig Young, and David Page
2015 Old River Bed Delta Geomorphology and Chronology. In *The Paleoarchaic Occupation of the Old River Bed Delta*, edited by David B. Madsen, Dave N. Schmitt, and David Page, pp. 30–60. Anthropological Paper No. 128. University of Utah Press, Salt Lake City.

Madsen, David B., and David E. Rhode
1990 Early Holocene Pinyon (*Pinus monophylla*) in the Northeastern Great Basin. *Quaternary Research* 33:94–101.

Madsen, David B., Dave N. Schmitt, and David Page
2015a Introduction and Research Perspectives. In *The Paleoarchaic Occupation of the Old River Bed Delta*, edited by David B. Madsen, Dave N. Schmitt, and David Page, pp. 1–21. Anthropological Papers No. 128. University of Utah Press, Salt Lake City.
2015b Integration and Synthesis. In *The Paleoarchaic Occupation of the Old River Bed Delta*, edited by David B. Madsen, Dave N. Schmitt, and David Page, pp. 237–256. Anthropological Papers No. 128. University of Utah Press, Salt Lake City.

Madsen, David B., Dave N. Schmitt, and David Page (editors)
2015 *The Paleoarchaic Occupation of the Old River Bed Delta*. Anthropological Papers No. 128. University of Utah Press, Salt Lake City.

Madsen, David B., and Thomas Williams
2019 The Upper Paleolithic of the Americas. *PaleoAmerica* 6(1):4–22.

Maguire, Leanna, Briggs Buchanan, Matthew T. Boulanger, Brian G. Redmond, and Metin I. Eren
2018 On the Late Paleoindian Temporal Assignment for the Honey Run Site (33-Co-3), Coshocton County, Ohio: A Morphometric Assessment of Flaked Stone Stemmed Lanceolate Projectile Points. *Journal of Archaeological Science: Reports* 20:588–595.

Mandel, Rolfe D., Laura R. Murphy, and Mark D. Mitchell
2014 Geoarchaeology and Paleoenvironmental Context of the Beacon Island Site, an Agate Basin (Paleoindian) Bison Kill in Northwestern North Dakota, USA. *Quaternary International* 342:91–113.

Mann, Henry B., and Donald R. Whitney
1947 On a Test of Whether One of Two Random Variables is Stochastically Larger than the Other. *The Annals of Mathematical Statistics* 18(1):50–60.

Manning, Cassandra R.
2011 The Role of Salmon in Middle Snake River Human Economy: The Hetrick Site in Regional Contexts. Master's thesis, Department of Anthropology, Portland State University, Portland, Oregon.

Manning, Sturt W.
2020 Comment on "Late Upper Paleolithic Occupation at Cooper's Ferry, Idaho, USA, ~16,000 Years Ago." *Science* 368(6487):4695.

Margold, Martin, John C. Gosse, Alan J. Hidy, Robin J. Woywitka, Joseph M. Young, and Duane Froese
2019 Beryllium-10 Dating of the Foothills Erratics Train in Alberta, Canada, Indicates Detachment of the Laurentide Ice Sheet from the Rocky Mountains at ~15 ka. *Quaternary Research* 92(2):469–482.

Marler, Clayton F.
2004 A Paleoindian Context for the Idaho National Engineering and Environmental Laboratory. Master's thesis, Department of Anthropology, Idaho State University, Pocatello.
2009 *Report on Trace Element Analysis of INL Obsidian Artifacts*. Idaho National Laboratory, Idaho Falls.

Martin, Erik P. J.
2019 An Examination of the Role of Costly Signaling and Projectile Point Optimization in Prehistoric Large Game Hunting in the Great Basin. PhD dissertation, Department of Anthropology, University of Utah, Salt Lake City.

Martin, Erik P. J., Daron Duke, and Andrew J. Hoskins
2018 Trends in Paleoindian Projectile Point Technology during the Pleistocene-Holocene Transition in the Northern High Plains and Old River Bed Delta. Poster presented at 83rd Annual Society for American Archaeology Meeting, Washington, DC.

Martin, Paul S.
1973   The Discovery of America. *Science* 179(4077):969–974.

Mason, Owen K.
2020   The Thule Migrations as an Analog for the Early Peopling of the Americas: Evaluating Scenarios of Overkill, Trade, Climate Forcing, and Scalar Stress. *PaleoAmerica* 6(4):308–356.

Matson, Richard G.
1991   *The Origins of Southwestern Agriculture.* University of Arizona Press, Tucson.

McDonough, Katelyn N., Jaime L. Kennedy, Richard L. Rosencrance, Justin A. Holcomb, Dennis L. Jenkins, and Kathryn Puseman
2022   Expanding Paleoindian Diet Breadth: Paleoethnobotany of Connley Cave 5, Oregon, USA. *American Antiquity* 87(2):303–332.

McGee, D., E. Moreno-Chamarro, J. Marshall, and E. D. Galbraith
2018   Western US Lake Expansions during Heinrich Stadials Linked to Pacific Hadley Circulation. *Science Advances* 4(11):eaav0118.

McGuire, Kelly R.
2002   Obsidian Production in Northeastern California and the Northwestern Great Basin: Implications for Land Use. In *Boundary Lands: Archaeological Investigations along the California–Great Basin Interface*, edited by Kelly R. McGuire, pp. 85–103. Anthropological Papers No. 24. Nevada State Museum, Carson City.

McLaren, Duncan, Daryl Fedje, Angela Dyck, Quentin Mackie, Alisha Gauvreau, and Jenny Cohen
2018   Terminal Pleistocene Epoch Human Footprints from the Pacific Coast of Canada. *PLoS One* 13(3):e0193522.

McLaren, Duncan, Daryl Fedje, Quentin Mackie, Loren G. Davis, Jon Erlandson, Alisha Gauvreau, and Colton Vogelaar
2019   Late Pleistocene Archaeological Discovery Models on the Pacific Coast of North America. *PaleoAmerica* 6(1):43–63.

Mehringer, Pete J.
1988   Clovis Cache Found: Weapons of Ancient Americans. *National Geographic* 174(4):500–503.

Mehringer, Peter J., Jr., and Franklin F. Foit Jr.
1990   Volcanic Ash Dating of the Clovis Cache at East Wenatchee, Washington. *National Geographic Research* 6(4):495–503.

Mehringer, Peter J., Jr., John C. Sheppard, and Franklin F. Foit Jr.
1984   The Age of Glacier Peak Tephra in West-Central Montana. *Quaternary Research* 21(1):36–41.

Meltzer, David J.
1989   Was Stone Exchanged among Eastern North American Paleoindians. In *Eastern Paleoindian Lithic Resource Use*, edited by Christopher J. Ellis and Johnathan C. Lothrop, pp. 11–40. Westview Press, Boulder, Colorado.

1995   Clocking the First Americans. *Annual Review of Anthropology* 24(1):21–45.

2002   What Do You Do When No One's Been There Before? Thoughts on the Exploration and Colonization of New Lands. In *The First Americans: The Pleistocene Colonization of the New World*, edited by Nina G. Jablonski, pp. 27–58. Memoirs of the California Academy of Sciences, No. 27. California Academy of Sciences, San Francisco.

2004   Modeling the Initial Colonization of the Americas: Issues of Scale, Demography, and Landscape Learning. In *The Settlement of the American Continents: A Multidisciplinary Approach to Human Biogeography*, edited by Michael C. Barton, pp. 123–137. University of Arizona Press, Tucson.

2006   *Folsom: New Archaeological Investigations of a Classic Paleoindian Bison Kill.* University of California Press, Berkeley.

2009   *First Peoples in a New World: Colonizing Ice Age America.* University of California Press, Berkeley.

2015   *The Great Paleolithic War: How Science Forged an Understanding of America's Pleistocene Past.* University of Chicago Press, Chicago.

2020   Overkill, Glacial History, and the Extinction of North America's Ice Age Megafauna. *Proceedings of the National Academy of Sciences* 117(46):28555–28563.

2021　*First Peoples in a New World: Populating Ice Age America*. 2nd ed. Cambridge University Press, New York.

Meltzer David J., Donald K. Grayson, Gerardo Ardila, Alex W. Barker, Dena F. Dincauze, C. Vance Haynes Jr., Francisco Mena, Lautero Núñez, and Dennis J. Stanford
1997　On the Pleistocene Antiquity of Monte Verde, Southern Chile. *American Antiquity* 62(4):659–663.

Meltzer, David J., and Vance T. Holliday
2010　Would North American Paleoindians Have Noticed Younger Dryas Age Climate Changes? *Journal of World Prehistory* 23(1):1–41.

Menounos, Brian, Brent M. Goehring, G. Osborn, Martin Margold, Brent Ward, Jeff Bond, Garry K. C. Clarke, John J. Clague, Thomas Lakeman, and Johannes Koch
2017　Cordilleran Ice Sheet Mass Loss Preceded Climate Reversals near the Pleistocene Termination. *Science* 358(6364):781–784.

Middleton, Emily S., Geoffrey M. Smith, William J. Cannon, and Mary F. Ricks
2014　Paleoindian Rock Art: Establishing the Antiquity of Great Basin Carved Abstract Petroglyphs in the Northern Great Basin. *Journal of Archaeological Science* 43(1):21–30.

Mika, Anna, Kat Flood, James D. Norris, Michael Wilson, Alastair Key, Briggs Buchanan, Brian Redmond, Justin Pargeter, Michelle R. Bebber, and Metin I. Eren
2020　Miniaturization Optimized Weapon Killing Power during the Social Stress of Late Pre-Contact North America (AD 600–1600). *PLoS ONE* 15(3):e0230348.

Miller, D. Shane, and Joseph A. M. Gingerich
2013a　Paleoindian Chronology and the Eastern Fluted Point Tradition. In *The Eastern Fluted Point Tradition*, edited by Joseph A. M. Gingerich, pp. 9–37. University of Utah Press, Salt Lake City.
2013b　Regional Variation in the Terminal Pleistocene and Early Holocene Radiocarbon Record of Eastern North America. *Quaternary Research* 79(2):175–88.

Miller, D. Shane, Vance T. Holliday, and Jordon Bright
2013　Clovis Across the Continent. In *Paleoamerican Odyssey*, edited by Kelly E. Graf, Caroline V. Ketron, and Michael R. Waters, pp. 207–220. Center for the Study of the First Americans, Texas A&M University Press, College Station.

Miller, D. Shane, and Ashley M. Smallwood
2012　Beyond Stages: Modeling Clovis Biface Production at the Topper Site (38AL23), South Carolina. In *Contemporary Lithic Analysis in the Southeast: Problems, Solutions, and Interpretations*, edited by Philip J. Carr, Andrew P. Bradbury, and Sarah E. Price, pp. 28–41. University of Alabama Press, Tuscaloosa.

Miller, G. Logan
2013　Illuminating Activities at Paleo Crossing (33ME274) Through Microwear Analysis. *Lithic Technology* 38(2):108–97.

Miller, Myles R.
2018　Archaic Transitions and Transformations in the Jornada Mogollon Region of Southern New Mexico and Western Texas. In *The Archaic Southwest*, edited by Bradley J. Vierra, pp. 119–144. University of Utah Press, Salt Lake City.

Miller, Myles R., and Tim Graves
2019　Chronological Trends Among Jornada Projectile Points. In *Recent Research in Jornada Mogollon Archaeology: Proceedings from the 20th Jornada Mogollon Conference*, edited by George O. Maloof, pp. 205–251. El Paso Museum of Archaeology, El Paso, Texas.

Mills, Wayne W., Michael F. Rondeau, and Terry L. Jones
2005　A Fluted Point from Nipomo, San Luis Obispo County, California. *Journal of California and Great Basin Anthropology* 25(2):214–220.

Minor, Rick
1984　An Early Complex at the Mouth of the Columbia River. *Northwest Anthropological Research Notes* 18(1):1–22.

Minor, Rick, and L. Spencer
1977　*Site of a Probable Camelid Kill at Fossil Lake, Oregon: An Archaeological Evaluation*. Prepared by the University of Oregon, Eugene. Submitted to the Bureau of Land Management, Lakeview, Oregon.

Moratto, Michael J.
1984　*California Archaeology*. Academic Press, New York.

Moratto, Michael J., Owen K. Davis, Shelly Davis-

King, Jack Meyer, Jeffrey Rosenthal, and Laurie Sylwester
2017   A Terminal Pleistocene/Early Holocene Environmental Record and Fluted Point from Twain Harte, California. *PaleoAmerica* 3(3):260–275.

Moratto, Michael J., Alan P. Garfinkel, Jon M. Erlandson, Alexander K. Rogers, Michael F. Rondeau, Jeffrey Rosenthal, Craig Skinner, Tim Carpenter, and Robert M. Yohe
2018   Fluted and Basally Thinned Concave-Base Points of Obsidian in the Borden Collection from Inyo County, Alta California: Age and Significance. *California Archaeology* 10(1):27–60.

Moreno-Mayar, J. Víctor, Ben A. Potter, Lasse Vinner, Matthias Steinrücken, Simon Rasmussen, Jonathan Terhorst, John A. Kamm et al.
2018   Terminal Pleistocene Alaskan Genome Reveals First Founding Population of Native Americans. *Nature* 553(7687):203–207.

Moreno-Mayar, J. Víctor, Lasse Vinner, Peter de Barros Damgaard, Constanza de la Fuente, Jeffrey Chan, Jeffrey P. Spence, Morten Allentoft et al.
2018   Early Human Dispersals within the Americas. *Science* 362(6419):eaav2621.

Morrow, Juliet E.
1995   Clovis Projectile Point Manufacture: A Perspective from the Ready/Lincoln Hills Site, 11JY46, Jersey County, Illinois. *Midcontinental Journal of Archaeology* 20(2):167–191.
2015   Clovis-Era Production in the Mid-Continent. In *Clovis: On the Edge of Understanding*, edited by Ashley M. Smallwood and Thomas A. Jennings, pp. 83–107. Center for the Study of the First Americans, Texas A&M University Press, College Station.
2019   On Fluted Morphometrics, Cladistics, and the Origins of the Clovis Culture. *PaleoAmerica* 5(2):191–205.

Morrow, Juliet E., Stuart J. Fiedel, Donald L. Johnson, Marcel Kornfeld, Moye Rutledge, and W. Raymond Wood
2012   Pre-Clovis in Texas? A Critical Assessment of the "Buttermilk Creek Complex." *Journal of Archaeological Science* 39(12):3677–3682.

Morrow, Juliet E., and Toby A. Morrow
1999   Geographic Variation in Fluted Projectile Points: A Hemispheric Perspective. *American Antiquity* 64(2):215–230.

Morrow, Toby A., and Juliet E. Morrow
1999   On the Fringe: Folsom Points and Preforms in Iowa. In *Folsom Lithic Technology, Explorations in Structure and Variation*, edited by Daniel S. Amick, pp. 65–91. International Monographs in Prehistory, Archaeological Series No. 12. Berghahn Books, New York.

Moss, Madonna L., and Jon M. Erlandson
1995   *An Evaluation, Survey, and Dating Program for Archaeological Sites on State Lands of the Northern Oregon Coast.* Report prepared by the University of Oregon Department of Anthropology for the Oregon State Historic Preservation Office, Department of Parks and Recreation, Salem.
2013   Waterfowl and Lunate Crescents in Western North America: The Archaeology of the Pacific Flyway. *Journal of World Prehistory* 26(3):173–211.

Mullineaux, Donal R.
1986   Summary of Pre-1980 Tephra-Fall Deposits Erupted from Mount St. Helens, Washington State, USA. *Bulletin of Volcanology* 48:17–26.
1996   *Pre-1980 Tephra-Fall Deposits Erupted from Mount St. Helens, Washington.* US Geological Survey Professional Paper P1563. Reston, Virginia.

Mullins, Daniel, and Nicole Herzog
2008   Protein Residue Analysis on Fluted Points from the Eastern Great Basin. Paper presented at the 31st Biennial Great Basin Anthropological Conference, Portland, Oregon.

Mullins, Daniel, Mark Karpinski, Jesse Adams, Elizabeth Karpinski, Nathaniel Nelson, Ashley Grimes, Jason Dabling, Nicole Adams, and Frank Parrish
2009   *Cultural Resources Survey of 100,000 Acres and 125 Miles of Fence-Line within the Milford Flat ESR Area, Millard County, Utah.* Technical Report No. 075417. Prepared by Logan Simpson Design, Salt Lake City, Utah.

Muñiz, Mark P.
2014   Determining a Cultural Affiliation for the CW Cache from Northeastern Colorado. In *Clovis Caches: Recent*

Discoveries and New Research, edited by Bruce B. Huckell and J. David Kilby, pp. 107–132. University of New Mexico Press, Albuquerque.

Munroe, Jeffrey S., and Benjamin J. C. Laabs
2013 Temporal Correspondence between Pluvial Lake Highstands in the Southwestern US and Heinrich Event 1. *Journal of Quaternary Science* 28(1):49–58.

Munyikwa, Kennedy, Tammy M. Rittenour, and James K. Feathers
2017 Temporal Constraints for the Late Wisconsinan Deglaciation of Western Canada Using Eolian Dune Luminescence Chronologies from Alberta. *Palaeogeography, Palaeoclimatology, Palaeoecology* 470:147–165.

Musil, Robert R.
1988 Functional Efficiency and Technological Change: A Hafting Tradition Model for Prehistoric North America. In *Early Human Occupation in Far Western North America: The Clovis–Archaic Interface*, edited by Judith A. Willig, C. Melvin Aikens, and John L. Fagan, pp. 373–388. Anthropological Papers No. 21. Nevada State Museum, Carson City.
2004 If It Ain't Fluted Don't Fix It: Form and Context in the Classification of Early Projectile Points in the Far West. In *Early and Middle Holocene Archaeology of the Northern Great Basin*, edited by Dennis L. Jenkins, Thomas J. Connolly, and C. Melvin Aikens, pp. 271–280. Anthropological Papers No. 62. Museum of Natural and Cultural History, University of Oregon, Eugene.

Muto, Guy R.
1976 The Cascade Technique: An Examination of a Levallois-Like Reduction System. PhD dissertation, Department of Anthropology, Washington State University, Pullman.

Nachar, Nadim
2008 The Mann-Whitney U: A Test for Assessing Whether Two Independent Samples Come from the Same Distribution. *Tutorials in Quantitative Methods for Psychology* 4(1):13–20.

Nakatsuka, Nathan, Iosif Lazaridis, Chiara Barbieri, Pontus Skoglund, Nadin Rohland, Swapan Mallick, Cosimo Posth, and Kelly Harkins-Kinkaid
2020 A Paleogenomic Reconstruction of the Deep Population History of the Andes. *Cell* 181(5):1131–1145.

Nakatsuka, Nathan, Pierre Luisi, Josefina M. B. Motti, Mónica Salemme, Fernando Santiago, Manuel D. D'Angelo del Campo, Rodrigo J. Vecchi et al.
2020 Ancient Genomes in South Patagonia Reveal Population Movements Associated with Technological Shifts and Geography. *Nature Communications* 11(1):1–12.

Nami, Hugo G., and Juan Yataco Capcha
2020 Further Data on Fell Points from the Southern Cone of South America. *PaleoAmerica* 6(4):379–386.

Nelson, Margaret
1991 The Study of Technological Organization. *Archaeological Method and Theory* 3:57–100.

Newby, Paige, James Bradley, Arthur Spiess, Bryan Shuman, and Phillip Leduc
2005 A Paleoindian Response to Younger Dryas Climate Change. *Quaternary Science Reviews* 24(1–2):141–154.

Newlander, Khori
2018 Imagining the Cultural Landscape of Paleoindians. *Journal of Archaeological Science: Reports* 19:836–845.

Norris, Sophie L., Lev Tarasov, Alistair J. Monteath, John C. Gosse, Alan J. Hidy, Martin Margold, and Duane G. Froese
2022 Rapid Retreat of the Southwestern Laurentide Ice Sheet during the Bølling-Allerød Interval. *Geology* 50(4):417–421.

O'Brien, Michael J.
2019 More on Clovis Learning: Individual-Level Processes Aggregate to Form Population-Level Patterns. *PaleoAmerica* 5(2):157–168.

O'Brien, Michael J., Matthew T. Boulanger, Briggs Buchanan, Mark Collard, R. Lee Lyman, and John Darwent
2014 Innovation and Cultural Transmission in the American Paleolithic: Phylogenetic Analysis of Eastern Paleoindian Projectile-Point Classes. *Journal of Anthropological Archaeology* 34(1):100–119.

O'Brien, Michael J., and Briggs Buchanan
2017 Cultural Learning and the Clovis Colo-

nization of North America. *Evolutionary Anthropology: Issues, News, and Reviews* 26(6):270–284.

O'Brien, Michael J., Briggs Buchanan, Matthew T. Boulanger, Alex Mesoudi, Mark Collard, Metin I. Eren, R. Alexander Bentley, and R. Lee Lyman
2015   Transmission of Cultural Variants in the North American Paleolithic. In *Learning Strategies and Cultural Evolution during the Palaeolithic*, edited by Alex Mesoudi and Kenichi Aoki, pp. 121–143. Replacement of Neanderthals by Modern Humans Series. Springer, Tokyo.

O'Brien, Michael J., Briggs Buchanan, and Metin I. Eren
2016   Clovis Colonization of Eastern North America: A Phylogenetic Approach. *Science and Technology of Archaeological Research* 2(1):67–89.

O'Brien, Michael J., J. Darwent, and R. Lee Lyman
2001   Cladistics Is Useful for Reconstructing Archaeological Phylogenies: Palaeoindian Points from the Southeastern United States. *Journal of Archaeological Science* 28(10):1115–1136.

O'Brien, Michael J., and R. Lee Lyman (editors)
2003   *Cladistics and Archaeology*. University of Utah Press, Salt Lake City.

Odell, George H.
1981   The Mechanics of Use-Breakage of Stone Tools: Some Testable Hypotheses. *Journal of Field Archaeology* 8(2):197–209.
1994   Prehistoric Hafting and Mobility in the North American Midcontinent: Examples from Illinois. *Journal of Anthropological Archaeology* 13(1):51–73.
1996   Economizing Behavior and the Concept of "Curation." In *Stone Tools: Theoretical Insights into Human Prehistory*, edited by George H. Odell, 51–80. Springer, Boston.

Odell, George H., and Frank Cowan
1986   Experiments with Spears and Arrows on Animal Targets. *Journal of Field Archaeology* 13(2):195–212.

Oetting, Albert C.
1994   Early Holocene Rabbit Drives and Prehistoric Land Use Patterns on Buffalo Flat, Christmas Lake Valley, Oregon. In *Archaeological Researches in the Northern Great Basin: Fort Rock Archaeology since Cressman*, edited by C. Melvin Aikens and Dennis L. Jenkins, pp. 155–169. University of Oregon Anthropological Papers 50. Eugene.

O'Grady, Patrick W., Michael F. Rondeau, and Scott P. Thomas
2011   New Fluted Artifact Finds at the Sheep Mountain Site (35HA3667), Harney County, Oregon. *Current Research in the Pleistocene* 28:69–71.

O'Grady, Patrick, Scott P. Thomas and Michael F. Rondeau
2008   The Sage Hen Gap Fluted-Point Site, Harney County, Oregon. *Current Research in the Pleistocene* 25:127–129.
2009   Recent Fluted-Point Finds in Eastern Oregon. *Current Research in the Pleistocene* 26:100–102.

O'Grady, Patrick, Scott P. Thomas, Craig E. Skinner, Jennifer J. Thatcher, Michael F. Rondeau, and John L. Fagan
2012   The Dietz Site: Revisiting the Geochemical Sourcing and Hydration Measurement Properties for Fluted and Stemmed Artifacts from 35LK1529, Lake County, Oregon. Paper presented at the 33rd Great Basin Anthropological Conference, Stateline, Nevada.

O'Grady, Patrick, Scott P. Thomas, Thomas W. Stafford, Daniel Stueber, and Margaret M. Helzer
2019   The View from the Trenches: Tying Paleoenvironment to Archaeology at Rimrock Draw Rockshelter, Oregon (35HA3855). Paper presented at the 84th Annual Meeting of the Society for American Archaeology, Albuquerque, New Mexico.

Ollivier, Aaron P., Geoffrey M. Smith, and Pat Barker
2017   A Collection of Fiber Sandals from Last Supper Cave, Nevada, and Its Implications for Cave and Rockshelter Abandonment during the Middle Holocene. *American Antiquity* 82(2):325–340.

Olson, Ronald L.
1930   *Chumash Prehistory*. University of California Press, Berkeley.

Orme, A. R.
2004   *Lake Thompson, Mojave Desert, California: A Desiccating Late Quaternary Lake System*. Monograph TR-03, US

Army Corps of Engineers, Engineering Research and Development Center and Cold Regions Research and Engineering Laboratory, Hanover, New Hampshire.

Orr, Phil C.
1960 Radiocarbon Dates from Santa Rosa Island. *Santa Barbara Museum of Natural History Department of Anthropology Bulletin* 3:1–10.
1968 *Prehistory of Santa Rosa Island*. Santa Barbara Museum of Natural History, Santa Barbara, California.

Oviatt, Charles G.
2015 Chronology of Lake Bonneville, 30,000 to 10,000 yr BP. *Quaternary Science Reviews* 110:166–171.

Oviatt, Charles G., David M. Miller, John P. McGeehin, Cecile Zachary, and Shannon Mahan
2005 The Younger Dryas Phase of Great Salt Lake, Utah, USA. *Palaeogeography, Palaeoclimatology, Palaeoecology* 219(3–4):263–284.

Page, David, and Steve Bacon
2016 *Browns Bench Predictive Modeling, Resampling, and Geochemical Characterization across Portions of Idaho, Nevada, and Utah*. Desert Research Institute, Reno, Nevada.

Page, David, and Daron G. Duke
2015 Toolstone Sourcing, Lithic Resource Use, and Paleoarchaic Mobility in the Western Bonneville Basin. In *The Paleoarchaic Occupation of the Old River Bed Delta*, edited by David B. Madsen, Dave N. Schmitt, and David Page, pp. 209–236. Anthropological Papers No. 128. University of Utah Press, Salt Lake City.

Pearson, Georges A.
2017 Bridging the Gap: An Updated Overview of Clovis across Middle America and Its Techno-Cultural Relation with Fluted Point Assemblages from South America. *PaleoAmerica* 3(3):203–230.

Pedersen, Mikkel W., Anthony Ruter, Charles Schweger, Harvey Friebe, Richard A. Staff, Kristian K. Kjeldsen, Marie L. Z. Mendoza et al.
2016 Postglacial Viability and Colonization in North America's Ice-Free Corridor. *Nature* 537(7618):45–49.

Pellegrini, Evan J.
2014 The Kammidikadi of Little Steamboat Point-1 Rockshelter: Terminal Early Holocene and Early Late Holocene Leporid Processing in Northern Warner Valley, Oregon. Master's thesis, Department of Anthropology, University of Nevada, Reno.

Pelton, Spencer R., Lorena Becerra-Valdivia, Alexander Craib, Sarah A. Allaun, Chase Mahan, Charles W. Koenig, Erin Kelley, George M. Zeimens, and George C. Frison
2022 In Situ Evidence for Paleoindian Hematite Quarrying at the Powars II Site (48PL330), Wyoming. *Proceedings of the National Academy of Sciences* 119(20):e2201005119.

Pelton, Spencer R., Marcel Kornfeld, Mary Lou Larson, and Thomas Minckley
2017 Component Age Estimates for the Hell Gap Paleoindian Site and Methods for Chronological Modeling of Stratified Open Sites. *Quaternary Research* 88(2):234–247.

Pelton, Spencer R., Marcel Kornfeld, Thomas Minckley, and Mary Lou Larson
2018 Component Age Estimates for the Hell Gap Paleoindian Site and Methods for Chronological Modeling of Stratified Open Sites—Response to Commentary by C. Vance Haynes. *Quaternary Research* 90(1):248–250.

Pendleton, Lorrane S.
1979 Lithic Technology in Early Nevada Assemblages. Master's thesis, Department of Anthropology, California State University, Long Beach.

Perreault, Charles
2019 *The Quality of the Archaeological Record*. University of Chicago Press, Chicago.

Perri, Angela R., Tatiana R. Feuerborn, Laurent A. F. Frantz, Greger Larson, and Ripan S. Malhi
2021 Dog Domestication and the Dual Dispersal of People and Dogs into the Americas. *Proceedings of the National Academy of Sciences* 118(6):e2010083118.

Perrotti, Angelina G., Christopher A. Kiahtipes, James M. Russell, Stephen T. Jackson, Jacquelyn L. Gill, Guy S. Robinson, Teresa Krause, and John W. Williams
2022 Diverse Responses of Vegetation and Fire after Pleistocene Megaherbivore Extinction across the Eastern US. *Quaternary Science Reviews* 294:107696.

Pettigrew, Richard M.
1984 Prehistoric Human Land-Use Patterns in

the Alvord Basin, Southeastern Oregon. *Journal of California and Great Basin Anthropology* 6(1):61–90.

Pettitt, Paul B., William Davies, Clive S. Gamble, and Martin B. Richards
2003 Palaeolithic Radiocarbon Chronology: Quantifying our Confidence Beyond Two Half-Lives. *Journal of Archaeological Science* 30(12):1685–1693.

Pigati, Jeffrey S., Kathleen B. Springer, and Jeffrey S. Honke
2019 Desert Wetlands Record Hydrologic Variability within the Younger Dryas Chronozone, Mojave Desert, USA. *Quaternary Research* 91(1):51–62.

Pilloud, Marin A., Derek J. Reaux, Geoffrey M. Smith, and Kristina M. Wiggins
2017 Using Fordisc Software to Assign Obsidian Artifacts to Geologic Sources: Proof of Concept. *Journal of Archaeological Science: Reports* 13:428–434.

Pinotti, Thomaz, Anders Bergström, Maria Geppert, Matt Bawn, Dominique Ohasi, Wentao Shi, Daniela R. Lacerda, Arne Solli, Jakob Norstedt, and Kate Reed
2018 Y Chromosome Sequences Reveal a Short Beringian Standstill, Rapid Expansion, and Early Population Structure of Native American Founders. *Current Biology* 29(1):149–157.

Pinson, Ariane O.
2007 Artiodactyl Use and Adaptive Discontinuity across the Paleoarchaic/Archaic Transition in the Northern Great Basin. In *Paleoindian or Paleoarchaic? Great Basin Human Ecology at the Pleistocene–Holocene Transition*, edited by Kelly E. Graf and Dave N. Schmitt, pp. 187–203. University of Utah Press, Salt Lake City.
2008 Geoarchaeological Context of Clovis and Western Stemmed Tradition Sites in Dietz Basin, Lake Country, Oregon. *Geoarchaeology* 23:63–106.
2011 The Clovis Occupation of the Dietz Site (35LK1529), Lake County, Oregon, and Its Bearing on the Adaptive Diversity of Clovis Foragers. *American Antiquity* 76(2):285–313.

Pitblado, Bonnie L.
2003 *Late Paleoindian Occupation of the Southern Rocky Mountains.* University Press of Colorado, Boulder.
2017 The Role of the Rocky Mountains in the Peopling of North America. *Quaternary International* 461:54–79.
2022 On Rehumanizing Pleistocene People of the Western Hemisphere. *American Antiquity* 87(2):217–235.

Pitulko, Vladimir V., Pavel A. Nikolsky, E. Yu Girya, Aleksander E. Basilyan, Vladimir E. Tumskoy, Sergei A. Koulakov, Sergei N. Astakhov, E. Yu Pavlova, and Mikhail A. Anisimov
2004 The Yana RHS Site: Humans in the Arctic before the Last Glacial Maximum. *Science* 303(5654):52–56.

Poinar, Hendrik, Stuart Fiedel, Christine E. King, Alison M. Devault, Kristo Bos, Melanie Kuch, and Regis Debruyne.
2009 Comment on "DNA from Pre-Clovis Human Coprolites in Oregon, North America." *Science* 325(5937):148.

Posth, Cosimo, Nathan Nakatsuka, Iosif Lazaridis, Pontus Skoglund, Swapan Mallick, Thiseas C. Lamnidis, Nadin Rohland et al.
2018 Reconstructing the Deep Population History of Central and South America. *Cell* 175(5):1185–1197.

Potter, Ben A., James F. Baichtal, Alwynn Beaudoin, Lars Fehren-Schmitz, C. Vance Haynes Jr., Vance T. Holliday, Charles E. Holmes et al.
2018 Current Evidence Allows Multiple Models for the Peopling of the Americas. *Science Advances* 4(8):1–8.

Potter, Ben A., Alwynne B. Beaudoin, C. Vance Haynes Jr., Vance T. Holliday, Charles E. Holmes, John W. Ives, Robert Kelly et al.
2018 Arrival Routes of First Americans Uncertain. *Science* 359(6381):1224–1225.

Potter, Ben A., Joshua D. Reuther, Vance T. Holliday, Charles E. Holmes, D. Shane Miller, and Nicholas Schmuck
2017 Early Colonization of Beringia and Northern North America: Chronology, Routes, and Adaptive Strategies. *Quaternary International* 444:36–55.

Prasciunas, Mary M.
2007 Bifacial Cores and Flake Production Efficiency: An Experimental Test of Technological Assumptions. *American Antiquity* 72(2):334–348.

Prasciunas, Mary M., and Todd A. Surovell
2015 Reevaluating the Duration of Clovis: The Problem of Non-Representative Radiocarbon. In *Clovis: On the Edge of a New Understanding*, edited by Ashley M. Smallwood and Thomas A. Jennings,

pp. 21–35. Center for the Study of the First Americans, Texas A&M University Press, College Station.

Prates, Luciano, and S. Ivan Perez
2021 Late Pleistocene South American Megafaunal Extinctions Associated with Rise of Fishtail Points and Human Population. *Nature Communications* 12(1):2175.

Pratt, Jordan E.
2021 Hasketts and Crescents: An Analysis of the Lithic Tools from Weed Lake Ditch, Oregon. Paper presented at the 86th Annual Meeting of the Society for American Archaeology, online.

Pratt, Jordan E., Ted Goebel, Kelly Graf, and Masami Izuho
2020 A Circum-Pacific Perspective on the Origin of Stemmed Points in North America. *PaleoAmerica* 6(1):65–108.

Price, Barry A., and Sara E. Johnson
1988 A Model of Late Pleistocene and Early Holocene Adaptation in Eastern Nevada. In *Early Human Occupation in Far Western North America: The Clovis–Archaic Interface*, edited by Judith A. Willig, C. Melvin Aikens, and John L. Fagan, pp. 231–272. Anthropological Papers No. 21. Nevada State Museum, Carson City.

Punke, Michele L., and Loren G. Davis
2006 Problems and Prospects in the Preservation of Late Pleistocene Cultural Sites in Southern Oregon Coastal River Valleys: Implications for Evaluating Coastal Migration Routes. *Geoarchaeology* 21(4):333–350.

Purdy, Barbara A.
1975 Fractures for the Archaeologist. In *Lithic Technology: Making and Using Stone Tools*, edited by Earl H. Swanson, pp. 133–141. Mouton, The Hague.

Raff, Jennifer
2022 *Origin: A Genetic History of the Americas*. Twelve Hachette Book Group, New York.

Raghavan, Maanasa, Matthias Steinrücken, Kelley Harris, Stephan Schiffels, Simon Rasmussen, Michael DeGiorgio, Anders Albrechtsen et al.
2015 Genomic Evidence for the Pleistocene and Recent Population History of Native Americans. *Science* 349(6250):aab3884.

Rasic, Jeffrey T.
2011 Functional Variability in the Late Pleistocene Archaeological Record of Eastern Beringia: A Model of Late Pleistocene Land Use and Technology from Northwest Alaska. In *From the Yenisei to the Yukon: Interpreting Lithic Assemblage Variability in Late Pleistocene/Early Holocene Beringia*, edited by Ted Goebel and Ian Buvit, pp. 128–164. Center for the Study of the First Americans, Texas A&M University Press, College Station.

Rasmussen, Morten, Sarah L. Anzick, Michael R. Waters, Pontus Skoglund, Michael DeGiorgio, Thomas W. Stafford, Simon Rasmussen et al.
2014 The Genome of a Late Pleistocene Human from a Clovis Burial Site in Western Montana. *Nature* 506(7487):225–229.

Rasmussen, Morten, Linda Scott Cummings, M. Thomas P. Gilbert, Vaughn M. Bryant, Colin Smith, Dennis L. Jenkins, and Eske Willerslev
2009 Response to Comment by Goldberg et al. on "DNA from Pre-Clovis Human Coprolites in Oregon, North America." *Science* 325(5937):148.

Rasmussen, Morten, Marten Sikora, Anders Albrechtsen, Thorfinn S. Korneliussen, J. Victor Moreno-Mayar, G. David Poznik, Christopher P. E. Zollikofer et al.
2015 The Ancestry and Affiliations of Kennewick Man. *Nature* 523(7561):455–458.

R Core Team
2020 R: A Language and Environment for Statistical Computing. R Foundation for Statistical Computing, Vienna, Austria. V. 4.0.3. PC. http://ww.R-project.org.

Reaux, Derek J.
2020 An Examination of Western Stemmed Tradition Settlement-Subsistence, Territoriality, and Lithic Technological Organization in the Northwestern Great Basin. PhD dissertation, Department of Anthropology, University of Nevada, Reno.

2021 Western Stemmed Tradition Settlement-Subsistence and Lithic Technological Organization in the Catnip Creek Delta, Guano Valley, Oregon, USA. *PaleoAmerica* 7(4):365–383.

Reaux, Derek J., Geoffrey M. Smith, Kenneth D. Adams, Sophia Jamaldin, Nicole D. George, Katelyn Mohr, and Richard L. Rosencrance
2018 A First Look at the Terminal Pleistocene/Early Holocene Record of Guano Valley, Oregon, USA. *PaleoAmerica* 4(2):162–176.

Redder, Albert J.
1985 Horn Shelter Number 2: The South End, a Preliminary Report. *Central Texas Archaeologist* 10:37–65.

Reddy, Seetha N., and Jon M. Erlandson
2012 Macrobotanical Food Remains from a Trans-Holocene Sequence at Daisy Cave (CA-SMI-261), San Miguel Island, California. *Journal of Archaeological Science* 39(1):33–40.

Reeder, Leslie A., Jon M. Erlandson, and Torben C. Rick
2011 Younger Dryas Environments and Human Adaptations on the West Coast of the United States and Baja California. *Quaternary International* 242(2):463–478.

Reeder-Myers, Leslie, Jon M. Erlandson, Daniel R. Muhs, and Torben C. Rick
2015 Sea Level, Paleogeography, and Archaeology on California's Northern Channel Islands. *Quaternary Research* 83(2): 263–272.

Reher, Charles A., and George C. Frison
1980 *The Vore Site, 48CK302: A Stratified Buffalo Jump in the Wyoming Black Hills*. Plains Anthropologist Memoir 16. Lincoln, Nebraska.

Reich, David
2018 *Who We Are and How We Got Here: Ancient DNA and the New Science of the Human Past*. Pantheon Books, New York.

Reich, David, Nick Patterson, Desmond Campbell, Arti Tandon, Stéphane Mazieres, Nicolas Ray, Maria V. Parra et al.
2012 Reconstructing Native American Population History. *Nature* 488(7411):370–374.

Reid, Kenneth C.
1997 Gravels and Travels: A Comment on Andrefsky's "Cascade Phase Lithic Technology." *North American Archaeologist* 18(1): 67–81.
2011 Updating the Age of the Clovis Culture and Western Stemmed Tradition in Idaho. *IPAC News: The Newsletter of the Idaho Professional Archaeological Council* 4(1): 24–39.
2014 Through a Glass Darkly: Patterns of Obsidian and Fine Grained Volcanic Toolstone Acquisition on the Southern Plateau. In *Lithics in the West: Using Lithic Analysis to Solve Archaeological Problems in Western North America*, edited by Douglas H. MacDonald, William Andrefsky Jr., and Pei-Lin Yu, pp. 97–119. University of Montana Press, Missoula.
2017 Idaho Beginnings: A Review of the Evidence. *Quaternary International* 444(B): 72–82.

Reid, Kenneth C., Richard E. Hughes, Matthew J. Root, and Michael F. Rondeau
2015 Clovis in Idaho: An Update on Its Distribution, Technology, and Chronology. In *Clovis: On the Edge of a New Understanding*, edited by Ashley M. Smallwood and Thomas A. Jennings, pp. 53–82. Center for the Study of the First Americans, Texas A&M University Press, College Station.

Reimer, Paula J., William E. N. Austin, Edouard Bard, Alex Bayliss, Paul G. Blackwell, Christopher Bronk Ramsey, Martin Butzin et al.
2020 The IntCal20 Northern Hemisphere Radiocarbon Age Calibration Curve (0–55 cal kBP). *Radiocarbon* 62(4): 725–757.

Renaud, Etienne B.
1942 *Reconnaissance in the Upper Rio Grande Valley of Colorado and Northern New Mexico*. Archaeological Series Third Paper. Department of Anthropology, University of Denver, Colorado.

Rhode, David, and Kenneth D. Adams
2016 *Landscapes in Transition: A Paleoenvironmental Context for Lincoln County, Nevada*. BLM Report No. 8111 CRR NV 040-16-2140. Desert Research Institute, Reno. Submitted to Caliente Field Office, Bureau of Land Management, Nevada.

Rhode, David, Ted Goebel, Kelly E. Graf, Bryan S. Hockett, Kevin T. Jones, Dave B. Madsen, Charles G. Oviatt, and Dave N. Schmitt
2005 Latest Pleistocene–Early Holocene Human Occupation and Paleoenvironmental Change in the Bonneville Basin, Utah–Nevada. In *Interior Western United States: Geological Society of America Field Guide 6*, edited by J. Pederson and C. M. Dehler. Geological Society of America, Boulder, Colorado.

Rhode, David, and Lisbeth A. Louderback
2007 Dietary Plant Use in the Bonneville Basin during the Terminal Pleistocene/Early Holocene Transition. In *Paleoindian or Paleoarchaic? Great Basin Human Ecology at the Pleistocene–Holocene*

Transition, edited by Kelly E. Graf and Dave N. Schmitt, pp. 231–247. University of Utah Press, Salt Lake City.

Rhode, David E., David B. Madsen, and Kevin T. Jones
2006   Antiquity of Early Holocene Small-Seed Consumption and Processing at Danger Cave. *Antiquity* 80(308):328–339.

Rhode, David, Geoffrey M. Smith, Eric Dillingham, Haden U. Kingrey, and Nicole D. George
2022   The Nye Canyon Paleo Site: An Upper Montane Mixed Fluted Point, Clovis Blade, and Western Stemmed Tradition Assemblage in Western Nevada. *PaleoAmerica* 8(2):115–129.

Rice, David G.
1972   The Windust Phase in Lower Snake River Region. PhD dissertation, Department of Anthropology, Washington State University, Pullman.

Rice, Harvey S.
1965   The Cultural Sequence at Windust Caves. PhD dissertation, Department of Anthropology, Washington State University, Pullman.

Rice, Sarah K.
2015   Analysis of Paleoindian Site Structure and Toolstone Procurement at the Overlook Site (26CH3413), Churchill County, Nevada. Master's thesis. Department of Anthropology, University of Nevada, Reno.

Richerson, Peter J., and Robert Boyd
2005   *Not by Genes Alone: How Culture Transformed Human Evolution*. University of Chicago Press, Chicago.

Rick, Torben C.
2008   An Arena Point and Crescent from Santa Rosa Island, California. *Current Research in the Pleistocene* 25:140–142.

Rick, Torben C., Jon M. Erlandson, Nicholas P. Jew, and Leslie A. Reeder-Myers
2013   Archaeological Survey, Paleogeography, and the Search for Late Pleistocene Paleocoastal Peoples of Santa Rosa Island, California. *Journal of Field Archaeology* 38(4):324–331.

Roberson, J., and E. Gingerich
2015   *Cultural Resources Inventory of 1,451 Acres in the Lead Mountain Training Area for Marine Corps Air Ground Combat Center, Twentynine Palms, California*. Report submitted to the Natural Resources and Environmental Affairs Division, Marine Corps Air Ground Combat Center, Twentynine Palms, California.

Roberts, Frank H. H., Jr.
1937   The Folsom Problem in American Archaeology. In *Early Man as Depicted by Leading Authorities at the International Symposium*, edited by George G. MacCurdy, pp. 153–162. Academy of Natural Sciences, Philadelphia. J. B. Lippincott Company, London.
1940   Developments in the Problem of the North American Paleo-Indian. *Smithsonian Miscellaneous Collections* 100:51–116.
1942   *Archeological and Geological Investigations in the San Jon District, Eastern New Mexico*. Smithsonian Miscellaneous Collections. Smithsonian Institution, Washington, DC.

Rogers, David B.
1929   *Prehistoric Man on the Santa Barbara Coast*. Santa Barbara Museum of Natural History, Santa Barbara, California.

Rogers, Malcolm J.
1938   Archaeological and Geological Investigations of the Cultural Levels in an Old Channel of San Dieguito Valley. In *Carnegie Institution of Washington Year Book* 37:344–345.
1939   *Early Lithic Industries of the Lower Basin of the Colorado River and Adjacent Areas*. San Diego Museum of Man Papers Vol. 3. Ballena Press, Ramona, California.

Rondeau, Michael F.
2006a   The Jakes Valley Fluted Points from White Pine County, Nevada: An Analysis. CalFLUTED Research Report No. 23. Rondeau Archaeological, Sacramento, California.
2006b   A Summary of Analysis on Selected Projectile Points from the Sunshine Well Locality, White Pine County, Nevada. CalFLUTED Research Report No. 29. Rondeau Archaeological, Sacramento, California.
2006c   Revisiting the Number of Reported Clovis Points from Tulare Lake, California. *Current Research in the Pleistocene* 23:140–142.
2006d   Analysis of Five Fluted Points on Display at the Nevada State Museum, Carson City,

Nevada. CalFLUTED Research Report No. 33. Rondeau Archaeological, Sacramento, California.

2008a Additional Studies on the Dietz Site Fluted Points and Associated Bifaces, Lake County, Oregon. CalFLUTED Research Report No. 39. Rondeau Archaeological, Sacramento, California.

2008b A Study of a Portion of the Early Points from the Campbell Collection, Joshua Tree National Park, Twentynine Palms, California. CalFLUTED Research Report No. 51. Rondeau Archaeological, Sacramento, California.

2009a Research on Additional Bifaces from the Borden Collection, Inyo County, California. CalFLUTED Research Report No. 69. Rondeau Archaeological, Sacramento, California.

2009b Fluted Points of the Far West. *Proceedings of the Society of California Archaeology* 21: 265–274.

2009c A Study of a Fluted Point Cast, Dietz Site, Lake County, Oregon. CalFLUTED Research Report No. 60. Rondeau Archaeological, Sacramento, California.

2009d Additional Artifacts from the Dietz Site and Other Fluted Points from Lake County, Lakeview BLM District, Oregon. CalFLUTED Research Report No. 61. Rondeau Archaeological, Sacramento, California.

2010 A Study of Additional Bifaces from the Campbell Collection, Joshua Tree National Park, Twentynine Palms, California: Report Two. CalFLUTED Research Report No. 68. Rondeau Archeological, Sacramento, California.

2013 Results of the 2012 Multi-Field School Surface Collection of the Dietz Site (35LK1529), Lakeview BLM District, Lake County, Oregon. CalFLUTED Research Report No. 102. Rondeau Archaeological, Sacramento, California.

2014 A Fluted Point from the Marine Corps Air Ground Combat Center, San Bernardino County, California. CalFLUTED Research Report No. 121. Rondeau Archaeological, Sacramento, California.

2015a Fluted Point Studies in the Far West. In *Clovis: On the Edge of a New Understanding*, edited by Ashley M. Smallwood and Thomas A. Jennings, pp. 39–51. Center for the Study of the First Americans, Texas A&M University Press, College Station.

2015b Finding Fluted-Point Sites in the Arid West. *PaleoAmerica* 1(2):209–212.

2016 A Study of Fluted Bifaces at the National Museum of Natural History, Smithsonian Institution, Washington, DC. CalFLUTED Research Report No. 148. Rondeau Archaeological, Sacramento, California.

2022 *Fluted Points of the Far West*. University of Utah Press, Salt Lake City.

Rondeau, Michael F., and Samuel Coffman

2007 A Study of Fluted Points and Similar Specimens from the Lake Tonopah and Mud Lake Portions of the Gary D. Noyes Collection, Esmeralda and Nye Counties, Nevada. CalFLUTED Research Report No. 37. Rondeau Archeological, Sacramento, California.

Rondeau, Michael F., and Nicole D. George

2017 An Evaluation of the Butcher Creek Fluted Point Cast, Idaho County, Idaho. CalFLUTED Research Report No. 158. Rondeau Archeological, Sacramento, California.

Rondeau, Michael F., Ted Goebel, and Mark B. Estes

2007 Fluted Point Variability in the Central Great Basin. *Current Research in the Pleistocene* 24:138–141.

Rondeau, Michael F., and Jerry N. Hopkins

2008 A Reevaluation of Reported Clovis Points from Tulare Lake, California. In *Ice-Age Tools from the San Joaquin Valley*, edited by Jerry N. Hopkins and Alan P. Garfinkel, pp. 99–108. Tulare Lake Archaeological Research Group, Redondo Beach, California.

Rondeau, Michael F., and Nathaniel Nelson

2013a Paleoindian Artifacts from 43MD2502 and 43MD2604, Milford Flat, Millard County, Utah. CalFLUTED Research Report No. 110. Rondeau Archeological, Sacramento, California.

2013b Additional Fluted Points from Millard and Tooele Counties, Utah. CalFLUTED Research Report No. 111. Rondeau Archeological, Sacramento, California.

2013c Two Fluted Points from the No Name Site, Milford Flat, Millard County, Utah.

CalFLUTED Research Report No. 112. Rondeau Archaeological, Sacramento, California.

Rondeau, Michael F., Geoffrey M. Smith, and John W. Dougherty
2017 Discriminating Black Rock Concave Base Points from Other Western Paleoindian Projectile Points. In *Plainview: The Enigmatic Paleoindian Artifact Style of the Great Plains*, edited by Vance T. Holliday, Eileen Johnson, and Ruthann Knudson, pp. 230–248. University of Utah Press, Salt Lake City.

Root, Matthew J.
2000 *The Archaeology of the Bobtail Wolf Site: Folsom Occupation of the Knife River Flint Quarry Area*. Washington State University Press, Pullman.

Rosencrance, Richard L.
2019 Assessing the Chronological Variation within Western Stemmed Tradition Projectile Points. Master's thesis, Department of Anthropology, University of Nevada, Reno.

Rosencrance, Richard L., and Katelyn N. McDonough
2020 Ten Thousand Years in the High Rock Country: New Radiocarbon Dates From Hanging Rock Shelter (25WA1502), Nevada. *Nevada Archaeologist* 32(1–2):30–52.

Rosencrance, Richard L., Katelyn N. McDonough, Justin A. Holcomb, Pamela E. Endzweig, and Dennis L. Jenkins
2022 Dating and Analysis of Western Stemmed Toolkits from the Legacy Collection of Connley Cave 4, Oregon. *PaleoAmerica* 8(3):264–284.

Rosencrance, Richard L., Geoffrey M. Smith, Dennis L. Jenkins, Thomas J. Connolly, and Thomas N. Layton
2019 Reinvestigating Cougar Mountain Cave: New Perspectives on Stratigraphy, Chronology, and a Younger Dryas Occupation in the Northern Great Basin. *American Antiquity* 84(3):559–573.

Rosenthal, Jeffrey S., Kim L. Carpenter, and D. Craig Young
2001 *Archaeological Survey of Target Area Buffer Zones in the Airport Lake, Baker, and George Ranges, Naval Air Weapons Station, China Lake, Inyo and Kern Counties, California*. On file, Naval Air Weapons Station, China Lake, Ridgecrest, California.

Rosenthal, Jeffrey S., and William R. Hildebrandt
2019 Acorns in Pre-Contact California: A Reevaluation of Their Energetic Value, Antiquity of Use, and Linkage to Mortar-Pestle Technology. *Journal of California and Great Basin Anthropology* 39:1–23.

Roth, Barbara, and Justin DeMaio
2015 Early and Middle Archaic Foragers in the Sonoran Desert: Investigations at the Ruelas Ridge Site. *Kiva* 80(2):115–136.

Rots, Veerle, and Hugues Plisson
2014 Projectiles and the Abuse of the Use-Wear Method in a Search for Impact. *Journal of Archaeological Science* 48:154–165.

Rowlands, Peter, Hyrum Johnson, Eric Ritter, and Albert Endo
1982 The Mojave Desert. In *Reference Handbook on the Deserts of North America*, edited by Gordon L. Bender, pp. 103–162. Greenwood Press, Westport, Connecticut.

Ruby, Allika, D. Craig Young, Daron Duke, and B. F. Byrd (editors)
2010 *Archaeological Data Recovery of 45 Sites within the Superior Valley Expansion Area, the National Training Center, Fort Irwin, San Bernardino County, California*. Report prepared for the Directorate of Public Works, US Army National Training Center, Fort Irwin, California.

Rudolph, Theresa
1995 *The Hetrick Site: 11,000 Years of Prehistory in the Weiser River Valley*. Prepared for Idaho Transportation Department by Science Applications International Corporation, Boise.

Russell, Dann J.
1993 Running Antelope: A Paleoindian Site in Northern Utah. *Utah Archaeology* 6(1):79–86.
2004 Running Antelope Revisited. *Utah Archaeology* 14:47–53.

Sanchez, Gabriel M., Jon M. Erlandson, and Nicholas Tripcevich
2017 Quantifying the Association of Chipped Stone Crescents with Wetlands and Paleoshorelines of Western North America. *North American Archaeologist* 38(2):107–137.

Sánchez, Guadalupe
2016 *Los Primeros Mexicanos: Late Pleistocene and Early Holocene People of Sonora*.

Anthropological Papers of the University of Arizona No. 76. University of Arizona Press, Tucson.

Sánchez, Guadalupe, and John Carpenter
2016 Tracking the First People of Mexico: A Review of the Archaeological Record. In *Stones, Bones and Profiles: Exploring Archaeological Context, Early American Hunter-Gatherers, and Bison*, edited by Marcel Kornfeld and Bruce. B. Huckell, pp. 75–101. University Press of Colorado, Boulder.
2021 Tales of the Terminal Pleistocene: Clovis in Northern Mexico and the First Mesoamericans. In *Preceramic Mesoamerica*, edited by Jon C. Lohse, Aleksander Borejsza, and Arthur A. Joyce, pp. 117–141. Routledge, New York.

Sánchez, Guadalupe, Vance T. Holliday, Edmund P. Gaines, Joaquín Arroyo-Cabrales, Natalia Martínez-Tagüeña, Andrew Kowler, Todd Lange, Gregory W. L. Hodgins, Susan M. Mentzer, and Ismael Sánchez-Morales
2014 Human (Clovis)-Gomphothere (*Cuvieronius* sp.) Association ~13,390 Calibrated yr BP in Sonora, Mexico. *Proceedings of the National Academy of Sciences* 111: 10972–10977.

Sanders, Paul H.
1982 A Lithic Analysis of the Windust Phase Component, Hatwai Site (10NP143), Nez Perce County, Idaho. Master's thesis, Department of Anthropology, University of Wyoming, Laramie.

Santarone, Paul
2014 New Insights into the Simon Cache. In *Clovis Caches: Recent Discoveries and New Research*, edited by Bruce B. Huckell and J. David Kilby, pp. 11–23. University of New Mexico Press, Albuquerque.

Saper, Shelby, Richard L. Rosencrance, and Katelyn N. McDonough
2019 Cascade Phase Context and Chronology at the Connley Caves, Oregon. Poster presented at 84th Annual Meeting of the Society for American Archaeology, Albuquerque, New Mexico.

Sapir, Edward
1916 *Time Perspective in Aboriginal American Culture: A Study in Method*. Canada Department of Mines, Geological Survey, Memoir 90, Anthropological Series 13. Ottawa.

Sappington, Robert Lee, and Sarah Schuknecht-McDaniel
2001 Wewukiyepuh (10-NP-336): Contributions of an Early Holocene Windust Phase Site to Lower Snake River Prehistory. *North American Archaeologist* 22(4): 353–370.

Sargeant, Kathryn E
1973 The Haskett Tradition: A View from Redfish Overhang. Master's thesis, Department of Anthropology, Idaho State University, Pocatello.

Sayles, Edwin B., and Ernst Antevs
1941 *The Cochise Culture*. Medallion Papers No. 29. Gila Pueblo, Globe, Arizona.

Scheib, Christina L., Hongjie Li, Tariq Desai, Vivian Link, Christopher Kendall, Genevieve Dewar, Peter William Griffith et al.
2018 Ancient Human Parallel Lineages within North America Contributed to a Coastal Expansion. *Science* 360(6392):1024–1027.

Schiffer, Michael B.
2011 *Studying Technological Change: A Behavioral Approach*. University of Utah Press, Salt Lake City.

Schiffer, Michael B. (editor)
2001 *Anthropological Perspectives on Technology*. Amerind Foundation New World Studies Series No. 5. University of New Mexico Press, Albuquerque.

Schillinger, Kerstin, Alex Mesoudi, and Stephen J. Lycett
2014 Copying Error and the Cultural Evolution of "Additive" vs. "Reductive" Material Traditions: An Experimental Assessment. *American Antiquity* 79(1):128–143.

Schmitt, Dave N., David B. Madsen, Charles G. Oviatt, and Rachel Quist
2007 Late Pleistocene/Early Holocene Geomorphology and Human Occupation of the Old River Bed Delta, Western Utah. In *Paleoindian or Paleoarchaic? Great Basin Human Ecology at the Pleistocene-Holocene Transition*, edited by Kelly E. Graf and David N. Schmitt, pp. 105–119. University of Utah Press, Salt Lake City.

Schroedl, Alan R.
2021 The Geographic Origin of Clovis Technology: Insights from Clovis Biface Caches. *Plains Anthropologist* 66(258):120–148.

Scott, Eric
2010 Extinctions, Scenarios, and Assumptions: Changes in Latest Pleistocene Large

Herbivore Abundance and Distribution in Western North America. *Quaternary International* 217(1–2):225–239.

Scott, Eric, Kathleen B. Springer, and James C. Sagebiel
2017 The Tule Springs Local Fauna: Rancholabrean Vertebrates from the Las Vegas Formation, Nevada. *Quaternary International* 443:105–121.

Sellards, Elias Howard
1952 *Early Man in America*. University of Texas Press, Austin.

Sellet, Frédéric
2011 Fallen Giants: The Story of Paleoindian Point Types on the North American Great Plains. In *Peuplement et Préhistoire en Amériques*, edited by Denis Vialou, pp. 383–396. Comité des Travaux Historiques et Scientifiques, Paris.
2013 Anticipated Mobility and Its Archaeological Signature: A Case Study of Folsom Retooling Strategies. *Journal of Anthropological Archaeology* 32(4):383–396.
2015 A Fresh Look at the Age and Cultural Affiliation of the Sheaman Site. *PaleoAmerica* 1(1):81–87.
2018 My Flute Is Bigger Than Yours: Nature and Causes of Technological Changes on the American Great Plains at the End of the Pleistocene. In *Lithic Technological Organization and Paleoenvironmental Change*, edited by Erick Robinson and Frédéric Sellet, pp. 263–279. Springer, Berlin.

Sellet, Frédéric, James Donohue, and Matthew G. Hill
2009 The Jim Pitts Site: A Stratified Paleoindian Site in the Black Hills of South Dakota. *American Antiquity* 74(4):735–758.

Shackley, M. Steven
2011 Sources of Archaeological Dacite in Northern New Mexico. *Journal of Archaeological Science* 38(5):1001–1007.
2019 *Energy-Dispersive X-ray Fluorescence (EDXRF) Whole Rock Analysis of Major, Minor, and Trace Elements for Archaic Period Artifacts from the Tularosa Basin, Southern New Mexico*. Report prepared for Cassandra Keyes, Department of Anthropology, University of New Mexico, Albuquerque.

Shennan, Stephen
2001 Demography and Cultural Innovation: A Model and Its Implications for the Emergence of Modern Human Culture. *Cambridge Archaeological Journal* 11(1):5–16.

Shillito, Lisa-Marie, Helen L. Whelton, John C. Blong, Dennis L. Jenkins, Thomas J. Connolly, and Ian D. Bull
2020 Pre-Clovis Occupation of the Americas Identified by Human Faecal Biomarkers in Coprolites from Paisley Caves, Oregon. *Science Advances* 6(29):eaba6404.

Sholts, Sabrina, Dennis J. Stanford, Louise M. Flores, and Sebastian K.T.S. Wärmländer
2012 Flake Scar Patterns of Clovis Points Analyzed with a New Digital Morphometrics Approach: Evidence for Direct Transmission of Technological Knowledge across Early North America. *Journal of Archaeological Science* 39(19):3018–3026.

Shott, Michael J.
1996 Innovation and Selection in Prehistory. In *Stone Tools: Theoretical Insights into Human Prehistory*, edited by George H. Odell, pp. 279–309. Springer, Boston.
2013 Human Colonization and Late Pleistocene Lithic Industries of the Americas. *Quaternary International* 285:150–160.

Shott, Michael J., Justin P. Williams, and Alan M. Slade
2021 Measuring Allometry in Dimensions of Western North American Clovis Points. *Journal of Archaeological Science* 131:105359.

Simons, Dwight D., Thomas N. Layton, and Ruthann Knudson
1985 A Fluted Point from the Mendocino County Coast. *Journal of California and Great Basin Anthropology* 7(2):260–269.

Sisk, Matthew L., and John J. Shea
2009 Experimental Use and Quantitative Performance Analysis of Triangular Flakes (Levallois Points) Used as Arrowheads. *Journal of Archaeological Science* 36(9):2039–2047.

Sistiaga, Ainara, Francesco Berna, Richard Laursen, and Paul Goldberg
2014 Steroidal Biomarker Analysis of a 14,000 Years Old Putative Human Coprolite from Paisley Cave, Oregon. *Journal of Archaeological Science* 41:813–817.

Sitton, Jase, Brett Story, Briggs Buchanan, and Metin I. Eren
2020 Tip Cross-Sectional Geometry Predicts the Penetration Depth of Stone-Tipped Projectiles. *Scientific Reports* 10(1):1–9.

Smallwood, Ashley M.
2010a Clovis Biface Technology at the Topper Site, South Carolina: Evidence for Variation and Technological Flexibility. *Journal of Archaeological Science* 37:2413–2425.
2010b Use-Wear Analysis of the Clovis Biface Collection from the Gault Site in Central Texas. Master's thesis, Department of Anthropology, Texas A&M University, College Station.
2012 Clovis Technology and Settlement in the American Southeast: Using Biface Analysis to Evaluate Dispersal Models. *American Antiquity* 77(4):689–713.
2015 Building Experimental Use-Wear Analogues for Clovis Biface Functions. *Archaeological and Anthropological Sciences* 7(1):13–26.

Smallwood, Ashley M., and Thomas A. Jennings (editors)
2015 *Clovis: On the Edge of a New Understanding.* Texas A&M University Press, College Station.

Smallwood, Ashley M., Thomas A. Jennings, Charlotte D. Pevny, and David G. Anderson
2019 Paleoindian Projectile-Point Diversity in the American Southeast: Evidence for the Mosaic Evolution of Point Design. *PaleoAmerica* 5(3):218–230.

Smith, Geoff M.
2003 Damage Inflicted upon Animal Bone by Wooden Projectiles: Experimental Results and Archaeological Applications. *Journal of Taphonomy* 1(2):105–114.

Smith, Geoffrey M.
2006 Pre-Archaic Technological Organization, Mobility and Settlement Systems: A View from the Parman Localities, Humboldt County, Nevada. Master's thesis, Department of Anthropology, University of Nevada, Reno.
2007 Pre-Archaic Mobility and Technological Activities at the Parman Localities, Humboldt County, Nevada. In *Paleoindian or Paleoarchaic? Great Basin Human Ecology at the Pleistocene–Holocene Transition*, edited by Kelly E. Graf and Dave N. Schmitt, pp. 139–155. University of Utah Press, Salt Lake City.
2008 Results from the XRF Analysis of Pre-Archaic Projectile Points from Last Supper Cave, Northwest Nevada. *Current Research in the Pleistocene* 25:144–146.
2009 Additional Results from the XRF Analysis of Pre-Archaic Artifacts from Last Supper Cave, Northwest Nevada. *Current Research in the Pleistocene* 26:131–133.
2010 Footprints Across the Black Rock: Temporal Variability in Prehistoric Foraging Territories and Toolstone Procurement Strategies in the Western Great Basin. *American Antiquity* 75(4):865–885.
2011 Shifting Stones and Changing Homes: Using Toolstone Ratios to Consider Relative Occupation Span in the Northwestern Great Basin. *Journal of Archaeological Science* 38(2):461–469.
2022 *In the Shadow of the Steamboat: A Natural and Cultural History of North Warner Valley, Oregon.* Anthropological Papers No. 137. University of Utah Press, Salt Lake City.

Smith, Geoffrey M., and Pat Barker
2017 The Terminal Pleistocene/Early Holocene Record in the Northwestern Great Basin: What We Know, What We Don't Know, and How We May Be Wrong. *PaleoAmerica* 3(1):13–47.

Smith, Geoffrey M., Alexander Cherkinsky, Carla Hadden, and Aaron P. Ollivier
2016 The Age and Origin of Olivella Beads from Oregon's LSP-1 Rockshelter: The Oldest Marine Shell Beads in the Northern Great Basin. *American Antiquity* 81(3):550–561.

Smith, Geoffrey M., Daron G. Duke, Dennis L. Jenkins, Ted Goebel, Loren G. Davis, Patrick O'Grady, Dan Stueber, Jordan E. Pratt, and Heather L. Smith
2020 The Western Stemmed Tradition: Problems and Prospects in Paleoindian Archaeology in the Intermountain West. *PaleoAmerica* 6(1):23–42.

Smith, Geoffrey M., Danielle C. Felling, Anthony W. Taylor, and Thomas N. Layton
2015 Evaluating the Stratigraphic and Chronological Integrity of the Last Supper Cave

Deposits. *Journal of California and Great Basin Anthropology* 35(1):99–112.

Smith, Geoffrey M., Danielle C. Felling, Teresa A. Wriston, and Donald D. Pattee
2015 The Surface Paleoindian Record of Northern Warner Valley, Oregon, and Its Bearing on the Temporal and Cultural Separation of Clovis and Western Stemmed Points in the Northern Great Basin. *PaleoAmerica* 1(4):360–373.

Smith, Geoffrey M., and David C. Harvey
2018 Reconstructing Prehistoric Landscape Use at a Regional Scale: A Critical Review of the Lithic Conveyance Zone Concept with a Focus on Its Limitations. *Journal of Archaeological Science: Reports* 19:828–835.

Smith, Geoffrey M., Stephen LaValley, and Craig Skinner
2011 Looking to the North: Results from the XRF Analysis of Pre-Archaic Projectile Points from Hanging Rock Shelter, Nevada. *Current Research in the Pleistocene* 28:81–83.

Smith, Geoffrey M., Emily S. Middleton, and Peter A. Carey
2013 Paleoindian Technological Provisioning Strategies in the Northwestern Great Basin. *Journal of Archaeological Science* 40(12):4180–4188.

Smith, Geoffrey M., Donald D. Pattee, Evan Pellegrini, Judson Bird Finley, and John L. Fagan
2014 A Flaked Stone Crescent from a Stratified, Radiocarbon-Dated Site in the Northern Great Basin. *North American Archaeologist* 35(3):257–276.

Smith, Geoffrey M., Sara Sturtz, Anna J. Camp, Kenneth D. Adams, Elizabeth Kallenbach, Richard L. Rosencrance, and Richard E. Hughes
2022 Leonard Rockshelter Revisited: Evaluating a 70-Year-Old Claim of a Late Pleistocene Human Occupation in the Western Great Basin. *American Antiquity* 87(4):776–793.

Smith, Heather L., and Ted Goebel
2018 Origins and Spread of Fluted-Point Technology in the Canadian Ice-Free Corridor and Eastern Beringia. *Proceedings of the National Academy of Sciences* 115(16):4116–4121.

Smith, Heather L., Jeffery T. Rasic, and Ted Goebel
2013 Biface Traditions of Northern Alaska and Their Role in the Peopling of the Americas. In *Paleoamerican Odyssey*, edited by Kelly E. Graf, Caroline V. Ketron, and Michael R. Waters, pp. 105–123. Center for the Study of the First Americans, Texas A&M University Press, College Station.

Smith, Heather L., Ashley M. Smallwood, and Thomas J. DeWitt
2015 Defining the Normative Range of Clovis Fluted Point Shape Using Geographic Models of Geometric Morphometric Variation. In *Clovis: On the Edge of a New Understanding*, edited by Ashley M. Smallwood and Thomas A. Jennings, pp. 161–180. Center for the Study of the First Americans, Texas A&M University Press, College Station.

Smith, Kevin N.
2021 A Technological Approach to Late Pleistocene and Early Holocene Aquatic Adaptations in the Far West of North America. PhD dissertation, Department of Anthropology, University of California, Davis.

Smith, W. G., and Judith A. Monte
1975 Marshes: The Wet Grasslands. *Geoscience and Man* 11:27–38.

Speer, Charles A., Kenneth C. Reid, Matthew J. Root, and Richard E. Hughes
2019 The Seagull Bay Site—Clovis Technology from American Falls on the Eastern Snake River Plain. *North American Archaeologist* 40(3):148–166.

Speth, John
2018 A New Look at Old Assumptions: Paleoindian Communal Bison Hunting, Mobility, and Stone Tool Technology. In *The Archaeology of Large-Scale Manipulation of Prey: The Economic and Social Dynamics of Mass Hunting*, edited by Kristen Carlson and Leland C. Bement, pp. 161–285. University Press of Colorado, Boulder.

Speth, John D., Khori Newlander, Andrew A. White, Ashley K. Lemke, and Lars E. Anderson
2013 Early Paleoindian Big-Game Hunting in North America: Provisioning or Politics? *Quaternary International* 285:111–139.

Springer, Kathleen B., Jeffrey S. Pigati, Craig R. Manker, and Shannon A. Mahan
2018 *The Las Vegas Formation*. Professional Paper 1839. US Geological Survey, Reston, Virginia.

Stanford, Dennis
1978 The Jones-Miller Site: An Example of Hell

Gap Bison Procurement Strategy. *Plains Anthropologist* 23(82):90–97.
2005 Paleoindian Archaeology and Late Pleistocene Environments in the Plains and Southwestern United States. In *Ice Age Peoples of North America*, edited by Robson Bonnichsen and Karen L. Turnmire, pp. 281–339. 2nd ed. Center for the Study of the First Americans, Texas A&M University Press, College Station.

Stanford, Dennis, and John Albanese
1975 Preliminary Results of the Smithsonian Institution Excavation at the Claypool Site, Washington County, Colorado. *Southwestern Lore* 41(4):22–28.

Steeves, Paulette F. C.
2021 *The Indigenous Paleolithic of the Western Hemisphere*. University of Nebraska Press, Lincoln.

Stephens, Carrie L., and Robert M. Yohe II
2012 A Paleoindian Surface Collection from Rose Valley, California. *Proceedings of the Society for California Archaeology* 26:179–191.

Stephens, David W., and John R. Krebs
1986 *Foraging Theory*. Princeton University Press, Princeton, NJ.

Stewart, Mathew, W. Christopher Carleton, and Huw S. Groucutt
2021 Climate Change, Not Human Population Growth, Correlates with Late Quaternary Megafauna Declines in North America. *Nature Communications* 12(1):965.

Stibbard-Hawkes, Duncan N. E.
2019 Costly Signaling and the Handicap Principle in Hunter-Gatherer Research: A Critical Review. *Evolutionary Anthropology: Issues, News, and Reviews* 28(3):144–157.

Story, Brett A., Metin I. Eren, Kaitlyn Thomas, Briggs Buchanan, and David J. Meltzer
2019 Why Are Clovis Fluted Points More Resilient than Non-Fluted Lanceolate Points? A Quantitative Assessment of Breakage Patterns between Experimental Models. *Archaeometry* 61(1):1–13.

Straus, Lawrence Guy, David J. Meltzer, and Ted Goebel
2005 Ice Age Atlantis? Exploring the Solutrean-Clovis "Connection." *World Archaeology* 37(4):507–532.

Stuart, David E,
2009 *The Ancient Southwest: Chaco Canyon, Bandelier, and Mesa Verde*. University of New Mexico Press, Albuquerque.

Stuart, David E., and Rory P. Gauthier
1996 *Prehistoric New Mexico, Background for Survey*. University of New Mexico Press, Albuquerque.

Stueber, Daniel, and Richard L. Rosencrance
2021 An Updated View from Redfish Overhang: Western Stemmed Technology and Chronology in Custer County, Idaho. Paper presented at 37th Great Basin Anthropological Conference, Las Vegas, Nevada.

Stueber, Daniel O., and Craig E. Skinner
2015 Glass Buttes, Oregon: 14,000 Years of Continuous Use. In *Toolstone Geography of the Pacific Northwest*, edited by Terry L. Ozbun and Ron L. Adams, pp. 193–207. Archaeology Press, Simon Fraser University, Burnaby, British Columbia, Canada.

Stuiver, Minze, and Henry A. Polach
1977 Reporting of 14C Data. *Radiocarbon* 19(3):355–363.

Stuiver, Minze, P. J. Reimer, and R. W. Reimer
2020 CALIB 7.1. Electronic program, http://calib.org, accessed March 10, 2020.

Suárez, Rafael
2017 The Human Colonization of the Southeast Plains of South America: Climatic Conditions, Technological Innovations and the Peopling of Uruguay and South of Brazil. *Quaternary International* 431:181–193.

Surovell, Todd A.
2009 *Toward a Behavioral Ecology of Lithic Technology: Cases from Paleoindian Archaeology*. University of Arizona Press, Tucson.

Surovell, Todd A., Sarah A. Allaun, Barbara A. Crass, Joseph A. M. Gingerich, Kelly E. Graf, Charles E. Holmes, Robert L. Kelly et al.
2022 Late Date of Human Arrival to North America: Continental Scale Differences in Stratigraphic Integrity of Pre-13,000 BP Archaeological Sites. *PLOS One* 17(4): e0264092.

Surovell, Todd A., Joshua R. Boyd, C. Vance Haynes Jr., and Gregory W. L. Hodgins
2016 On the Dating of the Folsom Complex and Its Correlation with the Younger Dryas, the End of Clovis, and Megafaunal Extinction. *PaleoAmerica* 2(2):81–89.

Surovell, Todd A., Judson Byrd Finley, Geoffrey M. Smith, P. Jeffrey Brantingham, and Robert Kelly
2009   Correcting Temporal Frequency Distributions for Taphonomic Bias. *Journal of Archaeological Science* 36(8):1715–1724.

Surovell, Todd A., Spencer R. Pelton, Richard Anderson-Sprecher, and Adam D. Myers
2016   Test of Martin's Overkill Hypothesis Using Radiocarbon Dates on Extinct Megafauna. *Proceedings of the National Academy of Sciences of the United States of America* 113(4):886–891.

Surovell, Todd A., and Nicole M. Waguespack
2008   How Many Elephant Kills Are 14? Clovis Mammoth and Mastodon Kills in Context. *Quaternary International* 191(1):82–97.
2009   Human Prey Choice in the Late Pleistocene and Its Relation to Megafaunal Extinctions. In *American Megafaunal Extinctions at the End of the Pleistocene*, edited by Gary Haynes, pp. 77–105. Springer, Dordrecht, Netherlands.

Susia, Margaret
1964   *Tule Springs Archaeological Surface Survey*. 12th ed. Nevada State Museum, Carson City.

Sutton, Mark Q.
2017   The "Fishing Link": Salmonids and the Initial Peopling of the Americas. *PaleoAmerica* 3(3):231–259.
2018a Paleoindian Colonization by Boat? Refining the Coastal Model. *PaleoAmerica* 4(4):325–339.
2018b From the Late Pleistocene to the Middle Archaic in the Mojave Desert: A Past Evolving. In *The Archaic of the American Southwest*, edited by Bradley J. Vierra, pp. 31–51. University of Utah Press, Salt Lake City.
2019   Reassessing the Paleoindian Witt Archaeological Locality, Tulare Lake, San Joaquin Valley, California. *PaleoAmerica* 5(3):276–299.
2021   Envisioning a Western Clovis Ritual Complex. *PaleoAmerica* 7(4):333–364.

Sutton, Mark Q., Mark E. Basgall, J. K. Gardner, and M. W. Allen
2007   Advances in Understanding Mojave Desert Prehistory. In *California Prehistory: Colonization, Culture, and Complexity*, edited by Terry L. Jones and K. A. Klar, pp. 229–245. AltaMira Press, New York.

Swanson, Earl H.
1972   *Birch Creek: Human Ecology in the Cool Desert of the Northern Rocky Mountains BC 9000 to AD 1850*. Idaho State University Press, Pocatello.

Swanson, Earl H., B. Robert Butler, and Robson Bonnichsen
1964   *Birch Creek Papers No. 2: Cultural Stratigraphy in the Birch Creek Valley, Eastern Idaho*. Occasional Papers of the Idaho State University Museum No. 13. Idaho State University, Pocatello.

Swanson, Earl Herbert, and Paul G. Sneed
1966   *The Archaeology of the Shoup Rockshelters in East Central Idaho*. Occasional Papers of the Idaho State University Museum No. 17. Idaho State University, Pocatello.

Tamers, M. A., F. J. Pearson Jr., and E. M. Davis
1964   University of Texas Radiocarbon Dates II. *Radiocarbon* 6(1):138–159.

Taylor, Amanda
2002   Results of a Great Basin Fluted Point Survey: Chronological and Functional Relationships between Fluted and Stemmed Points. Senior thesis, Department of Anthropology, Hamilton College, Clinton, New York.
2005   Great Basin Fluted Point Database. Electronic document, https://pidba.org/content/nevada/greatbasin_fluted pointsurvey_taylor2003.xls, accessed August 11, 2023.

Taylor, Amanda, and Charlotte Beck
2015   Artifact Analysis. In *Results of Data Recovery at the Bear Creek Site (45KI1839), King County, Washington, Volume I: Report*, edited by Robert E. Kopperl, pp. 131–208. Prepared by SWCA Environmental Consultants, Seattle, Washington.

Taylor, Anthony, Jarod M. Hutson, Vaughn M. Bryant, and Dennis L. Jenkins
2020   Dietary Items in Early to Late Holocene Human Coprolites from Paisley Caves, Oregon, USA. *Palynology* 44(1):12–23.

Taylor, Royal E., C. Vance Haynes Jr., and Minze Stuiver
1996   Clovis and Folsom Age Estimates: Stratigraphic Context and Radiocarbon Calibration. *Antiquity* 70:515–525.

Thatcher, Jennifer J.
2001 The Distribution of Geologic and Artifact Obsidian from the Silver Lake/Sycan Marsh Geochemical Source Group, South-Central Oregon. Master's thesis, Interdisciplinary Studies, Oregon State University, Corvallis.

Thomas, David H.
1981 How to Classify the Projectile Points from Monitor Valley, Nevada. *Journal of California and Great Basin Anthropology* 3(1):7–43.
1986 Points on Points: A Reply to Flenniken and Raymond. *American Antiquity* 51(3): 619–627.

Thomas, Kaitlyn A., Brett A. Story, Metin I. Eren, Briggs Buchanan, Brian N. Andres, Michael J. O'Brien, and David J. Meltzer
2017 Explaining the Origin of Fluting in North American Pleistocene Weaponry. *Journal of Archaeological Science* 81:23–30.

Thomas, Scott P., and Patrick O'Grady
2006 Fluted Projectile Points: A Close Examination of Finds from Burns District BLM Lands in the Northern Great Basin. Paper presented at the 30th Biennial Great Basin Anthropological Conference, Las Vegas.

Thomas, Scott P., Patrick W. O'Grady, and Michael F. Rondeau
2011 New Finds and Related Obsidian Studies at the Sage Hen Gap Fluted-Point Site, Harney County, Oregon. *Current Research in the Pleistocene* 28:89–91.

Thompson, Robert S.
1985 The Age and Environment of the Mount Moriah (Lake Mohave) Occupation at Smith Creek Cave, Nevada. In *Environments and Extinctions: Man in Late Glacial North America*, edited by Jim I. Mead and David J. Meltzer, pp. 111–119. Center for the Study of Early Man, University of Maine, Orono.

Thulman, David K.
2012 Discriminating Paleoindian Point Types from Florida Using Landmark Geometric Morphometrics. *Journal of Archaeological Science* 39(5):1599–1607.

Titmus, Gene L., and James C. Woods
1991a Fluted Points from the Snake River Plain. In *Clovis: Origins and Adaptations*, edited by Robson Bonnichsen and Karen L. Turnmire, pp. 119–131. Center for the Study of the First Americans, Oregon State University, Corvallis.
1991b A Closer Look at Margin "Grinding" on Folsom and Clovis Points. *Journal of California and Great Basin Anthropology* 12(2):194–203.

Tukey, John W.
1977 *Exploratory Data Analysis*. Addison-Wesley, Reading, Massachusetts.

Tune, Jesse W.
2020 Hunter-Gatherer Occupation of the Central Colorado Plateau during the Pleistocene–Holocene Transition. *American Antiquity* 85(3):573–590.

Tuohy, Donald R.
1968 Some Early Lithic Sites in Western Nevada. In *Early Man in Western North America*, edited by Cynthia Irwin-Williams, pp. 27–48. Eastern New Mexico University Contributions in Anthropology No 1. Portales.
1969 Breakage, Burin Facets, and the Probable Technological Linkage Among Lake Mohave, Silver Lake, and Other Varieties of Projectile Points in the Desert West. In *Miscellaneous Papers on Nevada Archaeology 1–8*, pp. 132–162. Anthropological Papers No. 14. Nevada State Museum, Carson City.
1970 The Coleman Locality: A Basalt Quarry and Workshop near Falcon Hill, Nevada. In *Five Papers on the Desert West*, edited by Donald R. Tuohy, Doris L. Rendell, and Pamela A. Crowell, pp. 143–206. Anthropological Papers No. 15. Nevada State Museum, Carson City.
1974 A Comparative Study of Late Paleoindian Manifestations in the Western Great Basin. In *Holocene Environmental Change in the Great Basin*, edited by Robert G. Elston, pp. 91–116. Research Paper No. 6. Nevada Archaeological Survey, Reno.
1988 Paleoindian and Early Archaic Cultural Complexes from Three Central Nevada Localities. In *Early Human Occupation in Far Western North America: The Clovis-Archaic Interface*, edited by Judith A. Willig, C. Melvin Aikens, and John L. Fagan, pp. 217–230. Anthropological Papers No. 21. Nevada State Museum, Carson City.

Tuohy, Donald R., and Amy J. Dansie
1997 New Information Regarding Early Holocene Manifestations in the Western Great Basin. *Nevada Historical Society Quarterly* 40(1):24–53.

Tuohy, Donald R., and Thomas N. Layton
1977 Towards the Establishment of a New Series of Great Basin Projectile Points. *Nevada Archaeological Survey Reporter* 10(6):1–5.

Turnbow, Christopher
1997 Projectile Points as Chronological Indicators. In *OLE Volume II: Artifacts*, edited by John C. Acklen, pp. 161–230. Prepared for TRC Mariah Associates and Public Service Company of New Mexico, Albuquerque.

Ugan, Andrew, Jason Bright, and A. Rogers
2003 When Is Technology Worth the Trouble? *Journal of Archaeological Science* 30(10):1315–1329.

Ugan, Andrew, and David Byers
2007 Geographic and Temporal Trends in Proboscidean and Human Radiocarbon Histories during the Late Pleistocene. *Quaternary Science Reviews* 26(25–28):3058–3080.

Van Klinken, Gert J.
1999 Bone Collagen Quality Indicators for Palaeodietary and Radiocarbon Measurements. *Journal of Archaeological Science* 26(6):687–695.

VanPool, Todd L., and Robert D. Leonard
2011 *Quantitative Analysis in Archaeology*. Wiley-Blackwell, Oxford, England.

Vellanoweth, René L., Melissa Lambright, Jon M. Erlandson, and Torben C. Rick
2003 Early New World Perishable Technologies: Sea Grass Cordage, Shell Beads, and a Bone Tool from Cave of the Chimneys, San Miguel Island, California. *Journal of Archaeological Science* 30(9):1161–1173.

Vetter, Lael
2007 Paleoecology of Pleistocene Megafauna in Southern Nevada, USA: Isotopic Evidence for Browsing on Halophytic Plants. Master's thesis, Department of Geoscience, University of Nevada, Las Vegas.

Vierra, Bradley J.
2012 Projectile Point Technology: Understanding Relationships between Tool Design and Hunting Tactics. In *Survey and Evaluation of 5,425.1 Acres in the Northern Maneuver Areas in Support of Engineering Training and New Firing Boxes, Doña Ana and Otero Counties, New Mexico*, edited by Bradley J. Vierra, C. G. Ward and T. P. Mills, pp. 275–290. Historic and Natural Resources Report No. 12–08. Submitted to the Directorate of Public Works, Environmental Division, Fort Bliss, Texas.

Vierra, Bradley J. (editor)
2018 *The Archaic Southwest: Foragers in an Arid Land*. University of Utah Press, Salt Lake City.

Vierra, Bradley J., Richard I. Ford, and Stephen S. Post
2018 Archaic Foragers of the Northern Rio Grande. In *The Archaic Southwest: Foragers in an Arid Land*, edited by Bradley J. Vierra, pp. 235–253. University of Utah Press, Salt Lake City.

Vierra, Bradley J., Margaret A. Jodry, M. Steven Shackley, and Michael J. Dilley
2012 Late Paleoindian and Early Archaic Foragers in the Northern Southwest. In *From the Pleistocene to the Holocene: Human Organization and Cultural Transformations in Prehistoric North America*, edited by C. Britt Bousman and Bradley J. Vierra, pp. 171–196. Center for the Study of the First Americans, Texas A&M University Press, College Station.

Villa, Paola
1982 Conjoinable Pieces and Site Formation Processes. *American Antiquity* 47(2):276–290.

Villa, Paola, Paolo Boscato, Filomena Ranaldo, and Anna Ronchitelli
2009 Stone Tools for the Hunt: Points with Impact Scars from a Middle Paleolithic Site in Southern Italy. *Journal of Archaeological Science* 36(3):850–859.

Villa, Paola, and Michel Lenoir
2006 Hunting Weapons of the Middle Stone Age and the Middle Palaeolithic: Spear Points from Sibudu, Rose Cottage and Bouheben. *Southern African Humanities* 18(1):89–122.

2009 Hunting and Hunting Weapons of the Lower and Middle Paleolithic of Europe. In *The Evolution of Hominid Diets: Integrating Approaches to the Study of Palaeolithic Subsistence*, edited by Jean-

Jacques Hublin and Michael P. Richards, pp. 59–85. Springer, Dordrecht, Netherlands.

Villa, Paola, Marie Soressi, Christopher S. Henshilwood, and Vincent Mourre
2009 The Still Bay Points of Blombos Cave (South Africa). *Journal of Archaeological Science* 36(2):441–460.

Wagner, Daniel P., and Joseph M. McAvoy
2004 Pedoarchaeology of Cactus Hill, a Sandy Paleoindian Site in Southeastern Virginia, USA. *Geoarchaeology* 19(4):297–322.

Waguespack, Nicole M.
2013 Pleistocene Extinctions: The State of Evidence and the Structure of Debate. In *Paleoamerican Odyssey*, edited by Kelly E. Graf, Caroline V. Ketron, and Michael R. Waters, pp. 311–319. Center for the Study of the First Americans, Texas A&M University Press, College Station.

Waguespack, Nicole M., and Todd A. Surovell
2003 Clovis Hunting Strategies, or How to Make Out on Plentiful Resources. *American Antiquity* 68(2):333–352.

Waguespack, Nicole M., Todd A. Surovell, Allen Denoyer, Alice Dallow, Adam Savage, Jamie Hyneman, and Dan Tapster
2009 Making a Point: Wood- Versus Stone-Tipped Projectiles. *Antiquity* 83(321):786–800.

Wallace, William J.
1955 A Suggested Chronology for Southern California Coastal Archaeology. *Southwest Journal of Anthropology* 11(3):214–230.

Wallace, William J., and Francis A. Riddell
1988 Prehistoric Background of Tulare Lake, California. In *Early Human Occupation in Far Western North America: The Clovis–Archaic Interface*, edited by Judith A. Willig, C. Melvin Aikens, and John L. Fagan, pp. 87–102. Anthropological Papers No. 21. Nevada State Museum, Carson City.

Warren, Claude N.
1967 The San Dieguito Complex: A Review and Hypothesis. *American Antiquity* 32(2):168–185.
1984 The Desert Region. In *California Archaeology*, edited by Michael J. Moratto, pp. 339–430. Academic Press, Orlando, Florida.
1991 Archaeological Investigations at Nelson Wash, Fort Irwin, California. Fort Irwin Archaeological Project Research Report No. 23. Coyote Press, Salinas, California.
2002 Time, Form, and Variability: Lake Mojave and Pinto Periods in Mojave Desert Prehistory. In *Essays in California Archaeology: A Memorial to Franklin Fenenga*, edited by William J. Wallace and Francis A. Riddell, pp. 129–141. Contributions of the Archaeological Research Facility No. 60. University of California, Berkeley.

Warren, Claude N. (editor)
1966 *The San Dieguito Type Site: M. J. Rogers' 1938 Excavation of the San Dieguito River.* San Diego Museum Papers No. 5. San Diego, California.

Warren, Claude N., and Robert H. Crabtree
1986 Prehistory of the Southwestern Area. In *Great Basin*, edited by Warren L. d'Azevedo, pp. 183–193. Handbook of North American Indians, Vol. 11, William C. Sturtevant, general editor. Smithsonian Institution, Washington, DC.

Warren, Claude N., and H. Thomas Ore
2004a Data Recovery at Pleistocene Lake Mojave: Sites CA-SBR-140, CA-SBR-6566, CA-SBR-264. In *Kern River 2003 Expansion Project: California Cultural Resources Data Recovery Project*, Vol. 2, edited by L. M. Blair, J. R. Wedding, S. F. Rose, J. E. Riddle, and A. J. Smith, pp. 39–56. Report submitted to the Federal Energy Regulatory Commission, Washington, DC.
2004b Geological Context of Lake Mojave Cultural Assemblages at Lake Mojave. In *Kern River 2003 Expansion Project: California Cultural Resources Data Recovery Project*, Vol. 2, edited by L. M. Blair, J. R. Wedding, S. F. Rose, J. E. Riddle, and A. J. Smith, pp. 57–77. Report submitted to the Federal Energy Regulatory Commission, Washington, DC.
2011 The Age of the San Dieguito Artifact Assemblage at the C. W. Harris Site. *Journal of California and Great Basin Anthropology* 31(1):81–97.

Warren, Claude N., and Carl Phagan
1988 Fluted Points in the Mojave Desert: Their Technology and Cultural Context. In *Early Human Occupation in Far Western North America: The Clovis–Archaic*

Interface, edited by Judith A. Willig, C. Melvin Aikens, and John L. Fagan, pp. 121–130. Anthropological Papers No. 21. Nevada State Museum, Carson City.

Warren, Claude N., and Anthony J. Ranere
1968 Outside Danger Cave: A View of Early Man in the Great Basin. In *Early Man in Western North American*, edited by Cynthia Irwin-Williams, pp. 6–18. Contributions in Anthropology, Vol. 1, No. 4. Eastern New Mexico University, Portales.

Warren, Claude N., and Joan S. Schneider
2017 *The Purple Hummingbird: A Biography of Elizabeth Warder Crozer Campbell*. University of Utah Press, Salt Lake City.

Warren, Claude N., and D. L. True
1961 The San Dieguito Complex and Its Place in California Prehistory. In *University of California Archaeological Survey, Annual Report*, pp. 246–291. University of California, Los Angeles.

Waters, Michael R.
2019 Late Pleistocene Exploration and Settlement of the Americas by Modern Humans. *Science* 365(6449):eaat5447.

Waters, Michael R., Steven L. Forman, Thomas A. Jennings, Lee C. Nordt, Steven G. Driese, Joshua M. Feinberg, Joshua L. Keene et al.
2011 The Buttermilk Creek Complex and the Origins of Clovis at the Debra L. Friedkin Site, Texas. *Science* 331(6024): 1599–1603.

Waters, Michael R., Ted Goebel, and Kelly E. Graf
2020 The Stemmed Point Tradition of Western North America. *PaleoAmerica* 6(1):1–3.

Waters, Michael R., Joshua L. Keene, Steven L. Forman, Elton R. Prewitt, David L. Carlson, and James E. Wiederhold
2018 Pre-Clovis Projectile Points at the Debra L. Friedkin Site, Texas– Implications for the Late Pleistocene Peopling of the Americas. *Science Advances* 4(10):eaat4505.

Waters, Michael R., Charlotte D. Pevny, and David L. Carlson
2011 *Clovis Lithic Technology: Investigation of a Stratified Workshop at the Gault Site, Texas*. Center for the Study of the First Americans, Texas A&M University Press, College Station.

Waters, Michael R., and Thomas W. Stafford
2007a Redefining the Age of Clovis: Implications for the Peopling of the Americas. *Science* 315:1122–1126.
2007b Response to Comment on "Redefining the Age of Clovis: Implications for the Peopling of the Americas." *Science* 317 (5836):320.
2014 Redating the Mill Iron Site, Montana: A Reexamination of Goshen Complex Chronology. *American Antiquity* 79(3): 541–548.

Waters, Michael R., Thomas W. Stafford, and David L. Carlson
2020 The Age of Clovis—13,050 to 12,750 cal yr BP. *Science Advances* 6(43):eaaz0455.

Waters, Michael R., Thomas W. Stafford, Brian Kooyman, and L. V. Hills
2015 Late Pleistocene Horse and Camel Hunting at the Southern Margin of the Ice-Free Corridor: Reassessing the Age of Wally's Beach, Canada. *Proceedings of the National Academy of Sciences* 112(14): 4263–4267.

Waters, Michael R., Thomas W. Stafford, H. Gregory McDonald, Carl Gustafson, Morten Rasmussen, Enrico Cappellini, Jasper V. Olsen et al.
2011 Pre-Clovis Mastodon Hunting 13,800 Years Ago at the Manis Site, Washington. *Science* 334(6054):351–353.

Watts, Jack L.
2013 The Culture of Santarosae: Subsistence Strategies and Landscape Use in the Northern Channel Islands from the Initial Occupation. PhD dissertation, Kellogg College, Oxford University, Oxford, England.

Wells, Stephen G., William J. Brown, Yehouda Enzel, Roger Y. Anderson, and Leslie D. McFadden
2003 Late Quaternary Geology and Paleohydrology of Pluvial Lake Mojave, Southern California. In *Paleoenvironments and Paleohydrology of the Mojave and Southern Great Basin Deserts*, edited by Yehouda Enzel, Stephen G. Wells, and Nicholas Lancaster, pp. 79–114. Special Paper No. 368. Geological Society of America, Boulder, Colorado.

Werner, Angelia, Kathleen Jones, G. Logan Miller, Briggs Buchanan, Matthew T. Boulanger, Alastair J. M. Key, Crystal Reedy, Michelle R. Bebber, and Metin I. Eren
2017 The Morphometrics and Microwear of a Small Clovis Assemblage from Guern-

sey County, Southeastern Ohio, USA. *Journal of Archaeological Science: Reports* 15:318–329.

Werner, Angelia, Andrew Kramer, Crystal Reedy, Michelle R. Bebber, Justin Pargeter, and Metin I. Eren
2018   Experimental Assessment of Proximal-Lateral Edge Grinding on Haft Damage Using Replicated Late Pleistocene (Clovis) Stone Projectile Points. *Archaeological and Anthropological Sciences* 11(11): 5833–5849.

White, Andrew A.
2013   Functional and Stylistic Variability in Paleoindian and Early Archaic Projectile Points from Midcontinental North America. *North American Archaeologist* 34(1):71–108.

Wigand, Peter E., and David Rhode
2002   Great Basin Vegetation History and Aquatic Systems: The Last 150,000 Years. In *Great Basin Aquatic Systems History*, edited by Robert Hershler, David B. Madsen, and Donald R. Currey, pp. 309–367. Smithsonian Contributions to the Earth Sciences No. 33. Smithsonian Institution Press, Washington, DC.

Wilke, Philip J., J. Jeffrey Flenniken, and Terry. L. Ozbun
1991   Clovis Technology at the Anzick Site, Montana. *Journal of California and Great Basin Anthropology* 12(2):242–272.

Wilkins, Jayne, Benjamin J. Schoville, and Kyle S. Brown
2014   An Experimental Investigation of the Functional Hypothesis and Evolutionary Advantage of Stone-Tipped Spears. *PLoS ONE* 9(8):e104514.

Wilkins, Jayne, Benjamin Schoville, Kyle S. Brown, and Michael Chazan
2012   Evidence for Early Hafted Hunting Technology. *Science* 338(6109):942–946.

Willerslev, Eske, and David J. Meltzer
2021   Peopling of the Americas as Inferred from Ancient Genomics. *Nature* 594(7863): 356–364.

Williams, John W., Bryan N. Shuman, Thompson Webb III, Patrick J. Bartlein, and Phillip L. Leduc
2004   Late-Quaternary Vegetation Dynamics in North America: Scaling from Taxa to Biomes. *Ecological Monographs* 74(2): 309–334.

Williams, Thomas J., Michael B. Collins, Kathleen Rodrigues, William Jack Rink, Nancy Velchoff, Amanda Keen-Zebert, Anastasia Gilmer, Charles D. Frederick, Sergio J. Ayala, and Elton R. Prewitt
2018   Evidence of an Early Projectile Point Technology in North America at the Gault Site, Texas, USA. *Science Advances* 4(7):eaar5954.

Williams, Thomas J., and David B. Madsen
2020   The Upper Paleolithic of the Americas. *PaleoAmerica* 6(1):4–22.

Willig, Judith A.
1988   Paleo-Archaic Adaptations and Lakeside Settlement Patterns in the Northern Alkali Basin. In *Early Human Occupation in Far Western North America: The Clovis–Archaic Interface*, edited by Judith A. Willig, C. Melvin Aikens, and John L. Fagan, pp. 417–482. Anthropological Papers No. 21. Nevada State Museum Carson City.
1989   Paleo-Archaic Broad Spectrum Adaptations at the Pleistocene–Holocene Boundary in Far Western North America. PhD dissertation, Department of Anthropology, University of Oregon, Eugene.
1991   Clovis Technology and Adaptation in Far Western North America: Regional Pattern and Environmental Context. In *Clovis: Origins and Adaptations*, edited by Robson Bonnichsen and Karen L. Turnmire, pp. 91–118. Center for the Study of the First Americans, Oregon State University, Corvallis.

Willig, Judith A., and C. Melvin Aikens
1988   The Clovis–Archaic Interface in Far Western North America. In *Early Human Occupation in Far Western North America: The Clovis–Archaic Interface*, edited by Judith A. Willig, C. Melvin Aikens, and John L. Fagan, pp. 1–40. Anthropological Papers No. 21. Nevada State Museum, Carson City.

Willig, Judith A., C. Melvin Aikens, and John L. Fagan (editors)
1988   *Early Human Occupation in Far Western North America: The Clovis–Archaic Interface*. Anthropological Papers No. 21. Nevada State Museum, Carson City.

Willis, Samuel C.
2005   Late Pleistocene Technological Organization on the Southern Oregon Coast: Investigations at Indian Sands (35CU67-C).

Master's thesis, Department of Anthropology, Oregon State University, Corvallis.

Wilmsen, Edwin N., and Frank H. H. Roberts Jr.
1978 *Lindenmeier, 1934–1974, Concluding Report on Investigations.* Smithsonian Contributions to Anthropology No. 24. Smithsonian Institution, Washington, DC.
1984 *Lindenmeier, 1934–1974, Concluding Report on Investigations.* Smithsonian Contributions to Anthropology No. 24. Reprinted. Originally published 1978. Smithsonian Institution, Washington, DC.

Wilson, Michael C., Stephen N. Kenady, and Randall S. Schalk
2009 Late Pleistocene Bison Antiquus from Orcas Island, Washington, and the Biogeographic Importance of an Early Postglacial Land Mammal Dispersal Corridor from the Mainland to Vancouver Island. *Quaternary Research* 71(1):49–61.

Wohlgemuth, Eric
2006 *Cultural Resources Inventory and Evaluation of Select High Probability Areas in the Southern Corridor Area, Fort Irwin National Training Center, San Bernardino, California.* Report prepared by Far Western Anthropological Research Group. Submitted to US Army National Training Center, Fort Irwin, California.

Wolfe, Allison L., and Jack M. Broughton
2020 A Foraging Theory Perspective on the Associational Critique of North American Pleistocene Overkill. *Journal of Archaeological Science* 119:105162.
2021 More on Overkill, the Associational Critique, and the North American Megafaunal Record: A Reply to Grayson et al. (2021). *Journal of Archaeological Science* 128:105313.

Wood, Janice, and Ben Fitzhugh
2018 Wound Ballistics: The Prey Specific Implications of Penetrating Trauma Injuries from Osseous, Flaked Stone, and Composite Inset Microblade Projectiles during the Pleistocene/Holocene Transition, Alaska, USA. *Journal of Archaeological Science* 91:104–117.

Woods, James C., and Gene L. Titmus
1985 A Review of the Simon Clovis Collection. *Idaho Archaeologist* 8(1):3–8.

Wormington, H. Marie
1939 *Ancient Man in North America.* Popular Series No. 4. Denver Museum of Natural History, Denver, Colorado.
1948 A Proposed Revision of Yuma Point Terminology. *Proceedings of the Colorado Museum of Natural History* 28(2):3–19.
1957 *Ancient Man in North America.* Popular Series No. 4. 4th ed. Denver Museum of Natural History, Denver, Colorado.

Wriston, Teresa A.
2003 The Weed Lake Ditch Site: An Early Holocene Occupation on the Shore of Pluvial Lake Malheur, Harney Basin, Oregon. Master's thesis, Department of Anthropology, University of Nevada, Reno.

Wriston, Teresa A., and Geoffrey M. Smith
2017 Late Pleistocene to Holocene History of Lake Warner and Its Prehistoric Occupations, Warner Valley, Oregon (USA). *Quaternary Research* 88(3):491–51.

Young, D. Craig
1998 Late Holocene Landscapes and Prehistoric Land Use in Warner Valley, Oregon. PhD dissertation, Department of Anthropology, University of Nevada, Reno.

Zancanella, John K.
1988 Early Lowland Prehistory in Southcentral Nevada. In *Early Human Occupation in Far Western North America: The Clovis-Archaic Interface*, edited by Judith A. Willig, C. Melvin Aikens, and John L. Fagan, pp. 251–272. Anthropological Papers No. 21. Nevada State Museum, Carson City.

Zeigler, Kate
2018 Geology of Lithic Artifacts Observed at 23 Archaeological Sites in the WSMR 414 Project Area, Southern White Sands Missile Range. In *Archaeology of the White Sands Missile Range: Evaluation of 36 Sites and Implementation of Site Protective Measures between Highway 70 and Nike Avenue, Otero and Doña Ana Counties, New Mexico, Volume 3: Analyses and Appendices*, compiled by Alexander Kurota, Evan Sternberg, and Robert Dello-Russo, pp. 49:1–10. WSMR Report No. 913. Prepared for William Godby, Department of the Army. Copies available from the Office of Contract Archaeology, Albuquerque, New Mexico.

Contributors

Pat Barker
Nevada State Museum
Carson City, NV

Charlotte Beck
Department of Anthropology
Hamilton College
Clinton, NY

Todd J. Braje
Museum of Natural and Cultural History
University of Oregon
Eugene, OR

Loren G. Davis
Department of Anthropology
Oregon State University
Corvallis, WA

Caitlin Doherty
Center for the Study of the First Americans
Department of Anthropology
Texas A&M University
College Station, TX

John W. Dougherty
PAR Environmental Services
Sacramento, CA

Daron Duke
Far Western Anthropological Research Group
Henderson, NV

Jon M. Erlandson
Museum of Natural and Cultural History
University of Oregon
Eugene, OR

Nicole D. George
Artemisia Archaeological Research Fund
Department of Anthropology
University of Nevada
Reno, NV

Kristina M. Gill
Museum of Natural and Cultural History
University of Oregon
Eugene, OR
Santa Barbara Botanic Garden
Santa Barbara, CA

Ted Goebel
Department of Anthropology
University of Kansas
Lawrence, KS

Amy E. Gusick
Natural History Museum of Los Angeles County
Los Angeles, CA

Amanda Hartman
Great Basin Branch
Far Western Anthropological Research Group
Carson City, NV

Andrew Hoskins
SWCA Environmental Consultants, Inc.
Reno, NV

Sophia Jamaldin
Cultural Resource Analysts, Inc.
Knoxville, TN

Dennis L. Jenkins
Museum of Natural and Cultural History
University of Oregon
Eugene, OR

George T. Jones
Department of Anthropology
Hamilton College
Clinton, NY

Cassandra L. Keyes
Carson National Forest
Taos, NM

Edward J. Knell
Division of Anthropology
California State University
Fullerton, CA

Joshua J. Lynch
Department of Behavioral Sciences
Arkansas Tech University
Russellville, AR

Katelyn N. McDonough
Department of Anthropology
Museum of Natural and Cultural History
University of Oregon
Eugene, OR

David J. Meltzer
Department of Anthropology
Southern Methodist University
Dallas, TX

Jordan E. Pratt
Center for the Study of the First Americans
Department of Anthropology
Texas A&M University
College Station, TX

Derek J. Reaux
Tennessee Valley Authority
Knoxville, TN

Torben C. Rick
Department of Anthropology
National Museum of Natural History
Smithsonian Institution
Washington, DC

Michael F. Rondeau
Rondeau Archeological
Sacramento, CA

Richard L. Rosencrance
Artemisia Archaeological Research Fund
Department of Anthropology
University of Nevada
Reno, NV

Geoffrey M. Smith
Artemisia Archaeological Research Fund
Department of Anthropology
University of Nevada
Reno, NV

Daniel Stueber
Department of Anthropology
University of Victoria
Victoria, British Columbia, Canada

Todd A. Surovell
Department of Anthropology
University of Wyoming
Laramie, WY

Mark Q. Sutton
Department of Anthropology
California State University
Bakersfield, CA

Index

Page numbers printed in *italic* type refer to figures or tables.

Agate Basin (Wyoming), 100, *200*, 201–2, *203–7*, *209–10*, 211, 222, 256
Agate Basin point style, 56, 80, 85–86, 91, 92, 99, 100, 102, 103, 109, 111, 199, *202*, *208*, *209*, 211, 215
Agogino, George A., 228
Aikens, C. Melvin, 5, 32, 116, 164
Alaska: and post-Clovis fluted point styles, 83, 184; and Haskett technology, 94, 95
Ames, Kenneth M., 154–55
Amick, Daniel S., 248
Amsden, Charles A., 94, 116, 117
Anasazi Origins Project (AOP), 221, 229
Ancient Man in North America (Wormington 1957), 165, 199–200
Ancient North Eurasian (ANE), and genetic studies of Ancestral Native Americans, 283
Antevs, Ernst, 3
Anzick site (Montana), *200*, *203*, *209*, 283, 286–87, *288*
Arlington Springs site (California), 264–65, 273
Arroyo Cuervo region (New Mexico), 221
atlatls: and hafting process, 86; and Lake Mojave type, 94; and Smith Creek Cave points, 151, 152
Aubrey site (Texas), 155, 166, 278
Awl site (California), *50*, 55

Baichtal, James F., 262, 283
Balter, Michael, 262, 297n10
Barbieri, Joseph, 94
Barger Gulch (Colorado), *200*, *204*, *209*, 211, 256
Barker, Pat, 136
Beacon Island site (North Dakota), *200*, *205*, *209*, 211
Beck, Charlotte, 6–7, 8–9, 12, 15, 23–25, 112n5–6, 117, 118, 126, 149, 150, 168, 169, 184, 227, 229, 234–35, 236, 252, 253, 255, 256, 260, 261n1, 261n4, 278, 279, 280, 284, 286, 287, 294, 295
Bedwell, Stephen F., 4, 12, 32, 33, 60, 90, 92, 175
Bement, Leland C., 256, 257n0

Bettinger, Robert L., 254
biased transmission, and social learning, 243
bifaces: and Clovis technology in Far West, 170–72, 183n3; reduction of and WST points in Far West, 246–55
Binford, Lewis R., 155
bison: Clovis and Folsom points from kill sites, 100, 102; and Clovis migration to Far West, 257; and design of projectile points, 258, 290, 297n11–12; extinct species of in Great Basin, 97
Bison Rockshelter (Idaho), 4
Blackwater Draw (New Mexico), 13, 163, 165, 166, 211, 290
Bølling-Allerød period: and extinction of megafauna in Great Basin, 96; and WST in Intermountain West, 37, 53, 57
Bonneville Basin, 96–97, 126, 137, *141*, 145, *146*, 149, 152
Bonneville Estates Rockshelter (Nevada), 8, 11, 22, 36, *41*, 45–46, *48*, *50*, 53, 54, 56, 88–89, 90, 94, 132, 147, *148*, 149, 152, 264, 280
Bonneville point style, 23, *26*, *27*, 36, 55, 57, *106*
Borax Lake (California), 198
Borden site (California), 114, 115, 117, 119, 123, 130
bow and arrow technology: adoption of in Far West, 254; and hunting of bison, 290
Boyd, Robert, 242, 243, 256
Bradley, Bruce A., 170, 172, 235, 236, 247
Braje, Todd J., 282
Brauner, David R., 160n2
Bryan, Alan L., 3, 6, 11, 14, 17, 23–24, 53, 86, 94–95, 132, 133–35, 152, 153, 240, 280
Buchanan, Briggs, 53, 100, 102, 244, 258
Buhl burial (Idaho), 54, 150
Bullion Mountains (California), 118
Bunny Pits complex (Oregon), 31, 32, 35, *49*, *51–52*
Bureau of Land Management, 185
Butler, B. Robert, 83, 84, 85–86, 91
Buttermilk Creek complex (Texas), 259
Byerly, Ryan, 119

CALIB Radiocarbon Calibration program, 137, 160n1
California, early stemmed points on southern coast of, 270–73. *See also* Northern Channel Islands
California Fluted/Lanceolate Uniform Testing and Evaluation Database (CalFLUTED), 186, 197
Callahan, Errett H., 139, 141, 246–47
Campbell, Elizabeth W., 3, 17, 94, 116
Cannon, Michael D., 180
Cardwell Bluffs (California), 266, 268
Carlson, Roy L., 56
Carter, Brian J., 256, 257
Carter/Kerr-McGee site (Colorado), 211, 228
Casper site (Colorado), 228, 229
Catnip Creek Delta Locality (Oregon), 62–63, 69, 70–71, 74, 76
Cavalli-Sforza, Luigi L., 242
Center for the Study of the First Americans (CSFA) (Texas A&M University), 13, 137
chaîne opératoire, and Haskett points, 80
Channel Islands. *See* Northern Channel Islands; Santarosae Island
Channel Islands Amol (CIA) and Channel Islands Barbed (CIB) points, 262, 266–70, 272, 273, 287, 297n10
Chapin, Nicolas, 222, 223, 227, 229, 236, 237–38
Charlie Range Basalt Ridge (California), 115
Charnov, Eric L., 178
chert: availability of on Columbia Plateau, 251; and Clovis points in Intermountain West, 103; and geographic variability of fluted points in Far West, 186, 194, 196; and Levallois-like points in Far West, 249; and morphology of projectile points from Mojave Desert, 123, *124*, 126, *128*; and raw-material procurement at Smith Creek Cave, 137; sources of for Northern Channel Islands, 268. *See also* toolstone
China Lake (California), 117, 119, 123, 125–26, 130
Christian, Leif J., 63
chronology: absolute and relative of stemmed and fluted points in Great Plains and Rocky Mountains, 199–215; of Clovis and WST in Far West, 164, 173–75, 277–81; of Jay type points, 222–23; "long" and "short" Clovis chronologies in Great Plains and Southwest, 155; of Paleocoastal assemblages from Northern Channel Islands, 269–70; and place of WST within debate on peopling of the Americas, 8–12; of WST in Intermountain West, 21–58.

See also Bølling-Allerød period; Early Archaic; Early Holocene; Pleistocene; Younger Dryas
cladistic analysis, of fluted points from Far West, 169
Clovis: chronological and morphological relationship between Western Stemmed, other Paleoindian techno-complexes, and, 277–81; chronology of in Great Plains-Rocky Mountains (GPRM) region, 56, 57, *203–205, 208, 209*, 211, 213, 214, 279; confusion of with other fluted point technologies, 115; cultural transmission and interaction of with WST peoples in Far West, 240–61; and history of fluted point research, 3–4, 7, 12–13; and parallels to Haskett technology in Great Basin, 79–111; as predated by WST in Columbia River Plateau, 153–60; predator-prey relationship and design of projectile points, 289; review of record in Far West, 163–83, 283–93. *See also* fluted technologies
Clovis-first hypothesis, for peopling of Americas, 176, 240, 263
"Clovis-like," use of term, 169, 261n4
Clovis Paleoindian Tradition (CPT), evidence for in Columbia River Plateau, 153, 155–59
Cochran, Bruce, 160n2
Cody complex, 198, 201–202, *203–207*, 208, *209–10*
Colby site (Wyoming), 83
Coleman site (Nevada), 92
Collard, Mark, 256
Collier Dune (New Mexico), 222
Collins, Michael B., 169–70, 172
Columbia River Plateau, comparative dates of Clovis and WST in, 153–60. *See also* Far West
conformist bias, and cultural transmission, 243
Connley Caves (Oregon), 4, 11, 31, 32, 33, *34*, 35, 39–41, *44*, 60–61, 65, 66–67, 69, *74*, 75, 90, 92, 173, *174*, 175
Connolly, Thomas J., 12, 35, 62
"contracting stemmed," use of term, 16, 27, 29, 35, 117, 136, 141, 159, 160n3, 220, 227, 266
Cooper's Ferry (Idaho), 1, 9, 10, 11, 14–15, 37, *38*, 53, 57, 59–60, 132, 153–60, 178, 181–82, 244, 249, 251, 259, 261n3, 278, 295
Coso Volcanic Field (CVF), 118, 123, 269
costly signaling, 82–83, 109, 110, 111, 297n11
Cougar Mountain Cave (Oregon), 11, 23, 33, *42*, *44*, 86, 89, 91, 92
Cougar Mountain point style, 25, *26, 27, 34*, 35, *47*, 54–55, 57, 86, 91, 149, 228, 242, 246, 260

Cowan, Frank, 142
Cowboy Rest Creek quarry (Nevada), *154*, 249
Crabtree, Don E., 84
Crescent Valley (Nevada), 244
crescents, 3, 12, 59, 60, 64, 115, 154, 163, 173, 263, 264, 273, 287; and the Paleocoastal Tradition, 9, 16, 262, 266, *268*, 271, 272, 274n1, 287, 297n10
Cressman, Luther S., 3, 8, 17, 62, 163–64
cryptocrystalline silicates (CCS). *See* chert
cultural resource management (CRM), and Mojave Desert projectile point database, 118
cultural transmission, and interaction of Clovis and WST traditions in Far West, 240–61
C. W. Harris site (California), 94
Cycyk collection (New Mexico), 219–20, 223, 225–26, 229–38

Daisy Cave (California), 265, 269
Danger Cave (Utah), 32–33, 35–36, *51*, 55, *174*
dates and dating. *See* chronology; radiocarbon dating
Daugherty, Richard D., 244
Davis, Emma Lou, 274n1
Davis, Loren G., 9, 10, 11, 14–15, 37, 94, 132, 154–55, 156, 183n3, 244–45, 249, 254, 255, 261n3, 282
Dawson, Jerry, 227
Debert site (Nova Scotia), 184
Debra L. Friedkin site (Texas), 95, 158, 211, 215n1, 259, 278
decision making forces, and cultural transmission, 243
Dent (Colorado), *200*, *203*, *209*
Desert Archaic, 179
Desert Culture concept, 4, 291
Dietz site (Oregon), 57, 92, 165–66, 185, 253, 259–60
direct bias, and cultural transmission, 243
Dirty Shame Rockshelter (Oregon), *34*, *44*, *49*, 54
distal shoulder angle (DSA), and Mojave Desert projectile point database, 119
DNA, direct dating of coprolites and chronology of WST, 9, 10. *See also* genetic studies
Dockall, John E., 142
dogs, and genetic studies on peopling of Americas, 286
Doherty, Caitlin, 137
Douglas, Charles L., 175
Dugway Stubby point style, 27
Duke, Daron G., 14, 23, 24, 54, 55, 75, 83, 92, 112n6, 150, 288, 290, 291, 297n11, 297n13
Dunas Altas (New Mexico), 222–23

Early Archaic, and interpretation of stemmed points in Southwest, 219–38
Early Holocene: and age range of Haskett technology, 87; and extinction of megafauna in Great Basin, 110; and WST in Intermountain West, 54–55. *See also* Terminal Pleistocene/Early Holocene
Early Human Occupation in Far Western North America: The Clovis-Archaic Interface (Willig et al., 1988), 5, 6
Eastern Nevada Comparative Collection (ENCC), 114, 126, 127, *128*, 129, 227–28
Eastern New Mexico University, 221
East Wenatchee Clovis Cache (Washington), 7, 153, 157, 160n2, 167, 171, 173, *174*, 175, 253
ecology, and ecological framework: and Clovis migration to Far West, 178–82; and similarity of sites with WST projectile points, 23. *See also* foraging theory; wetland localities
Edwards Air Force Base (California), 114, 117, 119, 120
Eerkens, Jelmer, 254
El Fin de Mundo (Mexico), 155, 184, 278
Elston, Robert G., 6
Eren, Metin I., 102, 183n3
Erlandson, Jon M., 9, 16, 262, 267–68, 297n10
Escalante Valley locality (Utah), 94
exchange: and models for spread of Clovis technology, 181; and toolstone sources for Paleocoastal assemblages, 269

Fagan, John L., 6, 170
Far West: cultural transmission and interaction of Clovis and WST peoples in, 240–61; geographic region, 2; geographic variability of fluted points in, 184–98; history of research on stemmed and fluted technologies in, 1–13; review of Clovis record in, 163–83, 283–93; use of term, 183n1, 296n2
Far Western Anthropological Research Group, 63
Far Western Fluted Point Database (FWFPD), 168, 253, 257
Far Western XRF Lab, 99
Fedje, Daryl, 95
Feldman, Marcus W., 242
Felling, Danielle C., 63, 260
Fenn Cache, 167, 170–71
Ferring, C. Reid, 155
fine-grained volcanics (FGV): and biface reduction of WST points in Far West, 246; and Cycyk collection, 225; and Haskett points

in Great Basin, 103; and morphology of projectile points from Mojave Desert, 123, *124*, 125, 126, *128*, 130; and toolstone conveyance at Smith Creek Cave, 145–49; and toolstone conveyance by WST in Great Basin, 59–77. *See also* toolstone

Fischer, Anders, 142

Fitzhugh, Ben, 151

Five Mile Flats (Nevada), *45*, 54

Fladmark, Knut R., 7

fluted technologies: absolute and relative ages of in Great Plains and Rocky Mountains, 199–215; conclusions summarized from discussions in volume, 277–96; and definition of fluting method, 190–91; geographic variability of in Far West, 184–98; history of research on in Far West, 1–13; overview of volume topics, 13–17; and post-Clovis point forms in Far West, 242, 256; and search for progenitors of earliest migrants to Americas, 281–83; and projectile points in Intermountain West, 55–57; terminal Pleistocene/Early Holocene projectile points in Mojave Desert, 113–31. *See also* chronology; Clovis; Folsom; Sunshine Fluted points; technology

Folsom (New Mexico), *200*, *204*

Folsom point style: and basal flaking characteristics, 194; and chronology of Haskett on Great Plains, 91; comparison of Sunshine points to, 256–58; and hunting of bison, 297n11; occurrence of in eastern Great Basin and Snake River Plain, 112n8; and radiocarbon database for fluted and stemmed points from Great Plains and Rocky Mountains, 202, *203–5*, *208*, *209*, 211

food residues, and WST sites, 60. *See also* DNA; faunal remains; hearths

foraging theory, and possible interactions between Clovis and WST peoples, 177–81

Fort Irwin (California), 93, 114, 117, 118, 119, 123, 125–26, 130

Fort Rock Basin (Oregon), 32, 60, *61*, 65, 66, 74–77, 92, 149. See also Fort Rock Cave

Fort Rock Cave (Oregon), 4, 62, 65, 68, *74*, 164

Fossil Lake (Oregon), 79, 98

fracturing and fracture mistakes, and phases of Haskett point production, 103

frequency-dependent bias, and cultural transmission, 243

Frison, George C., 86, 91–92, 97, 111, 229, 235

functional assessment, of stemmed points from Smith Creek Cave, 150–51, 152

Galm, Jerry R., 7, 248

Gault site (Texas), 158, 211, 215n1, 279

GAUSS analysis, 137

genetic studies, and research on peopling of Americas, 282–83, 286, 296–97n7–9. *See also* DNA

Geoarchaeological X-ray Fluorescence Spectrometry (XRF) Laboratory, 225

Gilbert, M., 259

Glacier Peak tephra, and dating of Clovis points, 155, 157, 160n2, 173, 175

Glassow, Michael A., 269, 270–71

Goebel, Ted, 9, 11, 35, 90, 135, 136, 138–39, 147

Gough, Stan, 7, 248

Graf, Kelly E., 7, 8, 31

Granite Point Locality (Washington), 29

Grayson, Donald K., 63, 95, 97, 98, 109, 292

Great Basin: description of Haskett technology and Clovis parallels in, 79–111; distribution of obsidian in eastern, *146*, 147; and morphological homogeneity of terminal Pleistocene/Early Holocene projectile points from Mojave Desert, 113–31; use of term, 183n1; WST and role of toolstone conveyance in chronology of early populations in, 59–77. *See also* Far West

Great Plains and Rocky Mountains (GPRM), relative chronology of fluted and stemmed points in, 15, 199–215

Green River Basin (Wyoming), 176

ground stone, and Early Archaic sites in Southwest, 237. *See also* milling stones

Guano Valley (Oregon), 62–63

guided variation, and cultural transmission, 243

Gulf Coast, and Clovis migrants, 176

hafting styles: of Haskett points, 86; and possible contacts of Clovis with WST peoples in Far West, 179

Hamilton, Marcus J., 244

Hanging Rock Shelter (Nevada), 4, 23, *34*, *45*, 47, 63, *72*, 74

Hartman, Amanda J., 25

Haskett point style: and chronology of WST projectile points, 4, 11, 14, 23, 56, 57, 260–61; compared to Ovate points, 227; compared to Lind Coulee points, *250*, 251, 260; description of technology and of Clovis parallels in Great Basin, 79–111; and hunting of megafauna, 288–89, 290–91; as primary technology in Great Basin during Younger Dryas, 53–54, 56; and projectile points from Connley Caves, 33, *34*, 35; and Smith Creek Cave points, 142, 149,

151; and Tule Lake Rockshelter points, 35; type specimens for, 26, 27
Haskett site (Idaho), 241, 249, 250
Hatwai site (Idaho), 154
Hawksy Walksy Valley (Oregon), 63, 70–71, 74
Haynes, C. Vance, Jr., 8
hearths, and dating of projectile points from Smith Creek Cave, 134, 135
Heil Pond site (Idaho), 173, 174, 175, 240, 253
Helen Lookingbill site (Wyoming), 92
Hell Gap point style, 56, 86, 91, 219, 228–38
Hell Gap site (Wyoming), 86, 201–2, 203–7, 208, 209–10, 211, 220, 222, 228–38
Henrikson, L. Suzann, 8
Henwood site (California), 115, 174, 175, 253
Heritage Research Associates, Inc., 32
Hetrick site (Idaho), 37, 47, 54
Heye, George G., 266
Hibbens, Frank, 296n1
Holliday, Vance T., 97
Honea, Kenneth, 219, 222, 227, 237
Hoppe, Kathryn A., 257
Horn Shelter (Texas), 211
Hoskins, Andrew J., 35
Howard, Edgar B., 163, 168, 281
Huckell, Bruce B., 173, 222, 236, 237
Hughes, Susan S., 102

ice free corridor (IFC), and debate on peopling of Americas, 176, 263, 278
Indian Creek (Montana), 211
indirect bias, and cultural transmission, 243
individual learning, and cultural transmission, 243
Intermountain West: chronology of WST in, 9, 16, 21–58; and megafauna in late Pleistocene, 291–92; use of vs. Far West, 1, 4, 13, 15
Irwin-Williams, Cynthia, 85, 219, 221–22, 223, 227, 228, 237, 238
Island Paleocoastal Tradition (IPT), 16, 263, 273

Jakes Valley (Nevada), 184, 185
Jamaldin, Sophia, 61, 62
Japan: and chronology of Tachikawa points, 37; dates for Jomon sites in, 273
Jay points (Oshara Tradition), 219, 220, 221–23, 226, 227, 228, 229–38
Jazwa, Christopher S., 11–12, 54
Jenkins, Dennis L., 8, 9–10, 33, 35, 90, 132, 286
Jennings, Jesse D., 3, 32, 36, 164
Jim Pitts site (South Dakota), 211
Jones, George T., 6–7, 8–9, 12, 15, 23–25, 76, 105, 112n5–6, 117, 118, 126, 136, 147, 149, 150, 169, 184, 227, 234–35, 236, 253, 260, 261n1, 261n4, 278, 279, 280, 284, 286, 287, 294, 295
Jones-Miller site (Colorado), 228, 229
Joshua Tree National Park (California), 118, 185
Judge, W. James, 222, 257–58
Justice, Noel D., 116–17, 269

Keene, Joshua L., 9, 11, 12, 90, 135
Kelly, Robert L., 177, 179, 180, 181
Kelvin's Cave (Idaho), 8
Kennedy, Jaime L., 10
Keyes, Cassandra L., 15–16
Knell, Edward J., 14, 116, 117, 122, 202
Kuehn, Stephen C., 173, 175

La Bajada (New Mexico), 222
Lafayette, Linsie M., 25, 101, 151
Lahontan Basin (Nevada), 92
Lakebed Locality (California), 115
Lake Chewaucan (Oregon), 60, 62, 65, 66, 68, 76–77, 149
Lake China (California), 117–18
Lake Mohave point style, 14, 23, 26, 27, 94, 106, 228, 251; chronologies compared, 56, 57; from Danger Cave, 36; described, 116–17, 122–31; frequency of by region, 119; radiocarbon dates, 50–51; summary data, 120
Lake Mohave (California), 26, 27, 50, 93–94, 114, 116–17, 118, 119, 123, 130
Lake Terreton (Idaho), 91, 112
Lake Tonopah (California), 92, 185
Lake Warner (Oregon), 260
Lassen, Robert, 261n5
Last Supper Cave (Nevada), 45, 46, 53, 63, 73, 74
Laurentide Ice Sheet (LIS), 176
Layton, Thomas N., 23, 55, 63
Lebow, Clayton G., 272
Lehner site (Arizona), 290
Leonard Rockshelter (Nevada), 44
Leonhardy, Frank C., 29, 31
Levallois-like system, and WST projectile points, 241–42, 244–46, 249
Lind Coulee point style, 26, 27, 37, 54, 56, 57, 182, 244, 250, 260, 261n3
Lind Coulee site (Washington), 4, 22, 43, 55, 89, 154, 241, 249, 250
Lindenmeier site (Colorado), 211
Llano-Plano type hypothesis, for WST origins in Columbia Plateau region, 158
Logan Simpson Design, 186
Lohse, Ernest S., 29, 31, 104, 172

Long, Austin, 8, 202
Long Valley (Nevada), 70, 72–73, 126, 149, 184, *241*
LSP-1 Rockshelter (Oregon), *34*, 46–47
Lubbock Lake (Texas), 211
Lyman, R. Lee, 257
Lynch, Joshua J., 11, 14, 53, 138–39, 142, 291

MacHaffie site (Montana), 211
Madsen, David B., 9, 108, 112n6, 282
mammoths: and Clovis population on northern Plains, 256–57; and Clovis points from kill sites, 83, 100, 284; and design of Clovis points, 289, 290; fossil record for in Great Basin, 96, 97, 110. *See also* megafauna
Mann, Henry B., 232
manos and metates. *See* milling stones
marginal-value theorem, 179
Marine Corps Air Ground Combat Center (California), 114, 118, 119
Marmes Rockshelter (Washington), 4, 29, *43*, *48*, 54, 154
McDonough, Katelyn N., 33, 91, 291, 296
McNine Cache (Nevada), 150, 248
megafauna: Haskett technology and evidence for in Great Basin, 79, 82, 83, 95–98, 110; and human occupation of Paisley Caves, 62; and Intermountain West in late Pleistocene, 291–92. *See also* bison; mammoths
Meltzer, David J., 97, 177, 180, 261n5, 262, 281
Mexico: Clovis sites in, 184; and Haskett technology, 95. *See also* El Fin de Mundo
migration, and dispersal of Clovis peoples into Far West, 175–77, 180–81. *See also* mobility
Milford Flat Locality (Utah), 185
Miller, D. Shane, 56, 139, 141, 150
milling stones, and Early Holocene assemblages from coastal California, 272. *See also* ground stone
Minor, Rick, 98
mobility: and Haskett sites in Great Basin, 108–109; influence of on projectile point morphology in Mojave Desert, 130; and Paleoindian sites on Great Plains, 293; and procurement distances for obsidian at Smith Creek Cave, 147, *148*, 149. *See also* migration; settlement strategies
Mojave Desert, morphological homogeneity of projectile points from Terminal Pleistocene through Early Holocene in, 113–31
Monte Verde (Chile), 95, 263
Moratto, Michael J., 175, 274n1
morphology. *See* basal morphology; technology

Mount Moriah occupation zone, of Smith Creek Cave, 133–36
Mud Lake (Nevada), 185
Muñiz, Mark P., 202
Musil, Robert R., 86
Muto, Guy R., 244

Naval Air Weapons Station China Lake (California), 114, 118
Nevada State Museum, 136, 185
Norris, Sophie L., 176, 240
Northern Channel Islands (California), and Paleocoastal assemblages, 7–8, 9, 262–73, 274n1–2, 287, 297n10
North Warner Valley (Oregon), 62, 69, *70–71*, 74
Northwest Research Obsidian Studies Laboratory (NWROSL), 64, 77–78n1–2, 137, 138
notch opening index (NOI), and Mojave Desert projectile point database, 119
Nye Canyon Paleo site (Nevada), 253

obsidian: availability of for WST in Great Basin, 59–77; and Clovis assemblages in Far West, 182; and geographic variability of fluted points in Far West, 186, 194, 196; and Haskett points in Great Basin, 103, 105, 107–9; and morphology of projectile points from Mojave Desert, 123, *124*, 125, 126, *128*, 130; and Paleocoastal technological tradition, 269; and raw-material procurement at Smith Creek Cave, 137–38, 145–49, 151. *See also* toolstone
Odell, George H., 142
O'Grady, Patrick W., 260
Ojito Dune (New Mexico), 222
Old River Bed Delta (Utah), 23, *26*, 75, 79, *80*, 91, 94, 100, 102, 103, 105, *106*, *107*, 114, 126, 127, *128*, 129, 130, 142, 147, 149, 152, 246, 249, 261
Orr, Phil C., 264–65
Oshara Tradition. *See* Jay points

Pacific Coast: and debate on peopling of Americas, 176, 264; recognition of Pleistocene sites and development of coastal migration theory, 7–8; and Upper Paleolithic lanceolate precursors, 95. *See also* Northern Channel Islands
Pacific Rim, and Late Pleistocene stemmed point types, 264
Paisley Caves (Oregon), 1, 3, 8, 9, 10, 11, *34*, 37, 38–39, *44*, 53, 57, 59–60, 61–62, 66–68, 69, 74, 75, 87, 88, 90, 92, 132, 153, 160n3, 163, 178, 181–82, 249, 250, 259, 278

PaleoAmerica (Waters, Goebel, and Graf 2020), 13
"Paleoarchaic": introduction and adoption of term, 6, 291; and use of term "Paleoindian," 8, 60
Paleocoastal assemblages, from Northern Channel Islands of California, 7–8, 9, 262–73, 274n1, 287, 297n10
"Paleoindian," and use of term "Paleoarchaic," 8, 60
Paleoindian or Paleoarchaic? Great Basin Human Ecology at the Pleistocene/Holocene Transition (Graf and Schmitt, 2007), 8
Paleontological Statistics (PAST) Software Package 3.24, 232
Parman Localities (Nevada), 26, 27, 61, 63–65, 69, 72–73, 74, 77
Parman point styles, 23, 228; from Connley Caves, 34; and dating, 45, 54–55; type definitions, 27; type specimens, 26
Paulina Lake site (Oregon), 31, 32, 34, 35, 48–49
Pendleton, Lorrane S., 6, 149
Peopling of the Americas: and Clovis-first hypothesis, 176, 240, 263; and coastal migration theory, 7, 278; and implications of WST variants on California's Northern Channel Islands, 263–64; and genetic studies, 281–83, 286; and interpretation of Clovis, 166; and timing of emergence of Western Stemmed points in Far West, 8–12, 132
Pettit, Paul B., 31
Phagan, Carl, 6
Pilcher Creek site (Oregon), 157, 160n2
Pleistocene: and chronology of Clovis era, 166; and recognition of archaeological sites on Pacific Coast, 7. *See also* Terminal Pleistocene/Early Holocene
Plisson, Hugues, 142
Polach, Henry A., 31
Potter, Ben A., 176, 262, 263, 269, 283
Powars II site (Wyoming), 211
Pratt, Jordan E., 282, 296n3
prestige bias, and cultural transmission, 243
prestige hunting, and comparison of Haskett and Clovis technologies, 110
prismatic blades, and Clovis technocomplex, 172
Pyramid Lake (Nevada), 79

Ranere, Anthony J., 4, 85
raw materials. *See* toolstone
Reaux, Derek J., 62–63, 75, 76
Redfish Overhang (Idaho), 44, 54, 89, 91

Reid, Kenneth C., 175
Renaud, Etienne B., 227
resharpening and reworking: and chronology of WST in Intermountain West, 24–25; of Haskett points, 84, 101; and interpretation of stemmed points in Southwest, 234–35; and morphology of projectile points from Mojave Desert, 123, 130
Rice, David G., 29, 31
Rice, Harvey S., 25, 29, 31
Richerson, Peter J., 242, 243, 256
Rimrock Draw Rockshelter (Oregon), 92, 112, *241*,
Rimrock Lake (Oregon), *241*
"Rio Grande Complex," 222
Rippeteau, B., 202
Roberson, J., 119
Roberts, Frank H. H., Jr., 277–78, 280, 296n1
rock art, and WST sites, 60
Rocky Mountains. *See* Great Plains and Rocky Mountains (GPRM)
Rogers-Buckhorn-Rosamond Lake (playa) system, 117
Rogers Ridge site (California), *50*, 55
Rondeau, Michael F., 15, 184, 185, 188
Rosamond Dry Lake (California), 117
Rosencrance, Richard L., 14, 24, 33, 54, 63, 87, 90–91, 287, 293
Rots, Veerle, 142
Running Antelope site (Utah), 94

Sadmat site (Nevada), 92, 149, 150
Sage Hen Gap site (Oregon), 171
San Pedro Valley (Arizona), 284
Santarosae Island (California), 264, *265*, 266, 274n2
Schillinger, Kerstin, 294
Schmitt, David N., 8, 112n5
Scottsbluff point style, 158, 199
Sentinel Gap site (Washington), 43, 86, 89, 91, 103, 154, 249
settlement strategies, and late Pleistocene sites on Great Plains, 293. *See also* ecology; migration; mobility
Shillito, Lisa-Marie, 10
Sholts, Sabrina, 248
Shott, Michael J., 284
SigmaPlot version 14, 119
Silver Lake (California), *50*, 116, 117, 129
Silver Lake point style, 14, 23; dating of, 55, 57; and Great Basin morphology, 126–31; morphological variance of Mojave desert examples, 113, 115, *116*, 120–21, 122; and raw

materials, *124*; type specimens compared, *26, 36*, 94, type specimens defined, *27*, 117
Simon Clovis Cache (Idaho), 3–4, 167, 176, 240
Sister's Hill site (Colorado), 228
size metrics: and comparison of Clovis and Haskett points, 99–101; and geographic variability of fluted points in Far West, 191–93, 195
skill level, required for Haskett and Clovis reduction strategies, 103–5
Smallwood, 139, 141, 150
Smith, Geoffrey M., 7, 13, 14, 24, 25, 53, 62, 63, 64, 101, 149, 151, 212–13, 260
Smith, H., 182
Smith Creek Cave (Nevada), 4, 6, 11, *41–42*, 53, 89, 90, 94, 132–52
Snake River Plain, 4, 15, 76, 84, 91, 95, 183n1, and evidence for Clovis dispersal, 176, 240, 248–49, 253
social learning, and cultural transmission, 243
social network analysis (SNA), of WST assemblages from Great Basin, 76
Society for American Archaeology (2019 meeting), 1
South America: chronology of fluted points in, 83; and Haskett technology, 94, 95. *See also* Monte Verde
Southwest, interpretation of stemmed points in, 219–38
Spencer, L., 98
Speth, John, 82, 292
Spirit Cave (Nevada), 286–87, *288*
Springer, Kathleen B., 93, 98
Stafford, Thomas W., *56*, 166, 201
stem length to total length ratio (STL/TTL ratio), and Mojave Desert projectile point database, 119
Stemmed Point Tradition, 5
stemmed technologies: absolute and relative ages of in Great Plains and Rocky Mountains, 199–215; chronology of projectile point forms at Cooper's Ferry, 159; conclusions summarized from discussions in volume, 277–96; history of research on in Far West, 1–13; interpretation of in Southwest, 219–38; overview of volume, 13–17; and search for progenitors of earliest migrants to Americas, 281–83; and Younger Dryas-aged points from Smith Creek Cave, 132–52. *See also* chronology; Haskett point style; Jay points; technology; Western Stemmed Tradition
stratigraphic superposition, of stemmed and fluted points in Great Plains and Rocky Mountains, 208, 211–12

Stubby point style, 23, *26*, 55, 57, *106*
Stueber, Daniel, 14, 54, 75, 104, 288, 290, 291, 297n11, 297n13
Stuiver, Minze, 31
Sudden Flats site (California), 272
Sunshine Fluted points: and interaction of Clovis and WST cultural traditions in Far West, 255–59; and morphology of fluted points in Far West, 12, 168, 169, 173
Sunshine Locality (Nevada), *45*, 54, 114, 126, 150, 173, *174*, 184, 185, 196, 251, 253, 256, 259
Surovell, Todd A., 15, 53, 91, 109, 279, 281, 294
Susia, Margaret, 92
Sutton, Mark Q., 14, 93
Swanson, Earl H., 12, 84–85, 91
SWL. *See* Sunshine Locality
Sylwester/Twain Harte site (California), *174*, 183n4

Tachikawa points (Japan), 37
tapering stemmed forms, classification and chronology of in Southwest, 220, 221–22
Taylor, Amanda, 168, 253, 261n1, 261n4
technology: and comparison of Clovis and Haskett projectile points, 79–111; and definition of Clovis technological complex, 166, 167–68; and geographic variability of fluted points in Far West, 186–88, *189–90*; and reduction of stemmed points at Smith Creek Cave, 149–50. *See also* atlatls; bifaces; bow and arrow technology; fracturing and fracture mistakes; resharpening and reworking; size metrics; toolstone; use wear
Terminal Pleistocene/Early Holocene (TP/EH), and projectile points from Mojave Desert, 113–31
Texas A&M University, 13, 137
textiles, at WST sites, 60
Thakar, Heather, 136
Thatcher, Jennifer J., 61
Thomas, Scott P., 111, 229, 253
Todd, Lawrence C., 177, 179, 180, 181
toolstone: and Clovis dispersal in Snake River Plain, 176; conveyance of and comparison of Haskett and Clovis technologies, 105, 107–9; procurement and conveyance of for stemmed points at Smith Creek Cave, 137–38, 145–49; role of conveyance in chronology of settlement in northwestern Great Basin, 59–77. *See also* chert; fine-grained volcanics; obsidian; technology; transport distances
trade. *See* exchange
transport distances: and lithic conveyance zones

in Intermountain West, 292; and raw material procurement at Smith Creek Cave, 138, 147, *148*, 149, 151; for toolstone conveyance at WST sites in Great Basin, 69, 74–75. *See also* toolstone

Tukey, John W., 232

Tulare Lake (California), 115

Tularosa Basin (New Mexico), 223, 224

Tule Lake Rockshelter (California), 11, 31, 32, *34, 35*, 42, 89, 91, 92–93

Tule Springs (Nevada), 98

Tuohy, Donald R., 3, 23–24

Two Moon Shelter (Wyoming), 211

unbiased transmission, and social learning, 243

University of California, Davis, 32

University of Georgia, Center for Applied Isotope Studies, 136

University of Nevada, Reno (UNR), 62, 63, 64

University of New Mexico, 219, 225

University of Oregon, 32, 60–61, 62, 185

University of Victoria, 13

use wear, of stemmed points from Smith Creek Cave, 142–45

Vail site (Maine), 184

Veratic Rockshelter (Idaho), 4, 85, 91

Vestuto, Matthew, 274n2

Vierra, Bradley J., 223

Wallman Bison site (Nevada), *48*, 97

Warner Mountains, and toolstone source sites, 75, 76

Warren, Claude N., 4, 85, 94

Waters, Michael R., 56, 83, 95, 155, 166, 201, 240, 259, 279

Weed Lake Ditch (Oregon), 11, 92

"Western Fluted," use of term, 155, 169

Western Pluvial Lakes Tradition (WPLT), 4, 92, 263, 274n1

Western Stemmed Tradition (WST): chronology of in Far West, 164, 277–81; chronology of in Intermountain West, 21–58; and Clovis record in Far West, 177–81; cultural transmission and interaction with Clovis peoples in Far West, 240–61; and description of Haskett points, 79–111; and Early Archaic period in Southwest, 227–28; and history of research on stemmed and fluted points in Far West, 1, 4, 7, 8–12; and morphological homogeneity of Terminal Pleistocene/Early Holocene projectile points from Mojave Desert, 113–31; overview of discussions in volume, 14–15; as predating Clovis in Columbia River Plateau, 153–60; toolstone conveyance and chronology of settlement in northwestern Great Basin, 59–77; variants of from Northern Channel Islands, 262–73

wetland localities: and Haskett point sites, 92; and Old River Bed Delta, 126; and Paisley Caves, 178; and Western Pluvial Lakes Tradition, 263; and WST peoples in Far West, 178, 179; WST projectile points associated with, 23, 60, 179, 181, 264. *See also* ecology

Wewukiyepuh site (Idaho), *42*, 53, 89, 91, 154

White Sands National Park (New Mexico), 223

Whitney, Donald R., 232

Williams, Thomas J., 215n1

Willig, Judith A., 5–6, 8, 116, 164

Willis, Samuel C., 244–45

Willow Leaf Bipoint Tradition, 94–95

Wilson Butte Cave (Idaho), 4

Wilson Workshop 1 (2018), 13

Windust Caves (Washington), 25, *26, 27*, 47–49, 198

Windust concepts, and chronology of WST, 23, 25, *28*, 29, 31, 57

Windust point style, *26*, 34, 36, 47–49, 54–57, 198, 263; defined, 27; summary of, *28, 29*, 31

Windust/square point style, *26*, 31, *34*, 55, 57

Wishbone site (Utah), 11, *42*, 89, 91, 94, 98–99, 108

Witt site (California), 273

Wood, Janice, 151

Wormington, Marie, 85, 165, 166, 199–200, 201

Wriston, Teresa A., 260

WST. *See* Western Stemmed Tradition

Wyoming State Historic Preservation Office, 201

Yesner, David, 262

Younger Dryas: and chronology of Clovis in Great Basin, 82; and megafauna in Great Basin, 95, 110; and stemmed points from Smith Creek Cave site in Nevada, 132–52; and WST in Intermountain West, 53–54, 56, 57

Yuma problem, and temporal relationship of fluted and stemmed points in Far West, 199–201, 212